District Gazetteers of India Series 182

PUNJAB DISTRICT GAZETTEERS

MULTAN DISTRICT
(1901-02)

District Gazetteers of India Series 182

PUNJAB DISTRICT GAZETTEERS

MULTAN DISTRICT
(1901-02)

BY

E. D. MACLAGAN

36 VOLUMES (IN 37 BINDINGS)

(VOL. 25th)

GYAN

Published by

Gyan Publishing House
5, Ansari Road
Daryaganj, New Delhi-110002
Phone: 011-47034999, 9811692060
E-mail: books@gyanbooks.com

Distribution Network
gyanbooks.com
India, USA, Canada, UK, Australia, France

ISBN: 978-93-6208-248-0 (Set) 36 Volumes (In 37 Bindings)
978-81-212-5835-7 (HB)

First Published, 1902

2nd Impression 2024

Printed at: Gyan Press, Delhi.

PUNJAB DISTRICT GAZETTEERS (VOL. 25th)
Author: E. D. MACLAGAN

LIST OF VOLUMES

S. NO.	ISBN NO.	VOL.	TITLE	AUTHOR	PRICE	PAGES
			ASSAM DISTRICT GAZETTEERS			
1	9788121286046	1st	Cachar	B. C. Allen	1200	300
2	9788121286039	2nd	Sylhet	B. C. Allen	1500	378
3	9788121286022	3rd	Goalpara	B. C. Allen	800	203
4	9788121286015	4th	Kamrup	B. C. Allen	1370	344
5	9788121286008	5th	Darrang	B. C. Allen	1450	364
6	9788121285995	6th	Nowgong	B. C. Allen	1120	280
7	9788121285988	7th	Sibsagar	B. C. Allen	1370	343
8	9788121285971	8th	Lakhimpur	B. C. Allen	1380	347
9	9788121285964	9th	Naga Hills and Manipur	B. C. Allen	1170	294
10	9788121285957	10th	The Khasi And Jaintia Hills, The Garo Hills And The Lushai Hills	B. C. Allen	1350	363
11	9788121285940	11th	The Sadiya and Balipara Frontier Tract	B. C. Allen	760	190
			BENGAL DISTRICT GAZETTEERS			
12	9788121218665	1st	Angul	L. S. S. O'Malley	500	168
13	9788121259644	2nd	Bakarganj	J. C. JACK	1350	194
14	9788121218689	3rd	Balasore	L. S. S. O'Malley	675	228
15	9788121259606	4th	Bankura	L. S. S. O'Malley	1390	199
16	9788121218368	5th	Bhagalpur	J. Byrne	580	194
17	9788121218283	6th	Birbhum	L. S. S. O'Malley	450	150
18	9788121259668	7th	Eastern Bengal and Assam - Bogra	J. N. Gupta	1320	188
19	9788121218344	8th	Burdwan	J. C. K. Peterson	680	227
20	9788121259545	9th	Calcutta District Gazetteer - Statistics, 1901 - 02		480	68
21	9788121218306	10th	Champaran	L. S. S. O'Malley	610	205
22	9788121259620	11th	Eastern Bengal District Gazetters - Chittagong	L. S. S. O'Malley	1500	216
23	9788121259569	12th	Chota Nagpur Tributary		180	26
24	9788121259422	13th	The Cooch Behar Gazette: Statistics		2040	292
25	9788121218405	14th	Cuttack	L. S. S. O'Malley	740	248
26	9788121261364	15th	Eastern Bengal District Gazetteers Dacca	B. C. Allen	800	207
27	9788121218429	16th	Darbhanga	L. S. S. O'Malley	540	180
28	9788121204965	17th	Darjeeling	L. S. S. O'Malley	500	248
29	9788121259460	18th	Eastern Bengal District Gazetteers - Dinajpur	F. W. Strong	1250	178
30	9788121259408	19th	Faridpur	L. S. S. O'Malley	980	140
31	9788121218467	20th	Gaya	L. S. S. O'Malley	810	270
32	9788121214025	21st	Bihar and Orissa District Gazetteer: Hazaribagh	E. Lister	950	234
33	9788121218320	22nd	Hooghly	L. S. S. O'Malley	1020	340
34	9788121218184	23rd	Bengal District Gazetteer Howrah	L. S. S. O'Malley	590	199
35	9788121259309	24th	Eastern Bengal and Assam - Jalpaiguri	John F. Gruning	1250	178
36	9788121259286	25th	Jessore	L. S. S. O'Malley	1340	192
37	9788121259248	26th	Khulna	L. S. S. O'Malley	1540	220
38	9788121259224	27th	Malda	G. E. Lambourn	940	134
39	9788121297912	28th	Manbhum	H. Coupland	1250	313
40	9788121218481	29th	Midnapore	L. S. S. O'Malley	750	252
41	9788121218580	30th	Monghyr	L. S. S. O'Malley	840	280
42	9788121259163	31st	Murshidabad	L. S. S. O'Malley	1750	250
43	9788121259583	32nd	Bengal District Gazetteers - Muzaffarpur	L. S. S. O'Malley	1300	188
44	9788121259149	33rd	Mymensingh	F. A. Sachse	1340	192
45	9788121259125	34th	Nadia	J. H. E. Garrett	1500	214
46	9788121259101	35th	Eastern Bengal and Assam - Noakhali	J. E. Webster	800	115
47	9788121218443	36th	Feudatory States of Orissa	L. E. B. Cobdenramsay	1180	395
48	9788121259088	37th	Pabna	L. S. S. O'Malley	990	142
49	9788121218504	38th	Palamau	L. S. S. O'Malley	570	190
50	9788121218627	39th	Patna	L. S. S. O'Malley	750	250
51	9788121218528	40th	Puri	L. S. S. O'Malley	980	328
52	9788121218740	41st	Purnea	L. S. S. O'Malley	660	220
53	9788121258944	42nd	Rajshahi	L. S. S. O'Malley	1500	216
54	9788121256674	43rd	Bihar and Orissa District Gazetteers: Ranchi	M. G. Hallett	1950	278
55	9788121258920	44th	Eastern Bengal and assam - Rangpur	J. A. Vas	1250	178
56	9788121218542	45th	Sambalpur	L. S. S. O'Malley	730	242
57	9788121214049	46th	Santal Parganas	L. S. S. O'Malley	1250	308
58	9788121218603	47th	Saran	L. S. S. O'Malley	570	190
59	9788121218641	48th	Shahabad	L. S. S. O'Malley	570	190
60	9788121256698	49th	The Gazetteer of Sikhim	H. H. Risley	2280	481
61	9788121218566	50th	Singhbhum, Saraikela And Kharsawan	L. S. S. O'Malley	840	280
62	9788121259446	51st	Eastern Bengal District Gazetteers - Tippera	J. E. Webster	1020	146
63	9788121259040	52nd	24 Parganas	L. S. S. O'Malley	1990	284

S. NO.	ISBN NO.	VOL.	TITLE	AUTHOR	PRICE	PAGES
			CENTRAL PROVINCES DISTRICT GAZETTEERS			
64	9789362085474	1st, Vol. A	Akola (Descriptive)	A. E. Nelson, C. Brown	1740	436
65	9789362087232	2nd, Vol. A	Amraoti (Descriptive)	S. V. Fitzgerald, A. E. Nelson	2100	524
66	9789362085191	3rd,Vol. A	Balaghat (Descriptive)	R. V. RUSSELL	860	216
67	9789362085986	4th, Vol. A	Betul (Descriptive)	R. V. RUSSELL	1220	306
68	9789362082039	5th, Vol. A	Bhandara (Descriptive)	R. V. RUSSELL	1170	292
69	9789362087713	6th, Vol. A	Bilaspur (Descriptive)	R. V. RUSSELL	1740	434
70	9789362084255	7th, Vol. A	Buldana (Descriptive)	A. E. Nelson	2170	543
71	9789362082107	8th, Vol. B	Chanda (Descriptive)	R. V. RUSSELL	940	234
72	9789362084576	9th	Chhattisgarch Feudatory State	E. A. De Brett	1760	440
73	9789362084873	10th	Chhindwara (Descriptive)	R. V. RUSSELL	1100	274
74	9789362086426	11th, Vol. A & B	Damoh (Descriptive and Statistical Tables 1891-1901)	R. V. RUSSELL	1660	414
75	9789362080240	12th, Vol. A	Durg (Descriptive)	A. E. Nelson	930	232
76	9789362080448	13th, Vol. A	Hoshangabad (Descriptive)	R. V. RUSSELL	1720	430
77	9789362080028	14th, Vol. A	Jubbulpore (Descriptive)	A. E. Nelson	1900	474
78	9789362088079	15th, Vol. A & B	Mandla (Descriptive and Statistical Tables 1891-1901)	R. V. RUSSELL	740	186
79	9789362086693	16th, Vol. A	Nagpur (Descriptive)	R. V. RUSSELL	1580	394
80	9789362085221	17th, Vol. A	Narsinghpur (Descriptive)	R. V. RUSSELL	1030	257
81	9789362086501	18th, Vol. A	Nimar (Descriptive)	R. V. RUSSELL	1200	299
82	9789362082145	19th, Vol. A	Raipur (Descriptive)	A. E. Nelson	1580	396
83	9789362085948	20th, Vol. A	Saugor (Descriptive)	R. V. RUSSELL	1140	285
84	9789362080318	21st, Vol. A	Seoni (Descriptive)	R. V. RUSSELL	930	232
85	9789362089625	22nd, Vol. A	Wardha (Descriptive)	R. V. RUSSELL	1210	302
86	9789362088468	23rd, Vol. A	Yeotmal (Descriptive)	R. V. RUSSELL	1110	277
87	9789362083500	24th, Vol. I, Pt. I	Gwalior (Text and Tables)	R. V. RUSSELL	1960	489
88	9789362081667	24th, Vol. I, Pt. II	Gwalior (Maps)	R. V. RUSSELL	790	198
89	9789362087478	24th, Vol. I, Pt. III	Gwalior (Village List)	R. V. RUSSELL	1620	406
90	9789362089731	24th, Vol. I, Pt. IV	Gwalior (Photos)	R. V. RUSSELL	2790	698
91	9789362088956	25th, Vol. II	Indore (Text and Tables)	C. E. Luard	2100	524
92	9789362088543	26th, Vol. III	Bhopal (Text and Tables)	C. E. Luard	1090	272
93	9789362082732	27th, Vol. IV	Rewah (Text and Tables)	C. E. Luard	1000	250
94	9789362087065	28th, Vol. V, Pt. A	Western States - Malwa (Text)	C. E. Luard	3050	762
95	9789362080707	29th, Vol. VI, Pt. A	Eastern States - Bundelkhand (Text)	C. E. Luard	1850	463
96	9789362086273	30th, Vol. VI, Pt. B	Eastern States - Bundelkhand (Tables)	C. E. Luard	1670	417
			GAZETTEER OF THE BOMBAY PRESIDENCY			
97	9788121283458	1st, Part I	History of Gujarat	Ed.: James M. Campbell	4500	644
98	9788121285599	1st, Part II	History of the Konkan Dakhan and Southern Maratha Country	Ed.: James M. Campbell	5870	840
99	9788121285575	2nd	Gujarat, Surat and Broach	Ed.: James M. Campbell	4150	598
100	9788121285551	3rd	Kaira and Panch Mahals	Ed.: James M. Campbell	2370	339
101	9788121285537	4th	Ahmedabad	Ed.: James M. Campbell	2600	372
102	9788121285513	5th	Cutch, Palanpur, and Mahi Kantha	Ed.: James M. Campbell	3330	478
103	9788121285490	6th	Rewa Kantha, Narukot, Cambay, and Surat States	Ed.: James M. Campbell	2030	290
104	9788121285476	7th	Baroda	Ed.: James M. Campbell	4550	652
105	9788121285452	8th	Kathiawar	Ed.: James M. Campbell	5300	758
106	9788121285438	9th, Part I	Gujarat Population - Hindus	Ed.: James M. Campbell	4450	636
107	9788121285414	9th, Part II	Gujarat Population - Musalmans and Parsis	Ed.: James M. Campbell	2120	304
108	9788121285391	10th	Ratnagiri and Savantvadi	Ed.: James M. Campbell	3500	501
109	9788121285377	11th	Kolaba and Janjira	Ed.: James M. Campbell	3550	513
110	9788121285353	12th	Khandesh	Ed.: James M. Campbell	4450	638
111	9788121285339	13th Part I	Thana	Ed.: James M. Campbell	2880	413
112	9788121285315	13th Part II	Thana	Ed.: James M. Campbell	2490	357
113	9788121285292	14th	Thana - Places of Interest	Ed.: James M. Campbell	4600	659
114	9788121285278	15th Part I	Kanara	Ed.: James M. Campbell	3250	468
115	9788121285254	15th Part II	Kanara	Ed.: James M. Campbell	2440	468
116	9788121285230	16th	Nasik	Ed.: James M. Campbell	4880	698
117	9788121285216	17th	Ahmadnagar	Ed.: James M. Campbell	5400	772
118	9788121285193	18th Part I	Poona	Ed.: James M. Campbell	4100	586
119	9788121285179	18th Part II	Poona	Ed.: James M. Campbell	3750	537
120	9788121285155	18th Part III	Poona	Ed.: James M. Campbell	3500	503
121	9788121285131	19th	Satara	Ed.: James M. Campbell	4840	692
122	9788121285117	20th	Sholapur	Ed.: James M. Campbell	3820	547
123	9788121285094	21st	Gazetteer of the Bomaby Presidency: Belgaum	Ed.: James M. Campbell	3590	514
124	9788121285070	22nd	Dharwar	Ed.: James M. Campbell	5880	841
125	9788121285056	23rd	Gazetteer of the Bombay Presidency:Bijapur	Ed.: James M. Campbell	4980	712
126	9788121285032	24th	Kolhapur	Ed.: James M. Campbell	3150	450
127	9788121285018	25th	Botany	Ed.: James M. Campbell	2850	408

S. NO.	ISBN NO.	VOL.	TITLE	AUTHOR	PRICE	PAGES
128	9788121284998	26th, Part I	Materials Towards a Statistical Account of the Town and Island of Bombay - History	Ed.: James M. Campbell	3525	504
129	9788121284974	26th, Part II	Materials Towards a Statistical Account of the Town and Island of Bombay - Trade and Fortifications	Ed.: James M. Campbell	3750	538
130	9788121284950	26th, Part III	Materials Towards a Statistical Account of the Town And Island of Bombay - Administration	Ed.: James M. Campbell	4840	702
131	9788121284936	27th	General Index	Ed.: R. E. Enthoven	2990	428
			MADRAS DISTRICT GAZETTEERS			
132	9788121258821	1st	Anantapur	W. Francis	1590	227
133	9788121258562	2nd	Malabar	C. A Innes & F. B Evans	4210	602
134	9788121258807	3rd	Bellary	W. Francis	2640	377
135	9788121258784	4th	Statistical Appendix For Chingleput		390	56
136	9788121258760	5th	Coimbatore	K. N. Krishnaswami Ayyar	4790	628
137	9788121232821	6th	Madras District Gazetteers District Gazetteer Cuddapah	C. F. Brackenbury	1950	285
138	9788121258722	7th	Statistical Appendix For Ganjam		510	73
139	9788121256759	8th, Vol. 1st	Godavari District Gazetteer	F. R. Hemingway	1280	320
140	9788121256797	8th, Vol. 2nd	Godavari District Gazetteer	F. R. Hemingway	340	83
141	9788121258685	9th	Statistical Appendix For Kistna		890	127
142	9788121258661	10th	Statistical Appendix For Kurnool		380	54
143	9788121258623	11th	Madura	W. Francis	2650	379
144	9788121258586	12th	Statistical Appendix For Madura		1040	148
145	9788121258647	13th	The Nilgiris	W. Francis	3060	437
146	9788121234283	14th	Madras District Gazetteers Gazetteer Of The Nellore District Brought Upto 1938			2110
386						
147	9788121258524	15th	North Arcot		830	118
148	9788121258500	16th, Vol. 1, Part I	Salem	F. J. Richards	2400	343
149	9788121258609	16th, Vol. 1, Part II	Salem	F. J. Richards	2520	360
150	9788121258463	17th	South Arcot	W. Francis	3360	480
151	9788121258487	18th	Statistical Appendix For South Canara		560	80
152	9788121258449	19th, Vol. 1st & 2nd	Tanjore: Main Volume and Statistical Appendix		2900	401
153	9788121258401	20th	Tinnevelly	H. R. Pate	3830	547
154	9788121258425	21st	Statistical Appendix For Tinnevelly		450	64
155	9788121258388	22nd, 1st & 2nd	Trichinopoly: Main Volume and Statistical Appendix	F. R. Hemingway	3410	487
156	9788121241960	23rd	Vizagapatam District Gazetteer	W. Francis	1520	385
			PUNJAB DISTRICT GAZETTEERS			
157	9788121255936	1st	Ambala District 1883-84		870	124
158	9788121255950	2nd	Amritsar		1650	236
159	9788121255974	3rd	Delhi		1820	260
160	9788121255998	4th	Ferozepore		1320	188
161	9788121256018	5th	Faridkot		490	70
162	9788121256032	6th	Gujranwala 1893-94		1780	254
163	9788121256056	7th	Gujrat	C. E. Luard	1590	228
164	9788121256070	8th	Gurdaspur 1891-92		1764	252
165	9788121256094	9th	Gurgaon 1883-4		1420	203
166	9788121256117	10th	Hazara	H. D. Watson	3200	458
167	9788121256131	11th	Hissar district and Lohar State		2570	367
168	9788121256155	12th	Hoshiarpur		1980	283
169	9788121256179	13th	Jhang		1490	213
170	9788121256193	14th	Jhelam		1410	202
171	9788121256216	15th	Jalandhar District 1883-84		750	108
172	9788121256230	16th, Vol. XIV-A	Jullundur District, with maps and Kapurthala		2786	398
173	9788121256254	17th, Pt. I	Kangra (Proper)		2030	290
174	9788121256278	17th, Pt. II	Kangra (Kulu, Lahual, Spiti)		2500	357
175	9788121256292	18th	Karnal		2700	386
176	9788121256315	19th	Kohat		2150	307
177	9788121256339	20th	The Lahore District 1883-84		1710	244
178	9788121256377	21st	Ludhiana and Maler Kotla		2350	335
179	9788121256391	22nd	Lyallpur		1029	147
180	9788121256414	23rd	Mianwali		1640	234
181	9788121256438	24th	Montgomery	P. J. Fagan	2230	318
182	9788121258357	25th	Multan (1901-02)	E. D. Maclagan	3360	480
183	9788121258692	26th	The Rohtak District 1883-84		1370	196
184	9788121258739	27th, Vol. III A	Dujana State 1904		600	16
185	9788121256476	28th	Shahpur District		2490	356
186	9788121256490	29th	Simla District		1110	159
187	9788121256513	30th	The Chamba State		2860	408

S. NO.	ISBN NO.	VOL.	TITLE	AUTHOR	PRICE	PAGES
188	9788121256537	31st	The Chenab Colony 1904		2170	310
189	9788121256551	32nd	Kalsia State		370	53
190	9788121256575	33rd	Suket and Mandi		1080	154
191	9788121256599	34th	Phulkian States, Patiala Jind And Nabha 1904		2898	414
192	9788121256636	35th	Simla Hill States		3100	443
193	9788121256650	36th	Sirmur		1280	183
			RAJPUTANA DISTRICT GAZETTEERS			
194	9789362089847	1st, Vol. I-A & B	Ajmer-merwara (Text and Statistics Tables)	C. C. Watson	1720	246
195	9789362088895	2nd. Vol. II-A & B	Mewar Residency (Text and Statistics Tables)	K.D. Erskine	2370	339
196	9789362087935	3rd, Vol. III-A & B	The Western Rajputana States Residency And The Bikaner Agency	K.D. Erskine	5000	718
			UNITED PROVINCES OF AGRA AND OUDH DISTRICT GAZETTEERS			
197	9789362080523	Vol. I	Agra	H. R. Nevill	3160	452
198	9789362084149	Vol. II	Aligarh	H. R. Nevill	1820	260
199	9789362081452	Vol. III	Allahabad	H. R. Nevill	2860	409
200	9789362085917	Vol. IV	Almora	H. G. Walton	2330	333
201	9789362089717	Vol. V	Azamgarh	D. L. Drake Brockman	2440	349
202	9789362089069	Vol. VI	Bahraich	H. R. Nevill	1970	281
203	9789362089670	Vol. VII	Ballia	H. R. Nevill	2450	350
204	9789362080974	Vol. VIII	Banda	D. L. Drake Brockman	2440	349
205	9789362082657	Vol. IX	Bara Banki	H. R. Nevill	2410	344
206	9789362089588	Vol. X	Bareilly	H. R. Nevill	2290	327
207	9789362088772	Vol. XI	Basti	H. R. Nevill	2250	321
208	9789362086556	Vol. XII	Benares	H. R. Nevill	3210	458
209	9789362089762	Vol. XIII	Bijnor	H. R. Nevill	2540	363
210	9789362087522	Vol. XIV	Budaun	H. R. Nevill	2650	378
211	9789362085665	Vol. XV	Bulandshahr	H. R. Nevill	2930	419
212	9789362080899	Vol. XVI	Cawnpore	H. R. Nevill	3090	442
213	9789362082237	Vol. XVII	Dehra Dun	H. G. Walton	2390	342
214	9789362089489	Vol. XVIII	Etah	E. R. Neave	2240	320
215	9789362086983	Vol. XIX	Etawah	D. L. Drake Brockman	1940	277
216	9789362081650	Vol. XX	Farrukhabad	E. R. Neave	2270	324
217	9789362083326	Vol. XXI	Fatehpur	H. R. Nevill	2640	377
218	9789362081018	Vol. XXII	Fyzabad	H. R. Nevill	2370	339
219	9789362086907	Vol. XXIII	Garhwal	H. G. Walton	1780	254
220	9789362085092	Vol. XXIV	Ghazipur	H. R. Nevill	2240	320
221	9789362083272	Vol. XXV	Gonda	H. R. Nevill	2310	330
222	9789362088185	Vol. XXVI	Gorakhpur	H. R. Nevill	2650	378
223	9789362082756	Vol. XXVII	Hamirpur	D. L. Drake Brockman	1940	277
224	9789362081780	Vol. XXVIII	Hardoi	H. R. Nevill	2350	336
225	9789362085641	Vol. XXIX	Jalaun	D. L. Drake Brockman	1650	236
226	9789362080998	Vol. XXX	Jaunpur	H. R. Nevill	2450	350
227	9789362088123	Vol. XXXI	Jhansi	D. L. Drake Brockman	2740	391
228	9789362081568	Vol. XXXII	Kheri	H. R. Nevill	2310	330
229	9789362088161	Vol. XXXIII	Lucknow	H. R. Nevill	2460	352
230	9789362081155	Vol. XXXIV	Mainpuri	H. R. Nevill	2440	348
231	9789362086839	Vol. XXXV	Meerut	H. R. Nevill	3040	434
232	9789362080400	Vol. XXXVI	Mirzapur	D. L. Drake Brockman	3400	486
233	9789362088666	Vol. XXXVII	Moradabad	H. R. Nevill	2660	380
234	9789362082213	Vol. XXXVIII	Muttra	D. L. Drake Brockman	3000	428
235	9789362083555	Vol. XXXIX	Muzaffarnagar	H. R. Nevill	3160	451
236	9789362080820	Vol. XL	Naini Tal	H. R. Nevill	2640	377
237	9789362087799	Vol. XLI	Partabgarh	H. R. Nevill	2180	312
238	9789362082022	Vol. XLII	Pilibhit	H. R. Nevill	2200	314
239	9789362085337	Vol. XLIII	Rai Bareli	H. R. Nevill	2250	322
240	9789362088901	Vol. XLIV	Rampur	H. R. Nevill	1640	234
241	9789362082664	Vol. XLV	Saharanpur	H. R. Nevill	3070	438
242	9789362088406	Vol. XLVI	Shahjahanpur	H. R. Nevill	2110	302
243	9789362089823	Vol. XLVII	Sitapur	H. R. Nevill	2220	317
244	9789362083913	Vol. XLVIII	Sultanpur	H. R. Nevill	1860	266
245	9789362081544	Vol. XLIX	Unnao	H. R. Nevill	2140	305

GAZETTEER

OF THE

MULTAN DISTRICT,

BY

E. D. MACLAGAN, Esquire, C.S.,

Settlement Officer.

1901-02.

Revised Edition.

Compiled and Published under the Authority

OF THE

PUNJAB GOVERNMENT.

LAHORE : "CIVIL AND MILITARY GAZETTE" PRESS.

1902.

PREFACE.

The present edition of the Multan District Gazetteer is based on the first edition, which was issued in 1884: but the material has been brought up to date, and has, in many cases, been entirely recast. Considerable use has been made of the information collected in Rai Hukm Chand's *Tawárikh-i-Multán*, which was published shortly after the Revenue Settlement of 1873-1880, and the Editor is under special obligations to several members of the staff of the recent Settlement (1896-1901) for help in the production of the present work.

September 1892.

TABLE OF CONTENTS.

CHAPTER I.—THE DISTRICT.

SUBJECT. *Page.*

CHAPTER II.—HISTORY.

CHAPTER III.—THE PEOPLE.

Section A.—Statistical—

Section B.—Social and Religious Life—

SUBJECT. *Page.*

CHAPTER III.—THE PEOPLE—*continued.*

Section B.—Social and Religious Life—*concluded.*

Section C.—Tribes, Castes and Leading Families—

Section D.—Village Communities and Tenures—

SUBJECT. *Page.*

CHAPTER III.—THE PEOPLE—*concluded.*

Section D.—Village Communities and Tenures—*concluded.*

CHAPTER IV.—PRODUCTION AND DISTRIBUTION.

Section A.—Agriculture, Arboriculture and Live-Stock—

SUBJECT.	Page.

CHAPTER IV.—PRODUCTION AND DISTRIBUTION—*continued.*

Section A—Agriculture, Arboriculture and Live Stock—*concluded.*

Section B.—Occupations, Industries and Commerce—

SUBJECT. *Page.*

CHAPTER IV.—PRODUCTION AND DISTRIBUTION—*concluded.*

Section B.—Occupations, Industries and Commerce—*concluded.*

Section C.—Prices, Weights and Measures, and Communications—

CHAPTER V.—ADMINISTRATION AND FINANCE.

Section A.—General—

SUBJECT. *Page.*

CHAPTER V.—ADMINISTRATION AND FINANCE—*continued.*

Section B.—Land and Land Revenue—

Section C.—The Canals—

I.—THE OLD INUNDATION CANALS.

II.—HAJIWAH CANAL.

III.—THE SIDHNAI CANAL.

SUBJECT. Page.

CHAPTER V—ADMINISTRATION AND FINANCE.—*concluded.*

Section C.—The Canals—*concluded.*

Table No. I.— Showing LEADING STATISTICS.

1	2	3	4	5	6	7	8
Detail.	District.	Detail of Tahsils.					
		Multan.	Shujabad.	Lodhran.	Mailsi.	Kabirwala.	
Total square miles (1899) according to village papers	5,948	934	683	1,061	1,660	1,610	
Cultivated square miles (1899) according to village papers.	1,569	356	363	280	308	362	
Culturable square miles (1899) according to village papers.	3,826	504	331	699	1,201	1,091	
Irrigated square miles (1899) ...	828	228	166	155	142	137	
Square miles under crops, average (1894-95 to 1898-99).	1,116	281	229	188	192	226	
Annual rainfall (April to March) in inches, average (1889-90 to 1899-1900).	7·96	7·96	5·76	5·12	5·90	6·64	
Total number of inhabited towns and villages (1901).	1,357	290	150	264	332	321	
Total population (1901) ...	710,626	232,126	124,907	113,359	109,727	130,507	
Rural population (1901) ...	601,975	144,732	113,878	165,657	1097 27	127,981	
Urban population (1901) ...	108,651	87,394	11,029	7,702	...	2,526	
Total population per square mile (1901).	119	249	183	106	66	81	
Rural population per square mile 1901).	101	155	167	99	66	79	
Hindus (1901) ...	133,560	55,117	20,882	20,871	16,296	20,394	
Sikhs (1901) ...	4,662	2,224	586	169	146	1,537	
Jains (1901) ...	134	134	...	...	...	...	
Musalmans (1901) ...	570,254	172,679	103,432	92,303	93,285	108,553	
Estimated average annual land revenue (new assessment).	13,39,844	3,67,282	2,74,391	1,61,018	1,49,789	3,87,364	
Average annual gross revenue (1895-1899*).	12,44,209	...	...	...	...	...	

* Land revenue, local rates, income tax, excise and stamps.

CHAPTER I.

THE DISTRICT.

Section A.—Description.

Chapter I.

Descriptive. Boundaries.

The Multan district lies between north latitude 29° 22′ and 30° 45′, and east longitude 71° 4′ and 72° 55′. It is bounded on the east, north and west by the districts of Montgomery, Jhang and Muzaffargarh, and on the south by the feudatory State of Baháwalpur. Roughly speaking, the Sutlej separates it from Baháwalpur, and the Chenáb from Muzaffargarh, but in the case of Jhang and Montgomery the boundary is an artificial one, running for the most part through desert country. The boundary with Montgomery has been maintained fairly consistently from the time of annexation, but the Jhang boundary has sometimes altered, always in the direction of increasing the Multan territories. The greater part of the Trans-Rávi tract was added to Multan in 1851, the river having previously formed the boundary. In 1880 five more villages on the lower Rávi were transferred, so that the whole of the area dependent for inundation on the Rávi might be included in the Multan district. Again, in 1898, eight more villages near the confluence of the Rávi and Chenáb were absorbed, with the object of facilitating certain extensions of the Sidhnai Canal system in that direction; and with the recent advent of the Chenáb Canal into the neighbourhood, it is possible that further changes in the district boundaries may take place. To the west, the deep stream of the Chenáb formed an ever-varying boundary until the year 1893, when it was laid down that specified villages should always remain portions of the Multan and Muzaffargarh districts respectively, whether they were on the right or the left bank of the river. The district of Multan as now constituted forms a rough triangle having as its basis the Montgomery line, and its apex the point of junction of the Chenab and Sutlej. The length of the base is about 60 miles; that of the Chenab line 100 miles as the crow flies and that of the Sutlej some 20 or 30 miles longer.

Area and general description.

The total area of the district, according to the village survey carried out in 1897 – 1899, is 5,948 square miles, of which 2,257 square miles are Government waste. The area, excluding Government waste, was thus 3,691 square miles, of which, again, only 1,572 were returned as cultivated, and of which only 1,237 were found to be on an average under crops. The cultivation

Chapter I.

Descriptive.

Area and general description.

was thus only 27 per cent. of the total area, whilst only 21 per cent. was actually under crop. The district is divided into five tahsils; and some leading statistics regarding the district and these tahsils are given in Table No. I. opposite the first page of this volume. The district contains one town of more than 10,000 souls, namely, Multan, with a population (including cantonments) of 87,394. The administrative head-quarters are situated at Multan, on the North-Western Railway, four miles from the left bank of the Chenáb, on about the middle point of the western boundary of the district. Multan stands 4th in order of area and 18th in order of population among the 32 districts of the province, comprising 6·3 per cent. of the total area, 3·5 per cent. of the total population, and 4·7 per cent. of the urban population of the British part of the Punjab territories. The latitude, longitude, and height in feet above the sea of the head-quarter station of each tahsil are shown in the margin.

	North latitude.	East longitude.	Feet above sea level.
Multan ...	30° 12′	71° 31′	402
Shujabad ...	29° 53′	71° 20′	380
Lodhrán ...	29° 32′	71° 41′	380
Mailsi ...	29° 47′	72° 15′	431
Kabírwála ...	30° 24′	71° 55′	437

Tahsils.

As will be gathered from the above statistics, the district is divided into five tahsils. The head-quarters of the Multan, Shujabad and Mailsi tahsils have been at those places from the beginning of British rule. Those of the Lodhrán* tahsil were for two or three years at Kot Pir Saadat until they were removed to their present situation on the high road from Multan to Bahawálpur. The head-quarters of the northernmost tahsil were at Sarai Siddhu till August 1889, when, in consequence of the changes caused by the Sidhnai Canal, they were transferred to Kabírwála. As regards the internal boundaries of these tahsils, there have, exclusive of small alterations, been three main changes made since annexation. Firstly, during the Settlement of 1856—1859 a large stretch of desert country lying between the old bed of the Bias and its old right-hand high bank were transferred from the Sarai Siddhu to the Mailsi tahsil. Then, in 1881, a series of changes were made with the object of enlarging the Shujabad and decreasing the Mailsi charge: under these arrangements the Shujabad tahsil, which formerly only reached to the old Biás, was extended southwards by the addition of 27 villages from Lodhrán, so as to include all the area ordinarily irrigated from the Chenáb river, and at the same time 60 villages in the neighbourhood of Kahror were transferred from the Mailsi to the Lodhrán tahsil. Even after

* This name, derived from the Lodhra tribe, is sometimes pronounced with the accent on the last syllable as though it were a Persian word, but in common parlance the accent is on the first syllable, and it is often spoken of among the people as Lodhre or Lodhreán.

Chapter I
Descriptive.
Tahsils.

these changes were made, however, the Mailsi tahsil was still found too unwieldly, and Shujabad too light a charge, and further alterations were made in 1897, by which the greater part of the remainder of the Jalálpur thána, consisting of 46 villages, was transferred from Lodhrán to Shujabad, while 104 villages to the east of Kahror were taken over from Mailsi in compensation.

The rivers.

The whole of the tract is an alluvial plain sloping gently from the north-east to the south-west, with a slight slope also from the north-west to the south-east. It is all of comparatively, and much of it of very, recent formation. The past physical history of the district is in fact the history of the rivers, which have made up the formation: and an exceedingly difficult history it is to unravel.*

The Rávi.

The Rávi would seem to have had three different courses within historical times. The earliest was in a straight line from Tulamba, that is, from shortly below the point of its entering the district, to the city of Multan. This route is indicated by a slight difference in the level of the land along a certain part of the tract of country lying immediately south of Tulamba and by some marked depressions in the country round Rashida and Tatipur. The next course adopted by the stream entailed the abandonment of its bed south of Tulamba for the extraordinary reach known as the Sidhnai (*i.e.*, the straight river), which is a perfectly straight cutting some ten or twelve miles in length from a little west of Tulamba to a little east of Sarai Siddhu. The origin of this wonderful reach is wrapt in mystery. The Hindús, who have a temple to Síta at Kachlamba at the head of the reach, and two to Rám Chandar and Lachman at Rám Chauntra and Lachman Chauntra at the tail, tell the story that Ráma and Lachman were bathing here, and having no one to watch their clothes, commanded the river to run straight on, which it did. Other variations of the legend explain that Síta was bathing at Kachlamba, and that the river straightened out to enable the brothers to see her from Rám Chauntra; or that some beautiful goddess (name unknown), who was bathing in the river, was pursued by the River-god, who, as she hid behind successive corners, straightened them out to obtain a view of her. The Muhammadans also have their own stories to tell. Some say that the Sidhnai reach was excavated by a Muhammadan king, whose name is no longer remembered. Others tell how, when Dára Shikoh was being pursued by Aurangzeb, one of his followers, to whom he entrusted his crown, threw it into the Rávi to prevent its falling into the hands of his pursuers, and how Aurangzeb, in order to recover the crown, diverted the Rávi by the

* Some attempts have been made in Cunningham's *Ancient Geography of India*, pp. 221-2, in Major Raverty's article on 'The Mihran of Sind and its Tributaries' (J. A. S. B., 1893, vol. lxi.), and in Surgeon-Major Oldham's article on the 'Lost River of the Indian Desert' in the *Calcutta Review*, July 1874.

Chapter I.

Descriptive.

Sidhnai reach into the Chenáb. From sober history we obtain as little aid as from these versatile fictions, for in no historical or geographical work does any clear indication appear to be given, either of the origin of this reach or of the date of its formation. Against the theory that the reach was artificially made, are the width of the bed and the absence of all traces of excavation : on the other hand, it is equally difficult to imagine the river cutting for itself a perfectly straight channel through the highest and hardest land in the neighbourhood. From whatever origin it has sprung, the reach as it now stands presents in flood time a most imposing and beautiful spectacle, probably not to be surpassed on any of the rivers of the Punjab plains ; either side being overhung with a rich growth of graceful trees, among which the date-palm is the most plentiful and prominent.* From the lower end of this striking reach the river used in former times to bend its course southwards, joining the older bed about Rashída, and passing on like the older river, to the neighbourhood of Multan. This course of the river lay almost through the centre of the area now irrigated by the Sidhnai Canal ; and in many of the Sidhnai villages the depressions which it has left are still spoken of as 'rávís.' From the banks of the river as it so ran were taken off a large number of canals and water-courses, the remains of which (known as *árás*,) are still prominent in the neighbourhood of Makhdúm Rashíd, Kádirpur Ran and other Sidhnai villages, but are slowly disappearing before the mattock of the cultivator. The presence of the Rávi at Multan is attested as early as A.D. 712, when the city was taken by Muhammad Bin Kásim; and though tradition states that when the Gardezis settled in Multan at the end of the 11th century the river had left the city, we find that in Tamerlane's time the Rávi joined the Chenáb below Multan. In 1502 A.D. we hear of the Rávi being adopted as the boundary between the Lodi and Langáh dominions, and of its being then only 20 miles from Shorkot†; a fact which would seem to indicate the existence of the Sidhnai reach, and possibly also the junction of the Rávi with the Chenáb (as at present) shortly below the reach. The statement of Abul Fazl,‡ that the Rávi and Chenáb at the end of the sixteenth century joined at Zafarpur (a place no longer identifiable), 27 *kos* from the confluence of the Chenáb and Jhelum, and 60 *kos* from that of the Chenáb and Indus, has been held to show that the Rávi and Chenáb then joined in much the same neighbourhood as at present; and this is not inconsistent with the other indications of the Ain, so far as these can be followed. In the days of Aurangzeb, however, there is no doubt that the Rávi again ran past

* Masson, who travelled along the reach about the year 1827, says ; 'The margins of the stream are fringed with groves of date-trees in which numerous wells are found, shaded by *pipals*. The opposite bank being embellished in like manner, the scenery up and down the river is fine and attractive.' (Travels i. 401)

†Ferishta iv. 393-5. Tab. Akb. Ell. v. 469.

‡ Ain ii. 326 (Jarrett's Translation).

Chapter I.

Descriptive.

The Rávi.

Multan: for we hear of the Emperor's camp being pitched in A.D. 1658 at Multan within 3 miles of the place where the Chenáb and Rávi met*; and the revenue village or *mahal* of Multan was divided in this same period into portions called *'tarafs,'* of which one, on the south-east of the city, retains the name of Taraf Rávi to this day. And writing as late as the end of the 18th century, the geographer Bernoulli † (depending, it is true, on sources of information which may have been somewhat out of date) remarks that the right bank of the Rávi was 2 or 3 miles from Multan, and that a branch of that river, known as the Monan, ran within a mile of the city. Even in comparatively recent years previous to the intervention of the Sidhnai cultivation, it was not unusual in flood time for a spill to pass from the Rávi down the old bed as far as the suburbs of the city; but as to the date on which the river finally diverted its course, so as to join with the Chenáb, as now, in the neighbourhood of Chauki Muhan,‡ it is impossible to make any statement. Indeed, it is very likely that the course of this river has undergone several marked alterations in either direction during historica times, and it is impossible to be sure without definite information as to the position which it occupied at any particular date.

The volume of water in the Rávi during the winter months has much decreased owing to the supplies taken off by the Bári Doáb Canal, and for the greater part of the cold weather its bed in this district is absolutely dry. When there is water in the river the whole of this is rendered available for irrigation by the dam at the head of the Sidhnai Canal; and the irrigation, owing to the rich quality of the silt in suspension, is of an excellent character. The river above the Sidhnai reach has of late years been straightening itself out, and has thus deprived many villages of the inundations on which they used to depend; while, at the same time, it has shown a marked tendency to scour its bed and thus reduce the surface level of the water. Although, therefore, in many ways the most interesting of the rivers of the district, the Rávi is also the most uncertain and the most disappointing.

The Chenáb.

The Chenáb,§ on the other hand, (or rather the united Jhelum and Chenáb) is, where it flows through this district, an imposing river, never dry, and never even fordable except in remarkably dry winters. It is not unlikely that the Chenáb originally flowed in a course some miles to the east of its present bed, passing, in fact, the same route as that above described as having at one time (*viz.*, after being abandoned by the Chenáb) occupied by the Rávi between Sarai Siddhu and

---

*Alamgírnama, pp. 200, *seq.*

†Desc. Ind. i. 116.

‡ This village derives its name from the fact of its being at the mouth of the Rávi.

§ Locally pronounced Chanha.

Chapter I.

Descriptive.

The Chenáb.

Rashída. While the Chenáb was in this bed, both Shorkot and Multan lay to the west of the river; and it is held by some authorities* that Multan lay to the west of the Chenáb as late as A.D. 1245, when the country was attacked by the Moghal Manguta. The river, however, flowed to the west of the city (as it now does) in the days of Albiruni, that is to say, in the 11th century, and it was also to the west of the city at the time of Tamerlane's invasion and at the time of the writing of the Ain-i-Akbari; and it is probable that Multan has lain east of the Chenáb for at least five centuries, if not longer. As it now runs the river has no very marked high bank, and the difference between the average level in January and the level of the highest floods is stated to be 13 feet. The damage which used to be done in years of excessive flood, such as 1893 and 1894, was very serious, the inundation at one time threatening even the safety of Multan itself; but steps have since been taken by a series of embankments, extending from Khatti-Chor in the Kabírwála tahsil to Dhundhun south of Shujabad, to protect the country from the possibility of such inundations in future. The Chenáb water, though less fertilizing than that of the Rávi, is more so than that of the Sutlej; and the people in the south-west of the district, whose lands receive water from both rivers, mark the difference by calling the Sutlej *nar* or male, and the Chenab *máda* or female. The stream is navigable throughout by country boats, and steamers used to ply upon it as far as Bandarghat until the breaking up of the fotilla some 20 years ago.

The Biás.

The Biás, which is known locally as the Viyáh, flowed, until comparatively recent times, in a bed, still very well marked, through the centre of the district from the neighbourhood of Pakhi Mián on the east to that of Tleh Kalán on the west. Although this bed is very small and narrow, the basin of the river in flood was fairly large, if we may judge from the remains of the right high bank, which are well marked along a great part of the course of the stream, running parallel to the old channel at a distance of several miles. On the left or southern side the old Biás has no high bank. The Biás was running in its old bed at the time of Tamerlane's invasion, and the country which it watered is described as full of supplies and prosperous towns. The river was also in its old bed in the days of the Ain-i-Akbari, and the pargana of Khai, which depended on this river for its prosperity, is described by popular rumour as a tract which yielded the traditional 'nine lakhs' of revenue. There are still remains of several canal cuts taking out from the Biás, both in the neighbourhood of Khai (near Mitru) and elsewhere; and these old canal cuts are still known to the people by their original names (Shekhwah, Lodanwah, Kálúwah, Gauharwah, etc.), though they have been out of use for many

* See Raverty (J. A. S. B., 1892, pp. 157, 159 and 165).

Chapter I.
Descriptive.
The Biás.

years. There is a story that the Biás deserted its original course because certain boatmen refused to carry a *fakir* across the stream, thereby entailing the curse of the *fakir* on everything concerned with the contretemps. As to the date at which the river left its bed to join, as it now does, with the Sutlej near Hari ka Pattan in the Lahore district, local accounts are very vague. People generally say that the event occurred some 200 years ago, and there are said to be some historical evidences of this. On the other hand, the stream is shown as flowing in its present course in Rennell's map of Hindustán, dated 1788, and there was a very old man living in 1889 who is said to have remembered the drying up of the stream in his youth.* The ordinarily accepted date for the change appears to be A.D. 1790 or 1796, † but it is possible that the process of change was only gradual.

The Sutlej.

The remaining river of the district is the Sutlej. The river is sometimes spoken of, especially in the upper part of its course, as the Níli, but the ordinary name for it is the Ghára; Satlaj or Sattluj being the '*sirkári nám*' employed in talking to officials only. This river, like the rest, has changed its course within historical times, but our information regarding its vagaries is somewhat uncertain. It is believed by some‡ that the Sutlej originally joined with a river known as the Hakra, but now lost, which used to flow through the Baháwalpur State at a distance of some 40 miles south of the present channel of the Sutlej. Abulfazl's description of the Sutlej and Biás is not very intelligible,§ but from the account given by him of the Suba of Multan, it is clear that the Sutlej in the time of Akbar ran in a bed not materially different from that which it now occupies. The river bed is narrower and more sharply defined than that of the Chenáb, and the depth of water during the cold weather seldom exceeds 12 feet, rising in flood to 18 feet. The river is in several places fordable in dry winters; and the difference between the average level in January and the level of the highest floods is only 9 feet, as compared with 13 feet on the Chenáb. The northern bank of the river is, moreover, far better defined than that of the Chenáb, and in ordinary years presents a sufficient barrier to the flooding beyond it. Near the confluence of the two rivers the intervening land is regularly flooded during the summer, but the floods come almost entirely from the Chenáb, the Sutlej, as a rule, only inundating the area below the high bank. As compared with the Chenáb, the Sutlej is very capricious in its inundations, and the area flooded varies very much from year to year. The stream is navigable throughout by

---

* *See* Raverty (J. A. S. B., 1893, p. 179); *see* also *Calcutta Review*, 1875, p. 337.

† *See* Dr. Oldham in *Calcutta Review*, July 1874, and Cunningham's *Ancient Geography*, p. 222.

‡ *See* Dr. Oldham's article referred to. This view is strongly opposed in another article by 'Nearchus' in *Calcutta Review*, 1875, p. 323, *seq.*

§ *See* Ain (Jarrett), ii. 326.

Chapter I. Descriptive. River discharges, etc.

country boats, and in the days of steam navigation steamers occasionally went up as far as Ferozepore.

There are no data to show the discharges of the Sutlej river in this district, but there are records for the Chenáb at Sher Shah since 1890, which give the following minimum discharges:—

Year.		*Minimum discharge.*	*Year.*		*Minimum discharge.*
1891-92	...	12,200	1896-97	...	11,600
1892-93	...	15,550	1897-98	...	10,100
1893-94	...	21,900	1898-99	...	5,900
1894-95	...	21,300	1899-1900	...	5,400
1895-96	...	20,300			

The question of the supply of water in the rivers is of considerable interest in connection with the canal-system of the district and with the complaints often made that the canals have suffered from the construction of the Sirhind and Chenáb Canals. The Sirhind Canal was opened in 1883-84, began to develop in 1887-88, and was in full working order in 1891-92; while the Chenáb canal was opened in 1887-88, began to develop in 1892-93, and was practically in full working order in 1897-98. The canals of this district begin to flow in the spring when the floods rise, and cease flowing in the autumn when the floods subside, so that the effect of canals above-stream would be felt mainly in the months of April and October. The average gauge readings on the rivers have been as follows*:—

	Chenab River.			Sutlej River.		
	For whole year.	For April.	For October.	For whole year.	For April.	For October.
1879—1883	391·13	390·78	390·04	370·96	369·79	370·46
1884—1888	391·84	392·51	390·07	371·22	369·76	371·27
1889—1893	391·80	391·96	390·55	371·25	369·95	371·33
1894—1898	381·13	382·18	379·24	370·23	368·45	369·64

* The Chenáb readings were at Bandarghát till December 1894, when the gauge was removed to Sher Shah. The Sutlej readings are at Adamwahan.

Chapter I.

Descriptive.

River discharges, &c.

The average annual period for which the canals were running are given below*: —

	Chenab River.			Sutlej River.		
	Average date of opening of canals.	Average date of closing of canals.	Period of running of canals.	Average date of opening of canals.	Average date of closing of canals.	Period of running of canals.
			Days.			Days.
1865—69 ...	26 April..	25 Sept....	152	19 April...	10 Oct. ...	175
1870—74 ...	17 " ...	27 " ...	163	3 May ..	9 " ...	159
1875—79 ...	22 " ...	28 " ...	159	13 April..	11 " ...	182
1880—84 ...	21 " ..	4 Oct. ...	166	2 " ...	17 " ...	199
1885—89 ...	24 " ...	22 Sept....	151	8 " ...	22 " ...	198
1890—94 ...	22 " ...	1 Oct. ...	162	20 " ...	9 " ...	174
1895—99 ...	29 " ...	1 " ...	155	7 May ...	8 " ...	155

The average areas irrigated (including failed areas) by the inundation canals, other than the Hájiwah canal, have been :—

	Chenáb Canals,	*Sutlej Canals,*
	Acres.	*Acres.*
1868-69 to 1872-73	101,353 ...	111,165
1873-74 to 1877-78	130,407 ...	137,249
1878-79 to 1882-83	154,380 ...	169,097
1883-84 to 1887-88	157,716 ...	173,706
1888-89 to 1892-93	164,531 ...	189,507
1893-94 to 1897-98	170,879 ...	171,119

Configuration of the district.

Strictly speaking, the district (if we omit consideration of the Trans-Rávi tract, which geographically is rather a portion of the Jhang district) consists of two main portions, *viz.*, (i) the high central plateau between the old bed of the Rávi and the old right bank of the Biás, a tract which is looked upon as the *bár* proper, though the term is also commonly applied to all lands outside the reach of the river; and (ii) a low alluvial plain sloping away from this central plateau towards the beds of the rivers. For practical purposes, however, it is more convenient to look on the district as composed of three distinctive tracts, namely, (*a*) the tract within the sphere of the direct influence of the rivers, (*b*) that reached by the canals, and (*c*) that beyond the reach of the canals.

The riverain.

The riverain tract, which is spoken of as the Hithár or the 'Kandha Daryá,' presents much the same features as similar tracts in other parts of the province. In the winter we find a straggling, sluggish stream, meandering between sandbanks,

* This relates to the four large Chenáb Canals (*viz.*, the Daurána Langána, Wali Muhammad, Sikandarabad and Gajjubatta), and to all the Sutlej Canals except the Hájiwah.

Chapter I.

Descriptive.

The riverain.

and along its sides long stretches of low tamarisk scrub, interspersed with long fields of gram. or wheat, or peas. In July come the floods (*chhal*), and the whole of the lower tract adjoining the river is inundated with water. Where there is an inlet towards the areas further from the river, or where the slope to the river bed is very gradual, the inundation spreads further inland, and (especially in the south-western corner of the district) penetrates by creeks and natural depressions to villages far distant from the river. Where the river is a full and vigorous stream like the Chenáb, the riverain villages are in many places protected by embankments against its encroachments, but the moisture will percolate much further inland than the actual floods themselves. Where the river is more feeble, as in the case of the Sutlej, its inundations are, as a rule, confined to the areas below the high bank; but the existence of the bank enables the zamíndárs to make more frequent use of *jhalárs* for conveying the river water on to the higher lands. The areas under the direct influence of the river are usually very bare of trees; but in the higher lands subject to the indirect benefit of the river moisture, trees and vegetation of all kinds are more luxuriant than in the tracts further inland.

The canal irrigated tract.

It is in the tract intervening between the riverain and the *bár* that the canals find their sphere of action. The canals of this district are (with the exception of the Sidhnai) inundation canals, running only when there is sufficient flood in the river to reach the level of their beds at the places where they take off from the river. An account of these canals will be given in Chapter V below; and meantime it will suffice to notice that the course of these canals and of their branches is generally manifested to the eye by a line of vegetation and a series of high spoil banks. The watercourses by which the water is taken from the canals to the fields, require, like the canals themselves, an annual silt clearance, and the banks on either side tend thus to grow higher year by year. The cultivation dependent on these canals is aided by an immense number of wells dotted over the tract under consideration, each with its Persian wheel attached and its cattle byres adjoining. The greater number of the cultivators live in houses round these wells in groups of three or four families to each well; but in many places there is some central well or other spot where the chief landowners, and artizans, and others are more especially congregated. Both the individual wells and the larger villages or *bastis* are, as a rule, distinguished to the eye by the cluster of trees that adjoins them, but elsewhere, except along the banks of canals and watercourses, this intermediate tract of country is marked by little in the shape of tree vegetation.

The bár.

There remains the third tract of high land beyond the reach of the canals, which is known by the general name of

Chapter I.

Descriptive.

The bár.

'the *bár*.' The high tract between the old banks of the Rávi and Biás is known properly as the Ganji *bár*. Between this and the Chenáb lies the Ráwa or Rávi *bár* (a term which for revenue purposes has been applied to the whole *bár* tract of the district); and to the south lie the Biás *bár* and the Nili *bár* on the old Biás and Sutlej respectively. The Ganji *bár* would be a comparatively sterile waste were it not for a scanty growth of *jand* and *jal* trees; as it is, water is obtained at depth of 40 to 48 feet, and is employed for drinking only, the tract being frequented only by camel breeders. Of the Ráwa proper or Rávi *bár* the greater part has been encroached upon by the irrigation of the Sidhnai Canal, and the remainder consists for the most part of a fairly thickly wooded tract, known as the *jhangar*, the more valuable portions of which have been set apart by Government as reserved forests for the production of firewood. The *bár* country to the south of the high bank of the old Biás, again, differs entirely in its features from the Rávi *bár*; the country being but slightly above the level of the Sutlej, and of comparatively recent alluvial formation, the upper soil is with the aid of water capable of producing good crops, and the country is here and there well wooded, but deep sand is met with a few feet below the surface;* and in the absence of water artificially supplied, the country for mile after mile is completely desolate and sterile without a trace of grass or other vegetation.

Rainfall.

There is a recording station for rainfall at each of the tahsil head-quarters, and the results of the records are shown in tables III, IIIA and IIIB of this Gazetteer. The average recorded rainfall of the district for the 10 years ending 1899-1900 is 6·27 inches, and the district shares very little either in the summer or in the winter rains.† The natives will say: "When we see a cloud, we exclaim, 'it has rained.'" The rainfall, besides being scanty, is very irregularly distributed, and heavy falls may occur in one place, while a village ten miles off may be left untouched. The town of Kahror considers itself especially badly treated in this matter; and the saying there is: "Ai Kahror di wári, há minh te thí gai andhári" that is to say, that when Kahror's turn for rain comes, the rain becomes a mere dust-storm. It is impossible to say whether the tahsil head-

* The sandy nature of the soil greatly increases the cost and difficulty of sinking wells, as it is necessary not only to have masonry sides but to line the masonry with wattles. The soil, too, is so yielding that it cannot (so the people say) bear the weight of buffaloes treading round the wells, and bullocks only can be used to work them.

† The traveller Albiruni, writing in the 14th century, says: 'The people of Multan used to tell me that they have no Varsha-Kála (rainy season).' (Sach 211). But the same author in contesting the supposed age of the idol of the sun at Multan wrote, 'How could wood have lasted such a length of time, particularly in a place where the air and soil are rather wet.' The immense damage done by the heavy rains during Tamerlane's invasion (A.D. 1397) is noted in Chapter II below. The most remarkable fall of recent times is probably that of the 28th-29th July 1892 when 8·48 inches fell at Multan within 48 hours.

Chapter I.

Descriptive.
Rainfall.

quarters, where the rain is registered, have higher or lower falls of rain than the average village; but in Mailsi, where the tahsil head-quarters lie at the southern corner of the tahsil, it is probable that the tahsil record falls short of the average of the tahsil. There are old zamíndárs, who will explain to you that the blessing of heaven cannot be expected to fall as copiously at places like tahsil head-quarters, where so much perjury is committed, as eleswhere; but we have at present no statistics to test this theory. The Canal Department have lately started some registering stations at their bungalows, which may at some future period shed further light on the subject. The rain, though so scanty in this district, is still of no little agricultural importance. There is, it is true, but little cultivation dependent on the summer rains, but the growth of grass, on which the welfare of the cattle hangs, is closely connected with the amount ot the summer rainfall. And although little or none of the rabi crop is sown with the aid of rain, a great part of it depends for its maturity very largely on the timeliness and quantity of the winter rain.

There are two sayings of the people on the subject of the rainfall which are worth noting, as showing the connection in their minds between rain and thunder. On the one hand they say:—

Awe to na bháwe ... ... Thukk hai us áwan kún
Kháwe to na máwe .. ... Thukk hai us kháwan kún
Gajje to ne wasse ... ... Thukk hai us Sáwan kún

'To come and not be welcome is a poor coming; to eat and not digest is a poor eating; to thunder and not rain is a poor July.' On the other hand, if they wish to point out that much talk means little action' they say, 'Jera gajje o wasse nahín.' 'If there is thunder, there is no rain.'

Climate.

The heat and dust of Multan are proverbial. The day temperature in the summer months is high, but this is counterbalanced by a comparatively cool night. Usually at night a breeze springs up, which prevents that feeling of suffocation felt in some other places where the actual temperature recorded may not be so high, but where the air is still. No doubt the high temperature is due to the comparative want of moisture in the atmosphere, which renders it diathermic, permitting the passage of the heat rays more freely than when it is laden with moisture. The soil, too, absorbs and reflects the heat to a high degree; yet once the sun goes down, the pure dry air allows of the rapid radiation of heat from the soil, thus giving as a compensation to the heat of the day a cool night. Table No. IV shows the average temperature of the three months, May, July and December, for the years extending from 1868-69 to 1898-99. The highest day temperatures are recorded in the end of May and beginning of June. The difference between the maximum and minimun temperatures in May is as much as 42 degrees.

Chapter I.

Descriptive.
Climate.

The climate of the district is not so bad as it is often painted. As elsewhere in the Punjab, the cold weather is delightful, and the hot weather, though a long one, is probably more endurable than that of most plain stations in the province. In March there are some hot days, but a storm or series of storms generally comes, and the mornings and evenings remain fairly cool till well into May. From then to the end of June it rapidly gets hotter, the last week or ten days of June being usually very oppressive. For some reason or other, although there seems to be only too much hot wind, tatties will not work in Multan. What the weather will be from the end of June to the beginning of the cold weather is a great chance. In favourable years a slight breeze sets in with the rains, and continues to blow on and off throughout July; in August there are generally some hot steamy days; in September the days are still hot, but the mornings and evenings become cool, and this coolness increases until the cold weather sets in, generally with a thunderstorm, about October 15th, but it is too hot to be pleasant in tents till the middle of November. This is the weather in favourable years; in unfavourable ones no breeze sets in, and as soon as the scanty showers cease the whole place begins to steam.

Health.

The district, as a whole, is healthy. The statistics regarding the births and deaths in the district will be found in Tables XI, XIA and XIB, and those for births and deaths in the towns in Table XLIV; and further remarks on the subject of these data will be found in Chapter III below.

Cholera is a rare visitant. In 1892 there was an epidemic causing 1,939 deaths; the next epidemic was in 1899, when there were 117 deaths. In the interval the disease was absent.

Malarial fevers are more or less prevalent, but the death-rate from this class of disease is considerably affected by the rainfall. In 1892, for instance, there was an enormous death-rate owing entirely to the increase of fevers in consequence of the heavy rainfall. The parts of the district near Jalálpur and Shujabad are subject to floods, and this detrimentally affects the health of the population. Spleen is common in this part of the district, and also asthma of a malarial origin—the two diseases often going together, and both being the result of repeated attacks of fever. Malarial fevers are most prevalent during the months of October, November, December and January. Speaking generally, however, there is not much fever in Multan: and there is a good deal of truth in the people's saying that 'Multan is healthy except when it rains—and it never rains.'

Eye diseases are rife, particularly those forms which affect the lids; large numbers of people being the subjects of granular ophthalmia in all its stages, from mere irritation to destruction of the eye as an organ of vision.

Chapter I.
Descriptive.
Health.

Stone in the bladder is also common, the actual cause being still undecided. This disease affects children as well as old persons. It is difficult to say whether it affects males and females equally, owing to the reluctance of the latter to undergo treatment.

The average death-rate per 1,000 for the period 1890—99 on the population of 1881 is 33·94; the birth-rate 47·41 per 1,000.

Geology.

The soil of the district is of an alluvial character, and sand is everywhere met at a short distance below the surface. The geology of the district has, however, been subjected to very little detailed enquiry; and readers are referred to the sketch of the geology of the Punjab as a whole, which was prepared by Mr. Medlicott, late Superintendent of the Geological Survey of India, and which has been published *in extenso* in the Provincial volume of the Gazetteer series, and also as a separate pamphlet.

Mineral products.

There was a certain amount of salt manufacture under native rule in places where *kallar* soil was prevalent, more especially in the Shujabad Tahsil, and the Nunars or salt workers have left their names attached to mounds, wells, &c., in various parts of the district, but such manufacture is no longer permitted under our salt laws. Even saltpetre is only manufactured in moderate quantities; in 1897-99 an average number of 13 licenses were granted per annum to cover an average manufacture of 5,000 maunds. A little *kankar* is also here and there found sparsely on the surface and a certain amount of *kankar* was at one time dug up from the bed of the Sidhnai reach in the Kabirwála tahsil.

Trees.*

The principal trees of the district are the Jand (*Prosopis spicigera*), Karril (*Capparis aphylla*), Farásh (*Tamarix articulata*), Van (*Salvadora oleioides*), Kikar (*Acacia arabica*), Sisham (*Dalbergia sissoo*), Ber (*Zizyphus jujuba*), Tut (*Morus alba*), Sirin (*Albizzia Lebbek*), Bohar (*Ficus indica*), Pipal (*Ficus religiosa*), Khajji (*Phœnix dactylifera*), Bhan (*Populus euphratica*), Amb (*Mangifera indica*), and the Ním (*Melia indica*). The first four are found all over the *bár*, and are in fact the only trees that flourish in the dry arid tracts of the district. The others prefer a fairly moist soil, and (with the exception of the last two) are met with on *sailâba* and irrigated lands, along canal cuts, and in depressions that are subjected to periodical inundations; while the two last named are generally found in gardens

* The information given below regarding the flora and fauna of the district has been kindly supplied by Mr. C. Rossiter of the Forest Department, who has been long and intimately acquainted with the natural products of Multan.

Chapter I. Descriptive. Trees.

The *kikar* is the most useful of those to the agriculturist. He roofs his house with its wood. His Persian water-lifts, carts and agricultural implements are generally made from it. The bark supplies him with tannin, and the leaves, twigs, and seed-pods with fodder; while the thorny branches are used for fencing in his fields and making sheep-pens, &c.

Next in point of importance is probably the *jand*, which, together with the *farásh*, *karril* and *van*, keep the local markets supplied with fuel. These four are the principal forest trees in the district. They are capable of withstanding long seasons of drought, and when properly cut, coppice freely. Camels, goats and sheep are very fond of their foliage, and when grass is scarce kine even browse off the plants with apparent relish The tender seed-pods of the *jand* are made into a sort of spinach, and are eaten by the people; and in times of famine even the ripe dry pods are used. On such occasions the seeds are removed from the pod, and the outer covering (which contains a soft fluffy substance) is ground into flour, and after being mixed with a little *átá* is baked into cakes. The wood burns well, and is without doubt the best wood fuel that can be produced in the district. *Farásh* and *karril* also burn well, and large quantities of these woods are cut annually for the supply of locomotive fuel to the railway. The annual output from the Government forests has of late amounted to as much as 17 lakhs cubic feet, the greater portion of which has been supplied to the railway.

Farásh and *karril* or *karính* are also used for building purposes. The wood of the latter much resembles the box, and is not attacked by insects. The flower and fruit of the *karril* are eaten by both man and beast—the unripe fruit being considered a great delicacy when prepared in the form of a pickle. A dye is obtained from the *farásh* galls, which are collected and sold in the *bazars*.

The *ván* is an evergreen shady tree, the fruit of which is largely eaten by all classes of natives. During the months of May and June, when the fruit ripens, most of the poorer people leave their homes and move on to the *ván* growing localities, where they remain for weeks, living almost exclusively on the fruit. Cattle are also very fond of the fruit, and so also are hares and deer. The dried fruit somewhat resembles the currant, both in form and flavour, and in good fruiting seasons large quantities of the fruit are preserved in a dry state for future use. The wood, which is rather soft and light, is not very good for either building or fuelling purposes, though it is used for both. It keeps pretty free from the attacks of insects, and when burnt smoulders away without producing much of a flame, and leaves a large quantity of ash, which when boiled in water forms a decoction that is used for killing mange and removing hair from mangy camels. The decoction has a wonderful effect in

Chapter I.
Descriptive.
Trees.

instantaneously removing hair, one application being enough to clean shave a beast in a few minutes.

The *sisham* is a well-known tree. It is valued for its wood, which is extensively used for all articles of furniture, cart and coach building, and all articles of wood-work that require strength and elasticity.

The *ber* under favourable conditions is a fast growing tree. It attains maturity in a few years, and bears the wild plum, which is much liked by natives. The wood is close grained and tough, and is used for well curbs, light rafters, door planks and charcoal making. The twigs and leaves are eaten by camels and goats, and the branches are used for making fences.

The *tút* or mulberry-tree begins to bear fruit at a very early age. It is found near wells and watercuts, and is grown as much for its shade as for its fruit and fodder. Its wood (which is very elastic) is used for axe and hoe handles, cot legs and other petty articles. Baskets are made from its twigs, and the leaves are used for fodder; the fruit being also eaten.

The *sirin* or *shavinh* is a tree that requires a little care. It grows rapidly during its infancy, but being thornless and weedy at that stage of its growth, requires more protection than the trees already described. It is grown chiefly for its shade, but its wood (which is of a dark reddish brown colour, and rather prettily marked) is used for oil pestles and mortars, posts, door *chaukhats*, and thick planks, &c.

The *bohar* and *pipal* are cultivated principally for their shade. Both trees are held in reverence by the Hindús. The wood is of very little use except for burning. The leaves are eaten by cattle; and the milky juice makes splendid birdlime. Charcoal made from the *pípal* is very inflammable, and in the absence of better sorts of charcoal may with advantage be used in the manufacture of gunpowder. The bark yields a reddish brown dye, and the fresh milk of the *bohar* is advantageously used for removing films from the eye.

The *khajjí* or Indian date-palm is well known to those who have been to Multan. It is grown chiefly for its fruit, large quantities of which are eaten and collected for export. It is a source of some revenue to the people, who look after the tree while it is in fruit, but take little interest in its improvement. The wood is used for beams, posts and water troughs, and the leaves are made into mats, baskets, ropes and hand fans. The leaf stalks are used for fuel, and when split up furnish material for basket making, &c. The fibrous matty covering which is found at the base of the fruit stalk is used for cordage, and the stalk itself is split up and made into chicks, cages, &c. Altogether the *khajji* is a very useful plant, and is deserving of better attention.*

* See also Chapter IV below.

Chapter I.
Descriptive.
Trees.

The *Bhan* is a tree that is found along banks and islands of the Chenáb and Sutlej. It is not much valued for its wood, which, though tough, is light and not very durable. It, however, is good enough for ridge-poles of sheds and other temporary structures, as well as for fuel and for making cot legs, &c. Camels, goats and sheep are very fond of the leaves, and the tender twigs are used as tooth-brushes by natives.

There are some good *mangoes* in the district. The best are probably the Sufeda, Shahpasand and the Tory, but there are not many trees of these varieties; and although some of the others are not bad eating, they are not nearly as good as those above named. The tree is cultivated for its fruit, which is eaten both in its ripe and unripe state; and when the tree gets too old to bear, it is cut down and used for fuel, planks, rafters, beams, &c.

The *nim* is another sacred tree that is cultivated as much for its medicinal properties as for its shade. It makes a splendid avenue tree, and is used in all sorts of medicines. The dried leaves when packed with warm clothing preserve the clothing from the attacks of insects.

Shrubs.

The *mallha* (Zizyphus numularia) is a thorny plant, much resembling the Ber in leaf and fruit, but not so tall of course, and growing more in the form of a bush. The leaves make an excellent fodder, but to collect them the plant has generally to be cut. The process of collecting is not a difficult one. The cut portions of the plant are dragged to a clear open spot, and when the leaves begin to wither they are knocked off by a few heavy blows from a stick, and are collected and stored away for future use. The clean straight stems make fairly good axe handles, and the branches and thorny portions are used for making fences and sheep enclosures, while the bark yields a tannin, and the wood is good for burning.

The *phog* (Calligonum polygonoeides) is found chiefly in the sandy portions of the district. It is eaten by camels and goats, and is used for fuel and charcoal making.

The *ak* (Calotropis gigantea) is another shrub that delights in sandy soils. It grows to a height of 5 to 8 feet, and is a very useful but much abused plant. Charcoal made from it is used in the manufacture of gunpowder. The milky sap is used in various ways and for all sorts of disorders. When applied to a splinter or thorn under the nail, or indeed in any part of the body, it has a wonderful effect in immediately loosening the splinter. The point of incision of the splinter should first be opened out with a needle, care being taken not to draw blood; and then a drop or two of the fresh milk should be allowed to fall into the wound, and in a few minutes, when the milk has dried, the splinter may be easily removed with a little manipulation of the

Chapter I.
Descriptive.
Shrubs.

needle. In cases of toothache it is applied to relieve pain, but if used frequently it destroys the tooth altogether, bringing it away in chips from the socket. Tanners use the milk for removing hair from raw hides, and people suffering from scabies use it for producing a healthy growth of flesh. Snake-charmers use the root, and it is believed both the flower and milk, in cases of snake bite; while the root bark is used in all sorts of preparations by hakims. The seed floss is used for stuffing pillows; and the inner lining of the green bark yields a strong silky fibre, which is not generally used, but which is capable of being spun into a strong glossy yarn.

The *kangán khár* (Haloxylon recurvum) is the plant from which sajji or barilla is made. It is cut early in the winter when the plant is in flower, and after being allowed to dry is burnt over a basin, shaped hollow, that is previously scraped in the ground; and as the plant burns it emits a liquid substance, which settling in the bottom of the pit, is stirred up with the living coals and ash, and then covered up with earth till it cools. On the third or fourth day the pit is dug up, and a large mass of barilla is found at the bottom. The revenue from the sale of Kangan Khár found growing in the district rakhs amounts to about Rs. 4,0C0 a year.*

An inferior description of barilla is also made from the *lana* (Salsola), two distinct varieties of which are found in the district. They are both much eaten by camels and goats; and where wood is scarce, are used also for fuel.

The *Láni* (Suaeda rudiflora) is another plant that yields an inferior sort of barilla, but which is not much used for that purpose. Camels are very fond of it, and so is the field rat.

The *khip* (Leptodenia spartium) is a plant that is chiefly used for heating ovens, stuffing pack-saddles, and making the walls and roofs of sheds. In its green tender state it is munched by cattle, but is not much relished by them. It yields an indifferent fibre, which can be twisted into ropes, but which is not much used for that purpose.

Lai.—There are two varieties of this plant. The *Tamarix gallica*, which is known as the Kokan or Gaddoh Lai, is generally met with on saline soils both near and long distances away from the rivers, while the *Tamarix dioica* is to be met with on alluvial deposits. The former grows more in the form of a deformed scraggy bush, while the latter (which is used for basket making and lining unbricked wells) takes the form of an erect leading shoot. Both plants are eaten by camels and goats, and are used for fuel. The former has been known to yield a sweet semi-transparent substance much resembling lumps of sugarcandy both in flavour and appearance. During the winter of 1899-1900

* See also the account of this product given in Chapter IV A. below.

Chapter I. Descriptive. Shrubs.

the plants in the Mailsi tahsil were covered with this substance, and crowds of people were to be seen collecting and eating it.

Búin.—This is a very useless plant. It is found in all sorts of soils, and is used chiefly for heating ovens.

Rasham (Pluchea lanceolata).—This is another very useless plant. It is eaten by camels and goats, but apparently not with any relish.

Jowasa or *Jawásh* (Fagonia arabica).—This plant grows abundantly on fairly moist soils. It makes its appearance early in spring, when it is most liked by camels and goats, and lasts till the end of the rains. It is a prickly shrub standing about 18 inches high, and is used occasionally by Europeans on tour as a substitute for khaskas in getting tatty screens prepared. It answers admirably for this purpose, as it works well even with a moderately light breeze, and is easily obtained in all parts of the district.

Dhamáhán (F. bruguiera).—This much resembles the Jowasa, but is not found in such abundance, and is used chiefly in medicines.

Climbers.

The *Van Vari*, *Bakrain* and *Kurkat* are the principal climbers that are found in the district. They are all eaten by camels and goats, and are generally found on Jand trees.

Grasses.

Of the many varieties of grasses that are to be found in the district, the following are most known; and the first six are considered the best for fodder:—

Khabbal	(*Cynodon dactylon*).
Dhaman	(*Pennisetum cenchroides*).
Palwahn	(*Andropogon annulatus*).
Kheo	(*Sporobolus orientalis*).
Sowank	(*Panicum colonum*).
Chimbar	(*Eleusine aegyptiaca*).
Girram	(*Panicum antidotale*).
Khavi	(*Andropogon iwarancusa*).
Dab	(*A. muricatus*)
Nonak	(*Sporobolus diander*).
Dila	(*Scirpus maritimus*).
Kura	(*Panicum helopus*).
Sar	(*Saccharum ciliare*).
Kánh	(*S. spontaneum*).

The two last named are tall coarse grasses that are much used for thatching purposes. They are found in great abundance on low-lying alluvial deposits and on the banks of watercourses and canals. Both plants yield a fibre, but the moonj fibre of the Sar is infinitely superior to the fibre obtained from the Kánh. The Sar reed, which is known as the Kána or Sarkanda, is extensively used for making chicks, stools, chairs, and for roofing houses, while the last, or rather uppermost, joint of the reed is used for making winnowing trays, screens, boxes and baskets.

Chapter I.

Descriptive. Grasses.

Altogether the Sar is a very useful plant, and is much valued by the agriculturist, whose needs in the matter of rope and cordage are all supplied from the fibre of this plant.

Other plants.

Some *Kúndar* (Typha angustifolia) is to be found in parts of the district. It is eaten by horned cattle, and is used for making mats, thick ropes, and baskets. The fruit (known as Búrí) is sometimes used for human food.

The *kanwal* or *pabban* (Nelumbium speciosum) is the lotus, the roots, stalks and seeds of which are eaten by natives. The roots (known as Bhen) are a common food in this part of the Punjab.

Tumma or *Kartumma* (Citrullus colocynthis).—The fruit, leaves and root of this creeper are all used medicinally. It is the colocynth mentioned in the Indian Pharmacopœia.

Kandiári (Argemone Mexicana).—This is a prickly little plant that bears a spherical little fruit which much resembles a miniature brinjál. The fruit, leaves and juice of this plant are used as medicines.

The *Kakora* or wild bitter gourd is found during the rains in well sheltered low-lying localities, and is eaten by both Hindús and Muhammadans.

Chibbhar.—This is a sort of a melon that trails along the ground. It bears a mottled oval-shaped fruit, about 1½ inches long, that is eaten by both man and beast.

The *Bhakra* (Tribulus terrestris) is found all over the district. It is the plant that is so often spoken of as having been freely eaten by people in times of scarcity. Camels, goats and sheep are very fond of it, and the powdered fruit is used in kidney and urinary disorders.

The *Bokhat* (Asphodelus fistulosus) and the *Leh* or milk thistle are two very troublesome weeds to the agriculturists. They prefer a fairly moist sandy soil but are found almost anywhere, and are very difficult to eradicate. The *Itsat* (Trianthema pentandra) is another very troublesome weed. It grows with great obstinacy during the rains, and requires a lot of weeding to be kept down. The two former are winter crop weeds, while the last named is one that asserts itself during the rains. It is used medicinally, and as a pot herb too, and is eaten greedily by camels and goats.

The *Khumb* or mushroom is found during the rains, and is eaten by all classes of people.

Wild animals: sport.

Multan is not a district that one would care to go to for purposes of sport, but to those who have to travel about the district it may be interesting to know that the rifle, rod and gun can all be used in their turn to break the monotony of camp life. Gazelle, hare and partridge (both grey and black) can be found in all the reserved forests; while snipe, duck,

Chapter I.
Descriptive.
Wild animals: sport.

geese and coolen can be had along the banks of the Sutlej and Chenáb during the winter. None of these are to be found in very large numbers, but they are sufficiently plentiful to induce an officer on tour to take his guns out with him. There are no nilgai or black buck, and the only descriptions of deer that are to be met with are the chinkara (Indian gazelle) and the hog deer; the latter is found mainly in the swampy belahs of the rivers. Pig are also to be found, but they never break cover in places where they can be ridden to the spear, and they must either be shot or (in the event of their being required for a run) netted and taken to the opén. Obárah and sand-grouse visit the district during the winter. In addition to these, there are the quail, plover, pigeon and curlew, which all add to the table fare and help to make camp life pleasant. As regards the curlew, the three varieties (red crested black, grey, and white) that are known in the Punjab are all to be met with. Foxes, hares and jackals are sufficiently plentiful to afford tolerably good sport with a bobbery pack.

Wolves are occasionally to be met with (generally in pairs), but they are not destructive to human life, and are seldom even known to attack people. Badgers and wild cats are also to be found, and some good rifle practice can be made on alligators that are often seen basking on the islands and sand-banks of the rivers.*

The Chuhras (people of the sweeper caste) shikar a lizard called the sáhna or sanda. This repulsive looking creature is about 10 inches long. It is gregarious in its habits, and is found in the bár, living in holes about 4 feet deep. The burrows slope to an angle of about 33° and are provided with two chambers, one just below the entrance of the hole and the other at the extreme lower end. The lower apartment is the nursery and is used also for the sáhna to lie up in during the dead of the winter, when he is in a semi-torpid state. The sáhna is gifted with a very keen sense of hearing, and is provided with a horny scolloped tail for purposes of defence. He is able to hold his own in cases of dispute between himself and the smaller varieties of snakes as to whether he is to give himself up, body and all, for the snake's dinner, or retain possession of his hole. He is most peculiar in his habits. From early spring to the commencement of winter he comes out of his hole daily, never leaving it, however, till the sun is fairly warm; and on retiring to rest, at about 5 or 6 in the evening, he carefully plugs up his hole with loose earth taken from the upper chamber and battered against the mouth of the hole with his head to keep it in position. In this way he protects himself fairly well from snakes; but if a snake

* Larger game was to be found within a comparatively recent period. Vigne travelling between Luddan and Multan in 1836 writes "Tigers are to be found in some parts of the jungle and on the banks of the rivers" (Ghazni, p. 14)

Chapter I.
Descriptive.
Wild animals: sport.

attempts to force himself into the hole (which they frequently do), the sáhna meets him at the hole, tail foremost, and, while carefully protecting his body by the walls of the hole, waggles his tail about and disputes his entrance. In the scuffle that ensues the snake as frequently comes off second best as victorious. The sáhna generally keeps his opponent at bay as long as he does not take a false step, either by allowing too much of his tail to protrude beyond the hole, or, on being intimidated, by retreating to a distance that may enable the snake to force himself between the sáhna and the sides of the hole. People who hunt the sáhna know how readily he comes up to defend himself from the attacks of snakes, and this knowledge has caused them to devise a plan for hunting him by imitating the rustling of a snake. They do this with a tuft of moonj fibre tied on to the end of a stick, about 5 feet long, in the form of a paint-brush. The holes are previously marked off by long straight lines, that are to serve as a guide to the shikári when he commences operations later on. On the sáhna retiring to rest, and before darkness sets in, the shikári approaches the hole very cautiously; and as he moves along with the brush well in advance of him, he trails it along the ground in a zigzag fashion till he gets up to the hole. He then quietly squats down, and at breaks of short intervals rustles the brush all around and over the hole till the sáhna, in his excitement and by constant waggling of the tail, dislodges the plug of earth which, in falling, still further excites the sáhna and causes him to poke it out to a distance that enables the shikári to lay hold of it. He is then speedily jammed against the side of the hole by a flat wooden peg that is inserted to keep him from struggling. This plan of shikár is practiced only in certain seasons and when a colony of sáhna happen to be within convenient reach of the chuhra's encampment. The usual mode of shikaring them is during the day, either before they have opened out their holes or immediately after they have plugged them up. The implements then used are a peg similar to the one already described and a mallet, shaped like a polo stick, about a foot long, with a 3-feet handle stuck in nearer towards the base than the apex. The mallet head tapers to a point about an inch in diameter, and is generally made of some hard wood. Armed with these instruments and a double cord-belt round his waist, the chuhra stalks out either before the sáhnas have left their holes, or immediately after they have retired; and as he moves along (always without shoes, and at a very slow pace) he keeps a sharp look out for the sáhna's hole, which he approaches very cautiously, almost on tiptoe; and when within striking distance of the hole, he brings his mallet down with such terrific force that with one blow of his mallet he sinks a shaft, about 4 inches away from the hole, that completely cuts off the sáhna's retreat, and rapidly inserting the wooden peg into the crumbled chamber, he secures his shikár, and breaking its

Chapter I
Descriptive.
Wild animals: sport.

spine just above the shoulders, he puts it between one of the twists of his cord-belt, and proudly marches off to the next sahna's hole. A chuhra, after a successful day's shikar, is a treat to see. His shoes (if he has any) are generally stuck into his pagri, and with his belt full of these repulsive looking sáhnas, all dangling around his waist, he brings to memory the pictures one sometimes sees of Adam and Eve after they had been driven out of the Garden of Eden. A third way of shikaring the sáhna is to suffocate the poor beast. This plan admits of all the members of the chuhra family participating in the sport. It is carried on during the rains (generally after a very heavy fall, when there is plenty of water available). The chuhra on such occasions goes out with all the spare members of his family, providing himself with a few pots and some sort of digging implements; they go to the nearest depression that has some water within convenient reach, and either drain water into the hole by an artificial cutting, or swamp it by filling it from their pots. As soon as this is done, the hole is plugged up with a tuft of grass or tender twigs; and after all the neighbouring holes are treated in a similar manner, the plugs are drawn out, and the poor swamped sáhna, that had been trying to force his way through the tuft, comes out cold in death, with his claws stiffened over the twigs that he had been trying to grasp.

Snakes.

Of venomous snakes, the cobra (*Naja tripudians*), the *Echis carinata*, and the krait (*Bungarus cæruleus*) are the most common. They are to be found all over the district, even at Multan; and are a constant source of danger during the summer. According to official returns for the years 1895 to 1898, sixty-nine persons on an average are reported to have died of snake bite each year; and rewards to the extent of Rs. 101 were paid annually for the destruction of 19 wolves and 218 snakes each year.

Fish.

The principal varieties of fish that are brought to the Multan market are the ráhu, bachwa, malli, tirkanda, doula, saul, moh, singi, chilwa, tengra, bam or eel, and the shrimp. They are mostly got from the Chenáb and Sutlej, though occasional consignments are received from the Indus. Of these, the best eating are the bachwa and the rahu—the bachwa being considered a particularly well-flavoured fish. From an angler's point of view, the doula and tirkanda afford the best sport—that is to say, they are plucky enough to take anything that comes in their way, and will not keep one waiting very long; while for a good run the ráhu is said to take the first place

CHAPTER II.

HISTORY.

Early History to 700 A.D.

Chapter II.

History.

The antiquities of the district are fully discussed by General Sir A. Cunningham in his Ancient Geography of India, pp. 219—241, and in Volume V of his Archæological Survey Reports, pp. 111—136. The chief information available regarding the early names of the city of Multan, the temple of the Sun, and so forth, will be found in Chapter VI below.

There is practically no history of Multan before the arrival of the Arabs in the 8th century A.D. It is nearly certain that Alexander passed through the district in the cold weather of B.C. 325—326, but it is almost impossible to trace his march with any definiteness. The accounts of his invasion are discussed in Sir A. Cunningham's books, in Bunbury's Ancient Geography and in the last edition of this Gazetteer, but the identifications are so utterly conjectural that it has been thought better in this edition of the work to quote as it stands the account given by Arrian, from which readers may draw their own conclusions. That historian, after describing how Alexander after reaching the confluence of the Chenáb and Jhelum rivers marched across a desert against the Malloi and stormed one of their cities (supposed by General Cunningham to be Kot Kamália). Arrian then continues :—

* Alexander having dined and allowed his troops to rest till the first watch of the night, began to march forward, and, having travelled a great distance in the night, arrived at the river Hydraôtês at daybreak. There he learned that many of the Malloi† had already crossed to the other bank, but he fell upon others who were in the act of crossing and slew many of them during the passage. He crossed the river along with them, just as he was, and by the same ford. He then closely pursued the fugitives who had outstripped him in their retreat. Many of these he slew, and he captured others, but most of them escaped to a position of great natural strength, which was also strongly fortified.‡ But when the infantry came up with him, Alexander sent Peithôn with his own brigade and two squadrons of cavalry against the fugitives. This detachment attacked the stronghold, captured it at the first assault, and made slaves of all who had fled into it, except, of course, those who had fallen in the attack. Then Peithôn and his men, their task fulfilled, returned to the camp,

Alexander himself next led his army against a certain city of the Brachmans,§ because he had learned that many of the Malloi had fled thither for

---

* The translation is that given by McCrindle in "The Invasion of India by Alexander the Great." Constable, 1893.

† The Malloi are probably the same as the Málavas mentioned in the Mahabharata.

‡ (χωρίον ὀχυρον καί τετειχισμένον)
Cunningham locates the position at Tulamba, where there are remains of a large mud fort. See also the account of Tulamba in Chapter VI below.

§ This, according to Cunningham, is probably the mound at Atári on the Kabirwála-Tulamba road.

Chapter II.

History.

Early period

refuge. On reaching it, he led the phalanx in compact ranks against all parts of the wall. The inhabitants, on finding the walls undermined, and that they were themselves obliged to retire before the storm of missiles, left the walls and fled to the citadel, and began to defend themselves from thence. But as a few Macedonians had rushed in along with them, they rallied, and turning round in a body upon the pursuers, drove some from the citadel and killed twenty-five of them in their retreat. Upon this Alexander ordered his men to apply the scaling ladders to the citadel on all its sides and to undermine its walls; and when an undermined tower had fallen and a breach had been made in the wall between two towers, thus exposing the citadel to attack in that quarter, Alexander was seen to be the first man to scale and lay hold of the wall. Upon seeing this, the rest of the Macedonians for very shame ascended the wall at various points, and quickly had the citadel in their hands. Some of the Indians set fire to their houses, in which they were caught and killed, but most part fell fighting. About 5,000 in all were killed, and, as they were men of spirit, a few only were taken prisoners.

He remained there one day to give his army rest, and next day he moved forward to attack the rest of the Malloi. He found their cities abandoned, and ascertained that the inhabitants had fled into the desert. There he again allowed the army a day's rest, and next day sent Peithôn and Demetrios, the cavalry commander, back to the river with their own troops, and as many battalions of light armed infantry as the nature of the work required. He directed them to march along the edge of the river, and if they came upon any of those who had fled for refuge to the jungle, of which there were numerous patches along the river-bank, to put them all to death unless they voluntarily surrendered. The troops under these two officers captured many of the fugitives in these jungles and killed them.

He marched himself against the largest city of the Malloi, to which he was informed many men from their other cities had fled for safety. The Indians, however, abandoned this place also when they heard that Alexander was approaching. They then crossed the Hydraôtês, and, with a view to obstruct Alexander's passage, remained drawn up in order of battle upon the banks because they were very steep. On learning this, he took all the cavalry which he had with him, and marched to that part of the Hydraôtês where he had been told the Malloi were posted; and the infantry were directed to follow after him. When he came to the river and descried the enemy drawn up on the opposite bank, he plunged at once, just as he was after the march, into the ford, with the cavalry only. When the enemy saw Alexander now in the middle of the stream they withdrew in haste, but yet in good order, from the bank, and Alexander pursued them with the cavalry only. But when the Indians perceived he had nothing but a party of horse with him, they faced round and fought stoutly, being about 50,000 in number. Alexander, perceiving that their phalanx was very compact, and his own infantry not on the ground, rode along all round them, and sometimes charged their ranks, but not at close quarters. Meanwhile the Agrianians and other battalions of light-armed infantry, which consisted of picked men, arrived on the field along with the archers, while the phalanx of infantry was showing in sight at no great distance off. As they were threatened at once with so many dangers, the Indians wheeled round, and with headlong speed fled to the strongest of all the cities that lay near.* Alexander killed many of them in the pursuit, while those who escaped to the city were shut up within its walls. At first, therefore, he surrounded the place with his horsemen as soon as they came up from the march. But when the infantry arrived he encamped around the wall on every side for the remainder of this day—a time too short for making an assault, to say nothing of the great fatigue his army had undergone, the infantry from their long march, and the cavalry by the continuous pursuit and especially by the passage of the river.

On the following day, dividing his army into two parts, he himself assaulted the wall at the head of one division, while Perdikkas led forward the other. Upon this the Indians without waiting to receive the attack of the Macedonians, abandoned the walls and fled for refuge to the citadel. Alexander and his troops

* This is the city usually identified with Multan. The identification is very probably correct, but that it is not without difficulties will be easily seen by a glance at the text above quoted.

Chapter II.
History.
Early period.

therefore burst open a small gate and entered the city long before the others. But Perdikkas and the troops under his command entered it much later, having found it no easy work to surmount the walls. The most of them, in fact, had neglected to bring scaling ladders, for when they saw the wall left without defenders they took it for granted that the city had actually been captured. But when it became clear that the enemy was still in possession of the citadel, and that many of them were drawn up in front of it to repel attack, the Macedonians endeavoured to force their way into it, some by sapping the walls, and others by applying the scaling ladders wherever that was practicable. Alexander, thinking that the Macedonians who carried the ladders were loitering too much, snatched one from the man who carried it, placed it against the wall, and began to ascend, cowering the while under his shield. The next to follow was Peukestas, who carried the sacred shield which Alexander had taken from the temple of the Ilian Athênâ, and which he used to keep with him and have carried before him in all his battles. Next to him Leonnatos, an officer of the bodyguard, ascended by the same ladder; and by a different ladder Abreas, one of those soldiers who for superior merit drew double pay and allowances. The king was now near the coping of the wall, and resting his shield against it, was pushing some of the Indians within the fort, and had cleared the parapet by killing others with his sword. The hypaspists, now alarmed beyond measure for the king's safety, pushed each other in their haste up the same ladder and broke it so that those who were already mounting it fell down and made the ascent impracticable for others.

Alexander, while standing on the wall, was then assailed on every side from the adjacent towers, for none of the Indians had the courage to come near him. He was assailed also by men in the city, who threw darts at him from no great distance off, for it so happened that a mound of earth had been thrown up in that quarter close to the wall. Alexander was, moreover, a conspicuous object both by the splendour of his arms and the astonishing audacity he displayed. He then perceived that if he remained where he was, he would be exposed to danger without being able to achieve anything noteworthy, but if he leaped down into the citadel he might perhaps by this very act paralyse the Indians with terror, and if he did not, but necessarily incurred danger, he would in that case not die ignobly, but after performing great deeds worth being remembered by the men of after times. Having so resolved, he leaped down from the wall into the citadel. Then, supporting himself against the wall he slew with his sword some who assailed him at close quarters, and in particular the governor of the Indians who had rushed upon him too boldly. Against another Indian whom he saw approaching, he hurled a stone to check his advance, and another he similarly repelled. If any one came within nearer reach he again used his sword. The barbarians had then no further wish to approach him but standing around assailed him from all quarters with whatever missiles they carried or could lay their hands on.

At this crisis Peukestas, and Abreas the[1] dimoirite, and after them Leonnatos, the only men who succeeded in reaching the top of the wall before the ladder broke, leaped down and began fighting in front of the king. But there Abreas fell, pierced in the forehead by an arrow. Alexander himself was also struck by one which pierced through his cuirass into his chest above the pap, so that, as Ptolemy says, air gurgled from the wound along with the blood. But sorely wounded as he was, he continued to defend himself as long as his blood was still warm. Since much blood, however, kept gushing out with every breath he drew, a dizziness and faintness seized him, and he fell where he stood in a collapse upon his shield. Peukestas then bestrode him where he fell holding up in front of him the sacred shield which had been taken from Ilion, while Leonnatos protected him from side attacks. But both these men were severely wounded, and Alexander was now on the point of swooning away from the loss of blood. As for the Macedonians, they were at a loss how to make their way into the citadel, because those who had seen Alexander shot at upon the wall and then leap down inside it, had broken down the ladders up which they were rushing in all haste, dreading lest their king, in recklessly exposing himself to danger, should come by some hurt. In their perplexity they devised various plans for ascending the wall. It was made of earth, and so some drove pegs into it, and swinging themselves up by means of these, scrambled with difficulty to the top. Others ascended by mounting one upon the other. The man who first reached the top flung himself headlong from the wall into the city, and was followed by the others. There, when they saw the king fallen prostrate, they all raised loud lamentations and outcries of grief. And now around his fallen form a desperate struggle ensued, one Macedonian after another holding his shield in front of him. In the meantime, some of the soldiers having shattered the bar by which the gate in the wall between the towers was secured, made their way into the city a few at a time, and others when they saw that a rift was made in the gate, put their shoulders under it and having then pushed it into the space within the wall, opened an entrance into the citadel in that quarter.

Upon this some began to kill the Indians, and in the massacre spared none, neither man, woman, nor child. Others bore off the king upon his shield. His condition was very low, and they could not yet tell whether he was likely to survive. Some writers have asserted that Kritodêmos, a physician of Kôs, an Asklapiad by birth, extracted the weapon from the wound by making an incision where the blow had struck. Other writers, however say that as no surgeon was present at this terrible crisis, Perdikkas, an officer of the bodyguard at Alexander's own desire made an incision into the wound with his sword and removed the weapon. Its removal was followed by such a copious effusion of blood that Alexander again swooned, and the swoon had the effect of staunching the flux. Many fictions also have been recorded by historians concerning this accident, and Fame receiving them from the original inventors, has preserved them to our own day nor will she cease to transmit the falsehoods to one generation after another except they be finally suppressed by this history.

The common account, for example, is that this accident befell Alexander among the Oxydrakai,* but in fact it occurred among the Malloi, an independent Indian nation. The city belonged to the Malloi and the men who wounded Alexander were Malloi. They had certainly agreed to combine with the Oxydrakai and give battle to the common enemy, but Alexander had thwarted this design by his sudden and rapid march through the waterless country, whereby these tribes were prevented from giving each other mutual help.

While Alexander remained at this place to be cured of his wound, the first news which reached the camp whence he had started to attack the Malloi was that he had died of his wound. Then there arose at first a loud lamentation from the whole army, as the mournful tidings spread from man to man. But when their lamentation was ended, they gave way to despondency and anxious doubts about the appointment of a commander to the army, for among the officers many could advance claims to that dignity which both to Alexander and the Macedonians seemed of equal weight. They were also in fear and doubt how they could be conducted home in safety surrounded as they were on all hands by warlike nations, some not yet reduced, but likely to fight resolutely for their freedom while others would to a certainty revolt when relieved from their fear of Alexander. They seemed besides, to be just then among impassable rivers, while the whole outlook presented nothing but inextricable difficulties when they wanted their king. But on receiving word that he was still alive they could hardly think it true, or persuade themselves that he was likely to recover. Even when a letter came from the king himself intimating that he would soon come down to the camp, most of them from the excess of fear which possessed them distrusted the news, for they fancied that the letter was a forgery concocted by his body-guards and generals.

On coming to know this, Alexander, anxious to prevent any commotions arising in the army, as soon as he could bear the fatigue, had himself conveyed to the banks of the river Hydraotês and embarking there he sailed down the river to reach the camp, at the junction of the Hydraôtês and the Akesines,† where Hêphaistion commanded the land forces and Nearchos the fleet. When the vessel which carried the king was now approaching the camp, he ordered the awning to be removed from the poop that he might be visible to all. They

* Also called Hydrakai, Sydracae and Syrakousai by various classical authors. Authorities are at variance as regards the proper Sanskrit equivalent which, is given as Suraka Asuraka, Sudra Sudraka, &c.

† i.e., of the Rávi and the Chenáb. As noted in Chapter I these rivers used up to a comparatively recent period to meet south of Multan.

Chapter II.

History.

Early period.

were, however, even yet incredulous, supposing that the freight of the vessel was Alexander's dead body, until he neared the bank when he raised his arm and stretched out his hand to the multitude. Then the men raised a loud cheer and lifted up their hands, some towards heaven and some towards Alexander himself. Tears even started involuntarily to the eyes of not a few at the unexpected sight. Some of the hypaspists brought him a litter where he was carried ashore from the vessel, but he called for his horse. When he was seen once more on horseback, the whole army greeted him with loud acclamations, which filled with their echoes the shores and all the surrounding hills and dales [!]

Alexander having received the submission of Malloi and Oxydrakai, proceeded down the Chenab to its junction with the Indus, leaving Philip as 'satrap' in charge. This Philip was shortly afterwards murdered by one Eudemus, who began to extend his power over the north and west of the province. In B.C. 327, however, the Macedonians were overpowered by Chandragupta, of Pataliputra, the Sandracottus of Megasthenes, and the family of this prince remained in power over Northern India till the beginning of the second century B.C., when the country was invaded by the Græco-Bactrian sovereigns who were at that time being ousted from their own Bactrian dominions. Then from about 30 B.C. to 470 A.D. the Kushan tribe of the great Yue-chi and their successors from a cognate race, the Little Yue-chi, were the predominant power; and from 470 to about 550 A.D. the Ephthalites or White Huns are supposed to have been in authority. The battle in which the White Huns are believed to have been finally defeated by a Hindu king Vikramaditya (about A.D. 544), is said by Alberuni to have been fought "in the region of Karúr between Multan and the castle of Loni," but the identification of this Karúr with the town of Kahror in the Multan district is very doubtful.

The next indication of events in the early history of Multan is derived from the writings of early Arab geographers* in which Multan figures as the capital of an important province of the kingdom of Sindh. At the time when the Arabs first penetrated the valley of the Indus, the country was ruled by Chach, a Brahman, who had usurped the throne on the death of Sahási Rai, the last monarch of a dynasty bearing the name of Rai. With regard to this dynasty no detailed information is extant.† The *Chachnáma*, however, relates that Siharas, father of Sahási Raj, had divided his kingdom into four provinces, the most northern of which had its capital at Multan, and extended as far as the borders of Kashmír.‡ The date of Chach's usurpation is fixed by Sir H. Elliot as A.H. 10, corresponding to A.D. 631. § Having seized upon Alor, the

---

* Collected in Elliot's "History of India," Vol. I.

† The *Chachnáma* mentions the names of three kings—Sahási Rai, his father Siharas, and his grandfather Sahási Rai I; the *Tufat-ul-kirám* mentions two additional names (see Elliot, Hist. Ind., I., p. 405). Another Arab History —the *Majma-i-wáridát*—assigns to the dynasty an antiquity of two thousand years.

‡ *Chachnáma*. Elliot, Hist. Ind., I., p. 139.

§ Hist., Ind., I., p. 414.

Arab rule.

capital of the Rai dynasty, he marched northwards into the province of Multan, which was held by Malik Bajhra, a relative of Saháši Rai. Crossing the Biás, which then had an independent course, he defeated the son of Bajhra, and having occupied the fort of Sikka, on the Rávi, opposite Multan, crossed over to the siege of the capital city. After a stout resistance Bajhra retired within the walls, and having made an unsuccessful application for help to the Rája of Kashmír, at last surrendered upon honorable terms. From Multan, Chach proceeded to subdue Brahmapur, Kahror and Ashahar, cities of the Multan province, and then marching northwards, and penetrating apparently into the lower Himalayas, there fixed the boundary between his kingdom and that of Kashmír.* Chach died in A. D. 671, and was succeeded by his brother Chandar, who is said to have been a zealous adherent of the Buddhist faith.† Chandar was succeeded in A. D. 679 by his nephew Dahir, son of Chach.

Towards the end of the year 641 A.D., while Chach was still alive, the Chinese pilgrim Hiuen Tsang came, *viá* Sindh, to Multan. The account of his travels merely states briefly that "leaving the right bank of the Indus, he arrived at the kingdom of Mu-lo-san-pu-lu" (Mula-sthána-pura), and continues with a short description of the Sun-temple in the city. Hiuen Tsang's account of the Punjab kingdoms of that day is not easily reconciled with the accounts given by the Arab historians, but deserves credit on account of his general truthfulness and accuracy.

Arab rule.—Circa 700—970 A. D.

One is apt to forget that when Hiuen Tsang visited Multan twenty years of the Hijra era had already passed, and that within twenty years of his departure the Arabs were knocking at the gates of Sindh The Arabs were, it is true, restrained by various considerations from any immediate incursions into India, and they had set about the conquest of Spain before they laid hands on the Indus valley, but in due time and within seventy years of the visit of the Buddhist pilgrim the Muhammadan conqueror stood in his footsteps at Multan. The piratical outrages of the Meds of lower Sindh had roused the spirit of the Caliph, and a victorious army led by a passionate general of eighteen years of age surged up the valley of the Indus, defeating the remnants of the dynasty of Chach and capturing fortress after fortress till Multan itself was reached.

Muhammadanism, having thus been introduced into Multan, was not again repulsed. It would be a mistake, however, to

* *Chachnáma.* Elliot, Hist. Ind., I., p. 144.
† *Ibid*, 152-53

Chapter II.
History.
Arab rule.

imagine that the district became at once the Muhammadan country that it now is. The invading force was but small in numbers, and far removed from its supports, so that the occupation of the district was in the main a military one The Governor himself lived in a cantonment some miles from Multan, and there appears to have been a subordinate Governor at Kahror, but the majority of the people of the district were, as before, Rájpút unbelievers. The conquerors must have been largely Arabs, but it was only by degrees that anything like a permanent immigration of true or nominal Arabs took place: there is no Syad or Kuresh family of note in the district that traces its advent from any date before the Ghaznavide invasion, and there is no tradition (other than that of the conversion of the Dhudis of Diwán Chawali Mashaikh) which points to any general conversions of the natives during the first three centuries of Muhammadan occupation. The Hindu populations, lying along the banks of the river, were left much to themselves, they were assessed to land revenue and the capitation tax, but their internal organization was not interfered with, and their religious institutions were, after the first flush of victory, left undisturbed.

As time passed on the power of the Caliphate began to weaken, and by the end of the 9th century Multan was, for all practical purposes, independent of Baghdad. How the local governors continued to maintain their power against the natives it is not easy to say: it is possible that, as Masúdi says, the possession of the Sun-temple was their safeguard, but more probably the Punjab and Delhi powers, though much renowned in story, were really too weak to have much effect on the Muhammadan garrison of Multan, while the Sáhí dynasties to the north were fully occupied in resisting Mussalmán aggression in the direction of Kandahar and Kábul. At all events we hear of no wars, and the district remained for three centuries the outpost of Islám in India, while practically the whole of the rest of what is now known as the Punjab remained under Hindu rulers.

Chronicle.

664. The Arabs invaded the Indus Valley. Firishta (Briggs i, 4) says that they penetrated to Multan, but Al Biladuri (Ell. i, 116) does not expressly state this to have been the case.

712. Muhammad Kasim marches triumphantly from lower Sindh up the Indus Valley, defeats Raja Dáhir near Sakkar, and presses on towards Multan. After taking Askalanda (supposed to be the modern Uch)*, he attacked Sikka (a fort lying apparently immediately opposite Multan on the south bank of the Rávi), and ultimately gained Multan itself.

---

* The Rávi then probably flowed south of the city of Multan. Askalanda (var. Alakanda, Akaslanda, A'dkanda, &c.) has been identified, very doubtfully, with Uch. The site of Sikka is unknown; possibly it was on the mounds south of the City Railway Station where the shrine of Mai Pákdáman now stands.

Chapter II.

History.

Arab rule.

The following is the account of the campaign given by Al Biladuri (d. A. D 892-3, Ell. i, 122):—

'Muhammad advanced towards Alsaka, a town on this side of the Biyás, which was captured by him and is now in ruins. He then crossed the Biás and went towards Multan, where, in the action which ensued, Zaida, the son of Umur, of the tribe of Tai, covered himself with glory. The infidels retreated in disorder into the town, and Muhammad commenced the siege, but the provisions being exhausted, the Mussalmáns were reduced to eat asses. Then came there forward an old man who sued for quarter and pointed out to them an aqueduct, by which the inhabitants were supplied with drinking water from the river of Basmad. It flowed within the city into a reservoir like a well which they call *taláb*. Muhammad destroyed this water-course, whereon the inhabitants oppressed with thirst surrendered at discretion. He massacred the men capable of bearing arms, but the children were taken captives as well as the ministers of the temple to the number of six thousand.'

The author of the Chach-nama, which was written before 750 A.D., gives a somewhat different account. (Ell. i, 203 *seqq.*) :—

'When he had settled affairs with Kaska, he left the fort, crossed the Biás and reached the stronghold of Askalanda, the people of which, being informed of the arrival of the Arab army, came out to fight. The idolators were defeated and threw themselves into the fort. They began to shoot arrows and fling stones from the mangonels on the walls. The battle continued for seven days, and the nephew of the chief of Multan, who was in the fort of that city, made such attacks that the army began to be distressed for provisions; but at last the chief of Askalanda came out in the night time and threw himself into the fort of Sikka, which is a large fort on the south bank of the Rávi.......Muhammad Kasim, with the army, proceeded towards Sikka Multan. It was a fort on the south bank of the Rávi, and Bajhra Taki, grandson of Bajhra (daughter's son) was in it. When he received the intelligence he commenced operations. Every day when the army of the Arabs advanced towards the fort, the enemy came out and fought, and for 17 days they maintained a fierce conflict. Bajhra passed over the Rávi and went into Multan. In consequence of the death of his friends Muhammad Kásim had sworn to destroy the fort, so he ordered his men to pillage the whole city. He then crossed over towards Multan at the ferry below the city, and Bajhra came out to take the field. That day the battle raged from morning till sunset, and when the world, like a day-labourer, covered itself with the blanket of darkness, the king of the heavenly host covered himself with the veil of concealment, and all retired to their tents. The next day when the morning dawned from the horizon, and earth was illumined fighting again commenced, and many men were slain on both sides; but the victory remained still undecided. For a space of two months mangonels and ghazraks were used, and stones and arrows were thrown from the wall of the fort. At last provisions became exceedingly scarce in the camp, and the price of an ass's head was raised to 500 dirhams. When the chief Gursiya, son of Chandar, nephew of Dahir, saw that the Arabs were in no way disheartened, but, on the contrary, were confident, and that he had no prospect of relief, he went to wait on the king of Kashmir. The next day, when the Arabs reached the fort and the fight commenced, no place was found suitable for digging a mine until a person came out of the fort and sued for mercy. Muhammad Kásim gave him protection, and he pointed out a place towards the north on the banks of a river. A mine was dug, and in two or three days the walls fell down and the fort was taken. Six thousand warriors were put to death and all their relations and dependents were taken as slaves. Protection was given to the merchants, artizans and the agriculturists...... When Muhammad Kásim had settled terms with the principal inhabitants of Multan he erected a Jama Masjid and minarets, and he appointed the Amir Daud Nasr, son of Walid Ummani its Governor. He left Kharim, son of Abul Malik Taman in the fort of Bramhapur, on the banks of the Jhelum, which was called Sobur (Shore ?). Akrama, son of Rihan Shami, was appointed Governer of the territory round Multan, and Ahmad, son of Harima, son of Atba Madani, was appointed Governor of the forts of Ajtahad and Karur.'

After this Muhammad Kásim had marched some distance northward when he was recalled by orders from the Caliph: the well-known story of this sudden recall and its tragic results is recorded in most histories of India.

Chapter II.

History.

The Karmatians.

After Kásim's death no further information is forthcoming, except that Multan was once more taken by the Arabs in the Caliphate of Mansur, 753—774 and once again in that of Mutasim billah (833—841) [Al Biladuri in Ell. i, 127—128].

In 871 the lower Indus Valley fell into the hands of Yakúb bin Lais, and shortly after that event we find two kingdoms established, one with its capital at Mansura near the present Haidarabad, and the other with its head-quarters at Multan.

915—916.—The Geographer Masudi visited Multan and in his "Meadows of Gold" he records:—'The king of Multan is a Koraishite, the crown of Multan has been hereditary in the family which rules at present, since ancient times, from the beginning of Islám.' 'Multan' he adds 'is one of the strongest frontier places of the Musalmáns, and around it there are 120,000 towns and villages, (villages and estates.)' (Ell. i, 22). Kanauj, he asserts, was then a province of Multan, 'the greatest of the countries which form a frontier against unbelieving nations.' (Ell. i. 454). He also says that Multan was under 'a Koreshi of the Bani us Samah' called Abu Lihab, and that it was 'the general rendezvous of the caravans which proceed into Khurasan.' (Raverty in J.A.S.B. 1892, page 190).

About 951, the Geographer Istakhri wrote his 'Books of the Climates' in which he says, 'Mansura is more fertile than Multan.' (Raverty J.A.S.B. 1892, page 190, translates 'Multan has a large *hisár* but Mansura is the more populous.') At half a parsang from Multan there is a large cantonment (lofty edifices—Raverty) which is the abode of the chief, who never enters Multan except on Friday when he goes on the back of an elephant, in order to join in the Prayer of that day. The Governor is of the tribe of Kuraish (Raverty adds—'the descendant of Sámson of Luwai who seized upon Multan') and is not subject to the ruler of Mansura, but reads the *khutba* in the name of the Khalifa. Samand is a small city, situated like Multan, on the east of the river Mihran; between each of these places and the river, the distance is two parsangs.* The water is obtained from wells. The people of Multan wear trousers, and most of them speak Persian and Sindhi as in Mansura.' (Ell. i, 28-29).

In 976 Ibn Haukal visited India for the second time, and gives very much the same account of Multan, as Istakhri does.

THE KARMATIANS IN MULTAN—A. D. 970—1206.

As the Caliphate grew weaker, the tendency to schism in Persia and elsewhere increased, and in 891, one Abdulla (called 'Karmat' from his using in confidential communications the minute Arabic writing so termed) came into notice as a follower of the Ismailians, one of the most dangerous of the Ali-ite sects in the East. This Abdulla started a doctrine that everything was allowable, and proceeded to carry out his views with violence. Syria was invaded, Basra and Kufa were taken, and even Mecca was pillaged, and the black stone removed. His followers were soon afterwards ignominiously defeated in Egypt and Irak, and appear gradually to have pushed themselves and their doctrines into the Indus Valley, where towards the end of the 10th century they seized Multan, destroyed the Hindu temple, and altered the site of the orthodox mosque. At that period a family of Lodi Patháns had obtained possession of the whole Punjab frontier from a little south of Peshâwar to Multan, and the governors of this family seem shortly to have come under

---

* The position of Samand or Basmad is not known. The cantonment referred to was known as Jandrud, Jandrár, Jandur, &c. See Ell. i, 380.

Chapter II. History. The Karmatians.

the Karmatian influence. Already owning a very loose allegiance to the Ghaznavide monarchs, they now became specially obnoxious to that zealous defender of the Faith, Mahmúd of Ghazni, who twice marched against them, and ultimately deported the governor Daud Lodi from Multan to Afghanistan. This Daud was shortly afterwards released by Mahmúd's successor Masaud, but Multan still continued to be steeped in heresy and we find among the Karmatians of the day a rája of the native Sumra family, who appears to have enjoyed considerable power in the district. The country, however, remained nominally subject to the Ghaznavides, until they in their turn were overthrown by Muhammad Ghori, who in the course of his expeditions passed several times through Multan and on one occasion is recorded to have 'delivered that place from the hands of the Karmatians.' This is the last we hear of this sect in Multan which had been more or less in their hands for two centuries.

The result of the sectarian wars appears to have been unfavourable to the prosperity of the city and the district; for when the Gardezi Syads first immigrated to Multan in the reign of Sultán Bairám Shah (1118—1152) the city is said to have been utterly deserted. The Gardezi Syads,—who, it may be noted, are to this day Shias—appear to have got possession of a good deal of land along the old course of the Rávi as far north as the middle of the Kabírwála tahsil and Sheikh Yusuf Gardezi, their chief, is the first of the great company of Muhammadan preachers of whom we hear so much in the next period.

Chronicle.

Circa 970 A. D.—Firishta says (Briggs i, 9) 'During the reign of the Samani kings the Afghans formed a barrier between the kingdoms of Multan and Lahore, and thus we find the Samani troops always limited their predatory excursions to Sind and Tatta. When the government of Ghazni devolved on Alaptagin, his general Sabuktagin frequently invaded the provinces of Multan and Laghman, carrying away its inhabitants as slaves in spite of the Afghans. Jaipal, the Raja of Lahore, concerted measures with the Bhattia Raja to obtain the services of Sheikh Hamid, an Afghan, who, being appointed Governor of Multan and Laghman, placed garrisons of Afghan troops in those districts.'

976.—'On the death of Alaptagin, Sabuktagin succeeded to his power: and Sheikh Hamid, perceiving that his own country would, in all probability, suffer in the incursions with which Sabuktagin threatened India, united himself with that prince. Sabuktagin from motives of policy avoided the district of Sheikh Hamid by every means in his power.' (Firishta, Briggs i, 9).

980.—The Karmatians under Jalam ibn Shaiban took Multan, destroyed the idol temple and built a new mosque in place of the old one. (Alb. Sach. i, 116).

1004.—Mahmud of Ghazni passed through the province of Multan on his way to Bhatia. The province of Multan appears to have extended up to the Salt Range, and Bhatia is supposed by Elliot to be Bhera (ii, 441). [Firishta Br. i, 38].

1005.—'Sheikh Hamid Lodi, the first ruler of Multan, had paid tribute (done homage) to Amir Sabuktagin, and after him his grandson Abul Fath Daud, the son of Nasir, the son of Hamid. Abul Fath Daud now having abandoned the tenets of the faithful had at this time shaken off his allegiance.'

Chapter II.
History.
The Karmatians.

He obtained the assistance of Anandpal of Lahore who was, however, defeated by Mahmúd, who then 'entered Multan by the route of Bhatinda.' Mahmúd besieged Multan for seven days, but hearing of an invasion of Herat, retired after receiving the submission of Abul Fath. (Firishta i, 41). The Tarikhi Yamini says 'he took Multan by assault and treated the people with severity.' (Ell. ii, 32). The Kamil-ut-tawarikh, (Ell. ii, 248), says the invasion was prompted by Abul Fath's inclination to heresy, and by his having induced the people of the country to follow his opinions: on hearing of Anandpal's defeat Abul Fath sent his property to Serandip and evacuated Multan. Mahmúd finding the people infatuated in this heresy besieged the place and took it by storm.

1010.—Mahmud was under the necessity of marching to Multan which had revolted, and having cut off a number of the infidel inhabitants and brought Daud, the son of Nasir, to Ghazni, he confined him in the fort of Ghurak (or Tabrak) for life. (Firishta i, 50.)

Hamid Ulla says 'Mahmud made war with Nawasa, (the grandson), ruler of Multan: conquered that country: converted the people to Islam: put to death the ruler of Multan, and entrusted the government of that country to another chief.' (Ell. iii, 65).

1011.—Mahmúd after taking Thánesar retired from that country because he had not yet rendered Multan a province of his own government. (Firishta i, 52). The Geographer, Alberuni, seems to have spent some time in Multan at this period. (J.A.S.B. 1892, p. 187).

1024.—Mahmud passed through Multan on his way to Somnath *via* Ajmer. He returned to Ghazni *vid* Sindh and Multan. (Firishta i, 69—78).

1027.—Mahmud, in order to fight 'the Jats who lived in the Jud mountains' (*i.e.*, probably the Salt Range) came to Multan, built a fleet of boats there and had a great naval battle with the Jats. (Firishta i, 82).

1030.—Masaud Ghaznavi released Daud, (Ell. i, 491). Masaud himself had at one time been Governor of Multan under his father. (Raverty Tab. Nas. 91).

1032.—In the sacred books of the Druses there is a curious letter written in 1032 by Baha-ud-din, the chief apostle of Hamza 'to the unitarians of Multan and Hindustan in general, and to Sheikh Ibn Sumar, Raja Bal in particular' bidding the latter 'arise and bring back Daud the younger into the true religion, for Masaud only delivered him from prison and bondage that you might accomplish the ministry with which you were charged against Abdulla, his nephew, and all the inhabitants of Multan.' The letter would seem to show that the Sumras were powerful in Multan at the time and were Karmatians. (Ell. i, 491).

1042.—Nami, grandson of Mahmúd Ghaznavi, was made governor of Peshawar and Multan: but Sultan Modud shortly afterwards sent a force to Multan against him, which attacked and slew him. (Firishta i, 116).

1049.—The Afghans seized on the Indus Valley, but were defeated by Ali bin Rabbia, who came to Peshawar from Ghazni, and 'having reduced Multan and Sindh, subdued by force of arms the Afghans who had declared their independence in that country.' (Firishta i, 129).

1118.—Muhammad Balin, the rebellious viceroy of Sultan Bairam Ghaznavi, advanced to oppose the king as far as Multan. A battle ensued: but 'the curse of ingratitude fell like a storm on the head of the perfidious rebel, who in his flight, with his sons and attendants sank into a deep quagmire wherein they all perished.' (Firishta i, 151).

1175.—Shahab-ud-din Muhammad Ghori having conquered Gardez, led his forces to Multan and delivered that place from the hands of the Karmatians who had regained possession of it some years previously. (Ell. ii, 293, Tab. Nas. Firishta i, 157, Rav. Tab. Nas. 449).

1176.—He again subdued the province of Multan and marched against Uch. (Firishta i, 169).

Chapter II.

History.
Moghal Invasions.

1178.—He again passed through Multan and Uch on his way to Guserat (Firishta i, 170).

1186.—Muhammad Ghori took Lahore and put it in charge of Ali Karmakh Wali of Multan. (Firishta i, 171, Rav. Tab. Nas. 454).

1192-3—Hindustan having rebelled, Muhammad Ghori advanced to Lahore *viâ* Multan, where he conferred titles and offices on all who had been firm to his interest. (Firishta i, 174).

1203.—Muhammad Ghori was defeated in Turkistan: then 'Aibak Bak, one of the most confidential servants of the State, an officer of high rank in the army, fled from the field of battle, and carried away the impression that by heavenly visitation the blessed person of the king had met with a misfortune and been slain. He fled with the speed of the wind to Multan, and on his arrival went immediately to Mir Dad Hasan, the lord of a standard,' (Raverty says Amir Dad, *i.e.*, Chief Justice, under Amir Muhammad, Governor of Lahore and Multan, Tab. Nas. 476), 'and told him that he had a private message from the king. Amir Dad Hasan retired with him into his closet where the assassin pretending to whisper into his ear, drew a dagger and stabbed him to the heart. He then ran instantly to the courtyard where he proclaimed aloud that he had killed the traitor Amir Daud in obedience to the king's command, and producing a false order and commission to assume the government, he was acknowledged by the army and the people.' (Taj-ul-Maasir, Ell. ii, 233, and Firishta i, 182). This led to an outbreak of the Khokhars who were then powerful between the Chenáb and the Salt Range, but 'Baha-ud-din Muhammad, Governor of Sangwan, with his brother who held lands (akta) within the borders of Multan, accompanied by many of the chief people of the city, marched out against them. Ultimately the Khokhars were thoroughly defeated on the Jhelum: but Muhammad Ghori was shortly afterwards (1205) assassinated by the Gakkhars, in the Ráwalpindi District.

THE MOGHAL INVASIONS—A. D. 1206—1528.

In 1218 Chingiz invaded Western Turkestan, and for the next three centuries the history of Multan is practically the history of the incursions from Western and Central Asia to which the Moghal invasion of Chingiz gave rise.

The centre of Muhammadan authority in India during the period was Delhi, and the normal condition of Multan was that of nominal subjection to the Delhi kings, but twice during the period Multan was for all practical purposes a separate kingdom independent of Delhi, *viz.*, in 1210—1227, when the energetic Slave Governor Nasir-ud-din Kubacha, ruled over Multan and Sindh, and again in 1445—1527 when the Langáhs governed the district independently of the Delhi Emperors. At times, too, the province was held by vigorous governors who, though unable to secure independence, were powerful factors in the dynastic changes of the time. Such were Malik Kabir Khan, who in 1236 joined in the conspiracy to put Razia Begam on the throne; Bahram Abia or Kishlu Khan who, in 1321, acted as the right hand man of Ghias-ud-din Tughlak in the latter's successful usurpation; and Syad Khizr Khan, who marched to Delhi in 1414 and there founded the Syad Dynasty which lasted 38 years. We get but little light from the historians as to the character of the government under each ruler, and the details given as regarding the various degrees of severity or ability with

Chapter II.
History.
Moghal Invasions.

which sovereigns like Ala-ud-din Khilji, Ghias-ud-din Tughlak, and Feroz Shah Tughlak administered their empires, can scarcely be taken as applying in any completeness to territories so far from Delhi as Multan and Uch. We may take it as very probable that the interior administration of the district was equally neglected by all or nearly all the numerous governors and kings that ruled it, and that their attention was mainly fixed on repelling the hideous and incessant ravages of the Moghal hordes from Khurasan and Central Asia.

There is an oft-quoted passage in the poems of Amir Khusrau which indicates the manner in which these pagan invaders were viewed by the Moslems of India. 'There were more than a thousand Tatar infidels,' he writes, 'and warriors of other tribes, riding on camels, great commanders in battle, all with steel-like bodies clothed in cotton; with faces like fire, with caps of sheep skin, with their heads shorn. Their eyes were so narrow and piercing that they might have bored a hole in a brazen vessel. Their stink was more horrible than their colour. Their faces were set on their bodies as if they had no necks. Their cheeks resembled soft leather bottles, full of wrinkles and knots. Their noses extended from cheek to cheek, and their mouths from cheek bone to cheek bone. Their nostrils resembled rotten graves, and from them the hair descended as far as the lips. Their moustaches were of extravagant length. They had but scanty beards about their chins. Their chests of a colour half black, half white were so covered with lice that they looked like sesame growing on a bad soil. Their whole body indeed was covered with these insects, and their skin as rough and grainy as shagreen leather, fit only to be converted into shoes. They devoured dogs and pigs with their nasty teeth.'

Such were the Moghals as they first appeared to the nations of Hindustan. As time went on the invading armies became less strange. numbers of them from time to time settled down in the country, they had gradually mixed with the inhabitants of Iran and Turan, they had adopted the tenets of Islam, and ultimately when the last Central Asian invasion placed Babar on the throne, the invaders were little, if it all, less civilized than the nations which they invaded. Without attempting to enter into the controverted questions regarding the ethnological relationship of Turks, Moghals and Tatars, it will suffice for us to notice that at least ten important invasions of the southern Punjab by these Central Asian hordes are recorded in the three centuries between 1221 and 1528. First there was the celebrated escape, described by Gibbon, of Jalal-ud-din Khwarizm Shah across the Indus pursued by the hosts of Chinghiz, an episode which drew upon Multan the hostility both of pursuers and pursued, (1221—1224). Then in 1239 another tribe, the Karlugh Turks, being ousted from Ghazni raided Multan, and were followed by a pursuing host of Moghals under Nuin Mungutah.

Chapter II.

History.

Moghal Invasions.

In 1257 the Moghals under Nuin Saleh were treacherously invited to Multan to aid the local Governor in his intrigues, and were only dissuaded from wholesale massacre by a handsome bribe. In 1284 the Moghal raiders, under Timur Khan, defeated and killed the Prince Muhammad, known as the Martyr Prince, who then ruled in Multan. In 1305 an invasion under Aibak Khan was repelled by the redoubtable warrior Ghazi Beg Tughlak, who is said to have twenty-nine times defeated the invading hordes. In 1327 a force under Turmsharin Khan overran the district, and only retreated on payment of a bribe. In 1397 came Tamerlane himself, whose troops occupied Uch and Multan, sacked Tulamba, raided the Khokhars of the Rávi Valley and passed on across the Biás to Pákpattan and Delhi. In 1430 Shah Rukh, the grandson of Tamerlane, dispatched a force against the province, which had advanced to the very gates of the city before it was defeated. Then in 1524-5 we find the Arghun Turks, who had been driven from Kandahar to Sindh, pressing up against the province, and after a long siege occupying and sacking the city. And finally in 1528 came the peaceful transfer of the province to the emissaries of the last great invader, Babar. For three centuries this unhappy district bore the brunt of the great racial disturbances caused by the Central Asian upheavals. The difficulties of the Khaibar route and (for a great part of the time) the powerful hostility of the northern Gakkhars, drove the majority of the invading hosts to attempt the Multan route to Hindustan, a route which, while the Gaggar and Sutlej still held their ancient courses, had much more to recommend it than in the centuries which followed. The Multan district, therefore, which in the ninth and tenth centuries constituted an outwork of Western Islam against Eastern Paganism, became in the thirteenth and fourteenth centuries the foremost barrier of Indian Muhammadanism against the paganism and barbarism which swept upon it from the West. That the district can have had any real prosperity during these prolonged periods of incessant raiding it is impossible to believe. The fact that an important commercial route ran through Multan gave a certain amount of intermittent prosperity to the city, but in the district there was probably little enough of cultivation, except in the strips of alluvial soil along the Chenáb, Biás and the Gharra.

As regards the races who cultivated the soil during these days of distress we have little or no information. Very few of the landowning races of to-day can trace their advent to a period before the establishment of the Langáh power in the fifteenth century. With the exception of the Langáhs themselves and of the Biloch tribes which joined them we find no notice of any invaders settling down upon the soil. The tribes of Moghal or Turk origin who from time to time became domiciled in the country, must have become absorbed among the people

Chapter II.

History.

Moghal Invasions.

and may be now represented by some of the numerous petty disjointed clans of the district which can give no account of their origin. The effect probably of the Moghal invasions was to break up and drive away the larger tribal units, especially on the western edge of the district, leaving the way open for the miscellaneous and haphazard colonization which forms the basis of the 'colluvies gentium' now presented to our eyes.

In one respect indeed the devastation of Khurasan and Western Iran was to the benefit of this part of India, for it led to the settling of a considerable number of pious and learned men, most of whom no doubt passed on towards Delhi but many of whom stayed to bless Multan with their presence. The preliminary disturbances of Ghori times had driven the Gardezi Syads to this district. A little later came a family of Kureshis from Khwarizm which settled at Kot Karor near Leiah and which gave birth to the famous Sheikh Baha-ud-din Zakaria or Bahawal Haqq, who, after traversing nearly the whole Muhammadan world, chose Multan as his place of residence. To Multan also about the same time came Pir Shams Tabrez from Sabzawar and Kazi Kutb-ud-din from Kashan: to Pákpattan came Baba Farid Shakarganj: to Delhi (by way of Multan) came Khwaja Kutb-ud-din Bakhtiar Kaki: and to Uch came Saiad Jalal, the founder of many sacred families in Multan, Muzaffargarh and Baháwalpur. In the same period arose Sakhi Sarwar, whose father had emigrated from Bakhara to Sakot in this district. These holy men, together with others too numerous to mention, would seem to have set themselves seriously to convert to Islam the remaining Hindu agriculturists and nomads of this part of India, and it is to their persuasion and reputation, rather than to the sword of any conqueror, that the people of the South-West Punjab own their faith in Islam. The lukewarmness of the population in previous times was roused into a keen fervour by the pagan invasions; an emperor's tomb was granted as the resting place of the body of the Saint Rukn-i-Alam, and from this time forward the holy men and holy shrines of Multan bestowed upon the city a unique reputation throughout the whole Mussalman world.

Chronicle.

1210.—Malik Nasir-ud-din Kubacha,* one of the trained slaves of Muhammad Ghori, and son-in-law of Sultan Kutb-ud-din, marched towards Sindh, and seized Uch and Multan. (Firishta i, 203, Tab. Nas. Ell. ii, 301-2). He was 'a man of the highest intelligence, cleverness, experience, discretion and acumen.' He set himself up as an independent sovereign, and issued coins with bilingual Hindi and Arabic inscriptions. (Thomas Path. Kings, p. 100-1), and his power at one time extended from Sirhind to Sindh.

1221.—Jalal-ud-din Mankbarni, Khwarizm Shah, was pursued by the armies of Changiz Khan to the banks of the Indus. Shortly afterwards the Moghal General Turtai advanced to Bhera and then to Multan, 'but as there were no stones there he ordered that the population of Bhera should be turned out to make floats of wood and load them with stones for the manjanicks. So they

* The name is said to be derived from the Turkish *kuba*, a short coat.

floated them down the river, and when they arrived at Multan, the manjanicks were set to work and threw down many ramparts of the fort, which was nearly taken, when the excessive heat of the weather put a stop to their operations.' (Jahankusha, Ell. ii, 392). The Rozat-us-safa says the Moghals were commanded by Bala Nuyan, and that owing to the excessive heat 'the Multanis escaped from that Bala (calamity).' (Ell. ii, 559). The Ain-i-Akbari gives the name of the general as Turmatai Novian, and says he actually took Multan, but that Kubacha by opening his treasury repaired the disaster. (Jar. iii, 344, see also Rav. Tab. Nas. 535). Howorth says that the army was commanded by two generals, Bela and Durbai (Hist Mong i, 90). Jalal-ud-din meantime found his progress opposed both by Shams-ud-din Altamsh in Hindustan and Nasir-ud-din in Multan; he accordingly joined with the Khokhars who were the enemies of the latter, and his general Uzbeg Pai fell suddenly on Nasir-ud-din at Uch. Kubacha fled to Bhakkar and then back to Multan, which Uzbeg Pai invested. Uzbeg Pai seems to have struck coins at Multan in anticipation of taking the city, (Thomas Path. Kings, p. 99), but the siege had to be raised. (Jahankusha, Ell. ii, 396-7). Jalal-ud-din passed through Multan territory again next year on his way to Sindh. (Do).

1224.—'After the victory of Nandana, Tari (or Toli, [or Turtai]), the Moghal prince, came with a large army to the walls of the city of Multan and besieged that strong place for forty days. During this war and invasion Malik Nasir-ud-din opened his treasures and lavished them munificently among the people. He gave such proof of resolution, energy, wisdom and personal bravery that it will remain on record till the day of judgment.' (Tab. Nas. Ell. ii, 303, and viii, xviii). [Possibly this is the same siege as that of Turtai recorded above; the accounts of this period are somewhat confused.] Firishta iii, 420, says Chaghtai Khan commanded the siege in person.

1227.—Shams-ud-din Altamsh of Delhi besieged and took Uch; and Nasir-ud-din was drowned, or as some say drowned himself, in the Indus (Tab. Nas. Ell. ii, 304, iv, 146, Firishta i, 210, iii, 420). Multan fell into the hands of Shams-ud-din, and a rare copper coin of this king records the fact of his rule in this city. (Thomas Path. Kings, p. 75). Malik Kabir Khan (also known as Izz-ud-din Ayaz) was made governor of Multan. (Raverty Tab. Nas. p. 725).

1236—Multan was apparently again in a troubled state for Shams-ud-din was starting from Delhi to march against it when he died. (Firishta i, 211 Others, *e.g*, Raverty Tab., p. 623, read 'Banian' not 'Multan' in connection with this incident). Malik Kabir Khan, governor of Multan, in the same year joined in the conspiracy to put Razia Begam on the throne; he became governor of Lahore, and was succeeded by Malik Karakash at Multan, but in 1239 Multan was restored to him. (Firishta i, 214—220, Tab. Nas. Ell. ii, 335, Raverty, 644). He shortly afterwards rebelled, and according to a local history, Razia Begam marched on and took Multan, where she bestowed much alms on the poor and gave villages in mafi to the Kureshi and Gardezi families.

1239.—The Karlugh Turk, Saif-ud-din Hasan, was driven this year from Ghazni by the Moghals and seized Multan. (Thomas Path. Kings, p. 93). He coined money in his own name. (Raverty in J.A.S.B. 1892, p. 157).

Meantime Kabir Khan assumed sovereignty at Uch, and after his death in 1241, his son Taj-ud-din several times attacked the Karlughs before the gates of Multan. (Raverty Tab. Nas. 656).

1245.—A Moghal army under Muin Mangutah attacked Uch; Saif-ud-din fled from Multan to Sindh; but the Moghals retired on hearing that the Delhi troops had reached the Biás. (Raverty Tab. Nas. 1154, Firishta i, 231).

1246.—The Delhi authorities made an effort to stem the tide of the Moghal advance by appointing Malik Sher Khan-i-Sunkar to a large frontier Government including Multan; which was taken from the Karlughs. (Firishta i, 235).

Chapter II.

History.

Moghal Invasions.

1249.—Malik Hasan Karlugh advanced from Banian; he himself was slain but the Karlughs under his son Nasir-ud-din Muhammad took Multan from Izz-ud-din Balban, who then held it. The Karlughs were very soon afterwards ousted by Sher Khan. (Raverty Tab. Nas. 684, 782—792).

1250.—Malik Izz-ud-din Balban, governor of Uch and Nagor, tried to take Multan from Sher Khan but failed. (Raverty J.A.S.B. 1892, p. 172). In the same year Akhtiyar-ud-din Kuroz, who held Multan for Sher Khan, captured a number of Moghals and sent them to Delhi (Raverty Tab. Nas. 688).

About this period the Sultan Nasir-ud-din visited Multan at least once, and as usual, showed great respect to the sacred families. (Firishta i, 238-9).

1254.—An insurrection in Sindh caused the loss of several forts in Multan, and Sher Khan was disgraced. Next year Izz-ud-din Balban was made governor of Multan. (Firishta i, 240, Raverty J.A.S.B. 1892, 173).

1257.—Izz-ud-din treacherously invited the Moghals; and Nuin Saleh, having arrived at Uch, sent a force against Multan. Multan was delivered to the Moghals and the defences of the citadel were destroyed. The Saint Bahawal Hakk had to pay down 100,000 dinars to save the place from being sacked, and one Chinghiz Khan was made Hakim of Multan. (Raverty J.A.S.B. 892, 175, Tab. Nas. 844 and 1201). D'Ohsson relates that the Moghals retired on hearing of the approach of Muhammad Sultan of Delhi, and adds that during the reign of Sultan Bahu (Balban 1265-87) Multan became the asylum of many Persian princes whose realms had been invaded by the Moghals (Hist. des Mongols, iv, 559).

1270.—Prince Muhammad, son of Ghias-ud-din Balban, was made governor of Multan. He twice invited Sheikh Saadi of Shiraz to his court at Multan, but the invitation was declined on the plea of age. The prince's intention was to build a Khankah for him in Multan, and to endow it with villages for his maintenance. Sheikh Saadi sent him a Gulistan and a Bostan written with his own hand; and Saadi's popularity in India dates from this event. (Firishta i, 259, Tar. Fir. Shahi, Ell. iii 110.) It is stated that although the prince was a noted patron of poets, he was on bad terms with Sheikh Sadr-ud-din, son of Bahawal Haqq.

1284.—The Moghals under Timur Khan invaded Lahore and Dipálpur and were met by Prince Muhammad 'on the banks of the river of Lahore* which runs through part of the Multan province. The Moghals were routed, but Muhammad while isolated from his followers was surprised and slain, (the incident led to his being known afterwards as the Khán-i-Shahid or Martyred Prince). Among the captives taken by the Moghals was the poet Amir Khusrau. (Firishta i, 269). The son of the deceased prince, Kai Khusru, succeeded his father in the Government of Multan, (Firishta i, 269).

1288 Circa.—Malik Jalal-ud-din Firoz, afterwards Sultan, was made governor of Multan, in order that he might preclude the possibility of any invasion by the Moghals. (Wassaf in Ell. iii, 38). In 1290 Firoz advanced to Delhi and seized the throne.

1292.—Arkali Khan, son of Sultan Firoz, was made governor of Multan. On Firoz's assassination in 1295, his family fled to Multan for protection against Firoz's nephew Ala-ud-din Khilji. The latter, however, sent 40,000 horse after them who besieged Multan for two months, until the citizens and troops betrayed the princes into their hands. (Firishta i, 325). Sheikh Rukn-ud-din, grandson of Bahawal Haqq, is said to have interceded for them, but on their arrival at Delhi they were blinded and imprisoned. Nasrat Khan was made governor of Multan, and he shortly afterwards defeated an invasion of the Moghals from Sevistan.

1305.—The Moghals under Kubák or Aibak Khan, an officer of Dua, the Chaghatai Khan of Máwarulnahr, ravaged Multan; they were defeated by Ghazi Beg Tughlak and perished miserably in the deserts. (Firishta i, 363. D'Ohsson, iv, 561. See also Oliver in J.R.A.S., 1888. p. 99.

---

* Probably the Rávi, but possibly the Biás, see Ell. iii, 520.

1321.—When Ghazi Beg of Lahore revolted, Moghaltagin, governor of Multan, jealous of precedence, refused to join him; he was accordingly cut off by Bahram Abia, 'a Moghal chief of some note in that quarter.' (Firishta i, 397). Ghazi Beg then usurped the power at Delhi under the name of Ghias-ud-din. He is said to have inscribed on the Jama Masjid at Multan the words, 'I have encountered the Tartars on twenty-nine occasions and defeated them; hence I am called Malik-ul-Ghazi.' (Thomas Path. Kings, p. 192, Ell. iii, 606). He is said to have left one Taj-ud-din as his governor at Multan.

1327.—A Moghal force under Turmushrin Khan subdued Multan, but was bribed by Muhammad Tughlak to withdraw. (Firishta i, 413).

1334.—Ibn Batuta of Tangiers arrived in Multan from Uch. He gives the following account of his journey :—

'From Uch I went to Multan. The city is the capital of Sindh and the Amir-ul-umara of the province lives there. Ten kos on this side one has to cross a river which is narrow and deep and impassable except by boats. Here travellers are interrogated and their property examined. At that time every merchant had to pay a fourth of his merchandise as toll as well as 7 dinárs per horse. Two years after I reached Hindustan the king abolished all this toll; and when the country was under the Abasside Caliph there had been no dues except the usar and zakát. I dreaded the examination of merchandise for my packages though containing little enough looked large, and I feared lest the whole should be opened: but Kutb-ul-Mulk sent a military officer from Multan with orders that my baggage should not be searched, for which I thanked God. We stopped that night on the river bank and early in the morning there came to me one Dahkán Samarkandi, a postal officer, who was the king's news-writer. After meeting him I went in his company to the ruler of Multan who in those days was Kutb-ul-Mulk, a great and accomplished ruler. When I came to him he got up to greet me and gave me a place at his side I offered as presents a slave, a horse, and raisins and almonds; these last do not grow in that country and are imported as curiosities from Khurasan. The Amir sat on a raised platform covered by a carpet and by him sat Salar the Kazi of the city and a Khatíb whose name I forget. To the right and left were the military officers and behind him stood armed men, while the army marched past in front. A number of bows were lying there, and any one in the army who wished to display his skill in archery took up a bow and drew it and if any one wished to display his skill in horsemanship, he ran his lance at a small drum that was attached to a low wall, or played *Chaughan* with a ball that was lying there. Men were promoted according to the skill shown by them on these occasions. When we had saluted Kutb-ud-din as I have described, he ordered that we should reside in the city with the dependents of Sheikh Rukn-ud-din, Kureshi, the rule being that the Sheikh could not entertain strangers without the governor's permission. Delhi is 40 days' march from Multan and there is cultivation all the way.'

Ibn Batuta says that he went to Delhi *viá* Abohar, Abibakhar, Pákpattan and Sarusti, but if the Abohar mentioned is the Abohar of the Ferozpore district, he has apparently forgotten the order of the towns. In another place also however (the passage quoted below) he has put Abohar near Multan, and possibly some site now disappeared is referred to. Abibakhar is not known, unless it *is* (as tentatively suggested by M. Muhammad Hussain) the shrine of Abubakar at Dhillun in Mailsi.

1340.—Muhammad Tughlak sent orders to Bahram Abia, governor of Multan (also known as Kishlu Khan) to have families removed forcibly to the new capital of Daulatabad in the Deccan, but the messenger, using insolent language, had his head cut off. Muhammad Tughlak defeated Bahram, and ordered a general slaughter of the inhabitants of Multan, which was only averted by the prayer of the saint Rukhn-i-Alam, who came bareheaded to the king's court and stood before him soliciting pardon for the people. (Firishta i, 421, Ell. iii, 242, vii, 136).

Ibn Batuta, however a more trustworthy authority, gives a different account. He says that Muhammad having flayed his nephew and sent his remains round the kingdom *in terrorem*, Kishlu Khan, governor of Multan,

Chapter II.

History.

Moghal invasions.

buried them: whereon Muhammad advanced against him. Battle was fought 'two days journey from Multan in the desert plain of Abohar', in which Kishlu Khan was killed. Muhammad then took Multan, flayed the Kázi and suspended Kishlu's head over the gate of the city. 'I saw it there,' says the traveller, 'when I arrived in Multan.' (Ibn Batuta, Ell. iii, 616). In this campaign the family of Bahawal Haqq sided with the king and were rewarded with 100 villages (see Muhammad Husain, Ibn Batuta, p. 153). If Ibn Batuta is correct the date of the rebellion given in Briggs' Firishta (1340) must be wrong as Ibn Batuta seems to have been in Multan once only viz. in 1334.

1341.—Bahzad Khan, governor of Multan, was defeated by some Afghans under Shahu, who 'poured down like a torrent on Multan,' and took the city. On the approach of the Delhi army the Afghans retreated. (Firishta i, 425, Tar. Fir. Shah, Ell. iii, 244).

1351.—Sultan Firoz who succeeded to the throne when he was in Sindh marched to Delhi *via* Multan and when in Multan behaved very liberally to the Sheikhs of the city. (Shams-i-Siraj, Ell. iii, 282).

1359.—Tatar Khan was made Shikkdar (governor) of Multan, (Ell. iv, 9). During this reign the converted Hindu Makbul, afterwards the Wazir Khan Jahan, and Ain Mahru, known as Ain-ul-Mulk, seem to have been governors of Multan (Ell. iii, 268—370). Afterwards the governors seem to have been Malik Mardan, Malik Shaikh, Malik Sulaiman and Khizr Khan, all of a Syad family. (Ell. iv, 46).

1396.—Sárang Khan, governor of Dipálpur, attacked Khizr Khan, and with the aid of Malik Mardan Bhatti seized the Shikk (province) of Multan. He then advanced against Delhi but was defeated and retired to Multan. (Firishta i, 482, Tar. Mb. Sh. Ell. iv, 32).

1397.—Pir Muhammad Jahángir, grandson of Tamerlane, invested Uch, and when Sárang Khan sent troops against him he advanced to the Biás and fell on the Multanis by surprise just after they crossed the river (apparently at a place called Tamtama or Tantana). He pursued them to Multan, which he invested for six months, so that therein 'nothing eatable, not even a rat or a mouse, remained alive.' At last Sárang capitulated, but meantime the excessive rains had caused a serious mortality among the horses of the besieging army, so that they had to shift their quarters from the camp into the city. The neighbouring zamindars seeing this began to get restive. (Fi. 482. Malf-i-Tim., Ell. iii, 399—417. Rav. J.A.S.B. 1892, 181, 279).

Meantime Tamerlane marching from the north encamped outside Tulamba (October 13th, 1398). After chastising some zamindars in the neighbourhood and seizing a large number of cattle he passed on leaving the fort uncaptured. He then halted at Jál (or, it may be, at a 'chál' or lake) on the Bias 'opposite Shahpur,' from which he marched out with a flying column to chastise Nusrat Khokhar, who was encamped in swampy ground on the bank of a lake. The 'unsanctified Indians' being defeated and 'the God-forsaken Nusrat' being slain, the army moved to Shahnawaz, a populous village on the Biás, 'where there was a great quantity of grain stored up.' On the 26th October, says Tamerlane, 'I set out from Shahnawaz on my return to the baggage and pitched my camp on the bank of the river Biyah, oppposite to Janjan, and gave orders that all my whole army and baggage should cross the river to Janjan (or Khanjan) and that they should set up my tent on a little eminence outside the town at the foot of which was a verdant garden.' At this place (which is stated to have been 40 kos from Multan, Rav., p. 283) Pir Muhammad, marching out from Multan, joined Tamerlane's army, and as the rains had killed his horses so that the soldiers went either on foot or bullocks, 30,000 new horses were provided for him. Leaving Janjan, Tamerlane marched to Sihwal: then on 3rd November to Arwán, then to Jahwál from which he passed on through Pákapttan to the conquest of Delhi.*

---

* Except Tulamba, none of the places in this district mentioned by Tamerlane are, so far as is known, identifiable.

Chapter II.

History
Moghal invasions.

(Malf. Tim. Ell. iii, 413—420; Zafarn. Ell. iii, 484-6; Fir. i, 487, Rav. J.A.S.B. 1892, 280—285). On his return from Delhi through the Punjab Tamerlane appointed Khizr Khan to be Governor of Multan. (Malf. Ell. iii, 475).

1405. The Delhi forces marched against Khizr Khan. 'At Tulamba they were opposed by Rai Daud, Kamal Khan Mai, and Rai Habbu, the son of Rai Ratti, chiefs in the northern provinces, who were defeated.' Near Pákpattan however, on November 18th, Khizr Khan was victorious, and in 1414 he seized on the power at Delhi, founding the dynasty of the Syads. (Fir. i, 501).

1427. Death of Malik Ala ul Mulk, Amir of Multan, (Ell. iv, 59).

1429. Malik Rajah Nadira Amir of Multan died and the fief was restored to Malik Mahmud Husain, Imad-ul-Mulk, who was sent to Multan from Delhi with a large army. (Tar. Mub. Shah. Ell. iv, 67, Fir. i, 524).

1430. Sheikh Ali, governor of Kabul, on behalf of Shah Rukh Mirza, son of Tamerlane, advanced against Multan Imad-ul-Mulk went out to Tulamba to oppose him, and Sheikh Ali moved off to Khatibpur. On May 8th Imad returned to Multan and Sheikh Ali crossed the Ravi and laid all waste along the bank of the joint Jhelum-Chenáb. (Firishta says the Rávi). At a kos distance from Multan he defeated and killed Sultan Shah Lodi who was sent against him, and on the 27th May he occupied Khairabad 'within six miles of Multan.' On June 18th a fight took place in the gardens outside Multan in which he was repulsed; and two days later he was again driven back. A reinforcement of royal troops came up, and on Friday, July 25th, 'approaching the prayer-house (namazgah) endeavoured to enter the kútela of Ala-ul-Mulk.' Sheikh Ali opposed them and a great battle ensued in which he was defeated and driven across the river (said to be the Jhelum, but either the Chenáb and Ravi is meant) towards Shorkot.

The Delhi authorities getting jealous of Imad had him recalled and the 'ikta' or fief of Multan was transferred to Malik Khair-ud-din Khani. The transfer was inconsiderately carried out and this led to troubles. (Tab. Akb. and Tar. Mub. Sh. Ell. iv, 70—72. Fir. i, 525—6).

1431. Sheikh Ali was induced by Jasrath Khokhar to attack Multan again. After taking Khatibpur he reached Tulamba and sacked the town ruthlessly. He does not however seem to have advanced further. (Ell. iv, 73).

1432. Saiad Mubarak Shah, Sultan of Delhi, advanced from the Montgomery district in pursuit of Sheikh Ali, and after crossing the Rávi near Tulamba put him to flight (Tar. Mub. Shah Ell. iv, 77, Fir. i, 528). After taking Shorkot the king made a detour to Multan to visit the tombs of the saints. (Fir. i, 529). In 1435 his successor, Muhammad Shah, paid Multan a visit for a similar purpose. (Tab. Akb. Ell. iv, 84). Shortly after this Bahlol Lodi seems to have been Governor of Multan. (Ain. Jar. ii, 388.)

1437. Disturbances arose in Multan owing to the discontent of the Langáhs who are represented by Firishta as a Pathan tribe recently arrived from Sibi (Ell. iv, 85. Fir. iv, 380). Their then habitat was Rapri (Cf. Ell. v, 306).

1443. Tired of anarchy the people of Multan selected a ruler 'one Sheikh Yusaf, a man of learning, wisdom and high character' of the tribe of Koresh (a descendant of Bahawal Hakk), and 'the public prayers were read, and money coined, in his name.' 'The prince fully repaid their confidence by re-organising the government and gaining the esteem and friendship of the surrounding zamíndars.'

1445. Rai Sahra, Langáh, father-in-law of Sheikh Yusaf, seized Multan and drove out Sheikh Yusaf to Delhi, The story of how he came to see his daughter in the town, and how having drunk duck's blood and taken an emetic he induced his son-in-law to let in some of his own people to tend him is given at length in Firishta iv, 381—2. Rai Sahra assumed the title of Kutb-ud-din Langah and reigned till 1469. (see Firishta; the names and dates in the Ain-i-Akbari differ somewhat, see Ain. Jar. ii, 234-5).*

* Mr. Dames in Punjab Notes and Queries ii, 514, observes that there are apparently no coins of the Langáh dynasty extant.

Chapter II.

History.

Moghal Invasions.

1469. Husain Khan Langáh, son of Kutb-ud-Din, succeeded. He attacked and took Shorkot and Chiniot; also the country round Kot Kahror and Dinkot, which he colonized with Dodai Beloches, who, being pressed by the Moghals in Kachi and Sindh, now appear for the first time in India. (Fir. iv, 386. J.A.S.B. 1848, ii, 560). His brother Shahab Din rebelled in Kahror but was taken and imprisoned. Then the Delhi troops advanced in aid of the exiled Sheikh Yusaf and had nearly reached Multan when Husain Khan, 'crossing the Indus' threw himself into the fort and routed the invaders, driving them towards Chiniot. About this time, too, a number of Sahnas emigrated from Sindh to Multan. (Fir. iv 387-8) and one of them called Jam Bayazid was granted Shorkot (cf. Punjab N. and Q. iii, 215).

1480 circa.—One historian relates that in the reign of Bahlol Khan Lodi of Delhi the Delhi troops marched through Multan to chastise a rebel called Ahmad Bhatti, but this is not mentioned in most histories. (Ell. v, 5). About this time, however, the Bhattis of Jesalmir established themselves between the Sutlej and the Biás (and even as far as Asinikot beyond the Biás) and were in constant conflict with the Langáhs, Khichís, Joyás and other tribes of that region. Rawal Chachik of Jesalmir was killed in a great fight with the Langáhs near Dunyapur (Tod Rájasthán, Calc. edn. 1894, ii, 110—113).

1483. A treaty was made between Husain Khan and Sikandar Khan Lodi of Delhi. (Fir. iv, 389).

1500 circa.—Firishta tells a story regarding the envoy whom Husain Khan sent to Ahmadabad and who said that the whole revenues of Multan could not build a palace like that at Ahmadabad. The prime minister consoled Husain Khan by saying that 'though India might be the country of riches yet Multan could boast in being a country of men.' Among the literary men of Multan he proceeded to enumerate 'Sheikh Yusaf Koreshi, Sheikh Baha-ud-din Zakaria, and others brought up in the philosophic school of Haji Abdul Wahab, besides Fatteh-Ulla and his disciple Aziz-Ulla, both inhabitants of Multan, and who had each thousands of disciples.' Husain Khan shortly afterwards resigned in favour of his son Firoz, but Firoz was poisoned by his minister, and Husain again assumed power. (Fir. iv, 389—391).

1502. Husain ousted his minister Imad-ul-Malk in favour of Jam Bayazid Sahna, and soon after died. (Fir.iv, 391; others put his death in 1497 or 1498.) His successor Mahmud was 'young and foolish withal,' and complaints were made to him that Jam Bayazid transacted public business at his private house on the bank of the Chenáb and insulted the dignity of revenue collectors. Jam Bayazid's son attempted to assassinate the king, and then fled with his father to Shorkot, where they submitted to the Delhi Lodis. A treaty was made by which the Rávi was recognized as the boundary between the Delhi and Multan kingdoms. (Fir. iv, 393-5, Tab. Akb. Ell. v, 469).

1520 circa.—Mir Chakar Rind, the famous Biloch Chief, tried to get a footing in Multan but was opposed by Sohrab Dudai and went on to Shorkot. (Taba Akb. Ell.v, 470. Fir. iv, 396). About this time Shiism is said to have been introduced to Multan by Mir Imad Gardezi—others say Mir Shahdad, son of Mir Chakar. (Do.).

1524. The Arghun Turks who had been driven out of Kandahar were induced by Babar to attack Multan and advanced to the Ghara. Sheikh Baha-ud din Koreshi, was sent from Multan to dissuade them but failed. The Langáh army composed largely of 'Beloches, Jats, Rinds and others' marched out, but at Beg, one or two marches from Multan, Sultan Mahmud died suddenly, probably poisoned either by Sheikh Shuja Bukhari, his minister, or by Langar (or Lashkar) Khan, a man of note. (Fir. iv, 39, Ersk. B and H. 456. Tab. Akb. Ell. v, 471. Tarkhannama. Ell.v. 314). Mahmud appears before his death to have sworn fealty to Babar (Fir. iv, 435).

His son Sultan Husain, a minor, succeeded him, and Sheikh Ba ha-ud-din seems to have persuaded the Arghuns to retire, leaving the Ghara as the boundary. (Ersk. Bab. and Hum., 391.)

1525. Anarchy prevailed in Multan. 'The leading chiefs and nobles retired each to his own tribe or jagir and strengthened himself there.' Langar Khan

The Moghal Emperors.

induced the Arghuns once more to attack Multan and the place was besieged. The besieged were reduced to great straits through the incapacity and rapacity of Shuja, the minister, and his factotum Jadah (or Juma) Machhi. (Ersk. 394).

1527. After the siege had lasted for a year and some months, the Arghuns took the fort by assault: 'having broken down the Lahore gate with axes and hammers.' Almost every one was massacred and even such as fled to the 'convent of the Sheikhs' did not escape, for this also was plundered and set on fire after being drenched in blood. The historians have preserved several detailed accounts of this siege, (see Erskine 395—6. Fir. iv, 899. Tab. Akb. Ell. v, 472—5).

Shams-ud-din who was left by the Arghuns with 600 men in charge of Multan committed great cruelties to extort money. Langar Khan on the other hand did his best to rebuild the desolated city, but had soon to retire in disgust to Babar at Lahore. (Ersk. 398).

1528. Some 15 months after the Arghuns took possession, a popular insurrection under one Shamsher Khan expelled Shams-ud-din. The Arghuns then resigned the province to Babar, who sent his son Askari with Langar Khan to take it over (Ersk. 398).

The Moghal Emperors—A. D. 1528—1752.*

Under the strong, centralized Government of the greater Moghal Emperors, Multan at last enjoyed a long period of peace, and it obtained in the documents and coins of the period the standing title of 'Dár-ul-amán' (the seat of safety). It may be said that for two hundred years from 1548 to 1748, there was no warfare in this part of the Punjab; a rebel or a fugitive prince once or twice flitted through the district, bringing no doubt a certain amount of temporary depredation in his train, but the country as a whole had settled down to peace. The cultivation probably remained as before for the most part confined to the riverain lands; the area immediately around and north of Multan was (for some reason not ascertained) available for settlers in Shah Jehan's reign and was colonized by men from all parts of North-Western India, but there was probably no very great extension of cultivation, and the figures for the provincial revenue, so far as we can follow them, do not indicate any very large development. The people, however, had peace and their status must in many ways have improved. Commerce at any rate seems to have flourished, and Multan itself became a noted emporium for trade between Hindustan and the Persian Empire. The city became the head-quarters of a Province, which covered the whole of the South-Western Punjab, and at times included also the whole of Sindh. The governors seem as a whole to have been intelligent and well behaved, and the Province—involving as it sometimes did the command of armies on the Kandahar frontier—was often confided to princes of the Royal House.

---

* For the information regarding this and the subsequent period I am indebted largely to a very interesting history of Multan prepared by Shah Yusaf, Gardezi, and most of the facts for which authority is not quoted below are related in that history. There are also some interesting details in a manuscript history of the Saddozai and Khudakka families entitled 'Tazkirat ul Muluk' in the possession of Nur Muhammad Khan, Khudakka, of Multan.

Chapter II.

History.

The Moghal Emperors.

Even when the Moghal power began to fall to pieces Multan at first escaped much of the devastation which visited other parts of India. The route to Delhi by Bhatinda and Abohar was now too dry for armies and the high road to Delhi from the west no longer lay through Multan but through Lahore. The armies of Nadir Shah and Ahmad Shah Abdali, with their awful attendant evils, left Multan unscathed, and it was only from minor and subsidiary contentions that this district suffered. In the later days of the empire, and more especially when the trans-Indus tracts had been cut off by Nadir Shah, the Multan Province became by degrees an appendage of Lahore. As the central power weakened, the government became more and more a government by contract, a money-making concern: it got into the hands of Hindus, and it is to the Hindu instinct that we owe the origin of those local farmings of revenue, which in turn led to that development of canal irrigation, that forms the one bright spot amid the general confusion of the succeeding period before the days of Diwan Sawan Mal.

Chronicle.

1528—1530.—Langar Khan, governor of Multan.

1530.—On Babar's death Mirza Kamran obtained the Punjab and recalled Langar Khan to Lahore.

1540.—Humayun, in his retreat from India, marched from Lahore into the territories of Bakhshu Khan Langáh. To propitiate this chief Humayun gave him the title of Khan Jahan, and Bakhshu Khan, though not attending the camp himself, gave all assistance to Humayun to help him to cross the Ghara (Ersk. Bab. and Hum. ii, 208).

1541.—Multan passed with Lahore into the hands of Sher Shah, Afghan. This sovereign is said to have erected three tiled mosques in Multan, *viz.*, at the shrines of Bahawal Hakk, Rukn-i-Alam and Shah Yusuf Gardezi.

1542.—Humayun in his wanderings came from Bhakkar to Uch, but Bakhshu Khan Langah put such obstacles in his way that he had to retire to Bikanir territory. (Ersk. ii, 238).

1543 Circa.—The Beloches had meantime continued their incursions, the Mazaris reached Tulamba and Mír Chakar Rind settled down at Satgara in Montgomery. Sher Khan sent Haibat Khan Niazi, governor of Lahore, against Chakar, and according to Beloch legend, Haibat having killed Chakar's son, roasted his ribs. Chakar however is said to have marched on Multan and thence to Sitpur; and legend (here at fault) says that Haibat was killed and his head made into a drinking cup. (Dame's Belochi Text book Stories, pp. 10-12. Temple's Legends of the Punjab, ii, 491).

One Fath Khan Jat, who was in rebellion at Pákpattan, was also attacked, by Haibat and his Afghans. He fled to a mud fort between Kahror and Fattehpur, when he held out for some time with the help of Hindu Khan Beloch, and Bakhshu Khan Langáh, but the fort was at last captured. Haibat Khan, on reaching Multan, restored it from the devastation done by the Belochis, and was ordered by Sher Shah to 'repeople Multan and to observe the customs of the Langáhs and not to measure the land but to take a share of the produce.' Fatteh Jang Khan was left in charge of Multan and under his benevolent rule Multan flourished more than under the Langáhs. He founded Shergarh. (Tar. Sher Shah, Ell, iv, 398—9). [Local Legend says that Malik Fatu'l Khan Joya, chief of Fattehpur, refused to pay his revenue to the Suba of Khai

Chapter II.

History.

The Moghal Emperors.

called Ali Husain who lived at Shitabgarh. Ali Husain attacked him and they met in single combat at Halim Khichi, and Ali Husain was killed. Another story locates the combat at Fattehpur and says that both were killed.]

About 1554 the Turkish Admiral Sidi Ali passed through Multan on his way from Uch to Lahore. In his Mirat-ul-Mamalik he wrote: 'In the beginning of Ramzan we came to the river Kara or Kere, which we crossed by means of a raft. The people of Sind gave us permission to proceed as far as the Machvara and the river was crossed by boats. On the other side we found 500 Jats awaiting us, but our fire-arms frightened them and they did not attack. We advanced unmolested and reached the town of Multan on the 15th of Ramzan. In Multan I only visited the graves of the Sheikhs Baha-ud-din Zakaria, Rukn-ud-din and Sadr-ud-din. I received a blessing from Sheikh Muhammad Radjva and after receiving permission to continue my journey from Sultan Mir Miran Mirza Hussain, we proceeded towards Lahore.' (Vambery's Translation, p. 45). [The Kara is apparently the Ghára or Sutlej and if so the Machvara must be the Biás].

1556—1605.—Reign of Akbar. We have some passing notices of the persons in power in Multan during this reign. In 1561, on the defeat of Bahram Multan was given in jagir to Muhammad Kasim Khan of Nishapur (Ain. i, 353). In 1570 Khan Jahan Lodi was made governor, (do. i, 503). Some time before 1577, Syad Khan Chaghatai was governor, (do. i, 331). Between 1580 and 1588 Sadik Khan was made governor, (do. i, 356). In 1586, Khwaja Abdussamad was made Diwan, (do. i, 495). In 1591, Khan-i- Khanan's jagir was transferred to Multan (do. i, 335), and in 1593, Multan, 'which is more than Kandahar,' was given in jagir to Mirza Rustam Safawi, (do. i, 314). In 1593, Mirza Jani Beg got the Suba of Multan as tayul. (do. i, 363), and in 1596 Muhammad Aziz Koka got Multan in jagir (do. i, 327). In 1602, Syad Khan Chaghtai was appointed to the province of Multan (do. i, 332). Multan in Akbar's time had a silver and copper mint (do. i, 31).*

In 1573, the family of the Mirzas, sons of Muhammad Sultan Mirza, rebelled against Akbar and passed through the Punjab towards Multan. Near Tulamba Ibrahim Husain Mirza, while returning from hunting, was attacked by the royal troops and his brother taken prisoner. Ibrahim Husain retired, and in trying to pass the Ghara was wounded in the throat with an arrow by certain Jhils [Jhabels] 'who are fishermen dwelling about Multan.' He was taken prisoner and carried to Multan. (Tab. Akb. Ell. v, 355, Ain. i, 463).

1605—1627.—Reign of Jahangir. In 1619 apparently Khan Jahan was made governor of Multan. (De Laet. Ind. 240. cf. Herbert's Trav., Ed. 1628, p. 90). In 1614 the Englishmen Still and Crowther passed through Multan on their way from Ajmir to Ispahan. (Wheeler's Early Travs., 63).

1627—1658. Reign of Shah Jahan. At first Kilij Khan was governor. When he was transferred to Kandahar, Multan was given in jagir to Shahzada Murad Bakhsh, who built the present city walls and the bridge outside the Lohari Gate, and who colonized and brought under cultivation a great deal of land in the neighbourhood. When he was transferred to the Deccan, Nijabat Khan, a mild and popular governor, came to Multan as subadar. After this Multan was given in jagir to Prince Aurangzeb, and in his time (1648) Kandahar being taken by the Persians certain Saddozai exiles came and settled in Multan and Rangpur. Prince Aurangzeb is said to have repaired the tombs of Zainul-ab-din at Sakot and Khalik Wali at Khatti Chor. After this Multan became part of the jagir of Dara Shekoh for a year and a half, but was again transferred to Aurangzeb. While Aurangzeb was occupied in the siege of Kandahar (1652), Multan was again given to Dara, who appointed Sheikh Musa Gilani as his Naib. In 1658 came the illness of the Emperor Shah Jahan, the defeat of Dara near Agra and the assumption of the sovereignty by Aurangzeb.

The Augustinian friar Manrique seems to have visited Multan twice during Shah Jahan's reign. (Itinerario, p. 378).

---

* The British Museum contains the following Moghal coins of the Multan Mint: Akbar, copper A. H. 1,000; Shahjahan, gold 1068; silver 1039, 1040, 1042, 1043, 1045, 1048. Aurangzeb gold 1075, 1077; silver 1070, 1073, 1076, Farrukh Siyar, silver 1125, 1126, 1130.

Chapter II.

History.

The Moghal Emperors.

1658—1707.—Reign of Aurangzeb. Dara Shekoh, fleeing from Lahore before Aurangzeb, came to Multan for a few days (5th to 13th September 1658), put his treasure on boats and marched himself by land to Uch, intending to go to Kandahar. He broke down behind him the bridges (probably boat bridges) on the Bias and Sutlej.* The vanguard of Aurangzeb's army sent out parties to Dunyapur, to see that Dara had not fled to Ajmir, but when it was clear he had escaped to Bhakkar, Saf Shikan Khan was sent in pursuit and Aurangzeb himself stayed at Multan. On 25th September 1658 the Emperor's camp was pitched three miles from the city at the place where the Chenáb and Rávi met and a day or two afterwards he paid his respects to the shrines. Shaikh Musa Gilani was dismissed, and Lashkar Khan, governor of Kashmir, was transferred to Multan, Khan Alim acting as Naib till Lashkar Khan should arrive. After staying five days, Aurangzeb heard of the movements of Shuja Khan in Bengal, and at once marched back to Delhi. (Alamgirnama, pp. 200 *seqq.* Khafi Khan, Ell. vii, 232. Dow iii, 252).

After two years Lashkar Khan gave place to Tarbiat Khan, and he afterwards to Saif Khan. Multan then became jagir to Prince Muhammad Azam, who stayed here a long time and seems to have made a good governor: he is said to have been accustomed to go in disguise through the city at night like Harun-al-rashid. After him the jagir went to Prince Muhammad Akbar. Then the Subadari was held jointly by Allayar Khan and Karam Khan. In 1694-5 Muizz-ud-din, afterwards Jahandar Shah, grandson of Aurangzeb, was governor and seems to have been fairly active. He refused to help the Daudputras of Bahawalpur on their opposition to the governor of Sindh (Irvine in J.A.S.B. 1896, pp. 176 and 208. Shahamat Ali Bahawalp. and Mult., p. 16).

1707—1719.—Reigns of Bahadur Shah, Jahandar Shah and Farrukh Siyar In 1712 Jahandar Shah is said to have appointed the dancer Niamat to be governor of Multan; the Wazir demanded in mockery a nazrana of 1,000 guitars and the Emperor cancelled the appointment. (Irvine in J.A.S.B. 1896, p. 167 The story is somewhat differently told in Shafi Khan, Ell. vii, 432).

Under Jahandar Shah Kokaltash Khan (Ali Murad) is said to have been Governor, with Sher Afkhan as his Deputy.

Under Farrukh Siyar the following were Subadars of Multan, *viz.*,—Nawab Khan Zaman, Sher Afkan Khan, Akidat Khan; and Sayad Hussain Khan. Sher Afkan Khan seems to have been only the Deputy of Kutbul Mulk the Wazir. (Irvine in J.A.S.B. 1898, p. 156).

1719—1748. Reign of Muhammad Shah. The following were Subadars. (1) Sher Afkan Khan, Iazuddaula. (2) Bakir Khan who built the Bakirabad mosque which stands near the Lahore road about two miles N.E. of the city. (3) Sayad Hasan Khan. (4) Sher Afkan Khan again. (5) Nawab Abdussamad Khan Turani; he held both Lahore and Multan, and built the Idgah. (6) On his death in 1735 his son Zakaria Khan (known as Khan Bahadur Khan) was granted both Subas, and lived sometimes in one, sometimes in the other. In his time all the trans-Indus part of the Multan province was transferred from the Delhi Empire to that of Nadir Shah. (7) On his death his son Hyat-ulla Khan, known as Shahnawaz Khan, who had previously been left in charge of Multan, was granted both Subas.

1748—1752. Reign of Ahmad Shah. On the death of Muhammad Shah Muin-ud-din Khan (Mir Mannu), son of the Wazir Kamr-ud-din Khan, was appointed to the Subas of Lahore and Multan. Kaura Mal, a low bred Kirar, who had obtained promotion under Shahnawaz, was employed by Mir Mannu to march against Shahnawaz. There was a fight outside Multan in which Jassa Singh Kalal, the founder of the Ahluwalia misl, aided Kaura Mal. At first Kaura Mal was defeated, but Shahnawaz hearing that Kaura Mal was with only a few attendants on an elephant near Daurana Langana, went against

* There is a local tradition at Shujatpur in the Shujabad tahsil that when Dara Shekoh had passed the bridge over the Biás there the inhabitants broke it down behind him to aid him in his flight and were consequently severely punished by Aurangzeb.

Chapter II.

History.

him with some horse and was shot while actually cutting with his sword at Kaura Mal's howda. Kaura Mal then took the 'ijara' of Multan as Nasim on behalf of Mir Mannu and assumed the title of Maharaja.

Pathan and Sikh rule.

Kaura Mal maintained a friendly intercourse with the Daudputras of Baháwalpur and bestowed on Bahawal Khan the perpetual lease of the Adamwahan taluka for Rs. 4,000 per annum. To improve the new acquisition Bahawal Khan built the Shahdara (Sardárwáh) canal. Kaura Mal used often to go to Lahore and on one occasion he left as Naib-Nazim one Zahid Khan Saddozai Khankhel; this man having disobeyed some order, Kaura Mal marched against him, but when the armies met at Matithal Zahid Khan's army deserted and he dismounted from his palki and fled, but was afterwards captured. On another occasion Kaura Mal left one Khwaja Ishaq as his Naib and this time Kaura Mal was killed, fighting against Ahmad Shah Abdali. (See Muhammad Latif's History of Punjab, 214, 315. Sh. Ali Sah. 83, 37 J.A.S.B. 1848, ii, 568—571).

In 1751 Mubarak Khan Daudputra* bought the land of Shini, Bakhri and Mudwàla (now in Muzaffargarh) from the zamindars of Tahir: also Bet (? Bet Moghal) and Dunawali from Sheikh Raju Gardezi and brought them under cultivation (J.A.S.B. 1848, ii, 568). In 1752 Ahmad Shah Abdali compelled the Emperor to cede the Punjab and Sindh to him.† His son Tamur Shah was left in charge with Jahan Khan as adviser.

Pathan and Sikh Rule.

After having been an outlying province of the Delhi Empire Multan in 1752 became a province owing allegiance, often very nominal, to the Afghan kings of Kabul. The country was ruled for the most part by Governors of Pathan extraction, and under the rule of the Saddozais of Kabul a marked change took place in the fortunes of those Pathan families, chiefly Saddozais, who from time to time had fled from Afghanistan to take refuge in this district. By degrees those families, known as the Multani Pathans, absorbed a good deal of power: the fief of Shujabad remained for some time in the hands of one of them, and ultimately under Nawabs Muzaffar Khan and Sarfaraz Khan the Multan Saddozais set up for themselves a kingdom which was for all practical purposes independent. Under their government lands were conferred freely on the Pathan families; and numbers of Badozais, Bamozais, Tarins, Babars, Khakwanis and others, who had previously been mere towns-people or soldiers of fortune, became large jagirdars and landowners.

The rule of this Pathan government has come down to us surrounded by a certain halo, partly on account of the heroic

---

* As the eastern half of the district was for a long time under the Daudputra rulers of Baháwalpur and one hears a good deal about them on travelling along the Sutlej it is thought convenient to append the following list of the more recent rulers of the Bahawalpur State:—A. D. 1727 Sadik Muhammad Khan I; 1746 Bahawal Khan I; 1751 Mubarik Khan; 1772 Bahawal Khan II; 1809 Sadik Muhammad Khan II; 1825 Bahawal Khan III; 1853 Sadatyar Khan; 1853 Fatteh Khan; 1859 Bahawal Khan IV; 1865 Sadik Muhammad Khan IV; 1899 Bahawal Khan V. Of these the best remembered in the district is Bahawal Khan III, our ally in the Multan campaign, who is always spoken of as Sakhi Bahawal Khan, *i.e.*, the generous. The Nawab of Baháwalpur for the time being is generally spoken of as 'Khan' simply.

†Ahmad Shah struck coins at Multan in A. D. 1752 and 1754.

Chapter II.

History.

Pathan and Sikh rule.

defence made by the Nawabs against the Sikh aggressions, and partly on account of the very valuable assistance given to the British arms by the Pathan families in 1848; but, as a matter of fact, the Pathan administration of the country seems to have been exceedingly lax, and the rulers, who were brave men in the day of battle, were slothful, luxurious and utterly unbusiness-like in the management of their territories in days of peace. The rule of the Saddozais extended over both sides of the Chenáb from the neighbourhood of Sarai Siddhu to about half way down the present Shujabad tahsil, and the revenue they collected was about 5½ lakhs per annum. Their army consisted in peace time of some 2,000 men and 20 guns, but the number could be raised on emergency by the calling out of 10,000 or 12,000 militia. Elphinstone, who passed through Multan on his way to Kabul in 1807, says of the Multani administration: 'Nothing could be worse than the government; all sorts of direct exactions were aggravated by monopolies, rapacious and ungovernable troops, and every other kind of abuse.' (Elph. Caubul, 23). The following account by Elphinstone of his reception by Nawab Sarfaraz Khan gives an idea of the Pathans' notions of discipline and order in matters of ceremonial:—

'The principal events of our stay were our meetings with the governor of the province. The name of this personage was Sarfaraz Khan, and, as his government was in India, he bad the title of Nabob. He was of an Afghan family, of the royal tribe of Saddozai, but his ancestors had so long been settled in Multan, that he had lost most of the characteristics of his nation. He seems to have been seized with a panic as soon as he heard of the approach of the mission and the whole of his behaviour to the end was marked with suspicion and distrust. He shut the gates of the city against us, and allowed none of our men or followers to enter without express permission. He also doubled his guards, and we heard, from good authority, of debates in his council, whether it was most probable that we should endeavour to surprise the city, or, that we should procure a cession of it to us from the king. He, however, agreed to visit me on the 15th of December, and a very large tent was pitched for his reception. One end of it was open, and from the entrance two canvass screens ran out, so as to form an alley about twenty yards long, which was lined with servants in livery, other servants extending beyond it. The troops were also drawn up in line along the road to the tent.

Mr. Strachey went to meet the governor, and found him mounted on a white horse, with gold trappings, attended by his officers and favorites, surrounded with large standards, and escorted by 200 horse and 3,000 foot. The dust, crowd, and confusion of the meeting are represented by Mr. Strachey as beyond all description. The governor welcomed Mr. Strachey according to the Persian custom, after which they joined and proceeded to the tent, the pressure and disorder increasing as they went. In some places men were fighting, and in others people were ridden down. Mr. Strachey's own horse was nearly borne to the ground, and only recovered himself by a violent exertion. When they approached the tent they missed the road, came in front of the line of troops, and rushed on the cavalry with such impetuosity that there was barely time to wheel back so as to allow a passage. In this manner the tide poured on towards the tent, the line of servants was swept away, the screens were torn down and trampled under foot, and even the tent ropes were assailed with such fury that the whole tent was nearly struck over our heads.

The inside was crowded and darkened in an instant. The governor and about ten of his companions sat, the rest seemed to be armed attendants and, indeed, the governor seemed to have attended to nothing but the number of his

Chapter II.

History.

Pathan and Sikh rule.

guards. He sat but for a very short time, during the whole of which he was telling his beads with the utmost fervency, and addressing us with: "You are welcome," as fast as he could repeat the words. At last said he was afraid the crowd must annoy me, and withdrew. Sarfaraz Khan was a good looking young man; he wore the Persian dress, with a cap and a shawl turban over it, and spoke very good Persian. His attendants were large, fair, and handsome Afghans, most of them very well dressed, but in no sort of order or discipline. On the same evening I returned his visit, and found him sitting under an awning, on a terrace in one of his gardens. He had a large company sitting with him in good order. They differed greatly in appearance from the natives of India, but were neither handsomely dressed, nor so decorous as Persians. The Nabob being now free from alarm was civil and agreeable enough.

Only a little less than half of the present Multan district was in the hands of these Pathans: the rest, consisting of the whole of the Mailsi and Lodhran tahsils, and the southern half of Shujabad, was in the hands of the Daudputra Chiefs of Baháwalpur, who had gradually acquired the various talukas in this tract on lease from the rulers of Multan. When the power of the Multan Nawabs grew feebler, the Daudputras ceased paying their rent for these tracts, but on the advent of the Sikh power the rent was again strictly exacted from them. Under the Sikhs the rent was enhanced largely, until ultimately in 1831 the Daudputras failed to pay it, and the whole country west of Sutlej then passed into the hands first of General Ventura and then of Diwan Sawan Mal. The Daudputra rule in the Sutlej tahsils had lasted, off and on, for some eighty or ninety years, and their management of the country seems to have been on the whole sensible and popular. Some of their kardars, such as Sirdar Muhammad Khan and Jam Khan, have left a name behind them for energy and justice, and it is to their management that we owe for the most part of the present system of canal irrigation in the district.

The earliest canals of which we can trace the origin were the Muhammadwah and the Sirdarwah which were made some time before 1750 to improve the Daudputra lands in the west of the present Lodhrán tahsil. The lands further to the east were then taken in hand, and in another five years the Daudputras had excavated the Bahawalwah, Sadikwah and Kabilwah. Further east again were constructed shortly afterwards, under the kardar Jam Khan, the two large canals, the Jamwah Kalan and the Jamwah Khurd, which are called after his name. And, finally, furthest to the east of all, when the Sikhs had taken the country, Ghulam Mustafa Khakwani built the canal Diwanwah, which he named after Diwan Sawan Mal. The success of these various irrigation schemes was great: large tracts of land were brought under cultivation, and tenants migrated eagerly from the Chenab lands to the Daudputra canals. The Pathans on the Chenab side were not slow in taking up the cue, and the Governor, Ali Muhammad Khan, started the digging of the large canal, still known after him as the Wali Muhammad, which irrigates the lands round Multan: but, with this exception, the attempts made to irrigate in the Chenáb tahsils were feeble and

Chapter II.

History.

Pathan and Sikh rule.

irregular, compared with the great works of the Daudputras on the Sutlej. Two small cuts, now the Shahpur and Durana Langana canals, were made at an early date. Another, now the Sikandarabad, was constructed by the powerful Khokhar family for the irrigation of its own lands. The Saddozais fostered their jagir in Shujabad by permitting the construction of the Gujjuhatta, Bakhtuwah and Dhundhun canals. And towards the end of their rule some small efforts were made to extend irrigation northwards by the construction of the Khadal, Tahirpur and Matital cuts. The Government, however, had little to do with the canal making on the Chenáb side; and, indeed, the cultivation carried on by these Chenáb canals seems to have been but small. Elphinstone, who notes the number of "large and deep watercourses" in the Sutlej tahsils, does not mention canal irrigation round Multan. He says that a good deal of the country in these parts was "most abundantly watered by Persian wheels," but "a large proportion of the villages were in ruins, and there were other signs of a well cultivated country going to decay." [Elph. Caubul, i, 28].

The chief factor in this picture of desolation was the continual warfare with the Sikhs of the north. From the time when the Bhangi Misl first appeared before the city in 1771 to the day when the army of Ranjit Singh stormed the Multan fort in 1818, the greater part of the Multan and Kabírwála tahsils was being constantly overrun by predatory armies, and the havoc thus wrought has left its traces to the present day. Even when Ranjit Singh had taken Multan, he contented himself for a time with putting in governors of the muharrir type, who were quite incapable of restoring the prosperity of the country or of coping with the robber bands that overran the Kabírwála "bar:" and it was not till 1821, when Diwan Sawan Mal was made governor, that the unfortunate district obtained any real peace or strong government.*

For 23 years the Chenáb tahsils, and for 13 years the whole district, was under the rule of Sawan Mal. The careless and disorganized happy-go-lucky administration of the Pathan aristocracy was now exchanged for a government conducted on the strictest of business principles. There was, it is true, very little system, as we understand it, in Sawan Mal's government: administrative boundaries were terribly confused and constantly changing, and his revenue arrangements still baffle us by their local and individual character; but want of system was atoned for by a most minute knowledge of personal and local matters, a precise attention to business and strong centralization of power. We hear little or nothing of Sawan Mal's kardars and his government was of the 'one-man' type. He

* So much have these Sikh incursions impressed themselves on the minds of the people that they still have a saying: 'Sáin, jo balá ándí hai uthiyou dí hai,' 'Misfortune is from the north.'

was constant and methodical in his kutcherry hours, and minute in his supervision, especially over matters of accounts. He was thus able in a remarkable way to make this district the most contented in India, and yet at the same time to make it yield every rupee of income that could be squeezed from it, and this result he achieved by a combination of strict justice with minute revenue management.

In his judicial work he was strict and impartial. Edwardes, who saw through the spectacles of his friends, the Pathan refugees, attributes this largely to Sawan Mal's own low origin, 'What in us,' he writes, 'is an imperfection in Sawan Mal amounted to a vice. He could not tolerate a gentleman. A low bred man himself, he hated any one who had a grandfather. Rich merchants he loved and called around him, for they earned their money as he did himself; but inherited wealth he regarded as contraband, a thing to be seized and confiscated whenever found. Thus the same man who would lend money to a Jat to buy a plough or dig a well, would keep a Multani Pathan out of his estate and think he did God a service. Between the poor he did justice with great pains and impartiality; but a rich man, even if in the right, never got a verdict from Sawan Mal without paying for it.'

So too in his revenue arrangements, which will be further described later on, he carried out the ideas of land nationalization to great lengths. His main principle was that if land was culturable and the owner did not cultivate it, another cultivator should be put in by the State, and the owner recouped by a small due or not according to circumstances. Each village was assessed in the way that gave the largest return to Government, but whenever possible that way was also the most suitable to the cultivators. If a man had not capital to build a well or to buy oxen, the State at once supplied the capital and recouped itself as best it could, not according to any system but by taking as much from the owner each year as he could spare without injury to the cultivation. The canals were diligently cleared out, the zealous zamindars being encouraged by rewards and honours, and the remiss being severely punished. The Hindu who wanted to invest money in land was given uncultivated land to reclaim, and when he had reclaimed it was made to pay a full annual revenue for it. Useless expenditure on jagirs and mafis was reduced to a minimum, and everything able to yield revenue was made to yield it. And yet the people, tired after long harassments and pleased with the substantial justice they received, were kept happy and contented as they have probably never been before or since.

Chronicle.

From 1752 to 1767 the most prominent person in the history of Multan was *Ali Muhammad Khan Khakwani*. This officer, who had accompanied Ahmad Shah in his expeditions, was appointed in 1752 to succeed Khwaja Ishak at Multan. He

Chapter II.

History.

Pathan and Sikh rule.

was at first a good ruler, but afterwards became avaricious and oppressive. In 1758 the Mahrattas, who had been invited into the Punjab by Adina Beg Khan, overran the district: Ali Muhmmad Khan had to retire beyond the Ghara, and the Mahrattas appointed one Salih Muhammad Khan as Nazim in his place.* After some two years, however, a fresh invasion of the Duranis caused the Mahrattas to retire and Ali Muhammad in 1760 came to his own again. Next year, however, he was suspended, and the province was committed to the joint rule of Abdul Karim Khan and Allayar Khan Bamezai. After another interval the province fell to Nawab Shuja Khan Saddozai Khankhel, son of the Zahid Khan who had previously been naib-nazim, and a fellow-clansman of the king Ahmad Shah Durani. About the end of 1766, however, Ali Muhammad Khan was again restored, and with the help of the Daudputras he seized the province of Dera. In return for this help he leased to them for Rs. 8,000 a year the ilakas of Khanwah, Kahlwan (Kalluwala?), Adamwahan, Imam-ud-dinpur (Mamdi Mahtam?) and Shekhwah: he also allowed Mubarak Khan to seize and build a fort in certain land belonging to the Mailsi tribe and to take the lands on lease in perpetuity for Rs. 400 per annum. The latter acquisitions were entrusted to Jam Khan, son of Mulla Ali Kihrani who at once began to build a canal for their irrigation, and the success of these Sutlej canals was insured by the immigration from the north induced by Ali Muhammad Khan's cruelties. Meantime Ali Muhammad Khan seized Shuja Khan and put him in prison. When Ahmad Shah advanced against Multan, Shuja Khan was relased but he had carefully kept the additional nails and hair which he had grown in prison and showed these to Ahmad Shah, who in his indignation seized Ali Muhammad Khan, had his belly ripped open and his body exposed on a camel through the streets of Multan. (See Sh. Ali, 49, 52—4 and J.A.S.B. 1848, ii, 569).

The years 1767 to 1770 are marked by what may be called the *Haji Sharif episode.* Although Nawab Shuja Khan was again appointed Subadar on Ali Muhammad's death, one Haji Sharif Khan Saddozai shortly afterwards got himself nominated from Kabul for the appointment, and Shuja Khan finding himself deserted by his army, had to retire to Shujabad. From Shujabad he sent a Hindu called Dharm Jas to Kabul with instructions to obtain the Subadarship either for Shuja Khan or for Dharm Jas himself: the Hindu did the latter, and sent one Mirza Sharif Beg, Taklu, a common chaprasi, as his naib to take over charge. Sharif Beg after seeing Shuja Khan at Shujabad advanced to Multan, entered the city by the Pak gate and then went into the fort by the Sikki gate. Haji Sharif Khan was having his beard dyed at the time in the Samman Burj of the fort; officer after officer was despatched by him to see what the disturbance was, but as none returned, his suspicions were roused and he escaped by the window. As he had been here so short a time, the people said of him 'Haji Sharif, na Rabi na Kharif,' *i.e,* he had not time to see either spring or autumn harvest. The naib Sharif Beg ruled well. When Dharm Jas came to take over charge, he summoned Sharif Beg to meet him at the Chenáb, but Sharif Beg refused and shut himself up in the fort, and while Dharm Jas was walking on the roof of a house in Diwan Mansa Ram's garden, a well directed ball from the fort killed him. Sharif Beg thereupon proclaimed himself ruler, and to protect himself from the anger of the king at Kabul he invited the assistance of the Bhangi Sikhs. A one-eyed general called Bahadur Khan Durani (called Bihra Khan in the Tazkirat-ul-Mulúk) was sent from Kabul to chastise Sharif Beg, and he took the city by undermining the walls, but failed to take the fort, and retired on the arrival of the Sikhs. Sharif Beg wisely refused to let his deliverers into the fort but one day, when he was at the Idgah, his Diwan allowed them in, whereon Sharif Beg fled to Sital Das' garden, and ultimately agreed to retire to his jagir at Tulamba where he built the present fort, and a few years later, he died. (See also p. 62, Sh. Ali where a somewhat different account is given; also J.A.S.B. 1848, ii, 571, where the dates differ a little).

From 1771 to 1779 the *Bhangi Sikhs* held and terrorized the whole of the north and centre of the district under their chiefs Ganda Singh and Jhanda Singh. Their general was Lahna Singh and the 'killadar' of the fort was Diwan Singh Chacchowalia. They failed to take Shujabad in spite of a three months siege: and Shuja Khan with his allies the Daudputras advanced against

* Apparently in subordination to a Mahratta Shamaji Rao (Muhammad Latif's History, Punjab, 231).

Chapter II.

History.

Pathan and Sikh rule.

Multan and seized the city, but failing to obtain the fort retired again. So too one Ali Muhammad Khan Durani who was sent from Kabul to expel the Sikhs was able to take the city only and failed to take the fort. In June 1773 Ahmad Shah Durani died and was succeeded by his son Taimur, who had hitherto been the nominal 'Nizam' of Multan.* So also in 1776 Nawab Shuja Khan died at Shujabad and was succeeded by his son Muzaffar Khan. The Sikhs had leased the country of Dipálpur, Kahror and Fattehpur between the Biás and Sutlej to Madad Ali Khan Daudpotra; but when the attack on Shujabad caused Muzaffar Khan to retire to Baháwalpur, the Daudputras espoused his cause and sent an army with him against the Sikhs. After besieging the city for 23 days they were admitted by the postern gate of the Gardezis on the west side of the town, and at once fell to indiscriminate looting, while the Sikh killadar, Diwan Singh, being shut up in the fort, sent expresses to Amritsar for aid. When Ganda Singh arrived from the Punjab the greater part of the Daudputra force were found to have returned to their homes in anticipation of sanction, and the Sikhs had little difficulty in driving Muzaffar Khan back to Shujabad. From Shujabad incessant appeals for help were sent to Taimur Shah, who then 'ordered Sirdar Bihru Khan with a proper force, experienced in war, to proceed and expel the Sikhs from Multan.' This general in 1778 had almost taken the fort when he was recalled. Another force under Sirdar Ali Maddad Khan was sent shortly afterwards, and this too had nearly taken the fort when it was withdrawn. In 1779 Taimur Shah himself advanced from Peshâwar to Dera Ghâzi Khan, and shortly afterwards a big fight took place between the two forces in the direction of Shujabad. The Shah's troops, numbering 18,000, under Zangi Khan, Kamalzai, are said to have been caught in a duststorm while facing the Sikh army; having obtained a Sikh drum, the Pathans began beating it, and the Sikhs, hearing their own war drum, began groping their way in small parties towards it and were cut down by the Pathans as they came up. Their heads were cut off and sent in kajawas on camels to Dera Ghazi Khan. The routed army was pursued by Taimur Shah in person to Multan; the Shah encamped at the Idgah and besieged the fort. By the intercession of Abdulkarim Khan, Babar, the Sikhs were allowed to surrender and march out with all the honours of war. Whereupon Taimur Shah took possession of the fort and after installing Muzaffar Khan as subadar, returned again to Kabul. (See J.A.S.B. 1848 ii, 566—7 Sh. Ali, pp. 62—4. Muhammad Latif's History, Punjab, 297—9.)

From 1779 to 1818 *Nawab Muzaffar Khan* Saddozai remained in power at Multan.

His relations towards the Kabul authorities were very varying and indefinite. In 1792 Taimur Shah took him to Kabul and was, it is said, intending to imprison him, when Taimur Shah died and was succeeded by Zaman Shah. Zaman Shah confirmed Muzaffar Khan, and we find coins of this king dated 1799 and 1800 which were struck at the Multan mint. Zaman Shah had summoned Muzaffar Khan to Kabul, and the latter had advanced as far as Tank when he heard that Zaman Shah had been blinded and deposed. Mahmud Shah set himself up as king in Kabul and Shah Shuja in Peshawar. At first the power of the former preponderated, and he confirmed Muzaffar Khan in his government, but his Wazir Fatteh Khan induced him to send Abdussamad Badozai in his place. Muzaffar Khan refused to recognize Abdussamad, and defeated him at Dinpur near Muzaffargarh. Meantime in 1807 Shah Shuja regained ascendancy in Eastern Afghanistan, and sent an expedition under the son of his Wazir Ata Muhammad Khan, but matters were compromised, and Shah Shuja duly confirmed Muzaffar Khan, associating with him in the government his son Nawab Sarfaraz Khan. In 1807, Nawab Muzaffar Khan went for nine months on a pilgrimage to Mecca, and during his absence Elphinstone's Embassy to Kabul passed through Multan, remaining in the district from the 5th to the 21st of December. Shah Shuja's power in these parts lasted till 1809, and we have gold coins of his struck in Multan in that year. The story is that when Shuja-ul-Mulk came to terms with Ranjit Singh in 1809, he promised to give Multan over to him, but afterwards he got him to agree to leave Multan with Muzaffar Khan, the revenue of S. Siddhu, Sirdarpur and

* Coins were struck by Taimur as Nizam in 1762—4 and 1770 at Multan, the device being 'Ba'alam yaft sikka Taimur Shah Nizam, ba hukm-i-Khuda wa Rasul,-i-anam,' and on the obverse 'San—zarb Dar-ul-aman Multan.' Coins were struck at Multan in the name of Taimur Shah as king in 1790 and 1791. (Dames,' Coins of the Duranis in Num Chron viii, 325, &c).

Chapter II.

History.

Pathan and Sikh rule.

Tulamba being assigned to Shuja-ul-Mulk for maintenance: and it is said that Shuja-ul-Mulk having visited his jagir and found the maintenance insufficient, went on to Lahore.* The unhappy monarch is said to have passed through Multan and while there to have been lodged in the Hazuri Bagh. His women were put up in the Nawab's Haram Sarai and afterwards in Ali Muhammad Khan's Haveli outside the Lohari gate; but the Nawab omitted all visits of courtesy. In any case after 1809 Muzaffar Khan was nominally subject to Mahmud Shah until he began paying tribute to the Sikhs; and the local coinage in his life-time and indeed after the Sikhs had taken Multan at the time of his death was in the name of Mahmud Shah (see J.A.S.B. 1848, ii, 570, Dames loc cit and Tazkirat ul-Mulúk).

In his relations with the Daudputras of Baháwalpur, who (it must be remembered) held the greater part of what are now known as the 'Sutlej Tahsils,' Muzaffar Khan was not at first very happy, and we hear of an unprovoked aggression on his part in 1779, followed by a skirmish in which his officer Abdulkarim Khan Babar was killed. After Zaman Khan's death, however, when other governors were sent from Kabul to oust Muzaffar Khan, the latter received the hearty assistance of the Daudputras under Bahawal Khan I, and in return helped that chief in his aggressions towards Dera Gházi Khan and Muzaffargarh. In 1807, when Muzaffar Khan went to Mecca, Sarfaraz Khan renewed the lease to the Daudputras of the tracts of Adamwahan, Khanpur, Shergarh, and Khai and the Daudputras 'brought them under fine cultivation.' In 1810, however, when certain rebels stood out against Muhammad Khan II Daudputra in the lands north of the Sutlej, Sarfaraz Khan seems to have in some way abetted them, and the Daudputras then ceased paying their annual rent for these lands. After this the two Nawabs remained on bad terms. In 1811 certain rebels from the Baháwalpur State were allowed by Muzaffar Khan to take refuge in Shujabad and make raids from thence. Shortly afterwards Muzaffar Khan sent his own army to oppose the Daudputra General Yakub Muhammad Khan, and the two forces met somewhere south of Shujabad, apparently near Panjani. The Multan force was defeated, and next day the bodies of their dead 'were transferred on hackeries to Shujabad by permission of the Daudputra commander.' The result of these contentions was that when the Sikhs attacked Multan, the Daudputras afforded the Pathans no kind of aid, (see Sh. Ali 65, 113, 120, 146, 166—7 J.A.S.B 1848, ii, 570 Muhammad Latif's History, Punjab, 385, Edwardes Year in Pb. Front iii, 417).

It was in his relations with the Sikhs that Muzaffar Khan ultimately failed to hold his own. After the Bhangis had been driven out of Multan, an attack was made on the town by the Hathianwalas but they were repulsed. Later on an army was sent by Muzaffar Khan to Kamalia under Khan Muhammad Khan Badozai who recovered that town from the Sikhs and gave it over to its hereditary rulers, the Rais of the Kharral tribe. In 1802, he first came in contact with Ranjit Singh when that chief, having marched into the Nawab's dominions, was induced to retire by the promise of a large 'nazrana.' In 1806, Ranjit Singh made his *second* invasion: he advanced as far as Kot Mahtam (now Khan Bahadargarh in the south of the Kabirwala tahsil), but on hearing that the Mahrattas under Holkar were on his eastern frontier he retired, accepting a present of Rs. 70,000. In 1807 the third invasion took place, Ranjit Singh being urged to attack Multan by Abdussamad Khan, Badozai, the unsuccessful claimant of 1803. Ranjit Singh accused Muzaffar Khan of harbouring and helping his enemy Ahmad Khan Syal of Jhang, and again marched his troops to Kot Mahtam. A truce was there made with Khudayar Khan, the representative of the local jagirdar, but was broken by Ranjit Singh in order that he might have an excuse for looting the kirars of the neighbourhood. An attempt was made to arrest Khudayar Khan, but that officer drew his sword, and was advancing against Ranjit Singh's elephant when he was cut down. The Sikhs then advanced on Multan. After 11 days the Pathans retired into the fort and after another 11 days, Ranjit

* One story is that Shuja-ul-Mulk found in Multan another refugee Shahzada Ahsan Bakht, brother of the Delhi Emperor, who was in receipt of an allowance from the Afghans; and that as the Shahzada's allowance was in the form of an assignment of the income from drugs, spirits and houses of ill-fame, Shuja-ul-Mulk was not much tempted to apply for similar pecuniary aid. The jagir actually given to him was purposely located in a direction where the raids of the Syals and Kathias rendered collection of revenue very difficult.

Singh, who had no siege appliances, accepted a nazrana of Rs. 70,000 (half of which was realized by the Nawab from the inhabitants of the town), and after exacting a further sum from the Daudputras returned to Lahore. In 1810 Ranjit Singh made his *fourth* attack, alleging as his ground for hostilities the non-payment of the subsidy promised by Muzaffar Khan. The Sikhs reached Multan on February 24th and took possession of the city the next day. A contingent of 500 horse was exacted from the Daudputra, and the fort was hotly besieged, but without success. The following is the account of the siege given in Muhammad Latif's 'History of the Punjab'—(see also Sh. Ali, 158).

Chapter II.

History.

Pathan and Sikh rule.

" The citadel of Multan was now closely besieged by the Sikh army, but the Pathans offered a stout resistance and the most strenuous attempts of the Sikh soldiers to carry the fort by assault signally failed. A heavy bombardment was kept up for several days, but without any effect. Batteries were then erected opposite the fort, and an incessant fire was maintained, but hardly any impression was made on the citadel. Recourse was at length had to mining; but the besieged successfully countermined. Ranjit Singh made the most solemn and lavish promises to the Chiefs who should distinguish themselves in the action by the earliest effective advance. He personally reconnoitred the enemy's position, examined his posts, and fixed his own, marking out the spots for the batteries, and assigning lines of approach to the different chiefs, whose sense of duty to their countrymen was appealed to with vehemence. Extensive transport arrangements were made both by land and water from Lahore and Amritsar, and the whole resources of the country were unreservedly placed at the disposal of the military authorities to secure this much coveted possession. The famous " Bhangi *top*," named " Zamzama," was broeght from Lahore to batter down the walls of the fort, but i tmade little impression on the besieged. It discharged a ball of $2\frac{1}{2}$ maunds (kachcha) or 80 lbs. in weight, but the appliances for working this huge piece of ordnance were wanting in the Sikh camp, while nobody possessed sufficient skill to make a proper use of it. Some little impression that was made on the ramparts of the citadel by the Sikh artillery had the effect only of redoubling the zeal of the besieged, who, in countermining, blew up the battery of Sardar Attar Singh, Dhari, close to the fort, killing the Sardar and twelve others, and severely wounding many more, among whom were Sardar Nihal Singh, Attariwala, and the youthful Hari Singh, Nalwa. Confused and panic-stricken the assailants fled, leaving their dead close to the fort, but the high-minded Pathans sent the bodies to the besiegers, that of Attar Singh being wrapped in a pair of shawls. The siege lasted for two months, during which the Sikh army was greatly reduced, and its best soldiers and generals killed or incapacitated. The most conspicuous of these was Attar Singh, Dhari, a favorite companion and confidential Sardar of the Maharaja. Nor did the Sikh army meet with better success in other quarters. Diwan Muhkam Chand, who had been sent to reduce Shujabad, found the fort impregnable. A general assault was made on the 21st of March, but the Sikh army was repulsed with considerable loss. The Diwan became dangerously ill, and the loss on the side of the Sikhs, in killed and wounded, was great. Another general attack was made on the 25th, but with no better result.

The protracted military operations now caused a scarcity of provisions in the Sikh camp, both in Multan and Shujabad, and the Maharaja, seeing his case to be hopeless, retired on the 19th of April, being forced to acknowledge himself completely foiled in his attempt, and having the additional mortification of finding himself compelled to accept now the very terms which he had on so many previous occasions rejected with scorn, namely, a tribute of $2\frac{1}{2}$ lakhs of rupees, twenty chargers and a contingent in time of war. Of the amount of the ransom Rs. 30,000 was paid in advance, while Abubakar Khan, brother-in-law of Muzaffar Khan, was delivered up as a hostage for the payment of the balance. The Maharaja's "amour propre" being in this way, to some extent, soothed, he returned to Lahore on the 25th of April, much depressed in spirits by the ill-success of his campaign, and throwing the blame on his Sardars and officers."

Shortly after this Muzaffar Khan began to correspond with the English in Calcutta, while Ranjit Singh approached Sir D. Ochterlony in Ludhiana, each hoping to receive English aid; but both parties were refused assistance. In 1812 the Sikhs appeared for the *fifth* time, commanded this time by Dal Singh.

Chapter II.

History.

Pathan and Sikh rule.

Some Rs. 50,000 of the promised subsidy was still due, but the Nawab having sold his jewels at Delhi made up the balance, the hostage was set free, and the Sikhs retired. In 1813 the Kabul troops threatened an attack on Multan by way of Trimmu Ghat, and Muzaffar Khan sent his Vakil, Ghulam Muhammad, to Lahore for help, with the result that troops were sent to Sarai Siddhu under Kanwar Kharrak Singh, and the danger averted. In 1816 the *sixth* Sikh invasion took place; Ranjit Singh advanced to Tulamba, besieged Ahmadabad, and camped at Salarwahan. An advanced column went on to Multan to enforce the subsidy demanded, and Phula Singh, Akali, intoxicated with bhang, suddenly stormed the town with some fanatics and got possession of part of the fort. The Nawab then paid down Rs. 80,060, promising to pay another Rs. 40,000 in a short time, and Ranjit Singh passed on to Mankera. In 1817 a *seventh* incursion was made under Bhawani Das, who was, however, compelled to raise the siege and retire, for which want of success he was fined Rs. 10,000 by his master. In 1818 came the *eighth* and last Sikh attack. It was felt that this was to be a war to the death, and immense preparations were made on either side. The Nawabs raised the cry of religion, and endeavoured to enlist the Mussalman sympathies of their neighbours, while the Sikhs endeavoured to detach them by all means in their power. An army of 25,000 men, fully equipped, was marched under Misr Diwan Chand into the trans-Chenab lands of the Nawab, and, after taking Khangarh and Muzaffargarh, appeared before Multan early in February. The city was taken after a few days, and the citadel was then bombarded. To quote Sir Lepel Griffin (Punjab Chiefs, p. 85) :—

"The Nawab had only a force of 2,000 men, and the fort was not provisioned for a siege, but he made a defence the like of which the Sikhs had never seen before. Till the 2nd of June the bombardment went on, and two large breaches had been made in the walls, for the great Bhangi gun, the Zam-Zam of Ahmad Shah, Durrani, had been brought from Lahore and had been four times fired with effect. More than one assault had been made by the Sikhs, but they were repulsed, on one occasion with the loss of 1,880 men. The gates were blown in, but the garrison raised behind them mounds of earth on which they fought hand to hand with the Sikhs. The defenders of the fort were at length reduced to two or three hundred fighting men, most of them of the tribe or family of Muzaffar Khan. The rest had either been killed or had gone over to the enemy, for they had been heavily bribed to desert their master, and many of them were unable to resist the temptation. At length on the 2nd June an Akali, by name Sadhu Singh determined to surpass what Phula Singh had done in 1816, rushed with a few desperate followers into an outwork of the fort, and taking the Afghans by surprise, captured it.* The Sikh forces seeing this success advanced to the assault, and mounted the breach at the Khizri gate. Here the old Nawab, with his eight sons and all that remained of the garrison, stood sword in hand resolved to fight to the death. So many fell beneath the keen Afghan sword that the Sikhs drew back and opened fire on the little party with their matchlocks. 'Come on like men' shouted the Afghans, 'and let us fall in fair fight,' but this was an invitation which the Sikhs did not care to accept. There died the white-bearded Muzaffar Khan, scorning to accept quarter, and there died five of his sons. Zulfaqar Khan, his second son, was also wounded severely in the face, and two others, Sarfaraz Khan and Amir Beg Khan, accepted quarter and were saved. Diwan Ram Diyal took Sarfaraz Khan upon his elephant and conducted him with all honor to his own tent. Few of the garrison escaped with their lives and the whole city was given to plunder."

What followed is thus described in Muhammad Latif's History (p. 412):—

"The city and fort were now given up to be plundered by the Sikh troops great were the ravages committed by the Sikhs on this occasion. About 400 to 500 houses in the fort were razed to the ground, and their owners deprived of all they had. The precious stones, jewellery, shawls and other valuables belonging to the Nawab were confiscated to the State, and kept carefully packed by Diwan Ram Diyal, for the inspection of the Maharaja. The arms were all

* Masson (Trav. i, 397) says of this siege: "The attack threatened to end, like former ones, in failure when an adventurer named Jones, in the Sikh service, took charge of the batteries, advanced them close to the citadel and breached it."

carried away. In the town many houses were set on fire, and nothing was left with the inhabitants that was worth having. Hundreds were stripped of their clothes. Outrages were committed on the women, many of whom committed suicide by drowning themselves in the wells, or otherwise putting an end to their lives, in order to save themselves from dishonor. Hundreds were killed in the sack of the city, and indeed there was hardly a soul who escaped both loss and violence. So great, in short, were the horrors inflicted upon the unfortunate inhabitants that the terrible incidents attendant on the sack of Multan are recollected to this day, and still not unfrequently form the topic of conversation. When all was over, Prince Kharak Singh made his triumphant entry into the fort, and took possession of all the State property and treasures belonging to the Nawab. The fort of Shujabad was then captured and sacked and booty estimated at 4,00,000 rupees, consisting of gold and silver utensils, and other valuables, fell into the hands of the victors. The first man who brought intelligence of the capture of Multan to Ranjit Singh, was a mace-bearer (chobdar) in the service of Sardar Fateh Singh, Ahluwalia. The Maharaja presented him with a pair of gold bracelets and a sheet of rich 'kalabatun' (cloth made of twisted silk and gold threads), and on the news being confirmed through official sources, great rejoicings were made at Lahore, which was the scene of festivities for eight days. The Maharaja having taken his seat on an elephant, moved about the principal streets of Lahore, showering down rupees to be scrambled for by the crowd.

Chapter II.

History.

Pathan and Sikh rule.

Thus ended the Pathan rule in Multan.*

Between 1818 and 1821 *the Sikh Governors* of Multan were often changed. At first Sukh Dyal Khatri was made Subadar, and he endeavoured to make the people settle down again to agriculture by liberal grants of taccavi. In September 1819 he was imprisoned for a deficiency in his remittances, and was succeeded by Sham Singh, Peshawria, who obtained the farm of Multan for 6½ lakhs, and who with his kotwal Nazar Ali did his best to put down robbery with a high hand. In 1819 Ranjit Singh came himself to Multan for three months, *viâ* Chiniot, and found cause to imprison Sham Singh. He was succeeded by Badan Hazari, a 'useless sycophant,' and in the charge of the accounts was placed Sawan Mal, a Khatri of Akalgarh, on a salary of Rs. 250 per mensem. (Ranjit Singh visited Multan again in 1822, and again when he was returning from his campaign against Fattah Khan Khattak). Badan Hazari and Sawan Mal having quarrelled, Shujabad was shortly afterwards given on contract to the latter; Tulamba and Sarai Sidhu, which had been in jagir to Khushal Singh, were given to Prem Ram of Aghapura, and Sirdarpur was given in jagir to Inayat Khan Syal. In 1820 Badan Hazari failed in his accounts, was confined and removed: in 1848 Major Edwardes wrote of this man that he was then alive and well, performing very indifferently the exalted functions of Magazine Store-keeper in the fort of Lakhi in Marwat for the consideration of Re. 1 per diem. 'He is as mean a little man to look at as I ever saw: of neither rank, parts, courage nor education, and one might suppose he was put into the government of Multan as a joke.' His place was given to Metha Mal, Shikarpuria, Jamadar Baj Singh being left in the fort to look after him. Very soon afterwards one Sewa Mal was appointed, and finally in 1821 the contract was given to Diwan Sawan Mal. All these changes had led to a great deal of lawlessness and robbery, and the jagirdars became insubordinate. (Muhammad Latif's History, Punjab, 419, J.A.S.B. 1848, ii, 571, Edw. Year ii, 29).

With the appointment of *Diwan Sawan Mal* a new state of things arose. He stopped the raids of the Kathias in the east of the district. His naib, Daya Ram, a native of Gujranwala suddenly attacked and killed Bakhu Langrial, a noted free booter in the neighbourhood of Tulamba. The zamindars were made to pay revenue punctually, and the Diwan's remittances to Lahore were always complete. By degrees other ilakas were added to the Diwan's contract until he held the greater part of the Dera Ismail Khan, Dera Gazi Khan, Muzaffargarh and Jhang districts in his charge. The Sutlej territories, however, remained outside his province till 1831: these were at first left in the hands of the Daudputras, the nazrana was raised every year, and every year the money had to be

* For the various attacks on Multan see Muhammad Latif, p. 359, 362, 368, 372, 386, 393, 398, 407, 410, and 412; also Shahamat Ali, p. 158.

Chapter II.

History.

Pathan and Sikh rule.

realized by the Sikhs at the sword's point. At last in 1831 General Ventura* occupied the country, 'posting thanas and offices at the different towns to regulate the police and collect the revenue.' And after this the Sotlej ilakas seem to have come within Diwan Sawan Mal's province. (Muhammad Latif 450. Sh. Ali, 206—7)

On Ranjit Singh's death in 1839, Diwan Sawan Mal was confirmed in the government of Multan, in spite of the hostility of the Jammu faction at Lahore. The Diwan was, however, summoned to Lahore by Kanwar Nao Nehal Singh. He obeyed the summons frankly and thereby not only saved his province from invasion, but obtained authority over the fort in Multan, which previously had been under a separate Governor. From this time forward he spent a good deal of money in strengthening the fort, and it is probable that he dreamed of throwing off allegiance to the Sikh darbar. (Edw. ii, 35—7).

The Diwan was assassinated in September 1844. Edwardes tells the story as follows :—' He had a good soldier who wanted to leave him, and whom he did not want to lose ; so he put him off at first by soft words and promises, but at last when the soldier demanded his pay and discharge, he got up a law suit against him and threatened to put him in prison. The soldier remonstrated and reiterated his demand. Sawan Mal got angry and told his guards as usual to "seize the rascal and take away his sword and shield." The soldier called out to the guards to lay hands on him at their peril, but stand back and he would give up his arms. He then pulled off his sword and shield and surrendered them. The guards asked if they should take him off to prison. "No," said the Diwan, "let him sit at the door that I may see him and have a few last words with him as I go out" They were his last indeed. The soldier had retained under his scarf a loaded pistol ; and burning with indignation at the shame that had been put on him after years of faithful service, he resolved to revenge himself if it cost his life ; so he cocked the pistol under cover of the scarf over his breast and shoulder and awaited the Diwan's coming. At last the Durbar broke up and Sawan Mal, with a smile of gratified malice, stopped before the arrested soldier, and commenced taunting him with the folly of resistance. In the midst of the abuse the soldier pulled the trigger and the contents of his pistol were lodged in the Diwan's left breast above the heart. The soldier was, I believe, cut to pieces by the guard. His victim bore up for about 10 days, and was apparently recovering when the wound broke out again, and caused instant death.' (Edw., ii. 32—3).

The following was the family of Sawan Mal :—

By Kishn Devi, daughter of Ganda Mal.			By Lachmi Devi, daughter of Tulsi Das of Haveli Bahadur Shah,		By Sat-bharai, sister of the last.
Ram Das, died before his father,	Mulraj,	Karm Narain, b. 1819.	Sham Singh, b. 1835.	Ram Singh, b. 1837.	Narain Singh.
Wazir Chand.					

During the Diwan's life-time Karm Narayan had been put in charge of Leiah, and Mulraj in Jhang ; the former was popular, the latter not, and the saying was that Multan got Sawan (the summer rains), Leiah got Karam (kindness) and Jhang got only Mula (an insect that eats the corn). On Sawan Mal's death *Diwan Mulraj* was confirmed on the same terms as his father, subject to a nazrana of 30 lakhs. He fell out with his family and divided with his brothers the private property left by his father, amounting to 90 lakhs of rupees. There was a delay about the payment of the nazrana and the Darbar on the mediation of the Governor-General's agent agreed in 1846 to reduce the amount due to 20 lakhs, on condition that Mulraj gave up all lands north of the Ravi and paid an increased revenue for the three years beginning with the Kharif of 1847. According to Sir John Lawrence, Mulraj

* The General stayed some time in Multan itself, occupying a house on the site of which the present District Jail is built. The remains of a canal called the Venturawah are also visible in the Mailsi tahsil. The General is said to have criticised Sawan Mal's schemes for the fortification of Multan and though his advice was followed it made Sawan his enemy.

Chapter II.
History.
The Multan Campaign, 1848—9.

"faithfully fulfilled his pecuniary engagements, but rendered himself obnoxious for neglect in not attending to the requisitions of the Resident when called upon by him to redress the complaints of his people. In fact," says Lawrence, "Diwan Mulraj is a ruler of the old school, and so long as he had paid his revenue he considered the province as his own to make the most of. He proved himself to be grasping and avaricious, with none of the statesmanlike views of his father, and few of his conciliatory qualities. The traders and agriculturists of the province had been complaining of his exactions." (Edw. ii, 40).

The appeals made to the Resident against his conduct rendered Mulraj discontented, and he was also rendered anxious by the fact that certain dues paid by his zamindars had been abolished in the rest of the Punjab. He therefore tendered his resignation. This was ultimately accepted, and it was arranged that Sardar Kahn Singh should be appointed Nazim in his place, in co-operation with Mr. P. A. Vans Agnew of the Civil Service and Lieutenant W. A. Anderson of the 1st Bombay European Fusiliers.*

The Multan Campaign, 1848—9.

The first Punjab war of 1845, though it led to the appointment of a Resident at Lahore and the despatch of officers to settle the revenue of various districts of the province, led at first to little or no change in the government of Multan, which continued as before under its Khatri ruler, Mulraj, the son of Sawan Mal. But when Mulraj determined to resign his charge and the English Officers sent to replace him were massacred by the populace at the Idgah in April 1848, Multan appeared at once in full revolt and the events of the next year are of the greatest interest. No one who cares about the local history should fail to read the entrancing account of this year which is given in the second volume of Sir Herbert Edwardes 'Year on the Punjab Frontier' or the clear description of the siege and campaign given in Gough and Innes' 'Sikhs and the Sikh Wars':† but for ordinary reference a brief abstract of the chief events will be found in the 'Chronicle' appended below. Roughly speaking, there were three phases in the campaign.

First, from 18th April 1848 to 18th August: during which Edwardes, Van Cortlandt and the Baháwalpur troops unaided by any British soldiers, drove in the Sikh forces from the south and practically confined Mulraj to the immediate vicinity of Multan: winning during the period two marked victories, one at Kineri in the Shujabad tahsil on June the 18th, and one at Siddhu Hisam, near the present Cantonment Railway Station on July 1st.

---

* Some interesting notes by 'Z. N.' on the state of the district in Sikh times will be found in the *Pioneer* newspaper issues of July 25 and December 17 1897; August 17, September 2, September 10, 1898, and October 13, 1899.

† The map in the latter work should, especially, be consulted. Other works of interest in connection with the campaign are Hugo James' 'Scramble through Scinde;' Dunlop's Illustrated Account of the Siege of Multan, and Siddon's description of the siege in the Corps Papers of the Royal and East Indian Company's Engineers (Vol. i, 1849-50). See also the 'Punjab Blue Book (Vol. 41, 1849). There is also an interesting vernacular account of the campaign written by Pir Ibrahim Khan, the Baháwalpur agent. A local vernacular poem on the same subject is printed below as an appendix to this volume.

Chapter II.

History.

The Multan Campaign 1848—9.

Secondly, from August 18th to December 10th. During this time a small British force under General Whish arrived and sat down before the city, but, being deserted on September 14th by the Darbar troops under Sher Singh, had at once to raise the siege and wait for the arrival of an adequate besieging force.

Thirdly, from December 10th, 1848, to January 22nd, 1849. The reinforcement having arrived from Bombay, the siege was renewed on December 27th. On January 2nd and 3rd the city was captured : and after a severe bombardment the fort was about to be stormed on the 22nd, when Mulraj in the nick of time surrendered.

The revolt of Mulraj—his action, it may be noted, was treated throughout as a revolt against the Darbar—was no doubt at first unpremeditated. It was primarily a revolt of the Sikh soldiery in Multan against anticipated English interference, and it was actively assisted by all the Hindu element of the district, which so largely profited under nearly 30 years of Khatri rule. On the other hand the movement was neither a national Sikh movement nor was it in any sense a rising of the people. Sawan Mal and his sons had kept so much aloof from Lahore politics that, when the rebellion broke out, none of the Sikh Sirdars, however disaffected, gave it any appreciable active help, and when the real Sikh insurrection gathered head in the north of the province, its leaders pursued their own game, leaving Mulraj to defend himself as best he could. The people of the District, moreover, who were almost all Muhammadans, had little sympathy with the revolt, and the Pathan nobility, who had been brought very low under Sikh rule, deserted almost *en masse* to the British side and assisted most actively in the suppression of the rebellion.

As regards the conduct of the campaign there can be no two opinions as to the admirable services rendered by Edwardes, then a young Lieutenant in political employ. But on two points there was at the time a good deal of dispute.

In the first place it was questioned whether a large British force should not have been sent against Multan in June 1848, in order to take the city at once and prevent disaffection from spreading. Edwardes thought this should have been done, Lord Gough and Lord Dalhousie were against it ; and the *pros* and *cons* of the question will be found fully set forth in Gough and Innes' book above referred to.

Secondly, when the siege had been commenced, it was a good deal disputed whether the bombardment should be directed on the fort or on the city : and at various times different views were adopted on this point. Ultimately, both

The Multan Campaign, 1848—9.

city and fort were breached, but Mulraj's timely surrender made it unnecessary to scale the breaches in the Fort.

Chronicle.

18th April 1848. Messrs. Agnew and Anderson arrived at Multan and encamped at the Idgah. They had a Sikh escort of 1,400 men, 600 Gurkhas, 700 Cavalry and 6 guns. Mulraj, who was living in the Am Khas less than a mile away, made two visits to the Idgah during the day, and it was arranged that he should make over the fort to the new Governor next morning.

19th April. Major Edwardes gives the following account of the events of the day :—

"Early on the morning of the 19th of April the two British officers and Sirdar Kahn Singh accompanied Mulraj into the fort of Multan ; were shown all over it ; received the keys ; installed two companies of their own Goorkha infantry in possession ; planted their own sentries ; mustered the Diwan's garrison, who seemed angry at the prospect of being thrown out of employment ; allayed their fears with promises of service ; and prepared to return home * * The cavalcade passed forth and entered upon the bridge over the ditch. Two soldiers of Mulraj's were standing on the bridge. One of them, named Umeer Chand, gazed for a moment at the two unarmed Englishmen, who presumed to ride in and out of the great fortress Sawan Mal had made so strong ; and brooding, perchance, over his own long services and probable dismissal, impatiently struck the nearest with his spear, and knocked him off his horse. Agnew, who was ignorant of fear, jumped up, and struck his assailant with the riding stick in his hand. The ruffian threw away his spear, and rushing in with his sword inflicted two severer wounds. He would probably have killed Mr. Agnew on the spot, had he not been knocked into a ditch by a horseman of the escort.

"The scuffle was now known ; the crowd pressed round to see what was the matter ; news was carried back into the fort that swords were out and going on the bridge ; an uproar rose within, and in another moment the whole garrison would come pouring forth. Mulraj made no attempt to stem the tide, and rescue the Englishman who had come down, at his invitation, to Multan. He either thought only of himself, or was not sorry for the outbreak ; and forcing his horse through the crowd, rode off to his garden-house at Am Khas. Nor was this all; his own personal sowars turned back half-way, and pursued Lieutenant Anderson, who had as yet escaped. Who can tell now who ordered them? * * What moved them we can never know ; but we know the fact that they sought out Anderson ; attacked and cut him down with swords, so that he fell for dead upon the ground, where he was found afterwards by some of his own Goorkha soldiers, who put him on a litter, and carried him to the Idgah.*

* For comparison with the above description is appended the account of the affair given by Mulraj's Judges in their written judgment :—

"About 7 o'clock on the morning of the 19th, the British Officers, Kahn Singh and Mulraj, visited the Fort. Mr. Agnew inspected the stores and magazines, harangued the troops of Mulraj who were to be retained or dismissed, and leaving the Fort in charge of two companies of the Goorkha Regiment prepared with the rest of the party to return home. The egress from the fort lay through an inner gate called Sikhi, and then an outer one Kumr Kotha. This last was connected with the glacis by a standing bridge over the deep fort ditch. At this point Mr. Agnew is said to have been riding on the extreme right, on his left was Mulraj, then Lieutenant Anderson, Kahn Singh being on the left flank. Somewhere near this bridge, for the spot is placed differently in different depositions, Mr. Agnew was struck with a spear by an assassin, fell from his horse and was wounded with three blows of a sword by the same man, who escaped by falling or getting into the deep ditch. Mulraj seeing what had taken place pushed on his horse. Lieutenant Anderson, too, rode off rapidly, while Kahn Singh stopped behind with Rung Ram, a relation of Mulraj by marriage, to take care of Mr. Agnew. From the bridge the distance to the city gate is less than the distance to the city gate (which has the name of Dowlut) from the Am Khas, the residence of Mulraj, and that is about 100

Chapter II.

History.

The Multan Campaign, 1848—9.

'Meanwhile Sirdar Kahn Singh, protected by the presence and assistance of Mulraj's brother-in-law, Rung Ram, whose honest deeds are the only witness worth a straw of the Diwan's good intentions, had extricated Mr. Agnew from the mob, lifted him on to his own elephant, and hurried away towards camp, rudely binding up Mr. Agnew's wounds as they rode along. The road lay properly by one end of Moolraj's garden, the Am Khas; but as soon as they emerged from the suburbs, between the fort and garden, a discharge of matchlocks from the latter warned them to come no closer; guns too were being dragged out of the garden gate; so they turned their elephant aside, and took another path; and as they went, a cannon shot from the guns behind them hissed over their heads. Mulraj who had gallopped on before, was in the garden at the time. * * * At last the two wounded Englishmen were brought back to the Idgah. A sad meeting for them, who had gone forth in the morning full of life and health, and zeal, to do their duty. The native doctor of the Goorkha regiment dressed their wounds. This done, Mr. Agnew proceeded to report these occurrences to the Resident at Lahore, and then addressed a letter to Diwan Mulraj expressing a generous disbelief in the Diwan's participation, but calling on him to justify this opinion by seizing the guilty parties, and coming himself to the Idgah. This was at 11 A. M. At 2 P. M. Mr. Agnew wrote off to General Cortlandt and myself for assistance. At 4 P. M. one of the Diwan's Chief officers, Raezadah Toolsee Das, brought an answer from Mulraj briefly stating "that he could neither give up the guilty nor come himself; that he and Rung Ram had already tried to do so, been stopped by the soldiers, and Rung Ram severely wounded for advising the visit; that all the garrison, Hindu and Muhammadan, were in rebellion, and the British officers had better see to their own safety." Mr. Agnew seems to have behaved with consummate calmness and heroism at this trying moment. He pointed out to Toolsee Das how grave a matter was in hand, and how absolutely indispensable it was for Diwan Mulraj to call on him, if he wished to be thought innocent. Toolsee Das returned with the admonition, but Mulraj never came. Why should he? The ambassador found the master, who had sent him on a message of peace, now presiding in a war council of his chiefs. The Pathans of the garrison were setting their seals to an oath of allegiance in the Koran; the Hindus in the Shastars, the Sikhs in the Holy Granth. The Sikhs were fastening a war-bracelet on the wrist of Mulraj himself! * *

---

paces, the road lying through a bazaar in the suburbs under the walls of the Am Khas to the Idgah, where Mr. Agnew was encamped. In taking, however, this the regular road, the elephant on which Mr. Agnew had been placed was compelled to go a bye-road to escape from the hostile demonstration of the soldiery, whose cantonment surrounds the Am Khas or rather with Mulraj's Palace composes it. Matchlocks were fired as if to warn the party from the direct route and guns were brought out of the cantonment. In the meantime Lieutenant Anderson had been severely wounded in his flight from the scene of the attack upon Agnew and was found beyond the Dowlut gate lying on the ground with seven wounds on himself and four on his horse. He was brought home by some of his own people, but the manner of his being cut down is not clear." Anderson apparently tried to get to the Idgah for help and was pursued by two sowars. It is said that, although he lost his way for a time, he out-distanced them and would have escaped if his horse had not fallen in attempting to jump a water-course somewhere between the Hazuri Bagh and the Idgah.

As regards the onslaught on Agnew the defence made at Mulraj's trial was that the soldier's spear accidentally ran into Agnew as the latter was riding past (p. 167, Trial). The Sikh proclamation of April 22, 1848, represents the assailant of Agnew as having acted without any sort of provocation (p. 150, Parly' Blue Book, Punjab, Vol. 41, 1849). Rumour however invented all sorts of stories, alleging provocation: one of these is given in the ballad reprinted at the end of this Gazetteer; another is that Amira was angry at being called to by Mr. Agnew to get out of the way.

The site of the incident is a few yards to the west of the well which lies on the left of the pakka road which leads from the circular road to the Prahladpuri shrine.

Chapter II.

History.

The Multan Campaign 1848—9.

On the evening and night of the 19th April the whole of the carriage cattle of the officers and their escort, which were out at graze, were carried off, camels, bullocks, elephants, every beast of burden. Thus was flight cut off, It was necessary for the little camp at the Idgah to face the stern emergency, and prepare for open hostility on the morrow. That night, under Mr. Agnew's personal direction, the six guns which had come from Lahore were mounted in three batteries, and all the soldiers and camp-followers of that luckless expedition were called inside the walls."

20th April. Major Edwardes continues :

" Morning broke, and Mr. Agnew made one last effort to avert the coming tragedy. Having failed with Mulraj, he now forwarded to Mulraj's officers and chiefs the parwanas of the Maharaja, ordering them to make over the fort to Sirdar Kahn Singh, and obey all Mr. Agnew's orders.

" The messengers found Mulraj again in council with his chiefs, preparing proclamations to the people of the province to rise and join in the rebellion. They had just agreed, too, to remove their wives and families into the fort before opening the guns. The messengers presented the Maharaja's letters. The chiefs and officers replied that Mulraj was their master, and they would only obey him. The messengers returned and extinguished hope. Mr. Agnew wrete off to Peer Ibraheem Khan, the British Native Agent at Bahawalpur, to bring troops to his assistance, intending to hold out in the Idgah till the reinforcement could arrive.

" All disguise was now thrown aside. The guns of the fort opened on the Idgah as did also the guns at the Am Khas which were dragged on to a high mound hard by. One round alone was fired in return from the six guns in the Idgah, after which the Lahore artillerymen refused to serve the guns. The fire of the rebels never slacked.

" And now arrived an embassy from Mulraj in return for Mr. Agnew's. Mulraj invited the escort to desert the British officers, and promised to raise the pay of every soldier who came over. One Goolab Singh, Commandant of the Ghorchurrahs of the escort, led the way and went over to Mulraj, who tricked the traitor out with gold necklaces and bracelets, and sent him back as a decoy. In vain Mr. Agnew bestowed money on the troops to hold out for three days only. It was honest money. The troops went over,—horse, foot, artillery—all had deserted by the evening, except Sirdar Kahn Singh, some eight or ten faithful horsemen, the domestic servants of the British officers, and the Munshis of their office.

" Beneath the lofty centre dome of that empty hall (so strong and formidable that a very few stout hearts could have defended it), stood this miserable group around the beds of the two wounded Englishmen. All hope of resistance being at an end, Mr. Agnew had sent a party to Mulraj to sue for peace. A conference ensued, and " in the end" says the Diwan's judges, " it was agreed that the officers were to quit the country, and that the attack upon them was to cease.' Too late ! The sun had gone down ; twilight was closing in ; and the rebel army had not tasted blood. An indistinct and distant murmur reached the ears of the few remaining inmates of the Idgah, who were listening for their fate. Louder and louder it grew, until it became a cry, the cry of a multitude for blood ! On they came, from city, suburbs, fort ; soldiers with their arms, citzens, young and old, and of all trades and callings with any weapon they could snatch.

" A company of Mulraj's Muzbees, or outcasts turned Sikhs, led on the mob. It was an appalling sight, and Sirdar Kahn Singh begged of Mr. Agnew to be allowed to wave a sheet and sue for mercy. Weak in body from loss of blood, Agnew's heart failed him not. He replied : 'The time for mercy is gone : let none be asked for. They can kill us two if they like ; but we are not the last of the English ; thousands of Englishmen will come down here when we are gone, and annihilate Mulraj, and his soldiers and his fort.' The crowd now rushed in with horrible shouts, made Kahn Singh prisoner, and pushing aside the servants with the butts of their muskets, surrounded the two wounded officers. Lieutenant Anderson from the first had been too much wounded even

Chapter II.

History.

The Multan Campaign, 1848—9.

to move: and now Mr. Agnew was sitting by his bedside holding his hands and talking in English. Doubtless they were bidding each other farewell for all time. Goodhur Singh, a Muzbee, so deformed and crippled with old wounds that he looked more like an imp than mortal man, stepped forth from the crowd with a drawn sword, and after insulting Mr. Agnew, with a few last indignities struck him twice upon the neck, and with a third blow cut off his head. Some other wretch discharged a musket into the lifeless body. Then Anderson was hacked to death with swords; and afterwards the two bodies were dragged outside, and slashed and insulted by the crowd, then left all night under the sky."

22nd April. The news of the outbreak reached Lieutenant Edwardes, the officer in charge of the Deraját, at Dera Fatteh Khan, 90 miles from Multan. He at once began to raise levies, and called for assistance from General Van Cortlandt at Dera Ghází Khan and from the Bahâwalpur State.

May. The Government of India decided that no British force should be sent against Multan, but that five columns of troops, belonging to the Sikh Darbar and the Baháwalpur State, should be ordered to converge on the district. In pursuance of this arrangement Edwardes, who was to command the Derajat column, received orders on May 9th to retire and stand fast on the west of the Indus.

6th June. The three columns from the north having all been much delayed, Edwardes received permission to cross the Indus and join the Baháwalpur column which was marching towards Shujabad *viâ* Jalálpur Pírwála,

17th June. The Baháwalpur column after a long halt at Jalalpur had advanced to Gawen, and the Sikh troops under Rang Ram were encamped across the high road, three miles south of Shujabad. In spite of orders to attack the Daudputras before they were joined by Edwardes, the Sikhs allowed Edwardes to reach the west bank of the Chenab opposite Panjani and only moved forward to Bagren on the evening of the 17th. Hearing of their intention Edwardes and the Daudputras agreed to converge at once towards the Kineri ferry which lay on the east bank of the Chenáb near Panjani.

18th June. Rang Ram finding the ferry occupied by the Daudputras took up a position at the abadi of Nunar, near some old salt pans, in the village area of Panjani. Edwardes himself crossed the river and reached the Daudputra camp about 8 A.M. in time to bring them into some sort of order. He sent orders for Van Cortlandt to cross with his guns as soon as possible, and spent the rest of the morning in waiting till this reinforcement should give him the necessary superiority. The forces were—Rang Ram, 8,000 to 10,000 trained troops: 10 guns. Daudputras, 8,500 troops: 11 guns. Edwardes, 5,000 irregular levies. Van Cortlandt, 1,500 trained troops: 15 guns.

By 2 p.m. the Daudputras had begun to retire and the enemy commenced moving after them. Edwardes, whose troops remained concealed among the jungle on the left of the line, tried to stave off the enemy by ordering a cavalry charge and about 3 p. m. the charge was successfully and gallantly carried out by his mounted levies under Faujdar Khan, Alizai. Before the enemy had recovered from the effect of this charge a considerable number of Cortlandt's troops and six of his guns arrived, and Edwardes at once pushed forward out of the jungle into the cultivation beyond. Then he came upon the enemy advancing through the 'long stalks of the sugar' (possibly jowar). Both forces at once commenced an artillery duel, and they were so close as to be able to use grape. As the enemy's fire slackened, one of Van Cortlandt's regiments charged to the front, followed by the whole line of infantry. The enemy retreated, but rallied again: and the battle was brought to a close by a wild rush on the part of the Pathan levies which sent the Sikh forces back in full retreat on Nunar. In this engagement (which Edwardes termed 'the Battle of Kineri'*) the enemy lost their whole camp and ammunition, together with 8 out of their 10 guns.

* The changes of the river have swept away all traces of the hamlet of Kineri. The Kineras are a tribe of weavers and hamlets called after them are not uncommon in the District. There is a Kaneriwala well close to the site of the battle.

Chapter II.

History.

The Multan Campaign, 1848—9.

(The story now told locally is that Mulraj's intention was to stand at Shujabad, but that the Babla money-lenders gave his commandant Jamiat Rai a large sum of money to move on so as to save their property near Shujabad. It is also said that the Pathans and indeed most of Mulraj's army, except the Gurkhas, were won over before the battle: and that they wore branches of tamarisk in their turbans to show they were friends. The actual hand to hand fighting was at the Ahmduwala well in village Panjani. A plan of the battle so far as it can be ascertained has been recently hung up in the Gawen rest-house).

22nd—25th June. The force encamped at Shujabad, a city which had given the rebels much encouragement. Edwardes writes: 'The chowdries, bankers and chief Kuthries (rebels to the backbone all of them) presented themselves and begged for kind treatment. This I readily promised though it is more than they deserve, for they have been supplying Mulraj largely with money, stores and encouragement from the Shastras. The rebellion indeed is a Bunyah rebellion, with a Sikh insurrection grafted on to it. One shroff alone of Shujabad, a mean looking little fellow, undertook to furish Diwan Mulraj with two months' pay for his army if he would only send them against the Nawab's troops, a circumstance I shall not forget when we are pressed for cash. Such moneyed men are invaluable in these times.'

26th June. The force advanced and took the fort of Sikandarabad.

27th June. The force reached Adibagh (village Taragarh).

28th June. March to Surajkund (village Kayanpur). Lieutenant Lake, in charge of the Baháwalpur troops, joined the camp this day.

1st July. As Mulraj had broken down the bridge on the Wali Muhammad canal at Surajkund, the force moved up the west canal towards Abid Khan ka bagh (village Langrial) and encamped in Tibbi Mansurpur. Meanwhile Mulraj, who had inteuded to attack at Surajkund, moved back his troops along the east side of the canal and having crossed them at the bridge south of the Lange Khan garden (the only bridge near the city then existing) marched them in the direction of the present cantonments. He took up a position round Siddhu-Hisam (called in the histories Saddosam), close to the place where the Cantonment Railway Station now is: and Edwardes' force turned out to oppose him. An artillery fire was kept up on both sides, but Edwardes had more guns than the Sikhs, and the latter had ultimately to turn and flee to the city, hotly pursued by Edwardes' troops. It is said that Mulraj having crossed the bridge over the canal with his artillery, planted two guns on it to stop his own soldiers from retreating. 'The majority of the enraged fugitives forced the barrier with some loss, but many of them tried to swim the nullah and were drowned.'

6th July. The Darbar's column under Sher Singh, which had marched from Lahore *viâ* Tulamba, Sirdarpur and Gagra, arrived and encamped at Surajkund. The fidelity of these troops was much suspected and Edwardes purposely arranged that he at Tibbi should be between them and the enemy.

10th July. Edwardes having asked for the immediate despatch of artillery to his aid, Sir F. Currie, the Resident at Lahore, decided on his own responsibility to send the required assistance, and orders were issued for the despatch of a division under General Whish containing two British regiments and a siege train: part were to go from Lahore by the Rávi and part from Ferozepore by the Sutlej.

16th August. Edwardes and Sher Singh exchanged encampments, the former moving to Surajkund, and the latter to Tibbi. This move was made in order that Edwardes might be in touch with General Whish's force, which was to encamp to the east of Surajkund.

18th-19th August. The Rávi and Sutlej column of General Whish's force joined and encamped at Mari Sital and awaited the arrival of the siege train.

1st September. Edwardes' troops moved across the canal to take up a position nearer General Whish. They dislodged the enemy from the Khuda Yar and Katti Bairagi gardens, from the Jog Maya temple and the village of Daira: and encamped 300 yards south of Jog Maya.

4th September. The siege train arrived from the Sutlej.

Chapter II.

History.

The Multan Campaign, 1848—9.

7th September. To prevent the enemy from flooding out the force by cutting the canal, steps had been taken by the Engineers to dam up the canal at its head, and this was completed by 7th September. On this day it was decided to attack the city from the S. E., and entrenchments were made between Katti Bairagi and the temple of Ram Tirath.*

9th September. A night attack was made on some gardens and houses in front of the entrenchments, but the attack was repulsed by Mulraj's troops.

12th September. General Whish made a general advance to clear his front. The troops under Van Cortlandt on the west assaulted and took the hamlet of Jamandon-ki-kiri, while the British troops on the east occupied a position known as the Dharmsala.† The capture of the latter made a great impression and is thus described by Edwardes; "Scarcely a man escaped to tell Mulraj how calmly the young English Engineer, Lieutenant Grindall, planted the scaling ladder in the grim faces of the defenders; how vainly they essayed to hurl it back; how madly rushed up the grenadiers of the 32nd; with what a yell the brave Irish of the 10th dropped down among them from the branches of the trees above; and how like the deadly conflict of the lion and the tiger in a forest den was the grapple of the pale English with the swarthy Sikh in that little walled space the rebels thought so strong. I myself, ten minutes afterwards, saw fully three hundred of Mulraj's soldiers in a heap in that enclosure."

14th September. Sher Singh, who had long been wavering, took over his troops *en masse* to the enemy. After this it was impossible for General Whish's force to continue the siege, and as the abandonment of our entrenchments left these works as cover for the enemy, it was decided to move the whole force to the west of the canal where it could guard the communications with Baháwalpur and the tracts which supplied food to the army. This change was executed on the 15th and 16th of September, the British troops encamping at Bakhar Arbi and Edwardes at Surajkund. Thus ended the first siege of Multan. During the siege Mulraj issued some rupees in gold which are now rather difficult to procure.

9th October. Sher Singh, who had been received with great distrust by Mulraj, determined to march away from Multan and join his father Chattar Singh, who was in open rebellion in the north. He accordingly left Multan, marching by Gagra and Sardarpur.

During the next three months both sides made strenuous preparations for the siege. The Diwan tried, in vain, to get assistance from outside. A British force assembled at Ferozpur to meet the main Punjab rebellion in the north and a Bombay army was ordered to advance to help in the siege of Multan.

7th November. The enemy having advanced in front of the British lines were attacked by Edwardes on the west, and General Markham on the east of the canal, and driven back with considerable loss.

10th December—21st. The Bombay column arrived. It included some British seamen who helped in working the guns.

25th-26th December. The Bengal force again encamped at Mari Sital: the Bombay troops between them and the canal: and Edwardes to the west of the canal. It was determined to attack the north-east angle of the Fort and as a preliminary to turn the enemy out of their positions along the eastern face of the city.

27th December. The real object of attack was the Am Khas and Sawan Mal's tomb and these were easily occupied by the right column, while two other columns were making serious diversions to the south. One of them after a struggle occupied the Mandi Ava, a large brickkiln standing on the left of the road from the Pak gate to Ram Tirath, and the other seized the Sidi

---

* A prominent landmark still existing on the left of the railway between the Mailsi and Basti Maluk roads.

† This building adjoins the Hindu burning ground, and is clearly seen from the railway train on the right as you approach Multan city fom Lahore The marks of the bullets are still visible. I have been told that the defen der were largely Gurkhas: these would be the remnants of the deserters who had formed Van Agnew's guard.

Chapter II.

History.

The Multan Campaign, 1848—9.

Lal Bhir, a high mound close by the present city railway station on the right of the road from the station to the city. These successes led General Whish to modify his previous plan and to direct batteries against the city walls as well as against the fort.

30th December. A shell from our batteries pierced the roof of the Jama Masjid in the fort which was used as a magazine and caused an enormous explosion, destroying 500 of the garrison and 40,000 lbs. of powder.

2nd January 1849. Breaches being reported practicable, a Bengal force was at 3 p.m. sent to attack the Delhi gate of the city, and a Bombay force to attack the Khuni Burj, or Bloody Bastion. The different fortunes of the attacking parties are thus described by Edwardes: "The storming party of the Delhi gate (which was led by a fine soldier, Captain Smyth of the Grenadier Company of Her Majesty's 32nd) had no sooner emerged from the suburbs than they found themselves on the edge of a deep intervening hollow; after crossing which under the heavy fire of matchlocks, they 'found to their surprise the city wall in front, about 30 feet in height, unbreached and totally impracticable,' which the hollow had hitherto concealed from both the breaching battery and the Engineers. They had the mortification therefore of retiring, but repaired at once to the breach at the Bloody Bastion to assist their more fortunate comrades in the city. The Bloody Bastion was assaulted by three companies of the 1st Bombay Fusiliers under Captain Leith. They found the breach easy to be surmounted, but it was retrenched inside and a most bloody struggle ensued for victory, in which the gallant Leith was severely wounded and carried off the field: but his place being taken by Lieutenant Gray, and Colour Sergeant John Bennet of the 1st Fusiliers having planted the colours of old England and stood beside it till the flag and staff were riddled with balls, the Fusiliers remembered the legends of their ancient corps, and closing with the rebels, soon made the city of Multan their own." All the southern gates were, in fact, occupied that same afternoon: and next morning the Delhi and Daulat gates were seized. Mulraj shut the gates of the fort, the streets of the city were occupied by the British, though not without resistance: and the remnants of the Sikh force 'scrambling over the western walls or issuing from the Lohari Gate, concealed themselves till night among the Afghan suburbs: then under cover of the darkness dispersed and fled, without gain or honour, to their distant homes.'

21st January. The siege of the fort having been continued with great vigour, two breaches were made, both of which are still clearly visible, one on the north-east near the tomb of Bahawal Haqq and the other on the south-west opposite the Husan Gahi. Orders were accordingly issued for these breaches to be stormed next morning.

22nd January. In a storm of wind and rain the troops prepared for the assault, but at 9 a.m. Mulraj surrendered at discretion; the entire garrison laid down their arms and became prisoners of war.*

---

* There is a brass in the north transept of the cantonment church which commemorates the names of the various regiments engaged in the siege of Multan as follows:—

Bengal Division.

Bengal Artillery, 4 Troops, 1st Brigade, and 4 Troops, 3rd Brigade, Horse Artillery; 2nd Company 2nd Battalion, 3rd Company 3rd Battalion, 4th Company 3rd Battalion, and 6th Company 7th Battalion, Artillery; and 2nd class siege Train.

Bengal Engineers, Head-quarters; 1st, 2nd and 3rd Companies, Sappers; 2nd and 3rd Company Pioneers.

Her Majesty's 10th and 32nd Foot.

11th Regiment Light Cavalry and 7th and 11th Irregular Cavalry, 8th, 49th 51st, 52nd, and 72nd Native Infantry, and Queen's Own Corps of Guides.

Bombay Division.

Bombay Artillery, 3rd Troop 1st Brigade Horse Artillery; 2nd Company 1st Battalion, and 4th Company 2nd Battalion, European (Foot) Artillery; 1st and 2nd Companies, 4th Battalion, Native (Foot) Artillery.

Bombay Engineers 1st and 2nd Company Sappers. 1st Her Majesty's 60th Rifles and 1st Bombay Fusiliers. 3rd, 4th, 9th and 19th Native Infantry. Indian Navy.

Baháwalpur Contingent.

Chapter II.
History.
British Rule.

Diwan Mulraj was 'taken to Lahore, charged with complicity in the murder of Agnew and Anderson, and found guilty but with extenuating circumstances.'* The view of the commission was that Mulraj had not procured by any overt act the attack on Agnew, but that in his subsequent conduct he was subject to no compulsion beyond the fear of a quarrel with some of his troops (Trial pp. 191—198). He spent in confinement the remainder of a life which was prolonged, only for a short time. He was taken to Calcutta and afterwards to Benares, where he died. His relations and descendants still live in the town of Akálgarh in the Gujránwála district and not a few have been in Government service.

BRITISH RULE.

Meantime possession of the district had been taken in the name of the British Government. Multan became the head-quarters both of a division and of a district.

The following account of the events of 1857 is taken from the Punjab Mutiny Report (pages 110—118):—

At the head-quarters of the division much anxiety was caused to Major Hamilton, Commissioner, and all the residents, by the presence of two corps of Native Infantry, of whom one, the 69th, was known to be thoroughly bad. The post was an important one, as commanding the only outlet the Punjab at that time possessed for communication with England, Bombay and Calcutta, &c. The troops were providently disarmed in time, and no outbreak took place. The station of Multan commands the passage down the river from Lahore, and the only post road whereby the Punjab could communicate with the rest of the world.

At the time of the outbreak it was occupied by the 62nd and 69th Native Infantry, 1st Irregular Cavalry, a native troop of horse artillery, and a company of European Artillerymen. The 69th was strongly suspected. The other native troops were considered staunch, and subsequent events verified the supposition in every case. It was necessary to provide a refuge in case of any disturbance. The old fort, which had lain in a ruinous condition since it had been battered and dismantled by the British army in 1849, was put in a position of defence, provisioned, and garrisoned by some men of Captain Tronson's Kuttar Mukhi police battalion. As those arrangements occupied some days, and the temper of the native troops could not be trusted from hour to hour, Lieutenant Etheridge of the Indian Navy, who happened to be at Multan with his vessel, was requested to detain the steamer until the fort should have become defensible. With this request Lieutenant Etheridge willingly complied, and the steamer lay off Multan until it was no longer requisite to trust to it as an asylum in case of need. In the early days of May a crowd of sepoys constantly thronged the Multan post office, eagerly asking 'for news,' and 'whether the mail had arrived,' and similar questions, in themselves unusual, and were accompanied by such language and demonstrations as were freely used tending to throw the whole establishment into bodily fear. Family remittances, which the soldiery had hitherto always made through the Government treasury, now ceased to be so made. The payments which the men had made on account of these remittances were boisterously demanded back in cash. The price of gold coin rose rapidly in the exchange markets, showing a large demand for portable wealth. Such symptoms of uneasiness (occurring too before any outbreak in the North-Western Provinces) could not but excite the gravest apprehensions in the minds of all European residents; they could not but lead to the conclusion that the soldiery were bent on some mischief, or, to say the least, that their confidence in our Government was gone, and they would rather trust their money in their own hand than in ours. When news of the outbreak in the North-Western Provinces reached Multan what had been inexplicable was at once explained, the mystery was revealed; these actions were seen to be part and parcel of a universal and determined design to subvert our rule.

---

* See 'the Trial of Mulraj, late Nazim of Multan, from authentic documents printed at the *Delhi Gazette* Press, by Kunniah Lal.' The commission for the trial were Mr. Mansel, C. S., Mr. Montgomery, C.S., and Colonel Penny. Mr. L. Bowring appeared for the prosecution and Captain Hamilton for the defence.

Chapter II.

History.
British Rule.

Colonel Hicks, commanding at Multan, failed to discover in the conduct of the regiments of native infantry any thing which could justify him in taking from them their arms. The Chief Commissioner, however, sent peremptory orders that they were to be disarmed, and on the morning of June 10th the minds of European and native residents were relieved, commerce was re-established, and our authority vindicated by the most successful disarming of the 62nd and 69th Native Infantry by Major C. Chamberlain, commanding 1st Irregular Cavalry. The peculiar character of this excellent move was that the European troops were but 48 atillerymen. The other auxiliaries were all natives, and one regiment, the 1st Irregular Cavalry, was composed of Hindustanis. During the whole day the townspeople flocked to the Commissioner, Major Hamilton, expressing their hearty congratulations on the success of the measure, and their own relief at the prospect of immunity from rapine and slaughter. On the 19th and two following days of June the left wing Bombay Fusiliers came in, and about three weeks afterwards the right wing arrived. The imperious requirements of the service, however, forbade the authorities to keep these troops here, and they as well as the trusty Punjabi troops who arrived from time to time were pushed on towards Lahore or Delhi; so that with the exception of the 1st Irregulars the company of artillery, and the police battalion, Multan had absolutely no military standby to resist the two full regiments of Native Infantry which were located there. It was an anxious time. If proof of the ill-will of the 69th be required, it is afforded by the facts that the chief native officer of the regiment and 10 men were blown from guns by sentence of court-martial for sedition and intended mutiny; that just before their execution they boasted of their intent and reviled each other for the cowardice displayed in their own past inaction; that when the regiment was disarmed it was found that the artillery (native) had laid the guns, in anticipation of a struggle, directly on the 69th, avoiding the 62nd; and that the demeanour of the corps throughout was insolent and rebellious to the last degree. On the 11th August the horse artillery was disarmed as a precautionary measure. On the same date the enrolment of men for the new 11th Punjab Infantry was commenced by transferring to it men from other regiments. The Gugera insurrection broke out little more than a month afterwards. The new men at Multan were still undisciplined, and could hardly yet be relied on as a serviceable field force. Most of them were left to guard the station, while Major Chamberlain led out his regiment, the 1st Irregular Cavalry (Hindustanis), with some 200 men of the new levies, against the insurgents. Another cause of anxiety at Multan had been the conduct of the preventive service on the Sutlej. Very many of the men employed in it were Hindustantis. They bolted at the first rise in Hindustan, and went off in numbers to join their kindred by blood and by disposition who were enjoying a transient glory over the smouldering ruins of Hánsi and Hissar. Men to take their place were raised in the district, and no serious damage was done to the Government interest by their defection. Under the orders of the Chief Commissioner a camel train was organized, having one of its depots at Multan. It was designed for the conveyence of private parcels, munitions of war and merchandize between Sind and the Punjab, and proved most useful. The care of it constituted one of the many miscellaneous duties entailed on Major Voyle, Deputy Commissioner. The duty of preserving the safety of part of the road between Lahore and Multan, especially during and after the Kharral insurrection, was another most anxious charge for him. The number of widowed ladies, wounded officers, and other travellers who passed down this way, and who were incapable of protecting themselves, made it very needful that the road should be defended. To this end the Deputy Commissioners of Lahore, Gugera and Multan were desired to locate extra police both horse and foot, at every road police station. The arrangement was vigorously carried out, and after the end of September, when the road was re-opened, every European traveller was provided with a guard. The mail-carts were also defended in their passage; for until routes opened up through Baháwalpur and Jhang the Punjab was as regarded communication with other localities hermetically sealed.'*

* An interesting account of the mutiny in Multan, with a plan showing how Major Chamberlain carried out the disarmament, will be found in Cooper's 'History of the Crisis in the Punjab.'

Chapter II.

History.
British Rule.

In Appendix IA will be found a list of the Commissioners and Deputy Commissioners who have controlled the fortunes of the district since annexation. Of the early Deputy Commissioners those longest in the district were Major Voyle and General Van Cortlandt, who between them held the district nearly continuously for 12 years. Of those that followed the longest tenures fell to Major Lang (four years and seven months), Mr. O'Brien (two years and nine months), Colonel Hutchinson (three years and nine months), and Mr. Meredith (two years). Of the previous generations of Deputy Commissioners those best remembered in the district are probably Mr. O'Brien and Colonel Hutchinson : the former for his knowledge of the people and his criminal administration, and the latter for his successful management of the colonisation of the Sidhnai Canal.

CHAPTER III.

THE PEOPLE.

SECTION A.—STATISTICAL.

Chapter III, A.

Statistical.
Distribution of the population.

Table No. V attached to this Gazetteer gives separate statistics for each tahsil and for the whole district, of the total area (cultivated, culturable and cropped), of the total population (urban and rural), of its distribution over area of the inhabited villages classified according to the population they contain, and lastly, of the number of occupied houses and resident families, which are given separately for towns and villages. The number of occupied houses in each town is given in Table No. XLIII. The total population of the towns at each of the last three enumerations was :—

	Census of		
	1881.	1891.	1901.
Multan City	57,471	64,265	74,627
Multan Cantonment	11,203	10,297	12,767
Total ...	68,674	74,562	87,394
Shujabad	6,458	6,329	5,880
Jalálpur Pírwála	3,875	3,884	5,149
Kahror	4,804	5,498	5,552
Dunyapur	2,041	2,101	2,150
Tulamba	2,231	2,792	2,526
Total ...	88,083	95,166	108,651

The statistics for the district, as a whole, give the following figures :—

			Census of		
			1881.	1891.	1901.
Percentage of total population who live in villages.		Persons ...	84·04	84·9	84·7
		Males ...	83·89	84·8	84·4
		Females ...	84·23	85·0	85·0
Average rural population per village ...		...	360	386	446
„ total population per village and town		...	427	452	524
Number of villages per 100 square miles		...	22	23	22
Density of population per square mile of	Total area	Total population...	94	106	120
		Rural population...	79	90	101
	Cultivated area.	Total population...	442	545	452*
		Rural population...	371	462	382*
	Culturable area	Total population...	100	165	215
		Rural population ..	84	97	182

*The term 'cultivated' in the revenue returns bears a different signification before and after 1897. (See para. 11 Settlement Report, 1901.)

Chapter III, A.

Statistical.
Distribution of the population.

		Census of 1881.	1891.	1901.
Number of resident families per occupied house.	Villages ...	1·18	1·10	...*
	Towns ...	1·49	1·05	...*
Number of persons per occupied house.	Villages ...	5·99	5·73	5·54
	Towns ...	5·42	5·42	4·56
Number of persons per resident family.	Villages ...	5·06	4·91	...*
	Towns ...	3·63	4·47	...*

The density of the population at various periods is shown by the following table :—

Date.	Population.	Number of persons per square mile.	Number of persons per square mile of area sown with crops.	Area sown in acres.†
1855 ...	411,386	70	595	442,828
1868 ...	472,268	80	607	* 408,179
1881 ...	551,964	94	638	564,204
1891 ...	631,434	106	545	741,448
1901 ...	710,626	116	608	748,214

The distribution of the population over the different physical divisions of the district was calculated at the recent settlement to be as follows (on the basis of the population figures of 1891) :—

	Persons per square mile.	Persons per square mile of cultivation.
The riverain circles (Hithar)	196	565
The canal circles (Utar)	146	500
The Sidhnai area	112	254
The central uplands (Rawa)	22	635
The whole district (excluding Multan City and Cantonments)...	94	464

Urban and rural population.

The proportion of the urban population to the whole was 16 in 1881, 15 in 1891 and 15 in 1901. The population of the present towns increased by 8 per cent. between 1881 and 1891 and by 14 per cent. between 1891 and 1901 : the corresponding increases in the rural population being 16 and 12 per cent., respectively.

---

* Figures for 1901 not available.

† The figures for 1855, 1881 and 1901 are those of the settlements which were in progress or just concluded at those dates.

Chapter III. A.

Statistical.

Urban and rural population.

The villages and towns are classified as follows in the successive enumerations :—

Population.				Number of towns and villages.		
				1881.	1891.	1901.
Over 10,000 souls	...	...	...	1	2	1
5,000 to 10,000	...	...	...	1	2	3
3,000 to 5,000	...	...	...	6	5	26
2,000 to 3,000	...	...	...	11	10	
1,000 to 2,000	...	...	...	88	108	132
500 to 1,000	...	...	...	189	210	240
Under 500	...	...	...	997	1,060	955
Total		...	...	1,293	1,367	1,357

The term 'village' employed in the above statistics means the revenue mauza, and the increase in the number of villages between 1881 and 1891 is due to the colonization on the Sidhnai canal from 1886 onwards. The two mauzas shown as having over 10,000 souls in 1891 are Multan and the Hajiwah estate; this latter has since been divided into eight villages.

Houses and families.

The statistics regarding houses and families are brought together below :—

				1881.	1891.	1901.
Number of persons per occupied house		...		5·89	5·56	5·36
" " per family		...	..	4·76	4·84	...*
" of families per occupied house		...		1·18	1·10	...*
Increase per cent. since last census in—						
Houses ...	Total	...	...		27	11
	Rural	...	...		28	10
Families ...	Total	..	...		13	...*
	Rural	...	...		19	...*
Number of rural houses per square mile		...	...		16	18
Rural population per village		...	...	360	386	446
Rural population per village and town			...	427	452	444

Birth-place and migration.

The percentage of persons born in the district was 90 in 1881, 87·2 in 1891 and 86·7 in 1901. The total number of immigrants compares as follows :—

Year.				Total.	Males.	Females.
1881		...	...	55,174	36,356	18,818
1891	...	...	...	80,846	50,397	30,449
1901	...	...	...	94,614	57,656	36,958

* Figures for 1901 not available.

Chapter III, A.

Statistical.

Birth-place and migration.

The figures in Table No. VI show the chief districts and States from which these immigrants have come, and the same table shows how the proportion of females among the immigrants tends to increase with the distance of the source of supply. The large proportion of females coming from the Native States (*i.e.*, mainly Baháwalpur and Bikanir) is somewhat striking. The proportion of female immigrants to males was 52 per cent. in 1881, 60 per cent. in 1891 and 64 per cent. in 1901.

The immigration is, of course, largely due to the attractions of the large city; but there has been a special form of immigration during the years 1886—1896, owing to the colonization of lands on the Sidhnai Canal with settlers from the Central Punjab and elsewhere. The area given to such settlers has not, however, been large, and a good deal of the land given out is tilled by local tenants, so that the immigration achieved by this colonization has not been as important or as extensive as is often supposed. This will be shown from the following figures :—

	1881.	1891.	1901.
Immigrants from the Amritsar, Siálkot, Lahore and Gurdáspur districts ...	6,063	8,811	13,580

The immigration into Multan exceeded the emigration from Multan within the province by 43,924 in 1881 and by 63,147 in 1891. The following are the figures showing the movement to and from the neighbouring State of Baháwalpur :—

	Emigration to Baháwalpur.			*Immigration from Baháwalpur.*		
	Total.	Males.	Females.	Total.	Males.	Females.
1881 ...	4,111	2,496	1,615	9,481	5,534	3,947
1891 ...	9,362	5,638	3,724	10,353	5,756	4,597
1901 ...	7,739	4,659	3,080	8,549	4,672	3,877

Increase of the population.

The boundaries of the district have not varied materially since annexation, and the following figures show with very fair accuracy, the increase in the population at the various enumerations :—

	Census.	Persons.	Males.	Females.
Actuals ...	1855 ...	411,386	229,423	181,963
	1868 ...	472,268	261,808	210,460
	1881 ...	551,964	304,517	247,447
	1891 ...	631,434	347,158	284,276
	1901 ...	710,626	388,570	322,056
Percentages ...	1868 on 1855 ...	114·8	114·1	115·7
	1881 on 1868 ...	116·9	116·3	117·6
	1891 on 1881 ...	114·4	114·0	114·9
	1901 on 1891 ...	112·5	111·9	113·3

The increase by tahsils is, owing to the change in the boundaries of the tahsils, less easily ascertainable. The popula-

Increase of the population.

tion of each tahsil, according to its present limits, by the enumeration of 1881 and 1891, was, however, worked out roughly at the recent settlement, and the figures compare as follows with those given by the enumeration of 1901 :—

Census.	Multan.	Shujabad.	Lodhran.	Mailsi.	Kabírwála.	Total.
1881 ...	260,189	109,036	109,665	85,749	80,012	544,651*
1891 ...	188,630	114,162	111,070	104,376	109,628	627,866*
1901 ...	232,126	124,907	113,359	109,727	130,507	710,626
Difference per cent. between 1881 and 1891...	+17·7	+4·7	+1·0	+21·7	+37·0	+15·3
Difference per cent. between 1891 and 1901 ...	+23·1	+9·4	+2·1	+5·1	+19·0	+13·2

Births and deaths.

Table No. XI shows the number of births and deaths of males and females in each year from 1880 onwards and the chief diseases by which the deaths were caused. The distribution of the total deaths from all causes and the deaths from fever over the twelve months in each year from 1895 onwards is shown in Tables Nos. XIA and XIB Further details as to births and deaths registered in individual towns will be found in Table No. XLIV.

The births and deaths in rural areas are recorded by the village watchmen, who come weekly to the police stations and report the births and deaths which have occurred during the last week in their several beats. For small villages the figures are fairly accurate, but for larger villages the omissions are more serious, and the watchman's memory does not prevent him from occasionally mixing up the births with the deaths. As is usual in the province the deaths are reported more fully than the births, and the births and deaths of males more fully than those of females.

The following figures show the birth and death-rates per 1,000 for 1881—1890, calculated on the population of 1881, and those for 1891—1900 calculated on the population of 1891 :—

	1881.	1882.	1883.	1884.	1885.	1886.	1887.	1888.	1889.	1890.	1891.	1892.	1893.	1894.	1895.	1896.	1897.	1898.	1899.	1900.
Birth-rate	17	18	34	43	35	41	41	41	41	41	34	34	32	38	45	45	48	38	52	47
Death-rate	15	20	30	36	31	25	27	27	32	35	30	55	29	28	30	25	33	28	27	28

* The totals ought to be 551,964 and 631,434, respectively, but as above noted in the text, the figures were only roughly calculated. In many cases, owing to changes in village boundaries, especially in the jungles and on the rivers, accuracy was impossible, and the above may be taken as a sufficient statement of the tahsil populations.

Chapter III, A.

Statistical.

Births and deaths.

The figures, roughly speaking, depend on the extent to which the autumnal fever prevails. In a year of bad fever there is a high death-rate, and the birth-rate in the succeeding year is low. The fever years again are the years in which the summer rains are heavy, so that against all the benefits of the summer rains we must set the 'green churchyards' and 'empty cradles,' which must also be ascribed to them.

The average birth-rate of the last ten years in the district at large is 40 per *mille*, and the death-rate 32 per *mille*. In the towns the corresponding figures are 71 and 56.

Ages.

The ages of the people, as indicated by the census returns of 1901, may be classified as follows :—

Age.	Number per thousand.			Number of females per thousand males of the same age.
	Males.	Females.	Total.	
0—1	34	38	36	935
1—	18	22	20	993
2—	30	34	31	950
3—	30	34	32	958
4—	32	36	34	911
Total under 5 years ...	144	164	153	945
5—	144	152	148	878
10—	117	106	112	747
15—	79	77	78	802
20—	78	86	82	916
25—	93	94	93	837
30—	86	84	85	809
35—	58	50	54	708
40—	58	58	58	826
45—	32	27	30	718
50—	41	38	40	766
55—	14	12	13	699
60 and over 60 years	56	52	54	777

Sexes.

According to the different censuses the proportion of males to females has been as follows :—

	1855.	1868.	1881.	1891.	1901.
Number of females per thousand males ...	793	804	813	819	830
" among Muhammadans...	...	...	827	831	842
" among Hindus ...	...	...	779	791	797

Statistical.
Sexes.

The figures for children are as follows:—

	Number of females per thousand males.					
	Under 1 year.			Under 5 years.		
	1881.	1891.	1901.	1881.	1891.	1901.
Muhammadans	960	941	944	962	938	945
Hindus	1,024	938	900	1,008	951	947
Total	972	941	935	966	941	945

The number of females to each thousand males in town and country in 1901 is shown as follows:—

	Villages.	Towns.	Total.
All religions	385	798	829
Muhammadans	844	826	842
Hindus	786	816	797

Conjugal condition.

The figures for conjugal condition are as follows:—

Years.	Proportion per thousand of all conditions.					
	Males.			Females		
	Single.	Married.	Widowed.	Single.	Married.	Widowed.
1881 ...	578	363	59	419	437	144
1891 ...	575	366	58	429	437	140
1901 ...	579	365	56	442	435	123

Religions.

The figures for 1901 for the different religions are as follows:—

	Proportion per thousand of all conditions.					
	Males.			Females.		
	Single.	Married.	Widowed.	Single.	Married.	Widowed.
Muhammadans ...	587	359	54	458	429	113
Hindus	545	391	64	375	458	167

The following shows the ages of marriage according to the census of 1901:—

	Number of single per thousand of all conditions under—					
	—10	10—14	15—19	20—24	25—59	60 and over.
Total	997	924	598	325	101	45
Muhammadans	998	944	631	331	96	39
Hindus ...	995	838	468	273	108	69

The number of married females per 1,000 married males is as follows:—

	1881.	1891.	1901.
Total	977	978	987
Muhammadans	1,003	998	1,006
Hindus	906	921	934

Chapter III A.

Statistical.

Infirmities.

Table No. XII shows the number of insane, blind, deaf-mutes and lepers in the district. The proportion per 10,000 of either sex for each of these infirmities is shown below :—

Infirmities.	Year.	Males per 10,000.	Females per 10,000.	Total per 10,000.	Actual number.
Insane	1881	12	7	10	526
	1891	5	3	4	264
	1901	8	6	7	514
Blind	1881	48	52	50	2,775
	1891	22	24	22	1,432
	1901	27	27	27	1,900
Deaf and dumb	1881	14	8	11	614
	1891	11	7	9	585
	1901	16	10	13	935
Lepers ...	1881	1	1	1	67
	1891	1	...	...	30
	1901	1	1	1	63

Christians and Europeans.

The figures given below show the composition of the Christian population in 1901 and the respective number who returned their birth-place and their language as European :—

	Details.	Males.	Females.	Persons.
Races of Christian population.	Europeans and Americans ...	1,393	249	1,642
	Eurasians	52	72	124
	Native Christians	124	74	198
	Total Christians ...	1,569	395	1,964
Language ...	English	1,427	307	1,734
	Other European languages ..	8	...	8
	Total European languages...	1,435	307	1,742
Birth-place...	British Isles	1,198	91	1,289
	Other European countries ...	5	5	10
	Total European countries ...	1,203	96	1,299

Chapter III, B.

Social and Religious Life.

Houses.

SECTION B.—SOCIAL AND RELIGIOUS LIFE.

The city houses are nearly all made of burnt brick, and are two or more stories in height; but the walls are narrower and the foundations weaker than in cities like Lahore and Amritsar, owing to the small amount of rainfall which they are calculated to withstand. Some of them have underground cellars, which are used for protection from the heat; but the fashion of having punkhas on the roof is gradually ousting that of sitting under ground. The newer class of building is more commodious and well ventilated than the old, but its materials are generally inferior. As in the Punjab proper, the Mahomedans have larger courtyards than the Hindús; the latter prefer high houses with many stories, and a number of small *kothís* or rooms in each. Mahomedan houses are generally surrounded by a high wall to ensure privacy for the women, and in both Hindu and Mahomedan houses the *baithak* or male portion of the house is kept separate from that reserved for females. Outsiders are received and entertained in the outer portion, but the female apartments can be entered by no males except those of the family. In a well-to-do establishment the receiving rooms are often well furnished according to European ideas, but this is seldom the case with the inner apartments. Both portions of the house are, as a rule, well kept; and in a Hindu house the most scrupulous cleanliness is observed in all things connected with the cooking.

In the villages a few rich zamindars and money-lenders live in brick houses, but the ordinary agriculturist or artizan lives in a house with mud walls and a thatched roof. The houses are not, as a rule, clustered together in one village site as in the central Punjab, but are scattered over the village land and grouped round the more important wells. Where there is a group of houses the drinking water of the village is not obtained from wells within the site, but from the nearest agricultural well. The houses in a hamlet or village are not built as closely together as in the Punjab, land being less valuable, and the tastes of the people all in favour of elbow-room. It is unusual to surround a courtyard with walls, and, if privacy is required, a screen of reed-thatch is all that is used. The houses themselves—especially those of the artizans—are usually kept pretty clean, but the courtyards are not attended to in this respect. The courtyard generally contains a tree or two, and the cattle are generally kept in separate byres *(bhána, dhára*)*. The village pond, which forms so marked a feature of Punjab villages, is here almost unknown. The house of a peasant consists of one room of a rectangular shape; the shorter pair of walls points up into a gable; the commoner classes of wood (karín or jál) are used for the roof tree; there are no windows

* A shed with mud walls is called a bhána; without wells, a dhára.

Chapter III, B.

Social and Religious Life.

Houses.

and only one door; and in the middle of the floor is a hole, where in winter the fire is lit, round which the family clusters for warmth. In summer the zamindars, rich and poor, arm themselves with hand fans; and outside each house, especially in tracts near the river, it is common to find a *mannha*, or raised platform, on which the whole family, male and female, sleeps together at night.

The common word for a house in this district is *jhugga*. If it has a flat roof it is known as a *makán*, and if it is of two stories it is a *mári*. Any house with a roof of thatch is known as *sálh*, and a shelter without walls as *chappri*.

Furniture and cooking utensils.

The furniture in a city house is very much like what is customary in the central Punjab, and many of the more advanced house-holders, both in the city and among the richer zamindars, have chairs and tables after the European fashion, and use table cloths, plates, glasses, &c., for their meals. In the ordinary peasant's house the catalogue of furniture is not a large one, and there are very few of the fancy articles and ornaments that are found in Punjab villages. The bed—which is used of course as a chair also—is the most important article, and more care is taken of it than of the bed-clothing. The latter in summer consists either of nothing at all or of a two-anna palm mat (parchh, phúri, traddi) of the coarsest description; the more fastidious zamindars substituting a *khes*, which is also used as a saddle-cloth. In the winter there is added to this the *sawwar* (leph, khindi) or rough homespun cotton quilt, which takes the place of the ordinary city *razai*. Besides the bed and its appurtenances, the country cottage contains a few reed baskets of various shapes, some mats and fans of date leaves, a cradle for the baby, and some spinning and churning apparatus for the women. There are also some large mud bins (kalhotás) for storing grain, and the cooking utensils of the family. Outside there will often be a swing. Almost always there is a *gharwanji* or four-legged wooden stand for the earthen pots, and a *nahila* or branched rack on which the pots are hung, face downwards. If the owner keeps fowls he has a little earthen fowl-house, known as *khuddi*, and a *tinga* or roosting pole in the immediate neighbourhood. The bhusa is also stored near the house in wattled stacks known as *pallas*.

In all houses the cooking utensils form an important part of the equipment. In Hindu houses these are most commonly of brass; among Mahomedans, of copper or bell metal, those manufactured in Bahawalpur and Multan being preferred. Among the poorer classes and in the villages earthenware largely takes the place of metal in the case of Mussalmans. The ordinary apparatus consists of the following, *viz.*, a cooking pot (majholá, deg, degchá, degchí, according to size, and kúnni

Chapter III, B.

Social and Religious Life.

Furniture and cooking utensils.

if of earthenware), a large open boiling pan (karhái), a parching pan (chattri or dángi), a flattish vessel for holding liquids (katorá or channa; if smaller, katori or mungrí; if covered, dhákwan), a deeper vessel with a neck to it (tamálú, or, if provided with a spout, wadná or karwá) several large plates (tás or táslá, or, if with no rim, khauncha), smaller plates (thál, tháli or rakebí), a spoon or two (karchi if large, chamcha if small, and, doí if made of wood), a large iron stirrer (kafgír), a pestle and mortar(ukhli mohla), some knives (chhura, káti or chhurí according to size), and a baking iron (tawwa, loh). The vessel known as a 'lota' in the Punjab proper is here called a 'tamálu' or, among Hindus, a 'gadwá' or 'gadwi'; the term 'lota' in this district being applied only to the earthenware pots (called tinds in the Punjab) on a Persian wheel. An earthen vessel called a 'dohwá' is always used to milk cows into; but the milk is stored or carried by Hindus in 'valtohas' 'valtohis,' and 'gágirs,' which are similar vessels made of brass.

In the villages the cooking of the Mahomedan population is often carried on during the whole summer by the Mácchi women at a large public 'tanúr' or oven; in the cold weather each family does its own cooking. The food is generally eaten by all the members of a family together, all of them sitting round a large earthen plate or a cloth (dastarkhwán) spread on the ground.

Hindus use an iron bucket or 'dol' as well as the brass 'gágir' for drawing water from wells. The use of 'mashaks' is common enough in towns, especially by servants of respectable Mahomedan families whose women are unable to carry water. In the villages water is always carried by the women in 'gharras' and the 'mashak' is unknown except among some of the Punjabi settlers on the Sidhnai. In the tracts where water is scarce, however, men on a journey will often provide themselves with a 'kúhní' or kid's skin, the form of a 'mashak' or with an earthen water-bottle (jhárí)

Food of the people.

Although the district has seldom suffered from acute famine, years of distress come round with considerable frequency and the question of 'our daily bread' is one of very vital concern to a large section of the people, more especially to the lower classes who are the first to feel the effects of scarcity. The people themselves recognize the peculiar liability of the lower classes to distress in their saying: 'Pahlí chikkí kál dí Mochi te Paoli.' They also appreciate the difference between a full and an empty stomach in the proverb; 'Pet bhariá rotián, te sabbhe gálhin motián; Pet na paián rotián, te sabbhe gáhlin khotián,' and in the following truly British sentiment: 'Kháwe ser kamáwe sher, khawe pá kamáwe swáh' ('He that eats a sér, works like a lion; he that eats ¼ of a sér works like wood-ashes.')

Chapter III, B.

Social and Religious Life.

Food of the people.

The staple food of the people consists of the kharif grains, the pulses, wheat and rice. The kharif grains, generally speaking, are sown in July and harvested in October; the pulses and wheat are sown in November and December and harvested in April. The proportion of wheat to inferior grains eaten depends very much on the means of the family : well-to-do people only eat wheat ; the very poor never get it at all. It depends also on the tract in which the family lives : in the Ráwa, for instance, where little but wheat is grown, little but wheat is eaten even by the poor. Rice is very little eaten in this district except at festivals : the rice grown locally is poor, and good rice for eating has to be imported from Baháwalpur or the Punjab. The ordinary poor zamindar eats jowár in the winter, diversified at times with bájra or china ; in the summer he takes wheat, or sometimes chiná or gram. The more prosperous landholders and the inhabitants of the towns take pulse and vegetables with the bread ; the ordinary zamindar does not always manage to do this. Their poorer people make free use of turnip stalks and roots, especially in bad years ; and the very poorest have to fall back for sustenance in years of distress on food like the ber-fruit, the fruit of the pilu, chopped methra leaves. the unopened buds of the karín (known as báta or dehlá), and so forth. The chapatis eaten in towns are generally much thinner than those eaten in the villages. During the investigations connected with the famine of 1879, the following estimate was made by the district authorities of the amount eaten per head*: —

"In an agricultural family the old person may be estimated to eat ¾ sér of átá, one chitak of dál or other pulses a day ; the wife the same as the old person ; the man one sér of átá and one chiták of dál ; the children would each eat half as much as the man : this seems a large allowance for them, but they eat much more often than adults. At the above rate the yearly consumption would be :—

Atá 3½ sérs a day = 1,277 sérs or 32 maunds a year.
Dál 4 chitáks a day = 91 sérs or 9 maunds 11 sérs a year.

The amount of vegetables and green food consumed cannot be definitely established. It depends on whether the family has a garden or not. The consumption of a non-agricultural family would be much the same as the above, but probably the man would eat ¾ instead of one sér of átá a day, and this would reduce the yearly consumption by 91 sérs or to about 30 maunds.'

Meat is very seldom eaten except by the better class, and except on occasions of rejoicing or by way of hospitality. Even for the better class the cooking is not done in the house, nor is the meat partaken of by the women. The ordinary dish is

* See also remarks on the same subject in Chapter IV, Section A, below.

Chapter III. B.

Social and Religious Life.

Food of the people.

goat; mutton and fowls being far less commonly eaten. Kirars, being better able to afford it, eat meat more commonly than ordinary zamindars, and in Multan city the greater number of the Hindus eat meat daily. Along the rivers the consumption of fish is not uncommon even among the lower castes. The salt water in which meat is boiled is often taken with the meat, and this practice gives rise to the saying (applied to men with unreasonable scruples) : 'Botián harám te shora halál' ('He refuses to eat the meat, but he drinks the salt water in which it is cooked.')

The use of gur and spices of various kinds is not unusual, but it is more common in towns than outside. Ghi is much more commonly used in the towns than in the villages. Salt is almost always used, whether the vegetables eaten with the food are of a saline character or not. Sweetmeats and sweet cakes are much sought after in towns, but to the ordinary labourer or peasant they represent a height of luxury to which he does not often attain. Of the man whose desires are unreasonable, he says : 'Ghar bhanejí átá nahín, Phúlka shokh pakáwe' ('In his niece's house there is not even flour, yet he calls for sweet-cake') ; or 'Ek piun khwáná, dújhá halwe dí khair' ('He is begging to avoid starvation, and yet he insists on having sweetmeats'); and he shows his idea of the luxuriousness of sweet things in the saying : 'Bhath piyá be-sharmi dá síra, jo ság sharma dá changá' ('The sweetmeat of dishonour goes bad, while the herb of honour tastes good)'. The sweetmeats sold in towns are the ordinary laddu. pera, ware, &c., of the Punjab. The town of Shujabad, in the proximity of which a certain amount of sugarcane is grown, is especially celebrated for the varieties of thin cake known as 'pápar' and the sweetmeat known as 'rewri'. There is also a special kind of sugar, of a crystallized kind, called sangrí misri or kujá dí misrí, which is said to be a speciality of Multan.

The ordinary drink in the towns is water, and in the country water or butter milk (lassi). Kirars and others who can afford it will drink milk ; and milk comes in for sale in Multan city from the nearer villages. The favourite milk in the city is cow's milk ; in the country buffalo's milk is preferred, being richer. In the bár camel's milk is drunk. There is no great consumption of spirits in the district : those who can afford them are comparatively few* ; and although many, both Mahomedans and Hindus, who drink to excess, are otherwise respectable men, the practice is looked with disfavour by both religions : and it is, of course, contrary to the strict precepts of Islam. The drinking

* The fact that the expense is the main deterrent is reflected in the saying Mukht di sharáb, Káziánbí nahin chhori ' ('If the liquor is to be got for nothing even the Kázis will not forego it.')

Chapter III, B.

Social and Religious Life.

of tea and coffee, so common in other Mahomedan countries is here practically unknown outside the town and cantonments.

Food of the people.

The usual plan for grown-up persons in the district is to dine once about midday, and again soon after dark. The peasants are, however, very irregular in their hours, and, if necessary, go without their morning meal altogether, without feeling the worse for it. In the ploughing season they often take a small repast (túkkur, kassá, lassí, and, in Kabírwála panráká) in the early morning.

Nearly every male, as soon as he can manage a hukka, smokes tobacco. Smoking among women is, however, rare, except in the lower castes. The ordinary tobaccos of the district, especially those with a special name, such as are grown in the Tulamba and Luddan tracts, are considered good smoking; and it is only a minority who prefer the more biting weed of Afghanistan. Cigars and cigarettes are affected by a few smokers in Multan, and by some of the officials outside; but otherwise the only form of smoking is by the hukka.* Snuff is taken as a preventive of colds in the head and so forth, and also fairly commonly as an ordinary indulgence; the snuff is generally kept in a small wooden box (dabbli) in the waistband or turban, and the tobacco employed is both country and Kábulí.

The drinking of 'post' is very little known, and the use of chandu is practically confined to the cantonment bazar. Opium is taken in the form of pills, but the practice is for the most part confined to men of bad character. Charas is little used outside Multan, and in Multan the tum-tum drivers, Sádhús and Brahmans, are said to be the chief victims of this form of indulgence. The drinking of bhang is very common among the fakir class, both Hindu and Mussalman; and among the villagers, too, a certain amount of bhang is said to be drunk with the excuse that this drink is suited to the climate of Multan. Hindus also use it frequently during the bathing season (dhaoni). Speaking generally, opium and hemp drugs, as forms of indulgence, are confined to the big towns and the cantonment bazar; outside they are chiefly used as medicines only.

The use of spirits or intoxicants is rare among women of any religion or any class in the district except during the Holí festival.

Dress.

The ordinary Mahomedan wears a 'patka' or 'pag' or turban on his head, and sometimes a 'kulla' or cap inside

* The Mohánas or boatmen, strangely enough, do not, as a rule, put water in their hukkas, and this has given rise to a proverb regarding people who have what others want and do not use it. 'Daryá dé Mohánе dá hukká sukká rahndá' ('The Mohána lives on the river, yet his hukka has no water').

Chapter III, B.

Social and Religious Life.

Dress.

In the towns a few wear the fez, but mainly as a substitute for the turban when indoors. In the cold weather a wadded cap coming over the ears (called a kannewalí topí) is commonly worn: a topí of this kind lasts for some six months, and as the hair is commonly oiled, the state of the head-gear at the end of that time can be easily imagined. This form of topí is higher and larger on the Sutlej border than elsewhere, and on that border a cloth topí is sometimes substituted. In buying cloth for a turban it is usual among Mahomedans to buy an uneven number of yards, such as 9, 11, 13, &c. The turban is tied in different ways, and that part which is the front elsewhere is in Kabírwála worn somewhat on one side. Its size varies according to its owner's taste, and his idea of his own importance: some of the Syads indulge in the most monstrous specimens. Turbans on the Baháwalpur border are larger than elsewhere, and the Mahomedan turbans are, as a rule, larger than those of Hindus. Hindus wear the pagri, and, to a certain extent, the kulla also; and though they usually tie the pagri in a different way to the Mahomedans, the difference is disappearing, especially in the towns. In the towns, too, it is common for them to wear a 'topí' or cap instead of the pagri when indoors.

The fashion of dress worn is said to be becoming much more uniform than formerly throughout the district, and local or tribal peculiarities are disappearing. The Biloches, for instance, no longer dress like their tribesmen across the Indus, and the greater number of the Pathans have discarded the shalwár or wide trousers of their ancestors. The Mahomedans, generally speaking, take more trouble about their dress and general appearance than the Hindus. The normal costume in the district consists of a waistcloth, a coat of some kind, and a plaid worn over the shoulder. The waistcloth (majhla or manjhla) is generally white or blue: among the Arains it is generally blue, and the Arains of Jalla in Lodhrán are known to their neighbours as the "nilí paltan," from their affection for the blue majhla. The Hindus substitute a dhoti for the majhla; and on the Sutlej side and the cities it is not uncommon for both Hindus and Mahomedans to wear the voluminous trousers known as shalwár or paijáma. Trousers, especially silk trousers of a red colour, were formerly the common wear of the district, but they are now seldom worn, except by Thakkars among Hindus, and Makhdums among Mahomedans, and even they are often laughed at by the people for wearing a feminine costume. Over the body it is usual to wear a chola or kurta; both are short coats, but the latter is closed by buttons, and the former by a loop: the latter is still in most places somewhat of an innovation. The long narrow-waisted coat, known as jáma, which was formerly worn by Hindus in the city, has now been generally abandoned in favour of the kurta or chola, but its place is sometimes taken by the angarakha, a tunic fitted with strings instead of buttons. The

Chapter III, B.
Social and Religious Life.
Dress.

angarakha is looked as a more respectable dress than the kurta, and when worn by Mahomedans is longer and lower than that worn by Hindus. Over all the other clothes is thrown, in the form of a plaid, the chadar of cotton : among the richer sort the plaid is a lungi or khes of better material: among the poorer it is often a coarse blanket, known as bhagal or lukar. Some add a rumál or large handkerchief of khaddar (coarse country cloth), which is worn hanging loose on the shoulder.

The women's dress consists of three parts, corresponding to the three items above described. Round the waist and legs are worn suthans (paijámas) or petticoats (ghaggra), the former being found mainly in the towns; and Hindu women, when cooking or washing, often substitute the majhla or dhoti for the petticoat. The Hindu petticoat is generally shorter and shows more ankle than that of the Mahomedan women. On the body is worn the short jacket, called kurti or choli, or a longer jacket, known as kurta or chola, often coloured in broad stripes of green, yellow, &c., and always fitted with very short sleeves. Over the jacket and over the head is worn the chadar or bhochhan, which is generally of white or red cloth; Hindu widows wearing white only. This head covering is sometimes dispensed with by the poorer castes, and is almost always discarded by all castes when indoors. The elaborate patterned plaids and silk-worked phulkaris, so common in the Central Punjab, are quite unknown among the peasantry here. The parda women of the Pathans, Syads, &c., wear, when in public, the long enveloping cloak, known as the *burka* : but the burka is not so commonly seen in Multan as in the Punjab proper. Generally speaking the women of this district, contrary to the practice of their European sisters, wear their best frocks when they are at home, and their worst when they go out.

The Hindus, as a rule, wear their hair shaved or very short, with the exception of the choti or scalp lock : the first shaving of a child's head is complete, but in subsequent shavings the scalp lock is left untouched. Both Mahomedans and Hindus generally wear the hair fairly short (so as not to fall perceptibly below the level of the lobe of the ear); but on the Sutlej side, and especially among Biloches and Daudpotras, the hair is allowed to hang over the shoulders. A common custom in both religions is to shave a rectangular space on the crown of the head; and officials or students often keep the hair quite short like Europeans, on the supposition that long hair interferes with the working of the brain. It is customary to wash the hair pretty frequently with Multani mitti or soap made of sajji, and, owing to the dryness of the climate, it is customary to anoint the hair frequently with oil, made of sarson, camphor and coriander. Among women the hair is not usually cut ; it is customary, especially among Mahomedans, for a girl's hair to be plaited up to marriage ; after marriage, it is (contrary to ordinary Punjab usage) worn loose. In the northern parts of the district the women sometimes wear the hair plaited and knotted on the top of the head.

Ornaments.

Men seldom wear ornaments : a few have bracelets or ear-rings or finger-rings, but the custom of men wearing ornaments is gradually disappearing. The ornaments worn by the women are much the same for Hindus as for Mahomedans, but the Hindus, being more wealthy, are able to afford a better stamp of ornament than the Mahomedans ; and while the Hindu woman will often wear her ornaments daily, the Mahomedan prefers to keep hers for special occasions. The usual complement of ornaments consists of ear-rings (murkián, wálián, jhumke, tukma), nose-rings (nath) or nose studs (laung), necklaces (katmálá or hassí), armlets (búzúband, tád), bracelets (chura, pourchí, kangan), plaques (takhtís), finger-rings (challe, mundrián), thumb-rings (ársi) and anklets (karián, anwatián, lachhe). The women in Kabírwála and the Khatri women in Multan also wear the 'choti-phul' on the top of the hair; but this is uncommon in the other tahsils. The ornaments are said to differ very little from those worn in the Central Punjab : but the solid anklets (karián) are said to be more common in Multan, and the chain anklets (lachhe) in the Punjab. The use of the nose-ring in towns is also being gradually abandoned. Generally speaking, the people of this district are poorer than in the Punjab proper, and the amount of jewellery possessed by them is probably very much smaller.

Birth customs among Hindus.

In Multan city the Aroras have a custom called 'aroe.' When a woman is in her first pregnancy, and has reached the fifth month, a kind of sweetmeat is prepared by the woman's parents : a little is put in her lap, and the rest is divided among the relations.

In the seventh or eighth month the custom of *kanji* is observed. In the villages the woman's relations send her clothes for herself and her husband, with trays of sweetmeat. The neighbours then collect together, and concoctions of flour, salt and ghi and sweet sherbet are distributed. This custom is observed in the first pregnancy only.

If a son is born, it is customary, some six days after birth, to call in the relations, and the mother, in the presence of the females of the family, gives the child the breast; this ceremony is known as *thanj pilána,* and it is accompanied with gifts and a certain amount of feasting. On the seventh day the mother is bathed ; so, again, on the thirteenth day, when she is further adorned with surma, &c., and food is distributed. Some time after, the child, who has hitherto been naked or in swaddling clothes, is clothed in a 'chola,' either at the shrine of some pír, or at Deví's temple, or in the house of the family. On this

Chapter III, B.
Social and Religious Life.

occasion sweetmeats are distributed, and the Brahman, after reverencing Ganesh, puts the 'chola' on the child.

Birth customs among Hindus.

At some interval after birth comes the ceremony of *Jhandian*, when the child's hair is shaved by the nai—sometimes at home, sometimes at some place by a well or under a pipal tree, and sometimes at the shrine of the Sitla Devi, or at that of Bahawal Hakk or Sakhi Sarwar. In some families the children's hair is shaved by turns on the suitable days, and sometimes a boy grows to a considerable age before the time comes for his hair to be cut; but if the ceremony is performed at the Ganges, all the children have their hair cut at once. Some people perform the ceremony four or five times a year. In the fifth year, on the day of Akhantrij, they begin to teach the boy lessons. When he is from 7 to 11 years old, they go on some favourable day to a river or canal, or to some shrine, Hindu or Mahomedan, and, having collected their relations, the Brahman puts on the janeo or sacred thread. The boy is then clothed in new garments, the old ones being given to the nai, his ears are bored, the Brahmans are again feasted, and presents of clothes, &c., are given to the boy.

Birth customs among Mahomedans.

During pregnancy a Mahomedan mother also observes the custom of *kanji*. From the fifth to the seventh month she neglects her appearance, omits to use henna, to cut her nails, to wear new clothes, &c. In the seventh month she calls in her friends and relations and gives a feast, at which the nai's wife sings, 'doras' or couplets, The woman is then washed and her forehead marked with sandal, after which she resumes her ordinary habits,

Soon after birth the child is washed by the dai, and the mulla or kází is at once called to whisper the 'báng'* in the child's ear. If the kází is not available then the duty is performed by some other man. The dai then proceeds to inform the neighbours, and receives a congratulatory present from each. The brotherhood are on the same day presented with a concoction of zíra and sugar cooked in ghi, which is known as *Phal zira*, and for some fifteen to twenty days there are rejoicings, with singing and dancing, up to midnight. On the third day the child's name is chosen; this is generally done on the advice of the mulla or of an astrologer, but sometimes the Koran is opened at random, and the first letter of the page is taken to intimate the first letter of the name to be adopted. As elsewhere, the child of poor parents is brought up by the mother; that of rich parents by the dai, Pathans generally employ Biloch women (camel graziers) as dais. On the sixth day (known as the *satthi*) the brotherhood is fed with milk and rice, with white sugar in it, and then the child's

* The meaning of the words used is,—Say, there is but one God, who is great and Muhammad is His Prophet. There is but one God.

Chapter III, B.

Social and Religious Life.

Birth customs among Mahomedans.

hand is washed in milk which is afterwards thrown away on some high spot of ground. On the seventh, ninth or eleventh day (but sometimes after three months or a year) comes the ceremony of akíka or '*jhand utárná,' i.e*, shaving the child's head: on which occasion (unless the parents are too poor) two goats are killed if the child is a boy, and one goat if it is a girl; or a he-goat for a boy, and a she-goat for a girl; and the bones of the slaughtered goat are buried. The mother is then washed and clothed in red clothes, and cakes are distributed. When the child's head has been shaved a present is sent to the nai. At birth there is generally an attendance of bards (bhánd), eunuchs (khusrá), quack doctors (kátímár and silmár) and fakirs of all sorts, who duly receive presents from the family.

There is no fixed rule as to the date for circumcision (khatna): some families have it done on the second or third day, while others put it off to the fifth or sixth year. The operator is always a Piráhin or follower of Sakhi Sarwar, and many come from Shakot in the Multan Tahsil, where Zain-ul-Abadin, the father of Sakhi Sarwar, is buried. The parents, if well off, generally arrange for a good deal of tom-tom beating for each of the two or three nights preceding the ceremony; and among the richer classes performances by dancing girls are added, though these are not favourably viewed by the stricter Mahomedans. On the night chosen food is distributed, and the child is then clothed in red and seated on a slab of wood or clay for the operation. When it is over the neighbours give their 'tambol' or presents. When the wound heals this is taken as the excuse for another distribution of food, &c., but on a smaller scale. The expenditure on circumcision ceremonies is, however, much less extensive than in the Punjab proper, and in ordinary families the expenditure ranges between 25 rupees and 4 annas.

Death ceremonies among Hindus.

A Hindu child dying within six months of birth is buried beneath a tree and a small cup for water is placed by the grave. If a child of less than five years old but more than six months old dies it is thrown into the river, unless the river is very far away. For persons over five years of age cremation is the rule.

When a man dies his relations are at once informed. His sons, grandsons and nephews shave their heads and perform the *kiria karm* according to the Shastras; the Jájaks and Achárajs put in an appearance; and the ceremonies are very similar to those in vogue in other Punjab districts. If the deceased is an old man the heir's pagri is tied on thirteen days afterwards, A certain degree of mourning (siápa) is maintained for a year. On the eighth or ninth day after death small gifts of coin are given to the daughters of the deceased, and the families whose

Chapter III, B.

Social and Religious Life.

daughters have married into the deceased's family also contribute something.

Death ceremonies among Musalmans.

After death among Mahomedans, a man's clothes are removed by the mulla; a woman's by the mulla's wife; and the corpse is washed and scented and then wrappd in a winding sheet. Women are generally (from feelings of delicacy) put in a coffin of palm-wood; but men are not given a coffin. The body is laid on a charpoy and covered with as valuable clothes as can be spared, and a copy of the Koran is also put with it. It is then carried out towards the cemetery and is halted at a convenient spot on the road, where Mahomedans who wish to do so present the dead man with so many readings of the Koran; that is to say transfer from themselves to the deceased the spiritual benefit of a whole or a part of the Koran reading which they have themselves undergone. When the funeral prayer has been said the bulk of the people disperse, the near relations only proceeding to the cemetery. After burial some wheat and salt are given in alms, and the mulla recites the 'bang' or call to prayer. The mourners then proceed to the house of the chief mourner: rice and salt is brought out, and after the chief mourner has partaken the rest do the same. This is known as *munh choli*. On the third day comes the '*kul khwáni*'; that is to say the whole of the Koran is recited in presence of all the near relations by a number of men who undertake separate parts, all reciting at one time. This being completed the chief mourner sends presents of rice and meat or pulse to every one of the mourners and the *dastúrbandi* ceremony, or formal recognition of the heir, is duly carried out. For forty days food is distributed daily: on Fridays the mulla receives sweetmeat, and on the day of the *kul khwáni* the relations give presents. On the *chihlam* or fortieth day cooked food is distributed to the relations and mullas; and the mullas are similarly treated on the Moharram and Shab-i-Barát following. During the forty days the women collect for lamentation every Saturday and Wednesday evening.

The prospect of a well-attended funeral has its attractions in Multan as elsewhere, especially among the women; and there is a proverb which says: 'Sadar kar moí. Te ghíl te satti ('She died with pleasure' (in expectation of a fine funeral), and they dragged her body out and threw it away.') A death at evening has its disadvantages, as people are then about to go to bed and will not stay up to mourn: 'Sawin sanje de murde kún kera rosi' ('If a man dies at evening, who will weep for him?') The bier is also introduced in proverbs as the emblem of human mortality: "Jihan takht jihan takhta" ('The bier levels kings and beggars').

Marriage customs among the Hindus.

If the proposal of marriage among Hindus comes from the girl's parents, no special ceremonies of betrothal are customary.

Chapter III, B.

Social and Religious Life.

Marriage customs among the Hindus.

If it comes from the boy's parents, some five or six of the boy's relations go on a favourable day to the girl's house, when they present a couple of rupees and a few vegetables, and sometimes some clothes. They then receive some small present in money, known as 'múra,' and the betrothal is complete. The cost of a betrothal seldom exceeds Rs. 15 in this district, whereas in the Central Punjab hundreds of rupees are squandered over it.

The next movement, known as the *Kaj Ganetra,* is on the part of the Brahman, who gives to each party a paper showing the exact date and hour which is auspicious for each part of the marriage ceremony. Shortly before the marriage the female relations of both sides join together for a formal grinding of a few grains of wheat; this is known as *chung;* and after this the near relations of the bride quarter themselves on the bride's house till the marriage is over. Then follows the *Deo Asthápan* or invocation of the manes, and the *Nawighri* or adoration of the planets. On the latter occasion food is distributed to the relations, and the males who receive food are supposed to return something by way of *tambol.* Meanwhile gifts, known as 'mura,' are constantly passing from the house of the bride to that of the bridegroom, and as the marriage day draws near the ceremony of anointing (*tel charhánáj* is gone through. The bridegroom's head is anointed, and the vessel containing the oil is then sent to the bride, whose head is also anointed forthwith.

On the marriage day the bridegroom has a silver crown, known as *mukat,* put upon his head, and he is mounted on a horse. In some cases he is also given a paper umbrella. Another boy, known as the sarbálá or sabálá (generally his brother-in-law), sits behind him, and the male relations follow. The procession, contrary to Punjab usage, generally includes women. As the procession starts the bridegroom cuts a branch of a jand tree with a knife, and then moves on to the bride's village. The bride's father advances a short distance and greets the visitors with the words 'Rám Rám:' hence this part of the ceremony, known in the Punjab as the 'Milni,' is here called the 'Rám Rám.' In some cases the bride is then brought out and made to pass under the horse's belly. Presents known as *ghál* are then given to the boy, and the boy, after dismounting, is respectfully greeted by his future father-in-law. A few of the relations follow the boy into the house, but the rest (contrary to the usage of the Central Punjab) return to their homes without partaking of any hospitality. Among the Aroras food, known as *junj*, is then distributed. It is then customary for the men of the bridegroom's party and the women of the bride's party to sing abusive songs against each other (dohá, sakhián, sitthrián). The boy and the girl are then confronted, the Brahman recites the formulas of marriage on behalf of both parties, and the bride and bridegroom join their right hands. The bride's father then recites the names of the three nearest male ancestors of the

Chapter III, B.

Social and Religious Life.

Marriage customs among the Hindus.

bridegroom and of the bride, and pours water into the bridegroom's hand. This is known as the *sankalp* or offering ceremony, and the bridegroom says : 'Svasti' in reply. The Brahman then utters some mantras, the bride's face is shown to the bridegroom, and the *hom* offerings are made to the gods. The parties then walk seven times round the fire, and the bridegroom having gone through a general conversation with the bride, the ceremony is brought to a close by the bride being placed in a palanquin and carried to her husband's house.

Later on the bridegroom's father goes with a small party to the bride's home, and then receives the dáj or dower : this visit is known as "wárísúí." The married couple then go to the bride's house to perform the ceremony of "phera," which is followed the next evening by the 'sirmel,' or completion of the marriage.

The Kirars have a sort of dance known as 'chhej' or 'gátkás' which they are fond of executing at a marriage. It consists of a company of men moving slowly round and clashing together small sticks, which they hold in their hands.

The Hindus of this district, though well enough off, are much more economical in their marriages than those of the Central Punjab ; and it is said that the total expenses of a marriage seldom exceed Rs. 500 or Rs. 600 to either party, even in the wealthiest families. The tambol given is any sum from Rs. 10 to Re. 1 and seldom exceeds the latter sum. Careful accounts are kept of the tambol given and received.

Marriage customs among the Mahomedans.

Betrothal (*mangna*) among Mahomedans takes place at any age. Very often a boy or young man becomes betrothed to some girl of the neighbourhood, not infrequently to a first cousin, much in the same way as in European countries : the selection being made either by the parents, or, if the youth is grown up, by the youth himself. The girl, too, has a greater say in the matter than is usual in India, and very often she has a very fair acquaintance with her future husband before marriage. Instances of girls refusing to marry the husbands selected for them are not uncommon. If there is no one suitable in the neighbourhood, some common friend is got by the boy's relations to arrange a betrothal with a suitable family, and the family, after making the necessary enquiries, send word that they agree. An auspicious day having then been fixed, the boy's male relations, and sometimes the female relations also, come in a body to the girl's family. Here they are fed with *patásá* and rice, and sometimes with milk and fruits also. The prayer of blessing (*fatiha-i-khair**) is then pronounced, and clothes and jewellery are put on to the girl. Poor people con-

* 'May God preserve this connection and may the bridegroom and bride prosper.'

Marriage customs among the Mahomedans.

tent themselves with putting on a ring, or a bracelet only; others give more numerous and more valuable gifts on this occasion. During the period of betrothal small presents of fruit are sent by the boy's relations to those of the girl every year at the Id. Children are betrothed at a much later age than in the Punjab proper, and the expenses incurred on the attendant rejoicings are comparatively small.

The betrothed girl is known as the *kwár*, and the boy as the *ghot*. When the time comes the parties arrange for a suitsble date for the wedding, and the relations on both sides are informed. This is done by sending round a thick coloured thread (called *mauli*), which is tied together at the ends.

Some ten days before marriage the ceremony of 'unplaiting the braids' ('*mendhi kholna*') takes place. Some days before the marriage the bride is kept in-doors and is rubbed by the *náin* or barber woman with a cosmetic called *watu*; this ceremony is known as *mangan*. On the night of the marriage, or a day or two before, both bride and bridegroom are marked with henna by the *mirásin*. On the marriage night the procession (*barát*) starts, composed not only of men (as in the Punjab proper), but of both men and women; a crown of flowers is put on the bridegroom's head, and an immense amount of tom-toming goes on. When the procession reaches the bride's house fireworks are let off, and the bride's women-folk throw flowers at the men in the procession. The procession, it may be noted, does not halt outside the village as is usual in the Central Punjab, but goes straight to the bride's house, and sometimes the bridegroom's party return without being even offered food. Then follows the answer of acknowledgment (*íjáb-kabúl*) which constitutes the marriage or *nikáh*. The girl is inside the house, while the bridegroom sits outside with his two witnesses and his vakíl (intermediary). The vakíl going to the girl asks her if she accepts the bridegroom for her husband, and her answer is communicated to the kází. Then the vakíl asks the bridegroom if he accepts the bride for his wife, and when he accepts the parties are congratulated. The *hakk mahr* or dower is also fixed (a sum which among ordinary zamindars averages about 35 rupees), and the *khutba* is recited.

When the service has been read (*nikáh khwáni*) *til* and brown sugar are distributed. The clothes of both parties are taken off and given to the nai, and fresh clothes are put on. A present of clothes and jewels (known as the *wari*) is then made by the bridegroom to the bride, and sometimes presents are made to the bridegroom's near relations also. Alms (*jhajri*) are then distributed to the bards, fakirs and the quacks in attendance, and to kamíns such as the Mirási, Kumhár, Chuhra, &c., who bring flowers. The bride is then taken to her husband's house not in a palanquin as in the Punjab, but on a camel,

Chapter III, B.

Social and Religious Life.

Marriage customs among the Mahomedans.

Some three to seven days after marriage occurs the '*satwara*'; that is to say, sweetmeats are taken by the bride's people to the bridegroom's house: the bride is then taken back to her house, the mírásin is called, and songs and feasting take place. Two or three days later the *putrete* (*i.e.*, the boy's mother or sister or near female relations) come to take away the bride, who is then dismissed from her home with more presents of food and clothing.

There is another custom in Multan which is not prevalent in the Punjab proper. It is known as *sir-mel*, or the joining of heads. Either at the marriage or a few days after, the náin and mírásin, singing together, take the bride and bridegroom into a closed room, where they place the bride's hand in that of the bridegroom and leave them alone. In this district the marriage is not considered complete until this ceremony has been gone through.

Marriage and the position of women.

Expenditure on marriages is, compared with that prevalent in the Central Punjab, quite small. An organisation was started some years ago, under the supervision of the Deputy Commissioner, to curtail such expenditure, but, except in the cities and among the more prominent families of the Sayads and Kureshis, there is not much inclination to extravagance; and in ordinary zamindar families the sum spent seldom exceeds Rs. 100. The food used is generally cheap; the ghi and rice cost comparatively little; and the custom of *sot* (by which small coins are thrown about over the head of the bridegroom) is unknown. Fireworks are only used in about 5 per cent. of the marriages, and dancing girls are very seldom invited, the dancing being often done by the women of the household. Dowries, too, are very small. The Khákwánís and other Pathans have the sense to spend very little on their circumcision and marriage ceremonies, and there is a proverb that a Khákwáni circumcision does not cost more than a pitcher of sherbet, and a Khákwáni marriage not more than a priest's fee.

There is not much polygamy in the district, but it is commoner than in the Punjab proper. The Hindus only marry a second wife when the first is barren; but a second wife among Mahomedans is by no means rare. It is of course pretty common among the richer classes, but one comes across instances of very poor men with several wives; and it is much easier for a man to get a second wife in Multan during the lifetime of the first than it is in the centre and east of the province. The bigger men when they marry two or more wives often provide them with separate establishments on separate wells or in separate villages, so as to prevent the discord which is apt to ensue when they are in too close proximity to each other. It is said, however, that co-wives live together in greater amity in Multan than is usual elsewhere.

Chapter III, B.

Social and Religious Life.

Marriage and the position of women.

The remarriage of widows is common enough among Mahomedans, though discouraged among the Makhdums and prominent Syad families. Among Hindus it is rare. The *karewa*, or marriage with a deceased husband's brother, is very uncommon in this district.

Among the bulk of the Mahomedans of the district the position of women is in some ways very free. Except in the cities and among Syads and Shekhs, they enter freely into conversation with men, greet them by shaking hands and are in many respects on a level with them. Marriage, too, is attended with few restrictions. The Syads, it is true, will not give their daughters to other tribes, and very few tribes will give their daughters to very lowest castes, such as Chúhras. By far the greater number of the tribes of the district however intermarry freely: marriage, as a rule, does not take place till the parties are grown up, and the woman in many cases has a distinct say in the matter.* This freedom has of course its other side. Where women are married unhappily, or married against their will, there is a good deal of immorality, and there are always a large crop of abduction cases before the courts. The injured husband seldom wishes to wreak vengeance on his wife, his love or his sense of propriety prevailing, as a rule, over his jealousy or sense of honour: and instances of blindly, infatuated husbands welcoming back the most impossible of wives are very common. There is none of that objection, so common in other parts of India, to marriage in the tribe or family. Under the conditions of family life prevailing in the district, the young men naturally see most of their near relations and cousins, and the marriage of cousins especially among the higher classes (where the preservation of the property in the family is a consideration), is remarkably common. The marriage of men of position with women of the more disreputable castes, such as the Pernís and the Kanjrís, is not infrequent; such unions do not escape a certain stigma which attaches to the offspring also: but not a few of the most prominent and intelligent men in the district are the result of marriages of this kind.

The authority of woman in the household, among both rich and poor, is very extensive; and most of the money transactions pass through her hands. It is she who decides what the family shall eat and how much the husband shall spend. The marriages, too, are mainly settled by her, and the men have merely to consent. The fact that the women grind corn and cook food with their own hands, even in the most respectable families, does not in the least militate against their superiority in household matters, such duties being looked upon as

* How little any one else has to say to it is indicated by the proverb 'Ghot kwár rází ke karesí Mullan Kází ? (If the bride and bridegroom want to be married, what can the clergyman do but marry them ? ')

Chapter III, B — Social and Religious Life. Marriage and the position of women.

proper accomplishments for women of all classes. Many a young man, too, separates from his parents and lives in a separate house at the instigation of his wife. And in most walks of life the Multání finds that 'hukm-i-jorúji bih az hukm-i-khudá') ('vox mulieris, vox Dei ').

Among the Hindus the women enjoy much less freedom than among the Mahomedans : they do not walk abroad unveiled, or talk with men in public, and are not supposed to talk even in-doors with their elder male relations. Their behaviour is much less open to comment than that of the Mahomedan women : any indiscretions which they may be guilty of are hushed up, and cases of abduction of Hindu women are exceedingly rare in the law courts

The proverbial philosophy of the district, much of which is the product of women's brains, is peculiarly rich in its allusions to women and to the married state. As is usual in other districts also, there are pithy comparisons between the points of a woman and those of a horse : the former should be tall, thin, straight and narrow in the waist, while the latter, should be none of these things—the latter should be short, with a thick barrel and wrinkled forehead, which things in the former are to be abhorred. A woman who stays at home has always the preference : 'Andar baithí, lakh dí; báhar gayí kakh dí' ('Who stays at home is worth a lakh ; who wanders out is worth a straw'). 'Treí kam kharáb : mard nún chakkí ; sandhe nún gáh ; ran nún ráh.' ('Three things are bad : grinding for a man, threshing for a buffalo, and travelling for a woman'). A woman is glad of any excuse to be away from home : 'Ran gaí syápe, ghar áwe tán jápe' ('If a woman goes to a mourning, one cannot tell when she will be home till she actually is home'). At the same time, no scandal can hurt a woman of real character : 'Ap takrí, kaun laí phakrí ?') ('If she is worth anything, who will say anything against her ?') The difficulty which mothers have in looking after their girls is compared to that of keeping lamps made of flour : 'Ata de diwe báhar rakhán tán kán ghinn vanjan ; andar rakhán tán chúhe khânwan' ('If you put them outside, crows fly off with them ; if you keep them indoors, rats eat them '). When the rich Copbetua marries the beggar maid, they say : 'Chundí áı tote, te án balhái kote' ('She used to gather sticks, and he placed her in a palace'). In praise of the 'whole duty of woman', they say : 'Saían bháni te kamlí bi siáni' ('If her husband is pleased, even the foolish wife shows intelligence'). Of the uxorious husband, they say : 'Bíbí múnh na láe, mián shakkar vandáe'. ('The lady hates the sight of him, yet her lord from sheer delight feasts his friends') In Multan, as elsewhere, the wife is a curtain lecturer : 'Ran sawwar da jinn' ('The demon of the bed-quilt'). And her master retorts with sayings such as : 'Ghore nún tallá, ran

Marriage and the position of women.

nún khallá' (' Grass for a horse, shoe-beating for a woman '), and 'Chor kún chattí, kutte kún gattí, ran kún chakkí; , A fine for a thief, a fetter for a dog and a millstone for a woman'). ' Ann dí thaggi khándian torí ; kapre dí thaggí handendian torí ; ran dí thaggi sárí mudd' (' Grain is only bad while you eat it ; clothes only bad while you wear them ; but a wife is bad for the whole of your life'). ' Ran milí kupattí ná márí gaí na sattí, ghaib dí chattí' (' He got a bad wife and could neither beat her nor divorce : this is one of God's mysterious visitations'). The slatternly housewife comes in for her share of blame : ' Ayá welá sotá, te kuchajji kunna dhotá ' (' It is time to go to bed, and the foolish woman begins to clean the cooking things'). ' Rotián pakáwe dún, angitián bhanne trae' (' To cook two loaves, she broke three cooking-grates '). The result of constant small extravagances is noted in : ' Haule aule chugge, sunj karende jhugge ' (' Slow pecking brings down the house.') The usefulness of marriage is indicated by the saying : ' Chhare karmán de sare, ap pakende rotian, ap bharendi gharre' (' The bachelor's lot is not a happy one : he has himself to cook the food, himself to lift the water-pots'). There are also the time-honoured jests about a woman in her husband's absence : ' Paiá nahín ghar, bíbí kún káin dá dar ?' (' When he is not at home, who is the lady afraid of ?'). If her husband displeases her, she has always her parents' house at hand : ' Ruthí kún pekián dá sanehâ' (' The moment she gets angry, a message comes from her father's house to fetch her'). ' Jihn de peke nere, oh pairán nál kahere.' (' If her father's house is near, she is constantly running over there.') ' Dhandí paundí pekian di dar te.' (' She is constantly at her father's house'*). Her own relations alone receive any, attention from her : ' Ayá zál dá sakká shatak máná pakká ; ayá mard dá sakka devis dharm da chikka'. (' When the wife's relation came, she at once cooked a loaf. When her husband's relation came, she said, " Push him out of the door.")

Games and amusements.

The games among children have a family resemblance to those known in other parts of the world, and girls have their dolls (gudian). Girls also amuse themselves with tossing up five bits of broken pottery off the back of the hand and recovering them again in the palm (fitián), and they take each other's hands and whirl ' round the mulberry bush' (chak chingal). They are fond of swings (pínhg). Boys play a kind of marbles (chidda) and also especially at night, a variety of hide-and-seek (akh di lukrí or lukkan-chappan). There is also a game, like fox and geese, which is played with bricks or potsherds on squares drawn with the finger in the dust : this game is known as ' The Lion and the Goat' (shinh-bakri). There is also

* The proverb is applied to persons who come to see you so frequently as to become a nuisance.

Chapter III, B.

Social and Religious Life.

Games and amusements.

tip-cat or gítí-dandá. Cricket has also become popular in the larger towns. Both boys and men are excited over kite-flying (guddí bází or patang-bází), but not so much as in the Punjab; and amuse themselves in the hot weather by diving into water feet foremost and swimming about; and boys amuse themselves by splashing water about in a game called 'dhí dhí.' Except in the Rawa nearly every male in the district can swim, owing to the constant bathing in canals and watercourses, as well as in the river. Men also amuse themselves, especially at fairs and festivals, by a kind of prisoners' base (pir kaudí or kaudí-kabaddí; another kind is known as doda), or by a slow dance with clapping of hands round a tom-tom (jhummar), or by playing flutes and singing songs. There is also a game known as 'tallián,' where one man presses his palm on the ground, and others try to pull away his hand from off the ground. At many of the fairs there is a rough kind of horse-racing (distance two to three hundred yards as a rule), and at a few there is tent-pegging: but this latter is not at all a popular form of sport. A few of the bigger men go in for sport as sport, but their ideas of what is fair shooting and what ought not to be shot differ somewhat from those of Englishmen.* Not a few of them get more amusement from having pigs netted, and then baited by dogs. In the towns there is a certain amount of cock and quail fighting; also ram-fights, which are said to be patronized mainly by dhobís, butchers, indigo-dyers, and so forth. Many of the idle and wealthier class, especially the Patháns, go in for pigeon flying (kabútar bází), the object being to join your flock with your adversary's and then to seduce as many as possible of your adversary's pigeons to your own roost. Wrestling by professionals for gate-money is also common, and the wrestling provided at the Sher Shah fair is said to be always good; wrestling is also carried on by young men throughout the district as a diversion of an evening, and some also exercise themselves with Indian clubs (munglián). In the city, chess (shatranj) and chaupat are common pastimes, and so are cards (tàsh): there are of course numerous varieties of the latter, such as pískot (a four-handed game), rang kí bází (a three-handed game), and so forth.

Fairs and festivals.

The number of fairs held in the district is very numerous. The most important are the following:—

---

* There is a kind of impression that sport is inconsistent with a respectable character. I once asked an old gentleman if he went in for shooting and he answered: 'Ne, main úbásh ádmi nahín hún.'

List of the more important Fairs in the Multan District.

1	2	3	4	5	6	7
Tahsil.	Name of fair.	Where held.	Why held.	Date.	Duration of fair.	Estimated attendance.
Multan ...	Sher Sháh ...	Sher Sháh ...	In honour of the shrine.	14th Sudi, Chet ...	3 days ...	20,000
	Makhdúm Rashíd ...	Makhdum Rashíd ...	In honour of the shrine.	First Thursday after 15th Har.	7 days ...	5,000
	Budha Sant ...	Dugrana ...	To celebrate New Year's Day.	1st Chet ...	3 days ...	30,000
	Suraj Kund ...	Kayanpur ...	A pleasure fair ...	Magh and Bhadon ...	1 day, twice a year.	10,000
	Shams Tabrez ...	Outside Multan city	To celebrate the Id	On the Friday following the Id.	1 day, ...	1,000
Shujabad ...	Pír Kattál ...	Jalálpur Pírwala ...	In honour of the Pir	In Chet, on every Friday (March—April).	4 days ...	14,000
	Pír Jiwan Sultan ...	Rappar ...	Ditto ...	In Chet, on the last Friday.	3 days ...	12,000
Ledhrán ...	Pír Ayub Kattál ...	Near Duniapur ...	Ditto ...	On 3rd Friday in Chet.	2 days ...	10,000

Chapter III, B.

Social and Religious Life.

Fairs and festivals.

List of the more important Fairs in the Multan District—concld.

1	2	3	4	5	6	7
Tahsil.	Name of fair.	Where held.	Why held.	Date.	Duration of fair.	Estimated attendance.
Mailsi ...	Abubakar Warák ...	Dhallu ...	In honour of the Pír	From last Saturday of Chet to the 3rd Baisakh.	8 days ...	5,000
	Diwán Chauli Mashaikh.	Diwán Chauli Mashaikh.	Ditto ...	26th and 27th of Ramzan.	2 days ...	1,000
Kabírwála ...	Ram Chautra ...	Ram Chautra ...	In honour of Raja Ram Chandar.	1st Baisakh ...	8 days ...	7,000
	Sháh Habíb ...	Baghdad ...	In honour of Sháh Habíb.	27th and 28th Sawan	8 days ...	5,000
	Abdul Hakím ...	Abdul Hakím ...	In honour of M. Abdul Hakím.	9th Har ...	4 days ...	4,000

Chapter III, B.

Social and Religious Life.

Fairs and festivals.

The fairs are mostly in connection with some shrine, and there are very few shrines of any importance to which some kind of fair is not attached. The guardians of the shrine generally receive some small offerings in cash or kind, but in most cases they also give out food, so that they retain little or no net income. In some cases the zamindars who own the land, or have influence in the neighbourhood, take a contribution either from the people at the fair or from the shopkeepers whom they allow to trade there. At some of the shrines the fair is a bathing fair (as at Ram Chautra, Ram Tírath, Suraj Kund, etc.); at others, as at Shahkot and Jagir Horián, the people have their children's hair cut: at others, as at Pír Ghaib in Halálwaja, the ailments of cattle are said to be cured. At Makhdúm Rashid the well, which is closed for the rest of the year, is opened, and the water, which has an aperient effect, is drunk by the people. At Jalálpur Pirwala devils are cast out of women. At Rappar, during the Moharram the people pass through two small doors in a small domed building, somewhat after the manner of the fair at Pákpattan; and the building is known as 'Bihisht.' Other fairs, too, have their own peculiarities: at Daud Jahánian's fair, for instance, in Mianpur, ulcers are cured, and at the Budha Sant fair in Dográna no flesh may be eaten.

Besides the fairs specially attached to shrines there are the ordinary seasonal fairs. The Baisakhi fair is celebrated with some circumstance at Rámpur near Multan and at Gwans near Mailsi, at Shahpur near Kahror, and at Paonta near Shujabad. The Dasehra or Ram Líla is observed in most large villages, and there are fine shows in Multan both in the cantonment and in the Dasehra ground near the Mandi Awa to the south-east of the city. There are fairs for the rainy season in Sawan, and several full moon fairs, as well as the ordinary Diwali and Holí. Among the Mahomedans there are great gatherings in large towns, and at centres of Shiism, during the Moharram for the carrying out of the Tazias. There are also gatherings at both the Ids, and the prayers at the Idgah in Multan are very numerously attended on the occasion of the Id uz Zuha. Except at the Id, the Mahomedans and Hindus join pretty freely in the festivals of each other's religion. This trait is unintentionally brought out in the common local proverb: 'Guzri' Holi Rahmat-ulla khede "The Holi is over, yet Rahmat-ulla goes on playing').

The fairs are chiefly for amusement, and the amusement is in the form of swings, merry-go-rounds, prisoners' base, juggling, wrestling, etc. At some of the fairs there is horse-racing and tent-pegging; and at the bigger ones there is dancing by professional dancers. At almost every fair, also, there are booths, where ordinary pedlars' wares and cloth are for sale, together with sweetmeats of various kinds. And at one or two of the gather-

Chapter III. B.

Social and Religious Life.

Faire and festivals.

ings there is some real buying and selling done among the people ; as, for instance, at Budha Sant, where mules and donkeys find a ready sale, and at Rappar and Dhallun, where young camels from Bikanir and Baháwalpur can be bought in large numbers. There is no cattle fair, and this is a serious want. A horse fair is held at Multan, under Government supervision, in the spring, and is very largely attended.

Hospitality.

Any sketch of the manners of the people would be incomplete without a refrence to the virtues of hospitality and liberality, which enter so largely into the ideal standard of a good life among the inhabitants of the district.. Among the Hindus there is naturally less hospitality than among the Mahomedans and their charity is more carefully regulated ; but from any ordinary standpoint, they, too, are extremely charitable, and during periods of drought, such as the years 1898 and 1899, their unostentatious contributions served largely to keep alive the numerous needy vagrants who wandered through the district. The hospitality of the Mahomedan, and his charity also, is on a more lavish and careless scale. The chief aim of the better class of zamindar is to be known as 'bará fayyáz,' or 'mahmán-nawáz,' and the more religious among them are nearly always the more generous. Rulers of a lavish character have a very solid renown, and few will be remembered longer in the Sutlej tract than the 'Sakhí Baháwal Khan,' of Baháwalpur. At the same time this profuseness—this *deredári* as it is expressively called—has brought many careless zamindars to ruin, and the virtue is apt to be carried to excess. There are also, no doubt, many zamindars, whose professions of liberality are louder than their acts, and many with whom liberality goes much against the grain ; but the existence of his virtue on so large a scale, and the large part which it plays in the people's standard of excellence cannot be too carefully remembered.

Although, however, the people fully appreciate a hospitable and lavish neighbour, they have a keen eye for all sorts of pretence to a station out of keeping with the facts ; 'Ghar topá, báhar hoká' ('Not a bushel of grain in the house ; yet he proclaims a feast outside.') 'Ghar dáng na, te medí badúk chái áwín. ('Not a stick in the house, yet he cries 'Bring me my gun') 'Dál mahori dí, dam pilao dá ' ('He has pulse of masar and blows on it as though it were a pilao'). 'Paisá na palle, te khísá pia halle ' ('Not a paisa in his purse, yet he keeps shaking his pocket.') 'Ushnák páolí, tab vichh narián ' ('The weaver sets up for a gentleman, yet his shuttles are sticking out of his pocket.") The grand names sometimes assumed come in also for their share of ridicule ; 'Diddhun bhukkí, Daulat Bibí nán ' ('Hungry belly, and her name Daulat Bibí') ; or 'Ghar vichh kutta nahín te nam Bahádur Khan ' ('Not a dog in his house,

Chapter III, B.

Social and Religious Life.

and he calls himself Bahádur Khan '); or 'Ghar vichh paisa nahin, te nán Lakhí Rám' ('Not a penny in the house and he calls himself Lakhí Rám '); or 'Do jhugge Mahtamán de, te nán Khairpur' ('Two Mahtam huts, and they are called Khairpur '). So, too, with those who pretend to a higher origin than they have: as in 'Má pinne, putr ghora ghinne' ('The mother begs; the son buys a horse'). 'Mán bhittiári, putr akkar khan' ('The mother a baker, and the son walks like a grand duke'). 'Mán pihnáyat, putr Fattah Khan' ('The mother grinds corn, and her son calls himself Fattah Khan'). 'Mán mar gaí pále, dhí dá nán Razai' ('The mother died of cold and the daughter calls herself Razaí'). 'Mán mari rukháwanen, dhi dá nán Chak-mak' ('The mother died of hunger, and the daughter is called Chak-mak'). The rise of a Hindu in the world is shown by the change in his name: 'Máyá ko tín nám' Parsú, Parsa, Pars Rám ('The world has three names—first Parsú, then Parsa, then Pars Rám').

Hospitality.

Crime and litigation.

Crime in the Multan district takes the form chiefly of cattle-stealing and of burglary. The latter is a comparatively late development, but its attractions for the criminal classes seem to be increasing. Cattle-lifting, on the other hand, is a practice of long standing, and with a large section of the population it constitutes a pastime rather than a form of crime. Apart from the actual cattle-lifters the offence is fostered by a number of receivers, known as 'Rassagírs', who pass the cattle from one hand to another with considerable rapidity over large tracts of country. The chief offenders in the matter of crime are found among the Tahíms, Hirajs, Joyas, Langriáls, Traggars, Sargánas, Pahors, Bilcches, Ghallus, Lángs, Saupáls, Káthias and Metlas; but the practice is confined to no particular tribe, and offenders are found in all classes. Usually the thieves are landowners or tenants, and the other landowners and tenants do what they can to shelter them. Apart from the offences above noted, the district is not noted for crime. Daring offences, such as murder and highway robbery, are not common; and there is no such animosity against the moneyed classes as is common in the central and northern Punjab. On the other hand, prosecutions for seduction of women are exceedingly common and show no signs of abating. Civil litigation is not serious, and revenue cases, other than suits for rent, are not numerous; but although litigation is ordinary, the fees of legal practitioners are high, owing to the number of large landowners whose means enable them to pay largely, and so to raise the standard.

On the subject of crime and criminal administration the proverbial philosophy of the people is not silent. Regarding excessive punishments for small offences, they say: 'Kharbúze de chor nún, lat muk káfi' ('For a man who steals a melon, a kick and a cuff are enough'); or 'Talí bádsháhán na jhalí'

Chapter III, B.

Social and Religious Life.

Crime and litigation.

('To pluck the ears of corn as you pass is a thing which even kings do not forbid'). On the subject of security, it is said: 'Na chikkiye káman, na pawiye záman' ('Draw not a bow and give not security'). The ways of witnesses are described in: 'Mámá gawáh to bhedán ápnián' ('He gets his uncle to bear witness, and the stolen sheep are proved to be his'); or 'Mulla chor te bánga gawáh' ('The múlla is the thief, and the muezzin is his witness'). So too: 'Chácha chor bhatríjá kází' ('The uncle the thief, the nephew the judge'). Men in authority are as great criminals as any; 'Nambardár da zor, dinh dá hákim rát dá chor' ('The lambardar's power is shown by his lording it by day, and thieving by night'). So with the sanctimonious: 'Munh mullah dá akkhín chor dián' ('The face is the face of a Mulla, the eyes are those of a thief'); or 'Tasbih phere, te jhugge here' ('He is fingering his rosary but at the same time he is spying out the houses to see where he can thieve'). Of which the Hindu equivalent is: 'Ram Rám japnán paráyá mál taknán' ('Muttering Rám Rám, eying other men's goods').

There are also sayings which illustrate the power of the local magnates and the hopelessness of contending against it; 'Chattí paí mahr te, te mahr pai shahr te' ('The squire was fined, so the squire fined the village'). 'Amir de aggon, te ghore de pichhon na lagiye' ('Go not in front of a great man, for fear he seize you for some forced labour; nor go behind a horse for fear it kicks you'). 'Jihn de hath vichh khalla, un dá jag vichh bhalá' ('He who has slipper in his hand, his is success in the world'). The great man's joke may cost the poor man much: 'Dádhe dá hása, gharíb dá bhajje pásá' ('The great man laughs, and the poor man's rib is broken'). And the great men's variances among themselves involve the ruin of those about them; 'Larin sáhn, patíjin búte' ('The bulls fight, and the shrubs suffer').

Characteristics of the people.

As will be seen by the information given in the preceding paragraphs, the habits of the people of Multan differ in many respects from those of the inhabitants of the Central Punjab. The character of the people also has certain peculiarities, and it may be said generally that they are more self-centered and, at the same time, less alert and less industrious than the ordinary Punjabi; but these qualities are mixed with some strange inconsistencies, and they have also redeeming traits of which one should not lose sight.

The Multani peasant lives on a well and not in a large village, and he marries a neighbour and not a woman from a distant district. He never enlists, and sees nothing of any district but his own. He has therefore a distrust of strangers. The proverb says; 'Safar-i-Multan tá ba Idgah" or 'The Multani travels no further than the Idgah.' It is only with great diffi-

Chapter III, B.

Social and Religious Life.

Characteristics of the people.

culty that even the educated classes are persuaded to leave the district: a Government servant will often refuse a transfer in spite of great inducements in the way of promotion, and even the better class of zamindars are as bewildered and unhappy in Lahore as a Highlander of the eighteenth century in London. To the ordinary peasant the effect of his isolated life is that his address is less pleasing and his demeanour more unsociable than that of a Punjabi agriculturist. He wants to be left alone; and though among friends he is cheerful enough, he lacks the real social instinct. He has little public spirit, and seldom looks at any one's interests but his own. The poorer zamindar cares nothing, for instance, about the assessment of his village, but is keenly interested in the revenue of his own holding. The richer men have no idea of spending money on works of public utility, and with one or two notable exceptions, there is scarcely a man in the district who has voluntarily spent a rupee on any public building or institution. As friends, too, the Multánís have a bad reputation; disinterestedness is said to be unknown, and a variant of the proverb above quoted says: 'Dost-i-Multán tá ba Idgah', which is as much as to say that a Multáni friendship has a radius of about a mile.

So, too, there is a pervading air of slackness about the inhabitants of this district. Both nature and man have been too strong for the Multani peasant. No one who has seen the cher labourers at work will say that the Multani is incapable of hard work, but there can be little doubt that he has a great disinclination for it. The prostrating effects of the fierce summer heats, and the absolute hopelessness of the agriculture in years when floods are scarce, have broken the heart of the peasant, and the size of his holdings has taken away a great incentive of minute cultivation. The inhabitant of Multán, though capable of exertion for a time, is, as a rule, easily discouraged. His efforts are by fits and starts; long continued energy is unknown to him; and he has not the instincts of discipline which mark the Jat of the Central Punjab. Though he is incapable of discipline (or rather perhaps because he is incapable of discipline) the Multani, having been since history began under the heel of one foreign conqueror or another, is peculiarly insensible to any display of authority which is not accompanied by force. A man, for instance, who is asked in an ordinary tone to show the road, will say he does not know it; but if addressed fiercely, will comply at once. A man who is reminded in the ordinary way that his revenue is due, will pay no attention; but if he is threatened with insult or imprisonment, will pay it with alacrity. This same want of stamina has rendered the peasant of the district a ready prey to unscrupulous officials: he believes stolidly that nothing can be done without a bribe, and he is ready to bribe any one to do any thing, merely because it is the custom to do so, and without any of the desire to obtain a *quid pro quo*, which characterizes the Jat of the Punjab proper.

Chapter III, B.

Social and Religious Life.

Characteristics of the people.

With all these drawbacks the native of the district is not without many good points. He has generally a strong, tall, well-nourished figure, and he is good natured and easy going to a degree. He is in his own careless way exceedingly hospitable. In his speech he is frank and outspoken, and his religious practices, as a rule, steer fairly clear both of indifference and bigotry. If he had more knowledge of outlying districts, more confidence in himself, and less distrust of his rulers; he would be a very favourable specimen of mankind.

Language.

The languages spoken by the people are detailed in Statement No VIII.* None of them call for notice except the two,—Punjabi and Jatki or Multáni,—which are spoken by far the larger part of the population. The distinction between these two languages in the census returns is quite arbitrary, and the bulk of the people in the district speak a language which, though a variant of the Punjabi spoken in the central Punjab, has greater affinities with the language of the Sind-Sagar and Jach Doabs than with that of Lahore and Jullundar. The language of Kabírwála and Eastern Mailsi is more intelligible to the stranger from the central Punjab than that of the tracts further south, and the characteristics of the local dialect are most marked in the extreme south of the district near Jalalpur and Lodhran. There is some difference, too, in the vocabulary used by Hindus and by Mussalmans, more particularly among the women; and the pronunciation also differs somewhat, especially in the matter of the palatal *r*. The language, as a whole, is softer, and its inflections better adapted for poetry than those of the standard Punjabi; and several of the best known poets and ballad writers of the central Punjab have made free use of Multani words and inflections in their works. The name given to the language of Multan by experts used to be Jatki or Multani, but of late years, since its affinities with the language of the Dera Ismail Khan and Shahpur districts have been carefully investigated, it has become usual to talk of it as a form of 'Western Punjabi.' To an outsider accustomed to the orthodox Punjabi of the Manjha, the chief peculiarities of the Multan language would probably appear to be (i) the use of the future in *s* (*e. g.*, karesán for karúngá); (ii) the passive in *í* (*e. g.*, maríndá hán for márá játá hún, and (iii) the use of the verb vanjan, 'to go,' in place of jáná both as an ordinary intransitive and as an auxiliary. There are of course, numerous other peculiarities, and the vocabulary is also very different, and contains a larger admixture of Persian and Arabic words. These latter are pronounced far more accurately than in the central Punjab.

* In the tenth century according to Istakhri most of the people of Multan spoke Persian and Sindhi (Ell. i, 28-9). In Akbar's time, the languages of Delhi, Multan and Sindh were unintelligible to each other (Ain. iii, 119.)

Chapter III, B.

Social and Religious Life.

Language.

The New Testament was printed at Serampur in the Multáni (or, as it is there called, the Uchhí) language as early as 1819; but the work must from the beginning have been of no value owing to its being printed in a particular form of shopkeeper's script, which would originally have been legible to very few, and is now becoming obsolete. Some rough notes on the 'Játake or Belochki Language' of Northern Sindh were put together by Sir Richard Burton, and published in the 'Transactions of the Bombay Branch of the Royal Asiatic Society' in 1851; and Mr. O'Brien, c.s., in 1880, published his admirable 'Glossary of the Multani Language,' which contains both a sketch of the grammar and a collection of the local sayings and proverbs prevalent in the Muzaffargarh and Multan districts. The Gospels also have been translated by the Rev. Dr. Jukes, of Dera Ghazi Khan, into a dialect closely resembling that of this district; and a series of detailed notes on the grammar of 'Western Punjabi' language were published by the Rev. Trevor Bomford, of Multan, in the 'Journal of the Asiatic Society of Bengal' for 1895. This was followed in 1898 by Mr. J. Wilson's 'Grammar and Dictionary of Western Punjabi as spoken in the Shahpur District,' and in 1900 by Dr. Jukes's 'Dictionary of the Jatki or Western Punjabi Language,' which is based mainly on experience of the Dera Ghází Khan district. It will be observed, therefore, that in the last few years a considerable interest has been taken in the class of dialects to which the Multan speech belongs; and it is to be hoped that further helps to the local student may shortly be forthcoming.

Of those who can read and write by far the greater number, whether Hindus or Muhammadans, write the Persian character. Hindus who know Sanskrit employ the Bháshá or Nagrí; while money-lenders and shop-keepers use the 'Bhábrí akhar' or the 'Multani akhar,' Tákre or Lande, both of which are known as 'Hindi.' There are varieties of this character known as Sirí, Sákri, and Siddha. The Gurmukhi character is understood by a few Sikh devotees, but by no one else.

Education.

Table No. XIII gives the main statistics regarding education as ascertained in the recent censuses. The figures in the margin show the number educated among every 10,000 of either sex according to census returns. For the rural population only, the corresponding figures are—

		1881.	1891.	1901.
Males ...	Under instruction ...	231	163	...*
	Able to read and write	698	819	1,013
Females	Under instruction ...	8·7	7	...*
	Able to read and write	14·5	21·8	36·6

* Figures not available; the figures of 1901 for those able to read and write include persons of all ages.

Chapter III, B.

Social and Religious Life.

Education.

		1881.	1891.	*1901.
Rural only—				
Males ...	Under instruction ...	155	...*	...
	Able to read and write ...	484	609	...
Females ...	Under instruction ...	4·4	...*	...
	Able to read and write ...	4·6	·11·1	...

Taking the religions separately we get the following figures per 10,000:—

		Hindus.			Mahomedans.			All Religions, excluding Christians.		
		1881.	1891.	1901.	1881.	1891.	1901.	1881.	1891.	1901.
Males	Under instruction.	546	489	...*	140	80	...*	226	163	...*
	Able to read and write ...	2,473	2,993	3,750	179	218	294	666	783	982
Females	Under instruction.	1	3	...*	6	5	...*	7	5	...*
	Able to read and write ...	6	26	95	3	10	10	4	13	2

The literate and those of the literate who know English were at the census of 1891 classified according to tribe and caste. The following figures show the chief of the tribes and castes concerned :—

Caste or Tribe.	Total number of caste or tribe.	Number able to read and write. Males.	Number able to read and write. Females.	Number of those in last column who know English. Males.	Number of those in last column who know English. Females.
Arain	28,582	13	...	...	...
Arora	82,331	327	5	...	...
Bhatia	1,478	657	...	9	...
Biloch	21,603	207	2	11	...
Brahman	5,310	1,182	20	57	...
Jat	146,082	1,811	82	22	...
Khatri	9,694	2,141	18	158	...
Pathan	7,069	249	20	13	4
Rajput	90,637	922	23	17	2
Sayad	15,392	642	25	12	...
Shekh	12,234	789	48	26	...
Christian	1,892	1,343	243	1,335	241
Other tribes	209,130	18,140	133	202	...
Total	631,434	28,423	619	1,862	247

* Figures not available. The figures of 1901 for those able to read and write include persons of all ages.

Chapter III. B.

Social and Religious Life.

Education.

Statistics regarding the attendance at Government and aided schools will be found in Table No. XXXVII, and these will be noticed further in Chapter V below.

The general attitude of the people towards modern education is one of even more apathy than in most other districts of the province. The Middle Government schools, and especially Middle Schools in the country towns, are fairly well attended by Hindu boys, who are sent there largely with the object of fitting them for Government employment; but among zamindars, although this is a district of large landowners, there is no general anxiety to secure education for the rising generation. A few of the richer and more prominent men have, it is true, shown praiseworthy foresight in the matter, but there is room for a good deal of improvement among the ordinary landowners. The want of energy in this matter is due largely to their stay-at-home habits and the very small degree in which the inhabitants of this district are enlisted in the public service.

Education of the old indigenous type is, however, fairly, though not remarkably, widespread among the people. The ordinary Jat is content if he knows the Kalama, the Azán and one or two of the ordinary prayers in the Arabic, and has a fair comprehension of their meaning; but it is not at all uncommon for the zamindars and others to proceed further in their studies. A boy or a girl, who is to undertake the pious duty of reading the Koran, is first taught by the mulla the elements of Arabic writing as entered in the 'Baghdádí Qá'ida': he or she then reads the first and the last sipárah of the Koran with the mulla, who, as they go along, explains the general meaning of the sentences; and unless anything urgent intervenes, they then proceed in the same way to read the rest of the sacred book. Some few go further and learn it by heart, and this knowledge by heart is not uncommon among blind men. Men who know the whole Koran by heart are known as 'Háfiz.' In reading the Koran, and indeed in some of the other branches of learning, the women are as adept as, if not more proficient than, the men; and they are often to be seen reading the book in the morning while the men are still fast asleep. The lithographed interlinear translations of the Koran are becoming popular; and although most persons in reading the volume are content to have some smattering of its general meaning, it has become more usual now to obtain a fairly precise idea of the meaning of the Arabic words.

If a boy is likely to be able to spare more time on education, it is usual for him to omit the complete reading of the Koran until he has obtained some knowledge of Persian. He begins with the Karímá of Sadí, then reads the Kháliq Bárí of Amír Khusrau, and then the Wáhid Bárí.

Chapter III, B.
Social and Religious Life.
Education.

Then follow the Gulistán and Bostán (both pronounced in this district with the accent strongly on the penultimate syllable) ; and a man who wishes to say that he has received an elementary Persian education will say he has 'read up to Gulistán-Bostán.' A boy with talent may then proceed to harder works, such as the Sikandarnáma of Nízámí, the Bahár-Dánish, the Ruq'át-i-Alamgírí, the Panjruk'a, Shabnam-i-shádáb and Dastúr-us-Síbíán.

In families where there is anxiety to gain proficiency in Arabic, the boys sometimes take up the study of that language ; the preliminaries being learnt from the better class of mullas in the villages and small towns, and the higher flights in some *dars* or school such as are established in Multan, Jalalpur and elsewhere. The fact of having passed through one of the Multan schools is not, however, a passport for the learned world of Islam such as a student obtains who goes through some of the more important training centres at Delhi, Lucknow, etc. The Arabic course begins with the grammar as taught in the Sarf Bihái, Sarf Mír, and Hidáyat un Nahv ; and continues through the Káfiah and the Sharah Mullá of Jámí. Logic (mantik) is taught from the Tahzíb 'Isá Ghojí, Qutbi and Mír Qutbi ; and Jurisprudence (fiqha) from the Tauzíh Talwíh and Hadáya If the student enters on the study of the Hadís or sayings of the Prophet, he learns the Mishkát.

Literature.

Multan, though it has been for so long the headquarters of important Governments, has not been in a literary sense a productive city. It is doubtful whether a single Multani author could be unearthed from M. Garcin de Tassy's copious Dictionary of Hindustani Literature, and in the higher flights of Arabic and Persian there are no distinguished names connected with this city. A fair number of religious works, mainly of a Sufistic tendency, have from time to time been issued by the descendants of Baháwal Hakk and by holy men of various kinds throughout the district. Several religious poems and amatory ballads, too, are attributed to Ali Haidar, of Kází Ghálib, who is said to have lived in the time of Aurangzeb, and to Salih Mahomed, the son of the saint Mai Sapuran, who is believed to have lived in the eighteenth century.* A number of Arabic works on physical science, medicine, etc., were composed in the time of Nawáb Muzaffar Khan by Maulvi Abdul Aziz, who seems to have enjoyed a certain amount of local celebrity ; and some further Arabic books of a similar character by Maulvi Mahomed Musa, of Multan, were issued in the middle of the nineteenth century. If we add to these the few local histories

* Ali Haidar composed the 'Se-harfí-ha' (Punjabi), the 'Nur-us-siraj, 'Diwán-i-Haidar,' 'Kasre Matin' (Persian), and a ballad of Hir (Punjabi) ; while Saleh Mahomed's works were 'The Miracles of Abdul Hakim' and the 'Diwán-i-Saleh' in Persian, and the ballad of 'Sohni Mahinwal, in Punjabi.

to which reference has been made in Chapter II above, we shall probably have exhausted the chief literary products of the district.

Literature.

Newspapers have occasionally sprung up in Multan city, but, as a rule, their life has been short, and the newspaper readers of this district have to content themselves with the Lahore journals. The ordinary Lahore papers, English and vernacular, find a public sale among the official class and a few non-officials, chiefly in Multan itself. The number of zamindars who take in a newspaper could probably be counted on the fingers of one hand.

Music and songs.

The music of this district is not particularly famous, but still a fair number of the people show a taste for it. The 'rágs' or modes most in favour are the Pahárí, Jog and Talang; but the following are also said to be popular modes, *viz.*, Kasúrí, Jangla, Jhanjhoti, Dhanásarí, Todi, Gauri rág, Kalián, Pilo, Kaunsia, Khamach, Kadárá, Bibág, Jaijaiwanti, Asa, Rámkalí and Bhairwin. The style of music, except in dealing with purely religious subjects, is the same among both Hindus and Mahomedans. In private and among friends men of all classes will sing and play, while the lower classes often sing aloud while at their work or walking along the road; but all the music on public occasions is provided by professionals, more especially by Kawwáls, Kanjrís, Pernis and Mirásís. The Kawwál of this district is said to be a poor performer compared with his brother in the Punjab proper and his performances are mostly confined to the recital of the class of songs known as 'káfís' on the occasion of a festival at some holy shrine or of some meeting of fakírs. The Kanjrís too are said to be less famous as singers than in the central districts, and their services as singers for a whole night do not cost more than Rs. 10 or Rs. 15. They seldom accompany marriage parties, but are sometimes employed for the festivities of the *rais* class; they mostly sing ghazals and dohrás (love odes or couplets), but at the end the audience always make a request for 'bols' or 'káfis' (songs of a sententious or Sufistic character, which are described below). The Pernís are a tribe of wandering acrobats, who also show some skill in singing; but their services are generally confined to the country districts, and they are seldom employed in the towns. Mirásís are far less common in Multan than is usual in the Punjab proper, and the Mirásí women, whose singing is most sought after here, are immigrants from the Shahpur district, and are known as Chinháwars.

The songs commonest in the district are *dohras* or rhymed couplets and *dholas* or blank verse poems, generally of an amatory character. The dholas of Míran are commonly sung by Jats, and the ordinary love tales of Hír Ránjha, Sassí Pannún, Sohni Mahínwál and Mirza Sáhiban are well known

Chapter III. B.

Social and Religious Life.

Music and songs.

But there is another class of poetry which is much in vogue known as the *káfi*, and this kind of poetry is a speciality of this part of the Punjab. These káfís are generally of a contemplative character, but by no means always so. They correspond roughly to what are known as 'bols' in the Punjab, and their versification does not follow the strict rules of prosody. As a rule, they relate to the transitory character of existence, and though they are often expressed in an erotic strain, they are of an allegorical and Sufistic character, and there is nothing improper about them. The best known, and it is said the first, writer of káfís was one Bulleh Sháh, who, though he was a native of Kasúr, employed the Multaní dialect for his poems: these have been collected in two volumes by M. Anwar Alí and published under the title of 'Kánún-i-Ishk.' Another well-known writer of káfís is Mian Ghulám Faríd, of Chachrán, in the Bahάwalpur State. The following short káfí of Faríd may be quoted as a specimen of this class of poetry :—

Samajh siání ghair na jání,	Be sure there is none else :
Sabh súrat hai ain zahúr ;	Every form sets forth God.
Rakh tasdík na thí awára.	Believe thou this nor wander away.
Ka'aba, kibla, dair, duára,	Ka'aba, kibla, temple,
Masjid girjá hikro Núr.	Mosque and church are but one Light.
Mulla púthre máne kadhde	The mullas interpret wrongly
Ayat Wáris hadís khabarde.	The Kuran and its commentaries.
Sirf sadá te tháí maghrúr.	They are puffed up with their own voices
Bhat gat rít rawash taklidi.	The path of imitation is useless ;
Ráh tahkíkí silk Faríd	The true path is that adopted by Faríd.
Kar manzúr te thí masrúr.	Accept it and be blessed.

Religions.

The proportion per cent. of the total population returned as belonging to the chief religions at successive censuses has been :—

Census of	Percentage of total population returned as				
	Hindus.	Sikhs.	Mahomedans.	Other.	Total.
1881	20·3	·4	79·0	·3	100
1891	19·4	·5	79·8	·3	100
1901	18·8	·7	80·2	·3	100

The percentage of each religion among the town population at the last three enumerations was as follows :—

	Hindus.	Sikhs.	Mussalmans.
1881 ...	44	8	50
1891 ...	46	1	51
1901 ...	45	2	51

Chapter III, B.

Social and Religious Life.

Religion of the Hindus.

Further details will be found in Tables Nos. VII and XLIII at the end of this volume.

There are practically no indigenous Jat and Rajput Hindus in this district as in the central Punjab; and the Hindus are almost entirely confined to non-agricultural castes, such as the Brahmans, Aroras and Bhatias.*

Outside the large cities the Shaiva side of Hinduism does not seem to be largely represented; the worship of Devi is less common than in Lahore and in the central Punjab, and there are not many Jogi establishments in the district. This class of worship is of course found to a certain extent in the big towns, such as Multan and Shujabad, and it is also prevalent in the direction of Kahror and Mailsi. The small vermilion-coated projections on the sides of shop-doors, which do duty for images of Bhairon, are, I think, more common in that direction, and there are said to be a good many Kirars of the disreputable Bám-margi sect in the neighbourhood of Mailsi itself.

Figures returned in	1891.
Shámjí	278
Shámjí ká Pujárí	26
Shám Shewak ...	133
Láljí	521

The prevalence of the Vaishnava tenets and practices in the Multan district is due very largely to a movement started by two reformers, Shámjí and Láljí, in the sixteenth century; a movement which received its main support from the Krishna centres of Mathura and Bindraban, and owed its origin to movements as remote as that of Chaitanya in Lower Bengal (see para. 66 of the Census Report of 1891). There are large temples of Láljí at Dera Ismail Khan and Dera Ghází Khan, and of Shámjí at Leiah, Dera Ghazi Khan and Dera Ismail Khan.

The Multan district is also traversed by pilgrims, who go by road from the central and eastern Punjab to Dwarka in Gujerat, and one often meets these pilgrims on their way to or from the Dwarka shrine.

A remarkable feature of the local Hinduism is the widespread river-worship prevalent in this district, more especially in the three southern tahsils. The river-worship is carried out mainly on Sundays, and the worshippers are known as Sewaks, their gurus being known by the name of Thakkars. The followers of the Thakkars are mainly Aroras, and there are Thakkars' places of worship in Multan city, Kasba, Shujabad and elsewhere. The Thakkars are themselves Aroras of the Dakhna section, and their original seat is at the shrine of Vadhera Lal at Sakhar in Sind; a shrine of which the guardians are said to be Mahomedans. The incarnation of Vadhera

*Kaempfer in his Amœnitates Exoticæ (p. 267) describes his meeting at Baku on the Caspian 'duo mercatores ex gente Multana omnium Ethnicorum religiosissimi.'

Chapter III, B.

Social and Religious Life.

Religion of the Hindus.

Lal is also known by other names such as Dulan Lal, Amar Lal, Zinda Pír, Darya Sahib, Ralbal Purak, etc., and the history of the incarnation is said to be fully described in a book called the 'Amargit.' The chief characteristics of the Sewak worship are the maintenance of lights (jots) before a pitcher of water or on the canals, the observance of a fast during the day on the second and fourteenth days of the moon, and the weekly bathing in the river. The more strict among the river worshippers go daily to the river, even if it may be four or five miles from their homes. The number returned as belonging especially to this class of Hindus (Darya Sewak) in 1891 was 8,485. The followers of *Ganjámáli* (887), who have a temple in honour of a Brahman saint of this name in Multan city and the followers of *Gopálji* (174), are sects very similar to the river-worshipping community. It is curious to note how this river worship has now quite superseded the sun worship for which Multan used to be so renowned (see Chapter VI, below). The fact, however, that the river worship is conducted chiefly by bathing festivals (dháonís) on Sunday (Adityawár, Itwár) may point to a historical connection between the two forms of worship.

Hindus of the Nának Panthi types of Sikhism are also very common in the district, and 4,504 persons returned this as their sect in 1891. Among the more remarkable offshoots of Nának's religion are the Sánwal Shahis (227 returned in 1891) who have shrines in Kasba and elsewhere. There are also dharmsalas and shrines connected with the Nirmalas, Sewapanthis, Kaladháris and similar sects at Multan, Kahror and other places.

The temples in the big towns are very much like what they are in the rest of northern India. In the smaller towns they are sometimes adorned with frescoes of a secular nature representing the stories of Hír and Ránjha, Sassi and Pannún, etc. Among the minor deities the cult of Saníchar, or the Saturday god, is very marked in this district: the centre of cross roads or streets, even in comparatively small villages, being very often taken up with a small mound in honour of this deity, over which weekly libations of oil are poured.

There is a branch of the orthodox Association, the Sanátan Dharm, in Multan city. The Brahmo Samaj has two meeting places in Multan city, and the Arya Samaj has branches both in Multan and at Mailsi: the latter, however, being mainly composed of officials.

Sikhs.

There are very few Sikhs in the district, other than foreigners who have come from the central Punjab or elsewhere on Government service, or on private business, or as colonists on the Sidhnai canal. A certain number of the Khatrís, Bhátias

Chapter III, B.

Social and Religious Life.

Sikhs.

and Aroras in Multan and Shujabad are Sikhs of the school of Nának, and have institutions of their own; and there is a shrine connected with Bábá Nának at the extremity of the district on the mound of Díwán Cháwali Mashaikh. In the days of the Sikh supremacy the pahul was more ordinarily taken, and children were more commonly given names ending in Singh than is now the case; but the Sikh tenets never acquired any very strong hold among the indigenous Hindús of Multan. The only Singh Sabhas in the district are in the cantonment bazaar, and their prosperity depends mainly on the presence or absence of Sikh regiments in the station.

Mahomedans.

Multan, lying as it does half-way between the fanaticism of the frontier and the listlessness of the down-country districts, shows Mahomedanism perhaps at its best. Although there is little religious antagonism between the Mahomedan and Hindu in the district, and although both religions often frequent the same fairs and honour the same shrines, the Mahomedan attitude is singularly free from the semi-idolatrous practices and superstitions which characterise its more eastern developments in this country. One finds of course the ordinary concomitants of Mahomedanism,—vows to saints, fear of supernatural agencies, use of amulets, and rosaries, and so forth,—but these are found in the form common to African and Central Asian Mahomedanism rather than with any Hinduised characteristics. Among the common people vows are frequently made in the name of some saint or shrine, either in connection with the birth of children or the sickness or loss of cattle, or some other household event; and way-side shrines are often hung with the offerings of the faithful in the shape of small swings, or of cattle bells or rags, etc. Charms (phul) for keeping off cattle disease are often put in earthern pots and swung on a rope over the entrance of the stall or pen; and charms for protecting the grain-heap are thrust into split sticks, and stuck upon the heap itself. The wearing of amulets both on the arms and round the neck is very common: there are witches who can extract a man's liver; and on dark nights the peasantry have a belief in jinns and other spirits, at which they will generally smile in broad daylight. * The more religious minded who attend with fair regularity the times of prayer † are known

* Regarding witches there is a proverb: 'Hik dáin baf tarak charhe' ('An ugly witch to start with and she rides a hyena'), of persons who add to their innate repulsiveness by additional horrors—a saying which used to be applied sometimes to the police constable and his uniform. The belief in spirits gives rise among Hindus to the following 'Shahr vasande deote, báhar vasande bhút' (The gods live in town, the devils in the country'); a counterblast to 'Man made the town but God made the country.'

†There is a time for all things and prayer at times not prescribed is useless. 'Vele dí namáz kuwele dián takrán' is a local proverb ('At the right time prayer is prayer: at the wrong time it is merely beating your head on the ground.')

Chapter III, B.

Social and Religious Life.

Mahomedans.

as 'nimází,' and many of these are equipped with rosaries (tasbih), which they keep constantly between their fingers. Almost every village, however small, has some kind of mosque or place of prayer; and it is a common practice for the more wealthy Mahomedans to mark their piety by building a mosque of masonry.*

One of the marked features of the local Mahomedanism is the practice of 'Pírí Murídí.' A disciple who for a time follows a particular man is known as a 'tálib'; but those who maintain a perpetual subservience to the teacher are known as 'muríds.' The teacher is known as the pír, and in many respects he takes the place of the Hindu guru. Practically every Mahomedan in the district has his pír;† he is not bound to adopt the same pír as his father, but he generally does so, and, once having adopted him, he keeps to him for life. The pír is in most cases a Syad, Koreshi or Khagga: he travels periodically among his muríds and is treated by them with great deference, and is supported by them with food and conveyance free of charge. In return for this he gives little or no religious teaching, but provides such charms and amulets as are required.

The following are the census figures showing the chief sects returned by the Mahomedans in 1881, 1891 and 1901:—

	1881.	1891.	1901 (males over 14)
Sunnis	431,656	495,629	177,109
Shias	3,830	5,787	2,153

The bulk of the people are of course Sunnís, and, so far as they come within any Sunní denomination, they may be said to belong to that of the Abu Hanifa, known as the Imám Azam. Some of the fisher and boatman tribes will describe themselves as followers of Imám Sháfi, mainly because of the greater latitude in feeding which the tenets of that teacher are supposed to allow. The number of persons returned in 1891 as belonging to this sect was 228. In 1901 39 males over 14 years of age were so returned.

Owing to intercourse with Persia, Multan has always been more or less open to schismatic influences. It has already been noticed in Chapter II how Multan was for several centuries a strong hold of Karmatian heresy, and in later years there has always been a nucleus of Shias in the district. Under the great Mughals and under the Duranis, however the Shias were forced outwardly to conform with Sunni practices, and it is only of late

* Some of the traditional views of religious history are worth noting. When, for instance, a man fails to understand something, he will say: 'Likhe Músá parhe Khudá' ('What Moses wrote, God alone can read'). When a man tries to escape from what is inevitable they say: 'Isá nathá maut tún, agge maut kharí' ('Jesus fled from death (to escape from the Jews), but death stood before him')

†To be without a pír and a mír (*i.e.*, a mírási) is practically to be an outcast. The word 'be pír' is used as a term of reproach.

Mahomedans.

years that, with increasing tolerance, the Shias have more openly proclaimed themselves as such. In several Shia families a marriage would, until quite recent years, be celebrated both publicly in the Sunní fashion and privately after the Shia rites. There is no organized proselytizing, but every now and then a man is by conversation or by the loan of books induced to change his sect, and there seems no doubt that conversions from Sunnism to Shiism are more common than *vice versâ*. There is no bar to marriage between the two sects, but a woman who marries a Shia is deemed *ipso facto* to become a Shia herself. The chief Shias in the district are found among the more prominent Syad and Koreshi families, such as the Gardezis of Multan and Salarwahan, the Syads of Kuranga and Dhrúharwahan and the Koreshis of Multan, among the Kazzilbash and Persian immigrants, and among one or two families of the Khakwani Pathans. Others, such as some of the Syads of Kahror, have a leaning towards Shiism and are known to their neighbours as 'Ním Shias,' or 'Khafíf Shias.' The Shia observances are more strictly carried out in the towns than in the villages, and in Multan the Shias maintain maulvis, who give fatwas on matter of doubt. They do not use the same mosques as the Sunnís, having their own mosques and imámbaras. They have colloquies at the mosques on Fridays, but not, as a rule, set sermons like the Sunnís and Wahábís. They are careful in the observance of the mourning in Moharram; and although Sunnís join freely in the tázia procession, such observances are practically unknown, except in quarters where there are Shias to start and organize the shows. Generally speaking there is very little bitterness between the Sunní and Shia sects in this district, and in the ordinary intercourse of life there is little to distinguish the two.

The Ahl-i-Hadís or Wahábís are not very numerous; and though they have no doubt increased in numbers, their attitude towards the other sects is less truculent than it used to be some years ago. They are still looked on with some suspicion by co-religionists, and a man is often described as a 'sakht Wahábi' with the hint that he is in the eyes of the speaker little, if at all, better than an atheist. The Wahábís are found mainly in Multan city and among the Khojás of Jalalpur Pírwála; but there are also scattered Wahábís elsewhere, as in Amirgarh in Kabírwála, in Alamgir and Kayanpur in Multan, in Shahpur Ubbha in Shujabad, and so forth. The chief points on which the Wahábís in this district differ from their co-religionists are in their objection to tázias; their repudiation of all pilgrimages except that to Mecca; their abhorence of shrines, and certain peculiarities in their attitudes at prayer. In Multan they have their separate mosques, but in the villages they use the same mosques as others, and are said to pray with other Mahomedans more commonly now than was formely the case.

Chapter III, B.

Social and Religious Life.

Mahomedans.

The important pilgrimage for the Sunnís is that to Mecca and Medina. The Wahábi goes only to Mecca. The Shia goes also, if he can, to Kerbela and to Meshed. Pilgrimages of all kinds are not uncommon. For a man of the Rais class a pilgrimage is a serious undertaking, as he is generally accompanied by a considerable company of women and dependants, and the expenses increase accordingly. For a man in ordinary circumstances, who travels by himself, the pilgrimage is not very expensive. A poor man will often beg part of his journey, and for a man who pays his way, and uses discretion, the expenses of a pilgrimage to Mecca and Medina do not exceed 300 rupees. In all parts of the district one finds a few zamindars who have done the 'Hajj,' but the artizan castes such as the Machhis, Charhoas, etc., supply almost as many pilgrims as the zamindars themselves.

It is difficult to say how far Súfí tendencies are spread among the Mahomedan population. Hitherto they have been chiefly prominent among the fakírs and the literary classes. Some of the more daring actions of the fakírs excite nothing but distaste among the ordinary Mahomedans. I came across the case once of a village in Mailsi, where a fakír had settled, who found himself so advanced in spiritual progress that he tore a Koran into fragments: the zamindars at once banished him from the village, and after collecting the fragments gave them reverent burial.

There is a branch of the Anjuman Islamia at Multan.

It is a very common practice for Mahomedans to go on Thursday evenings to pay their respects to some neighbouring shrine or to light lamps on some grave. On Fridays ordinary work is carried on till 12 or 1 o'clock by most Mahomedans, though some of the more devout abstain entirely from business on that day. At noon, or soon after, it is usual to attend prayers, and after prayers those who can afford it very frequently close their shops or otherwise cease from work. This custom is said to be growing, and no doubt will continue to grow as intercourse with the western forms of Mahomedanism increases.

Conversions from Hinduism to Islam.

There is little or no active proselytizing by the followers of Islam in this district; but one occasionally comes across cases of conversions to that faith. The conversions are generally confined to men of somewhat inferior status, and they are in many cases prompted by the desire of marriage with a Mahomedan woman.

Native Christians.

The number of Christians in this district, other than Europeans and Eurasians, was returned in 1881 as 42, in 1891 as 41

Chapter III. B.

Social and Religious Life.

Native Christians.

and 1901 as 198. The chief agency for the superintendence and instruction of the native Christian community is the Church Missionary Society, which began its operations in 1855, and which now counts among its converts some 79 persons in Multan, Muzaffargarh and Baháwalpur, of whom the greater number are Hindustanis and men from the eastern Punjab. The Church Mission School at Multan is the oldest in the district, having been opened in 1856, and the number of scholars in 1900 was 180. A school was also maintained at Shujabad until 1887, when it was abandoned. Attached to the Multan school, outside the Husain Gáhí, is a church built in 1887, where service is conducted every Sunday in Urdu. Preaching is also done in the bazars and in the district. The Mission staff in 1900 consisted of three clergy (one native), four catechists, four Christian and ten non-Christian teachers, and six zanana workers. A female hospital has been started near the cantonment bazar under the auspices of the Mission, and a book-shop in connection with the Punjab Religious Book Depot at Lahore has been maintained in the city for the last seven years: it is situated just outside the Haram Darwaza. The first Multani Christian was baptized in 1870, and he was ordained priest in 1899.

The only other Society working among native Christians in Multan is the American Methodist Episcopal Mission, which was established in 1893. The staff consists of one clergyman and his wife (who is in charge of the zanana work), two local deacons, six local exhorters and five Bible women. There are five Sunday schools and a day school. Services are conducted in a hired house, and for the military in the garrison prayer-room.

Shrines to saints.

The district is thickly dotted with shrines of various degrees both of age and of sanctity. The shrines of Multan, with that of Bahawal Hakk at their head, are described in detail in Chapter VI of this Gazetteer. Outside the city and its environs there are many others of more or less note, but the most renowned are those* connected with the celebrated shrine of Sayad Jalál at Uchh in Baháwalpur, namely, the shrines of Sher Shah and Jalálpur Pírwala. The former of these was built in honour of Shah Ali Mahomed Husain, who came from Meshed in A.H. 905 (A.D. 1499), and the latter in honour of Sultan Ahmad, Kattal, who, after converting the Lakhweras and Salderas of the Mailsi tahsil, came to Jalalpur in A.H. 990 (A.D. 1582). Both of these are fine buildings, and the latter is especially worth seeing on account of its remarkable coating of tile work.

---

* Sayad Jalál is in some ways the premier saint in this part of the Punjab, and his miracles are proverbial. 'Dhai man khoti, te panj man bár, kyá karesi Sayad Jalál?' (If an ass can bear $2\frac{1}{2}$ maunds only, and a load of 5 maunds is put on it, what can Sayad Jalál do? Even he cannot make the ass fit to bear 5 maunds.')

Chapter III. B.

Social and Religious Life.

Shrines to saints.

In the Kabírwála tahsil there is at *Rampur* a shrine of Jati Abdál, or Abdál the Chaste, a servant of Dara Shekoh. No women are admitted into the shrine, and the river has hitherto scrupulously avoided diluviating it. At *Aroti* is the tomb of Mian Rahmán, a saint of Aurangzeb's time, and at *Baghdád* is that of Sháh Habíb, a miracle worker of the days of Sháh Jahán. In *Abdul Hakím* is the shrine of the saint of that name, a charhoa or dhobi by caste, who died in 1732 A.D. : the tomb is revered by the rulers of Bikanir because of a miracle worked on the bitter Bikanir wells by some followers of the saint. Among the disciples of Abdul Hakím was a woman, a Nunari by caste, called *Mai Sapuran*, whose tomb is in the village of that name : she was able to spread out her prayer carpet on the waters of the Rávi and to kneel for prayer upon it, and both she and her descendants could cure the bites of mad dogs. At the large mound outside Tulamba, which Cunningham identifies with the 'strongly fortified position' taken by Alexander in this neighbourhood, is the shrine of *Mámán Sher*, who was martyred with Dátá Ganj Bakhsh at Lahore, but rode back without his head to the place where his body is now buried. Near *Sarai Siddhu* is the shrine of Arjan Sher, who rode on a tiger with a snake in his hand and destroyed a terrible jinn, who used to feed on the children of the neighbourhood. At *Sirdarpur* is a shrine in honour of Talib Sháh Bukharí, who came from Uchh some 500 years ago.

In the Multan tahsíl there are, besides the shrines of Multan and that of Sher Sháh, four or five more or less well-known shrines. One is that of Sháh Ali Akbar at *Sura Miani*, which is described in Chapter VI below. Another is that of Isa and Musa at *Fatuhalpur* : this Musa was a wonder-worker from Delhi : when he shook hands with Sháh Ali Mahomed, of Sher Sháh, their hands stuck together. Besides the above, there is the tomb at *Shakot* of Zain-ul-abdin, father of Sakhi Sarwar : a tomb with some good tile-work and a handsome gateway, which is worth seeing ; also the shrine of Makhdúm Abdurrashid or *Makhdúm Rashid* on the Mailsi road. This saint was cousin of Baháwal Hakk ; and the actual shrine consists of a pillar of brickwork, some four feet high, surmounted by a long pole and set off by a picturesque background of jál trees, but the chief feature of the place is the brackish well outside the village site. Another curious shrine is that of Budhla Sant at *Dograna*, with its adjacent tank ; this saint was a Hindu weighman who wrought miracles, and finally disappeared into a jál tree, round which the present shrine is built.*

* This saint was one day weighing out the corn, and as he did so, he used the words 'Kul únwíá.' A passing fakír said : 'Does he mean Kul unwí' (19 in all) or does he mean 'Kul un wiá' ('Go also to HIM, *i.e.*, God').

Chapter III, B.

Social and Religious Life.

Shrines to saints.

In the north of Shujabad tahsil are some small shrines, such as that of Pír Ghaib in Halalwaja, Mahomed Isa in Khánpur, and Sháh Rashid at the gate of Shujabad itself. The chief shrines are, however, towards the south of the tahsil. At *Lutfpur* is the chauki or the resting-place of Pír Dand Jahánian, a herdsman of the Muzaffargarh saint Makhdúm Jahánian; this Pír Daud made a dead stick blossom in a shisham tree, and sand from his shrine, if warmed and applied to a boil, is a sovereign remedy. Near *Bahadarpur* is the roofless tomb of Pír Aulia Ghori, which is said to date from Humáyún's time, and in which used to grow a talking melon which spoke the words 'Salaam alekum': this tomb is now a common resort for persons bitten by mad dogs and jackals. At *Naurájabhutta* lie the bodies of Hásil and Wásil, two holy men who were martyred there; and at *Umarpur* lie the remains of Shaikh Ismail, a disciple of Baháwal Hakk, who appears in a dream to deter any one that tries to make his tomb 'pukka'. Lastly, there is the shrine of Shah Mihr Ali at *Darabpur*, a mud-built tomb of a saint who disappeared miraculously some three hundred years ago.

In Lodhrán there are a few fairly well known shrines. Among these are the Gardezi tomb at *Adamwáhan*, now falling into considerable disrepair, and the shrine of Pír Múla at *Maulri Sikandar*, built in the time of the Emperor Mahomed Sháh. At *Lahori* rests the body of Pír Fattehulla: this saint lived some three hundred years ago. When a child he was found weeping at the thought of the grave, and received a promise that he would never be buried: accordingly when he died two coffins came down from heaven: they are both in the shrine and can be seen from outside, but no one knows in which of them the pír lies. At *Kahror* are the shrines of Ali Sarwar and Pír Burhán, which are described in Chapter VI below. At *Rappar* is the tomb of Pír Jíwan Sultan, a saint of Shah Jahán's time, and in the middle of the desert east of *Dunyapur* is the khánkáh of Sultan Ayúb Kattál, the grandson of Makhdúm Rashíd, a saint who was a special adherent of Khwája Khizr, and is said to have died in A.H. 766 (A.D. 1364.)

In Mailsi are one or two Hindu shrines of local celebrity: including that at *Nagarkot*, near Fadda,—a comparatively modern shrine of Devi, the vicinity of which is haunted, because some centuries ago two girls were at this place set upon by dacoits and killed. The mound of *Díwán Chawali Mashaikh* is named after one of the very early converts to Islam, and on this site there are several curiosities, *viz.*, the tomb of the Díwán and of his sister, the staff of the Díwán, the shrine of his Wazír Shekoh Sáhib, the jál tree from which the Díwán sprang out as a tiger, the well in which Bábá Farid hung head downwards for twelve years, the tombs of Bábá Farid's three sons, and, lastly, a shrine and Darbár Sáhib in commemoration of Bábá Nának. At *Dhallu* is the shrine

Chapter III, B.

Social and Religious Life.

Shrines to saints.

of Abubakar Warák, lately restored with considerable taste, a building of distinct beauty: this saint was connected with the Chishtís of Ajmir, and he was called Warák because he used every day to give his disciples a leaf of paper (wark), on which he wrote something and bade them take it to the river, where a mystic hand would be stretched out to take the 'wark' and give another 'wark' in exchange. This saint was a particular friend of Khawája Khizr; and lately when the shrine wanted repair, and no timber long enough for the roof could be found, the river brought down logs of the required size and deposited them near the tomb. Outside is a remarkable carved stone, evidently at one time a part of some Hindu temple, which is pointed out as the alms' bowl of the saint. At *Dhruharwahan* are the shrines of another Abu Bakar and his son and grandson: this Abu Bakar came here early in the fourteenth century; and hard by is the tomb of his brother Ahmad Sultán, where women who are possessed with devils get cured.

Ruined religious buildings.

The shrines above mentioned are all in more or less good repair; but there are three buildings worth noticing, which are now uncared for and in a state of comparative ruin. One of these is the fine tomb of Khálik bin Walíd, usually known as *Khálik Wali,* near Khattíchor in Kabírwála. Khálid is said to have been a Koreshi, who came from Arabia in 1015 A.D.: the present shrine is said to have been built in the fourteenth century and to have been repaired by Sháh Jahán. This emperor also built a sarai here, and Khálik Wali appears in the old geographies under various disguises as one of the stages on the road between Multan and Lahore. Some camel-owners offended the saint, and no camel's milk will give butter in this neighbourhood. There is a white stone in the middle of the dome, which is said to be made of camels' butter: a drop is said to fall from time to time, and when the last drop falls the day of judgment will come.

Another and, perhaps, still more remarkable ruin is that of the incomplete mosque at *Malikwahan* in the Mailsi tahsil. The mosque is situated on a high mound picturesquely surrounded by trees, and it still bears considerable fragments of exquisite tile-work, including some in colours not ordinarily found elsewhere. These remains, like many others in the Mailsi tahsil (*e.g.*, at Shergarh, Lakhan, etc.), probably date from the flourishing days of the seventeenth century.

Another remarkable monument, of a different character, is the small tomb of *Sayad Kabír,* situated in a somewhat inaccessible position in the jungle west of Sarla on the eastern boundary of the Lodhrán tahsil. The design is a curious mixture of Saracenic and Hindu types, and there are inscriptions, moulded on the brick, both in Persian and in Nagri characters.

Chapter III. C.

Tribes, Castes and Leading Families.

Grave yards.

One of the proverbial characteristics of Multan city is the prevalence of graveyards; and in the district at large the graveyards (goristán or gustán) are a marked feature in the landscape. They are generally on ground too high for irrigation or cultivation, often on ruined 'bhirs', and are entered somewhat pathetically in the revenue records as 'makbúza ahl-i-Islám'. It is common to bury in the neighbourhood of some saint's grave, and in such cases the wood round the grave is allowed to grow, it being considered profanity to lay hands upon it. Though most of the graveyards are bare unlovely spots, there is a tendency, where possible, to find a shady place for graves. The grave is generally of mud; often a couple of bricks are set at the head, leaning against each other, to shelter the lamp ; or else a small chamber is built for this purpose, or else the lamp is left unsheltered. Sometimes there are small earthen ornaments at the four corners of the grave. Sometimes at the head or foot there is a coloured tile containing the words 'Yá Allah' or the name of the deceased. Women are buried in tombs of the same shape as the men's : pardah women have generally a special portion of the graveyard allotted to them, but otherwise men and women are buried indiscriminately. Children sometimes have separate graveyards (there is one such in the village of Wahí Channar in Lodhrán), and, in the villages at least, Hindu children are buried without objection in Mahomedan graveyards.

At the period of the Moharram it is the custom for surviving relatives to repair the tombs of their dead and to pour water over them ; and on the tenth day of that month it is the practice to spread branches of plam-trees or masúr over the graves.

For the grave of a pír or saint considerable outward reverence is shown : it is salaamed from a distance and shoes are taken off in its vicinity. But ordinary graveyards are treated without much sentiment. They are generally unfenced in any way. Dhobís find the graves convenient places for spreading out clothes to dry. I have even during the course of settlement measurements seen the measuring chain being taken through a graveyard and notches being cut in the graves to keep the chain level.

SECTION C.—TRIBES, CASTES AND LEADING FAMILIES.

Statistics for tribes and castes.

Table No. IX gives the figures for the principal castes and tribes of the district, with details of sex and religion. Many of these are found over all the Punjab and most of them in many other districts, and their representatives in Multan are distinguished by no local peculiarities. Most of them are described in Chapter VI of the Census Report of 1881. In the census of 1881 the figures for tribes and castes were tabulated for the district

Chapter III, C.

Tribes, Castes and Leading Families.

Statistics for tribes and castes.

only, so that no information is available as to their distribution by tahsíls and villages in 1881, but in 1891 this information was tabulated, and is available on reference to the vernacular census tables of that census. On the other hand, the numerous sub-castes and clans returned were tabulated for the district in 1881, and the results were printed in divisional lists of tribes, etc., which are now somewhat hard to obtain; but in 1891 the names only and the localities (by districts) of these sub-castes and clans were tabulated, the number under each head being ignored, and the results of the tabulation are printed in a provincial list at the end of the 3rd volume of the report on that census. The sub-castes and clans are not of much importance in this district, except as regards some of the Jats, and as a certain number of sub-tribes of the Patháns, Bilochís, Jats and Rájpúts were fully tabulated in 1891 and 1901 we have figures for some of the Jat clans though not of all. The figures for the more numerous tribes by tahsíls were in 1901 :—

Caste.	Multan.	Shuja-bad.	Lodhran.	Mailsi.	Kabír-wala.	Total.
Aráíns ...	6,974	5,478	8,712	9,127	2,124	32,410
Arorás ...	30,468	14,330	17,699	11,064	15,426	88,987
Bilochís ...	6,265	6,420	6,298	2,804	2,701	24,488
Brahmans (including Muhiáls) ...	2,835	1,017	643	380	704	5,579
Chúhras ...	4,093	983	425	2,262	3,424	11,187
Dhobís ...	4,277	2,616	2,841	2,635	2,313	14,682
Jats ...	49,597	29,811	23,192	15,662	22,053	140,315
Juláhas ...	11,786	1,761	4,416	4,043	5,226	27,232
Khatrís ...	9,072	461	536	358	450	10,877
Khokhars ...	5,227	1,813	956	1,664	1,946	11,606
Kumhárs ...	4,309	2,765	2,647	3,514	5,592	18,827
Lohárs ...	1,173	538	605	562	896	3,774
Máchhís ...	2,606	981	1,364	3,312	4,166	12,429
Malláhs ...	1,916	2,842	1,052	200	1,736	7,745
Mochís ...	6,991	3,620	3,836	3,961	5,736	24,144
Náís ...	2,239	1,531	1,322	1,544	1,802	8,438
Patháns ...	4,564	1,507	836	767	577	8,251
Rájpúts ...	19,133	12,988	9,348	20,997	29,050	91,516
Sayads ...	3,296	1,944	2,019	1,774	1,534	10,567
Sheikhs ...	3,022	1,141	517	654	1,492	6,826
Sunárs ...	841	393	476	551	560	2,821
Tarkháns ...	6,068	2,777	3,234	2,255	3,022	17,356

We may now proceed to notice such of the tribes as call for consideration; taking them in the following order—(i) Hindu castes, (ii) prominent Mahomedan tribes, and (iii) inferior and artisan tribes or castes.

Chapter III, C.

Tribes. Castes and Leading Families.

Hindu castes and tribes.

Among the Hindus four castes only are numerous, *viz.*, the Brahmans, the Khatrís, the Aroras and the Bhátias.

The *Brahmans* are for the most part confined to the towns, and such landed property as they possess is owned generally in connection with shrines and dharmsálas of which they are the incumbents. The Brahmans held a city in the north of Kabírwála in Alexander's time (see Chapter II); and there is some temptation to connect that city with Tulamba, where the most prominent landholding families are still Brahmans. The Brahmans of the district are mainly Sársuts, but Pushkarna Brahmans are also not uncommon, especially in Shujabad, where they are the parohits of the Bhátias. They are commonly spoken of as 'pandits', and there are proverbs here, as elsewhere in India, at their expense; such as, 'Bhat, Brahman, Bakrí : vele mul na pakrí' ('The bard, the Brahman and the goat, at the right time are of no earthly use').

1881	...	4,183
1891	...	5,310
1901	...	5,571

The *Khatrís* are mainly confined to the town of Multan, and very few own any land. They are largely immigrants from the Punjab proper and often in Government service. The Khatrís of this district are chiefly Mirhotras, Khannas and Kapúrs. They include the family of Raizada Ram Chand Sahigal, Honorary Magistrate, Malik Rám Chand, Vijh, and one or two other prominent families, most of which attained their present status under the Sikh *régime*.

1881	...	9,798
1891	...	9,694
1901	...	10,873

By far the largest number of Hindus in the district belong to the *Arora* caste; and there are more Aroras in Multan than in any other district of the Punjab. They are also called Karárs—a term which in this district is practically synonymous with Arora, though somewhat more derogatory in its application. They constitute the bulk of the trading, shop-keeping and money-lending element; they enter freely into Government service, and they possess in proprietary right, or on mortgage a vast amount of land. They are mainly of the Dakhna section, though Utrádbís and Dahras are not uncommon. The three sections do not intermarry, but the *gots* within each section are, as usual, exogamous. The most prominent families among the landowning Aroras are the Bajájs of Sikandarabad, the Jáwas of Traggar, the Munjals of Ubaora, the Batras of Khanpur, the Tanejas of Garhí Khichían, the Talejas of Wahi Salamat Rai, the Chughs, Gands, and Relans of Tulamba.

1881	...	76,842
1891	...	82,331
1901	...	88,987

The Karár being the peasant's creditor and natural enemy comes in for as much proverbial abuse as the attorney in England. 'Bhuke Karár wahían pharole' ('If a Karar is hard up, he turns over his account books (to fish up forgotten debts'): or 'Kan, Karar, kutte da, visáh na kija sutte da' ('A crow, a Karár and a dog should not be trusted even if asleep'), or 'Jat waddhe tán

Chapter III. C.

Tribes Castes and Leading Families.

Hindu castes and tribes.

ráh baddhe, Karár waddhe tán Jat baddhe' ('If a Jat prospers, he blocks the road (by extending cultivation); If a Karár prospers, he blocks the Jat'); or 'Dhátá Karár te bhuká bhagiár' ('A Karár after his morning bath is as cross tempered as a hungry wolf'). Or again: 'Karár dandálí te Khoja pháwara' ('The Khoja is a hoe, but the Karár is a rake, *i.e.*, he destroys wholesale').

The chief clans of the Aroras in this district are:—*Dakhnas,* Bajáj, Taneja, Raheja, Batra, Gera, Sadána, Chopra, Kukar, Lulla, Munjál, Ghakkar, Saneja, Khaneja, Juneja, Doreja, Mehndiratta, Giddar; *Utrádhís,* Khorána, Cháwala, Nángpál, Thakrál, Sethí, Kukreja, Thareja; *Dahras*—Sachdev, Nángpál, Ichhaláni. The existence of what appear like totem clans (such as Kukar and Giddar, from which the villages of Kukar Hatta and Sabz Giddar obtain their names) may be marked.* The Aroras (especially in the villages) are not very orthodox, and remarriage of widows is not unknown among them.

There remain the *Bhátias,* who, though one of the smaller Hindu tribes, are remarkable for the firm hold they have got on the land in the neighbourhood of Shujabad. They belong to the same tribe as the Bhátias of the lower Indus, and are believed to have been originally Rájpúts. This chief clan in this district is the Babla, which traces its origin to an ancestor of this name, and which had its original seat in this district at Mári Nún, a few miles east of Shujabad. The chief members of this clan made themselves exceedingly useful to the Multan Nawábs, and took full advantage of the opportunities which Sáwan Mal's *régime* gave to capitalists for the acquisition of land. The leading men among the Bablas and other Bhátia clans are known as Chaudhrís, and the Chaudhrís of Shujabad are renowned for their enterprise, business-like habits and successful agriculture. The Bhátias are rather strict Hindús, they eschew smoking and widow remarriage and abstain from meat and spirits.

1881	...	1,995
1891	...	1,478
1901	...	2,718

Mussalman tribes.

Syads, Koreshis, etc.

The *Syads* are, properly speaking, the descendants of Ali, who married Bíbí Fátima, the daughter of the Prophet; but it is impossible to say how many of the persons claiming to be Syads can establish their descent. The Syads in this district mostly belong to the more important families—the Gilánís, Gardezís, and so forth, who are described further on in this chapter; but many are men of comparatively obscure position. In addition to the families there mentioned, there is a family of Syads now

1881	...	8,908
1891	...	11,006
1901	...	10,567

* Other such clans are the Nángpál, Nangrú, Gahlar, Gera, Mehndiratta, Cháwala, Pabreja, Taneja and Kataria. The Kukars are said to avoid eating poultry, the Nángpáls to avoid killing snakes, the Mehndirattas, to avoid planting henna, and so forth: but these rules are by no means strictly observed.

Chapter III, C.

Tribes, Castes and Leading Families.

Syads, Koreshís, etc.

settled at Kotla Saadat in the Multan tahsil who, about the end of the seventeenth century emigrated to Multan from Kaniguram in the Mahsud country on account of a blood feud: the chief men of this family are at present Wazír Sháh and Lál Sháh. There are also several families in the neighbourhood of Kahror, who are called Jabli Syads, after some mountain (Jabl) in Arabia. The Syads are held in considerable reverence by the people, who salute them with respect and look up to them as pírs. They most of them own lands, but are seldom found actually handling the plough. Members of the sacred and semi-sacred tribes of this part of the Punjab generally have names ending in 'Sháh' (as 'Sher Sháh,' etc.); and though this practice is not uncommon among the Koreshis, Khaggas, Chishtís, etc., it is almost invariable among the Syads.

Closely allied to the Syads are the *Koreshís*, who numbered according to the census of 1881 some 6,100 souls and in 1901, 7,797; they were not separately tabulated in 1891, being included among Sheikhs. The Koreshís claim descent from the tribe to which the Prophet belonged, and the Koreshís of the district are confined mainly to the families of the Makhdúms of Baháwal Hakk in Multan, the guardians of the shrine at Makhdum Rashid, and their immediate connections. The *Shekhs*, who also claim Arab descent, are largely men of inferior status, and include a certain number of Hindu converts, who nearly always assume this appellation. Among the more prominent Shekh tribes are the Ansáris (1,539 in 1881), to whom several respectable families in Multan belong. There are also certain tribes claiming to be *Arabs*, such as the Arbís, who used to hold several villages in the Multan tahsil, but have now fallen into decay. The Arabs of the census return of 1891 are, however, mainly strangers,—Jews and others from Mesopotamia,—who assumed that title for the census night.* Among the tribes claiming an Arab or semi-sacred status are the *Háns, Khagga, Nekokára* and *Jhandír*, who have all been tabulated in the census as Shekhs. The Háns are found mainly on the Montgomery border; the Nekokára and Jhandír, though found also in Mailsi, are chiefly conspicuous in the direction of Jhang; the Khaggas own land both in the Multan and Mailsi tahsils, and in Pakka Háji Majíd, near Tulamba. All these tribes are looked on with a certain amount of respect. In the troublous days before Sáwan Mal, if any one was distressed he took refuge with a Khagga: and any marauder who entered a Khagga's house was miraculously struck blind.

Shekhs, including Kureshis.

1881	...	12,649
1891	...	12,234
1901	...	14,623

Arabs.

1881	...	475
1891	...	81
1901	...	...

Patháns.

The first settlement in the district of *Patháns* in any numbers took place during the reign of the Emperor Sháh Jahán, after the ineffectual efforts made by the Princes Aurangzeb and

1881	...	9,067
1891	...	7,069
1901	...	8,251

* There were Jews in Multan in the 18th century (p. 21, Gentil's Memoires sur l' Indoustan, 1822).

Chapter III, C.

Tribes, Castes and Leading Families.

Pathans.

Dara Shekoh to recover Kandahar from Persia (A.D. 1649—53). The Pathan adherents of the empire then flocked in some numbers into India, and many of them were located by royal grants in this and the neighbouring districts. The position of the refugees was subsequently much improved by the accession of one of their number, Záhid Khan, to the post of Náib-Názim of Multan. From this time for more than a century and a half Afghán influence was predominant throughout the Multan province, and the members of the tribe largely profited by its political predominance. But when Multan fell before Ranjit Singh in 1818, their position became much altered. Naturally Muzaffar Khan had found his most devoted adherents among his own tribe, and these, equally naturally, were objects of special dislike to the Sikh agents who took over charge of the province. During the first two years, accordingly, of Sikh rule many Patháns left the district, finding their claims lightly regarded by the new rulers. Under Sáwan Mal, however, their position again improved. He enlisted them in large numbers into his army, and many who had left their estates after the fall of the city were encouraged to return. During the revolt of Diwan Mulraj they sided for the most part with the British power, and after annexation great efforts were made by them to become reinstated in their former position. The Multani Pathans, as might be expected from their history, belong mostly to clans of the Abdáli or Duráni stock, which, coming from the country round Kandahar and Hirát, are little known in the northern frontier districts. The Abdális are said to be divided into two branches with five main clans in each,* *viz.* :—

Popalzai branch.	*Panjpao branch.*
1. Popalzais.	6. Khákwánis.
2. Bádozais.	7. Alizais.
3. Bámozais.	8. Mákús.
4. Ismailzais.	9. Nurzais.
5. Saddozais (including Khudakkas).	10. Addozais.

Of the above, Nos. 1, 4, 8, 9 and 10 are not found in this district; but families of the remaining clans are fairly common. Besides the above, there are the Taríns, who are an older branch of the stock from which the Abdális are descended, and whose chief sub-clans in this district are the Mallezais and Jamunds: their chief habitat is the Pishin valley. Apart from either of the above are the Bábars, a clan of uncertain origin, but who are said to be Garghushti Pathans and not Afghans proper.

* The names differ from those given on page 205 of Ibbetson's Punjab Ethnography, and on page 96 of Volume II of Elphinstone's Caubul, but I give them as given to me by one of the Multani Pathans. It should be explained that in the Popalzai branch the eldest son is said to have always started a new sept of his own, while the younger sons continued the name of their father; *e.g.*, *Bádo* was the eldest son of Popal, Bamo of Bádo, and so on.

Chapter III, C.

Tribes, Castes and Leading Families.

Pathans.

The Pathans of this district live very largely in Multan city or as fairly large landowners in the villages; they are seldom found following the plough. They alone of any Mahomedan tribe in the district show any taste for Government service, and a certain number are enlisted in Cureton's Multani Horse, the XVth Bengal Lancers. The bulk of that regiment has for some time past been recruited in Dera Ismail Khan and other districts,* but it maintains a certain hold on this district, where several retired native officers and men of the regiment are proprietors of land. Some of the more prominent officers have considerable grants, such as Abdulla Khan at Kot Abdulla in Kabirwála, Rabnawáz Khan in the neighbourhood of Multan, Mahomed Nawáz Khán at Bibipur and Bákirpur near Multan, the sons of Nawáb Kale Khan at Bahádurpur in Shujabad, and so forth, while a fair number of the non-commissioned officers and men were recently provided for in a village on the Báwan rajbaha, some six miles out of Multan. The Pathans in this district are, as a rule, men of gentlemanly manners, even if in a lower position in life, but many of them are reckless and extravagant, and they make, as a rule, poor managers of property. The people have a proverb: Pathán dá pút, kadáhin jinn kadáhin bhút ('A Pathan's son is sometimes a devil, sometimes a demon'), that is to say he is never anything but bad though some are worse than others. This saying is probably a reminiscence of the oppressions practised in the palmy days of Pathan supremacy: for the Pathan, as he now is, it seems a bit hard.

Besides the indigenous Pathans there are a certain number of immigrants, chiefly from the Ghazni direction who come every cold weather and wander about the district, either as builders of walls or as pedlars of fruit, cloth and indigo. They are looked on as excellent workmen, but are a bit turbulent in exacting their dues. They live on the proceeds of begging, and take away with them in the spring the whole of their earnings for the winter. They almost always leave their women behind them in "kirris" in the Derajat, and this accounts for the small proportion of Pathan women returned in the census.

---

* The composition of the XVth Bengal Lancers (Cureton's Multanis) was on 1st January 1900 as follows :—

		Multan.	*Other Cis Indus Districts.*	*Trans-Indus.*	*Total.*
Multani Pathans	...	21	14	61	96
Other Pathans	...	4	45	94	143
Bilochis	...	1	76	108	185
Miscellaneous	...	2	112	86	200
Total	...	28	247	349	624

The Multani Pathans were of the following clans—Alizais, Khákwánís, Bádozais, Bábars, Addozais, Jamunds, Khalils. Ismailzais, Bámozais, Nurzais, Tarins, Khajakzais, Saddozais, Popalzais and Khalafzais. No members of the eight clans last mentioned were inhabitants of the Multan district.

Chapter III C.

Tribes, Castes and Leading Families.

Pathans.

The Pathans in this district, even those of the ragged wall-building species, are commonly addressed by the people as 'Khán' or 'Khán Sáhib.' Of the settled Pathan families very few have any knowledge of Pashto, and they maintain little or no connection with their fellow-tribesmen on or beyond the border, having in most cases intermarried freely with the native races of the district.

Bilochis and Daudpotras.

1881	...	18,547
1891	...	21,603
1901	...	24,488

The *Bilochis* first obtained a footing in the district during the latter half of the fifteenth century, when the Dodais and afterwards the Rinds made incursions into the district, in some cases enlisting as mercenaries under the Langáhs, and, in others, settling down as agriculturists. They are now found for the most part in the Lodhrán tahsil and its immediate neighbourhood; and though they own no very prominent men, they include several sturdy agricultural families of a good stamp in villages such as Wahi Jugguwala, Haveli Nasir Khan, Chauki Sobha Khan, etc. The Biloch villages in the east of Lodhrán are mostly called chaukís; the story being that the Bilochís were settled there as outposts in former days to protect the boundary of the neighbouring desert, which is still known as the Chit Dáin or Desert of Terror. The Bilochís of the district are chiefly Rinds and Korais. They have long been, for practical purposes, ordinary Jats, having forgotten their old language, disused their old costume and intermarried freely with the neigbouring population. They not uncommonly, however, still wear their hair long and among the Rinds the married women wear white clothes only.

1881	...	1,315
1891	...	942
1901	...	670

The *Daudpotras*, though claiming a separate origin, are commonly looked on as Bilochís. They are of the same family as the Nawáb of Baháwalpur, and those found in this district are mainly descendants of men who obtained a footing in the Sutlej tahsils during the days of Baháwalpur supremacy. In appearance they resemble the Bilochís. They are mainly tenants and labourers, and own very little land.

Moghals.

1881	...	4,601
1891	...	10,843
1901	...	8,038

Of the so-called *Moghals* of the district but few are real Moghals: the assumption of Moghal clan names, such as Chughatta, etc., being a very common practice among the lower castes. The census figures regarding this tribe are therefore specially untrustworthy. Considering the enormous number of Moghal invasions from which the district has suffered, there are remarkably few families in Multan which can show Moghal or Turkish descent. There is a tribe called Kaum, near Mitru, which is said to have come from Central Asia, and at Wahind Sarmani, near Kahror, there are Aibaks: these Aibaks, however, say they are not Turks but Joyas. Possibly some of the innumerable so-called Jat tribes of the district may represent fragments of the

Chapter III C.

Tribes, Castes and Leading Families.

Moghal invasions; but after five or six centuries of free intermarriage, it would probably be difficult to find now many undoubted descendants of the Moghal invaders. Such few Moghals as there are among the peasantry look on themselves as merely a kind of Jats.

Aráíns and Kambohs.

The *Aráins* of the central Punjab attribute their origin to Multan, and the Aráíns of Multan almost invariably say that they came from the central Punjab or from Hindustan, so that our knowledge of the origin of this tribe is obscure. Possibly both statements are true. They are often found in this district in their usual position of cultivators and market gardeners, but as proprietors they hold two main clusters of villages round Jalla in Mailsi and round Kabírpur in Multan, and are also prominent at Jalla in Lodhrán and elsewhere. As proprietors they are looked upon as fully the equals in rank of the other tribes. Their leading men are called *mullán*. Of the Aráín as a tenant, the people say: 'Aráín tama tain,' which signifies that the Aráín will stay with you as long as you satisfy his greed by advances of money, etc. The Aráíns of Jalla in Lodhrán have a character for high-handedness, which is represented in the local proverb: 'Jalle de Arain ápe chor ápe sain' ('The Arains of Jalla are thieves and judges in one'). The Aráíns are scarcely ever found in this district as sellers of vegetables or greengrocers, professions commonly adopted by them in the Punjab proper but monopolized here (except near Multan city) by Hindus.

1881 ...	23,981
1891 ...	28,582
1901 ...	32,410

The *Kambohs* in this district are an unimportant tribe, with very little property. They often cultivate vegetables, and those so occupied are not uncommonly called Aráíns by the people.

1881 ...	687
1891 ...	1,318
1901 ...	1,953

Jats and Rájpúts.

The *Jats* and *Rájpúts* of the district may conveniently be considered together. The term Jat is to a certain extent recognized as the name of caste or race as it is in the central Punjab, but it is also freely used to include all whose profession is agriculture or pasturage, and to distinguish indigenous tribes of this character from the immigrant Syads, Pathans, Koreshís and others of a similar social status. The word is also used as a common noun to signify a cultivator*; so that it will be readily understood how the tribe 'Jat' does not include a very definite body of men, and how the number recorded as Jats at the various censuses is subject to considerable variations. The term is often found to include on the one side menial or other lowly castes which have taken to agriculture, and, on the other, clans with

	Jats.	*Rájpúts.*
1881 ...	102,952	59,627
1891 ...	146,082	90,687
1901 ...	140,315	91,516

* As when one asks at a well, 'Who is the owner? and who is the Jat?'

Chapter III, C.

Tribes, Castes and Leading Families.

Jats and Rájpúts.

pretended or undoubted Rájpút origin. There are no indigenous clans in the district who call themselves in common parlance Jat or Rajpút : each clan is known by its own name, and its classification as a Jat or Rájpút clan is a matter left for the mirási or other outsider to consider. The number of these petty clans is immense (368 such clans were returned in 1881 under the head of "Jat" alone), and attempts to classify them are almost hopeless, as by far the greater number of them are confined to one or two villages, and are quite unable to give any account of themselves or of their relations with any other clan. The chief of the Jat and Rajput clans in the district are—

Siáls,	Núns,
Thahíms,	Drigs,
Traggars,	Langáhs,
Wainses,	Joyas,
Bosans,	Mitrus,
Khokhars,	Khichís,
Marrals,	Langriáls,

and an account of these clans is given below.

Among the less distinguished Jat and Rájpút tribes we find in *Kabírwála* the Sahus, Khaks, Pahors, Dahas, and Pándas; in *Multan*, Kheras, Athangals, Metlas, Buches, Mahotas, Chhajjras, Ráns, Kálrus, and Hammars; in *Shujabad*, Khákis, Jhakkars, Rids, Lángs, Ruks, Pannûhans, Shajras, and Jais; in *Lodhrán*, Channars, Ghallus, Utherás, Kánjuns, and Kuliárs; in *Mailsi*, Dhudhis, Sandhals, and Wasírs.

The Jat is the backbone of the agriculture in the district and his boorish habits, his clannishness, his insolence in prosperity, all come in for their share of notice in the sayings of the people: 'Jat ke jánen rah?' ('What does a Jat know of roads? he cuts across country'). 'Jat názuk te sirdá tarorá' ('However particular a Jat may become, he still ties a blanket on his head as a pagri'). 'Jat bhukká kutta, te rajjiá súr'. ('If a Jat is empty, he is a dog; if full, a pig'). 'Jat te phat, baddha change' ('A Jat and a wound should be tied up'). 'Jat pinne te kandh kolon bí ghinne' ('If a Jat begs. he insists on getting something even from a brick wall'). Jat Jatán de sáleh, kar lainde ghála mále' ('All Jats are closely related to each other, and carry out deceitful practices to protect each other'). And yet, after all, a Jat wife is the best and most economical: 'Rau Jatti te hor sab chattí' ('A Jat wife for me: all the rest are a mere waste of money').

The *Siáls* with their various sub-divisions occupy nearly all the villages on both banks of the Rávi in the Kabírwála tahsil. The sub-divisions best known in the district are the Sargána, Hiráj, Thiráj, Sanpál, Dáduaná, Duána, Kamlána, Panjuána, Sasrán,

1881	...	27,482
1891	...	30,909
1901	...	30,995

Chapter III, C.

Tribes, Castes and Leading Families.

Jats and Rájpúts.

Daulatána* and Mirálí. They all take their names from various descendants of the common ancestor, Seo or Siál, whose pedigree table is given in Appendix III of Sir Charles Roe's report of the second Regular Settlement. Siál is said to have been a son of Rai Shankar, a Panwár Rájpút. He migrated to the Punjab, and was converted to Islam by Bábá Farid of Pákpattan in the time of the Emperor Ala-ud-din Ghori, or about 1250 A.D. He married the daughter of Bahádur Khan, a local chief, and his sons established themselves in Chauntra, and then across the Chenáb in Jhang, which they ruled more or less independently down to the time of Ranjit Singh. Ahmad Khan, the then chief, was direct descendant and male representative of Siál; after repulsing one or two attacks, he was at length defeated by the Maharaja and his country annexed. He was, however, granted a jâgír, and his descendants still reside and hold land in Jhang. During the period of the Siál supremacy and the breakdown of the Moghal power large bands of this tribe appear to have passed down southwards and to have settled in their present habitat along the banks of the Râvi. Amongst the Sargánas the leading men at present are Salábat of Kund Sargána and Ahmad of Bágar; there is also a branch of this clan settled in the Mailsi tahsil. Among the Hirájs there is the Chauki Muhan family described below, and the family of Nur Mahomed of Chauki Siág. The Siál clans of the Rávi above Tulamba (especially the Sanpáls and Panjuánas) have a bad name for cattle-lifting; they contain several zamindars who are possessed of energy and strong character, but none of any eminence.

1881	...	2,821
1891	...	4,300
1901	...	4,540

The *Thahíms* appear from the Ain-i-Akbari to have been a common tribe in the district in the days of Akbar. The bulk of the present Thahíms, however, are said to have immigrated from Chiniot at the time of the Siál upheaval in the eighteenth century; and there are still Thahíms in Chiniot and its neighbourhood. The Thahíms claim Arabic descent, and they say that their immediate ancestor, Sámbhal Sháh, came to Multan seven hundred years ago, killed the local chief, and reigned in his stead for forty years. The tribe is now found mainly on the Chenáb in the south-west of the Kabírwála tahsil, where they have a bad name for crime. They are also found in other parts of the district especially in the tract between Lodhran and Kahror. The chief Thahím family in the district is that of Pír Bakhsh, of Mamdál. Among the remarkable men whom the tribe has produced are Sadullah Khan, the Prime Minister of the Emperor Sháh Jahán, and Shekh Jalál, one of the learned men of Agrá in the days of Humáyún. The tribe, therefore, was not always a purely agricultural one, and there may be something true in

* To be distinguished from the Joya Daulatánas of the Luddan tract in Mailsi.

Chapter III, C.

Tribes, Castes and Leading Families.

Jats and Rájpúts.

their claims to Arabic extraction. The Báni Tamím are a large tribe in Arabia, and the Báni Taím are a Koreshi clan to which the first Caliph belonged.

The *Traggars* hold a few villages on the Chenáb next the Thahíms. They say they are Bhatti Rájpúts, and take their name from their ancestral home at Traggar in Bikanír. They first immigrated to Jhang, but about one hundred and fifty years ago, on account of quarrels with the Siáls, they left that district and settled under their leaders, Hasta, Mulah and Salábat, on the banks of the Chenáb, where they hold a few villages both on the Multan and on the Muzaffargarh side of the river.

The *Vains* clan hold two villges on the extreme north of the Multan tahsil, and their leading man is Kádir Bakhsh, zaildar. They are also found in the north of the Shujabad tahsíl. They say they are Hajua Rájpúts, and that their ancestor Vains came to Multan from Sakesar in the days of Firoz Sháh. The *Bosans* headed by Núr Mahomed Khan Bosan, hold the villages south of the Vains; their ancestor is said to have come from Haidarabad in Sindh as a disciple of Baháwal Hakk, and to have received from his master some of the land which the latter obtained from the ruler of Multan.

1881	...	8,895
1891	...	17,612
1901	...	11,606

The *Khokhars* of the district are not a very important clan, except for the one family described further on this chapter. The Khokhars are sometimes looked on as a distinct tribe, with Awán or with Arab origin, and sometimes as a clan of the Jats or Rájpúts. The figures in the margin included all the Khokhars returned at the census, but the large rise between 1881 and 1891 is not easily accounted for, unless it be due to the inclusion of menials under this name. The Khokhars themselves generally attribute their origin to one Kutb Sháh, who came from Ghazni to Sakesar with the conquerer Mahmud, and from whom the Awáns also are said to be descended. Writing on the census of 1891, Maulvi Mahomed Hussain notes as follows regarding another story of their origin :—' The author of the Jawáhir Farídi, a book written in 1016 by one of the descendants of Báwa Faríd, gives the Khokhars an Arab origin, but he gives us no detail. I think this authority cannot be relied on, because the descendants of Báwa Faríd took their wives out of the Khokhar families of Pákpattan; and this fact might have induced them to give an Arab origin to the Khokhars.' The Khokhars, from whatever origin descended, were a considerable power in the tract between Jhelum and Multan at the time of the invasion of Tamerlane; but their history has been somewhat obscured owing to their being constantly confused in the written records with the Ghakkars.

Chapter III. C.

Tribes Castes and Leading Families.

Jats and Rájpúts.

The *Marrals*, like the Khokhars, are for the most part represented by a single family only. They are said to be by descent Rájpúts, and were the founders of the village of Kasba in the Multan tahsil. Abdul Nabi, Rai Baman and Rai Khair Mahomed are said to have come from Karnál some four hundred years ago. Their chiefs afterwards dropped the title of Rai, and are now spoken of as Chaudhri. Chaudhri Sultan Bakhsh, the grandfather of the present Chaudhri, Sher Bakhsh, was reckoned one of the greatest zamindars of the district, as he was able to afford to keep horses. Sher Bakhsh, the present head of the family, is a notorious spendthrift, and the race has of late much degenerated. In the time of Akbar the Marrals were the principal tribe of the Islampur and Ismailpur parganas, and there are still traces of their former power in many villages in the south of the Multan and the north of the Shujabad tahsil.

In the north of Shujabad the predominant clan is that of the *Núns*, who are said to be a sub-division of the Bhatti Rájpúts, and to have migrated from some place called Thánewáhan, which is said to have been in the direction of Delhi. The date of the immigration appears uncertain, but they say that their ancestor Rájwaddan was converted by Makhdúm Jahánian of Uchh, or, as others say, by Saiyad Jalál. They first settled at Bhangála in Shujabad, and afterwards extended over the greater part of the north of the tahsil, and their villages benefited greatly by the opening of canals in the times of the Nawábs. They are now somewhat decaying, but still hold a good deal of land. Rána Pallia, Rána Khudáyár, Rána Fatteh Mahomed and Rána Mahomed Ali are their chief men. The Núns are said to be connected with the Jais, Jhakkars and Uteras : Jai and Uterá being represented as brothers of Nún, and Jhakkar as son of Jai. The Jakkars, who live immediately north of the Núns in the Shujabad tahsil retain, like them, the old title of Rána. I have also seen a manuscript genealogy in which Utherá, Kánjun and Kuliár (the names of three well-known tribes in this district) are represented as the brothers of Nún and the sons of Rájwaddan above mentioned.*

The *Drigs*, who are found along the banks of the Chenáb, attribute their origin to 'Kech Makran', and like other tribes who came from the direction of Sindh they are known by the appellation of 'Jám.' They are thought to be Rájpúts from Sindh who were driven out from that country in the end of the fifteenth century by the oppression of the ruler of Thatta.

---

* In the following rhyme the Channars also are added :—

Jhakkar Channar Kánjun Nún te Uterá,
Hin Ráne Shaitán de panje bújh bhará.

All five clans assume the title of Rána, and all five would seem to have given cause of offence to the maker of the couplet.

Chapter III C.

Tribes Castes and Leading Families.

Jats and Rájpúts.

1881	...	4,491
1891	...	2,402
1901	...	2,927

The *Langáhs* hold villages in various parts of the Shujabad tahsil, but are in chief strength towards the south. The figures given for this tribe in the various censuses differ a good ideal, possibly owing to their being confused with the Lángs, a smaller tribe of the same neighbourhood. The Langáhs, as has been noticed in Chapter II above, furnished a dynasty of rulers who were supreme in Multan for about eighty years, from 1445 to 1526 A.D. The Langáhs of that dynasty are said by Firishta to have come from Sibi, and he is quoted as ascribing to them an Afghan origin.* The people themselves, so far as they know about their original habitat, locate it at Delhi, and some persons throw doubt on the identity of the present Langáhs and those of the old reigning dynasty; but as Fírishta gives Rappri (a small village on the Chenáb in the south of the Shujabad tahsil) as the original home in this district of the Langáhs whom he mentions, and as the Langáhs now resident in the district own large areas of land, it seems only reasonable to suppose that the Langáhs, now extant and those of Fírishta are one and the same race.† In former times the Langáhs owned several villages which are now in other hands. It is not unlikely that the Langáhs were Rájpúts from Sindh, and some say that they were Panwárs, and that they are allied to the Bhuttas, Kharrals, Harrals and Laks. It is also stated by mírásís that Langáh, Bhutta, Dahar, Shajrá and Naich (all now represented by tribes in this district) were five sons of one Mahlí, and this may reflect some original connection between those various clans.‡ Some of them claim Arabic descent according to the fashion prevalent in this part of the Punjab (where Rájpút descent is thought of little account), and say that Shujaat Khan, who founded the village of Shujaatpur, came from Arabia six hundred years ago. The chief man of the tribe is now Lál Khan, who lives at Shujaatpur but Ghulám Mohamed, of Jahánpur, and Yáran Khan, of Rukanbatti, are also well to do, and respectable members of the tribe. The chief Langáh clans are Sanpál, Raizáda, Jore,

---

* The Lucknow edition of Fírishta describes Rai Sahra as 'Sardár-i-jumá 'at-i-Afghán Langáh'; but there seems to be some doubt about this. The Langáhs ordinarily have names ending in Khán, like the Pathans of this part of the Punjab.

† The following rhyme, recited by a mírási of Rukanbatti, can scarcely refer to any one but Husain Khan, Langáh :—

Khán Husain takht baithá, kabr that chauchakk,
Hikk dháwaní Multan gioso nál súm sarakk.
Takár Tátár dharm mánge: líkkadi nakk
Khán Husain pái vaddi bhág bakhatt.

'Khan Husain sat on the throne and wide was his fame; he went with one dash to Multan in great wrath; he took an oath from the Turks (?) and Tartars: they drew a line in the dust with their noses: Khan Husain obtained great rank and fortune.'

‡ The verse runs :—

Sagli jihándi dá[illegible], Sodí jihán dí ma.
Mahlí jái panj putr—Dahr, Bhutta, Langáh, Naich, Shajrá.

Chapter III C.

Tribes, Castes and Leading Families.

Jats and Rajpúts.

Jabuje and Jahankhánia. There are also some families of Langáhs at Rath Mammar in the Mailsi bár: these men are fakírs and do medicine work, and are said to have no connection with the other Langáhs.

1881	...	5,532
1891	...	5,649
1901	...	7,212

The *Joyas* hold most of the land along the Sutlej in the Mailsi tahsil. Cunningham would identify them with the Yaudhias, who are thought to have been in the same tract of country before the Christian era. The Joyas themselves say that they are Rájputs from Bikanir, and Mr. Morris, the Settlement Officer of 1858, states that they came from Sindh. They are said to have been converted by Ruku-i-Alam in the fourteenth century, but their own account places their conversion earlier. They say that eight hundred years ago Rai Jalál-ud-din and Rai Kamál-ud-din, two brothers, and Fatteh Khan were sent by the Delhi emperor against Khar, a Bhatti chief then ruling in Kahror, and that after defeating Khar they held his land in farm from the Delhi sovereign. As noted in the description of Kahror in Chapter VI, below, there is reason to believe that this Khar or Kahr lived not earlier than the fourteenth century, and the first immigration of the Joyas probably dates from then. Jalál-ud-din remained at Kahror, while Fatteh Khan settled at Fattehpur. In the time of Akbar the Joyas were the predominant tribe of the Mailsi and Lodhran tahsils. Then, or soon after, probably, the four brothers—Jágan, Mangan, Luddan and Lál—colonized the country round Luddan; and, as time went on, fresh bands came over the Sutlej. In the latter days of the empire the Joyas were a turbulent element in the population, but were kept somewhat in order by the Daudpotras. They contain a vast number of sub-clans, of which at present the Daulatanas, the Salderas and the Lakhweras are the most prominent. The chief family among the Joyas was, till lately, that of Dín Mahomed Khan, of Kahror: but Dín Mahomed died in 1891, leaving two young sons, who are still minors, and the widow has allowed the family property and position to decay. The chief men, among the Joyas at present are Ghulám Mahomed, of Luddan, and his only son, Ghulám Kádir, who are held in great respect throughout the tahsil on account of their energy and liberality. There is also a fairly well-to-do family at Saldera formerly headed by Fatteh Khan, but the family has decreased in importance under Fatteh Khan's son, Ghulám Mahomed Saldera.

1881	...	3,046
1891	...	1,269
1901	...	1,558

The *Khichís* are a branch of the Chauháns and are said to be descended from one Khichi Khan, who was ruler in Ajmir, and afterwards obtained possession of Delhi, from which he was driven out by the Mahomedans. His descendants, Sísan and Vadan, migrated to Multan in the time of the Moghal

Chapter III C.

Tribes, Castes and Leading Families.

Jats and Rájpúts

sovereigns: Sísan founded Faddah and Vadan Shergarh. They fought with the Joyas, then paramount in this direction, and the names of Rai Lúna Khichi, of Sakhi Dalel and of Ali Khan are still remembered among them. There is a tale, too, to, the effect that the Bilochís of Khaí having in Moghal times become rebellious, the Khichís were sent against them under two brothers, Husain Khan and Háji Fatteh; but there is no indication of the date of this event. The Khichís fought also against the Sikhs under Jhanda Singh and Ganda Singh, and were discomfited. The tribe still holds several villages round Mailsi: their chief men are Núr Mahomed, of Fadda, and Azam Khan, of Aliwah. The variations in the numbers returned at the various censuses are due probably to the Khichís being in some cases classed as Chauháns, and in others separately enumerated.

The *Mitrús* own a small circle of villages to the north of Mailsi. They say they are Bhatti Rájpúts, and that their ancestor Mitrú came from Bikanír two hundred years ago and founded the village of Tibba. When this village decayed about a century later, one Saran set forth and founded Mitru. The chief man among the Mitrús at present is Nasír Bakhsh.

1881	...	...
1891	...	2,375
1901	...	3,174

The *Langriáls*, who inhabit the whole of the eastern bár country, are a comparatively new tribe in the district. The tribe is found in Ráwalpindi and Siálkot also, where they claim a Solar Rájpút descent. It is sometimes stated that the Multan Langriáls claim descent from a Brahman of Bikanír, but an inspection of their *kursi náma*, shows that it is only their mírásí who claims this descent: the Langriáls themselves, like many other converted tribes, say they are from Arabia and are Koreshís; and that they held power for some time in Tatta in Sindh under one Ghiás-ud-din, who from the extent of his public kitchen (langar), obtained the clan name of Langriál. Ghiás-ud-din is said to have been a contemporary of Shaháb-ud-din Ghori, and to have gone with him to Delhi; after which the tribe is found wandering *via* Kashmir to Sháhpur, and then driven from Sháhpur to Gariála in Jhang. From this they went to the Kamália iláka in Montgomery, from which they removed in the time of Shuja Khan to their present habitat in the country formerly held by the Háns tribe round Kamánd. Their two chiefs were Wága and Rahmán. Máchhia, the descendant of Wága, lives at Kamánd and Bákir, the descendant of Rahmán, at Sharaf. Both hold jágirs in return for services in 1857 against the Káthias and the mutinous Multan regiments. The Langriáls are by nature nomads, and by habit cattle-lifters; but they are by degrees settling down to more stable and reputable means of living.

Chapter III C.

Tribes, Castes and Leading Families.

The inferior tribes.

Of the more lowly castes which are sometimes found engaged in agricultural pursuits, those mentioned in the margin are the most prominent.

	1881.	1891.	1901.
Jhabels ...	1,868	1,154	2,954
Kehals ...	232	27	78
Labánas ...	307	475	222
Mahtams ...	4,193	3,802	5,127
Ods ...	3,459	2,362	3,782
Pakhíwáras ...	727	866	1,053

The *Jhabels* and *Kehals* are fishing tribes who live by the bank of the river. They both say they came from Sindh, and the Kehals are said to be given to polygamy on a large scale. The *Labánas* in this district are vagrants, who make ropes and mats, and who are usually spoken of (with some contempt) as 'Sikhs,' without further designation; being as a rule Monâ Sikhs and not Mahomedans. The *Mahtams*, who are found in larger, numbers, are both Mussalman and Hindu the former being mainly cultivators (and good ones); the latter clearers of jungle, hunters of pig and so forth. They have a dark complexion, say they came from Sindh, and claim a Rájpút origin. Some of the Mahtams near Multan city are said to be really Jats, who were called Mahtams from having settled on the homes and lands of an old Mahtam colony. The Mahtams are looked down upon, and the local proverb says: 'Do jhugge Mahtamán de te nán Khairpur' ('Two Mahtam huts and the village called Khairpur'). A village in Kabírwála was known for many generations by the name of Mahtamán; but when the Sidhnai canal was extended to it, and it was colonized by Dabs from Jhang, the name of the village was by special request altered to Khan Bahádurgarh. The *Ods* are wandering caste, mostly Hindus, living by earthwork and carrying their grass huts and other belongings with them on donkeys from place to place. Occasionally (as in Dera Buddhu Malik near Multan) they are found in settled houses. The *Pakhíwáras* are also vagrants: Mussalman by religion and owing their name to the *Pakhís* or reed huts in which they dwell. A wandering tribe of somewhat thievish propensities, called Márath, is also found, mainly in the northern part of the district.

Chapter III, C.

Tribes, Castes and Leading Families.

The menial castes.

The figures for the menial castes as returned at the censuses are shown in the margin. The workers in leather are in this district entirely Mussalmans and are known as *Mochís,* not as Chamárs. The scavengers also are mainly Mussalmans and are spoken of as *Kotánas,* Kurtánas or Mussallís. In the same way, the washermen are known as *Charhoas* and the weavers as *Paolis,* and both these castes are also almost entirely Mussalman. The remaining menial castes are much as the central Punjab. Oil-seeds not being plentifully grown *Telis* are fewer than in the centre and east of the province ; but, as might be expected, Malláhs and Kassábs are much more common. Generally speaking, the distinction between the menial and agricultural castes is far less marked in this part of the province than in the centre and in the east. Owing to the lack of village sites, the menials are very often found as tenants or farm-servants, and are in such circumstances spoken of and treated as ordinary Jats. With certain restrictions, too, the intermarriage of menials with the agricultural tribes is comparatively common. The Kotánas are distinguished from the other menial castes by their catholicity in the matter of food ; they eat anything clean or unclean ; (always excepting snakes, rats, spiders jackals and pigs) ; but in other respects are outwardly Mahomedans, going to the mosques, being married by nikáh and burying their dead. They very commonly call themselves Khokhars, just as the Náís commonly call themselves Bhattís. The sweeper in bad years is a humble individual, but when his wants are satisfied there is no holding him ! ' Palli vichh dáne kuddan kutáne' ('Grain in bin ; the Kutána leaps in his

	1881.	1891.	1901.
Chamárs and Mochís (leather-workers) ...	18,542	15,864	24,894
Chúhras (sweepers) ...	29,489	32,026	*37,720
Charhoas (washermen) ...	11,875	9,209	†14,682
Kassábs (butchers) ...	5,914	4,978	3,817
Kumhárs (potters) ...	13,716	12,478	18,823
Paolís (weavers) ...	23,753	28,545	27,232
Lohárs (ironsmiths) ...	2,768	2,553	3,774
Machhís and Jhínwars (watermen)	9,913	9,989	13,287
Malláhs or Mohánas (boatmen)	6,011	5,916	7,746
Mírásís (bards)	7,510	7,699	10,767
Náís (barbers)	6,035	6,149	8,438
Tarkháns (carpenters) ...	11,915	10,427	17,356
Telís (oilmen)	484	1,228	1,119

* Including Kutánas.
† Returned as Dhobi.

Chapter III, C.

Tribes, Castes and Leading Families.

The tribes as landowners.

pride'). He is indispensable for winnowing, and the winnowing-fan is, as it were, the emblem of his race: 'Chuhre kún chhaj di vadáí' ('The winnowing-fan is the sweeper's boast'). He also makes ropes, especially for wells.

The following figures show the area in acres held by each main caste or tribe at the Settlement of 1873—1880 :—

Tribes.	Multán.	Shujabad.	Lodhrán.	Mailsi.	Kabírwála.	Total.
I.—Hindus.						
Brahmans, Karárs and Gosáíns	2,155	2,623	4,596	5,403	1,382	16,159
Rájpúts	67	...	...	...	...	67
Khatris	8,308	67,497	4,395	95,924	672	309,997
Kirárs and Sunárs ...	36,793		91,842		2,566	
Other Hindus	50	532	378	23	...	983
Total Hindus ...	47,373	72,652	101,211	101,350	4,620	327,206
II.—Mahomedans.						
Syads and Koreshís ...	65,867	12,354	37,403	60,165	37,759	213,548
Pathans	32,548	3,918	5,079	51,824	953	124,135
Bilúchís...	78		19,735			
Rájpúts	199	...	...	...	...	199
Jats	193,747	96,222	242,189	391,605	106,859	1,030,622
Other Mahomedans ...	1,224	716	3,466	...	1,837	7,243
Total Mahomedans ...	293,663	113,210	317,872	503,594	147,408	1,375,747
III.—Village Servants ...	2,815	1,983	5,068	1,803	342	12,011
IV.—Miscellaneous. (*i.e.*, Government, Companies, Europeans) ...	38,606	3,889	15,767	10,010	74,063	142,335
Grand Total ...	382,457	191,734	439,918	616,757	226,433	1,857,299

Similar figures were not compiled in the recent Settlement, but the percentage of area held by each of the more prominent groups in each tahsil is noticed in the Assessment Reports. Of the whole proprietary area 26 per cent. is now held by Hindus, most of whom are Karárs; and 74 per cent. is held by Mahomedans, the majority of whom are Jats, to whom, however, the Syads and Pathans bear a good proportion. The holdings of the Karárs and Syads are scattered all over the district; so, too, are the Pathans and Bilochís, who, however, are most numerous in Mailsi and Lodhrán, and very few in Kabírwála. The localities of the Mahomedan Jats are very distinctly marked.

Chapter III, C.

Tribes, Castes and Leading Families.

The tribes as landowners.

The banks of the Rávi are held by the Siáls, including their sub-divisions of Hirájs, Sargánas, Daduánas, Panjuánas, etc. Along the Chenáb to the borders of the Multan tahsil the villages belong mainly to Thahíms and Traggars. In Multan the predominance of any one tribe of Jats is not so clearly marked; but in Shujabad, the Khokhars, Núns, Khákhís, Lángs, Kachálas, and Langáhs are found in more or less solid groups. In Lodhrán again the groups are not so very well marked; but in Mailsi the Joyas, with their sub-divisions, hold almost all the Sutlej lands. Behind these come extensive groups of Khichís, Aráíns, Syads, Pathans and Mitrus, whilst the *bár*, as far as it is habitable, is occupied mainly by Langriáls.

In each of the assessment reports of the recent Settlement there is a map showing roughly the distribution of these various landowning tribes.

History of tribal immigrations.

If the history of the various tribes is investigated, it will be found that there is scarcely a single important tribe now found in the district which has not immigrated within the last five or six hundred years. The whole population for many centuries has been in a state of constant flux, and it is of very little use trying to discover who the original inhabitants or the inhabitants in pre-Mahomedan times can have been. In Kabírwála the Khaks, Pándas, Pahors and Sahús have locally the reputation of being the four most ancient tribes in the tahsil; but there are traditions that the Khaks came from Jammu in the seventeenth century, and we find the Sahús still immigrating from Márwár in Akbar's time and the Pahors still immigating from Bikanír in the time of Jahángír. The earliest landmark in the immigrations of the district is the arrival of the Gardezi Syads in the twelfth century, when they received large grants along the old Rávi in the Kabírwála and Multan tahsils. In the thirteenth century came the Koreshís, and their proselytizing movements throw some further light on the tribal arrangements of the day. The Dhudhís, for instance, were at that time established in the extreme east of the Mailsi tahsil; and the Aráíns of the Multan tahsil appear to have begun immigrating about this time from Lahore. The Kheras, north of Multan, would seem to have arrived about this time from the direction of the Lakhi jungle. In Tamerlane's time we find the Khokhars in considerable power in the north of Kabírwála, but their settlement in their present habitat dates from the time of Humáyún. Shortly after this we find the Langahs, who had arrived from Sivi, in sufficient power to start a local dynasty, and during the time of Langáh supremacy began the incursions of the Bilochís from the south.

When the Ain-i-Akbari was written the Sahús held the country round Tulamba, and Sandas already occupied the present mouth of the Rávi near Khatpur Sanda. Over a good deal of the Multan

Chapter III, C.

Tribes, Castes and Leading Families.

tahsíl, and in other parts of the district also Thahíms were then in force; but this tribe is now mainly confined to a group of villages on the Chenáb north of Multán, and the colonization of those villages probably dates from a later period than that of Akbar. The country immediately south of Multán was in the hands of the Marrals. The Ghallus and Channars were in much the same area as they now occupy in the south-west corner of the district; and the Joyas were in considerable force all along the Sutlej. The Utherás, too, were settled round Dunyapur, and the Khichís were in possession of their present haunts north of Mailsi.

History of tribal immigrations.

According to tradition, it is to Akbar's time that we must ascribe the arrival of Tángras and Dheds to the neighbourhood of Sirdárpur, and of the Drigs from Kech Makran to Amanullapur and Bet Kech, and of the Lángs to the banks of the old Biás in the centre of the Shujabad tahsíl. About this time, too, apparently the Núns settled down in the north of Shujabad, and in the time of Jehángír the Khákís from Bhatner settled between the Núns and the Chenáb river. In Moghal times, also came the Khádals and Athangals from Jammu to the north of the Multán tahsíl, the Jánglas of Wán Chatta from Jhang, the Ráns of Ran Labidarya from Delhi, the Vainses from Sakesar, the Mahotas of Ináyatpur from Umarkot, the Ganwens of central Shujabad from Delhi, the Kánjuns from Delhi, the Panrúhans of southern Shujabad from the south, the Mitrús from Bikanír and the Arains of Lodhrán and Mailsi from Lahore. In the same period came the Arbis,—it is said from Arabia,—who were treated with consideration and given several villages round Multán, on which they have now to a large extent lost their hold. But the chief feature of this period is the large colonisation scheme carried out by Shahzáda Murád Bakhsh, who was governor of Multán in the time of Shah Jahán. It appears that for some reason or other—a change in the course of a river or the extirpation of some rebellious tribe—a large tract between the old Rávi and the Chenáb north of Multán was then available for settlement, and under the supervision of the State a number of foreign tribes were introduced into this tract: the Kálrú employés of Shah Jahán's army were rewarded with the land where Nawábpur and other Kálrú villages now stand; Mahe pilgrims from Jammu were given the site of Sharífpur, Saleh Mahe and Bahádurpur; Metlas from the north country settled at Basti Raza Khán; Sandílas from Delhi acquired Binda Sandíla; Buches got Buch Mubárik, and Suras from Delhi founded Alamdi Sura and Tindni.

In the reign of Aurangzeb arrived the Pathán refugees from Kandahár, who were afterwards so largely to affect the fortunes of the district; and with the break up of the empire in the early part of the eighteenth century still greater changes commenced. The upheaval of the Siáls in Jhang drove a

Chapter III, C.

Tribes, Castes and Leading Families.

History of tribal immigrations.

body of Thahíms from Chiniot into the west of the Kabírwala tahsíl, and an influential family of Syads from the same place to the tract north of the Rávi. These were followed later by the Siáls themselves, who established themselves firmly along the Sidhnai reach. About the middle of the century the Daúdpotras crossed the Sutlej and occupied the Mailsi and Lodhrán tahsíls; and with the drying up of the Biás and the starting of the new canal systems, a good deal of local shifting took place among the tribes of the district, more especially among the Khichís and other tribes formerly dependant on the Biás for their livelihood. The wars of the latter part of the eighteenth and the beginning of the nineteenth centuries gave a further impetus to change, and amid the devastation which overtook the district (and more particularly that part of it between Multán and Tulamba, which was so constantly crossed by the Patháu and Sikh armies), tribes were constantly leaving the desolated areas for new homes in safer tracts; and at the close of this period occurred the last great tribal immigation—that of the Langrials from Kamália to the eastern *bár* of Mailsi.

After the advent of the Sikh power there was no marked immigration from outside; but the colonization of the Diwánwáh and the constant grants of property to Hindu capitalists gave rise to a great deal of local shifting. Under the British rule the chief changes in the local population have been due to the starting of the three great canals—the Durána Langána, the Hájíwáh and the Sidhnai. The Durána Langána, which was formerly a comparatively small cut, was greatly enlarged and extended so as to colonize a large part of the western Ráwa of the Multán tahsíl. The Hájiwáh, constructed by the Khákwáni Pathans, resulted in the attraction of a large number of tenants especially from the Rávi, to the irrigated areas of Mailsi. And finally the Sidhnai canal has caused the immigration, not only of owners and tenants from a radius of 100 miles around, but also of Sikh and other settlers from the central Punjab, such as the Kambohs and Nain Jats from Chunián, Badheches from Amritsar and Batála, and Rájpúts from Jullundur. Of late years, however, the attractions of the Sidhnai have had to compete with those of the Chenáb canal; and it is probable that in time a large number of the inhabitants of the Rávi riverain will permanently immigrate to the happier areas of stable irrigation.

Honorary titles.

In connection with the tribal constitution of the district, it is of some interest to note the honorary titles of respect affixed by the people to the names of the more prominent men. The Bablas of Shujabad and some of the Aroras are spoken of as *Chaudhri*; Aroras of position, especially in the east of the district, are called *Mahta*; Brahmans are known as *Pandit* or *Misr*; traders from Shikarpur, etc., as *Seth* or *Bhai*; and there are Khatri families in Multán which are addressed as *Malik* or *Raizáda*.

Chapter III C.

Tribes, Castes and Leading Families.

Honorary titles.

Among Mahomedans the term *Malik* is applied to the chief men among the Khokhars, Vainses and some other clans. The Hirájs are called *Mahr* ; the Marrals, *Chaudhri* ; and the Aráíns, *Mullán*. The Núns, Utherás and Jakkhars retain the old Hindu title of *Rána*, and the Drigs, Lárs, Samejas and Mohánas the title of *Jám*. Patháns and Daúdpotrás are spoken of as *Khán Sáhib*, and Syads as *Sháh Sáhib*. Syads are also called *Pír*, and the Bhutta family of Khairpur is addressed as *Pírzáda*. The title *Nawáb* is applied sometimes by the people to members of prominent Pathán families, such as the Khákwánís and Bádozais ; but the only persons connected with the district who are entitled to this appellation are Nawáb Alladád Khan Saddozai and Nawáb Rabnawáz Khan Alizai, both of whom live in Dera Ismail Khan. The title *Makhdúm* is applied to the actual guardians of the shrines of Baháwal Hakk, Sher Shah, Shah Yusaf Gardezi, Sultán Ahmad Kattál and Músa Pák Shahíd, and it is sometimes extended to one or two of their immediate relations. The title is one of considerable honour, and its use is jealously reserved by those who are traditionally authorized to enjoy it.

Darbáris.

The following is a list of the Raises in the district who in June 1902 had places assigned to them in the Provincial or Divisional Darbárs :—

Provincial Darbaris of the Multan district.

1. Makhdúm Hassan Bakhsh, Koreshi of Multán.
2. Mahomed Yár Khan, Khákwáni, Pathán of Multan.
3. Makhdúm Sadr-ud-dín Shah, Syad of Multán.
4. Ashik Mahomed Khan, Badozai, Pathán of Multán.
5. Haidar Shah Gardezi, Syad of Salárwáhan.
6. Diwán Sultan Ahmad of Jalálpur Pírwála.

The following being Honorary Magistrates were entitled to a seat in the Lieutenant-Governor's Darbár by virtue of their office :—

1. Lala Netsi Das.
2. Makhdúm Shekh Rájú.
3. Lala Shiva Rám.
4. Mahomed Yár Khan.
5. Raizáda Ram Chand.
6. Syad Hassan Bakhsh, Gardezi, Khan Bahádur.

(Nos. 1–6: Multán City.)

7. Makhdúm Hassan Bakhsh.
8. Lala Tola Rám.
9. Syad Ghulám Rasúl Shah, Kuranga.
10. Shekh Riáz Hussain, Honorary Extra Assistant Commissioner.
11. Mahar Allayár, Honorary Magistrate.
12. Khan Bahádur Rabnawáz Khan, Multán.
13. Diwán Sultán Ahmad, Jalálpur, Pírwála.

Chapter III C.

Tribes Castes and Leading Families.

Leading families.

The following were entitled to a seat in Divisional Darbárs :—

Divisional Darbáris.

1. Shekh Riáz Husain, Koreshi of Multán.
2. Makhdúm Shekh Rájú, Gardezi of Multán.
3. Syad Hámid Shah, Gardezi, Syad of Multán (dead).
4. Rabnawáz Khan, Khákwání of Multán.
5. Khan Bahadur Hassan Bakhsh, Gardezi Syad, of Multán.
6. Munshi Asa Nand, Bagai of Multán, retired Extra Assistant Commissioner.
7. Zulfikár Shah, Gardezi of Multán.
8. Núr Mahomed Khán, Khuddaka Pathán, of Multán.
9. Mahomed Afzal Khan, Khákwáni Pathán, of Multán.
10. Diwán Sultán Ahmad, Syad of Jalálpur.
11. Mubárak Ali Shah, Syad of Sher Shah.
12. Faizullah Shah, Koreshi of Ghauspur.
13. Syad Habibullah Shah, Syad of Baghdád.
14. Ghulám Rasúl, Bhutta of Khairpur.
15. Mahomed Bakhsh, Bhutta of Khairpur.
16. Risáldar Ghulám Haidar Khán, Bábar Pathán of Multán.
17. Máchia, Langriál of Kamánd.
18. Mahar Allah Yar Hiráj of Chauki Mahan.
19. Lál Khán, Langah of Shujaátpur.
20. Seth Tek Chand, Shikarpuri of Multán.
21. Cháudhri Asa Nand of Shujabad.
22. Ghulám Rasúl Shah, Syad of Kuranga.
23. Ináyat Khan Sargána of Kund Sargána.
24. Karm Khán, Daha of Khanewál.
25. Malik Faiz Bakhsh, Khokhar.
26. Sirdár Sháh of Ghauspur.

The following have been approved by the Commissioner as entitled to the courtesy of a chair :—

Kursi Nashins.

1. Seth Gopál Sahai of Multán.
2. Ghulám Mahomed Khán, Daulatána of Luddan.
3. Seth Hákim Rai, Tálwar of Multan.
4. Maulvi Shams-ud-din, Koreshi of Multán.
5. Mahomed Makbúl, Bhutta of Khairpur.
6. Dost Mahomed Khan, Khákwáni, Durpur.
7. Chaudhri Shám Singh, Chawla, of Shujabad.
8. Khálikdád Khán, Pathán of Núrgarh.
9. Chaudhri Ram Kishán, of Sikandrabad.
10. Taj Mahmúd, Záildar of Boróna.

11. Ghulám Kádar Khan, Daulatána, Zaildár of Luddan.
12. Chaudhri Narain Singh of Shujabad.
13. Mahmúd Shah of Thath Ghalwán.

Leading families.

It is impossible to give an account of all the persons included in the above lists. Below, however, will be found a brief description of the more prominent of these, as well as some other families well known in the district. The families described are :—

The Syads.	The Hirájs of Chauki Multan.
The Koreshís.	The Khokhars.
The Bhuttas of Khairpur.	The Babla Chaudhrís of Shujabad.
The Patháns.	

The Syad families.

The traditional genealogical connection of the chief Syad families of the district is shown in the following table :—

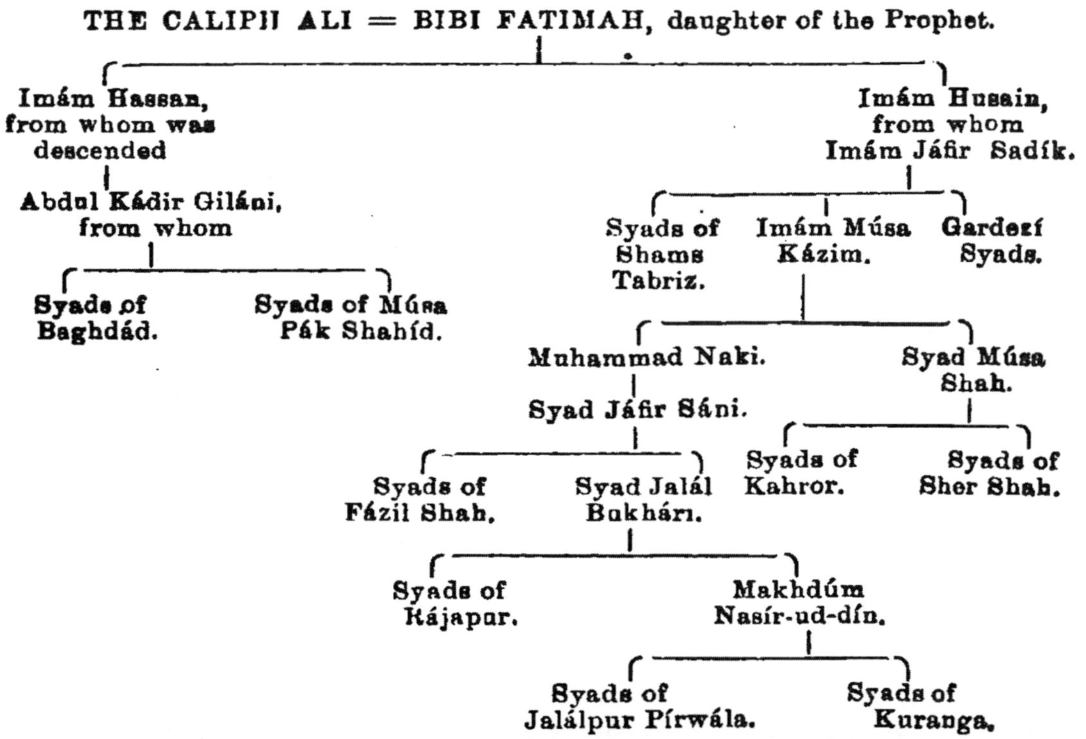

The above table includes ten separate families, some of whom possess considerable wealth, while others have little income beyond the precarious offerings of their disciples. In the following account they are taken in their genealogical order :—

i.—*The Baghdád Syads.*—The immediate ancestor of this branch was Sháh Habíb, who is said to have immigrated from Baghdád some three hundred years ago, and to have founded the village of Baghdád at the commencement of the Sidhnai reach in Kabírwala, where his shrine is still extant and forms the centre of a considerable fair in the month of August. His descendants once possessed considerable jágírs, but these were

Chapter III, C.

Tribes, Castes and Leading Families.

The Syad families.

resumed in the Nawábs' time, and they now hold only a small grant in their own village, outside of which they are little known. Their present representative, Syad Habíbulla Sháh, retains, however, a right to a seat as a Divisional Darbárí.

ii.—*The Syads of Músa Pák Shahíd.*—This family, like that above described, is known as Husan Husainí or Gílání. The latter name is derived from Gílán, the province in Persiá from which their ancestor Abdul Kádir, otherwise known as Pírán Pír, sprung; and although some point to the common use of the title Shekh among their ancestors and deny their claims to be Syads, they are generally looked upon and addressed as Syads in this district. Shekh Jahán Bakhsh *alias* Shekh Muhammad Ghaus, tenth in descent from Abdul Kádir, migrated from Baghdád to Uchh in the middle of the fifteenth century, and his son was the Músa Pák Shahíd, of whom an account has been given in Chapter VI, below. The descent of the family is shown in the following table :—

MUSA PAK SHAHID.

- Hámid Ganj Bakhsh.
  - Syad Músa Pák Dín.
    - Shekh Abdul Kádir, from whom in the ninth generation the present Makhdúm Sadr-ud-dín Shah.
      - Ghulám Yasin Shah.
      - Mustafa Shah.
      - Muhabbati Shah.
      - Murtaza Shah
    - Hámid Jahán Bakhsh, from whom in the fifth generation Makhdúm Hámid Shah.
      - M. Shams-ud dín Shah.
        - M. Hámid Shah.
      - Abdul Kádir Shah.
        - Alla Bakhsh Shah.
- Syad Bakshi.
- Inayat Wiláyat.
- Ján Muhammad.

There is considerable dispute between the two branches of the family, as to whether Shekh Abdul Kádir or Hámid Jahán Bakhsh was the elder son of Músa Pák Dín. The former branch of the family is in possession of the main shrine, but both branches hold jágírs—the former in Háfizwala and the latter in Lár, Chak, Mubárikpur and Gáwen. Makhdúm Sadr-úd-din Shah, the head of the former branch, is a Provincial Darbári. In this branch of the family the Makhdúms take in succession the three names of Hámid Ganj Bakhsh, Muhammad Abdul Kádír and Muhammad Ghaus; the present Makhdúm's official title is Makhdúm Muhammad Ghaus.

Chapter III, C.

Tribes, Castes and Leading Families.

The Syad families

iii.—*The Syads of Shams Tabriz.*—The origin of this family is traced to the saint Shams Tabriz, whose blue-domed shrine lies outside the city of Multán near the tahsíl. An account of the saint and his shrine is given in Chapter VI below. His descendants are the custodians of the shrine : they are Shías, and their present head is Isan Shah.

iv.—*The Syads of Fázil Shah.*—This branch of the family, like the last, is not of any great consequence. Their immediate ancestor, Hisám-ud-dín, came from Bokhára to Uchh, where he is buried. His son Násir-ud-dín immigrated to Nawábpur in the Multán tahsíl, and the family lived there for some time : in fact, some of his descendants still live there and in the villages near. His great-grandsons, Fázil Shah and Dost Muhammad, came from Nawabpur to the Kabírwala tahsíl, where they founded the villages of Fázil Shah and Muhammad Shah. Fázil Shah became a fakír and a disciple of the Syad of Kot Adu in Muzaffargarh, but his shrine is in his own village. His disciples are numerous, but the family hold no jágírs. The late lambardár of Fázil Shah, Rájan Bakhsh, was a well-behaved and influential landowner.

v.—*The Syads of Rájapur.*—These, like the Syads of Jalálpur and Kuranga, trace their descent to Syad Jalál Bukhari, who is said to have come from Bukhára to Uchh in A. D. 1235 and to have died in A. D. 1283. Mírán Syad Ghulám Ali, a descendant of his eldest son, migrated to Rájapur near Lodhrán, where his descendants have lived in obscurity ever since. Amir Haidar Shah, the present representative of the family, was once a zaildár, but his conduct necessitated his retirement into private life.

vi.—*The Syads of Jalálpur Pírwála.*—These are descended, like the last, from Syad Jalál Bukhári, but their immediate ancestor was Syad Sultán Ahmad Kattál, of whom an account has been given in the description of the town of Jalálpur in Chapter VI below. He left three sons, Syad Ibn-ud-dín, Shekh Alam Pír and Diwán Shah Ismail. The eldest settled at Alipur, near Jalálpur, and his descendant, Abdul Hádi Shah, died as lately as 1900 A.D. The other two brothers remained in Jalalpur, and the elder called the younger his Diwán. The younger branch has become extinct in the male line, but the daughter of the last Diwán married the representative of the elder branch. Their son was Shekh Muhammad Ghaus, who died in 1898, and who called himself Díwán Muhammad Ghaus to commemorate the union of the two branches of the family. His son Díwan Sultán Ahmad, a comparatively young man, is the present head of the family, and has married into the family of Diwan Abdul Hádí, so that he practically represents all the three sons of the original Sultán Ahmad Kattál. The members of the

Chapter III C.

Tribes, Castes and Leading Families.

The Syad families.

family are the hereditary guardians of the Jalálpur shrine, and assume in alternate generations the name of Muhammad Ghaus and Sultán Ahmad. They are held in considerable respect in the neighbourhood on account of their saintly descent, and have a good deal of influence in Muzaffargarh and Baháwalpur, as well as in this district. Sultán Ahmad holds no jagirs in this district, but is a zaildár both in Multán and in Muzaffargarh and is a Provincial Darbari and Honorary Magistrate.

SULTAN AHMAD KATTAL.

Alam Pír, from whom in the 7th generation Díwán Muhammad Ghaus died 1898; M. dter. of Syad Hassan Bakhsh.	Ilm-ud-din, from whom in the 8th generation Syad Hassan Bakhsh.
Díwan Sultán Ahmad.	Díwan Abdul Hádi Sháh died 1900 without male issue.
Ghulám Rasúl.	

vii.—*The Syads of Kuranga.*—The family are descended from Syad Ismail, who immigrated from Uchh to Chiniot. His descendants subsequently entered the country immediately north of the Rávi, and, after halting for some time at Pír Mahal, settled at Katálpur and Kuranga in the north-west corner of the district. Mehr Shah, a man of great influence, owned considerable tracts of land in the north of the tahsil, and was succeeded some twelve years ago by his son Pír Ghulám Rasúl Sháh, who is a zaildár and an Honorary Magistrate. He holds a grant of land on the Chenáb canal, considerable grants on the Sidhnai system, and half of a lease near Tulamba, as well as a good deal of property scattered through the Rávi tract.

viii.—*The Syads of Kahror.*—This family is descended from a branch of the Syads who lived for a long time at Mashhad. It is said that a dispute arose between two brothers, Háji Fakír-ud-dín and Syad Muhammad Shah, regarding the possession of certain relics of the Prophet, which were then carefully preserved in a chest, and it was agreed that whoever could open the chest should take them. Háji Fakír-ud-dín succeeded in doing so, and from this his descendants have taken the name of Kufálís (sc. Kuflálís). Fearing the enmity of his brother, he left Mashhad and came to Multán, where he is buried near the Bohar Gate. Five generations after this, his descendant, Syad Muhammad Zinda Pír accompanied the great Rukn-i-Alam on an 'itineration' to Kahror, where they converted the Joyas. The descendants of Zinda Pír have a certain amount of landed property in the neighbourhood of Kahror, and are at present represented by Syad Násir Shah, who is zaildár, and member of the

The Syad families.

District Board. The following shows the present members of the family:—

MUHAMMAD SHAH.

- Roshan Sháh.
  - Muhammad Sháh.
    - Waláyat Sháh.
      - Ghulám Sháh.
        - Muhammad Sháh.
          - Altáf Husain.
        - Sháh. Nawáz.*
      - Hámid Sháh.
        - Roshan Sháh.
- Nizám Sháh.
  - Ahmad Sháh.
    - Fateh Sháh.
      - Násir Sháh.
        - Ahmad Sháh.
        - Akbar Sháh.
        - Riáz Hussain.
      - Nizám Sháh.
        - Abbás Sháh.

ix.—*The Syads of Sher Sháh.*—This family, like the last, had its origin in Mashhad, from which its immediate ancestor, Sháh Ali Muhammad, migrated in 1533 A.D. to Uchh, where he enrolled himself as a disciple of Makhdúm Muhammad Ghaus, father of Músa Pák Shahíd. He afterwards moved on to the present village of Sher Sháh, then called Ratanwáhan and held by the Hammar Jats. His shrine is at Sher Sháh, the residence of the present Makhdúm. It is well endowed with jágírs, and has a large annual fair in its honour in the month of Chet. The late Makhdúm who died in 1901 had held that position ever since annexation, and was an old man of exceedingly refined appearance and gentlemanly manners. He had, however, suffered a good deal from family dissensions, and his expensive tastes had led to his estate being brought under the Court of Wards. His family is as follows:—

MAKHDUM SHAH ALI MUHAMMAD.

- (By elder wife).
  - Syad Mubárik Sháh, born about 1845. Lives in Jhang District.
- (By younger wife).
  - Syad Pír Sháh, born about 1879.
  - Syad Amír Sháh born about 1881.

The question of the succession to the 'gaddi' is still (June 1902) in dispute between Mubárik Sháh and Pír Sháh.

x.—*The Gardezi Syads.*—The Gardezi Syads were once the most wealthy and influential in the district, and owned nearly the whole of the part of the Kabírwála tahsil through

Chapter III, C.

Tribes, Castes and Leading Families.

The Syad families.

which the Lahore road now passes. The comparative ruin of that part of the country, owing to the change in the course of the Rávi, has led to their decay, but they still possess a very considerable influence and position. They are also known as Husainís, from their descent from Imám Husain and their attachment to the Shiah faith. The family formerly lived at Baghdád, and they were then known as 'Baghdádi.' Their immediate ancestor was Syad Muhammad Dibal, great-great-grandson of Imám Husain. It was his son, Syad Muhammad Ali, who migrated from their original home at Medina to Baghdád. His great-grandson, Abdullah, removed from Baghdád to Gardez, and his great-grandson again, Shekh Muhammad Yusaf, who was born at Gardez in A.H. 450 (A.D. 1058), made a further move to Multán in A.H. 481 (A.D. 1088). He immediately acquired great reputation for sanctity and miracles, and received large grants of land. He died in A.H. 531 (1137 A.D.) Shekh Muhammad Yusaf the Second, eighth in descent from his namesake, died without male issue, and his daughter married Makhdúm Syad Muziz-ud-dín, a descendant of Zaid Shahíd, another grandson of the Imám Husain. Hence the family are sometimes called Zaidis. Most of the Gardezi jágírs were resumed by the Sikhs, but large estates are still held by various branches of the family. The chief of these branches are the following;—(*a*) In Multán the family of Makhdúm Shekh Rájú, the head of the family, who is an Honorary Magistrate, and much respected in the city for his uprightness and generosity. His brother, Amír Haidar Sháh, lives a good deal in Amírpur in the Kabírwála tahsil, where he is held in considerable esteem : he is a careful and intelligent agriculturist. (*b*) In Korai Biloch, in the Kabírwála tahsil, there is a group, of whom the most important member was Murád Sháh, at one time Chief Judge of Baháwalpur. Murád Sháh died some years ago, and his son, Hassan Bakhsh, resides in Multan, where he is an Honorary Magistrate, and has been Vice-President of the Municipal Committee : he is a Khan Bahádur and has a seat in the Divisional Darbár. Hassan Bakhsh is a gentleman of considerable education, literary tastes and good manners, and he has travelled a good deal in Persia and elsewhere. (*c*) In Salárwáhan Kohna in Kabírwála there is a branch of the Gardezís headed by Haidar Sháh, an old and much respected zaildár. (*d*) In Multan there is another family, at one time represented by Hámid Sháh, a portentous spendthrift, who in the course of his life absolutely ruined a magnificent series of estates, most of which fell into the hands of Rai Mela Rám, contractor, of Lahore. Hámid Sháh died without male issue in August 1900, and his brother, Fatteh Sháh, now represents this branch of the family. (*e*) At Adamwáhan there is another branch, in somewhat reduced circumstances, now represented by Ahmad Sháh, son of Muhammad Sháh, late zaildar. (*f*) There is also a small branch at Murádpur, between Kahror and Mailsi, headed by Mustafa Sháh, a man who has known better days and was once zaildar, but is now an ordinary zamindar. Most of the Gardezi families are Shiahs.

Koreshi families.

There are two Koreshi families of repute in the district, that of the Makhdúm of the Baháwal Hakk shrine in Multan and that of Ghauspur in Kabírwála. They are both descended from the saint Bahawal Hakk, of whom an account has been given in Chapter VI below. In the sixth generation from the saint the family split into two branches : from the elder of these branches (which was founded by Shekh Yusaf, who was ruler of Multan in A.D. 1453-55), sprang the original race of Makhdúms, and also (from a subsequent division) the Koreshís of Baghdád. From the younger of the branches sprang the present Makhdúms, who succeeded to the gaddi by marriage on the failure of heirs in the original line in the first part of the nineteenth century. A full history of the family is given in Massy's "Punjab Chiefs."

The following table shows the relationships in the family of the present Makhdúms :—

SHEKH HASSAN SHAH.

- Makhdúm Sháh Mahmúd, died 1869.
  - Makhdúm Baháwal Bakhsh, died 1896 without heirs.
  - Makhdúm Hassan Bakhsh, born 1859.
    - Muríd Husain, born 1878.
    - Shekh Kabír, born 1880.
- Shekh Pír Sháh, died 1897.
  - Shekh Riáz Hussain.
    - Bhawan Sháh, born 1880.
      - Manzúr Hussain.
    - Wiláyat Husain, born 1881.
    - Murtaza Husain.
    - Pír Sháh.

The present Makhdúm, Hassan Bakhsh, has precedence of all other unofficial Viceregal Darbárís in the district, and is thus the 'premier peer' of Multan. He possesses land in various parts of the district, especially at Hitháran on the Sidhnai canal, and also has a grant on the Chenáb canal ; but is unfortunately a good deal involved in debt. His cousin, Shekh Riáz Husain, is an Honorary Extra Assistant Commissioner, who has done good service both in Multan and on the frontier : he has land in Kotla Abulfatteh, at Lohárwála, at Riázabad on the Sidhnai, and elsewhere. The family is much respected in the south-west of the Punjab and in Sindh as descendants of, and guardians of the shrine of, the saint Baháwal Hakk. The shrine enjoys considerable grants of revenue in Jalíl, Fatuhalpur, Lábar, and many other villages in this district.

Chapter III, C.

Tribes, Castes and Leading Families.

Koreshi families.

The Ghauspur branch of the family is shown in the following table :—

- SADR-UD-DIN.
  - Hyát Sháh.
    - Rukn-ud-dín Sháh, died 1900.
      - Sardár Sháh.
        - Muhammad Husain.
        - Barkhurdár.
        - Dost Ali.
    - Roshan Chirágh.
      - Irshád Ali.
      - Alladád.
    - Ibráhím Sháh.
      - Karm Sháh.
      - Rahím Sháh
      - Ata Husain Sháh.
  - Murád Sháh.
    - Ghulám Bahá-ud-din.
      - Madad Ali
      - Habíb Ulla.
    - Faiz-ulla Sháh.
      - Imám Sháh.
      - and 4 others.
    - Daulat Sháh.
      - Alla Ditta.
      - Abdul Hakk.

Both Hyát Sháh and Murád Sháh rendered valuable assistance to Government in 1857 and received suitable rewards. This branch of the family consists of fairly well-to-do, but not wealthy, zamindars, and its members do not affect the style or habits of raises.

The Bhuttas.

At Khairpur near the Multan cantonment, there is a family of Bhuttas who may, perhaps, be said to be in the transition stage towards becoming Syads. They came originally from the Chiniot tahsil of the Jhang district, and settled about a century ago in the neighbourhood of Muhammadpur Ghota, where the elder branch of the family, represented by Muhammad Bakhsh, now mainly reside. Amír Bakhsh, however, and after him his son Murád Bakhsh, obtained other lands also by sale and by grant from Government, and gradually accumulated a fine property in the village of Khairpur. Murád Bakhsh did good service in 1849 and 1857, and was generously rewarded. He was a pushing man, and dropped the appellation of Bhutta, substituting that of Pírzáda. He left a family of four sons, two (Ghulám Rásul and Muhammad Makbúl) by one wife, and two (Karim Bakhsh and Amír Bakhsh) by another. They are all intelligent and masterful men and good thrifty zamindars; but the two sets of brothers have not always got on well with each other. Ghulám Rasúl is a zaildar at Nurabba in Mailsi, where he has acquired a fair property, and he is a Divisional Darbári ; while Muhammad Makbul is a zaildar in Multan and entitled to a chair. Their cousin, Muhammad Bakhsh, is also a zaildar and

The Bhuttas.

Darbári, and the family, generally speaking, has provided well for itself. The relationships are shown as follows :—

AMIR BAKHSH.

- Chirágh Bakhsh.
  - Ghulám Sarwar.
    - Muhammad Bakhsh.
    - Maula Bakhsh.
    - Ghulám Murtaza.
    - Ahmad Bakhsh.
    - Muhammad Ibráhím.
    - Muhammad Ismail.
- Murád Bakhsh.
  - Ghulám Rasúl.
  - Muhammad Makbúl.
  - Karím Bakhsh.
  - Amír Bakhsh.

The Pathan families.

There are three well-known families of Pathans—the Khudakkas, the Bádozais and the Khákwánís—residing in the district, together with others of less note among the Bábars, Taríns and Bámozais. And there are certain other well-known families who, though not residing in Multan, own or used to own land or jágírs in the district, and are thus frequently brought to the notice of the District authorities, *viz.*, the descendants of the Saddozai Nawábs of Multan, the Nawábs of Dera, the Alizai family of Nawáb Faujdár Khan, the family of Nawáb Kalle Khan, the Saddozai family of Alla Bakhsh Khan of Dera Ghází Khan, and the Jáfir family of Khwája Alla Bakhsh of Taunsa.

Khudakkas.

The Khudakkas.—The ancestor of the Khudakkas was Khuda Dád Khan, the son of Khizar Khan, ancestor of the Khizar Khel, and the grandson of Saddu Khan, the founder of the Saddozai family. His descendant, Sultan Haiát Khan, being defeated by the Shah of Persia, came to Multan to obtain the help of the Emperor of Delhi. He was promised assistance and received a jágír of Rs. 15,000. He lived near the Shísh Mahal in Multan. He died in A.H. 1114 (A.D. 1702), and was succeeded by his son Bákar Khan, who died in A.H. 1173 (A.D. 1759). Bákar Khan was first succeeded by his brother Abdul Aziz Khan, whose descendants live in Dera Ismail Khan. On the death of Abdul Aziz Khan the succession reverted to Muhammad Sharíf Khan, son of Bákar Khan, who died in A.H. 1189 (A.D. 1775), and was succeeded by his son Dín Muhammad. Dín Muhammad restored Sultán Haiát's house, and made the family garden, which is still kept up. He died in A.H. 1221 (A.D. 1806), and was succeeded by his son Ali Muhammad Khan, an educated and cultivated man, who held a jagír of Rs. 3,000 in Multan and Rs. 2,000 in Dera Ghází Khan. His property was plundered on the taking of Multan, but Ranjít Singh gave him a jágír of Rs. 1,800 and a pension of Rs. 1,200. He died in A.H. 1256 (A.D. 1840), and was succeeded by his eldest son, Muhammad Bairám Khan, who was confirmed in his father's

Chapter III, C.

Tribes, Castes and Leading Families.

The Pathan families.

jagírs. On annexation half of the jágírs were resumed, and the remaining half converted into a cash pension; but Bairám Khan was taken into Government service and he was Tahsildar and Superintendent at the Regular Settlement. He made the pilgrimage to Mecca, and built a fine mosque at Multan. At the end of 1876 he divided his property amongst his sons and retired to Mecca for good. He was a man of very high character, but he kept rather himself in the background from the feeling that the fortune of the family was hardly equal to its descent. The family owns some land in Sadarpur in tahsil Multan and elsewhere. The only member of the family now holding a public position is Núr Muhammad Khan, who is Sub-Registrar in Multan city.

Badozais.

The Bádozai family.—So full an account of the family is given in "Punjab Chiefs" that it is only necessary to mention here the most prominent facts in its history. The first of its members to permanently settle in Multan was Muhabbat, whose father, Bai Khan, accompanied Nádir Sháh in his expedition of A.D. 1738. His great-grandson, Sháh Muhammad Khan, greatly distinguished himself in A.D. 1772 and 1779 in the service of the Nawábs of Multan, for which he was rewarded with a jagír in Dera Dinpanáh and Dera Ghází Khan. He was succeeded by his son, Muhammad Sarfaráz Khan, who was soon afterwards killed in battle, and left no issue. He, however, left two brothers, Abdul Samad Khan and Háfiz Muhammad Sarbuland Khan, who immediately began to quarrel about their inheritance. The ruler of Kabul, to whom they appealed, directed that it should be divided equally, but Sarbuland Khan could only succeed in obtaining the Multan estates. Sarbuland Khan was a faithful servant to the Multan Nawábs and afterwards of the Sikh Governor, and he was active and loyal throughout the campaign of 1848-49. He died in A.D. 1853, and was succeeded by his son, Sadik Muhammad Khan. Sadik Muhammad Khan was born in 1814, and was employed at an early age in important duties by Diwán Sáwan Mal. On the breaking out of Mulraj's rebellion, he distinguished himself by refusing the oath of allegiance to him, and he rendered signal service throughout the campaign, at the close of which he retired on a pension of Rs. 2,000 a year, besides receiving other substantial marks of Government's favour. He again came forward in A.D. 1857, and after the close of disturbances re-entered for a time Government service, acting as Tahsildar in the different tahsils of the Multan district. After he retired his pension was exchanged for a jágír, the most valuable portion of which was the village of Lutfabad, about eight miles from Multan. Sádik Muhammad Khan died in February 1883, and one-half of his jágír was continued for life to his second son, Ashik Muhammad Khan, as being the most worthy representative of the family. Ashik Muhammad Khan (who in popular parlance

Chapter III, C.

Tribes, Castes and Leading Families.

The Pathan families :

often receives the title of Nawáb) is a discreet, well educated man of literary tastes. He served for a time as a Naib Tahsildar but has for some time past lived a quiet life mainly in the city of Multan. He is a Provincial Darbári, being fifth on the district list. The members of the present family are shown below :—

SADIK MUHAMMAD KHAN, died 1883.

- Muhammad Sherdil Khan, born 1829.
  - Khuda Bakhsh, born 1873.
- Ashik Muhammad Khán, born 1850.
  - Abdul Kádir, born 1881.
  - Sháh Husain, born 1892.
- Dost Muhammad Khan, born 1849.
  - Sher Muhammad, born 1871.

(*See* also pp. 90—99, Volume II, Griffin's "Panjab Chiefs," new edition).

Khákwánís.

The Khákwáni family.—The Khákwánis say that they derive their name from Khákán, a village in the neighbourhood of Hirat*; others derive it from an incident connected with the hunting of the boar (khok). The first branch of the family to appear in Multan was that of Malik Sháh Pal, who with his brothers accompanied Hamáyún some four hundred years ago. His descendant, Ali Muhammad Khan, served under Ahmad Shah Abdáli, and was made Subadár of Multan, a post which he held till A.H. 1181 (A.D. 1767). It was he who constructed the Wali Muhammad canal. He was dismissed for oppression, but he refused the order deposing him, and seized and imprisoned Nawáb Shuja Khan, who had been appointed to succeed him : for this he was put to death by Ahmad Sháh. There are no descendants of this branch in Multan. The ancestor of the present Khákwánís was Lál Khan, who came from Ghazni some three hundred years ago. His son, Háji Ali Muhammad Khan, was Governor of Sikandarabad under Nawáb Muzaffar Khan. Mustafa Khan, the son of Háji Ali commenced his career in the Baháwalpur State, but he soon became one of Sáwan Mal's Kardárs, and on Mulraj's rebellion he took the side of the English and supported it to the utmost of his power. He again did good service in 1857, when he was Tahsildar of Mailsi. For this he received considerable grants of land and other rewards.

He died in 1869, and was succeeded by his son, Ghulám Kádir Khan, who followed in his father's footsteps as a loyal adherent of Government. Ghulám Kádir Khan completed the Hajiwah canal, which had been begun by his father, and in 1880 he was granted an area of 60,000 acres in proprietary right, subject to certain conditions which were embodied in a formal deed of grant executed in 1886. At his death in 1888, he left

---

* Elphinstone (Caubul ii, 99) speaks of the Khákwánís as a small clan living partly at Kandahar and partly mixed with the Nurzais.

Chapter III, C.

Tribes, Castes and Leading Families.

The Pathan families.

Khákwánis.

four sons—one, Muhammad Yár Khan by one mother, and the remaining three, Ahmad Yár Khan, Khuda Bakhsh Khan and Hámid Yar Khan, by another. The two sets of brothers immediately began to quarrel among themselves, and the canal was taken over by Government. All the brothers live in Multan, and enjoy very considerable wealth. Muhammad Yár Khan, the eldest, is a Provincial Darbári, and he has throughout the troubles about the canal looked to Government for protection from his brothers. He is a man of somewhat retired habits, with no taste for business. His younger brother, Ahmad Yár Khan, on the other hand, is a man of considerable intelligence who is fully alive to his own interests, and has spent considerable sums in suing Government for reparation in connection with the assumption of control over the canal. The genealogy of the family is shown below :—

- Muhammad Amín Khan.
  - A daughter = Ghulám Kádir Khan, died 1888 (see below).
  - A daughter = Hakúmat Khan.
    - Muhammad Afzal Khán.
    - Muhammad Aslam Khan.
- Ghulám Mustafa Khan, died 1869.
  - Ghulám Kádir Khan, died 1888 (= A daughter of Muhammad Amín Khan).
    - By first wife.
      - A daughter = Khwája Alla Bakhsh Khan of Taunsa.
        - Mian Mahmúd Khan.
      - Muhammad Yár Khan.
        - 3 children. 1 Ghulám Muhammad Khan. 2 Ata Md. Khan. 3 Faiz Md. Khan.
    - By second wife.
      - Ahmad Yár Khan.
        - 4 children. 1 Faiz Md. Khan. 2 Dost Md. Khan. 3 Ata Md. Khan. 4 Dur Md. Khan.
      - Hafiz Khuda Bakhsh Khan.
        - 3 children. 1 Abdul Karím Khan. 2 Muhammad Aslam Khan. 3 Alla Wasaya Khan.
      - Háfis Hámid Yár Khan.
      - A daughter = Abdulla Khan Khákwáni.
  - A daughter = Abdurrahmán Khan Khákwáni.
    - Rabnawáz Khan.
      - Abdul-Kádir Khan.
    - Abdulla Khan.

Considerable areas on the Hájiwáh canal were bestowed by gift on his relations by Ghulám Kádir Khan; and are now held by Mián Mahmúd Khan and Muhammad Afzal Khan.

A second cousin of Ghulám Kádir Khan, named Ata Muhammad Khan, owned lands at Durpur near Tibba in the Mailsi tahsil. His son, Dost Muhammad Khan, is zaildar in this tract and lives the life of an ordinary landowner. He is a man of considerable energy and intelligence, and enjoys

The Pathan families.

the privilege of a chair. This branch of the Khákwánís are Shias: the Hájiwáh branch being Sunnís.

Another member of the same family, Muhammad Rabnawâz Khan (shown in the above table), has, along with his brother, considerable landed property in Jhok Gámun near Kasba in the Multan tahsil.

Bábars.

The Bábar families.—Amongst the Afghans of lesser note are four families of the Bábar clan. (i) The first is that now represented by Fattehulla Khan. His grandfather, Muhammad Yár Khan, took service under Nawáb Sarfaráz Khan, but on the capture of Multan by the Sikhs retired to Mánkera and entered the service of the Nawáb of that place. Muhammad Yár Khan's son, Ghulám Haidar Khan, on the taking of Dera Ismail Khan, first went to Sindh, but eventually took service under Sáwan Mal, on whose death he went to Bahâwalpur. On annexation he joined a cavalry regiment as jamadar, and was promoted to rasáldár for his services in 1857. On his retirement he soon afterwards received a pension of Rs. 300 a year and a lease of five hundred acres near Chauki Sobha Khan in Mailsi. He died at a ripe old age in 1900. His son, Fattehulla Khan, is somewhat afflicted in mind, and his grandson, Habíbulla, is not likely to maintain the prestige of the family. (ii) Another branch, represented by Khalikdád Khan, Tagge Khan and others, lives at Khángarh in the Muzaffargarh district, but also owns land at Nurgarh near Tibba. Their ancestor, Abdul Karím Khan, came with Ahmad Shah and acquired considerable estates in Multan and Muzaffargarh, which they lost at the Sikh conquest, but partially recovered under British rule. (iii) Another branch, now represented by Khan Bahadur Rabnawaz Khan, came to Multan in the time of Shuja Khan, and, like the branch above described, owns most of its land in Muzaffargarh. Haknawáz Khan was a rasáldár in the 5th Bengal Lancers, and his son, Rabnawáz Khan, after serving in the same regiment and doing excellent political work on the Turkistan border, was made Assistant Political Agent in Chitral, and retired in 1898 covered with wounds and decorations. He was in 1900 granted one hundred and thirty acres of land on the Sidhnai canal, and now resides in Multan, where he is an Honorary Magistrate.

Tarins.

There are a few families of the *Tarín* tribe, but none of them are of any great mark. One of them is that of three brothers—Habíb-ulla Khan, Hyát-ulla Khan and Faujdár Khan—who own land in Akbarpur and Umarpur of tahsil Multan and Hyátpur of tahsíl Kabírwála; their ancestor came to Multan from Kandahar as a merchant in the time of Ahmad Sháh. The other is that of Ahmad Yár Khan, of Wahi Daúd Khan in Lodhrán. Another Tarín family lives at Siddha near Gelewála in Lodhrán, and another at Cháhán Míráu Khan in Shujabad. The only remaining Afghan family of any position is that of Rahmat-ulla Khan *Bámozai*. His ancestor, Abdul

Bamozais.

Chapter III C.

Tribes, Castes and Leading Families.

The Pathan families:

Bámozais.

Karim Khan, came from Khorasan in the time of Ahmad Shah; two of his sons settled in Dera Ismail Khan, and the third, the ancestor of Rahmat-ulla Khan, in Multan. The Multan branch prospered, and is said to have acquired ten villages in Multan and fifteen in Muzaffargarh, but it lost them all at the Sikh conquest, and at annexation it only succeeded in recovering in Multan the villages of Kachur and Basti Nau. The lands in Basti Nau have been since lost.

Outside Pathan families:

Nawábs of Multan.

In addition to the families resident in the district, there are, as above noted, certain Pathan families connected, historically or otherwise, with Multan, of whom a short notice here may be useful, *viz.*, (i) the family of the Nawábs of Multan, (ii) the Nawábs of Dera, and (iii) the family of Nawáb Faujdár Khan.

The family of the Saddozai Nawábs of Multan have now no connection, direct or indirect, with the district, and they live mainly in Lahore, to which the family retired after the catastrophe of A.D. 1818 (see Chapter II, above). The genealogy of the present members is:—

- NAWAB ZAHID KHAN, died 1749.
  - Nawáb Shuja Khan, died 1776.
    - Nawáb Muzaffar Khan, died 1818.
      - Nawáb Sarfaráz Khan, died 1851.
        - Firozdin Khan died 1855.
          - Kásim Ali Khan.
            - Azam Ali Khan.
              - Four sons.
          - Sádik Ali Khan.
            - Barkat Ali Khan, born 1887.
        - Ahmad Ali Khan, died 1884.
          - Sádat Ali Khan, born 1878.
          - Muzaffar Khan, born 1882.
      - Zulfikár Khan, died 1847.
        - Muhammad Khan, died 1861.
          - Yusaf Ali Khan, born 1860.
            - Five sons.
        - Khan Ahmad Yár Khan, died 1899.
          - Muhammad Akbar Khan, born 1859.
            - Ináyat-ulla Khan, born 1875.
      - Shahnawáz Khan, died 1818.
        - Nawáb Abdul Majid Khan, died 1890.
      - Haknawáz Khan, died 1818.
        - Rabnawáz Khan, born 1830.
          - Wazir Khan, born 1839.
            - Alla Ditta Khan.
            - Abdurrahmán Khan.
      - And four others.

Chapter III C.

Tribes Castes and Leading Families.

Outside Pathan families:

Nawábs of Multan.

Of the above, Nawáb Abdul Majíd Khan, C.S.I, was a much respected and loyal gentleman, who served for some time as Vice-President of the Lahore Municipal Committee. Several members of the family draw political pensions from Government, and some from the Baháwalpur State, where some branches of the family reside. A few have studied in the Chiefs' College at Lahore. and one Ináyat-ulla Khan, is Názir in the Commissioner's office at Lahore. (A full account of this family will be found at page 73 *seqq.* of Griffin's "Punjab Chiefs" new edition, Volume I).

Nawábs of Dera.

The family of Nawáb Alladád Khan, Saddozai, is decended from a cousin of Nawáb Muzaffar Khan of Multan, and this family held the whole country round Dera Ismail Khan until Sikh times. Nawáb Sarfaráz Khan rendered many useful services to Government on the frontier, and his son Alladád Khan, the present head of the family, was for many years an Extra Assistant Commissioner. This family own large jagirs in Firozpur, Jakkharpur and other villages of the Multan tahsil. The following are the present members:—

NAWAB SARFARAZ KHAN, C.S.I., died 1889.

- Nawáb Alladád Khan, born 1843.
  - Ahmad Nawáz Khan, born 1879.
  - Haknawáz Khan, born 1884.
- Hakdád Khan, born 1850.
  - Muhammad Khan, born 1877.
  - Muhammad Hyát Khan, born 1886.
- Abdul Rahmán Khan, born 1876.
  - Abdul Jabar Khan, born 1894.
- Ghulám Kádír Khan, dead.
- Abdulla Khan, died 1878.
  - Ahmad Khan, born 1876.

Family of Faujdár Khan.

The Alizai family owes its present position to the excellent services rendered by Nawáb Faujdár Khan as Assistant to Major Edwards in the war of 1848 and as our representative at Kabul during the mutiny. The present Nawáb, Rabnawáz Khan, served during the mutiny in the Multani Horse, and afterwards held the posts of Inspector and Assistant District Superintendent of Police. His brother, Muhammad Nawáz Khan, a risáldár in the XVth Bengal Lancers, was appointed in 1900 to serve as our representative at Kabul. The family has jágírs and property in Bákirpur, Bíbípur and elsewhere in the Multan tahsil; but with the exception of Muhammad Nawáz Khan they are a good deal involved in debt. Muizz-ud-din Khan, son of Nawáb Kalle Khan, who is a risáldár in the XVth Bengal Lancers, and holds part of a grant of land in Bahádurpur in

Chapter III. C.

Tribes, Castes and Leading Families.

Outside Pathan families :

Family of Faujdár Khan.

tahsil Shujabad, is nearly connected with this family. The following table shows the present descendants of Nawáb Faujdár Khan* :—

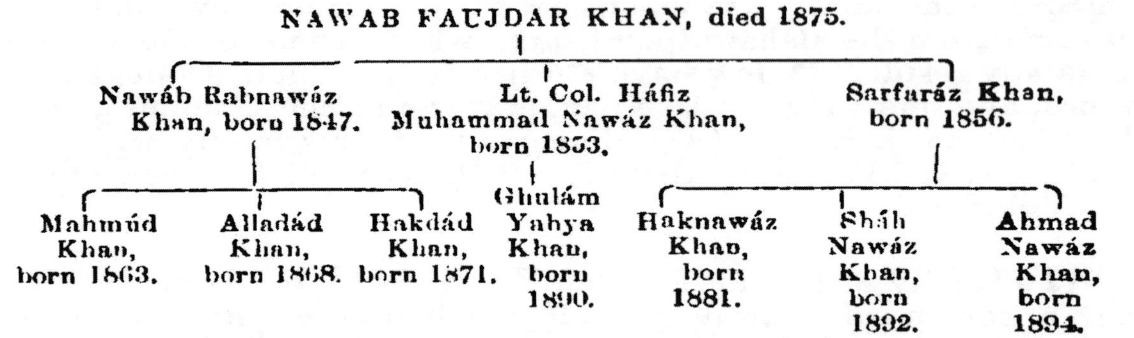

The Hirájs of Chauki Múhan.

The Hirájs of Chauki Múhan, an offshoot of the Siáls, came into prominence under Sultán Hiráj, a zaildar and large cattle owner of the last generation. Sultan gave good assistance to Government in connection with the transport required for the Afghan war of 1879-80, and was liberally rewarded with grants of land. He has been succeeded by his son Alla Yár, who during the famine of 1899-1900 held an honorary post under Government in the Hissár district and is now an Honorary Magistrate. The family is a large one, and there are sometimes disputes between the members, which the following table may help to elucidate. Bahádur, the senior representative is a wealthy land and cattle-owner and a member of the District Board.

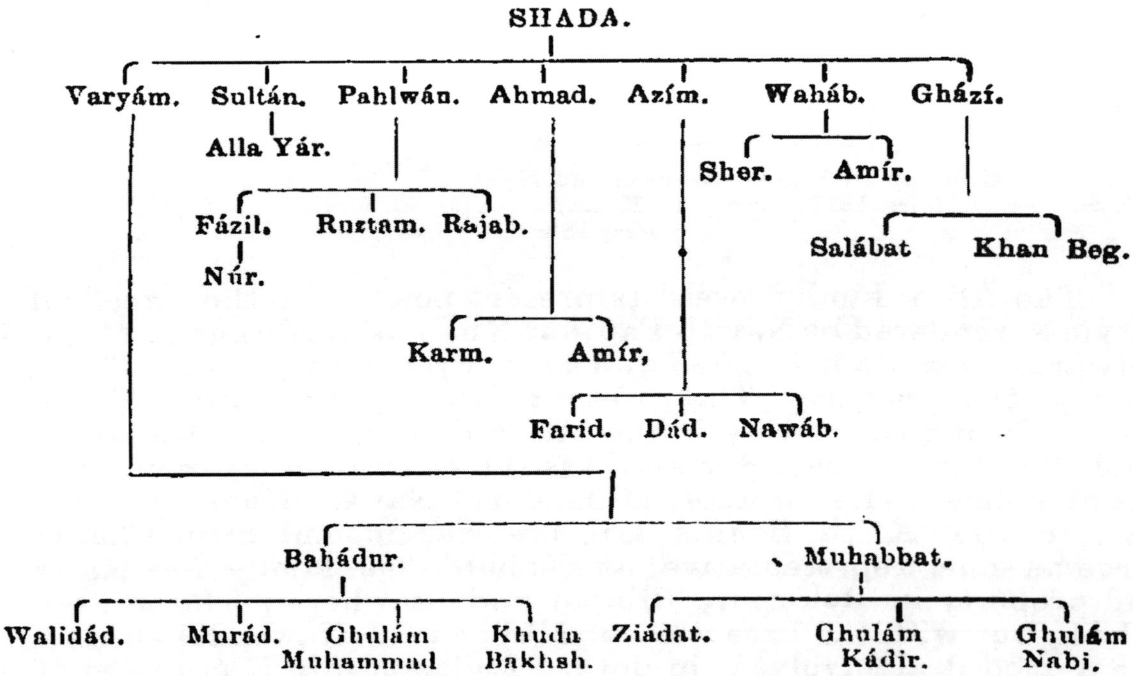

* For a more detailed account of the Saddozai and Alizai families, see pp. 531—571 of Massy's "Chiefs and Families of note in the Punjab" (1890).

The first of the Khokhar family to come into Multan was Básí, who founded Balel in the time of Hamáyun, and subsequently other villages in its neighbourhood. Under the Moghals the family extended their estates very considerably, but they lost them nearly all under the Pathán Nawábs. In the time of Ranjít Singh, Malik Piára, father of Malik Umr Ali, by giving through Sardár Hari Singh, Nárua, a nazrana of Rs. 3,000 and two horses, obtained an order for the restoration of all the villages the Khokhars had held under the Moghals, and in accordance with it he recovered several estates. But it was pointed out by the local officers that if the orders were fully carried out it would create a revolution; consequently an amended order was passed that the Khokhars were to retain the estates they had already recovered, but that the work of restoration was to go no further. They thus retained the villages they still hold. The descent of the family from Malik Piara is as follows:—

MALIK PIARA.

- Umr Ali, died 1873.
  - Khuda Bakhsh, died 1898.
    - Faiz Bakhsh.
  - Alla Bakhsh, died 1899.
    - Kádir Bakhsh.
    - Baháwal Bakhsh.
      - Subah Sádik.
  - Sultán Bakhsh.
    - Rahim Bakhsh.
      - Wáhid Bakhsh.
        - Karím Bakhsh.
        - Hassan Bakhsh.
  - Karím Bakhsh.
    - Rahím Bakhsh.
  - Amir Bakhsh.
    - Nasír Bakhsh.
  - Muhammad Bakhsh.
    - Ahmad Bakhsh.
  - Kádir Bakhsh.
- Háji.
- Nijábat.
  - Iláhí Bakhsh.

Umr Ali was a man of energy and intelligence, and rendered good services both in 1849 and in 1857. His sons were by three wives—the eldest three by the first wife, Karím Bakhsh and Amír Bakhsh by the second and the two youngest by the third. At the Settlement of 1880 Khuda Bakhsh, Alla Bakhsh Karím Bakhsh and Iláhí Bakhsh were all made zaildars, the villages of the south of the Multan and the north of the Shujabad tahsil being parcelled out among them. The only zaildar in the family now is Karím Bakhsh. Khuda

Chapter III, C.

Tribes, Castes and Leading Families.

The Khokhars.

Bakhsh received from Government a special inám of Rs. 270 per annum, of which Rs. 200 have been continued to Faiz Bakhsh. Iláhí Bakhsh also holds a small inám in consideration of the reduction of his zail in 1900. The members of this family are for the most part intelligent, prosperous men, and good zamindars, and they are very frequently under the notice of district officers. Unfortunately there is a good deal of smouldering dissension among them, which every now and then breaks out into open quarrelling.

The Babla Chaudhris.

The chief Hindu family of the district is that of the Babla Chaudhrís of Shujabad. Their late genealogy runs as follows :—

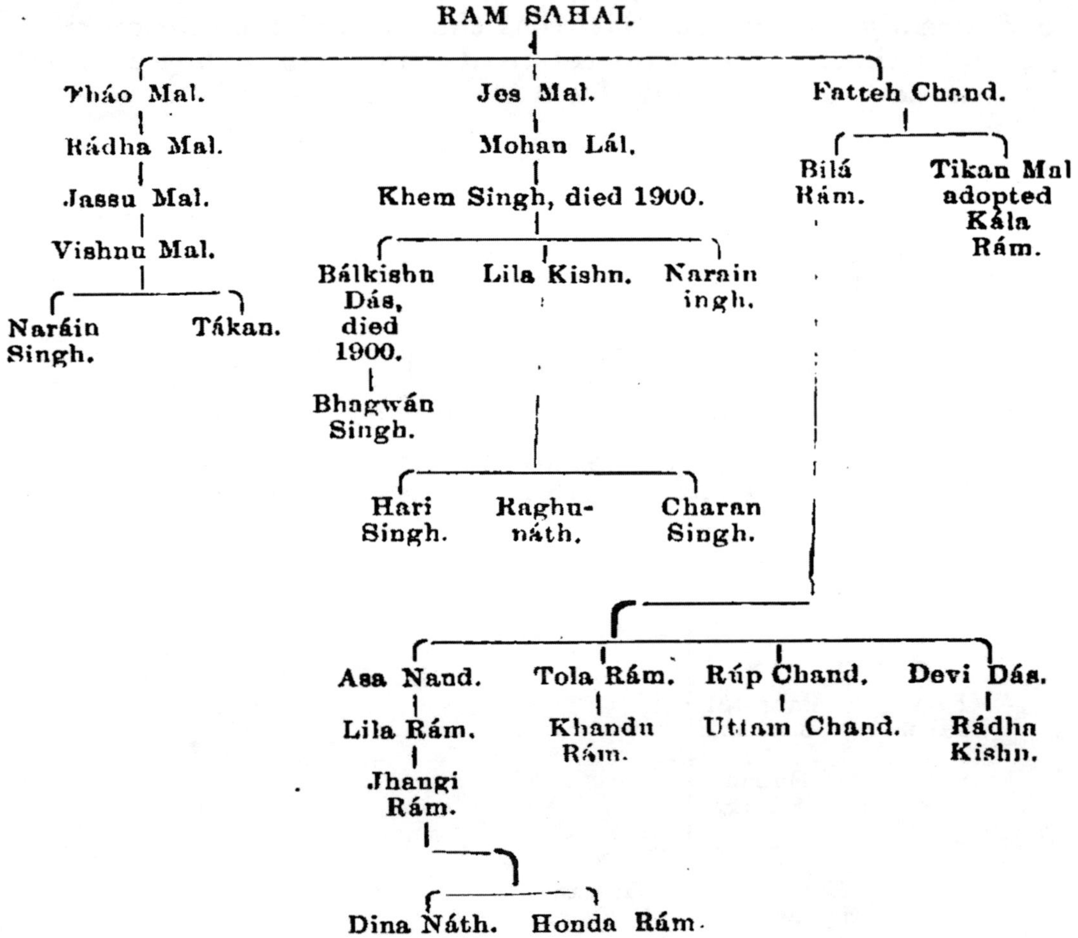

This family owns a large amount of landed property, chiefly in the north of Shujabad, and its members are, for the most part, shrewd, intelligent and exacting landlords. The late head of the family, Chaudhri Khem Singh, was a Provincial Darbári and enjoyed a special inám of Rs. 200 per annum which has been continued to his grandson Bhagwán Singh. The most prominent members of the family after Khem Singh are Asa Nand and Hoa Rám, of whom the former is comparatively nearly related to Khem Singh, and the latter is a more distant connection.

SECTION D.—VILLAGE COMMUNITIES AND TENURES.

Chapter III, D.

Village Communities and Tenures.

The village community in Multan.

In the case of the greater number of the villages of the district, the village community, in the ordinary acceptation of the term, can scarcely be said to exist; they being for the most part mere aggregations into a fiscal circle of independent plots of cultivation, having no further bond of union than that of joint responsibility for the revenue imposed by the British Settlement system. Of this nature are all the estates of the interior. In the immediate neighbourhood of the rivers, communities are found which fall naturally under the definitions applied to the upper part of the province. In the remainder of the district cultivation is found only where wells have been sunk or means provided for canal irrigation, and is therefore scattered for the most part in isolated plots, each of which was independently cleared by its occupant, and under native governments bore its own assessment without reference of any kind to neighbouring plots. Under these circumstances it was not without protest from officials of influence that at the time of the first regular Settlement joint responsibility for the revenue was generally imposed. The question was, however, settled in favour of maintaining the usual procedure. The opinion of Mr. Cust, Financial Commissioner, upon the subject is given as follows, in his letter forwarding Mr. Morris' report for sanction:—

"Another question of interest, on which the Commissioner (Colonel Hamilton) holds very decided opinions, is the alleged absence in this district of village communities which would justify the enforcement of our village system of revenue administration. This is a very important subject; and divergence from fixed principles at this period would leave a permanent trace and hamper the Deputy Commissioner in his collections. Mr. Morris classes his villages in the well-known families of zamindari and bhayachara, sometimes a little complicated from the changes of possession, but still maintaining the chief characteristics. I am glad to find that along the rivers, where population and cultivation have attained a degree of permanence, 'common land' exists and regular communities: here we have thus proof that there is nothing in the physical features of the country or in the customs of the people to render this development impossible. As we retire from the rivers and approach the *bár*, or barren dorsal ridge, we lose all trace of these communities. Each well has its separate owner unconnected with its neighbour—often a separate hamlet or hut, with no common land, interests or homestead, no ties of race, religion or kindred. But this is just what we should expect: these people are the pioneers of civilization, the squatters of the primeval forest. Gradually, however, the ramparts of a municipality will be formed round them; we have now given them a defined village area, and a joint property in the jungle, to the exclusion of others. The owners of patches and wells are represented by headmen;

Chapter III. D.

Village Communities and Tenures.

The village community in Multan.

the ties of fellowship and mutual advantage will draw them together; the law of joint responsibility will bring with it the right of pre-emption. As cultivation, population, and wealth extend, these infant communities will develop themselves on one of the well-known types—perhaps streaked by some local peculiarities. Such has been the mode by which in the old settled tracts of the Gangetic valley the village community has come into existence, and by an innate vitality has survived empires and dynasties."

As yet the change here anticipated has not occurred, and indeed the tendency in Multan, as in the rest of the province, is all in the opposite direction. Mr. Roe wrote in 1880:—

"In the tracts near the rivers the lands generally belong to Jat tribes, and here are found regular village communities, some of which still hold their land in common, whilst others have divided it, and in most cases lost all trace of the original shares. Away from the rivers the villages are generally merely a collection of wells, which have been sunk in the neighbourhood of a canal or in the more favourable spots in the high lands. In these there has never been any community of interest; in very many cases there is not even a common village site; each settler has obtained his grant direct from the State, sunk his well, and erected his homestead on it. Under our Settlements the waste land between these wells has been recorded, as a matter of course, *shamilat deh,* but originally the well-owners had no claim to it whatever."

Hakk zamindari.

But whilst this is the origin of many or most of the villages, there were other tracts where a particular tribe or family was undoubtedly recognized as holding a zamindari or proprietary right over all the lands, cultivated or uncultivated, which we call a mauzah or village. This right was not, however, recognized under native rule as an exclusive one. If the zamindar could not bring his waste under cultivation the State had no hesitation in authorizing outsiders to do so; but the new settler had to pay a quit rent to the zamindar of half a ser in the maund as hakk zamindari or wajah zamindari and if the zamindar was a strong man he exacted an installation fee in addition. It often happened that the zamindar would himself introduce outsiders and allow them to sink wells; in this case, too, the quit rent was fixed at the rate of half a ser in the maund, and an installation fee, under the name of *jhuri, lúngí,* or *siropa* was almost invariably taken.

Hakk mukaddami.

The hakk zamindari described in the preceding paragraph is closely connected with a similar due which was known as the hakk mukaddami. We have seen how outsiders were introduced, either by the zamindar himself or by the State, and how they had to pay hakk zamindari. But it often happened when the zamindari family was numerous, and their land limited, that no

Chapter III, D.

Village Communities and Tenures.

Hakk mukaddami

outsiders were introduced. The various members of the family divided the lands amongst themselves, or, as was more commonly the case, each man brought what he could under cultivation without regard to any regular shares. Each became full proprietor of his own holding, but he had to pay half a ser in the maund as hakk zamindari or mukaddami to the head of the family. Sometimes, however, where the head was weak, or there was a dispute, the due was not levied. There can be little doubt that the zamindari and mukaddami are one and the same due, that the original form was the mukaddami, and that this was somewhat the same as our lambardar's fee. Indeed, this is admitted by most men who are not directly interested in maintaining the contrary. This due would originally be collected by the headman from all the proprietors, but when the number of outsiders became sufficiently great to give the headman a fair income from them alone, he would cease to collect from the proprietors of his own tribe. He would also do so when he was weak and required their support: for instance, when a young man wished to succeed his father to the exclusion of a richer or more powerful uncle; and in extreme cases he would promise not only to exempt his kinsmen, but even to divide amongst them the due collected from others. When this last practice has become firmly established, the due has ceased to be a mukaddami or headman's fee; it has become the property of a whole family or zamindari hakk; and the family speak of themselves as zamindars or ála máliks, in distinction to the settlers of other tribes, who are adna máliks or chakdárs. Along the Chenáb and in the west of Lodhrán this change has been complete, and the half ser in the maund is always spoken of as hakk zamindari. But in the greater part of Mailsi it is still sometimes spoken of as the mukaddami and in more than one village the Settlement Officer in 1873—1880 was asked to abolish it on the ground that it was merely a lambardar's fee, and as such had been superseded by our pachotra. But whatever may have been the origin of the due, it has been levied ever since the introduction of English rule separately from the pachotra, and it has now become by prescription a zamindari right; so that the hakk zamindari and hakk mukaddami are no longer distinguished in the revenue records.

Hathrakhai.

In connection with the hakk zamindari, it is necessary to notice the arrangement known as hathrakhai, or 'placing under protection.' The zamindari was usually levied by the zamindar or his tribe from outsiders whom he or they had admitted. But sometimes a community of zamindars, to obtain a lighter assessment, would voluntarily create this right against themselves in order to put themselves under a man of power and influence. By a fictitious sale they professed to sell him their entire village; he became the nominal proprietor, and by his influence obtained a light assessment: this was paid by the villagers, and the new proprietor received from them the usual hakk

Chapter III. D.

Village Communities and Tenures.

Hathrakhai.

zamindari of half ser in the maund, but beyond this he had no right in the village. On the establishment of English rule these nominal proprietors made great efforts to become real ones. Where their true position was known they were of course unsuccessful; but it occasionally happened that the court trying the claim was not very well acquainted with the peculiar features of the Multan tenures, and that the piece of paper on which the hathrakhai arrangement was recorded was taken literally and accepted as a full deed of sale. When this was done the evil was past remedy; the 'proprietor' had obtained decree after decree on the basis of the original order, but the old zamindars had for a long time fought against what they considered his encroachment, and much confusion and ill-feeling was the result.

Chakdars.

The settlers introduced by the State, or by the zamindar himself, into a zamindar's village, are known as chakdárs. The name is also applied to those proprietors of the zamindar's tribe who have continued to pay the hakk zamindari or mukaddami to their chief or chief's family, and it is sometimes even extended to settlers who have sunk wells under direct permission of the State in tracts where there has never been any one to claim a zamindari due. Thus when Diwán Sáwan Mal made his new canal, the Diwánwáh, through the Mailsi bar, he gave direct grants to settlers, proclaiming at the same time that if any one could establish a claim to zamindari it should be allowed; no such claim was established, but still the settlers were generally described as chakdárs. The supposed connection of the name with the wood-work of the well* and the payment of the zamindari gave rise to the idea that the chakdar owned the well only; in fact that he was a capitalist who had sunk a well for the zamindar who remained the true owner of the soil, and could buy out the chakdár on repaying him the money expended. This idea was still further encouraged by the fact that the chakdár sometimes did not cultivate himself, but let his well to tenants, and it occasionally happened that the tenant was one of the old zamindars. There was consequently rather a tendency at the commencement of our Summary Settlements to regard the chakdár as an interloper who, by the power of money, was ousting the old family from its original rights. But this was quite a mistake; the chakdár, whether he got his title from the zamindar direct or through the State, always held his land in full proprietary right, subject only to the payment of a quit rent in the shape of the hakk zamindari. Of course if he abandoned his land it reverted to the zamindar, but this was because the latter was the owner of all the waste land and not in virtue of any contract entered

* As a matter of fact the chak is the plot of land round the well, and the wood-work of the well is never in this district spoken of as 'chak.' A reference to the sanads quoted in Chapter V will show that the word 'chakdar' was in use as early as the time of Sháh Jahán, and was not, as is sometimes alleged, introduced by Sáwan Mal.

Chapter III. D.

Village Communities and Tenures.

Chakdars.

into at the time of purchase. On the other hand any right of cultivation enjoyed by the zamindar was acquired by a distinct contract beween him as tenant on the one side, and the chakdar as proprietor on the other; the terms of this contract might vary from that of a tenancy-at-will on a full rent to that of a permanent occupancy on a quit rent, but the original rights of the zamindar in no way influenced his position as tenant.

Kasúr Khwárs.

Under native rule the revenue or *mahsúl* was taken in kind and as the rate approached in many cases that of a full rent there remained, after deducting the cultivator's and the State share, but a small fraction for the non-cultivating proprietors. This fraction was called kasúr (the plural of kasar, and meaning 'fractions'). When this fraction was small it would be hardly worth the proprietor's while to go perhaps some distance to personally superintend the division of the crops; the rent he received from the cultivator with one hand was immediately almost entirely paid away with the other in the shape of the Government revenue, and he would remain responsible for any balances. Hence the custom would naturally spring up of the chakdar allowing his tenant to pay the Government share direct to the Government official, and to give the chakdar a fixed allowance in lieu of the actual balance. It is this fixed allowance which is now, and has for some time been, generally known as the hakk kasúr; and its general rate is two sers in the maund, or one-twentieth of the gross produce.* The chakdar who received this allowance is called the kasúr-khor, or kasúr-khwár, the eater of the kasúr, but the word is often corrupted into kasúr-khwáh. From his kasúr the kasúr-khwár has to keep in repair the brick-work of the well, and pay the hakk zamindari of half a ser in the maund if there is one. Uuder the system of fixed cash assessment the permission to engage direct for the Government revenue has grown into a very valuable right; the chakdar finds that he cannot recover his former position, aud the only right left to him is the nominal ownership of the well, and the right to receive kasúr. This chakdar who has lost his right to engage is now the person generally meant by kasúr-khwár, and this position has frequently been conferred as a compromise on a man who has claimed a well of which he or his ancestor was undoubtedly the original proprietor, but from all possession of which he has long been excluded. When the Multani Pathans were allowed on annexation to bring forward claims which would ordinarily have been barred by the law of limitation, in cases in which the claim was made out, it was almost invariably compromised in this way. The word kasúr is, however, still used occasionally in its original sense of the profits

* Under native Governments a lessee of waste land would often contract to give half the kasúr to Government (see the deed of 1816 quoted in Appendix to Chapter V below).

Chapter III, D.

Village Communities and Tenures.

of the chakdar, who pays the revenue himself, and such a man is also occasionally known as *Kasúr Khwár*.*

Present aspect of proprietary rights.

The account of the proprietary tenures above given explains the terms commonly in use among the people during the early years of Britsh occupation. Some of these terms are still in common use, but both the terms and the things which they represent are gradually becoming merged into the ordinary terminology and practice of the province at large. The hakk mukaddami is no longer recorded; the class of owners known as kasúr-khwárs is confined to a very small number of villages chiefly near Multan; the zamindar is to all intents and purposes an ála málik, and is entered as such in our records, while the chakdar is entered as an adna málik. The over-proprietary or ála malkiát tenure is no doubt much more common in this part of the province than in most other districts, but its incidents are practically the same as elsewhere, and old over-proprietary rights are by degrees disappearing, being merged by sale or other forms of transfer in the ordinary under-proprietary or chakdar class of rights.

Prescribed classification of village tenures.

The figures in Statement XV show the village tenures classified according to the prescribed sub-division of zamindari and pattidari or bhayachara. There are exceedingly few villages of the pattidari class, so that all the villages are practically either zamindari or bhayachara. The figures include what are known as jungle villages in which the whole or the greater part of the proprietary right belongs to Government; if we exclude them we find that 209 estates are held on the zamindari and 1,085 on the bhayachara or pattidári form of tenure. There are, besides, 11 estates which, though owned by Government, are at present given out entirely on lease to private individuals.

Historical classification of village tenures.

It will be seen from the above remarks, however, that the ordinary classification of tenures into zamindari, pattidari and bhayachara quite fails to show the real manner in which land was originally held in this district. Here we may rather divide the villages into two main groups :—

I. Unconnected with a zamindar, *i.e.*, villages founded by groups of settlers who have received grants direct from the State.

II. Originally owned by zamindars.

---

* The kasúr is in fact the mahsul after deducting the revenue, and this sense of the word survives in the phrase 'súd kasúr barábar,' which is applied to an ordinary usufructuary mortgage. The term kasúr is now generally used to denote the share in the produce taken by a person who without owning the land provides part of the means of cultivation. It is most commonly applied to the share taken by owners of water-courses in return for water supplied to lands owned by other persons. In the neighbourhood of Luddan, too, it is not unusual to find a well sunk by a man in land in which he has no proprietary right, but from which he takes a share of the produce (known as kasúr sil cháh) in return for the irrigation supplied by his well.

Chapter III, D.

Village Communities and Tenures.

Historical classification of village tenures.

The last group would contain many sub-divisions. First are the villages which are still, and always have been, held entirely by the members of the old tribe; next to these are the villages in which outsiders have been admitted, but the old tribe has retained an undoubted supremacy, levying the hakk zamindari and maintaining an exclusive right to the waste outside wells; the third group would be the villages in which this supremacy has been considerably weakened, many of the chakdárs have become independent, the zamindari is only taken from a few wells, and the exclusive right to the waste has been lost. This last result has been chiefly caused by our system of record; we have treated all waste outside wells as shamilat deh as a matter of course: we have accepted it as an undoubted axiom that all shamilat deh land must be divided amongst all the khewatdars 'hasb rasad khewat,' and by khewatdars we have meant all men paying direct to the lambardar a portion of the cash jama. The fourth and last group of villages would be those in which both the hakk zamindari and special claims to the waste have entirely disappeared.

Common land.

The well area is in most cases the unit of proprietary right, and in Sikh times all land outside this belonged either to the State or to some zamindar (ala malik) who had some vague claim over it. When under English rule boundaries were regularly demarcated, a certain portion of the waste outside wells was included in the village areas. In villages where the ála máliks had a claim to the waste, this was recorded as their common property, but elsewhere it was entered as shamilat deh. The present common village land is thus for the most part a creation of our rule, and, compared with districts in the central Punjab, Multan presents comparatively few cases of village shamilat; common village land being found in only 249* villages in the district out of 1,451. Where such land exists, it is now dealt with under the general rules applicable to the enjoyment and partition of common land.

The number of shareholders in private jointly-owned land varies greatly: on the one hand, there are large estates owned by individual proprietors; on the other, there are holdings which, owing to the action of Mahomedan law and other causes, are owned in the most confusing and minute of shares: some such holdings there are in a village on the Rávi, where the common denominator of the shares runs to over 175,000. As a whole, however, the shares are comparatively large, and the number of shareholders is not excessive. As a rule, too, a well estate is held in common, and it is the exception to find well estates partitioned. The joint tenure of land has, no doubt, its advantages, but it gives the lazy or spiteful shareholder a tremendous power of retarding improvement; and it is often used by

* In many of these villages, too, the only common village land consists of water-course, road or other unculturable unit.

Chapter III, D.

Village Communities and Tenures.

money-lenders as an engine for bringing their agriculturist co-sharers under their power. Generally speaking, therefore, the partition of a holding leads to nothing but good.

Customary Law of Succession.

In matters of inheritance, enjoyment of property, and so forth, the law directs the courts to follow local custom when this is established; and failing that, the Mahomedan or Hindu Law, except in cases where these have been superseded by Acts of the Legislature. The customs in force on such points were investigated and recorded at the second Regular Settlement during the years 1875—1877; and the results of this enquiry are accepted as a general guide by the courts. A revised edition of the English abstract of the record then made has been lately issued, giving information as to decisions which have been passed by the higher courts since the issue of the first edition in 1879. It is found that, as a general rule, all sons succeed equally, and that succession is regulated *per capita* and not *per stirpes*. Where there are sons the daughters occasionally take a share, but not usually; where there are no sons, instead of being excluded, as she usually is elsewhere, the daughter very often succeeds or at least gets a share of the property. As regards widows, the custom generally is for the widow to succeed on a life-tenure if there are no sons, and to receive maintenance only if there are sons. The possessor of property has, as a rule, power to alienate a reasonable amount in reasonable ways, and is not tramelled so closely by the claims of the agnates as is usual elsewhere in this province. Speaking generally the rights of individuals, as contrasted with the rights of families or clans, are far more freely recognized than in the Punjab proper; and this peculiarity is due partly to the proximity of the frontier and the influence of Mahomedan Law, and partly to the absence in the greater part of the district of anything like communal village cultivation. There are very few families who actually follow the Mahomedan Law of Succession in its entirety, but a fair number of families are under the impression that they follow it, and a great many, though not following it in detail, are actuated very strongly by its principles in regulating the succession of the family property.

Riparian custom.

There are three main methods by which the rights to lands affected by alluvion and diluvion are determined:—

(i) the deep-stream rule, pure and simple (bánd banna or dhár kalán), under which the deep-stream is accepted as the boundary between the villages;

(ii) the modified deep-stream rule, under which land carried away by avulsion, without alteration of its features, remains the property of the original proprietors, although separated from their other property by the deep-stream; and

Riparian custom

(iii) the fixed boundary, or give-and-take rule (known as len den), by which the proprietary boundaries remain unchanged and are not affected by any changes in the river.

During the Settlement of 1873—1880 the custom of each river was duly recorded. On the Rávi it was found that most villages followed the modified deep-stream rule; while on the Chenáb a certain number of villages, mostly towards the north, followed the unmodified deep-stream rule, and the rest followed the fixed boundary rule. On the Sutlej about a quarter of the villages, mostly at the two ends of the district, were recorded as following the modified deep-stream rule while the remainder were entered as following that of the fixed boundary.

It has now been generally recognized that the least objectionable of the three systems is that of the give-and-take or fixed boundary. Efforts were therefore made in 1897 to persuade all the villages on the Rávi and Chenáb which were not hitherto governed by that rule to accept a fixed boundary, and these efforts were successful in all these villages except Akbarpur in Multan and a group of twelve villages near Tulamba in Kabírwála The greater number of the proprietors concerned signed stamped agreements accepting the fixed boundary. This boundary was adopted in the measurement papers, and the facts were stated in the wajib-ul-arz. Meantime Act No. I (Punjab) of 1899 was passed, and under orders of the Financial Commissioner, passed in 1900 and 1901, a fixed boundary was authoritatively laid down under the Act for all villages on the Ravi and Chenab which had not hitherto enjoyed a fixed boundary.

On the Sutlej matters are in a less satisfactory state owing to the fact that the district along the whole of this river marches with the Baháwalpur State and the custom on this river has had a curious history. The original rule all along the river appears to have been that of the fixed boundary; but in the absence of maps this gave rise to a good deal of dispute, and in 1850 the Board of Administration ordered the introduction of the deep-stream rule. This was followed in 1860 by orders from Government of India, ordering that so far as jurisdiction is concerned, the modified deep-stream rule should be observed. At the Settlement of 1873—1880, however, as has above been noted, only a quarter of the villages observed the modified deep-stream rule, yet by 1896, when the third Settlement commenced, it may safely be said that the modified deep-stream rule prevailed universally all along the river, both in matters of jurisdiction and in those of private rights. This rule has led to an intolerable series of petty disputes, and negotiations are now in pro-

Chapter III, D.

Village Communities and Tenures.

gress for the introduction, so far as jurisdiction is concerned, of a system of fixed boundaries along the Sutlej as along the other rivers of the district.

Rights in irrigation

No record having been made of rights in irrigation, it is a matter of some importance to understand the present position of affairs regarding the rights of irrigators on the Inundation canals in the water which they receive. The main canals were made in pre-annexation days by the people themselves working under the orders of the ruler of the day, and thewater-courses made from the canal to private lands were made by private persons with the permission of the ruler. Awater-course having been made, the person who made it was no doubt considered as much its owner as the persons who made a well was the owner of the well : he could dispose of the water as he pleased ; could put up dams and jhalárs, and could if he desired sell the whole or a part of the right to irrigate from the water-course ; this being all, of course, subject to any orders emanating from the ruler of the day or from powerful men depending on the favour of that ruler.

When we took over the country we found persons constantly quarreling as to the right to use water-courses and jhalárs on outlets, etc. ; and, in order to help in deciding these disputes, a statement was prepared in 1860 by Syad Mohsan Ali Shah, Extra Assistant Commissioner, showing very briefly the water-courses, etc., then in existence, and in certain cases, the names of eth owners and other details. This has hitherto been the only record of the kind in existence, but it has become utterly out of date and no longer of any value. The Government meantime has been gradually exercising more and more control over the distribution of the water. The Canal Act was passed in 1873, and these canals were shortly afterwards brought under its operation, the general rules under the Act being applied in 1878. In 1873—1880, when the district was under re-settlement, the Settlement Officer refrained from making any record of irrigation rights, partly from the dread of stirring up unnecessary disputes, partly to avoid stereotyping transitory rights, and partly for fear of placing on record anything which might fetter the power of distributing water possessed by the canal officers under the Act. By the time the present Settlement was commenced, the Government had obtained a considerable degree of control over the water ; but partly from want of establishment and partly from proper respect for the traditional feelings of the people, this control is still a good deal weaker than on most Government canals. The richer and stronger men, who own water-courses or shares in water-courses, still sell or barter water, and control the supplies of their weaker neighbours in a way which would not be allowed elsewhere. The ques-

Chapter III, D.

Village Communities and Tenures.

Rights in irrigation.

tion whether a record of irrigation rights was the proper remedy for this state of things was mooted, but it was felt that all the objections urged against such a record at the last Settlement still held good; and it was decided by the Settlement Commissioner, in September 1898, that no such record should be prepared. The revenue records will always show the actual use and practice in respect of irrigation; and the best system of ensuring satisfactory distribution would appear to be one by which the canal officer, while possessing these data for his guidance, is in other respects left as little hampered as possible. The introduction of a system of occupier's rates, moreover, in place of chher labour, though not in theory in any way necessarily entailing this change, is looked upon by the people as betokening, and will no doubt in practice lead to, a still further developement of Government control in the distribution of water.

Size of holdings.

The question of *morcellement*, which forms so prominent an item in the agricultural aspect of many Punjab districts, is not a pressing one in Multan. The size of the holdings, as calculated at the recent Settlement for the various tahsils, is shown in the following table :—

		Multan.	Shujabad.	Lodhrán.	Mailsi.	Kabírwála.
Total acres ...	per holding	40	21	55	84	48
	per owner	37	21	33	38	30
Cultivated acres	per holding	21	9	14	32	22
	per owner	20	8	9	14	15

The holdings are smallest in the Tarafs of Multan and in the southern part of Shujabad. They are largest in the Sutlej tahsils, and the average in Mailsi is swollen by the presence of the large Hájiwáh estate, where some 50,000 acres are held in two holdings by four owners. In Multan and Kabírwála many of the holdings are Sidhnai grants of 90 acres each.

Chapter III, D.

Village Communities and Tenures.

Tenants.

Statistics regarding the cultivating occupancy of land are given in Statement XVI, from which it will be seen that the cultivated area of the district is held as follows:—

	Per cent.
By owners	25·0
By occupancy tenants	2·6
By tenants-at-will	72·1

The percentage of area cultivated by owners is less than in most Punjab districts. The proportion is highest in Kabírwála, where there are a number of comparatively small landholders on the Sidhnai canal; and in Shujabad, where the percentage is swollen by considerable areas cultivated round Shujabad by Hindu landlords through hired servants. In Mailsi and Lodhrán, where the holdings are more extensive and the Sahukar element among the proprietors is larger, the proportion cultivated by owners is lower than elsewhere.

The tenants are very migratory, and the proprietors sometimes excuse their evictions by saying that they wish to prevent the tenants from acquiring a right of occupancy in the land. At the first Regular Settlement, it is true, a certain number of tenants seem to have been recorded as holding occupancy rights on the ground of twelve years' possession; but since the Regular Settlement—that is, during the last forty years—there have been no creations of occupancy rights by executive order. The occupancy tenancies of the district owe for the most part their origin to one of the three following causes, *viz.*: (i) recognized custom, whereby the breaker up of waste is given fixity of tenure, the rights in such case having been recorded at the Regular Settlement, or by special decision or agreement since then; (ii) an arrangement known as *adhlúpí*, by which an owner of land agrees with an outsider, generally a capitalist or successful artizan, that if the outsider builds a well in his land the outsider will acquire the proprietary right in half the well area and a right of occupancy in the other half; (iii) judicial or executive orders giving occupancy right to men who were found at annexation in proprietary possession of lands which had shortly before been abandoned by their rightful owners*; (iv) arrangements by

* The most common case of this kind was that of the Pathan villages; lands which had been seized by the Pathans and held by them for many years, but from which they were ousted under the Sikh supremacy. At annexation we found their lands occupied by the tenants or by the old owners, while the Pathans, who had been our valuable allies in the war, clamoured for re-instation. In some cases the Pathans were given a kind of over-proprietary right (as, *e.g.*, in Fírozpur); in others they were given a full proprietary status, while the cultivators were given occupancy rights (as in Bákirpur, Lutfabad, etc.).

Chapter III, D.

Village Communities and Tenures.

Tenants.

which lessees holding under Government in the Sidhnai or in the Mailsi *bár* have been given an occupancy status. Owing to the migratory character of the tenants and the certainty of obtaining employment, the occupancy status has not hitherto been fully appreciated, and in many cases it is abandoned with a light heart. At the same time the owners steadily press for the extinction of the rights of their tenants at every favourable opportunity; so that the area under old tenancies of this character has a tendency to decrease. At the same time, new occupancy tenancies are created from time to time by *adhlápí* agreements, and under the arrangements recently sanctioned on the Sidhnai canal the number of occupancy tenants in the district has already begun to increase, and will increase very rapidly in future. The general result has so far been a slight net increase in the area held under occupancy, which has risen from 20,991 acres in 1381-82 to 23,911 acres in 1898-99.

All other tenants are strictly tenants-at-will, and have been so recorded in the revenue records. A partial exception has, however, been made in favour of the *god-kash* tenants of the Sutlej border. These are tenants who have cleared the jungle, and are generally recognized as having rights corresponding to those of an occupancy tenant: if any outsider cultivates the lands they have cleared, they obtain from the cultivator a due, known as *bhoang*, and the right to receive this due is transferable. It was therefore thought advisable in cases where the title of the tenant to be a *god-kash* was undisputed to enter him as such in the records.

Rents.

Cash rents are paid in ·4 per cent. only of the rent-paying area, and they are for the most part of one or other of the three following kinds:—(i) Firstly, ordinary lump cash rents. These are distinctly rare, except in the immediate vicinity of Multan city. (ii). Secondly, payments made under the mortgage-lease system. Under this system the mortgagor takes a lease (mustajiri) of his land from the mortgagee, promising to pay the latter a lump sum at each harvest. This lump payment is, as a rule, fixed quite independently of the value of the land; and the object of the arrangements is to secure for the mortgagee a safe interest on his investment. This class of contract is found mainly in the Multan and Shujabad tahsils, and the practice has spread very rapidly of recent years. (iii). Thirdly, there are the cash rents in the form of land revenue, with or without an addition by way of malikana. The figures under this third head include the tenants of Government under the bár-báráni and khám tahsil arrangements described in Chapter V, but they also include a fair number of private tenancies under the same conditions. The most common form of revenue paying tenancy is that prevalent in the southern corner of the district, whereby the tenant (generally an occupancy tenant, and often an

Chapter III, D.

Village Communities and Tenures.

Rents.

adhlápidar) pays the revenue, and the owner receives a certain small proportion of the gross produce (generally from $\frac{1}{10}$th to $\frac{1}{17}$th) under the name of *lichh*.* The returns of rent under the second and third of the above heads are of course useless as indications of the letting value of agricultural land; and even the returns under the first head are of comparatively little value unless means are taken to eliminate all cases in which the land concerned contains fruit-trees and other special products, and to ascertain the conditions prevailing in each lease as to the payment of menials, the responsibility for clearing the water-courses or providing for the canal clearances, and so forth. The records of this district, therefore, provide no data for determining the true cash rent per acre over any but a very inconsiderable area. Zabti rents or cash rates per bigha on particular crops are practically unknown.

Ninety-three per cent. of the rented area pays rents in kind; and the figures in Statement XVI show the shares of the produce paid. These figures, however, need a good deal of explanation. In the first place, the whole of the produce does not come under division: certain areas are always allowed to the tenant for fodder, and very often the owner also takes a small share of the fodder crops. From the grain heap actually divided the dues of the superior proprietor and those of the village menials have to be provided before the landlord and tenant get their share. Then the recorded or nominal share varies a good deal according to the incidents of the tenancy. In some cases the landlord receives certain extra dues or cesses, and the recorded share is thus less than the actual. Or he may have advanced seed or bullocks, or money to the tenant, so that the recorded rental is really more than the actual return received. And as regards the maintenance of the well, the clearing of the water-courses, the contribution for the clearances of the Government canals, and so forth, the conditions vary considerably. The general rule of the district may, however, be said to be that the landlord maintains the well and clears the water-courses while the tenant provides for the clearances of the Government canals.† This latter is in most cases the most important item to consider, and accordingly, in order to get a fairly clear and uniform view of the kind rents in force, it is sufficient to take the recorded rents for all cases in which the tenant provides for the clearance of the Government canals. In such circumstances the

* The term is also sometimes applied to a due paid by adna máliks to ála máliks in addition to the hakk zamindari: in such cases it is said to be a survival of the time when the adna máliks were really tenants.

† The figures of Statement XVI were prepared before the system of cash occupier's rates in lieu of chher labour was introduced (see Chapter V below).

Chapter III, D.
Village Communities and Tenures.
Rents.

share of the divisible produce taken (after deducting menials' dues and fodder) is as follows :—

Average rent rates in kind.

Soil.		Area in acres paying					
		Half.	Two-fifths.	One-third.	One-fourth.	One-fifth.	Average per cent.
Cháhi	...	8,609	573	7,029	9,489	2,724	34
Cháhi-nahri	Sidhnai Circles	42,487	2,588	3,375	1,577	16	47
	Others* ...	12,273	46,321	73,940	30,664	1,294	34
Nahri	Sidhnai Circles	108,093	859	628	164	12	50
	Others* ...	22,128	24,087	36,996	2,680	75	39
Cháhi-sailáb	...	11,406	3,235	9,135	1,477	...	41
Abi	...	1,073	395	2,234	284	...	38
Sailáb	...	37,273	6,801	23,120	486	...	43
Báráni	...	223	81	2,960	119	169	34
Total	...	243,565	84,940	259,417	46,920	4,290	40

* Where the tenant provides the chher for canal clearances.

It may be said, roughly, that the ordinary rate on sailáb land is one-half, on canal lands one-third, and on pure well lands one-fourth or less. On canal lands, if the owner provides for the canal clearances, one-half is taken instead of one-third.* Whether the rent rates are, on the whole, increasing or not is uncertain, and the statistics on the subject require so many qualifications that no certain grounds for a conclusion are forthcoming. Speaking generally, however,

*Among other rents commonly in use are two-fifths (bhá-didh-bhá, *i.e.*, one share and one and-a-half share) and four-ninths (náwín sam, the extra 'ninth share' going to the tenant).

Chapter III, D.

Village Communities and Tenures.

Rents.

from experience of individual cases, it can probably be said that, as regards lands enjoying the same advantages both now and twenty years ago, the tendency has been towards a slight, but a very slight, increase in the share taken by the owner. The balance of power between owner and tenant varies in different parts of the district, but, as a whole, it is at present fairly even, and the changes being effected by time are in favour of the owner, who will no doubt gradually increase his rents as the competition for tenancies becomes keener.

Proprietary dues.

Allusion has been made above to the extra dues which are in some cases paid to the owner by the tenant. These dues, to a large extent, represent the old cesses exacted by native Governments over and above their share of the produce, and they are found recorded with considerable minuteness in cases where the rents of occupancy tenants were determined shortly after occupation. They are, however, commonly found in all classes of tenancies. A common due of this kind is that known as *jholi*, which means, literally, the skirt of the coat; it having been the custom for the proprietor after partition of the grain to hold out his skirt for the tenant to fill. A similar due under the name of *dalla*, or a child's skirt, was sometimes taken, and also that known as *tobra*, or the horse's nose-bag, representing the free feed of corn given by the tenant. In some villages *kiráyá* was taken, on the ground that the tenant was bound to convey the proprietor's share of the produce home for him. Sometimes the proprietor would claim to have his share weighed at 42 sérs to the maund, and this exaction was known as bitálah, from bitálís (forty-two). If the proprietor lived near he would take 2 or 3 marlas of green crop for fodder, and this was called kíára. Sometimes amlána or munshiána would be taken as a contribution for the pay of the proprietor's accountants, and sometimes, but much more rarely, a charitable contribution or *bhik* was demanded, or a fixed sum was taken per well under the name of *malba*. The above dues are of course not taken in every case or by all proprietors, and they are naturally largest and most numerous where the proprietors are strong and the tenants weak. In former days officers used often to represent that these dues were voluntary gifts from the tenant, and that the owner was not entitled to have them recorded as dues. There is, however, little voluntary about them, and where they exist they are now regularly entered in the record as constituting part of the payments actually made by the tenant.

Agricultural labour.

The employment of field labour, other than that of the proprietors or tenants themselves, and the system of agricultural partnerships, are thus noticed in answers furnished by the district officer and inserted in the Famine Report of 1879 (pages 718-19):—

"Hired labourers are employed by all the richer zamindars, who are above following the plough themselves, for their khud-

Chapter III, D.

Village Communities and Tenures.

Agricultural labour.

káSht lands. They are employed for all farming operations, and receive wages sometimes in kind, sometimes in money, sometimes in both, amounting to from Rs. 3 to Rs. 5 a month. They are of all classes, except Syads and Brahmans: they cannot be said to form a class apart: they are the outskirts of the tenant-at-will class. A tenant loses his bullocks, or gets into trouble, and he works as a labourer till he can recover himself. On the other hand, a zamindar takes a fancy to a labourer who has worked for him for some time, and he gives him some lands, advances him money for bullocks, and sets him up as a tenant. Sometimes, too, a small proprietor meets with a temporary diffculty in the Rawa: in long continued drought cultivation is impossible: the proprietor then sends his cattle to graze in the bár, and goes to work as a labourer until better times return. These labourers generally live on their wages with ease; they may run up petty scores for food in the bazar, but they cannot get into serious debt. But their condition is inferior to that of poorer tenants, inasmuch as it is generally when a tenant is ruined that he becomes a day labourer. As long as a man is a tenant, he has no want of the actual necessaries of life, nor has the labourer, as a rule; but he may have at any time—at least there is the possibility of this, but I have never known it to occur particularly. The demand for labour has always been in excess of the supply, and the agricultural labourers work on steadily all the year round."

The wages of labour prevailing at different periods are shown in Table No. XXVII, though the figures refer to the labour market of towns rather than to that of villages.

Zaildars.

The zaildarí system was introduced into Multan at the conclusion of the Settlement of 1873 to 1880. The zails were marked out, as far as possible, in accordance with the tribal distribution of the people, regard being had, at the same time, to the personal circumstances of the zaildars and the villages in which their properties lay. The zaildars received one per cent. of the revenue of their zails: this one per cent. being collected in Kabírwála as a cess in addition to the revenue, and being in the other tahsils deducted as a drawback. On the Sidhnai canal in both Kabírwála and Multan it was collected as an extra cess.

In 1900 several changes were made in the zaildarí arrangements. The zails were made larger, and were reconstituted so as to fit in with the limits of thanas and tahsils. The zaildars, too, instead of being remunerated according to the revenue of their zails, were classed in three grades, receiving Rs. 250, Rs. 200 and Rs. 150 per annum, respectively; this remuneration being calculated so as not to exceed an average year, one per cent. of the district revenue.

Chapter III, D.

Village Communities and Tenures.

Zaildars.

The appointments in each grade sanctioned for the different tahsils are :—

Grade.	Multan.	Shujabad.	Lodhrán.	Mailsi.	Kabírwála.	Total.
1st grade at Rs. 250 per annum ...	2	2	2	2	2	10
2nd grade at Rs. 200 ,, ,, ...	8	6	6	6	9	35
3rd grade at Rs. 150 ,, ,, ...	5	3	3	3	5	19
Total	15	11	11	11	16	64

The duties of the zaildars are defined by rules under the law, and consist chiefly in rendering assistance in the prevention and detection of crime and the supervision of the work of village officers in the circle or zail.

Inamdars.

In the years following annexation a certain number of revenue assignments were made under the title of zamindar mafis to zamindars who had been holding similar assignments under the previous Government. At the second Settlement of 1873 to 1880 the question was raised whether, in villages which contained more than one headman, chief headmen or ála lambardars should be appointed under the system adopted in the central Punjab. It was decided that the ála lambardar system was not called for, but that a small proportion of the revenue should be devoted to the payment of cash grants to the more prominent among the zamindars under the title of zamindari inams. Persons enjoying existing zamindarí mafis were offered the choice of continuance of the mafi or an exchange to one of the new cash inams ; and they all elected the latter course.

At the third Settlement the system was continued, but in a somewhat altered form. The list of inamdars was revised, and the terms on which they held were assimilated to those prescribed by rule for the province at large. They each receive Rs. 25 or Rs. 30 per annum; and their duties are similar to these of the zaildars.

Village headmen.

The village headmen are appointed on the same system as in the rest of the province. They are responsible for the collection of the land revenue, and are bound to assist in the

Chapter III. D.

Village Communities and Tenures.

Village headmen.

prevention and detection of crime. In two respects, however, the lambardarí arrangements in this district differ from those of most Punjab districts. In the first place, owing to the predominance of large landowners who own land in many villages, a large proportion of the lambardars are necessarily absentees and have to work through substitutes. And in the second place, owing to the scattered nature of the cultivation and the migrating habits of the people, the duties of a village headman, in respect both of the collection of revenue and of the detection of crime, are infinitely more heavy than in districts where the whole village lives within a stone's throw of the lambardar's house. In most villages the position is valued, but in not a few it is recognized as rather a burden, and often it is impossible to find any one willing to take up the post. The headman receives the same remuneration as in the Punjab at large, *viz.*, 5 per cent. on the collections of land revenue and 3 per cent. on those of occupier's rates. Previous to 1897 each separate holding in the jungle villages had its own lambardar, and constituted for revenue purposes a separate estate; but since the jungle villages were reconstituted in that year, the holdings there have been grouped under village lambardars in the ordinary way. There is usually one lambardar for each village, but in many villages there are more than one, and in a few (especially round Shujabad) there are not less than seven or eight. The number of lambardars in 1900 was as follows :—

Tahsils.	Number of estates.	Number of lambardars.	Number of estates with					
			One lambardar.	Two lambardars.	Three lambardars.	Four lambardars.	Five lambardars.	More than five lambardars.
Multan	297	422	204	60	22	8	...	...
Shujabad	153	286	86	29	24	6	4	4
Lodhrán	276	370	202	58	13	2	1	...
Mailsi	387	410	366	19	2	...	...	...
Kabirwála	338	448	247	73	17	1	...	...
Total ...	1,451	1,936	1,105	239	78	17	5	4

Patwaris or village accountants.

The patwari is a revenue official who is responsible for the maintenance and preservation of all village records affecting the land revenue in his circle. His circle comprises a number of villages, which varies according to the size of the

Chapter III, D.

Village Communities and Tenures.

Patwaris or village accountants.

several estates, the number of fields, the amount of revenue work entailed, and so forth. The number as sanctioned in 1900 is as follows :—

		Multán.	Shujabad.	Lodhrán.	Mailsi.	Kabírwála.	Total.
Patwaris, 1st grade, at Rs. 14 ...		30	25	24	18	27	124
" 2nd " at " 12 ...		30	25	24	24	28	131
" 3rd " at " 10 ...		13	15	12	10	15	65
Assistants at Rs. 6		4	4	4	4	4	4
Average per Circle	Total acres ...	7,950	6,739	11,262	20,643	14,773	11,880
	Cultivated acres	3,212	2,521	2,963	4,025	3,144	3,142
	Fields	3,898	2,890	3,729	3,724	3,785	3,609

The total cost is thus Rs. 48,936 for one year, which, together with the incidental expenses of the establishment and the maintenance of part of the supervising agency, is met by a cess of 6¼ per cent. on the land revenue. In January 1901 72 of the patwaris of the district were Mahomedans, and the rest Hindus. The establishment is for the most part recruited from towns where there are Middle schools, such as Multan, Shujabad, Tulamba, Sarai Siddhu, Kahror, etc., and a very small proportion of the patwaris at present are agriculturists in the true sense of the word.

Village watchmen.

Most villages have one or more watchmen (chaukidars), the smaller ones, which are near one another, often having a chaukidar between them. The number of these village servants in each tahsil are :—Multan 122, Shujabad 91, Lodhrán 111, Mailsi 88, and Kabírwála 110, total 522. In large villages there is a dafadar. The ordinary pay of a chaukidar is Rs. 3 per mensem, which is levied as a cess upon the inhabited houses of the village.

Village servants.

The village servants may conveniently be classed under two heads, *viz.*, (A) those necessary for the maintenance of the agriculture ; (B) others.

In the first group, again, there are three classes of servants, *viz* :—

(i) The carpenter, potter, blacksmith and míráb. The carpenter or *tarkhán*, besides repairing houses, looks after the

Village servants.

well gear and the plough; the *kumhár* or potter makes the water-pots of the well, as well as those for domestic use; the *lohár* or blacksmith makes the ploughshares; and the *míráb* distributes the canal water. The carpenter is used almost everywhere, the kumhár is used wherever there are wells, and the míráb where there are canals; and these three servants almost always receive dues in grain at harvest time. The lohár, on the other hand, is very often paid by the job. The míráb has never been employed on the Sidhnai and Hájiwáh canals, and he is gradually being ousted from the other canals, his place being taken by the canal chaukidar, who is paid by Government.

(ii) The weighman or *dabír* and the *mohassil* or crop watcher constitute a group by themselves; and are often classed as 'muta'lik málik' or the owners' kamíns, their dues being often paid in the first place to the owner, who not infrequently remunerates them by a fixed stipend, and pockets the difference, if any. The dabír is kept by all but the smallest landholders, and his duty is to weigh the grain at harvest, and to keep the accounts of the various payments made. He is generally an Arora; and several of the largest landowners in the district owe the origin of their prosperity to the profits of dabíri. The mohassil is only entertained by the larger owners, and both he and the dabír are almost invariably paid by a share of the produce, generally half a sér in the maund. A watcher kept by the tenant is known as *rákhá*.

(iii) *Laihárs* or reapers are employed for reaping such crops as are grown in large quantities and need to be cut at one time; the laihár generally receives three sheaves in every hundred as his remuneration. A *gahera* is also often used to drive the bullocks at threshing time, and when so employed receives, as a rule, half a ser for every maund threshed. And a *chháji* or winnower, generally a low caste man, is almost universally employed and receives generally about a ser for each maund winnowed.

In the second or non-agricultural group of village servants we may class the *mochi* (currier or shoemaker), the *nái* (barber), the *mirási* (bard), the *kotwál* (messenger and general servant), the *máchhi* (baker), *kutána* (sweeper and thatch-maker), the *charhoa* (washerman), the *deora* (camel grazier), and the *mohána* (ferryman). Of course these are not all found in every village; the deora, for instance, being only found in villages where camels are kept, and the mohána in villages where the villagers have occasions to cross the river. This class of servants is also generally paid at harvest time by donations of grain; and many of them also receive customary dues on occasions of marriages and festivals.

In addition to these inevitable payments, there is another drain on the resources of the grain heap, in the shape of

Chapter III. D.

Village Communities and Tenures.

Village servants.

religious offerings. Mullas or teachers almost always get something, and so do men of the sacred tribes such as the Koreshís or Jhandírs. Local shrines, especially the more famous ones like those of Baháwal Hakk, or Makhdúm Rashíd, or Diwán Chaoli Mashaikh, are also propitiated with a due known as *lota*, and the mulla also receives the dues known as jakh or rasúl-arwáhí in return for his charms and other spiritual services. If there is a Hindu shrine near, a few sérs are given as 'Ganesh', without much distinction as to the creed of the owners of the grain heap. These dues are generally set aside before the heap is divided, and they are not subject to any special limit in each case.

In the calculations made in connection with the recent Settlement, it was estimated that the percentage of the gross produce (after deducting fodder taken by the tenant), which was consumed by the agricultural class of kamíns alone, amounted to 12 per cent. The percentage varies according to the class of cultivation; and the figures for the district, as a whole, came to 6 per cent. on báráni, 7 per cent. on sailâb, 13 per cent. on cháhi-nahri and 12 per cent. on other soils.

Petty village grantees.

Petty grants of land to village menials or to local shrines, etc., are far less common here than in the central Punjab. They are, however, found in some villages in the shape either of small holdings gifted in absolute proprietary right or of exemptions from fixed land revenue, the land revenue thus remitted being distributed over the remainder of the village.

Village cesses.

No official record has been made of the village cesses in force in this district, and there are only two cesses of this kind which are at all common. One is known as *dharat,* and it is confined mainly to a few large villages in the Mailsi tahsil, where it is the custom to levy fees on all weighments made within the village. The proceeds of these fees are appropriated by the owners (or, if the lambardars are strong, by the lambardars) for general village purposes; and where (as is often the case) the right to collect the fees is sold by auction very good prices are sometimes fetched. The other due referred is that called *jhajhri,* which is a contribution sometimes levied by the landowners of a village on the occasion of a marriage from the bridegroom's party.

A cess known as *malba* or *gaon-kharcha* is realized in all villages from the revenue payers for the purpose of meeting common village expenses, such as the maintenance of boundary pillars, the payment of watchmen's uniform, the reception of travellers and fakirs, and so forth. This cess is recognized by Government, and the rates at which and the conditions under which, it is leviable in each village are entered in the Administration Papers prepared at the Settlement.

Chapter III. D.

Village Communities and Tenures.

Poverty or wealth of the proprietors.

The Hindu proprietors are almost all well off and some, such as the leading men among the Bablas of Shujabad, own immense possessions. Nearly all the Hindu landowners combine landowning with money-lending and some 10 or 15 per cent. only are in any way distressed for a living in bad years. Among the Muhammadans there are men of every type. Compared with most Punjab districts the number of landowners with large rent-rolls is very considerable, but in most cases their expenses are made to exceed their incomes. A few of them, more especially among the Aráíns, the Bhuttás, the Khokhars, the Bosans and the Langáhs, keep a reasonably careful eye on their properties and live in comparative comfort. The majority, however—and most markedly the Syads, Koreshís and Pathans—are exceedingly careless or exceedingly extravagant, so that although they live ostensibly in comfort they are bound sooner or later to come to grief. The mass of the landowners, the men with moderate and uncertain rent-rolls, enjoy in some cases a certain amount of mild luxury, such as the possession of a riding camel, or a pony or two, or a spare wife, but the majority live in a state of equilibrium in good years and have to contract their enjoyments or increase their debts in years when crops fail. The class below this—that of the very small owner or tenant or farm labourer—lives more or less from hand to mouth and in years of scarcity is forced to migrate elsewhere or to submit to a period of penury.

Indebtedness.

Almost every Muhammadan landowner has an account with a banker and about half of the accounts would probably, if a balance were struck, display a deficit against the depositor. The causes of debt are much the same as in other Punjab districts, *viz.*, extravagance, profligacy and litigation among the bigger men; carelessness, high interest, dishonest bankers, loss of cattle, bad seasons and the like among the smaller. The rates of interest on a loan (udhárá) vary a good deal, but on ordinary security 12 per cent. is looked on as a reasonable rate, provided it is not enhanced as it usually is by compound interest. Grain loans are generally repayable in a year at 25 per cent. interest, and on these loans also compound interest is not uncommon. In either form of loan it is usual for the lender to retain $\frac{1}{16}$th or $\frac{1}{32}$nd of the nominal loan or to enter up as the capital lent an amount considerably exceeding the actual sum given out. The landowner is also, it is true, able to borrow money from Government for agricultural purposes at $6\frac{1}{4}$ per cent., but the formalities and the punctual repayments required generally deter him from this expedient.

Alienation of land.

For any large loan the proprietor has to offer land as security and the mortgages in this district are of two main classes. In one of these (known as Súd-mahár-barábar or sud-panálá-barábar), the purchaser is put in proprietary possession of the land, arranges for the cultivation, pays the revenue

Chapter III. D.

Village Communities and Tenures.

Alienation of land.

and accepts the net profits as the equivalent of the interest due on the loan. In the other (known as lekha-mukhi) the proprietary profits of the land, either after or before payment of revenue, are handed over to the creditor who puts them to the credit of the debtor, debiting him at the same time with the interest due on the original capital of the loan. In either class of mortgage it is not unusual for the mortgagor to remain in possession as tenant; and in lekha-mukhi mortgages the mortgagee sometimes takes full possession and sometimes contents himself with receiving the net profits. It is not uncommon, and the practice has increased of late years, for the mortgagor to take the land on lease (mustájiri) from a mortgagee with possession at a fixed sum per annum, thus securing to the mortgagee an assured interest in the form of rent. Alienations in the form of conditional sale (bai-bil-wafa) are not common, but are less rare than they used to be. Nor are alienations by way of collateral mortgage very common, though by no means unknown. The mortgagees in almost all cases are Hindús, as the receipt of interest is opposed to the strict precepts of Islám: but a certain number of Muhammadans, especially among the Aráíns, take land on mortgage, and the prejudice against it seems to be less strong than it was.

The zamindars in most parts of this district prefer to mortgage their land before proceeding to sale: in some parts however it is customary to sell certain areas rather than mortgage the whole of a property. In any case sales are not uncommon, and though sales were known in Moghal and Sikh times they have only become common since the establishment of British rule and the increase in the value of landed property. Statistics regarding the sales and mortgages of land will be found in Table No. XXXII and the figures showing the operations of the Registration Department in Tables Nos. XXXIII and XXXIII A. From these it will be observed that the area mortgaged in the quinquennium ending 1897-98 was more than twice as large as in the quinquennium ending 1877-78, and the area sold four times as large. The area under mortgage at the Settlement of 1896-01 was 272,574 acres or 50 per cent. more than the area (180,675 acres) under mortgage at the Settlement of 1873-80. The area sold in the 20 years between the 1st and 2nd Settlements was 95,251 acres; that sold in the 20 years between the 2nd and 3rd Settlements was 301,542 acres or more than three times as much. Of the land under mortgage at the 3rd Settlement 89 per cent. was in the hands of money-lenders, and of the land sold between the 2nd and 3rd Settlements 61 per cent. was sold to the same fraternity. Hindus who owned 17 per cent. of the propietary area at the 1st Settlement, had at the 2nd 20·3 per cent., and at the 3rd 26·8 per cent., so that they now own more than half as much land again as they did 40 years ago.

CHAPTER IV.

PRODUCTION AND DISTRIBUTION.

SECTION A.—AGRICULTURE, ARBORICULTURE AND LIVE STOCK.

Chapter IV, A.

Agriculture, Arboriculture and Live-stock.

Area under cultivation.

In Table No. XIV will be found the recorded figures regarding the areas under cultivation at various periods; but the statistics of cultivation in this district are beset with many intricacies and difficulties, which render the figures there quoted to a large extent meaningless. The term 'cultivated area' was, until the new measurements of 1897—1899 commenced, taken to mean the area actually under crop during the year; and in a district like Multan, where the area under crop varies so much from year to year, it is of little avail to compare the figures of any particular year with those of other years. Until 1884, moreover, the establishment for supervising the record of cultivated areas was insufficient, and the figures previous to that date are not very trustworthy. At the new measurements again, another system was adopted, under which, according to the practice of the province at large, the term 'cultivated area' was applied not only to lands actually under crop, but also to lands recently cropped or ploughed for a subsequent crop. But this latter form of entry, though suitable in some ways for comparison with other districts, has its defects, as, owing to the extreme variations in the seasons and the abundance of land, the 'cultivated area' does not always reflect truly the actual state of the cultivation. For purpose of comparison with the past it is best to adopt the present record of the sown area, *i.e.*, the area cropped *plus* the area failed in an average of years, and on this basis we find the average sown area of the five years preceding the new assessments to be 748,214 acres as against a cultivated area of 564,204 at the previous Settlement (1873—77). The failed areas were not recorded previous to 1885, and have only of late years been recorded with any degree of completeness; but for comparison with future records of cultivation there can be no better starting point than the recorded average matured (excluding failed) area of crops cultivated in the five years 1894-95 to 1897-98, which was 713,969 acres, or in the five years preceding the new assessments,* which was

* *i.e.*, 1893-94 to 1897-98 in the three western tahsils and 1894-95 to 1898-99 in the two eastern tahsils.

Chapter IV, A.

Agriculture, Arboriculture and Live-stock.

Area under cultivation.

728,488 acres. According to the measurements of the present Settement, 9 per cent. of the total area of the district is taken up by reserved forests and other tracts not available for cultivation, 38 per cent. by unappropriated Government waste, and the rest by culturable village lands, of which about half (or 26½ per cent. of the whole area) is recorded as 'cultivated.'

Soils.

The whole district is one of comparatively recent alluvial formation, and the composition of the soil is, within certain limits, of a very uniform character. Everywhere there is sand at a greater or less distance from the surface, and the main soils are distinguished from each other according to the greater or less admixture of the clay with the sand.

The sandiest soil of all is known as *retli*, and the soil which consists of a thin layer of alluvion above a sandy substratum is called *dramman*. The ordinary light loam prevalent in the greater part of the district is the *gas*; a good average soil requiring a fair amount of irrigation, but capable of bearing most of the ordinary crops. *Gas* which grows drab grass or harmal is not as good as that which grows jál or karíl bushes; and this, again, is inferior to that which grows the jand. A somewhat richer *gas* is known as *phambi*, and the best soil of all is the *milk*, a reddish soil of a soft texture, with very little sand and retentive of moisture.

The ordinary hard clay soils are known as *mal* or *pakki zamin*. Harder than these and more difficult of cultivation are the soils known as *kappar* and *rappar*. Both these terms are used by zamindars for very hard soils, in which, as a rule, nothing but rice or sawánk will grow; they often distinguish between the two soils, but the points of distinction as given by different zamindars do not always agree; and all that can be said is, that on the whole rappar is somewhat better and more culturable than kappar, which is almost, if not entirely, unculturable.

Kallar, kallar shor and *kalaráchhi* are all varieties of the saline soils so well known in other districts of the province. The surface of the soil is generally a soft snowy white, but this superficial defect does not necessarily imply any radical impracticability in the soil; on the contrary, some of the best cultivation in the district round Sher Sháh and elsewhere is in immediate proximity to the *shor*. So long, no doubt, as the efflorescence remains the land is unculturable, but this can be removed by irrigation or by digging it away. This ordinary shor is known as 'chittá shor'; but there is another variety known as 'kála shor,' which presents a black, clammy looking appearance, and which it is practically impossible to eradicate: it is espe-

Chapter IV, A.

Agriculture. Arboriculture and Live-stock.

Soils.

cially prevalent in the tract near Gawen in Shujabad. The general attitude of the agriculturist towards kallar soils is shown by the proverb: 'Bhanne de pichhon múl na bhajjín; kallar bíj na hári' ('Do not run after a man who is running away; and do not waste your seed on kallar land').

In the riverain tracts one finds special names attached to the soils usually found in places subject to flood. The sticky, uneven soil caused by the long standing of water in places where new alluvial matter has been deposited is known as *gap daryai*. When it dries and cracks into huge blocks with miniature crevasses between them it is known as *treranwalí*. There is also a special form of injury caused by excessive percolation from the river: this is known as *soman*, and it has the effect of water-logging the soil and stunting the growth of the crops. It was very markedly prevalent in the neighbourhood of Shujabad after the heavy floods of 1893 and 1894; and though the trouble has now largely abated, this excessive percolation had the effect of driving out, to a very large extent, the sugar and indigo cultivation which was formerly so luxuriant in that neighbourhood.

So, too, in the bár or Ráwa areas, there are special names applied to particular tracts or soils. Good soil, if supplied with water, is spoken of as 'Ráwa sohāwa,' and, if deprived of water, as 'Ráwa rund': the epithets being expressive of the 'married' or 'widowed' state of the tract. In Kabírwala the well wooded tract south of Tulamba, which was once part of the Rávi bed and is now mostly occupied by reserved forests, is known as the 'Jhánghar' (from 'jhang,' a clump of trees); and the land near Kachha Khuh and Khánewala is spoken of as 'jhábra' from the jál trees, of which people pluck the fruit (jhámban). The high tract between the railway and the old Beás is known as 'ganji,' from its 'bald' and sterile appearance not as some commentators wrongly interpret, from its having once been a 'Ganj' or 'granary' of luxuriant cultivation); the good, moist soil along the old Biás goes by the name of the 'bár viyáh', and the Mailsi bár between the Biás and Sutlej is spoken of as the 'bár-báráni' tract.

Means of irrigation.

When all is said, however, that can be said regarding the differences of soils, it remains that in a district like Multan all these distinctions fade into very little as compared with the distinction between irrigated and unirrigated land, and the composition of the soil has much less to do with the produce than the amount and character of the irrigation received. The soil has on this account been always classed in the Government records according to the method of irrigation, and the area

Chapter IV, A.

Agriculture, Arboriculture and Live stock.

Means of irrigation.

under cultivation at the third Settlement (1896—1901) was classified as follows :—

	Acres.	Per cent.
Wells, unaided	45,164	4·5
Wells aided by canals	454,443	45·4
Wells aided by river floods	41,759	4·1
River floods and lift from rivers	126,209	12·5
Canals	311,133	30·9
Rain land	27,025	2·6
Total	1,005,773	100·0

Wells.

The only form of well found in this district is that known as the 'Persian wheel' well. It is generally made of masonry, but occasionally in the river lands (more especially on the Chenáb) the masonry extends only as far as the water level, and in such cases the well is known as a 'kharora.' Kachha wells, made entirely without masonry, are very uncommon.

The value of a well depends on the quality of the water, on its depth from the surface, and on the continuity of the supply.

Wells are occasionally found in which the water is brackish (khára) and unfit for drinking. A marked line of such wells extends, more or less continuously, from Dunyapur in the centre of the district to Jalálpur Pírwála in the south-west. When a brackish well is fully aided by canal water, the brackishness has no serious effect on the crops; but if the crops depend on such a well alone without further help, they are apt to suffer considerably.

The depth of the well depends mainly on its distance from the river : and as the whole of the district is within reasonable distance of the river, we do not find any wells of extraordinary depth, although those in the centre of the *bár* tract are deep enough. The average figures for the district, as ascertained at the Settlement of 1896—1901, are shown in the margin. The agriculturist often calculates the

	Average depth to water.
Hithar	16
Utar and Sidhnai	25
Ráwa	33

Chapter IV, A.

Agriculture, Arboriculture and Live-stock.

Wells.

depth of water by the number of well-pots (lota) required, and, roughly speaking, some six well-pots go to each *háth* of depth. With the extension of canal irrigation the water level has a tendency to rise, though not of course to the same extent as in tracts where permanent canal irrigation is introduced. Taking, for instance, ten villages in various parts of the area now irrigated by the Sidhnai canal, we find that since 1879 the average depth to water has decreased from 44·7 to 40·1 feet; and, in the same way, the subsidence of the river causes lowering of the water level, as for example, in the Rávi riverain circle, where the water level which in 1877 was 16 feet, is now 26 feet, below the surface.*

The third requisite in a well is the constancy of the supply afforded by the sub-soil water. There is everywhere a stratum of water-giving sand, which is known as the *sachh*, and which it is the object of the well-sinker to reach. As he goes down below the surface, the first water he meets is a trickling and dirty moisture, which is known as *soman*, and which is of a fluctuating character. The real permanent supply (or 'shauh páni' as it is called) is found in the *sachh* only, and the diver knows by examining the soil which he brings out whether he has reached the desired stratum or not.

The agriculturist about to build a well first chooses a suitable spot, if possible a little above the level of the area he wishes to irrigate. He then traces the circle of the well, and he sets the labourers to work, under the supervision of the village carpenter, to dig the cylinder or *bhár* down to the water level. The wooden base of the brick-work (known as *talwang*) is then hoisted in with the aid of a large crowd of neighbours and fixed in its place at the bottom. On this the brick-work is carefully built up, the bricks being joined with mud (*gára*) instead of mortar, and the masonry cylinder is completed to the level of the ground or to a height of some three or four feet above the level of the ground. On to this cylinder is then attached an apparatus known as the *pal*, which consists of transverse sticks and thick ropes of twisted *sar* grass (called 'wat') arranged so as to hold the earth taken up from the well and to act as a heavy weight to depress the masonry cylinder. The diver or tobi now begins his operations, working with a huge mattock (*kahí*) attached to a rope, which he from time to time fixes into the subsoil, and which is in turn withdrawn and hauled to the top of the well. The diver's work is exceedingly hard owing to the physical strength required and the cold dampness of the air he has to live in, but he is fed on the best during his term of

* In dealing with these figures, it must be remembered that the depths of wells at this Settlement were taken when the river and canals were not running whereas we do not know what rule was observed at last Settlement.

Chapter IV, A.

Agriculture, Arboriculture and Live-stock.

Wells.

labour. As he works, the cylinder slowly subsides until it reaches the true water stratum, which is generally some 10 to 15 feet below the place where it first touched the water. The *pal* is then removed, and the *nál* or cylinder is completed by the addition of the *gadohar* or upper portion and the *gal*, which is the portion projecting above the ground.

The cost of a well differs considerably, not only according to the depth of the well, but according also to the degree to which the zamindar can supply materials, (such as timber, fire-wood, bricks, etc.,) from his own resources. The cost of digging the cylinder both below and above water is generally put at Re. 1 per háth (about two feet), and that of the bricks, if bought, at Re. 4 per thousand : these latter can, however, be made at Rs. 2-4 0 per thousand if the owner can provide the firewood and the clay himself. The average cost of a masonry well (apart from the removeable fittings) may be taken, roughly, at Rs. 400 in the Hithar, Rs. 500 in the Utar, and Rs. 600 in the Ráwa and Sidhnai circles : and in granting advances for wells it will generally be safe to adopt this standard. Generally speaking, about a half of the cost goes in the purchase and carriage of the bricks, and the rest in the brick-laying, digging and diving, the construction of the *pal*, and occasional bursts of free feeding.

The well cylinder, if carefully constructed and made with good bricks, lasts for an unlimited length of time ; and *dals* or old disused wells of previous centuries are often dug out again and made fit for use at small expense. A good well will need cleaning out once in every five years or so ; a bad one oftener. This is done by attaching a rope and mattock to a revolving arrangement in the form of a capstan (known as a dol or úrá), by which the extraneous silt at the bottom of the well is gradually cleared out. A well, however, is subject to various forms of disrepair and weakness, and when suffering from these is spoken of as being ill (bímár). If the original sinking was not carried to the right point, the well soon begins to run short of water (chora ho vendá). If the bricks at the side of the cylinder begin to give way ; the well's 'waist' is said to break (kamr trut vendi) ; or if a large hole is formed in the cylinder, an outlet is said to be formed (mori nikal paí) : in such cases the damage is known as bhattha (bhattha pai gaí). To avert disaster from such accidents, it is usual to insert a wooden cylinder fitting closely inside the circle of the well, and some six to ten feet in height ; if laid below the tilwang to prevent the intrusion of sand, the framework is known as a *kothi ;* if laid above the tilwang to support the sides of the masonry cylinder, it is known as a *ghanda*. Such a framework costs some Rs. 4 per háth to make, apart from the cost of fixing it in, and it may keep a well going for ten or twelve years longer; but to use a well repaired is proverbially looked on as the equivalent of wearing old clothes that have been stitched together.

The wood-work of the well (chob chakkal) is constructed in the same way as in the rest of the Punjab, though the nomenclature in some respects varies. The chief parts of the framework are the horizontal wheel (chakkal), the vertical pole on which it revolves (bhurjal), the horizontal beams below and above those (bhurní and kánjan), the pillars on which the upper beam rests (munnán), the seat on which the driver sits (gádhí), the shaft connecting the two wheels (lath), the vertical wheel (chakli), the vertical apparatus for drawing up the water (bair), the ropes (mahl), the sticks connecting the ropes (rerián), the earthen pots (lote), the wooden projection to keep the ropes in its place (sútarlar); the cog (tháka), the splash-board to prevent earth from falling into the well (chaman), the small conduit into which the pots pour the water (parchha), the longer conduit which takes the water further into the cistern (nisár), the log on which this conduit rests (jhal) and the cistern into which it pours the water (khádá).* The cost of the whole apparatus varies a good deal according as tahli, kikar or ukánh wood is used; but, speaking roughly, the average cost of the whole is about Rs. 40 or Rs. 50 if the materials have to be bought. Generally, however, the constructor of a well has the wood growing on his own lands, and has to pay for the construction only; the cost of which comes to about half of the figures above quoted.

The area irrigated by a well varies a good deal, not only according to the state of the well cylinder, but also according to the amount of aid received from canals or sailáb, and according to the degree to which the soil retains moisture. The average areas under irrigation and the average areas matured in a year from a well in each circle in the district are as recorded below:—

Per well in use.	Hithar.	Utar.	Rawa.	Sidhnai.	All circles.
Average area under cultivation ...	26	35	31	32	32
Do. matured ...	11	21	18	11	18

The rate at which well irrigation can be carried on of course varies immensely, but a normal rate of irrigation would

*Which gives rise to the local saying: 'Khúh gahra te kháda sáf' ('The well is dirty, but the cistern clean.')

Chapter IV. A.
Agriculture, Arboriculture and Live-stock.
Wells.

seem to be a little over one-fourth of an acre of ploughed land in twenty-four hours, the well being worked hard all the time. Wheat irrigated during winter by an ordinary well probably receives water at the rate of some three or four days to the acre.

The following figures show the wells in existence in 1899-1900:—

Aided by canals	...	In use	13,423	out of use	1,546
Aided by sailáb	...	In use	1,833	out of use	291
Unaided ...	...	In use	2,027	out of use	780

Well cultivation.

The wells in the greater part of the district are unused during the summer months, the areas which they serve being in those months as far as possible irrigated by canal water or submerged by river floods; and the well cattle are thus during those months available for ploughing. The land which is cultivated for the rabi is during the latter part of the summer soaked as much as possible with water from canals or floods, and when the rabi has been ploughed and sown the effects of this soaking in many tracts suffice to bring the crop to maturity, especially if aided by a little winter rain. As a rule, however, the crop requires some further irrigation, and it is the function of the wells to supply to these winter crops the further irrigation that they need. The people, therefore, are busy all the winter, and especially towards the end of the winter months, in doing all they can to supply the necessary well water to each part of their holdings in succession. The months when the wells are working are in some ways the busiest months; and is a saying: Jinhán jutte khúh, unhán de sukh na sutte ruh' ('One whose well is working gets no peace or sleep.')

Where the wells are unaided either by canals or sailáb—as in large parts of the central or Ráwa tracts—the system of well cultivation has special peculiarities. The wells are, it is true, often abandoned there also in the summer, owing to the intense strain on the cattle which the working of the wells in the blazing heat of these unsheltered tracts entails, but generally a little jowár and cotton is sown to keep things going; and as the autumn begins the well is worked to aid the rabi ploughings. The wheat sowing continues for a longer period on the unaided wells than on the aided wells. Each portion of ground is moistened, ploughed and sown in turn, whereas on the aided wells the whole area must be ploughed and sown before the effects of autumn drenching have passed off. These unaided wells are generally deeper than the others and they require a superior breed of cattle to work them; and tenants for such wells are less easy to procure than for others. On the other hand, the areas attached to them are large, the harvests are so alternated that there is no fear of exhaustion and the produce per acre is often surprisingly good.

Chapter IV, A.

Agriculture, Arboriculture and Live-stock.

Well cultivation.

As a rule, however, the well in this district is looked on as a pis-aller in the absence of canal or sailáb irrigation; and the word *páni* is often used by the people. in the sense of canal water only. A well is said to have no *páni* when it is not aided by canals; such a well is also spoken of as *kura* or waterless.

The well is of considerable importance in the agricultural economy of the district, and the landed property is for the most part divided into 'wells,' that is into well estates or areas attached to wells; and the well thus serves as a unit of proprietorship. The lands that are attached to no well are known as ghair-ta'alluk lands.*

Canal cultivation

It will be seen from the figures quoted at the beginning of this chapter that some 76 per cent. of the cultivation of this district is dependent either entirely or partly on the canals, and the canal cultivation constitutes the main characteristic of the agriculture of the district. A more detailed account of the canals themselves will be given in the succeeding chapter; but in respect of their relation to the local agriculture, attention may here be drawn to the character of the cultivation on the inundation canals and the Sidhnai canal, respectively.

The inundation canals take their rise in cuttings made in the banks of the rivers, and flow only when there is sufficient flood-water to pass over the bed-level of these openings; that is to say, generally speaking, from the end of April to October. When the rivers are in full flood from June to August there is always plenty of water in the canals, and the difficulty is to arrange by means of regulators and escapes for the harmless disposal of superfluous water. It is at the beginning and end of the season, when the rivers are rising or falling, that the conditions of irrigation become critical. The success of the kharif crops does not depend on the volume of water received by them during the season, but upon the length of time during which supplies can be assured; and the success of the rabi sowings depends not on the amount of water available during the summer, but on the amount, if any, available at the end of the season. It is, therefore, in respect of its position towards these early and late waterings that the chief differentiation between village and village, or between holding and holding, consists. A water-course with a good slope and a head whose level is well below the flood-level of the canal will run earlier and longer than others; and the village supplied by it will, *ceteris paribus*, be better off than others. So, too, if a village is dependent for its kharif on indigo, a late rise in the river will ruin

* Some lands so termed have become subsequently irrigable from wells, but continue to be entered in the revenue records as '*ghair-ta'alluk*,' so that one sometimes hears lands incongruously described as 'unattached lands attached to such and such a well.'

Chapter IV, A.

Agriculture, Arboriculture and Live-stock.

Canal cultivation.

its harvest, or, if it depends on cotton, an early fall will seriously damage it. Some villages are so situated that they are sure of supplies for the whole of their rabi sowings; others are thankful if they can sow any of their wheat at all without using their wells. Some holdings are assured of flow throughout the summer, and such are readily taken up by tenants. Other holdings have to eke out their supplies by working jhalárs in the earlier and later months, and on such the tenants look askance. Some water-courses, owned by rich men, are fully cleared in the winter so as to run throughout the summer: others, owned by the poorer or less united zamindárs, are not cleared, or are cleared imperfectly; so that they run in flood time only or silt up altogether.

A glance at the tables of crop returns will generally indicate pretty clearly the position of a village in respect of a canal irrigation. The choicest class of village is that in which the whole kharíf crop is nahri flow, and the whole rabi is cháhi-nahri, that is to say, in which the small supply in the hot months is so continuous and assured that the wells need not be used either for sowing or maturing the kharíf, and in which the number of wells is amply sufficient to protect and to mature in the winter the crops which have been sown by the aid of canal water in the autumn. The more a village deviates from this standard the less satisfactory is its position. A village will sometimes have some pure nahri gram and peas in the rabi, especially if there be much rice land on which these crops can be sown without further watering, and such a village is not necessarily inferior to the best; but if there be any considerable amount of nahri wheat, the wells are clearly insufficient and the outturn will be inferior. If there is much pure cháhi cultivation in the rabi, or if any part of the kharíf is cháhi-nahri, the village has obviously received an inadequate supply of canal water, or portions of it must be too high to be properly commanded. Worse still is the village which has any pure cháhi cultivation in the kharíf, for with canals in the immediate neighbourhood a tenant requires great inducements to work a well in the summer. And in each class of village things are made worse if the canal irrigation is by lift and not by flow: for the tenant objects to the 'lote ká páni' on the canal, almost as much as he objects to it in the case of a well. If the village is near the head of a canal, its irrigation will be mainly dependent on lift; if at the tail, the water runs short when supplies in the canal are low. It is to considerations such as these just noticed that the native of this district addresses himself in estimating the value of a holding, far more than to considerations of soil; but the poorer a village or holding may be as regards irrigation, the more important does difference of soil become. When canal water is abundant, it matters little whether the ground be 'thirsty'

Chapter IV. A.

Agriculture, Arboriculture and Live-stock.

or 'cold'; but the more the crop is dependent on wells, the more does it concern the cultivator to have a soil which retains the little moisture he can from time to time supply.

Canal cultivation.

In the normal village in the normal year the cultivator looks for the arrival of the canal water about the end of April. If he wishes to grow indigo on his holding he at once floods his lands in order to plough and sow for that crop. If cotton is to be grown, its cultivation has to be undertaken with little delay, and the sowings are generally over by the middle of June. If rice is cultivated, the seedlings are transplanted about the end of the same month. The kharíf jowár is sown in July, the bájra follows shortly, and then the til. All these crops are sown and grown with canal water only; the indigo and rice are cut before the canals cease to flow; and the cultivator will think himself hardly used if he is unable to use the canal for the final watering of the others. While the water is still in flood, he begins the 'rauni' or preliminary waterings for the rabi crops; and the more waterings and ploughings he can give to his wheat the better chance he has of a good outturn. Before the canals subside, he puts in his peas, turnips and gram, and towards the end of October, shortly after the canals have ceased to run, the wheat sowings commence. The turnips and wheat will receive some three or four waterings from the well during the winter, and the others will get such water as can be spared. From December onwards the turnips are taken up for cattle, and with the spring the peas begin to be similarly utilized. Then the gram is harvested, and the operations of the year culminate finally with the wheat cuttings in April.

On the Sidhnai canal the circumstances, though similar, differ in some respects. The agriculturist on that canal generally counts on the canal beginning to flow in March. If supplies are scanty, they are used to save the nahri wheat; if, however, an adequate amount of water is available, it is employed to help in the cotton ploughing, and to irrigate the vegetables and early chína of the zaid rabi. By the end of April he may be pretty certain of regular supplies, and he then begins his khárif sowings, or if any portion of his land is kappar he will try to lay down some rice. As soon as supplies are assured he ceases to work his well (if he has one), and it is quite exceptional for any well water to be used for the kharíf harvest. Not only are rice, indigo and til grown on purely nahri lands, but cotton, chari, jowár and chína are also almost entirely grown without well water. In August and September the cultivator puts down the late chína and sathri which the autumn flowing of this canal allows him to interpose between the kharíf and the rabi. Then as the chances of supplies failing increase, he hastens to sow his turnips and to plough for the wheat. The area which he puts under wheat depends

Chapter IV, A.

Agriculture, Arboriculture and Live-stock.

Canal cultivation.

almost entirely on the amount of water available during the autumn months; if supplies cease early in October the area will be comparatively small, but if supplies continue more and more land is brought under the plough, the maximum being reached (except as regards well areas) when supplies last on to the middle of December. As a rule, however, the zamindar cannot look for water after the first few days of November, and all cultivation thereafter is dependent on wells. If rain fails during the winter the zamindar who has no well begins to feel the want of it; and if the canal does not begin flowing till late the nahri wheat harvest runs great risk of destruction. With a well in use judicious waterings are bestowed on the turnips and wheat within reach; so that these crops are duly saved and their outturn promoted, but should the canal run all through the winter there is every temptation to leave the well alone and to trust entirely to canal irrigation. The chabi-nahri irrigation of the rabi in fact varies pretty nearly in inverse proportion to the duration of the winter supplies in the canal.

The critical time with the Sidhnai agriculturist is the period when the supplies are short. If all the rájbahas cannot be fed at once, they run in turns, and everything depends on the period elapsing between two supplies thus meted out to one rájbaha. Both in spring and in autumn there are crops to sow and crops to mature, and the zamindar is often in a strait, when water is scarce, as to whether his scanty supply shall be used for sowing or maturing; and bad judgment or bad luck in this respect may have serious consequences.

Sailab cultivation.

The character of the floods on the three different rivers—the Rávi, Chenáb and Sutlej—has been described in Chapter I above; and the cultivation naturally is affected by the character of the flooding in each case.

The Rávi riverain for the first ten miles from the district border is a thin strip of country, mostly covered with sand and small tamarisk scrub; it is bounded, as a rule, on either side by a bank, which displays at times a solitary jhalár, and at times the gaping mouth of some disused canal cut. At places the bank shelves away, and here, especially if the river is on the turn, a little sailáb may flow inland and give rise to a few acres of cultivation. Occasionally, too, there is an old river branch which penetrates the bank and rejoins the main river below; and through this branch the flood waters may flow in summer, and on its bed some gram or wheat crops may be grown in winter. As it approaches Tulamba, the riverain widens out and the sailáb improves; but even here the tract which is sure of inundation is comparatively small, and large areas slope up on either side which can only hope occasionally to be flooded. Outside the land directly reached by the floods there lies on either side of the river a higher tract which looks for sustenance to the numerous river-cuts made by the zamindars. A large part of the area recorded in our papers as sailáb in this riverain is land which receives the floods in this indirect manner. The wells, lying as they do for the most part in the higher tracts, have been built in the expectation of helping this indirect inundation; not a few, also, have been made in positions where direct flooding is received, but scarcely one has been constructed with the intention that it should subsist on its own resources. When floods begin to fail, the wells are for a time kept up in the hope of better things to come: then as this hope is disappointed the inferior wells drop out of use, and their owners migrate elsewhere; better wells and those in the hand of stronger men last on; and as the water is not far from the surface, and oxen are plentiful, the zamindars gradually become used to the new condition of things and cease to look for any help from the river.

Chapter IV, A.

Agriculture, Arboriculture and Live-stock.

Sailáb cultivation

On the Chenáb there are, roughly speaking, three classes of riverain cultivation. Immediately adjoining the river is the low land on to which the river is almost certain to overflow every year; the soil here is exceedingly variable not only from place to place, but also from year to year; and the fine rich river-bed wheat soil of this year may in a year or two be reduced to mere sand or swept away altogether. Above this lower area and divided from it by a rise of level more or less well defined is the tract of secondary sailáb, which, as a rule, the high floods only penetrate, and where but little silt is deposited; the soil in this tract is less liable to violent change, but the area inundated fluctuates greatly from year to year. When the floods come down in June and July, their tendency is to spread vaguely inland as far as the surface levels will permit, and (especially in the southern corner of the district). to penetrate by creeks and natural depressions to villages far distant from the river. This tendency to spread inland, having in many cases led to widespread destruction of crops and other property, has in the Multan tahsil, and in the northern part of Shujabad been artificially checked by a series of embankments; but the areas immediately within these embankments, though protected from direct flooding, are often subject to indirect influence from the river by means of percolation, and in such areas is found a kind of cultivation which may be classed as a tertiary form of sailáb. This again exhibits itself in two forms which are found not only within the embankments, but also outside them in lands to which the actual flooding does not reach. In the north of Multan on the one hand, where the soil is favourable, the cropping on lands reached by percolation is as rich as that of the flooded areas, and being much safer is much sought after. On the other hand, in the south of Multan and north of Shujabad, where the soil is worse

Chapter IV, A.

Agriculture, Arboriculture and Live-stock.

Sailáb cultivation.

and more tainted with salts, the water oozes freely through the earth, and in the summer months (especially since the big floods of 1893 and 1894) often stands so deep and so long on the canal commanded area as to retard the cultivation of the rabi and to prevent or seriously injure that of the kharif. This oozing of water is known as soman, and it forms the subject of much complaint; but complaints are equally loud when owing to a change of the course of the river, or for some other reason, it ceases altogether and the land is left without moisture. The general result, however, in the villages affected has been the substitution of rabi crops for kharíf, and of less valuable crops for the more valuable. A favourable flood season is one that begins early in June, and ends early in August. If the floods go down in time, the higher lands available are sown with til, and the lower with másh; but the floods are more powerful and of longer duration in the south than in the north, and the proportion of kharíf cropping decreases markedly as one goes further south, from 21·2 per cent. in the Kabírwála Hithar to 17·8 per cent. in Multan and only 1·3 per cent. in Shujabad. The general riverain cultivation in the two latter tahsils begins in September, when the peas, masar, methra and gram are put into the ground, to be followed in October by the wheat. The wheat is the main staple of the river lands, and all the energies of the zamindars, especially in the extreme south, are directed towards its successful cultivation. Manure, however, is seldom used; and although the sailáb cropping is particularly impeded by noxious weeds, weeding is practically unknown. There is, moreover, little or no attempt at rotation, and the broad wheat lands of southern Shujabad have borne the same crop year after year ever since they were reclaimed from jungle. Of the wells which are dotted about the landward portions of the sailáb area very few are used for the production of an autumn crop; for if the floods reach the well area in the summer, the standing water, will, as a rule, prevent the kharíf ploughing; and if the floods in any year fail to reach the well, the soil is generally too dry and too light to make unaided kharíf watering profitable. The main function of the wells is to mature the wheat and to ensure the supply of water to this crop when the moisture introduced by the summer flood begins to disappear. The sailáb wells are shallower: their cylinders, as a rule, are narrower; and the number of cattle required for working them is smaller, than in the canal tracts. Being to a great extent deserted in the summer months, they are very often devoid of the usual accessories—the trees and the adjoining homestead—of the upland wells; the people and their cattle live less upon their wells than elsewhere: and are often congregated in high plots of ground in groups of thatch-roofed byres and cottages, sometimes surrounded by a small embankment, and sometimes half hidden among clumps of palm-trees. As autumn comes on many of the cultivators move out to their fields and live for the winter in rough wattled sheds, which they run up alongside of their cultivation.

Sailáb cultivation.

On the Sutlej there is comparatively little cháhi-sailáb cultivation; the river seldom penetrates beyond the high bank, and in the tract below the high bank there are very few wells. The high bank, at the same time, limits the influence of the river in the way of percolation. The river floods come down in July and August. If the floods are strong, they work up to the high bank or beyond it; if weak, they leave large stretches untouched even on the lower levels. As a rule, the water stands too late in all but the higher parts of the riverain lands to allow of any kharíf being cultivated, but occasionally a little til or jowár is sown in July in the immediate neighbourhood of the water. The main agricultural operations, however, begin in the latter part of September, when the floods have subsided. For wheat the zamindar will plough twice; for other crops, such as peas, or grain, or masur, or methra, he contents himself with a single ploughing, or at times dispenses with ploughing altogether. In new land he will for a year or two grow the inferior crops, and will then proceed to grow wheat. As the spring advances numbers of cattle migrate from the higher tracts to graze in the moister river lands and to feed upon the peas and other fodder crops which their owners purchase for them. In April comes the wheat harvest: the cattle are then let loose among the stubble, and by the middle or end of June, before the floods begin to rise, the grain heaps are removed to the higher and more secure grounds; the cattle and the cultivators follow, leaving the temporary sheds in which they have spent the winter; and the fields are abandoned once more to the mercy of the river.

Jhalárs.

Irrigation from an open surface of water by means of the Persian wheel or jhalár is found both on the rivers and on the canals. The jhalárs are of several kinds. The *oral* or *baharbadi* is a small contrivance, having a few pots only, but of a large size; it is worked by one bullock only, and is the common form in use round the city of Multan. The *tangan* or *utangan* is used when the water is at a medium distance, and the wheel of a tangan contains about fifty to sixty pots. The *beghar* or double jhalár is used when the distance from the water is very great, one wheel conveying the water to an intermediate reservoir into which the second wheel plays. A *jung* or *do charkhi* jhalár is one in which there are two wheels playing into the same reservoir.

On the rivers the jhalárs are only employed where the banks are not liable to erosion, and consequently they are uncommon on the Chenáb. They are most frequently found on the Sutlej and on the Sidhnai reach of the Rávi, and the

Chapter IV, A.

Agriculture, Arboriculture and Live-stock.

cultivation which they irrigate is entered in the revenue records as 'abi'. Sometimes water is lifted out of ponds or depressions in the same way, and this also is classed as 'abi.'

Jhalar cultivation.

In the canal irrigated tracts the jhalárs are found both on the canals themselves and on the water-courses taking out of them. They are used with two objects, *viz.*, either to irrigate lands on to which canal cultivation cannot flow, or to prolong the period of irrigation in cases when the full supplies of the canal or water-courses reach the land but not the lower supplies received at the beginning and end of the season. In this latter case they serve as an intermediary between the canal flow irrigation of the summer and the well irrigation of the winter. The presence of a jhalár generally indicates a difficulty in irrigation, and rent rates paid on jhalár lands are usually less than on flow lands; but of course in the second of the two sets of circumstances above mentioned, *viz.*, in lands fairly well commanded by flow, a holding that has a jhalár has a distinct advantage over one which has not.

Báráni cultivation.

Rain cultivation is of no importance, except in the Mailsí tahsil, where in years of good rainfall a considerable amount of scattered cultivation is carried on, chiefly in the depressions (dhoras or toas) found in the Government waste. This cropping is both kharíf and rabi, but for the most part the latter. The rains generally come too late for much kharif cropping other than til, but they admit of considerable wheat sowings; and the crop once having been sown, reliance is placed on the extraordinary moisture of the soil of these depressions and on the possibility of winter rains to bring the crop to maturity.

Ploughing.

There is only one description of plough in use in the district, though ploughs are made heavy or light to suit different soils. It is constructed, generally of kikar wood, by the village carpenter, the phála or share being supplied by the blacksmith. The fields are divided into portions by preliminary lines, and in turning up the intervening space the plough always turns in narrowing circles from right to left. The act of ploughing is not looked on with much respect, and there is a proverb which says, 'Halán dá ke waháwan hai? Picchon lagá jáwan hai' ('What does ploughing consist of? Merely walking behind the plough'). The task of ploughing, which in most districts is entrusted to grown up men, is here largely left to boys and young lads. Before ploughing the land has always to be moistened, and the kharíf ploughings are often much delayed when the canals fail to run early. It is very common for neighbouring tenants to join their resources for ploughing, and several pairs (sometimes as many as 8 or 9 pairs) of bullocks follow one another, ploughing each a furrow inside the one in

Chapter IV, A.

Agriculture. Arboriculture and Live-stock.

Ploughing.

front. Male buffaloes are sometimes seen in the yoke, especially in the Chenáb tahsils, and camels are sometimes employed for ploughing in the *bár* in Mailsi. Some crops can occasionally be grown without ploughing, such as gram on suitable depressions by the river, or indigo on the stubble of wheat. Some receive ploughings after the seed is sown as well as before, such as wheat, in lands where it is sown broadcast; and some, such as cotton, are occasionally ploughed between the plants to get rid of weeds.

Sowing.

The grain used for sowing generally comes from the previous year's crop, or if that is exhausted, it is taken on loan from the money-lenders. Very often the landlord lends the seed to the tenant, against the harvest, without interest; but in cases where the landlord is also a money-lender, he lends the seed on heavy interest, seldom less than 25 per cent. Some crops, such as indigo and turnips, are made use of before they seed, and for these a special area is set aside to mature to seed. In the case of indigo, however, it is very common to purchase imported seed from Sukkur, or Khairpur, or the districts near Delhi. There is not much care taken about the selection of grain for seed; but in some tracts, more especially among the Aráins round Jalla in Lodhrán, wheat seed of a particularly good description is available for purchase.

When the surface of the ground has been recently moistened, as is the case in most of the kharíf crops and in that of those rabi crops which are ploughed for with the aid of well water, the sowing is usually done broadcast (chhatt). If, however, some time has elapsed between the watering and the sowing, the seed is put in by drill (náli); and this is the common practice on the sailáb lands. When the seed is small it is sometimes mixed with earth before it is sown; and cotton seeds (pewe) are smeared with cowdung and dried before being sown. Sugarcane is grown from seed canes; and some crops, such as rice, tobacco and onions are first raised in nurseries (paníri), and afterwards transplanted.

Rolling and levelling.

After ploughing, the land is usually smoothed down by means of a heavy wooden roller (mehra). The roller is required for the double purpose of breaking the clods and of keeping in the moisture (wattar) which otherwise evaporates. Where the clods have already been broken, and it is desired merely to smooth the soil, a lighter variety of roller known as the 'ghíhal, is also in use, and sometimes a couple of ploughs lashed together serve the same purpose.

Where the land is new, or where cultivation is being extended the land requires levelling by the removal of earth from one place to another. This operation is known as 'ken kashi', as it is done with the aid of an instrument called a 'ken,' which is a

Chapter IV, A.

Agriculture, Arboriculture and Live-stock.

Rolling and levelling.

screen of wattles with a rake at the bottom. It is pulled by bullocks, and guided by a man in much the same way as a plough. The process of ken kashi is also employed to remove earth from one part of a field to another, so as to get a fresh stock of soil and so improve the production of the field.

When canal water is given to the fields before ploughing (rauni), it is not usual to have any partitions made in the field, except on the Sidhnai. When, however, the canal water is applied after the seed has been sown, and when well water is applied, whether before or after sowing, it is usual to make *kiárís* or compartments in the field, and this is done by banking up the earth to the height of about six inches with the aid of a jandra or large wooden rake.

Weeding.

All crops, especially in the sailáb and moister canal soils, are liable to be troubled with weeds. Such are the uthpairara, a common weed with a fan-shaped leaf, which is supposed to resemble a camel's foot ; rárí, a vetch-like creeping plant which grows among the rabi crops ; pápra, a small plant about a foot high, with purple flowers ; vanverí, which is like a small convolvulus ; chiratta, like a dandelion ; the bhaira, with a lilac-coloured bell-like flower ; and the harmal, with a white flower, which comes out in March. There are also the bhúí, with its yellow bunches of blossom ; the jowán, with its purple cruciform flower ; the bughát, with its white bells : the bhuenphor, with its waxy unwholesome looking flowers ; the leh, kander and lút, which are like thistles ; the juság, the jaudal (wild oats), and many others which are collectively spoken of as 'gandí bútí.' Weeding (godi or chokí) is done with a spud (ramba), but, except in small fields of superior crops (tobacco, sugar and vegetables) and near wells, it is unusual for any attention to be paid to the weeding of the crops.

Manure.

Sailáb and pure nahri lands seldom receive manure, which is confined, as a rule, to crops round the wells. Special crops, like tobacco, vegetables and sugarcane, are always manured and turnips nearly always get some manure. Owing to the plentifulness of the wood supply, it is less necessary than in the central Punjab to sacrifice the cattle dung as fuel, and owing to the scattered character of the farmsteads it is easier to get the manure on to the ground ; so that, on the whole, the crops of this district receive a fair share of manure compared with those of many other districts. The manures employed are of various kinds. First there is the ordinary cattle manure, the whole of which goes on to the land : while it is on the well it is called páh, and when it is put on the land it is known as kallur or áhl. Then there are the indigo stalks (wal), which form excellent manure, especially for wheat fields. The droppings of goats and sheep (mengan) are also much prized, especially for tobacco,

Chapter IV, A.

Agriculture, Arboriculture and Livestock.

Manure.

and the owners of flocks are induced to place their animals near wells in return for special payment, or for leave to graze them on the kikar loppings. In some tracts camels are in the same way stationed near wells, and their dung is valuable: it is a powerful manure, but it is said to render the land saline, and much water is required to counteract this effect. The owner of a local shrine, if also a landowner, gets a good deal of camels' dung for nothing, as it is usual for camel owners to locate their cattle for a night (generally Thursday night) round the shrine of some saint in order to protect them from illness. Another useful manure is the soft soil found at the roots of jál trees, and a manure very commonly used is the *at* or silt of canals and watercourses. The zamindars, indeed, say that to make land fertile three things are needed: 'yá phatte yá satte yá atte;' that is to say, 'ploughing, or fallowing, or manuring with silt.' Manure ashes are sometimes used for seed beds. Some zamindars scatter pulverized manure over the young crops in Magh (January-February); and thus have a saying: 'Poh na wattrí, Máh na kallri, na hákimán vandde, na sáinán phallre' ('If you do not irrigate in Poh, or manure in Magh, there will be no share for the Government and no rent for the owners'). In the neighbourhood of Multan the sewage and street sweepings are also very fully utilized, and the sale of these brings in a large sum of money to the municipality and cantonments. Almost every cultivator within a radius of two or three miles from the city has a bullock (pothi) specially set apart for the purpose of being sent in daily (from the nearest wells twice daily) to fetch the manure required. The present arrangement is that wells lying within municipal limits pay Re. 1-8-0 per mensem, and those lying outside those limits Re. 1 per mensem, for the privilege of fetching the sweepings in this way.

Watching.

Jowar and bajra need to be watched during the day for a month or two; when the grain is ripening, in order to keep off the birds. The watchman sits on a high platform, called *mannha*, which is raised on four stakes some ten or twelve feet from the ground: seated on this eminence he slings pellets from a 'khábáni' or cracks a rope (trat), or merely emits howls. Fruit trees need to be watched in the fruiting season in much the same way as jowar; the chief destroyers of the fruit being parrots. Scarecrows are sometimes put up to keep off birds: these often take the shape of waving stalks of sarkana.* In the Rawa precautions are taken against the depredations of chinkára, either (i) by putting up scarecrows—sticks with clothes on them—or a row of sarkana stalks; or (ii) by putting up sticks and con-

* In the months of Phaggan and Chet, Hindus are said to celebrate no marriages, and in those months there are no crops for the birds to eat. Hence the proverb: 'Dhirin ghar ujaria, chirian ujaria khet: Do mahine sulakhine, hikk Phaggan to duja Chet.' ('Daughters destroy a house as birds destroy a crop: two months alone are lucky, namely Phaggan and Chet).'

Chapter IV, A.

Agriculture, Arboriculture and Livestock.

Watching.

necting them with ropes along the side of the field from which the deer come; or (iii) by making holes in the ground and sitting in them at night with a gun. The chinkára chiefly attack the turnips and young wheat. Jackals and foxes do also damage, and are kept off by putting down some dry karil stalks along the side of the field which they frequent. Pig also commit depredations along the river, and it is necessary in some sáilab lands to watch the wheat, when ripening, against pigs both by day and night.

Fencing.

It is not usual to fence a field in any way, but in some parts a rough fence of dry kikar or karíl branches (lorha) is put round the field or round that part of it which most needs fencing, or sometimes merely across the paths leading through the field. In the south of Shujabad this class of fence is firmly and thickly made, and entrance to a field can often only be obtained through a small gate. In lands round the towns or big villages it is not uncommon to have fields walled in; and rough fences often protect those parts of fields which adjoin some frequented road.

Reaping.

Cotton and pepper are picked by hand, but all other crops are reaped with the datri or small sickle. The work of reaping (kapi) is done in a squatting position, and the crops are cut near the roots; in the case of bajra, however, the heads alone are cut off (lápar), because the stalks are not stored for fodder. The tenant does a certain amount of the reaping, but for several crops, especially those of which a large area has to be cut within a short period of time, outside reapers (láwas or laibára) are employed, and these men get three sheaves (múhan, kahín) in every hundred. The ordinary láwa cuts about two kanals of wheat in the day, but sometimes men are found who can get through much more than this. The cotton is picked by women who proceed to the work in large bands, and who receive about one-eighth of the produce as their hire: the cotton (phutti) is not cleared from the husk (sangli) of the pods (dehnu) as it is picked, but the pods are taken to a corner of the field and the cotton picked out of them there.

Threshing.

Corn, when reaped, is gathered into stacks, which are afterwards taken to a hard, clean piece of ground (pir), where the threshing (gah) takes place. There are two kinds of threshing, known as 'munniwala gah' and 'pharsawala gah.' If the amount to be threshed is not very large, a stake (munni) is fixed in the middle, the crop is laid in a circle round it, and one or more yoke of cattle, having been tied by a rope to the stake, are driven round and round over the crop. When, however, wheat is being threshed in large quantities, a heavy mass of wood and straw (pharsa) is yoked behind each pair of cattle, and these are

Chapter IV, A.

Agriculture, Arboriculture and Livestock.

Threshing.

driven round and round, commencing from the outside of the circle and working gradually inwards. The cattle are driven by a 'gahera,' who is often a hired man, employed for this purpose only. Almost all kinds of crops (including rice, jowar, peas, etc.) are threshed by cattle; but when the amount is small, it is often beaten out by hand with sticks (kúdan). Til is held upside down and shaken by hand (jharan or chhangan); and china is often threshed by being beaten by hand against the sides of a hole in the ground.

Winnowing.

When the grain has been separated and the straw broken, the stuff is tossed into the air with a pitchfork, and then further cleaning is done by shaking the grain and chaff still left in a winnowing basket (chajj), held up aloft in a man's hand, above his head to catch the breeze. The more breeze there is, the quicker the work is finished. The winnower is almost always a Chúhra or man of low caste; but the villagers sometimes do the work themselves.

Storing.

The grain, when ready, is stored in stacks called 'palla,' which are circular erections with sides made of munj grass or other suitable material; the grain, after being put in these, is plastered at the top, and the whole is generally raised from the ground on bricks in order to allow air to circulate and keep off weevils (ghun). Big landowners in the Multan and Shujabad tahsíls have granaries (bhanda) of brick, in which the grain is stored in bulk. Grain required for household use is stored in plastered bins known as 'kalhota.'

Carts.

Carts as a means of conveying agricultural produce are practically unknown. The figures given in Statement No. XXII would *primâ facie* lead us to suppose that the number of carts had greatly increased of late years; but the explanation probably is that the earlier figures did not include the *ghurlas*, or rough field carts, which are very commonly used in the Lodhran and Mailsi tahsíls for the conveyance of indigo from the fields to the vats, and for conveying manure and jowar stalks; they are also used for taking parties of women to local fairs. These ghurlas are made for about Rs. 20, including the wood, or Rs. 10, excluding the wood: the wheels are generally each in one block of wood, and the whole contrivance is of the roughest possible description. Carts are not used for taking produce to the market, except by a few of the more enterprising zamindars in the Multan and Shujabad tahsíls. The letting of carts on hire is unknown, except among a few Aráíns in these tahsíls.

Cropping.

In Table No. XX will be found the areas under matured crops for each year from 1888-89 to 1898-99, and also the average for each tahsíl during the five years ending 1898-99. The per-

Chapter IV, A.

Agriculture, Arboriculture and Livestock.

Cropping.

centage of the matured area under each of the more important crops during this five-year period was—

Rice	2·7	Sathri	·6
Wheat	43·5	Ussun	1·1
Barley	1·4	Sugarcane	·2
Jowar	9·3	Cotton	9·4
Bajra	1·8	Indigo	4·3
China	1·5	Tobacco	·3
Gram	2·7	Methra	1·6
Peas	5·2	Turnips	6·3
Til	3·2		

We have in the third book of the Ain-i-Akbari a list of the crops grown in Multan three centuries ago, and it is interesting to compare the names with those of the crops now grown. Rice, wheat, barley, jowar, til, cotton, indigo and methra are all in Abul Fazl's list; so also is china, under the name of arzan, and masur under that of adas. The ordinary sugarcane is in his list, but no *pona* cane. We do not of course find tobacco, and it may be noted that the list does not contain bajra, ussun, sathri, peas, gram or turnips.

Sugarcane.

Sugarcane (kamand) is not an important crop in this district, and the area grown decreased from 3,672 acres at the second Settlement to an average of 1,760 acres in the five years ending 1898. The crop is grown mostly round Multan city and near Shujabad; but the percolation (soman) caused by the river, especially since the floods of 1893-94, has driven it very largely out of the latter locality. The variety grown near Multan itself is the *pona*, which is eaten in its natural state; that grown elsewhere is generally the *katha*, or thin, reddish kind of cane, required for the preparation of gur. The pona is generally sold standing, and in the suburbs of Multan it fetches about Rs. 100 per acre. The katha is believed to produce about 16 to 18 maunds of gur per acre, which sells usually for something like Rs. 3-10-2 per maund.* The cost of cultivation is, however, extremely high. The seed canes are preserved from the previous harvest, and buried during the cold weather. They are then planted in February or March in ground which has been specially prepared by constant ploughings and abundant manure. The crop then receives a succession of canal waterings, interspersed with hoeings and weedings and further manurings. The cutting begins in October, and goes on through the cold weather.

Indigo.

A detailed account of the cultivation of indigo (nil) as it stood in 1858 was prepared by Mr. Morris, the Setttlement

* These were the figures adopted at the third Settlement. For a discussion as to the outturn of the crop, see Mr. Gordon Walker's note attached to the Shujabad Assessment Report of the second Settlement, and Mr. Roe's remarks on the note in the body of the Report.

Chapter IV. A.

Agriculture, Arboriculture and Livestock.

Indigo.

Officer, and will be found reprinted as Appendix A to the last edition of this Gazetteer. This crop, which at the second Settlement (1875—1888) occupied 10 per cent. of the cropped area, now represents only 4·3 per cent. of the cropping. It is little grown upon the Sidhnai lands, but is common wherever there is flow irrigation from inundation canals. The most famous is that of the Sardárwah tract in Lodhran and Shujabad; but there is good indigo elsewhere also. The outturn assumed for assessment purposes at the present Settlement was 10 or 11 sers per acre; and the price obtained by the cultivator, though subject to large fluctuations,* averages about 10 chitaks to the rupee, or Rs. 64 per maund.

This crop is seldom grown on lands near the river; it requires a good average loam in the soil, and, above all things, an early and plentiful supply of water. The crop being cut early in the autumn, an early stoppage of the canals does not affect it; but it is essential that the canals should not begin to run too late. Well or jhalar water is very seldom applied, and the crop is practically always irrigated by canal flow. The crop is cut down to about six inches from the ground after the first year, and produces a further crop on the same stalks in the second year; the first year's crop is known as *sarop* and the second year's as *mundhí*. Third year indigo is looked on as unlucky, and is practically unknown. The outturn of sarop and mundhí is much the same; but if the original sowings were early in the season the sarop will be slightly more productive than the mundían and *vice versâ* if the sowings were late. The mundhí require earlier waterings than the new crop; so that sometimes when the canal water comes somewhat late the mundhí crop is lost but sarop can be sown.

The ploughings for the first crop begin as early in the year as is feasible, and the more ploughings there are the better: the crop, however, is often made to follow wheat, and in this case ploughing is often dispensed with altogether. Canal water ought to be put on the land by the third week in May, and the seed, generally some twenty sers to the acre, is sown broadcast. After this some eighteen to twenty waterings are required, but great discrimination has to be used in applying the water. While the plants are young the water is given sparingly and at night, so that they may not rot from standing in water heated by the sun. Manuring is seldom resorted to, and weeding is generally done by letting sheep and goats graze among the plants. Mundhían are ready to cut from the 1st August; sarop from the middle of August to the end of September.

---

* The people say that a maund of indigo fetches what a camel fetches; that is to say, anything from Rs. 5 to Rs. 100.

Chapter IV, A.

Agriculture, Arboriculture and Livestock.

Indigo.

Then follows the vatting or *valori*. The vats (hauz) are built in sets of three, two large ones on each side and a smaller one in the middle; they are spoken of as "jori," and cost from Rs. 30 to Rs. 40 per set to construct. The people estimate the outturn by the area which a set of vats will serve daily: this is put for an average crop at about one-eighth of an acre: and if we put the period of croppings at twenty-four days, this gives about three acres for each pair or set of vats. Each pair of vats produces about 1 ser of indigo daily, or about 32 sers each season. If, however, there are mundhí in the same field, the time available is longer and the acreage served is larger. The plant, when cut, is tied up in bundles, and at once taken to the larger vats, in which they are placed upright, with the stalks downwards: each vat contains eight to ten bundles: at evening water is let in sufficiently to cover the plant, which it is kept pressed down by heavy beams of wood placed across it. It is of importance that this steeping takes place as soon as possible after the plant is cut, otherwise it dries up and is spoilt. After the plant has been steeped from twenty-four to twenty-six hours, it is taken out, leaves and all, leaving only the liquid in the vats, which the second workman now begins to churn up with an instrument like a large paddle: this lasts about four hours, and is an art requiring great practice. It is called 'vilorna,' the object being to assist the indigo or sediment to precipitate, which it does in about an hour after the churning is over. The clear liquid is then drawn off, leaving the sediment or pulpy water at the bottom of each large vat; this is then transferred to the smaller vat and allowed to settle all night. In the morning the water is again drawn off from the smaller vat; the sediment carefully collected, tied up in a cloth, and drained on a heap of sand; finally it is dried in the sun, kneaded into a paste with the hand, and made up into small balls; a little oil being added to heighten the colour. The peculiar circumstances of indigo are such that it is impossible to give any part of the crop in charity to the poor, and I have known a zamindar abstain from cultivating the crop because, as he said, 'it had not the name of Allah in it.'

Besides the ordinary dye of commerce, the leaves supply a hair dye, and the stalks (val), after steeping, afford an excellent manure, especially for wheat.

The cultivation and vatting are, as will be seen, of a very different type to that usual in Behar. Attempts to introduce scientific methods of production have been occasionally made. A factory with two wells and a garden was started in 1862-63 in Wahi Riki, in tahsil Shujabad, by a European; in 1869 it was sold to another European; in 1876 he, in his turn, became insolvent and sold the concern to another European. The expenses, however, again proved too great, and in 1882-83 the factory was

Chapter IV, A.

Agriculture, Arboriculture and Livestock.

abandoned. There are extensive remains of large vats also at Hámidpur Kanora, in the Multan tahsíl. The concern at Hámidpur was started by a Major Tulloch about 1884-85, and financed by Gillanders, Arbuthnot & Co., but it appears to have come to grief owing to the untrustworthiness of the manager, and the buildings had to be sold up a few years later in satisfaction of decrees.

Indigo.

The indigo of this district goes chiefly to Afghánistan, Bokhara and Yarkand. The export is, to a large extent, *viâ* Batum, freights being obtained cheap in the returning oil steamers.

Cotton.

Cotton (vanwár, vár or váran), which only occupied about 7 per cent. of the cropped area at the second Settlement, now represents 9·4 per cent. of the cropping, a result which is largely owing to its popularity on the Sidhnai canal. It is found in all circles, and, indeed, except on the river, on almost every holding. As a rule no particular care is taken in selecting varieties for seed, but a few agriculturists (especially on the Sidhnai) have experimented in some of the special varieties introduced in other districts. The people generally speak of two main kinds of cotton, namely, the *bagga*, or white, and the *narma*, or dark leaved plant; the former of which gives one-fourth weight of cleaned cotton and three-fourths of seeds; the latter one-third of cleaned cotton and two-thirds of seeds; the latter is less commonly found in the Sutlej tahsíls than in the west part of the district. The normal outturn is from 3 to 4 maunds, and the price obtained by the cultivator for his uncleaned cotton (phutti) is in an ordinary year about 10 sérs to the rupee, or Rs. 4 per maund.

The practice of growing second year cotton is practically unknown. The crop requires a soil of ordinary character, and very often follows turnips or wheat. It is seldom found on sailab: but is commonly grown with well or canal water, or with both. The usual form of cultivation is by canal water alone, but very often a well is at hand to supply water if the canal fails. On canal lands the cultivator generally defers preparation of the soil until the canals begin to flow, and if the canals begin late the time left is often too short to enable the crop to be sown in time. Generally two ploughings suffice before sowing, and the land is sometimes, but very seldom, manured. The seed is sown at the rate of 6 or 8 sérs per acre. The sowings are carried on during May, and for a week or two in June; and when the shoots appear some ploughing or light hoeing between the plants is sometimes undertaken. Except for this a crop is seldom weeded, and on rich canal lands the grass on the cotton fields sometimes nearly conceals the crop. Waterings continue every month or fortnight during the summer until the canals dry. If the crop has been sown early it is sufficient

Chapter IV, A.

Agriculture, Arboriculture and Livestock.

to water up to the end of September, but where sowings have been late, the crops suffer if water is not given in October. Pickings (chunai) commence from the 1st October and continue to about the middle of December. Most of the cotton of the district, which is not used for home consumption, goes to the factories at Multan.

There is some trade in cotton seeds (pewe), but they are mostly used for feeding the cattle. The stalks, which are of so much use in the Punjab, are here of little value owing to the large supply of firewood.

Rice.

Rice (dhánj) occupies 7·7 per cent. of the cropping. It is grown abundantly in certain of the Sidhnai villages and in the tract between Multan and Shujabad, but is practically unknown in the Lodhran and Mailsi tahsíls. The common red rice is known as *satthra*, and the white rice as *baggi*. There are many other varieties, of which the *saunfia* and the *kalanga*, which are both late growing rices, are the best known. The outturn is generally about 10 maunds to the acre, and the unhusked produce is sold by the cultivator in an average year at 26 sérs to the rupee, or Re. 1-8-7 per maund. The quality of the outturn is very inferior to ordinary Punjab rice, and there is practically no export of any rice grown in the district.

The soils most suited to this crop are the hard clayey bottoms, unculturable for most other staples; but rice, here, as elsewhere, requires immense supplies of water. On the Sidhnai the seed is sown broadcast; elsewhere the seedlings (bíja) are usually transplanted from seed beds (panírí). The cultivation is dependent entirely on the canals, well water being used only for the development of the seed beds. The ploughing begins when the canals begin to run, and after two or three ploughings the seedlings are transplanted, generally during June and the early part of July. Manure is seldom used, except for the seed beds, and there is no weeding. Water has to be continually supplied every few days until the plant ripens in September.

Jowar.

The jowar of this district, whether grown for food or for fodder, is spoken of as *jowar*; but of late years the crop, when grown for fodder, has been entered in the revenue returns as *chari*. The distinction is not, however, as yet satisfactorily made, and the two crops must be considered together. The total area under both crops averages about 70,000 acres, and it was assumed in the calculations connected with the last assessments that 45 per cent. of this was utilized as fodder for the agricultural cattle, so that at least this proportion falls to be matured. The crop is common everywhere; it produces, when matured, 5 or 6 maunds of grain per acre, and in an average year the cultivator sells his grain at 27 sérs per rupee, or Re. 1-7-8 per maund. The crop appears both in the zaid rabi harvest and in the kharif.

The seed is sown at the rate of about 12 sérs to the acre, and the crop receives some four waterings. The earlier crop is sown, as a rule, on well waterings and matured by canal: the later crop is both sown and matured on canal irrigation.

Bajra.

Bajra, or as it is more usually called bajri, represents 1·8 per cent. of the cropping of the district: it is found in all tahsíls, but is most common in Mailsi. The produce per acre is ordinarily 5 to 6 maunds, and the price obtained by the zamindar in ordinary years is 24 sérs to the rupee, or Re. 1-10-8 per maund. The crop is one of the later kharíf crops, and is cultivated in much the same way, and at much the same time, as til. Some 4 or 5 sers of seed are sown per acre, and the sowings generally take place in August, and the crop is cut in October and November. The stalks are always decapitated near the top, and this process is known as *láparná*.

Maize.

Maize (makki) as a food crop is practically unknown, except on the Sidhnai, where it is grown by Punjabi settlers. The only maize cultivation of importance is that of the suburbs of Multan, where it is grown as a fodder crop for sale to horseowners and to the Commissariat. The early or jethi maize, which is the commoner form, is sown in July and cut in September; the late or kanjhi maize is sown in October and cut in January. In either case the crop is sold standing, and the average price fetched is not less than Rs. 40 an acre.

Til.

Til or sesamun (generally spoken of in the plural as tillán) represents 3·2 per cent. of the cropping, and the area under the crop has extended greatly since 1880. It is mainly a nahri crop, though found also in the Mailsi barani lands and on the sailab lands of the upper part of the Chenab river. The outturn is from 3 to 3½ maunds per acre, and the produce fetches to the zamindar some 10 sérs to the rupee, or Rs. 4 per maund. The crop gives fair returns and costs less to cultivate than most, as it can do with a light soil and moderate moisture, can be sown late, and requires very little looking after. The sowings take place in July, and the crop is cut in November. It is liable, when grown on the river side, to be destroyed by floods. When the crop fails the stalks are sometimes browsed by camels; they are no use as fodder for cattle.

China.

China is a crop which has nearly trebled in area since 1880 and now represents 1·5 per cent. of the cropping of the district. This increase is entirely due to its popularity on the Sidhnai canal, where it has been extensively grown both in the zaid rabi and in the kharíf harvest, about one-third being shown in the revenue records against the former, and two-thirds against the latter harvest. The crop is mainly used for food, but a certain portion of the zaid rabi is employed as fodder also. As a food the grain

Chapter IV. A.

Agriculture, Arboriculture and Livestock.

China.

is inferior: the produce averages some 6 or 7 maunds only per acre, and sells on an average year for 34 sers to the rupee, or about Re. 1-2-10 per maund. The crop requires a good soil, some manure, and plenty of water; and in view of these requirements the cultivators often pay a lower rent for china than for other staples. On the other hand, it only occupies the land for a comparatively short time, the cultivation for the zaid rabi crop beginning in January, and that for the kharif in August: and it provides the poorer classes with a cheap, if somewhat distasteful, food.

Wheat.

Wheat (kanak or pl. kanakán) is the most important crop in the district, occupying 43·5 per cent. of the cropping. The area under wheat has increased considerably since 1880, but the proportion of the whole cropping under wheat is slightly less than in 1880. This crop is grown on all soils—well, canal and river; but unless circumstances are favourable it is the better for being matured in all cases by well irrigation. The crop now grown seems, so far as one can judge, to be chiefly composed of varieties of white wheat, though red wheats are also common, especially on the river sides, and it is generally said that the cultivation of red wheat is now more common than it used to be. The varieties one hears most mentioned are the 'ramak' or true white, the 'satthra,' the 'kanjári' and the 'dhúdi.' The 'ramak' is looked on the best as regards both the flour and the straw; the 'satthra' is said to give a large outturn of grain, but an inferior straw; the 'dhudi' is small-eared white wheat; and the 'kanjári' is the bearded red wheat, which is grown especially on the riverain lands because of the aversion shown by pigs to this variety. Other wheats, such as kunj, pamman, vadának, mendianwali, etc., are also grown, but not in appreciable quantities. The wheat is never intentionally sown with barley, but barley seeds, to a certain extent, get mixed in wheat, and, except the Arains, few of the zamindars take the trouble to separate the two at reaping so as to keep the seeds distinct. The best class of wheat seed is said to be obtained from the Arains of Jalla in the Lodhran tahsíl. Wheat is often sold before it reaches maturity, and such advance sales are known as 'boli.' They are chiefly customary in the western tahsíls, and are not so common in Lodhran and Mailsi. The outturns vary a good deal in different tracts, and, generally speaking, the sandy sailab soil gives a lower outturn than the lands sown by canals, but on an average an acre of wheat, according to the calculations made at the recent Settlement produces 8·7 maunds of grain, or about 12 bushels, and the price received by the cultivator for his grain may be taken now-a-days to average at least 21 sers to the rupee, or Re. 1-14-6 per maund.

On canal lands the ploughings begin from the middle of June onwards, and on sailab lands they begin as soon as the soil is

Chapter IV, A.

Agriculture, Arboriculture and Livestock.

Wheat.

sufficiently dry. On wells they do not begin till later than on the canals, but if there is any summer rain advantage is at once taken of the moisture supplied by it. The ploughings and harrowings should be as frequent as possible, but they are naturally fewer on sailab lands, where the time allowed is short, than elsewhere. Sowings begin in October, and can be carried on in well lands up to near the end of December, but elsewhere they must be finished in November, because the moisture supplied by the rivers and canals is insufficient to mature the crop if sown later. The amount sown is, roughly, a maund an acre; but the later the sowings the more is the amount required. The seed is generally sown by drill (*nálí*), as the moisture supplied by canals or the river has generally sunk somewhat by the time sowings commence: if, however, well irrigation is available and the upper soil is moist, the seed is often sown broadcast (*chatta*). After the sowings are completed the land is generally left unwatered for a month or two, but after that it is watered as frequently as can be arranged. Manure is used where available, and the stalks of the indigo plant are a very favourite kind of manure. This crop is very seldom grown as a mixed crop with others. It is, however, largely employed in the spring as a fodder crop when the turnips have been exhausted. It is calculated that on an average year between 7 and 8 per cent. of the crop is so employed, but in bad years the proportion is very much higher, mounting as high in some tracts as 25 or 30 per cent. The harvesting commences on the 1st of Baisakh (middle of April). Wheat is said to give the largest yield in the same year in which the ber-tree yields most plentifully: '*Berín ber kanakán dher.*'

The wheat straw (*bhoh* or *bhúu*) is collected in stacks (*palle*), and surrounded with wattles or cotton stalks and daubed over with mud. It is given out to the cattle mixed with green fodder, or, if green fodder is not available, by itself. The outturn of straw per acre is much the same, speaking generally, as that of the grain: the price varies of course a good deal according to the proximity of the market, and only a small proportion of the straw is sold, but on an average it probably fetches four to six annas a maund. It will keep for about two years; after that it becomes red and sour.

The root of the plant is known as *muddh*, the stalk as *nár*, the leaves as *pattr*, the ear as *sitti*, the husk as *ghúndí*, the grain as *dána*, and the beard as *kanjár or kíh*.

Barley

Barley (*jau*) occupies 1·4 per cent. of the cropping, and the area now grown is nearly twice as large as it was twenty years ago. The crop is grown in all soils and in all parts of the district, mainly in small patches near wells, and under much the

Chapter IV, A.

Agriculture, Arboriculture and Livestock.

Barley.

same conditions as wheat. There is a dark variety grown which is known as indarjan. The crop is generally grown on wells, and it is chiefly used as fodder for horses. It is very seldom intentionally mixed with any other crop, but owing to carelessness, a good deal of barley grows up along with the wheat. The grain is reaped a fortnight or so before the wheat, and the outturn is much the same as that of wheat. The price, however, is much lower, and the average price received by the cultivator in an ordinary year is now-a-days 29 sers per rupee, or Re. 1-6-1 per maund.

Gaam.

Gram (channa) is grown in 2·7 per cent. of the cropped area. It is common as a nahri crop throughout the district; as a sailab crop it is found chiefly in the upper course of the Chenab and on the Ravi. The crop produces, as a rule, some 5 maunds to the acre, but the quality of the produce is very inferior, and the price received by the cultivator in an ordinary year at harvest time is 28 sers the rupee, or Re. 1-6-10 per maund. The crop is grown, as a rule, in depressions with hard bottoms, or it follows rice in hard clays which have been drenched with canal water during the summer. Only one or two ploughings are required, and well water is seldom, if ever, given; but the crop is the better for rain in the winter. Ploughings begin in September, and the crop is ripe early in April. Manure is never used. Gram is liable to damage if the frosts are hard, and if thunder occurs when it is in pod. It is often grown along with turnips or peas, but is usually a separate crop. It is not unfrequently used as fodder, especially when mixed with other crops.

Peas.

Peas (mattar or charál) occupy 5·2 per cent. of the cropping, and they are found mainly as a riverain crop, and their cultivation is especially common on the Sutlej in Mailsi. The peas of this district are nearly always used as fodder, especially for cows and she-buffaloes. They are, as a rule, sold standing, and the price received in an average year may be taken as Rs. 10 per acre. In years when fodder is scarce the crop fetches prices much higher than this. The soil affected by this crop is much the same as that which is suitable for gram; the mode of cultivation is very similar, and the two crops are often grown mixed. Peas are also grown along with methra. Peas can, however, be sown somewhat later than gram, and are usually pulled somewhat earlier They are subject to the same complaints as gram, and the straw of the matured plant is utilized as a fodder.

Methra.

Fenugreek or methra is a crop not unfrequently seen in the district, where it occupies 1·6 per cent, of the cropping. It is found in all parts of the district, chiefly in the neighbour hood of wells, where its presence is detected by its peculiar 'pig-sty' smell. It is used entirely as a fodder crop. The land is ploughed for methra about October, and about half a maund of seed is used to the acre. The crop should get four or five waterings during the winter, and is fit for use in February.

Tobacco.

Tobacco (tabákún) is found all over the district, and the cultivation is almost always carried on by well irrigation. In the suburbs of Multan, where this is a popular crop, two kinds are commonly grown, *viz.*, the country tobacco and the Kandahári. For country tobacco the seed beds are prepared in October or November, and the land is ploughed several times, beginning from October onwards; in February or March the transplanting takes place, and the leaves are ready in July. The Kandahari tobacco is an earlier crop, being commenced in January and cut in June. The produce is best if the soil is slightly saline; and the wells of the Lodhran and Shujabad Rawa are said to produce excellent tobacco, mainly on this account. Half a ser of seed will furnish a seed bed sufficient to plant an acre of crop. Tobacco needs a great deal of manure and plenty of water The outturn on an ordinary well will average some 4½ to 5 maunds per acre, and the average price obtained when it is sold may be put at 11 sers to the rupee, or Rs. 3-10-2 per maund. In the suburbs of Multan the outturn and price are both higher, and the crop there will generally be soid standing at an average price of some Rs. 50 per acre.

Ussun and Satthri.

Very litte rape is grown in the Multan district and practically no linseed; their place as oil-seeds being taken largely by ussun (tárámíra) and satthri (toria). Ussun is a rabi crop, being sown about the end of September and reaped about the beginning of April; while satthri is in a way intermediate between the kharíf and rabi, being sown about the end of August and maturing in November. Ussun does not require much moisture; it is grown on pure canal or barani cultivation, and is chiefly found in the Lodhran and Mailsi tahsils. It is, often found in the outer reaches of well estates, where it will get well water if there is any to spare, but will survive well enough if there is none. It is also often grown with turnips. An acre of ussun will on an average produce about 3 maunds of oil-seeds, which will be sold by the cultivator at about 20 sérs to the rupee, or Rs. 2 per maund. Satthri (the greater part of which is counted in the revenue records as a kharíf crop) is not grown as a separate crop to any great extent outside the Sidhnai area, where it is a very popular staple. Outside this area it is mainly grown along with turnips, and forms, when so grown, a green fodder which is available for the cattle earlier than the turnips. Satthri as a separate crop is nearly always grown on pure nahri land: it requires a good deal of water after sowing, and is generally irrigated once a fortnight until the canal dries up. It is believed to give on an average some 5

Chapter IV, A.

Agriculture, Arboriculture and Livestock

maunds per acre, and the zamindar sells it at about 25 sérs to the rupee, or Re. 1-10-0 per maund.

Turnips.

The Multan district grows more turnips (gonglu or ság) than any district in the Punjab, and probably more than any district in India. This crop represents 6·3 per cent. of the cultivation, and its function is to keep the cattle alive when the jowar fodder is finished, until the wheat and the wheat straw are available. It is used to a small extent as food—the stalks (gandal) being cooked and the roots being eaten either raw or cooked,—but it is not cultivated with this object. There are two varieties, the red and the white, of which the white are said to be the better and the more widely cultivated. The crop needs a fair amount of water, and is seldom found outside the reach of well irrigation. It is common in all parts of the district. The ploughings begin in July, and the seed is sown shortly after. The crop receives six or seven waterings during the autumn and winter: it is manured if possible, and sometimes weeded. The roots are not taken up at one time and stacked, but are pulled from time to time, from the end of November onwards, and given at once to the cattle. As a rule the tops and roots are given together, but sometimes the tops are cut and fed off separately, while the roots remain in the ground. The plants are never thinned or transplanted. The crop is sometimes grown along with other crops, such as methra, gram, satthri and ussun. Considering the way in which the produce is treated, it is difficult to give any reliable estimate of the outturn; and as the crop is very seldom sold, it is not easy to estimate its ordinary price. For sowing some 2 or 3 sérs of seed are required per acre, and some 2 or 3 marlas are kept in each acre for seed. Plants required for seed are allowed to grow on till April.

The better class of turnips, whether kept for seed or intended for consumption, are taken up about February, and the roots are subjected to the process of 'dakk.' There are two varieties of this process: the first, which has the best results, consists in taking out the root, cutting off about one-third from the bottom and replacing it in new soil; the other, known as 'dátriwala dakk,' consists in taking out the root, making an incision with a sickle, and then replacing it in its old position. The latter, though giving inferior results, renders the root more immune from 'tela,' and is for this reason often adopted in preference to the other. The seed of turnips is sometimes, but not often, sold for oil or mixed with flour to make oil-cakes for cattle.

Miscellaneous crops.

Múng and moth are nearly unknown in this district, and másh is confined mainly to the upper part of the Chenáb riverain tract. In this tract, too, the cultivation of rawán (vigna catiang) is not uncommon, especially as a catch crop after the

Chapter IV, A.

Agriculture, Arboriculture and Livestock.

Miscellaneous crops.

rabi. Chillies (mirch) are very little grown, and hemp (bhang) is only grown in small patches near fakirs' dwellings. Henna (mehndi) is grown in the immediate neighbourhood of Mailsi, and is not much found elsewhere. Vegetables of all kinds are grown round Multan city, all small plots of vegetables are commonly found on wells, especially those with Arain owners or tenants. Onions (vasal) are very commonly grown in such plots. In Fatehpur, in the Mailsi tahsil, the soil and conditions are especially suited to the cultivation of garlic (thom), and considerable areas round the village site are there cultivated with this crop at high profits. A crop very commonly grown is the bátaun or egg plant, of which there are two kinds— the Lahori, which is ready in April, and the desi, which is ready in June. Dhania (coriander) with its white flower and the blue-flowered kásni (endive) are also fairly commonly seen on wells. Melon-fields (vári) are also common near Multan, and their cultivation gives rise to a curious proverb on the various fortunes of mankind: 'Várí vichh kharbúze rahde, apo apni já Kai gore kai sánvle. Rabb wadda be parwá!' ('You may sow melons in a field, each in its proper place; some come up white, some red. God is mighty careless!')

Diseases of Crops.

Some of the diseases experienced by crops have been already noticed, but some of the more prevalent and general of the crop diseases may be referred to here. Tela is an insect which chiefly attacks methra, turnips and tobacco, and many other crops: it makes its appearance both when the crop is young and when it is nearly ripe. White ants (siwi) attack the young crops or the roots of maturing crops in dry soils when there has been a lack of water: the injury they cause is also spoken of as *múla*. A common cure for this disease is to get hold of a Kirar, called Múla, and to hit him frequently until he leaves the field: he is afterwards appeased with a few vegetables. Various kinds of 'worms' (kíra) attack jowar, indigo, gram and other crops. The 'worm' that attacks indigo appears when the crop is young and is green in colour. A similar 'worm' did great damage to the cotton crop in 1899 and 1900, appearing in the flower when the crop had begun to flower. Wheat is also subject to rust (ratti or kungí) if the spring is cloudy; and smut (kani) is also common in wheat and other grain crops. Hard frosts (pála) are injurious to gram, ussun, tobacco and peas; and gram is said also to be damaged by lightning. Field rats gnaw the roots of ussun, wheat, etc., especially in sandy soils: crops so damaged are said to suffer from 'toka' (from tukan, to eat or bite). The injuries done by pigs, deer, &c., are noted in pages 209-210 above. Hailstorms are not very frequent, but occasionally crops are destroyed by visitations of this nature. Locusts do great damage to almost all kinds of crops: the extent and character of the damage they do depends on the stage of growth in which the crops and the locusts, respectively, are.

Chapter IV. A.

Agriculture Arboriculture and Livestock.

Produce and consumption.

The total consumption of food grains within the district was estimated in the Famine Report of 1878 to be 3,095,291 maunds, as shown in the margin. The figures are based upon an estimated population of 471,563, and this gives an average consumption per head of nearly 6½ maunds per annum. Now the present average produce of the district, according to the estimates made at the recent Settlement, is as follows :—

GRAIN.	Agriculturists.	Non-agriculturists.	Total.
	Mds.	Mds.	Mds.
Wheat	583,374	1,096,225	1,679,599
Inferior grains ...	526,056	602,966	1,199,022
Pulses	88,774	127,896	216,670
Total ...	1,268,204	1,827,087	3,095,291

	Maunds.
Wheat and barley	2,976,230
Pulses (gram, moth, mung and másh)	137,628
Other grains (jowár, bájra, maize, kangní, chína and rice)	679,388
Total ...	3,793,246

If this is divided among an estimated population of 7 lakhs, the average production per annum comes out to $5\frac{3}{7}$ maunds per head. And the railway returns at the same time show for the two years ending 1st June 1899 an average export of 288,600 maunds of food stuffs.* It is, of course, impossible for all these figures to be correct. The figures for the net exports by rail may, perhaps, be taken, for want of further information, as representing fairly well the actual net exports from the district: they include, on the one hand, a certain amount of produce which comes into Multan stations from the Jhang and Muzaffargarh districts, but they exclude, at the same time, the produce which goes down the river by boat. If this is accepted, then either our estimates of produce at the Settlement are too low, or our estimates of the annual consumption of food grains is too high. Probably both these conclusions would be, to a certain extent, correct; and the true figures, so far as we can venture to give any definite form to our data, might be said to be as follows :—

	Maunds.
Total food produce of the district	3,955,000
Amount locally consumed at 5¼ maunds per head by 7 lakhs of population	3,675,000
Balance exported	280,000

* The estimate in the Famine Report of 1878 was 492,000 maunds.

Chapter IV. A.

Agriculture, Arboriculture and Live-stock.

We are probably justified in reducing the average consumption of grain to 5¼ maunds a head, owing to the various extraneous forms of food available, such as turnips, dates, berries, fruits, flesh, vegetables, and so forth ; but it is difficult to speak with any kind of certainty on the subject.

Fruit gardens.

The Multan and Shujabad tahsils contain a number of fine gardens which bring in considerable incomes to their owners. There are three methods of garden culture: the owner may elect to plant the garden himself and to water it by a special small well worked by a servant ; or he may plant the garden himself and pay the tenant of the neighbouring well a certain amount each year in money or fruit in return for the tenant's supplying water ; or he may give out the whole planting and construction to a tenant (then called a násib) in return for a share of the produce, generally a half. The most common fruits planted are mangoes and pomegranates, but apples, oranges, limes, vines, horse-radish, fálshá and kachnál trees are also common. The mango fruits after six or eight years costs very little to keep up, and is said to last for fifty or one hundred years. The pomegranate fruits after four or five years, and lasts for fifteen to twenty-five years. The mango fruits in June and July ; but there are some special kinds, found mainly in the south of Shujabad, which fruit as late as August, and are known as bhadri. Pomegranates fruit in February, and oranges in March. The Shahpasand and Sufeda mangoes of Multan and the Tori of Shujabad are well known ; and in the early days of annexation while communication with Bombay was still undeveloped, one of the luxuries of the hot weather among Europeans in Lahore used to consist of Multan mangoes. Locally, a white pulp and a small stone are looked on as the points of a good mango. Good edible mangoes sell in the season for three or four rupees the sér and there is a very considerable export in the Lahore direction. A preserve and a kind of vinegar are made from mangoes. The produce of a garden unless used by the owner for home consumption, is nearly always sold by auction to *baikhars* ; and there is a custom by which the owner after the auction is allowed within a certain time to sell to a higher bidder on condition that he pays to the original purchaser one-fourth of the difference in the bids. It is also customary for the owner to be allowed to take for his own use one sér of fruits for each rupee of the purchase. The purchaser in the case of mangoes pays half down and half in July or August ; for pomegranates or oranges one-third is paid down in July, and one-third in December. In some cases, where the outturn is apt to vary, the purchase includes the fruit of two successive years. The purchaser employs a servant, generally on Rs. 4 per mensem, to watch the garden for two or four months before the crop ripens.

Fodder crops.

In an ordinary holding in this district the well cattle will be fed in April on peas or methra, and as the wheat is cut they get

Chapter IV, A.

Agriculture. Arboriculture and Live-stock.

Fodder crops.

grazing in the stubble ; in May and June they graze in the wheat stubble or get fed on china or pea-straw ; in July they get the early jowár, and wheat straw is also available ; from August to December they get jowár or green grass or bájra stalks ; and when green food is not available, then wheat-straw or dried jowar is given to them. With December begins the turnip season, and as the turnips give out, green wheat is supplied as far as necessary, or the cattle receive peas and methra until the wheat crop is cut in April. During a large part of the year, therefore, the well cattle are stall fed ; and it is, as a rule, only when there is wheat stubble or peas or fresh grass on the ground that they get any thing like sufficient grazing. In addition to the peas, wheat, chína, jowár and turnips above mentioned, there are several other crops used wholly partly for fodder, such as rawán, másh, massar, gram, senji, methra and sawánk. Sometimes crops, such as jowár and turnips, shrivel up when young and become actually poisonous to cattle : this is called 'patha lagna.' Cattle can graze freely among indigo plants, so long as they have not begun to seed, without injuring the crop.

The date-palm.

The date-tree (khajjí) is one of the most remarkable products of the district.* It is almost everywhere self-produced, and it is exceedingly rare to see date-trees artificially cultivated. The only treatment of any kind which they receive is a little lopping (chángi) in the spring. They are to be found in almost all areas where there is a large amount of natural moisture in the soil : they do not grow in tracts subject to flooding and in the higher tracts away from the rivers. Their chief habitats are the lower Rávi and the Chenáb riverain near Multan ; on the Sutlej they are comparatively rare, except in a cluster of villages near Fattehpur and Kahror. The date-trees are for the most part female (máda), but a certain proportion are male (nar) and a few neuter (khassi). These last bear only small shrivelled dates without stones (gitak), or with very small stones. The males and females are exceedingly difficult to distinguish when the female is not in fruit ; and though the zamindars will detail to you many points of difference, their statements generally fall through when applied in practice. Experienced men will often give absolutely different decisions as to the sex of a tree ; and as the Government revenue is taken on the females only, the enumeration for Government purposes has to take place in the fruiting season (June to August). A date-palm begins to fruit in about five years, but does not give a full produce for some ten years longer. How long a tree lasts altogether is not known to the people, but their existence certainly exceeds an ordinary human lifetime. The female is never, so far as I can ascertain, artificially fertilized in this district ; but the rate of increase by natural

* In the following account use has been made of the account, so far as it applies to this district, of the Muzaffargarh date given in Mr. O'Brien's Muzaffargarh Settlement Report.

Chapter IV. A.

Agriculture. Arboriculture and Live-stock.

The date-palm.

reproduction is very rapid; and if the revenue statistics are to be trusted, the number of female trees exceeding 10 feet in height from the ground to the base of the leaves rose from 235,522 in the second Settlement to 330,544 in the third—an increase of 40 per cent. in about twenty years. A tree is sometimes charred by lighting a fire against it with the object of increasing its production. The spathes (sipí) of the palm begin to issue in February from the terminal cluster of leaves. As the spathe opens, clusters of tendrils (known as gosha) emerge covered with little white waxy balls (búra), which are the flower buds. In April the fruit is the size of a pea, and is spoken of as gandora. In June and July the fruit has attained its full size and is called doka, and the unripe dates, which are to be ripened by being salted are then gathered. Dates which fall from the tree are called 'phus.' In July and August the fruit ripens, and is then called pind. The ordinary practice is for the owner to sell his produce in advance to an outsider, who is known as the *baikhar,* and after the sale the expenses connected with the date harvest fall on the baikhar. It is usual to entertain a watchman (rákhá) for some five months from April to September: he receives about Rs. 4 a month and a small number of dates, and he attends, taking one month and one locality with another, some 300 trees. It is his duty to keep off birds, and various subsidiary means are employed to this end, such as the enveloping of the clusters in bags (bindi) and the attaching of kerosine oil tins at the end of a rope, which is constantly shaken. When the dates ripen pickers (chárha) are hired, who receive for about two months a remuneration averaging some Rs. 4-8-0 per month, together with certain perquisites in kind. A picker looks after about fifty trees. He uses for climbing a thick rope (kamand), which he passes round the tree and under his seat, his feet press against the overlapping bark (chhonda) of the trunk, and he jerks the rope gradually higher. There are not many accidents to pickers; but the fact that the occupation has its dangers is reflected in the local proverb, which says: 'Ahmak na howan há, tán pind koi na kháwe há.' ('If there were no fools to climb the trees none of us would have dates to eat').

It is difficult to say what the average produce of a full-grown tree may be. At the recent Settlement the produce recovered by the owner or baikhar, after deducting payment in kind and miscellaneous losses, was assumed to be 30 sérs of green dates in Kabírwála and 20 sérs in the other tahsils. The outturn is injuriously affected by severe rains; and there is a green caterpillar, similar to that which attacks gram, from which date-trees sometimes suffer severely. The produce is eaten in four ways:—(i) As salted dates (luni pind): these are picked when unripe, and are rubbed with salt and kept for a day in a closed jar. They get good prices, as they are available early in the season. (ii) As picked (van de pind), that is

Chapter IV, A.

Agriculture, Arboriculture and Live-stock.

The date-palm.

to say, fresh (táza) as taken from the tree. (iii) Dried (shangist). In this case the better class of dates are exposed to the sun for a few days, after which they will keep good for some three or four months. (iv) Chirvin-pind or split dates. Inferior dates are split open, and the stone is taken out and the dates dried. The refuse fruit (gadr) at the end of the season is given to cattle: it is boiled in water and then fried in a little oil; or else it is given as it stands. Fruit that remains unripe to the end is called 'kokan,' and dates which are pressed together into a lump are spoken of as 'pinn.' Dates lose about two-thirds of their weight in dryage; and dry dates sell in the season for some Rs. 2 to Rs. 2-8-0 per maund. The chief date markets are Tulamba, Multan, Shujabad, Jalálpur and Fattehpur; each of these supplies the country round, both inside and outside the district, and there is also a certain amount of export to Lahore and Amritsar. The dates are of innumerable varieties (nalli, garma, richh, moghal, chawára, etc., etc.), and in some places the produce of each clump has a special name and fame of its own. Attempts are said to have been made some fifty years ago at the instigation of Mr. Edgeworth, the Commissioner, to extract sugar from the dates of the district: the experiments were conducted by natives of Jessore in Bengal: but the outturn of sugar was not equal in value to that of the fruit lost. The uses of a date-tree are, however, by no means confined to the food obtainable from it. The leaf stalk (chari) is in bad years cut up and given to the cattle with the whea straw as fodder. The charís are also used for making light fences, frames, etc., etc., and the fibre from them is employed in making ropes. The pinnæ (bhútra or phara) are used for mats, baskets, fans and ropes. The network fibre which is found at the base of each petiole is called kabál; and this forms a good light firewood. The fruit stalk, with the fruit on it, is called gosha; after the fruit is off it is called buhára, and is often used as a broom. The stem of the tree is called 'mundh,' and it is used for rafters and, when hollowed out, for cattle-troughs or for acqueducts on wells and jhalárs. The wood, however, is soft and does not last long. A cluster of stems springing from one stool is called 'thadda' or (in Kabírwála) 'chopa.' Where dates are valuable, each clump, and in some cases each individual tree, has its name by which it is known in the neighbourhood. The cluster of leaves at the top of the palm is called gáchá, and in the heart of it is the terminal cabbage head called gari, which is edible. The date-stone is called gitak or gakkar.

Attempts to cultivate foreign date-palms have occasionally been tried, but with moderate success. Native gentlemen who go on pilgrimage to Karbala sometimes bring back stones from Baghdád, which they cultivate in their gardens, but not apparently with any marked results. Government also in the year 1888 started the cultivation of some Arabian dates. The Canal

The date-palm.

Department has small plantations of these at Sidhnai head-works, Shujabad, Lodhrán, Kahror, and the Abbanwali syphon and the Goth-bahar bridge on the Muhammadwah canal; but the numbers are not large, and only a few of the trees have yet begun to fruit. It is said that the fruit withers and dries up while yet unripe. There are also some plantations under the District Board at Lodhrán and Kabírwála, but in neither case have the trees so far exceeded 4 or 5 feet in height.

Sajji (barilla).

Another interesting plant (occasionally cultivated, but almost always found growing wild) is the lána, from one variety of which the sajji is produced. A short reference to the sajji plant has already been made in Chapter I; but the following note, prepared in 1899 by Mr. C. A. Barron, Officiating Settlement Officer, for the Reporter on Economic Products, gives some further details:—

There are four varieties of the sajji plant known more or less generally in the Multan district by the name of 'lána.' They are (1) sajji or khar, (2) láni, (3) lána, (4) gora lána. All the plants are eaten by camels and goats, while 'láni' is also eaten by sheep, and 'sajji' by cattle in times of scarcity.

From the 'sajji' plant alone is 'barilla' manufactured. The plant is cut at the time of flowering in the month of Katik (October 15th to November 15th). It is then left for fifteen days to dry. A spherical hole, 1 foot deep and 3 feet broad, is dug in the ground, and round this the sajji is piled up to a considerable height. The pile is then set fire to, and the juice of the plant runs into the hole. When the hole is full, the juice is stirred for a couple of hours with a stick called 'ghusa,' after which a little earth is sprinkled on the top, and the produce is allowed to cool down into a hard mass called a 'khangar'

The manufacture is carried on by 'chuhras' (menials of the sweeper caste). They cut and boil the plant, receiving as pay a share of the value of the outturn varying from one-fifth to one-eleventh, according as the total outturn is small or large. Occasionally the labourers are paid by time at the rate of 5 or 6 annas per diem, the head labourer or overseer getting Re. 1 a day for supervising the work.

The plant grows wild on the 'bar' and as a rule, the monopoly of manufacture is farmed out over large tracts of waste land. A contractor for an area of about 6 square miles in the Multan tahsil pays Rs. 2,400 per annum. Sajji grows to the height of 2 feet 6 inches or so at the time of cutting. When sold green as fodder it fetches Rs. 2 per camel-load. From 15 camel-loads about 10 maunds of the soda salt is obtained.

The salt (also called sajji as well as the plant) sells wholesale at the time of cropping at Re. 1-8-0 per maund, at other times at Re. 1-12-0, and retail at Rs. 2 per maund. It is used for washing and for making coarse kinds of soap. The best kind is the white, which sells at Re. 1-12-0, the black being the poorest quality and selling at Re 1-10-0 per maund. The third specimen is of medium quality, valued at Re. 1-11-0 per maund.

Government land.

Table No. XVII shows the areas of Government waste lands in the district. These lands are administered for the most part through the agency of the Forest Department, and are of two classes, *viz.*, (1) the reserved forests and (2) the protected waste.

Chapter IV, A.

Agriculture, Arboriculture and Live-stock.

Reserved forests.

The reserved forests of the district are those shown in the following table :—

Tahsil.	Name of reserve.	Area by latest settlement measurements in acres.
Kabírwála ...	Makhdum Vanoi ...	24,641
	Akil	16,142 measured together
	Dangra	and named Bura Kotla
	Bura Kotla	Akil
	Pakka Háji Majid ...	2,072
	Rajuana ...	8,847
	Pír Mahal ...	14,494
Multan ...	Arbi ...	354
Shujabad ...	Shujatpur ...	996
	Ubaora ...	650
	Kot Walak ...	507
	Nauraja Bhutta ...	1,178
	Jalálpur ...	1,475
Lodhrán ...	Khanwah ...	1,278
	Lodhran ...	1,140
Mailsi ...	Sharaf ...	5,196
	Tajwana ...	2,039
	Chak Kaura ...	1,578
	Sahuka ...	20,963
	Total ...	98,850

The following account of the establishment and working of these reserves was furnished by Mr. C. Rossiter, District Forest Officer, in 1901 :—

The idea of forming separate reserves in the Multan district originated before the year 1872, but was completed much later. In this district (as in so many others) the area of waste or rakh land at the disposal of Government was enormous, and at a very early date it was felt that it was both useless as well as impossible to attempt any thing like forest conservancy over the whole. A few of the better wooded tracts had been roughly marked off as "Jangal Sarkari," and although a small establishment with a rakh darogha at its head had been maintained, the duties of this establishment were practically confined to collecting the dues on wood cutting and grazing. All the rakhs were open to grazing of the most destructive character; all the villages paid a certain annual rate per head of cattle, and thenceforward were free to graze when and where they pleased, irrespective of limits.

The continuance of such a system, if the production of wood fuel on a large scale was desired, was impossible. It was therefore determined to commence a survey which should have for its object the selection and demarcation of a few compact blocks of the best wooded rakhs to form permanent reserves. As the main object of such reserves would be to supply the great cities, the cantonments, and the Railway with fuel, it was necessary that they should be near the Railway line or within easy access of some cheap means of conveyance. With this object in view 5 reserves were formed in the Kabírwála tahsil close to the Lahore-Multán branch of the Sindh, Punjab and

Chapter IV, A.

Agriculture, Arboriculture and Live-stock.

Reserved forests.

Delhi Railway, now forming part of the North-Western line. Four others were selected in the south-east corner of the Mailsi tahsil close to Luddan and not far from the Sutlej, while 7 others were selected lower down between Lodhrán and Jalálpur. These reserves were gazetted between the years 1879 and 1881, but they were not found to be sufficient, and later on as the demand for fuel and fodder increased 3 others were selected—one in the Multan tahsil and two in the north-east corner of Kabírwála. These two latter were formed with the object chiefly of meeting the demand for fuel on the Khánewál-Lyallpur line, which has recently been constructed, and their reservation dates from the year 1899. There are thus 7 reserves in the Kabírwála tahsil, 1 in Multán, 4 in Mailsi, and 7 in what formerly constituted the Lodhrán tahsil; the aggregated area covered by them being about 158 square miles.

They have all been demarcated and many of them have been divided into compartments, which serve to define the limits of the different modes of treatment that may be applied to each. As a rule, they are all closed to grazing during the rains (camels and other browsers being excluded throughout the year); and when a block or compartment is felled, the felled area is closed for reproduction, and only grass cutting allowed.

Since July 1897 a working plan has been sanctioned for the south Kabírwála and Mailsi reserves. The principal feature of the plan is the regulation of the fellings, so as to form coupes of a series of age classes that may again be felled on a rotation system of 22 to 24 years.

Wood and grass are the chief products; the revenue from the former being about eleven times as much as that obtained from the latter during the last 5 years. In 1881 (after the first 15 reserves were formed) the revenue from all sources amounted to Rs. 6,965. In 1891 it rose to Rs. 79,153, and the revenue for the current year (1900-01) has been estimated to amount to about Rs. 93,000. The expenditure has similarly increased. In 1881 it was Rs. 6,795. In 1891 it rose to Rs. 29,639, and it is likely to amount to Rs. 50,000 during the current year.

Protected forests.

In addition to the reserved forests there are some 2,260 square miles of 'protected' waste belonging to Government. These waste lands which were formerly counted as 'unclassed waste,' have since 1899 been shown on the books of the Forest Department, and they were declared to be Protected Forests by Punjab Gazette Notifications 312, dated 7th June 1901, and 618, dated 18th November 1901. These lands lie partly within the boundaries of ordinary villages, and partly in separate jungle estates of their own. At the survey of 1857 the waste land of the district was divided up into a number of imaginary units to which numbers (Takra No. I, No. 53, etc.) were given. In 1897, however, this system was done away with, and fresh boundaries, represented for the most part by actual physical limits, such as roads, were adopted and fresh names given to the jungles. In the east portion of Mailsi, however, where the Barbarani Settlement of 1893 had more or less stereotyped the old imaginary boundaries, the old boundaries were, as a rule, retained. The Government land is not, however, entirely in the possession of Government, and considerable areas have from time to time been given out to private persons, who now hold on various tenures, *viz.*, (i) 'darkhwasti,' held on full proprietorship; (ii) lands held on the Sidhnai terms of lease; (iii) lands held on ordinary long-term leases; (iv) lands held on occupancy tenure under the Barbarani Settlement in Mailsi; (v) lands held under the same Settlement on non-occupancy tenure; (vi) lands let

Chapter IV, A.

Agriculture, Arboriculture and Live-stock.

Protected forests.

out on cultivation leases for one harvest only; and vii) small areas occupied by inhabited sites or by water-courses, etc., for some of which malikana is paid to Government, and for some not. Further particulars regarding most of these tenures will be found in Chapter V below. The Government also receives an income from its waste lands from other sources, *viz.*, (i) the tirni or cattle-grazing tax; (ii) the sale of the right to collect máin or the galls of the ukánh tree; (iii) the sale of the right to collect sajji or the barilla plant; (iv) the sale of the right to cut wood. The income from these three latter sources is credited to the Forest Department, and amounted in 1898-99 to the sums noted in the margin.

Sajji ...	Rs.	3,933
Máin ...	„	42
Fuel ...	„	9,729

Arboriculture.

The arboriculture of the district rests mainly in the hands of the District Board and of the Canal Department, a little being also done by the Multan Municipality. There were in 1898-99 thirty acres of nurseries under the District Board and 11 acres under the Canal Department. There were in the same year 174 acres of plantations under the Canal Department. The avenues maintained by the District Board were 234 miles and those maintained by the Canal Department were 675 miles in length. In the district there was an income of Rs. 3,794 against an expenditure of Rs. 12,035; and on the canals an income of Rs. 14,008 against an expenditure of Rs. 10,839. The difficulties in the way of water-supply are very great, and all the more accessible places have now been planted.

Statistics of stock

The agricultural stock of the district has been enumerated at various times; but a glance at the figures in Statement No. XXII will show that the method of enumeration has not been uniform. The figures sometimes include and sometimes exclude young stock, and they sometimes extend to the whole area of the district and sometimes to the village lands only. The fact that the tirni assessments fell on certain classes and ages and not on others has had a good deal to do with this confusion. The figures for 1898-99 are, however, believed to be, as far as such data can be, complete, including as they do the whole area of the district and animals of all ages. According to these figures the stock in the district was:—

Bulls and bullocks	186,645
Cows	154,918
Male buffaloes	6,606
Cow buffaloes	38,765
Young stock of above	152,226
Sheep	318,972
Goats	374,236
Horses and ponies	11,635
Mules	610
Donkeys	31,505
Camels	25,858

Chapter IV, A.

Agriculture, Arboriculture and Live-stock.

By 'young stock' in the above table is meant animals under two years of age. It was calculated at the recent Settlement that the annual income made by the people from the sale of ghi, wool, hair, hides and stock, and from camel hire, came to close upon seven lakhs of rupees per annum.

Civil Veterinary Department.

The agricultural stock of the district, more especially the horses, are under the supervision of the Superintendent, Civil Veterinary Department, South Punjab, whose head-quarters are at Amritsar. The organization of the Department is still in its infancy. In 1901 the establishment under its control consisted of one zilladar on Rs. 40 per mensem and 3 Veterinary Assistants on Rs. 20 per mensem each, travelling allowance being granted to all at the rate of 4 annas per day. There are no Civil Veterinary Dispensaries at present in this district.

Cows and bullocks.

The plough cattle of the village lands were separately enumerated at the first and second Settlements; and as there are few such cattle outside village lands, the figures may be compared more or less satisfactorily with the figures now available for bulls and bullocks, and they show that the number has risen from 103,460 in 1858 to 170,954 in (say) 1878, and from that to 186,645 in 1898. The increase is no doubt slightly exaggerated for reasons which need not be detailed here; but the figures, no doubt, reflect an actual increase of considerable magnitude. The same cattle are used for the plough and for the well; and in either case the turning is always from right to left, and the inner bullock must in either case be the stronger. At the well it is said that three-fifths of the whole strain falls on the inner bullock, and two-fifths on the outer. There is a good deal of breeding done locally, but most of the better class of cattle come from outside the district. There are, generally speaking, four breeds recognized, *viz.*, (i) the Bhágnári, a tall, very expensive animal, usually found in the higher lands of the Shujabad and Multan tahsils; (ii) the Massuwáh (from Dera Gházi Khan), a small, strong breed, costing about Rs. 50 or Rs. 60 a piece; (iii) the Dájal, which are looked on as slightly inferior to the Massuwáh; and (iv) the locally bred cattle (tal de), which are mostly of an inferior description. The Bhágnári cattle have generally to be paid for in cash; the other classes of foreign cattle are bought on a year's credit. The dealers come round in the autumn or spring; after selling a beast they go away for a year, and return at the expiration of that period to demand its price. The Government at one time provided Hissar bulls for improving the local cattle, but the experiment was not a success, and they were withdrawn. The class of cattle found in the lower lands near the river,—*i.e.*, where the well water is near the surface and the jungle scarce, —is poor in quality and size: they are for the most part locally

Chapter IV, A.

Agriculture, Arboriculture and Live-stock.

Cows and bullocks.

bred (tal de). Their size is from 10 to 12 hands, and they cost Rs. 10 to Rs. 30 a piece. In the higher lands, where the wells require stronger cattle and the grazing is more abundant, the animals are almost always imported and are of a much finer class, being large, white, heavy animals with short horns. About 60 per cent. of them are castrated, and their price runs from Rs. 40 to Rs. 100 each. A bullock is generally purchased for use about his fourth year, and he will usually continue capable of work until his eighth or tenth year. The bullock at various ages is spoken of by the following names:—while suckling it is called gábá or vachha ; from suckling to puberty, vábar ; and when full grown, dánd. While it has milk-teeth it is called khíra ; when two teeth, dunda ; when four, chauga ; and when six, chhigá. The age is told (as the above expressions indicate) by the teeth ; and there is a proverb, which says: 'Jinhan dá jam sahí, un de dand kyá dekhnen,' which means that that there is no object in looking at the teeth when you have known the animal from birth. Another saying illustrates the familiar terms on which the people live with their cattle; 'Ghar jam te búhe dhíngar' ('It was born in the house, and yet the owner puts thorns at the door to keep it out !'') The loss of its hump by the ox in days of scarcity is alluded to in the following saying: 'Burre tún burra kurra : na dánd dí kuhárd, na jowán dá turra' ('Great are the evils of famine : the bullock loses its hump, and the young man the projecting end of his pagri').

Cows are kept everywhere for breeding purposes, and the owners drink the buttermilk (chhá) and eat the ghí obtained from them. In the neighbourhood of Multan city there is a constant and good demand for the milk (khír) for sale, but elsewhere the milk is seldom sold. The ordinary peasant's cow gives comparatively little milk, and the best milkers are the cows kept by Gujars and Ahírs in the cantonments and their immediate vicinity.

Buffaloes.

Female buffaloes (manjh) are very commonly kept by the people owing to the large amount of milk which they give. The milk and ghí are both considered inferior in quality to the produce of the cow; but on the riverside the people profess a partiality for the milk of the buffalo. These animals are found especially along the river banks, and the buffalo is as much at home in the water as on land. A proverb says: 'Manjhin kún budná mehná he,' which implies that a buffalo must be exceptionably stupid to get drowned. Male buffaloes (sánh) are comparatively few; and though they are occasionally castrated and used at the plough or on the well, their extra strength is not sufficient to make up for the extra expense of their keep as compared with oxen, and they are of no use for work when the weather gets hot. The people still to a large extent—though not so much as formerly—make a practice

Chapter IV, A.

Agriculture, Arboriculture and Live-stock.

Buffaloes.

of killing the male offspring of buffaloes as soon as born; whence the saying: '*Wáh majhín de dil, jo putr' kohávan te khír duhávan*' ('Bravo for the spirit of the she-buffaloes! they have their sons slain before their eyes and yet give milk to the slayers'). This practice is, however, being gradually abandoned in the Chenáb tahsils, as the people have begun to find a market for their male buffaloes in the central Punjab. It is less common among the Sidhnai settlers than elsewhere in the district. A buffalo-calf is spoken of as *katá* or *katí*, according to the sex. A female buffalo sells, as a rule, for about 50 or 60 rupees.

Diseases of cattle and buffaloes.

The diseases from which cattle and buffaloes chiefly suffer are four in number, *viz.*, rinderpest (*mái-rání, mátá, mátá rání*), foot and mouth disease (*mahára* or *munh-khur*), gloss anthrax (*ghut* or *galghotú*), and a form of sudden death called *sáng*. Of these, foot and mouth disease is perhaps the most common, especially in the early summer, but it is not generally fatal; while rinderpest is both very prevalent and very fatal.

Ghí.

The amount of milk obtainable from a cow in the district, of course, varies a good deal; but though some may be found milking well for a time, the ordinary peasant's cow cannot be said to give more than 1½ sers for six or nine months of the year or about 1 ser per day on an average. A buffalo-cow will give, in the same way, about 2 sers a day. One ser of cow's milk gives 1 oz. (½ chitak) of butter and 1 ser of buffalo's milk 2 ozs. (1 chitak). The weight of ghí is put on an average at about ¾ lbs. of the weight of the butter from which it is extracted; so that, on the whole, a cow may be said to give an average of 8 sers of ghí per annum, and a she-buffalo an average of some 34 sers. Taking the usual price of ghi at 1½ sers to the rupee, this gives for a cow an outturn of Rs. 5 and for a buffalo Rs. 23 per annum. Taking into consideration the proportion of cows out of milk and the proportion not kept for profit, it was calculated at the recent Settlement that the annual income made by the people of the district from ghí was at least Rs. 1,60,000. The ghí of the cultivated tracts is mostly consumed locally, but from the *bár* there is a certain amount of export.

Hides and bones.

There is a considerable net export in hides, averaging in the two years 1896—1897, 5,381 maunds in weight. The hides of cattle sell at about Rs. 2, and those of buffaloes at about Rs. 4 a piece. The price in the case of a goat is about 6 annas, of a sheep 5 annas, and of a camel 8 annas. The hides of animals that are slaughtered fetch more than those of animals which die by disease; and these latter are generally handed over to the village mochi for disposal. It was calculated at the recent

Chapter IV, A.

Agriculture, Arboriculture and Live-stock.

Settlement that the income made by cattle-owners from the sale of hides came to not less than Rs. 33,500.

Hides and bones.

Bones and horns are also collected by the Chuhras, and other low caste tribes, who sell them for about 14 annas a maund. The average net export of these articles in 1896-97 was 8,254 maunds.

Camels.

Camels are found all over the district, but are especially common in the Mailsi and Kabírwála tahsils, where there is most jungle for grazing. The camels are of two kinds—one kept mainly for riding, and other mainly for pack transport. The riding camels are mostly from Baháwalpur and Bikanír, but there is also said to be a good breed in Shujabad. The pack camels are mostly bred locally. The riding camel is the better bred animal, but he is an exotic, and is more liable to ailments than the pack camel. There are fairs for the purchase of young stock at Dhallu in Mailsi, at Rappar and Sultan Ayub Kattál at Lodhrán, which are patronized by camel-owners from Baháwalpur who wish to sell their young stock. Camels are very seldom castrated, and the services of the stallions are usually provided gratis by their owners. The best pack camels are those of the Kabírwala and Mailsi tahsils, those in the south of the district being rather poor in size and quality. In the two northern tahsils there are several large owners of camels among the Langriáls, Hirájs and other tribes; but elsewhere they are mostly in the hands of small owners. A zamindar of any position generally keeps a camel to ride upon; but the bulk of the pack camels are not kept by zamindars, but by Biluchis and other miscellaneous tribes whose hereditary occupation is camel breeding, and who are known collectively as Dakhnas. Pack camels sell for any price from Rs. 30 to Rs. 100 each; the average being probably about Rs. 50. Camel hire is generally about 1 anna per maund for a stage of sixteen miles or so.

The female camels (dáchí) are not usually laden, being kept entirely for breeding and for milk: they and the young camels are driven from place to place by the Dakhnas, Biluchís and others through the large wastes of the district.

The camel until he is one year old is called toda; from then till two years, mazát; from two to three years, trihán; and from three to four years, chhatr. A camel under three or four years old is also called lihák. At four years old camels lose their milk-teeth and the permanent teeth come; so after this age they are named according to the number of their teeth, *viz.* doak, chaugá, chhigá and nesh, according as they have two, four, six or eight teeth. A camel becomes capable of bearing loads when he has four teeth, that is to say, when he is about six years old. The camel eats almost anything, but is chiefly grazed on kikar

Camels.

branches, on the camel-thorn shrub, on jál and karil trees, and on láni or khár. The proverb says: 'Uth je kanken chhoriye, watt jawáhán khá; kuttá ráj batháiye, chakki chhattan já.' ('Though you leave a camel in the wheat, he will still eat camel thorns. If you put a dog on the throne, he will still run and lick the mill-stone'). So, too, the fact that the camel grazes on the jál is generally evident to the nostrils, and the local equivalent for 'plain as a pikestaff' is 'uth de munh vichhon jál di bo' ('the smell of the jál from the mouth of the camel'). The camel is so conspicuous an object in the life of the people that sayings connected with it are very common. Such are 'Uth da náz kajáwá trutte' ('If the camel is pleased with you and begins to frisk, crash go the kajáwas'); or 'Uthín phar na áwe, te borín latta máre' ('He cannot stand up against the camels, so he kicks the camel's loads') or 'Uth dí laháí charháí, har do la'nat' ('Mounting a camel or dismounting, one is as damnable as the other').

The camel is shorn usually once in the year, and from its hair (millass) ropes (mahár) and coarse sacks (borís) are made: the hair is seldom sold, but if sold it would seem to fetch about 6 sers to the rupee: and a camel provides on an average about a ser of hair in the year. From the camel's hide are made the kuppas or large jars which are used for carrying ghí. The milk of the camel cannot be made into butter, and it is mostly drunk by the breeders, and camelherds themselves: with persons not accustomed to it, it acts as a violent purgative.

The principal diseases to which a camel is subject are fever (maror), loss of hair (pán), trembling of the legs (kamorí), paralysis (shímak), and a kind of rheumatism (ákra).

Sheep.

Sheep are found all over the district, and are owned by the landowners themselves or by the tenants and the village menials. They are generally grazed along with the goats. No special breeds are said to be grown and no particular care seem to be taken about the breeding; but a distinction is made between the hornless (ghoni) and the horned (singlí) varieties of sheep. The male lambs are generally killed and eaten a day or two after birth, and those that are left are never castrated. Sheep are shorn twice a year, at the beginning and the end of the hot weather, and each sheep gives about three-eighths of a ser of wool each time it is sheared. The wool sells generally for about Rs. 20 a maund, and there is a considerable demand for it in Multan for export. Full grown sheep are very seldom killed for meat, except for European consumption. An ordinary wether (ghatta) in the district sells for about Rs. 2; a ewe (bhed) for a little more; and lambs (lela, leli) for much less. Sheep, besides suffering from rinderpest and foot and mouth disease are especially liable to pleuro-pneumonia (phepri) and to violent diarrhœa (rikhi).

Goats.

There are more goats than sheep in the district, the excess in the number of goats being very marked in the Mailsi and Lodh-

Chapter IV. A.

Agriculture, Arboriculture and Live-stock.

Goats.

rán tahsils. The goat is, indeed, in some ways, a more valuable animal than a sheep. It is only shorn once a year, and its hair (jatt), of which about three-eighths of a ser is obtained at each shearing, sells at 7 or 8 rupees only to the maund. But the she-goat provides milk to the peasants and is in milk for five or six months at least in each year. Goats, too, are commonly killed, by those who can afford it, for human food, and goat's flesh is preferred, as a rule, to mutton. Goat's hair makes excellent ropes and is used for horses' nose-bags. A good milking she-goat sometimes sells for as much as Rs. 10, but an ordinary goat will fetch on an average about Rs. 2. Two breeds are recognized, *viz.*, the desi or common goat, and the barpari. The latter is reddish in colour, very lightly built and provided with good horns. Goats of this breed are said to be obtained originally by putting a chinkára to a she-goat. The goat is a voracious feeder, and is especially destructive to young trees. In the early spring it gets fodder, and when disparaging a 'Jack-in-office,' the people say : 'Dhai diháre Chetr de, kudde bakarwár' ('The goatherd leaps in his pride for two and a half days in Chetr'). The goat is subject to much the same diseases as sheep.

Poultry.

Cocks and hens (kukkar, kukri) are kept by all conditions of men, but much less interest is taken in them than is usual in the central districts of the province. Two classes are recognized, namely, the tarra or ordinary variety, and the gauri, which is bigger and stronger. A peasant of moderate standing who has a guest to feed will sometimes kill a hen in his honour ; and the eggs are eaten, both by Muhammadans and Hindús, in a fried condition with ghí, vegetables, etc. ; they are never boiled. The insufficiency of the fowl for a real feast is indicated by the saying : 'Kukkar kutthí ; gawándhin rutthi, ('I killed a fowl ; but the neighbours were dissatisfied').

Dogs.

The peasants live in partial isolation on separate wells ; each well, as a rule has one or more dogs to keep watch, and the dogs, though mostly uncared for, are, as a rule, private property. 'Manda kutta,' it is said, 'khasmen gálh' ('A bad dog and its owner gets abused'). One occasionally comes across in the villages a dog of an unmistakeably English type, and some of the raises have pure or half-bred dogs for show or sport. The partiality of an owner for his dog is reflected in the saying : 'Andha kutta wá kún bhaunke, sáin de lekhe tází' 'The dog is blind and barks at the wind, but his owner thinks him a smart animal.' In the *bár* there are some dogs which have been bred from wolves ; they are said to be strong, useful animals, but endowed with an unfortunate relish for goat's flesh.

H orses and poni

There are about ten thousand horses and ponies in the district exclusive of those in the cantonment ; but the district is only moderately prominent as a ground for horse breeding. There are far fewer horses in the Sutlej tahsils than in the western parts of the district. There are usually six Government stallions and three District Board stallions in the district, generally Arabs and thoroughbreds. The stallions, when the system was first introduced, were more numerous and were entrusted to the zaildars or to the Deputy Inspectors of Police; but of late years they have been confined to the tahsil head-quarters and to one or two other suitable centres, such as Sarai Siddhu, Kadirpur Ran and Kahror. No fees are taken for the services of either the Imperial or the District Board stallions. There is also a privately owned stallion at Chauki Muhan which has been passed as fit by the Civil Veterinary Department. In addition to these, there are a number of private stallions of an inferior description, the owners of which let out their services in return for a few rupees. The mares kept by the bigger zamindars are sometimes of good class and run from 13-2 to 14-2 hands. A few are imported from Dera Gházi Khan, but most are bred locally; and the zamindars are very averse to selling their mares. The chief breeds known to them are the Biluchi, Hárni and Topra. They keep the mares for riding and breeding, and sell the colts at one or two years old or use them for loads. The poorer class of landowners, etc., also employ them for riding purposes.

There is a horse fair at Multan about the beginning of March in each year. The following statement shows the number of horses exhibited and sold, and the prizes awarded :—

Statement showing the number of horses exhibited and sold and the prizes awarded at the Multan Horse Show.

YEARS.	Number exhibited.	Number sold.	Prizes awarded by Government.	Prizes awarded by District Board.
			Rs.	Rs.
1879	556	24	825	...
1880	959	59	1,500	...
1881	440	24	2,000	...
1882	648	18	2,000	...
1883	771	33	2,000	...
1884	731	48	2,000	...
1885	548	163	2,000	...
1886	506	192	2,000	...
1887	404	150	2,000	...
1888	405	145	2,000	...
1889	395	198	2,000	...
1890	469	147	1,900	...
1891	454	194	1,900	...
1892	328	225	1,800	345
1893	261	113	1,550	100
1894	348	180	1,500	315
1895	309	185	1,075	150
1896	436	120	1,000	150
1897	418	162	1,200	165
1898	355	189	1,200	300
1899	414	226	1,200	350
1900	910	226	1,200	350
1901	915	210	1,200	350

Chapter IV, A.

Agriculture, Arboriculture and Live-stock.

Horses and ponies.

The fair is followed by some tent pegging, horse racing, and camel racing. The horses sold at the fair for remounts fetch prices averaging about Rs. 300; but taking the whole of the horses and the ponies of the district into consideration, the average price obtainable in the district is probably not over Rs. 50.

The figures in Statement No. XXIIA show that there were in 1898-99 five hundred and seventy-nine branded mares in the district which had been passed as fit to be served by Government stallions. In the same year 449 mares were served by Government and District Board stallions, and 134 castrations were effected by Government agency.

The following list includes the names of the zamindars of the district who take any interest in horses. The interest on some of them is lukewarm enough, but the list may be of use to officers making enquiries regarding the horse-breeding capacities of the district :—

List of persons taking most interest in horse-breeding.

Tahsil.	Name.	Tribe.	Place of abode.
Kabirwala.	Amír Haidar Sháh ...	Syad ...	Amírpur.
	Mahr. Allah Yár Khan...	Hiráj ...	Chauki Muhan.
	Mahr. Bahádur	Do. ...	Do.
	Salábat	Do. ...	Do.
	Karam	Do. ...	Do.
	Khán Hiraj	Do. ...	Sada Hiráj.
	S. Ghulám Rasúl Sháh ...	Syad ...	Kuranga.
	Chiragh Sháh	Do. ...	Katalpur.
	Daulat Sháh	Koreshi ...	Ghauspur.
	Mahomed Khán ...	Sial ...	Narhal.
	Mahmud Sháh Khagga...	Khaga ...	Bhaironwála.
	Sháh Nawáz Sháh ...	Syad ...	Solgi.
	Karam Khán Daha ...	Daha ...	Khanawal.
	Hashmat Khán	Tangra ...	Jawahari.
	Salábat	Sargana ...	Kund Sargana.
	Ghulám Mahomed ...	Sial ...	Fakir Sial.
	M. Karam Husain ...	Syad ...	Gagra Kalandar Jahanian.
	Nur Mahomed ...	Hiráj ...	Nuri Siag.
	Ghulám Mahomed ...	Langrial ...	Mankot.
	Haidar Sháh	Syad ...	Salarwahan Kohna.
	Amir	Daduana ...	Daduána.
	Pahlwan	Dawána ...	Hájí Dawana.
	Sháh Mahmud ...	Syad ...	Fázil Sháh.
	Murad	Pahor ...	Makhdúmpur.
	Baháwal	Chaddhar ...	Baháwalpur.

List of persons taking most interest in horse-breeding—(concld).

Tahsil.	Name.	Tribe.	Place of abode.
Shujabad.	Lál Khán	Langáh ...	Shajaátpur.
	Ch. Lila Kishan ...	Babla ...	Shujabad.
	Malik Abdullah	Panuhan ...	Mochi Panuhan.
	Jam Hamíd	Wagha ...	Bet Kech.
	Fateh Mahomed... ...	Biluch ...	Jagguwála.
	Ghulám Mahomed Khan	Langáh ...	Jahánpur.
	Sewa Rám	Munjal ...	Ubaora.
	Rana Pallia	Nún ...	Nasírpur.
	Ch. Howá Rám	Babla ...	Shujabad.
	Allah Bakhsh	Khakhi ...	Panjáni.
Multan.	Dargahi	Athangal ...	Mati Tal.
	Nur Mahomed	Bosan ...	Bosan.
	Kádir Bakhsh	Vains ...	Jhok Vains.
	Mahomed Makbúl ...	Bhutta ...	Khairpur.
	Mián Faiz Bakhsh ...	Khokhar ...	Khokhar.
	,, Karím Bakhsh ...	Do. ...	Do.
	,, Kádir Bakhsh ...	Do. ...	Do.
	Rahím Bakhsh ...	Hammar ...	Sultánpur Hammar.
	Ch. Luddu Mal	Jawa ...	Traggar.
	Gobinda Mal	Do. ...	Do.
	Mullan Khan Mahomed...	Aráin ...	Kabírpur.
	Abdulla Sháh	Syad ...	Muzaffarabad.
	Saifal Khan	Luthar ...	Luthar.
	Sher Bakhsh	Maral ...	Kasba.
	Kádir Bakhsh	Aráin ...	Firozpur.
	Wazir Shah	Syad ...	Kotla Sádát.
Lodhran.	Nazar Mahomed Khan ...	Biluch	Haweli Nasir Khan.
	Amar Ditta Mal... ...	Arora	Jamraniwah.
Mailsi.	Dost Mahomed Khan ...	Afghán ...	Durpur.
	Mián Ghulám Rasúl ...	Bhutta ...	Nurabba.
	,, Ghulam Mahomed...	Daulatána ...	Luddan.
	Amír Sháh	Syad ...	Hasan Sháh.
	Ahmad Yár Khan ...	Khákwáni ...	Hájiwáh.

The people have some sayings about horses which are perhaps worth recording, such as: 'Ghora te phora hath pheriá waddhda hai' ('Stroking with the hand increases the size of a horse and of a wound'), and 'Randar dá putr, saudágar dá

Chapter IV, A.

Agriculture, Arboriculture and Live-stock.

Horses and ponies.

ghorá: kháwe bahun, chale thorá' ('A widow's son and a merchant's horse eat much and work little'). And when a man being refused a big demand, makes a small one, he will say: 'Terá tappan chhoriá: chalen hí chal' ('If you won't jump, at any rate walk.')

Horses are pastured on grass in the summer, and afterwards on jowár stalks (tánda). When the green wheat appears they get some of this or some nihárí; and if the owners grow barley, the horse gets barley and barley-straw in the spring. Gram is very seldom given. Mares and geldings are often allowed to graze freely in the fields and jungles during the six months following the wheat harvest: the chief crops then ripening, indigo and cotton, being in no way damaged by them; but in the winter they are tied up. Some of the zamindars used to keep horse runs (lohra); but there are no horse runs now in the district. A considerable number of young ponies are bought in this and the neighbouring districts by Purbia dealers from Oudh, and it is not an uncommon sight in the spring to see droves of some fifty or sixty of these being driven along the road towards the north.

Mules.

One very seldom sees any mules in the district. According to the enumeration of 1898 there are 610 mules in the district, of which, however 415 are in the Multán tahsil, and most of these latter are Government animals belonging to the Transport. There are usually 9 Imperial donkey stallions and District Board donkey stallions in the district (including Cyprus, Italian and country-bred animals). The figures given in Statement XXIIA show that a fair number of mares are served by donkey stallions, but the proportion of successful coverings is not satisfactory; and it is not improbable that a certain number of the zamindars purposely bring in their mares too early or too late. Mules are generally sold as yearlings to the dealers: they are not, as a rule, kept for use in this district, but are only bred for the purpose of being sold to agents from Jhelum and elsewhere, who, after keeping them for a year or two, sell them to the Government.

Donkeys.

There were by the enumeration of 1898 thirty-one thousand five hundred and five donkeys (khotá) in the Multán district, and they are fairly well distributed over all parts of the district. They are generally small and weedy; and only about 4 per cent. of them are said to be fit for a two-maund load on a long march. In spite of the presence of donkey stallions in the tahsils, very little is done to improve the breed of the animals. They are mostly owned by Kumhárs (potters), who use them for carrying pots to and from the kiln, and by Kirárs (petty shop-keepers), who use them for

Chapter IV, B.

Occupations, Industries and Commerce.

Donkeys.

riding and for carrying small stores from the market towns. The name 'Khotá Mal,' so common among Kirárs, is said by some to be adopted in honour of the faithful ass: but the donkey in this district generally meets with the same measure of contempt that is usually bestowed on him elsewhere, and the local equivalent for 'Pearls before swine' is 'Gaddán de gal lál' (Pearls on donkeys' necks'). When, in spite of a change made things are much the same as before, the people say: 'Gaddán oho dá oho, athar byá' ('The saddle was different, but the donkey was the same'). A donkey on an average sells for about seven or eight rupees.

SECTION B.—OCCUPATIONS, INDUSTRIES AND COMMERCE.

Occupations of the people.

The occupations of the people as returned at the census of 1901 are detailed in Statement XXIII, but the figures for occupations are not altogether satisfactory, and they must be taken subject to certain limitations and explanations which need not be detailed here. The returns are classified in the margin with the grouping adopted in the Census Return of 1901. The figures classed under 'Agriculture,' however, include only such part of the population as are agriculturists, pure and simple, and exclude not only the considerable number who combire agriculture with other occupations, but also the much larger number who depend in great measure for their livelihood upon the yield of agricultural operations.

	Total actual workers and dependents.	ACTUAL WORKERS.		Dependents, both sexes.	Per cent.
		Males.	Females		
Government ...	16,823	7,529	14	9,280	2·4
Pasture and agriculture.	308,217	97,639	1,865	208,713	43·4
Personal services	28,151	10,581	773	16,797	4·
Preparation and supply of material substances.	197,276	60,451	10,740	126,085	27·8
Commerce, transport and storage	39,705	12,725	115	26,865	5·6
Professions ...	18,074	5,560	622	11,892	2·5
Unskilled labour not agricultural	68,486	23,225	3,021	42,240	9·6
Means of subsistence independent of occupation.	33,894	14,124	2,586	17,184	4·7
Total ...	710,626	231,834	19,736	459,056	100

The course and nature of trade.

The trade of the district is practically synonymous with the trade of Multan town, and the chief figures relating to the imports and exports of the town and the articles subject to octroi are given in Chapter VI below. As regards the district as a

Chapter IV, B.

Occupations, Industries and Commerce.

The course and nature of trade.

whole the following figures give a very fair indication of the course and nature of the trade :—

Total imports and exports by rail for the Railway Stations of the Multan District, average of the two years 1896 and 1897, in maunds.

Article.	Import.	Export.	Article.	Import.	Export.
Cotton seed ...	280	137,021	Salt	19,164	291
Cotton, loose ...	31,272	16,500	Kerosine oil ...	9,088	66
Cotton, pressed ...	475	168,102	Common oil ...	5,802	424
Wool, raw ...	40,170	19,799	Dried fruits ...	16,297	11,484
Gunny-bags ...	17,176	14,468	Fresh fruits ..	136	3,260
Edible grain (excluding wheat).	1,92,288	136,364	Bones	489	8,743
Wheat	98,690	414,962	Hides and skins ...	2,006	25,383
Rice	37,654	2,738	Iron	27,788	1,228
Oilseeds ...	27,266	796	Piece goods ...	26,101	...
Sugar, refined ...	58,600	610	Piece-goods, Indian	7,098	270
Sugar, unrefined ...	10,115	...	Indigo	512	2,345
Gur	130,210	7,143	Multani Mitti* ...	552	...
Ghi	15,074	682	Sajji	260	2,876

From the above figures it will be seen that the district is an importer of rice, oilseeds, oil, sugar, gur, ghi, iron and piece-goods, and an exporter of wheat, cotton, indigo, bones, hides and sajji. There is an excess import of raw wool, but cleaned wool is a staple of export.

The district is not well suited for sugarcane or for the better class of oilseeds and rice, so that considerable quantities of these products have to be imported from other districts. So too the supply of ghi in the district does not meet the demands of the city and large imports are made from Jhang and Montgomery. Iron and piece-goods have of course to be imported from Europe.

The larger exports of the district are almost entirely to Europe except in the case of indigo, the chief part of which

* This article really comes from Sindh and not from Multan.

Chapter IV, B.

Occupations, Industries and Commerce.

The course and nature of trade.

goes to Central Asia or (of late years) to Japan. The chief staples of European trade are wheat, cotton and wool and the exporting agencies in 1901 were :—

Messrs. Ralli Brothers.

Messrs. Sandy Patrick and Co.

Messrs. Volkart.

Messrs. Clements and Co.

Messrs. McHinch and Co.

Multán has long been a well-known centre of wheat trade, but of late years it has had to contend with new centres such as Lyallpur, which have somewhat impaired its prosperity in this respect. As a cotton centre it has had its ups and downs since the ginning factories were first started in 1893-94 in the neighbourhood of the city. The number of gins rose in a few years to over 60 and in 1895-96 exporters handled about 2½ lakhs of maunds of raw cotton from these gins, which was baled in hydraulic presses (of which there were 4 working in 1900), but owing to smaller outturns in subsequent years and the establishment of factories at other places the number of gins out of work since 1896 has been considerable and the trade had, by 1901, fallen considerably. The wool exported previous to 1895 was sent to Karachi as it stood without further manipulation, but since that date over 30 wool-washing godowns and several hydraulic presses have been started, enabling producers to transmit cleaned and pressed wool direct to Liverpool and thus to save the freight and other charges which the old system entailed.

Principal industries and manufactures.

The chief statistics regarding the factories working in the district are given in Table XXIV. All the factories in question are, with the exception of the Railway workshops, cotton ginning or pressing factories, and all except two are situated in the immediate vicinity of Multan city.

Village industries consist mainly in the weaving of coarse cotton cloth and the preparation of ropes, mats, etc., from the sarkana or date. In some of the villages and country towns there are some special industries which have a local reputation. In Tulamba and Kahror, for instance, stamped cloths for bed-covers are made somewhat after the Kamalia type. At Thatta Paolian, Jalálpur and Obáona chequed saddle-cloths and other forms of cloth-work are prepared. At Shujabad various kinds of sweet confections, such as *pápar* and *reorian*, have a local celebrity. At Wachha Sandila ordinary wood-work such as cot-legs, etc., is well turned out. At Jalálpur Pírwála there are the remains of what was once a very flourishing paper trade.

Chapter IV, B.

Occupations Industries and Commerce.

The following note on the special industries of the district was furnished for the first edition of this Gazetteer by Mr. Lockwood Kipling, then Principal of the Lahore School of Art, and the account therein given has been brought up to date by Mr. Percy Brown, the present Principal :-

Glazed pottery.

The industries for which the town of Multan is noted are glazed pottery, vitrous enamel, ornaments in silver, cotton and woollen carpets, silk fabrics, mixed textures of cotton and silk, cotton printing in colour (formerly more extensively practised than now), wood painting and metal-work.

The glazed faience is a relic of the time when mosques and tombs were covered with this beautiful material. There are many such buildings at Multan and Muzaffargarh, as elsewhere in the province. Until a comparatively recent period, the work was exclusively architectural, and consisted of tiles painted in dark and light blue with large geometrical patterns for wall surfaces, finials for the tops of domes, the Mahomedan profession of faith painted in bold Arabic characters for tombs, and panels of various sizes for lintels, door jambs and the like. There is here no ornamentation of earthern vessels for domestic use (except perhaps of the *hookah* and *chillum* as at Peshäwar. The European demand has developed a trade in flower-pots, large plateaux for decorative purposes, and many varieties of the comprehensive word 'vase.' The work differs technically from the pottery of Sindh, which had the same origin ; in that its decoration consists solely in painting in two or three colours on the glaze or enamel, the use of coloured or white "slips," which gives a raised appearance to the patterns on Sindh ware, being unknown or at least not practised. The colours used are a dark blue from cobalt, and a very fine turqoise from copper. A manganese violet and a green with other colours have been recently tried, but with no great success. The "biscuit" and "glost" firing are done at one operation, *i. e.*, the article is made in clay, sun-dried, covered with glaze, and painted at once. The green glaze is said to require that preliminary burning of the clay which is invariably given in European practice. The demand for this ware is greater than the supply, and it is to be regretted that more enterprise and intelligence are not brought to bear on a craft which has to begin with first-rate materials and good traditions. Architectural objects are still better understood, and more satisfactorily treated, than are the vases and other wares made for the European mantelpiece. No more suitable material for internal wall-decoration could be devised, but little use has been made of it for this purpose. A tomb by one of the potters now practising at Multan, and copied from an original in the neighbourhood, occupies a place of honour in the National Ceramic Museum at Sevres.

The glaze which is used now is said to be not so durable as that on the old work, some of the recent productions being very brittle and easily washed off with soda-water. The present method of making the glaze is as follows :—One part of powdered limestone and two parts of powdered soda are mixed with water and made into balls. These are dried for fifteen or twenty days in the sun. They are then burnt in an earthen vessel in a smokeless fire till they become quite white. Again it is melted in a strong fire for twenty-four hours and put into cold water to set. When required for use it is powdered in a mill and mixed with water to the required consistency. It is not applied with a brush, but is poured over the article, which is kept on the move until the whole surface is covered.

Enamel.

The enamel on silver of Multan probably owes its preservation to the continued use of vitrified colour in the local pottery. The dark and light blues of the tiles are as identical in their nature with, as they are similar in appearance to, the colouring of a Multan brooch or necklace. Black, red, and yellow, the difficulties of the potter all the world over, are easier to manage in the small scale on which the silversmith works. But they are not nearly so good in Multan enamel as the blues. In larger objects, such as cups and some forms of bracelets, the work might be described as *champlevé* enamel. The ground on which the colour is laid is graven out precisely as in Europe, but in the case of the studs, solitaires, brooches and other objects which form the staple of the trade, a more expeditious and mechanical plan is adopted. The threadlike lines of silver which

Enamel.

bound the pattern are engraven on a steel or bronze die or *thappa* into which the silver is beaten. The result is a meagre and mechanical raised line within which the enamel is laid. Copper is added to the silver to the extent of nearly half its weight to enable it, so the workmen say, the better to resist the heat of the fire. The ordinary price varies from Re. 1 to Rs. 2 per *tola*; to which, for enamel in two colours, 4 annas per rupee is added for workmanship. When three or four colours are introduced, a rupee per *tola* is added. The reason for the enhanced price is the additional firing requisite to bring up reds and yellows to the proper tone. There is no contrivance at all resembling the muffle kiln used by enamellers in Europe and elsewhere, and the work is practically roasted in an open charcoal fire, protected by shards or by a wire cage. Rough as this process may appear, and deficient in design as much of the Multan enamel work is when compared with the best of which India is capable, it is undeniable that it is growing in popularity. and that it compares very favourably with the Algerian, Parisian and Syrian articles of the same class which are extensively sold in Paris. There are several good workmen who can be trusted to produce excellent work at a fair price. The prices of the articles rise very rapidly with their size, as the difficulty of evenly firing a piece six inches in height is very much greater than in the case of buttons, studs, etc. The Multanis, unlike the Kashmirís, have a notion that enamel cannot well be applied to any other metal than their modified silver, and have no inclination to work on brass or copper, cheaper materials which might doubtless be largely brought into use. The largest objects to which enamel is applied in the district are the *mokabbas* or covered dishes that come from Baháwalpur, where the practice is similar to that of Multan, excepting that in addition to the opaque enamels, a semi-translucent sea green and dark blue are a pplied, while the silver is frequently heavily gilded. These are both points of superiority. Mr. B. H. Baden Powell in his Handbook of Punjab Manufactures quotes a local legend, ' that the first maker was one Nantu, who worked four hundred years ago, and that since then the art so increased in excellence that Multan enamelled ware was highly esteemed and exported to other districts.

Woollen carpets.

Multan is probably the only town in the province which can claim woollen carpet-weaving as an independent, if not absolutely indigenous, manufacture. It seems likely that rugs and carpets brought over from Turkestan in the course of its large and long-established Pawindah trade may have served as the original inspiration. The patterns have a decidedly Tartar air. They are excessively bold and yet not clear in detail. The unusual size of the stitch, together with a peculiar brightness in the white, and their rather violent red and yellow, give them a somewhat aggressive and quite distinctive quality of colour. The cost ranges from one rupee per yard upwards; and, though looser in texture than good jail carpets, they are durable and serviceable. The larger sizes are always, to European eyes, disproportionately long for their width, a peculiarity noticeable in all carpets that come from countries like Persia and Turkistan, where wood for roofing timber is small, and apartments in consequence are long and narrow.

[The competition of Amritsar and Lahore, where huge carpet factories under European supervision have of late years sprung up, has had a deleterious effect on the woollen carpet weaving of Multan, so that this industry has very much decayed. The weavers now principally live by making foot-mats for carriages and Hindu prayer-carpets.]

Cotton pile carpets.

The cotton rugs and carpets are sometimes parti-coloured like the woollen ones, but the typical Multan cotton carpet is an exceedingly strong and substantial fabric coloured entirely in a bright blueish white and blue. There would seem, indeed, to be a sort of unity in local treatment of pottery, enamels and rugs. They are sometimes made in large sizes, but always, unless specially ordered, long in proportion to their width. The colouring is vivid, but not unpleasant, in effect: and the texture, notwithstanding its large stitch, is substantial and serviceable. The Multan carpets, on the whole, are very respectable productions; and although the original *motif* of the pattern has been merged by dint of many repetitions in vague masses of colour, its fabric remains stout and good; forming in this respect a strong contrast with the Mirzapore rug, another survival which has not only lost its pattern, but become flimsy and loose in workmanship.

Chapter IV, B.

Occupations, Industries and Commerce.

Silks.

The traveller Vigne, quoted by Mr. Baden-Powell in his Handbook, wrote :—'Seven hundred maunds of raw silk are brought to Multan every year by the Lohánis, chiefly from Bokhára and Turkistan; these are manufactured in one hundred and fifty workshops. One man will finish an ordinary *khes* or silk scarf in six days, perhaps three yards long and a foot and a half wide, taking eight days previously for the arrangement of the weaving apparatus. A very handsome *khes* is finished in sixteen days. That of the red colour is most valuable; it is dyed with cochineal, which is brought from either Bombay or Bokhára; that from Bombay is a rupee a ser—about a shilling a pound.' The trade still continues, and Multan silk-weaving is probably the best in the province. At Amritsar and Delhi there is a more varied use of the staple, and at Lahore there is perhaps more variety in the European style of pattern; but the Multan *daryai*, plain self-coloured silk, the *dhúpchhán* or shot silk, and the *khes*, a sort of checked, damasked fabric are better finished and more agreeably coloured. All Indian silks are deficient in lustre to European eyes, but those of Multan are decidedly less " cottony " in appearance than others. These fabrics are chiefly worn by native ladies, and are therefore little known to Europeans. The combination of cotton with silk to make the latter lawful for Muhammadan wear (*Musaffa*, pure), has given the name of Sufi to a mixture of a cotton warp with a silk weft, which is very well made at Multan. *Shujá kháni* is another name for these mingled goods, for which Bahawalpur is perhaps better known than Multan, where, however, they can be produced in equal perfection. Gold thread is frequently worked into the variegated stripes for these cloths, and it is also wrought into the borders and ends of the *lungis*, turbans, *khes* and *iklais*. One of the best features of this manufacture is the great durability and wearing power of the fabric. The fashions of the zanána do not change, and their inmates are keen and accomplished critics, who would quickly detect the presence of jute or any other adulteration.

[The fashion of wearing silk fabrics is rapidly dying out, and now both native ladies and gentlemen wear chiefly European-made cloths, so that this trade has decreased considerably; the chief articles now being made are *patkas* with gold edges, which are exported in fairly large numbers.]

Cotton printing.

Cotton-printing, though it is well done at Multan, can scarcely be called a flourishing industry, for the brighter and cheaper wares of Manchester have here, as elsewhere, seriously depressed a once extensive trade. The staple article of to-day is the *abrá*, a piece of cotton cloth usually 8 feet long and 5 feet wide, printed with a broad border all round, and a centre field of a different colour. It is used for the *razái* or cotton-stuffed quilt, which forms at once a cloak and bed-cover during the cold months. Large floor-cloths elaborately printed were formerly more extensively made than now, in response to the Hindu preference for cotton. A Rája or Sardar will often cover a rich woollen carpet with a cotton print. This is said to be the invariable practice at the Kashmiri court. Besides the *jázam* or floor-cloth, the *divar gir*, " wall veil " or continuous lengths of print about 3 feet 6 inches wide for wall lining, and a variety of *rumals* (handkerchiefs) and dopattás (scarves) were formerly much more largely made than now. It is noticeable, too, in examining a cotton-printer's graven blocks, that but few have the appearance of being newly cut. If there is a peculiarity in the Multan prints, it is an almost lake-like depth in the red derived from madder, which contrasts strongly with the brick-red in inferior work from other places. The greens, light blues and light yellows are not fast colours. Good cotton prints are made at Tulamba, which, indeed, is often spoken of as the best place for these fabrics.

[English chintzes have now entirely superseded the once famous ones made at Multan, and this industry is practically extinct. A few *abrás* are still made for quilts for the country people, as they wear better than the English cloth. Susis and tislías of cotton are made in quantities for the poorer class of people who cannot afford silk. They are made in imitation of the silk articles.]

Ivory.

In addition to the handicrafts of common life practised at Multan as in every Indian town of its size, is a peculiarly local one of turned ivory *churis* or bangles. These are merely large rings, sometimes coloured red, and in no way artistic, interesting or commercially important. The price of ivory has everywhere risen, so rapidly that it was at one time thought that this use of the material, to which it is not particularly applicable, must shortly cease. The increased demand, however, for ivory bangles in preference to gold and silver ornaments has caused the ivory industry to become quite a flourishing one at Multan, so that the supply falls short of the demand.

Wood-painting.

[The trade in wood painting is practically extinct, only a few bowls and charpoy legs being turned out.

Metal-work.

Within the last ten years one or two tinsmiths from Karachi have settled in Multan and have introduced the manufacture of cash-boxes and despatch-cases. This industry is rapidly growing.]

System of book keeping.

The wealthier and more business-like bankers and shop-keepers keep the following account-books (called vahís by the Multánís and Shikarpurís, and bahís by the Marwarís and men of the eastern Punjab) *viz*, (1) The day-book. This is known in the Chenáb tahsils as súhr or roznámcha, and in the Sutlej tahsils as kharra, and in this day-book all transactions are recorded day by day, as they occur. Where a number of transactions are settled within the day, it is usual to record these on a kachha súhr, hath-rakha or takhti, and to omit them from the súhr itself. (2) The ledger or kháta vahi in which each client's account is shown separately. The entries from the súhr are transferred to the kháta vahi once a month, or, where transactions are large, once a week or once a day, according to the custom of the house. In this ledger the receipts are shown on the right side, and the disbursements on the left; and a balance is struck, not necessarily every year, but only when the requirements of the Limitation Law necessitate it. In the *kháta vahi* some shops show the items in detail, with dates, etc.; others merely enter the amounts with a reference to the page (panna) of the súhr concerned. (3) The cash-book or rokir bahi, in which all cash transctions are entered as they occur, in addition to the entries made of such transactions in the súhr, and a day balance is struck showing the cash in hand. Transactions settled within the day are often omitted from the book, and some houses omit transactions in copper money. Money taken out by one of the partners is entored as an outgoing (ghar da kháta) and the further account of such monies is kept by the partner concerned at his private house. Any deficiency in the balance is entered as a batta or vatta kháta, and the recorded balances are made to agree with the cash in hand to start the next day.

The smaller shop-keepers and money-lenders are not, however, very regular in their book-keeping, and generally only keep a kháta vahi and a kachha súhr, and entries in both of these are made in a very casual manner. The leaves, instead of being numbered as in the better shops are left plain; and as a ledger consists merely of leaves stitched together there is plenty of room for subsequent fraud even when the original entries have been honestly made.

Chapter IV, C.

Prices, Weights and Measures. and Communications.

SECTION C.—PRICES, WEIGHTS AND MEASURES, AND COMMUNICATIONS.

Rent rates and wages.

The information available regarding the rates of rent prevalent in the district has been already given in Chapter III D above. The normal prices of labour as entered in the annual returns are reproduced in Statement No. XVII; and though the prices there quoted cannot be taken as trustworthy in detail, yet they may be accepted as reflecting roughly the degree in which the price of labour and the hire of animals has risen during the last thirty years. The rate of unskilled labour, which thirty years ago ranged from 2 annas to 4 annas, now lies between 4 annas and 5 annas.

Prices of agricultural produce.

The prices quoted for the agricultural produce in the district are of three kinds:—

Firstly, there are the wholesale prices prevailing at head-quarters. These will be found in Statement No. XXVI A below, and they represent the following averages: for rabi produce, average of prices of 15th June and 1st July; for kharíf produce, average of prices of 1st December and 1st January; and for gúr the average prevailing from 1st to 31st January.

Secondly, there are the retail prices prevailing at head-quarters. These are shown in Statement No. XXVI below. It is not known to what dates the prices previous to 1886-87 relate; those for subsequent years represent the prices entered for the 1st January in the retail price register maintained at head-quarters.

Thirdly, there are the prices actually received by the average producer immediately after the harvest. It is a common custom for the chief zamindars and money-lenders of each tract to determine after each harvest what shall be the standard rate adopted for transactions in each staple for that tract; and the figures which are quoted below represent the average of the rates so fixed at the chief country towns of the district. As a matter of fact, the ordinary zamindar who is in a debt to his banker does not receive these prices in their entirety, as the money-lender reduces the credits by various forms of discount, and it was calculated at the recent Settlement that, roughly speaking, the prices actually received by zamindars of this class were 5 per cent. lower than the figures quoted below. In the last column of the statement below have been added the prices adopted for the valuation of the produce in the calculations connected with the recent Settlements :—

Prices of agicultural produce.

Table of prices obtained by the producer for agricultural produce.

Crops.	Five-yearly period.										Accepted for Settlement purposes.	
	A.D. 1853 to 1857.	A.D. 1858 to 1862.	A.D. 1863 to 1867.	A.D. 1868 to 1872.	A.D. 1873 to 1877.	A.D. 1878 to 1882.	A.D. 1883 to 1887.	A.D. 1888 to 1892.	A.D. 1893 to 1897.	A.D. 1898 to 1900.	A.D. 1873 to 1879.	A.D. 1896 to 1900.
Wheat	36	28	19	22	24	18	21	18	20	17	31	21
Barley	17	39	28	31	33	26	30	27	26	24	43	29
Gram	45	31	24	24	27	21	24	23	22	18	39	28
Tobacco	16	14	11	11	10	9	8	8	8	8	14	11
Sarsaf	31	23	18	18	17	16	15	14	14	13	25	14
Taramira ...	47	33	27	23	28	24	21	20	20	17	...	20
Peas	65	44	30	35	36	30	35	30	32	15	48	37
Masur	46	34	25	29	33	25	24	27	25	21	41	29
Sugar	17	11	10	11	11	10	11	11	11	10	14	11
Indigo	$\frac{27}{32}$	$\frac{21}{32}$	$\frac{48}{80}$	$\frac{10}{16}$	$\frac{10}{16}$	$\frac{9}{16}$	$\frac{9}{16}$	$\frac{17}{32}$	$\frac{9}{16}$	$\frac{10}{16}$	$\frac{11}{16}$	$\frac{10}{16}$
Cotton	14	11	10	10	12	11	11	10	10	9	14	10
Jowár	47	34	22	28	27	25	27	25	27	21	42	27
Bájra	40	29	19	25	27	24	26	23	22	22	40	24
Rice	51	30	28	36	31	29	33	29	27	20	40	26
Til	22	15	13	12	13	11	11	10	10	9	20	10
Másh	31	20	16	19	18	15	17	14	14	15	28	20
China	49	36	27	31	35	31	33	31	30	22	45	34
Moth	45	27	22	26	24	16	22	18	19	12	23	24

At the recent Settlement the following prices, adopted for the Mailsi tahsil, differ from those accepted for the rest of the district: wheat 24 sers, cotton 12, and jowár 30.

Rise in the prices of agricultural produce.

From the figures above given the statistics in the following table have been drawn, showing (*a*) the comparative value of the different crops in the district at different periods ; (*b*) the comparative value of agricultural produce generally in the various tahsils and in the district at large at various times. From the latter it will be seen that the general rise between 1868—77 and 1883—95 was 12 per cent., and this was the rise assumed in the recent Settlement.

Chapter IV. C.

Prices, Weights and Measures, and Communications.

Rise in the prices of agricultural produce.

(a) Value of various classes of produce at different periods.

Crop.	Assumed produce in maunds of average in 5 years before present Settlement.	Detail.	1853 to 1857.	1858 to 1862.	1863 to 1867.	1868 to 1872.	1873 to 1877.	1878 to 1882.	1883 to 1887.	1888 to 1892.	1893 to 1897.	1883 to 1895.	Rise per cent. Between 1853 to 1862 and 1883 to 1895.	Rise per cent. Between 1868 to 1877 and 1883 to 1895.
Rice ...	1 82,646	Rs.	1,14,717	2,38,881	2,25,695	1,66,890	1,94,575	2,22,136	1,76,714	2,84,449	2,91,224	2,28,896	29	26
		p. c.	100	208	198	146	171	195	155	249	254	200		
Jowár ...	220,952	Rs.	2,02,087	2,87,984	4,45,185	3,34,580	3,13,871	3,54,482	3,20,609	3,41,834	3,51,975	3,29,834	34	2
		p. c	100	142	221	165	155	175	158	169	174	163		
Bájra ...	72,337	Rs.	71,400	95,922	1,40,761	97,760	1,05,757	1,28,361	1,14,735	1,25,864	90,071	1,20,714	45	19
		p. c.	100	134	197	137	148	180	160	176	126	169		
Chína ...	70,560	Rs.	60,858	89,781	1,23,090	98,000	87,222	1,03,634	90,213	87,265	85,026	86,148	15	7
		p. c.	100	147	202	162	143	171	149	143	139	142		
Másh ...	13,358	Rs.	14,586	28,621	32,132	27,736	28,474	34,795	28 486	32,985	34,795	30,320	41	8
		p. c.	100	197	220	190	195	240	196	227	240	208		
Moth ...	1,162	Rs.	645	1,076	1,320	1,599	1,210	1,815	1,320	1,613	1,528	1,448	68	1
		p. c.	100	166	205	248	187	281	205	250	237	224		
Til ...	70,207	Rs.	1,27,096	1,78,800	2,19,520	2,21,965	2,19,788	2,50,552	2,58,024	2,89,483	2,74,781	2,76,768	82	25
		p. c.	100	140	173	174	173	197	203	228	216	218		
Gúr ...	31,755	Rs.	55,791	87,574	96,332	82,757	85,734	99,970	82,757	85,734	1,18,449	1,06,958	50	27
		p. c.	100	157	173	148	154	180	148	154	212	192		

Chapter, IV C.

Prices, Weights and Measures, and Communications.

Rise in the price of agricultural produce.

Value of various classes of produce at different periods.

Crop.	Assumed produce in maunds of average in 5 years before present Settlement.	Detail.	1853 to 1857.	1858 to 1862.	1863 to 1867.	1868 to 1872.	1873 to 1877.	1878 to 1882.	1883 to 1887.	1888 to 1892.	1893 to 1897.	1883 to 1895.	Rise per cent. Between 1853 to 1862 and 1883 to 1895.	Rise per cent. Between 1868 to 1877 and 1883 to 1895.
Indigo ...	8,535	Rs.	2,67,925	3,05,457	3,70,147	5,53,877	5,44,433	6,24,181	5,96,042	6,25,801	6,08,073	6,28,253	119	15
		p. c.	100	114	138	207	203	233	223	233	227	234		
Cotton ...	276,631	Rs.	8,22,786	11,18,599	11,47,712	11,32,059	10,18,139	10,60,726	10,38,903	11,82,841	11,63,273	11,15,434	15	4
		p. c.	100	136	139	138	124	129	126	144	141	135		
Wheat ...	2,651,970	Rs.	29,46,620	39,67,216	56,03,485	47,44,420	44,63,622	59,94,840	51,38,061	60,15,473	56,49,944	51,98,273	50	13
		p. c.	100	135	191	161	152	204	174	204	192	176		
Barley ...	79,261	Rs.	62,819	85,888	1,15,793	1,02,221	96,005	1,26,830	1,06,247	1,15,689	1,20,872	1,09,925	48	11
		p. c.	100	137	184	163	153	202	169	184	192	176		
Gram ...	289,324	Rs.	2,48,171	3,76,611	4,72,918	4,66,682	4,10,736	5,95,265	4,77,683	5,19,345	4,72,051	4,79,297	54	10
		p. c.	100	152	190	188	165	239	192	209	190	193		
Tobacco ...	9,469	Rs.	24,135	28,380	33,822	34,178	40,494	42,134	46,333	51,864	49,549	48,310	84	29
		p. c.	100	117	140	141	168	175	192	215	205	200		
Sarshaf ...	52,076	Rs.	69,972	97,299	1,15,650	1,07,670	1,07,686	1,03,430	1,29,468	1,30,596	1,30,470	1,30,160	56	22
		p. c.	100	139	165	154	154	148	185	187	186	186		
Masúr ...	27,695	Rs.	26,712	34,923	48,157	40,404	34,755	50,846	41,072	45,510	44,235	41,226	34	10
		p. c.	100	131	180	151	131	190	155	171	165	154		
Peas ...	280,052	Rs.	1,69,779	2,70,263	4,08,847	2,69,878	3,33,763	3,85,659	3,24,773	3,91,270	3,82,185	3,62,033	64	20
		p. c.	100	159	241	159	197	227	191	230	225	213		

Chapter IV. C.

Prices, Weights and Measures and Communications.

Rise in the prices of agricultural produce.

(b) Value, at different periods, of the assumed produce of average cropping in five years before present Settlement.

Tahsil.	Detail.	1853 to 1857.	1858 to 1862.	1863 to 1867.	1868 to 1872.	1873 to 1877.	1878 to 1882.	1883 to 1887.	1888 to 1892.	1893 to 1897.	1883 to 1895.	Rise per cent. Between 1853 to 1862 and 1883 to 1895.	Rise per cent. Between 1868 to 1877 and 1883 to 1895.
Multan ...	Rs.	15,95,488	21,55,420	27,16,900	24,14,676	23,48,985	29,77,002	26,21,382	29,59,046	27,99,909	27,21,071	45	14
	p. c.	100	135	170	152	148	187	164	185	175	171		
Shujabad	Rs.	11,14,979	16,20,503	21,81,835	16,75,090	17,14,746	22,14,608	18,84,961	22,31,530	19,92,695	17,95,986	31	6
	p. c.	100	146	106	151	154	200	169	200	179	161		
Lodhrán ...	Rs.	6,64,317	9,09,114	12,16,414	12,05,085	12,18,464	13,79,793	13,17,885	15,09,609	15,83,275	14,38,980	83	19
	p c.	100	137	181	181	183	208	198	227	238	216		
Mailsi ...	Rs.	7,42,043	8,27,102	12,60,068	13,21,635	11,71,627	14,15,768	12,85,748	14,68,793	14,39,670	13,67,561	74	10
	p. c.	100	111	169	170	158	191	173	198	194	184		
Kabírwála	Rs.	11,69,282	17,81,136	22,25,349	18,66,790	16,32,442	21,92,485	18,62,064	21,58,638	20,52,952	19,70,399	34	13
	p. c.	100	152	191	160	140	187	159	185	176	169		
TOTAL ...	Rs.	52,86,109	72,93,275	96,00,566	84,83,276	80,86,264	1,01,79,656	89,72,940	1,03,27,616	98,68,501	92,93,997	48	12
	p. c.	100	138	182	162	153	192	171	195	187	148		

Chapter IV, C.

Prices, Weights and Measures, and Communications.

Price of land.

The figures compiled at the recent Settlement to illustrate the sales of land give the following data regarding the price of land:—

Period.	Average price paid per acre.	Percentage of acres sold which was cultivated.	Incidence of the total price on the cultivated area, per acre.
	Rs.		Rs. a. p.
1878—83	22	47	45 2 7
1884—88	27	46	58 5 7
1889—93	33	45	74 8 8
1894—98	36	45	80 7 7
Total ...	31	46	68 6 11

In the calculations made in 1899-1900 of the value of leased lands for the purposes of assessing malikana, the following were the figures adopted as guiding rates in the tracts concerned:—

Tahsil.	Tract.	On cháhi land.	On cháhi-sailáb land	On chahi-nahri land.	On nahri land.	On sailáb land.	On báráni land.	On uncultivated land.
Kabírwála ...	Trans-Rávi (mostly Rawa)	30	30	...	..	27	27	5
	Cis-Rávi east of Tulamba (mostly Rawa). ...	31	31	...	...	28	28	6
	Cis-Ravi west of Tulamba (mostly Utar)	33	33	...	...	29	29	7
Shujabad ...	All leases	40	40	...	..	32	...	12
Multan ...	Utar	35	...	35	28	...	28	8
...	Rawa	32	...	32	25	..	25	7
Lodhrán ...	In canal limits	32	...	32	24	...	24	6
...	Outside canal limits ...	28	...	28	...	...	...	5
Mailsi ...	In canal limits	32	...	32	24	...	24	6
...	Outside canal limits ...	27	...	27	...	...	20	5

These prices relate to lands situated for the most part away from the more cultivated areas or along the fringe of the cultivated tract. The prices obtained in highly cultivated tracts are of course much higher.

Chapter IV, C.

Prices. Weights and Measures. and Communications.

Measures of time.

The following is the ordinary manner in which the time of day is described—watches and clocks being, of course, practically unknown outside the towns. The first approach of morning, the time when people have to get up to eat food during Ramzán, is known as the 'sahúr.' The very early dawn is 'tarka,' 'wadda wela' or 'namáz wela.' The dawn is 'subah,' 'savere' and 'paraphát' (parbhát). 'Pahur din charhe' is about 9 a.m., and noon is 'dopahara,' 'dopra' or 'roti wela.' At 2 p.m. they say, 'Dopahar dhalle' or 'pichhawan dhal gayá.' 'Peshí wela' is about 3 p.m., and the late afternoon is 'lahndá wela,' digar wela' or 'tarkála.' Evening is 'shám,' 'namáshan,' and (among Hindus) 'sandhia wela.' Nine p.m. is 'asha' or 'pahur rát,' and midnight is 'ádhí rát.' The twenty-four hours are divided into eight *pahars* or watches, of which four are from sunset to sunrise and four from sunrise to sunset, so that the length of a *pahar* varies at different times of the year.

The days of the week are :—

Aitwár (Sunday).	Buddh (Wednesday).
Sowár (Monday).	Jummarát or Khamís (Thursday).
Mangalwár (Tuesday).	Jumma (Friday).

Chhanchan (Saturday).

The months commonly referred to by the people are those of the Sambat or solar year of Vikramaditya : each of these begin about the middle of an English month :—

Month.	Corresponding English month.	Month.	Corresponding English month.
Chetr* ...	March-April.	Assun ...	September-October.
Visákh ...	April-May.	Kattak ...	October-November.
Jeth ...	May-June.	Mangghar ...	November-December.
Hár ...	June-July	Poh ...	December-January.
Sáwan ...	July-August.	Mángh ...	January-February.
Bhádron ...	August-September.	Phaggan ...	February-March.

For calculating the feasts and fasts of the Muhammadan year, the lunar calendar of the Muhammadans is followed.

The whole year is divided into two seasons, *viz.* the summer months (hunála) and the winter months (siála). The rains are not recognized as a separate season.

Measures of length.

The usual measures of length employed in measuring cloth, etc., are :—

3 ungals or finger breadths = 1 girah.
10 girahs = 1 hath or cubit.
2 haths = 1 gaz or yard.

* The Multan astronomers previous to the 11th century used to begin the year in Mangh. (Alberuni Sach. ii. 9).

Chapter IV, C.

Prices, Weights and Measures, and Communications.

Measures of length.

The 'hath' is of two kinds, the 'angrezi' and the 'pakka.' The former is understood to be the length from the elbow to the tip of the middle finger; the latter is the length of one 'angrezi' hath, *plus* the length of the middle finger repeated. There are consequently two yards: the English of 36 inches, and the pakka gaz of about 45 inches.

For measuring wood the table is :—

2 angals = 1 tasu.
2 tasus = 1 shárak.
4 sháraks = 1 pá.
2 pás = 1 hath.
2 haths = 1 gaz.

The gaz in this case being 3 feet 10 inches.

For linear measurement of land the basis is the karam of two paces. The indigenous karam is, generally speaking, about 57 or 58 inches; but one finds now in almost universal use the recognized Government karam of 66 inches. The koh or kos is an indefinite distance, amounting, as a rule, to something like a mile and a half.

Measures of area.

The main unit of area is the bigah, which is constituted as follows :—

9 sarsahis or square karams = 1 marla.
20 marlas = 1 kanál.
4 kánals = 1 bigah.

The bigah has for many years been presumed to be exactly half an acre, and the revenue records are kept in marlas, kanáls and acres. The indigenous bigah and the bigah referred to in old sanads is somewhat smaller than half an acre; but for all practical purposes the bigah now recognized by the zamindars is the half acre bigah prescribed by the Government. The people never use the terms biswa or ghumao

Measures of weight.

For small weighments made by goldsmiths, bankers, etc., the weights are:—

2 cháwals = 1 dána.
4 dánas = 1 ratti.
8 rattis = 1 másha.
12 máshás = 1 tola.

The standard tola is the weight of one rupee, but in local business the tola used is $\frac{12}{11}$ths of the standard tola.

For larger weighments the following are used :—

1¼ tola = 1 shai.
4 shais or sarsais = 1 chitak.
4 chitaks or sháraks = 1 pa.
4 pás = 1 ser.
4 sers = 1 dhari.
40 sers = 1 man or maund.

Chapter IV, C.

Prices, Weights and Measures, and Communications.

The 'man' usually employed is the standard maund of $82\frac{2}{7}$ pounds avoirdupois. In the tarafs round Multan city vegetables are sold by a maund of 54 sers and fruit by a maund of 54 sers.

Measures of capacity.

In dealings between grain-dealers among themselves and in all sales of grain for value, the grain is sold by weight according to the standard above given. In purely grain transactions, however, and in dividing the produce of land, various measures of capacity are generally used.

In the Multan tahsil grain transactions are now generally carried on by weight alone. In 1884, when the last edition of this Gazetteer was published, the following measures of capacity were said to be in force:—

4 thúlas	= 1 paropi.	20 páis	= 1 bora.
4 paropis	= 1 topa.	2 boras	= 1 kharwár.
4 topas	= 1 pái.	2 kharwárs	= 1 mání.

And the weight of a topa was tried in the following kinds of grain with the following result:—

	sr.	*ch.*		*sr.*	*ch.*
Barley	1	8½	Sarson	1	8½
Gram	1	14½	Til	1	6½
Bájra	1	14½	Maize	1	14
Jowár	1	14	Chína	1	10
Wheat	1	12	Rawán	1	14½
Ussún	1	14			

In portions of the Sidhnai tract in this tahsil which are occupied by immigrants from other areas, the following measures are found:—

4 thúlas = 1 paropi.
4 paropis = 1 topa (2 sers).
16 topás = 1 maund (32 sers).

In the Kabírwála tahsil the chief standards are, as was formerly the case in Multan, the paropi (4 thúlas), the topa (4 paropis), and the kharwár (160 topas) ; but the weight of a topa

Measures of capacity.

of wheat varies in different parts of the tahsil, so that the measures expressed in weight are as follows:—

	Weight in wheat of			
	Thúla.	Paropi.	Topa.	Kharwár.
	Chitaks.	Chitaks.	Sers.	Maunds.
To the east of Ghauspur (inclusive) south of the Rávi.	$2\frac{1}{2}$	10	$2\frac{1}{2}$	10
To the east of Kachlamba (inclusive) north of the Rávi; also in the parts of village Fakir Syal and Kot Kathia lying beyond the Chenáb.	$2\frac{1}{4}$	9	$2\frac{1}{4}$	9
In the rest of the tahsil	2	8	2	8

In the northern part of the Shujabad tahsil, lying to the north of the village of Jhangi, measures of weight alone are used as in the Multan tahsil. In the rest of Shujabad there are five different sets of measures of capacity employed in five different tracts. The various tracts may roughly be defined as follows :—

		Weight of 1 topa of wheat in sers.
Tract I.	River villages near Panjani	4
" II.	Villages round Mansurpur	$3\frac{1}{4}$
" III.	Villages west of Jalálpur, including the ... villages from Miri Malla to Nauraja Bhutta	5
" IV.	Villages round Bahadarpur	3
" V.	Villages round Thath Ghalluan ...	3

And the table of measures in each tract is as follows :—

Tract I.	Tract II.	Tract III.	Tract IV.	Tract V.
4 thúlas.*	4 thúlas.	4 thúlas.	4 thúlas.	4 thúlas.
4 paropis.	4 paropis.	4 paropis.	4 paropis.	4 paropis.
4 topas.	4 topas.	4 topas.	4 topas.	4 topas.
	4 páis			
4 páis.	12 choths.	4 pais.	4 páis.	4 páis.
4 choths.	1 máni.	4 choths.	2 choths.	3 choths.
4 boras.	(24 maunds 15 sers.)	2 boras.	$1\frac{1}{2}$ tokas.	4 boras.
1 path.	...	2 mánis.	4 boras.	1 máni.
(25 maunds 24 sers.)	...	1 path.	2 mánis.	(14 maunds 16 sers).
...		(32 maunds)	1 path.	...
			(28 maunds 12 sers.)	

* i.e., 4 thúlas = 1 paropi, 4 paropis = 1 topa, etc., etc.

Chapter IV, C.

Prices, Weights and Measures, and Communications.

Measures of capacity.

In tahsil Lodhrán the ordinary standard is the topa of 2½ sers, and the measures are as follows :—

4 thúlas = 1 paropi.	10 páis = 1 toka.
4 paropis = 1 topa.	5 tokas = 1 máni (12½ maunds).
4 topas = 1 pai.	

In the Hithár villages there is also a 'dhari' of 10 paropis, and in the centre of the tahsil 16 páis are spoken of as a 'bora.'

In the western part of the tahsil, including Lodhrán itself and all the villages west of the railway, the topa is of 3¼ sers, and the measures are :—

4 thúlas = 1 paropi.	8 páis = 1 toka.
4 paropis = 1 topa.	12½ páis = 1 bora.
2 topas = 1 dhari.	3 boras = 1 máni (16 maunds).
2 dharis = 1 pai.	

In Mailsi there are five separate sets of measures in five different tracts, *viz.* :—

		Weight of a topa of wheat in sers.
I.	Iláka Khai, *viz.*, the north-west part of the tahsil	4⅝
II.	The south-west part of the tahsil	2½
III.	The villages round Luddan	3⅛
IV.	The villages round Sahuka	3½
V.	The tract lying in the eastern part of the Hájiwah	3
VI.	The villages round Saldera	3¾

The detailed measures are :

Tract I.	Tract II.	Tract III.	Tract IV.	Tract V.	Tract VI.
4 thúlas.	4 thúlas.	4 thúlas.	4 thúlas.	4 thúlas.	4 thúlas.
4 paropis.	4 paropis.	4 paropis	4 paropis.	4 paropis.	4 paropis.
4 topas.	4 topas.	4 topas.	4 topas.	4 topas.	4 topas.
6¼ páis.	10 páis.	4 páis.	4 páis.	8 páis.	4 páis.
8 tokas*.	5 tokas.	12½ mans.	12½ mans.	6¼ boras.	12½ mans.
1 máni.	1 máni.	1 pakka máni.	1 pakka máni.	1 máni.	1 pakka máni.
(22 maunds.)	(12½ maunds.)	(12 man = 1 kachha máni.)	...	(15 maunds.)	...

* This is known as the pakka toka Khaiwála.

It will be seen, therefore, that there are fifteen different measures in the district for grain transactions. As, however, sales are made almost everywhere by weight, the confusion

Chapter IV. C.

Prices, Weights and Measures, and Communications.

caused is less than one might otherwise have expected. It would appear, too, that the practice of substituting weight for measure is gradually extending.

Communications.

The figures in the margin show the communications of the district as returned in Table No. I of the Administration Report of 1898-99. Table No. XLVI of this Gazetteer shows the distances from place to place as officially recognized for the purpose of calculating travelling allowance, and Table No. XIX shows the area taken up by Government for communications in the district.

	Miles.
Navigable rivers ...	344
Railways	130
Metalled roads ...	68
Unmetalled roads ...	1,220

The external communications are extremely good. Railways converge on Multan from the Sind-Ságar Doáb, from Karáchi, from Lahore and from Wazírabad. In addition to these, there are the rivers Chenáb and Sutlej, on which a certain number of boats ply, and the Southern Punjab line just beyond the southern boundary of the district is of some value along the Sutlej. The internal communications are also fairly good in the cold weather, though capable of improvement when the canals are running and the rivers are in flood. Roads are numerous; and the fact that they are not metalled is of little consequence in a tract like this when both rain and wheeled traffic are practically non-existent. All the traffic is on camels or donkeys or pack-bullocks, and the roads are good enough for these throughout the cold weather. The numerous canals and water-courses are, however, insufficiently bridged, and in places, such as the southern part of Shujabad, where the roads are exposed to inundation, further improvements are needed before the roads can be depended on throughout the summer.

The main roads are for the most part under the management of the District Board. Those within municipal limits are looked after by the municipalities concerned, and those in the cantonments are repaired by the Military Works Department under instructions received from the Cantonment Committee. The following roads are maintained by the Provincial Public Works Department, *viz.*, (i) the metalled road from Multan to Shah Shah; (ii) four miles of metalled road from the District Jail to the river; (iii) the metalled road from the Central Jail to the neighbourhood of the City Railway Station.

The old customs line.

The description of the communications of the district would not be complete without a reference to the old customs line, which was at one time a serious impediment to free communication in the district. The old preventive customs line, which ran through northern India from Leia to Khandwa, lay in this district a distance of some 10 miles from and

Chapter IV. C.

Prices Weights and Measures, and Communications.

The old customs line.

parallel to the Sutlej river. The road along which the prevention posts were situated is still known as the 'Permitwali Sarak'; it ran from Jalálpur to a point a few miles north of Lodhrán, and thence through Kahror, Mailsi, Karampur and Luddan. The whole line was furnished with a hedge (lohra) made of brushwood and sarkana, which was passable only at certain gates, distant a mile or so apart, each of which was guarded by a chaukídar. At every three miles or so there were 'chaukís' containing one sergeant and four constables for patrolling purposes; and at larger intervals there were bungalows for the inspecting officers. The Collector of Customs had his head-quarters at Kahror. Shortly before the Settlement of 1873—1880, the western part of the line was altered so as to run a good deal more to the north, within some eight or ten miles of Shujabad; the area covered by this latter road has since been disposed of, and is now largely under cultivation; the head-quarters of the department were at the same time transferred to Multan. On 1st April 1879 the preventive line was abolished, the establishment reduced, and the materials of the hedge sold by auction. It had originally affected a large amount of merchandize of various kinds, but in the latter years of its existence the traffic touched by it was that in salt, gur and sugar only. The import of salt from the south was entirely prohibited, while gur exported southwads was charged 6 annas per maund and sugar Re. 1 per maund.

River communications.

The Sutlej river is navigable for country craft throughout its length in this district and for steamers of light draught; the only steamers now to be seen on it, however, are small vessels owned by the Nawáb of Baháwalpur. The Chenáb is similarly navigable, but steamers are no longer to be seen on it since railway communication with Karáchi and Muzaffargarh became established. Small country boats are seen in the hot months on the Rávi, but there is little or no traffic on that river. The principal river traffic of the district, as stated in the Famine Report of 1879, is shown in Table No. XXV, but the extent and variety of the traffic has, owing to the extension of railways, fallen off a good deal since 1879. On the Chenáb a certain amount of grain, stores, etc., is brought down from the Jhang district to be enrailed at Multan, and there is also some small trade between the southern parts of Shujabad and points such as Sukkur on the lower Indus. On the Sutlej there is much less trade than on the Chenáb, and, generally speaking, the only commercial use now made of the rivers as means of communication is to bring goods from places on their banks which are far from the railway to other places on their banks which are near to the railway. The Rávi can be crossed by the dam at the Sidhnai head-works. Of the three railway bridges in the district (at Adamwáhan, Sher Sháh and Bátian) that at Sher Sháh alone is available for any traffic except that of the railway itself.

Chapter IV, C.

Prices, Weights and Measures, and Communications.

River communications.

The ferries of the district have since 1896 been managed by the District Board, who pay to the Government a fixed sum of Rs. 11,000 per annum in return for the income derived therefrom. The system is for the boats and the men to be provided by the local boatmen; these boatmen charge travellers at the rates fixed by Government, and of the proceeds half on the Rávi and Chenab and three-fifths on the Sutlej goes to Government, the rest being taken by the boatmen themselves. On the Chenáb the whole proceeds of each ferry go to one or other of the opposite districts: on the Sutlej, the Baháwalpur State and the Multan authorities each levy a toll on each ferry for all persons coming *into* their respective territories. The Government share is leased out annually by the District Board to contractors. The leases for 1900-01 fetched Rs 9,290, but in the days before the completion of the railway system the figures reached were much higher; previous to 1877 the income to Government from this source averaged Rs. 18,500, but since the completion of the bridges at Adamwahan and Sher Sháh the use of ferries for through traffic has much diminished. The ferries near Multan have especially fallen off, owing to the fact that they used to lie on the direct route of the Powinda traders from Dera Ismail Khan, who now use the railway instead. The following is a list of the ferries of the district.

List of Ferries.

1	2	3	4
River.	Stations.	Distance in miles.	Income for 1898-99.
			Rs.
CHENAB	Muhanwala	...	625
	Traggaranwala	8	550
	Alipur	4	575 (Alipur and Jatoi)
	Jatoi	5	
	Chuhepur Arewala ...	6	410
	Pipli Rájghat	6	1,300 (Pipli Rájghat and Hamandwala)
	Hamandwala	7	
	Bulewahan	7	*
	Dhaulanwala *alias* Somanwala	5	*
	Dhundhun	4	*
	Tibba	7	*
	Ganga	7	*
	Manakwali	1	*
	Shahpur	2	*
	Shahr Sultán	2	*
	Nahranwala	2	*
	Shihni	2	*

* These ferries belong to the Muzaffargarh district.

Chapter IV, C.

Prices, Weights and Measures, and Communications.

River communications.

List of Ferries—concld.

1	2	3	4
River.	Stations.	Distance in miles.	Income for 1898-99.
			Rs.
SUTLEJ	Sahuka	...	100
	Lakkha Saldera	4	262
	Mehru Baloch	6	95
	Fatteh Sháh	4	70
	Sharaf	4	130
	Kalia Sháh	7	125
	Nurpur	3	640
	Azimpur	5	640
	Murádpur	4	640
	Nekokara	4	310
	Fattehpur	7	323
	Khurrampur	6	230
	Durpur	4	
	Dera Lala	4	144
	Gulpur	4	
	Goth Sháh Muhamadwala	3	75
	Tibbi Lal Sohara	2	38
	Golanwala	5	35
	Mír Muhammadwala ...	3	48
	Mangwanewala	4	45
	Chanewala	3	32
	Moranwala	3	136
	Gudpur	3	126
	Laiwahan	2	83
	Bindra	3	681
	Sirahatta	2	
	Samasatta	5	73
	Nahranwala	3	111
	Bandwala	3	1,150
	Aliwahan	4	
	Aimananwali	3	
	Pailadpur	3	
	Kot Imám Din	2	
RAVI	Fazil Sháh	3	230
	Nur Mirali	4	
	Báti	3	
	Shakruwala	5	32
	Sarai Siddhu	3	250
	Ram Chauttra	5	65
	Sai Sahu *alias* Buchanwala	4	60
	Baghdád	5	150
	Ghauspur	2	165
	Tulamba	4	13
	Sanpalanwala	5	21
	Nusratwala	3	15
	Nakreri	6	15

Chapter IV. C.

Prices, Weights and Measures, and Communications.

River communications.

The fees leviable are as follows :—

	Rs.	a.	p.
On every four-wheeled carriage	2	0	0
On every two-wheeled carriage	1	0	0
On every ekka	0	4	0
On every hackery on springs...	0	2	0
On every cart and hackery not on springs drawn by eight bullocks, buffaloes, horses, ponies, asses or mules, if laden	1	8	0
Ditto ditto, ditto if not laden...	0	8	0
On every cart or hackery drawn by six bullocks, buffaloes, horses, ponies, asses or mules, if laden ...	0	12	0
Ditto ditto, if not laden ...	0	6	0
On every cart or hackery drawn by four bullocks, buffaloes, horses, asses or mules, if laden	0	8	0
Ditto ditto, if not laden	0	4	0
On every cart or hackery drawn by two bullocks, buffaloes, horses, ponies, asses or mules, if laden	0	4	0
Ditto ditto, if not laden ...	0	2	0
Buffaloes or bullocks, per head, if laden	0	1	0
Ditto ditto, if not laden	0	0	6
On every elephant	1	8	0
On every camel, if laden	0	4	0
Ditto, if not laden	0	2	0
On every horse, if laden or ridden	0	1	6
Ditto if unladen or led	0	0	9
On every tattoo or mule, if laden or ridden	0	0	9
Ditto ditto, if unladen or led	0	0	6
On every ass, if laden or ridden	0	0	6
Ditto, if unladen or led	0	0	3
On every sheep or goat or pig	0	0	1
On every palanquin, dooly, palki or tonjon, with 8 bearers	1	0	0
Ditto ditto, with 6 ditto...	0	12	0
Ditto ditto, with 4 ditto...	0	8	0
Ditto ditto, with 2 ditto..	0	4	0
On every foot passenger	0	0	3

N.B.—Animals drawing any vehicle, for which toll can be demanded. are not to be also charged with toll.

In addition to the income from tolls on ferries there is a small income (amounting in 1900-01 to Rs. 361) from the lease of the right to collect dues from boats using the Government landing stage at Bandarghát near Multán. The establishment maintained out of the ferry income consists of a jamadár on Rs. 10 per mensem and four peons at Rs. 5 per mensem each, whose duty it is to watch the goods laying at the Bandarghát wharf, and to see that the prescribed ferry dues on the Chenab are not exceeded.

Chapter IV, C.

Prices Weights and Measures, and Communications.

Railways.

The North-Western Railway runs through the district from the north-west to Multán, and then south towards Baháwalpur, passing the following stations :—

	Miles from Lahore.	Miles from last station.
Chhannu	150	...
Kachha Khúh	164	14
Khanewala	177	13
Rashida	187	10
Tatipur	195	8
Multán City	207	12
Multán Cantonment	208	1
Muzaffarabad	215	7
Sher Sháh	218	3
Buch	222	4
Chak	228	6
Shujabad	232	4
Gelewala	246	14
Miranpur	252	6
Lodhran	261	9
Adamwahan	267	6

Muzaffarbad, Chak and Miranpur are flag stations only and there are disused stations at Tulamba Road, Pirewala and Wahi Rája Rám. Gelewala is commonly spoken of as Chitwala, and the Multán City Station as Begi ká Bágh.

Besides this main line there are two branches which start in this district. One of these runs from Khanewala to Wazirabad through Lyallpur, and has the following stations in the district :—

	Distance from Khánewal.	Distance from last station.
Makhdúmpur Pahoran	9	...
Abdulhakím	19	10
Darkhana	29	10

The other runs from Sher Sháh to Lala Músa by way of Muzaffargarh, Bhakkar and Khushább, and passes out of this district a few miles after leaving the Sher Sháh junction.

The railroad from Lahore to Multán was opened in 1865, and was extended to Muzaffarabad in 1870, further communication southwards being carried on by steamer. A railway from Karáchi to Kotri was built in 1861, and this was extended to Multan in 1878, but goods and passengers had to be ferried across the river at Sukkur until the Sukkur bridge was opened in 1889. The Sind-Sagar line towards Muzaffargarh was opened in 1887, and the branch from Khanewal to Lyallpur in 1900.

Chapter IV, C.

Prices, Weights and Measures, and Communications.

Roads.

The chief roads of the district are the following:—

Main roads—From Lahore to Sher Sháh through Tulamba, Kabirwala and Multán.

„ Multán to Uchh through Shujabad and Jalálpur.

„ „ to Baháwalpur through Lodhran.

„ „ to Kahror through Dunyapur.

„ „ to Mailsi through Tibba, with a branch from Tibba to Karampur.

„ „ to Shorkot through Matital, Narul and Lalera (with an alternative route by the river through Mamdal).

„ Khanewala to Shorkot through Kabirwala and Sarai Siddhu.

„ Jalalpur to Pákpattan *viâ* Lodhran and Maílsi.

Cross roads—From Fazil Shah to Channu *viâ* Sarai Siddhu and Tulamba,

„ Channu to Luddan *viâ* Pakhi Mián.

„ Shujabad to Mailsi *viâ* Basti Maluk and Dunyapur.

For convenience of reference the roads have in the table below been classified in a somewhat different way, and further particulars are added regarding the distances, and the conveniences for travellers at each halting place:—

List of Roads in the Multán District.

Name of road.	Halting station.	Distance.	Has it an encamping ground?	Has it a bungalow?	Has it a sarai?
Multan to Jhang ...	Matital ...	10	Yes	No	No.
	Narul ...	14	Yes	Yes	Yes.
	Lalera ...	7	Yes	Yes	Yes.
Multan to Lahore ...	Kadirpur Ran ...	14	Yes	Yes	Yes.
	Kabirwala ...	14	Yes	Yes	Yes.
	Makhdumpur ...	11	Yes	Yes	Yes.
	Tulamba ...	12	Yes	Yes	Yes.
Fazil Shah to Shorkot ...	Sarai Siddhu ...	10	Yes	Yes	Yes.
	Kuranga ...	6	Yes	Yes	No.

Chapter IV. C.

Prices, Weights and Measures, and Communications.

Roads.

List of Roads in the Multan District—concld.

Name of road.	Halting station.	Distance.	Has it an encamping ground?	Has it a bungalow?	Has it a serai?
Multan to Kahror ...	Faridkot ...	16	Yes	Yes	Yes.
	Dunyapur ...	15	Yes	Yes	No.
	Kahror ...	16	Yes	Yes	No.
Multan to Sakhar ...	Adhi Bagh ...	10	Yes	Yes	No.
	Shujabad ...	9	Yes	Yes	No.
	Ganwen ...	13	Yes	Yes	Yes.
	Jalalpur Pirwala	13	Yes	Yes	Yes.
Multan to Bahawalpur ...	Lar ...	13	Yes	No	No.
	Basti Maluk ...	13	Yes	Yes	No.
	Aliwala ...	18	Yes	No	No.
	Lodhran ...	8	Yes	Yes	Yes.
	Adamwahan ...	6	Yes	Yes	No.
Jalalpur to Mailsi ...	Kureshiwala ...	13	Yes	Yes	No.
	Lodhran ...	13	Yes	Yes	Yes.
	Dhanot ...	8	No	No	No.
	Kahror ...	10	Yes	Yes	No.
	Miranpur ...	12	No	Yes	No.
	Mailsi ...	6	Yes	Yes	Yes.
Multan to Sher Shah ...	Sher Shah ...	14	Yes	No	No.
Sarai Siddhu to Khanewal	Jodhpur ...	8	No	Yes	No.
	Kabirwala ...	7	Yes	Yes	Yes.
	Khanewal ...	8	No	No	Yes.
Mailsi to Tibba ...	Lal Sag ...	13	No	Yes	No.
	Tibba ...	9	Yes	Yes	No.
Mailsi to Sahuka ...	Karmpur ...	13	Yes	Yes	Yes.
	Luddan ...	12	Yes	Yes	No.
	Sahuka ...	18	Yes	Yes	Yes.
Luddan to Pakhi Mian ...	Ratta Tibba ...	4	No	Yes	No.
	Pakhi Mian ...	12	Yes	Yes	Yes.
Karmpur to Tibba ...	Mitru ...	17	Yes	Yes	No.
	Tibba ...	11	Yes	Yes	No.

Bungalows and rest houses.

The following is a list of the public bungalows in the district. The Multán dâk bungalow is the only one in which any khansama is maintained. At the Lodhran, Mailsi and Kabirwala district bungalows the ordinary crockery and kitchen requirements are found, in the rest only the necessary furniture is provided. Generally speaking the canal bungalows are cleaner and better fitted up than the others.

Chapter IV, C.

Prices, Weights and Measures and Communications.

Bungalows and rest houses.

List of Canal, Police and Civil Bungalows in the Multán District.

1	2	3	4	5	6	7
No.	Tahsíl.	Town or village.	Class of rest house.	Size.	In whose charge.	Remarks.
1	Multán ...	Multán Cantonment ...	Staging bungalow ...	Large ...	Deputy Commissioner (District Board).	
2	Do. ...	Nawábpur ...	Canal bungalow ...	Do. ...	Executive Engineer, Chenab Canals.	
3	Do. ...	Rashída ...	Do. ...	Do. ...	Ditto ditto.	
4	Do. ...	Kadirpur Rán ...	Do. ...	Do. ...	Ditto ditto.	
5	Do. ...	J. Basti Maluk ...	Police rest house ...	Small ...	District Superintendent of Police.	
6	Do. ...	Ilampur ...	Canal bungalow ...	Large ...	Executive Engineer, Chenab Canals.	
7	Do. ...	Miani Rawa ...	Do. ...	Small ...	Ditto ditto.	
8	Do. ...	Billiwala ...	Do. ...	Large ...	Ditto ditto.	
9	Do. ...	Kasba ...	Do. ...	Do. ...	Ditto ditto.	
10	Do. ...	Lillipur ...	Do. ...	Do. ...	Ditto ditto.	
11	Do. ...	Mobarikpur ...	Do. ...	Do. ...	Ditto ditto.	
12	Do. ...	Taragarh (Adibágh) ...	Do. ...	Do. ...	Ditto ditto.	
13	Do. ...	Makhdum Rashid ...	Police rest house ...	Large ...	District Superintendent of Police.	
14	Do. ...	Mirzapur ...	Canal bungalow ...	Do. ...	Executive Engineer, Chenab Canals.	

Chapter IV. C.

Prices, Weights and Measures and Communications.

Bungalows and rest houses.

List of Canal, Police and Civil Bungalows in the Multán District—contd.

1	2	3	4	5	6	7
No.	Tahsil.	Town or village.	Class of rest house.	Size.	In whose charge.	REMARKS.
15	Shujabad ...	Shujabad ...	Canal bungalaw ...	Large ...	Executive Engineer, Chenab Canals.	
16	Do. ...	Satburji ...	Do. ...	Small ...	Ditto ditto.	
17	Do. ...	Ganwen ...	Police rest house ...	Do. ...	District Superintendent of Police.	
18	Do. ...	Jalálpur ...	Canal bungalow ...	Large ...	Executive Engineer, Sutlej Canals Division.	
19	Do. ...	Jugguwala ...	Do. ...	Do. ...	Ditto ditto.	
20	Kabírwala ...	Bágar ...	Do. ...	Do. ...	Executive Engineer, Chenab Canals.	Head works of Sidhnai Canal.
21	Do. ...	Serai Siddhu ...	District rest house ...	Do. ...	District Board.	
22	Do. ...	Tulamba ...	Do. ...	Do. ...	Ditto.	
23	Do. ...	Kuranga ...	Canal bungalow ...	Do. ...	Executive Engineer, Chenab Canals.	
24	Do. ...	J. Arjániwala ...	Do. ...	Do. ...	Ditto. ditto ...	Called Bati Bungalow.
25	Do. ...	Jodhpur ...	Do. ...	Do. ...	Ditto ditto.	
26	Do. ...	Jhandir ...	District rest house ...	Very small ...	District Board ...	Called Narúl Bungalow.
27	Do. ...	Amrana ...	Police rest house ...	Do. ...	District Superintendent of Police.	
28	Do. ...	Mohri Jhandir ...	District rest-house ...	Do. ...	District Board ...	Called Lalera Bungalow.
28a	Do. ...	Khutpur Sandha ...	Canal bungalow ...	Large ...	Executive Engineer, Chenab Canals.	
20	Do. ...	Binda Sargana ...	Do. ...	Do. ...	Executive Engineer, Chenab Canals.	

Chapter IV. C.

Prices, Weights and Measures, and Communications.

Bungalows and rest houses.

List of Canal, Police and Civil Bungalows in the Multán District—contd.

1	2	3	4	5	6	7
No.	Tahsil.	Town or village.	Class of rest house.	Size.	In whose charge.	REMARKS.
30	Kabirwala ...	Kukar Hatta ...	Canal bungalow ...	Large ...	Executive Engineer, Chenab Canals.	
31	Do. ...	Kabírwala ...	District rest house...	Do. ...	District Board.	
32	Do. ...	Makhdúmpur ...	Do. ...	Small ...	Ditto.	
33	Do. ...	Channu ...	Do. ...	Do. ...	Ditto.	
34	Lodhran ...	Lodhran ...	Canal bungalow ...	Large ...	Executive Engineer, Sutlej Canals Division.	
35	Do. ...	Do. ...	District rest house...	Do. ...	District Board.	
36	Do. ...	Koreshiwala ...	Police rest house ...	Small ...	District Superintendent of Police.	
37	Do. ...	Do. ...	Canal bungalow ...	Do. ...	Executive Engineer, Sutlej Canals Division.	
38	Do. ...	Dunyapur ...	Police rest house ...	Do. ...	District Superintendent of Police.	
39	Do. ...	Kahror ...	Canal bungalow ...	Large ...	Executive Engineer, Sutlej Canals Division.	
40	Do. ...	Chelawahan ...	Do. ...	Do. ...	Ditto ditto.	
41	Do. ...	Haveli Nasír Khan ...	Do. ...	Do. ...	Ditto ditto.	
42	Do. ...	Mianpur ...	Do. ...	Do. ...	Ditto ditto.	
43	Do. ...	Bukanpur ...	Do. ...	Do. ...	Ditto ditto.	Called Basantpur.
44	Do. ...	Adamwahan ...	Railway bungalow...	Do. ...	Executive Engineer, N.-W. Railway, Multán.	

Chapter IV, C.

Prices, Weights and Measures and Communications.

Bungalows and rest houses.

List of Canal, Police and Civil Bungalows in the Multán District—concld.

1	2	3	4	5	6	7
No.	Tahsil.	Town or village.	Class of rest house.	Size.	In whose charge.	REMARKS.
45	Mailsi ...	Miranpur ...	Canal bungalow ...	Large ...	Executive Engineer, Sutlej Canals Division.	
46	Do. ...	Mailsi ...	District rest house ..	Do. ...	District Board.	
47	Do. ...	Khanpur ...	Canal bungalow ...	Do. ...	Executive Engineer, Sutlej Canals Division.	
48	Do. ...	Karampur ...	Police rest house ...	Do. ...	District Superintendent of Police.	
48a	Do. ...	Do. ...	Canal bungalow ...	Do. ...	Executive Engineer, Sutlej Canals Division.	
49	Do. ...	Luddan ...	District rest house ...	Do. ...	District Board.	
50	Do. ...	Islam Deh ...	Canal bungalow ...	Do. ...	Executive Engineer, Sutlej Canals Division.	
51	Do. ...	Mitru ...	Do. ...	Do. ...	Ditto ditto.	
52	Do. ...	Tibba ...	District rest house...	Small ...	District Board.	
53	Do. ...	Sahuká ...	Do. ...	Do ...	Ditto.	
54	Do. ...	Pakhi Mian ...	Police rest house ...	Do. ...	District Superintendent of Police.	
55	Do. ...	Lál Saggú ...	Canal bungalow ...	Large ...	Executive Engineer, Sutlej Canals Division.	
56	Do. ...	Ghafúrwah ...	Do. ...	Small ...	Ditto ditto.	Called Ratta Tibba.
57	Do. ...	Allahabad ...	Do. ...	Do. ...	Ditto ditto.	

Chapter IV. C.

Prices, Weights and Measures, and Communications.

Telegraph and Telephone.

Multán is provided with a second class telegraphic communication to the rest of India, and is connected with Lahore, Sukkur, Quetta, Ráwalpindi and Dera Ghází Khan. The head office is a private building rented by Government and fairly situated in a central position near the Railway Station and Post Office. The building affords accommodation for the Telegraph Master in charge and a Deputy Telegraph Master, both of whom live on the premises. The office consists of one third-grade Telegraph Master in charge, one Military Deputy Telegraph Master and six Military Signallers. There is a sub-office at Multán city, which is worked by the Postal Department, and consists of two Native Signallers. The sub-office is in connection with the Multán Government Telegraph Office and with Lahore. There are also Telegraph Offices at Lodhran and Shujabad, as well as at the Railway Station.

There is a telephone system for the Municipal Police; the Exchange at the Kotwali is in communication with all the police stations in the city, and is worked by the police. There is also a telephone connection between the Central Jail and District Jail through the police lines, and the Exchange is also connected with the District Superintendent of Police's office and the Police Lines at the Kutchery building.

Post Office

The postal service in the Multán district is good. Outside Multan itself there are six sub-offices and thirty-eight branch offices. There are also five town sub-offices (three in the City; one in the Sadr Bazar, and another at the Kutchery). The letters for the city are delivered through the city sub-post office twice daily, except on Sundays and other post office holidays, when only one delivery is made.

The General Post Office is situated near the Cantonment Railway Station. Delivery of letters, etc., in cantonments is made four times daily through this post office, except on Sunday, when only one delivery is made. There are eleven letter boxes placed in different quarters of the city and eight in the cantonments. There is also a branch office at the Multan City Railway Station, and letters for Railway quarters are delivered through that office. The work done by the Post Office in the district in the eight years ending 1898-99 is shown in detail in Table XLVIII.

The sub-offices and branch offices in the district in 1900 were: Adamwahan, Bagren, Bahadurpur, Basti Maluk, Channu, Darúharwahan, Dunyapur, Fatehpur, Gogran, Jalálpur, Jallah, Jhokwains, Kabírwala, Kádirpur, Kahror, Karmpur, Khanbela. Khanewal, Khanpur. Khokhar, Lodhran, Luddan, Mailsi Makhdumpur, Makhdum Rashid, Matotli, Mitru, Multán Chawk Bazar, Multán City Railway Station, Nawabpur, Pakhi Mian, Qasba, Rashida, Sarai Siddhu, Sardarpur, Sher Shah, Tulamba, and Shujabad.

Chapter IV, C.

Prices, Weights and Measures, and Communications.

All have Money Order Offices, except Nawabpur, and all have Postal Saving Banks, except Bahadurpur, Bagren, Basti Maluk, Dharúharwhan, Dunyapur, Fatehpur, Gogran, Jallah, Jhokwains, Kadirpur, Karmpur, Khanbela, Khanpur, Makhdumpur, Makhdum Rashid, Matotli, Nawabpur, Pakhi Mian, Qasba, Rashida, Sadarpur, and Sher Shah.

CHAPTER V.

ADMINISTRATION AND FINANCE.

SECTION A.—GENERAL.

Chapter V, A.

General Administration.

Executive charges under native rule.

In the organization of the Moghal kingdom described in the Ain-i-Akbari, Multán was the headquarters of one of the subas or provinces. It then contained properly three sirkars or divisions, Multan itself, Dipálpur and Bhakkar, but the newly annexed kingdom of Thatta with five more sirkars was also counted as part of the Multan suba. The sirkar of Multán itself contained the whole of the present district and some little area outside it, and it was divided into five parganas, as follows*:—

(1).—Bast Jullundur Doab (between the Ravi, Sutlej and the Bias), with nine mahals, *viz.*, Adamwahan, Jalalabad, Dunyapur, Rajapur, Shergarh, Fatehpur, Kahror, Khai Buldi and Ghallu Ghara. This last was probably the lowest part of the Doab where the Ghallu tribes live near the Ghara or Sutlej river.

(2).—Bari Doab (between the Bias and the Ravi), with eleven mahals—Islampur (along the Chenab on the south-west of the Multán tahsíl, probably near Kasba), Ismailpur (site unknown), Balda (country near Multán to the north and east), Tulamba, a part of Chaukhandi (now in Montgomery), Haveli (the Chenab riverain, north of Multán), part of Khatpur (probably Khatpur Sanda, now an insignificant river village near Fazil Sháh), part of Deg Ravi (now in Montgomery), Shah Alampur (proably in the south-east of the Multán tahsíl), part of the Khai Buldi, and Metla (site unknown, but possibly Mianpur Metla on the Bias).

(3).—Rechnab Doab (between the Ravi and Chenab) with six mahals—Irajpur and Deg Ravi (in Montgomery), Chaukhandi (in Montgomery), Khatpur, Dalibhatti (site not known), and Kulamba (*i.e.*, the trans-Sidhnaí tract north of Tulamba).

* A short paper on this subject will be found in J. A. S. B. for 1901.

Chapter V.*A.

General Administration.

Executive charges under native rule.

(4).—Sind-Sagar Doab (between the Chenab and the Indus), with four mahals, none of which come in this district.

(5).—Birun-Panjcad (outside the five rivers)—it must be remembered the Indus probably joined the Chenab above Uch—with seventeen mahals, of which only one (Rappar) can be said with certainty to have been within the present limits of the district.

In later Moghal times the district was divided into the following parganas for revenue purposes :—

Kulamba.	Alampur.
Tulamba.	Ghazipur.
Haveli.	Bahadurpur.
Balda.	Kahror.
Islampur.	Khai.

Fatehpur.

In Shah Jahán's time the taluka of Sarai Siddhu was formed out of Tulamba and Haveli.*

In the Sikh times the following talukas or kardaris are mentioned, *viz.*, :—

Sidhnai ... Tulamba ... Sarai Siddhu ... Sardarpur ...	In tahsil Kabirwala.
Tarafs ... Sair Miani ... Shahpur ... Sikandarabad ... Kotli Nijabat ... Shujabad ... Dhundbun ... Jalálpur Panjani ... Kotli ... Ghazipur ... Bahadurpur ...	In tahsils Multán and Shujabad.
Sirdarwah ... Kahror ... Khai ... Mailsi ... Luddan ...	In tahsils Lodhran and Mailsi.

These were not necessarily each confined to one ring fence and villages belonging to one taluka were often scattered about

* In sanads of Muhammad Shah's time parganas Dunyapur and Ghallu Ghara are also mentioned.

Chapter V. A.

General Administration.

in other talukas. The number of kardaris and their boundaries were also constantly being changed.

Executive charges under native rule.

The list given by Edwardes of the kardaris existing at the time of annexation is (" Year on the Punjab Frontier," Volume II, 13) :—Luddan, Tibbi, Mailsí, Kahror, Nala Sadarwah, Bahadurpur, Kotli Adil, Panjani, Ghazipur, Multan, Khanpur, Khai, Shahpur, Sikandarabád, Shujabad, Sardarpur, Sidhnai and Tulamba.

Executive staff under native rule.

The ruler of the suba was known as subadar or suba ; but in the eighteenth century the title of názim appears to have been gradually substituted. Under the subadar in Moghal days was an enormous host of officials and semi-officials : mutsaddis or clerks of innumerable departments, ijáradars or revenue contractors, jagirdars or revenue assignees, kárdárs of the parganas, and so forth. For the repression of crime there were the barkandázes under their faujdárs, thánadárs, kotwáls and jamadárs. The civil work was mainly in the hands of the kázis and muftis ; and the practical work of securing the Government revenue was in the hands of innumerable village dabírs, patwaris, tappadárs, karoris or bakhshis, whose accounts were controlled by a large staff of kanungos, who, again, were accountable to kárdárs of the parganas.

Under Sawan Mal the number of subordinates seems to have been much diminished. There was still a pretty strong central office of clerks at Multan, but their work was very strictly supervised by Sawan Mal, who had himself risen from the lower grades of the administration. At the same time the vast number of scattered officials, such as the kanungos, etc., was much curtailed. For each kardari—equalling, perhaps, in average area, the ordinary modern thána—the staff allowed was one kardar and one munshi ; and the kardar was paid from Rs. 15 to Rs. 30 a month. At stated times he had to produce his accounts, and if there was complaint of exaction he was fined. For criminal offences the common punishment was fine (chatti) ; sometimes, however, mutilation was resorted to, and sometimes imprisonment ; but the last could always be commuted to a fine paid by the prisoner or his relations. For ordinary murders the punishment was not necessarily severe ; but for cattle theft the ordinary sentence was death by the sword. The extreme severity shown towards cattle thieves by the Diwan is often spoken of by the people, and contrasted with our present methods. One tale that is often told is that of Ali Dángra, one of the Diwan's assessors, who ventured to plead on behalf of a handsome young robber who was under trial, with the result that under the Diwan's express orders the robber was hung at Ali Dángrá's own door. Prisoners, both in Moghal and Sikh times, were confined in the various forts (kots or thuls), and had to beg their bread, as no food was provided by Government. The repression of crime, which under the Moghals is believed to

Chapter V, A.

General Administration.

have been entrusted to a more or less distinct staff, was under the Sikhs carried out by the members of the regular army. On the other hand the kazis, who, under the Moghals, were judicial officers, were now superseded by Government officials, known as adálatis, and their functions were strictly confined to the registration of documents and other formal duties.

Present executive staff.

Under British rule the district was originally under the administrative control of the Commissioner of Multán, whose headquarters were in the station itself, but in the reorganization of 1884 the Multan Commissionership was abolished, and the district was transferred to the control of the Commissioner of Lahore. In 1901, however, concurrently with the formation of the N. W Frontier Province, the Commissionership of Multan was reconstituted. The ordinary headquarters civil staff of the district now consists of a Commissioner, a Deputy Commissioner (who also is Magistrate of the District, Collector and Registrar), one Assistant Commissioner, and four Extra Assistant Commissioners, of whom one is the Revenue Assistant and another the Treasury Officer. The other Assistants perform criminal, revenue and miscellaneous executive work under the control of the Deputy Commissioner, and also whatever civil judicial work may be made over to them by the District Judge. There are, as noted in Chapter I, five sub-collectorates or tahsils, and each tahsil is in subordinate charge of a Tahsildar, who ordinarily exercises the criminal powers of a second class Magistrate, the civil powers of a Munsiff of the third grade, and on the revenue side the powers of a second grade Assistant Collector. Under him are two Naib-Tahsildars with or without civil powers, and with criminal powers of the third class only. The village record staff, working under a sadr kanungo with two assistants, was in 1900 of the strength shown below :—

Tahsil.	Office kanungos.	Field kanungos.	Patwaris.	Assistant patwaris.
Multan	1	4	73	4
Shujabad	1	3	65	4
Lodhrán	1	4	60	4
Mailsi	1	4	52	4
Kabírwála	1	4	70	4
Total ...	5	19	320	20

The revenue accounts are kept at the outside tahsils by a siáha-nawís and a wásilbáki-nawís, and at the headquarters tahsil by a wásilbáki-nawís ; and the accounts are checked a headquarters by a sadr wásilbáki-nawís and his assistant.

Judicial.

The chief judicial officer is the Divisional Judge, who sits at Multan, and is also Sessions Judge, exercising civil and

Chapter V. A.

General Administration.

Judicial.

criminal powers within the jurisdiction of the Multan Sessions Division, which includes the districts of Multan, Muzaffargarh, Dera Gházi Khán and Montgomery. The District Judge ordinarily does only civil judicial work, original and appellate, but is also employed to help in the criminal administration. There are two Munsifs for petty civil work, each of whom sits at Multan and exercises second class Munsif's powers, with jurisdiction over the whole district.

Cantonment Magistrate and Canal Magistrates.

The staff is supplemented by a Cantonment Magistrate in the cantonments, who exercises criminal powers of the first class within cantonment limits, and also some civil powers as well. The Executive Engineers of Canals, and Deputy Collector of Canals have also second class criminal powers to try cases relating to breaches of canal rules.

There is at the present time at Multan itself Sheikh Riaz Hussain, an Honorary Extra Assistant Commissioner, exercising first class civil and criminal powers. He also has powers of an Assistant Collector of the second grade on the revenue side. There is also a bench of Honorary Magistrates who have criminal powers of the second class within municipal limits. The bench consists of eight members,—four Muhammadans and four Hindus, and they sit daily in benches of two, one of whom is a Hindu, and the other a Muhammedan. The same bench sits ordinarily for one month, when it gives place to another until all the Honorary Magistrates have served. There are four other Honorary Magistrates *viz.*, Pír Ghulám Rasúl Shah, of Kuranga, Mahr Allayár, of Chauki Mohan, Khán Bahádur Rabnawáz Khán of Multán, and Díwán Sultán Ahmad of Jalálpur Pírwála.

The number and value of civil suits regarding moveable and immoveable property and the number of revenue cases in the last ten years are given in Table No. XXXIX, and details of criminal trials in Table No. XL.

Police.

The police force is controlled by the District Superintendent of Police, aided, as a rule, by one Assistant. The strength of the force on the 1st of January 1900 was as shown in the margin, the totals there given including 3 Inspectors, 22 Deputy Inspectors or Thanadars, 97 Sergeants and 674 Constables. In addition to this force there are 2 Daffadars

Class of Police.	Total strength.	Distribution.	
		Standing guards.	Protection and detection.
District	503	39	259
Municipal ...	252	...	252
Cantonments ...	41	...	41
Total ...	796	39	552

Chapter V, A.

General Administration.

and 6 town watchmen on Rs. 6 and 5 per mensem in Tulamba and Dunyapur.

Police.

The police force is distributed at thanas, out-posts, and road-posts. The thanas are as follows:—

First class thanas—

Multán City.	Kahror.
Multán Cantonment.	Mailsi.
Multán Sadr.	Mitru.
Alpa.	Luddan.
Shujabad.	Tulamba.
Jalálpur Pirwala.	Sarai Siddhu.
Lodhran.	Kabirwála.

Second class thanas—

Basti Maluk.	Pakhi Mian.
Makhdúm Rashíd.	Sábuka.

The jurisdiction area of each thana is confined to the tahsil in which its head station lies, except in the cases of Alpa and Basti Maluk, of which each lies in two tahsils.

There are out-posts at Kureshiwala, Aliwala, Souru, Makhdúmpur, Pír Mahal, Adamwahan, Nawábpur, Dunyapur; and road posts (for forwarding persons under custody) at Faridkot, Tibba, Kuranga, Kadirpur Rán, Lír, Gáwen Sher Sháh and Amrána.

There are cattle pounds at each thana, and also at Kureshiwala and Souru.

The police force is supplemented by the services of the village watchmen or chaukídars, 522 in number, of whom an account is given in Chapter III, Section D, above.

The district lies within the western police circle of the province, under the control of the Deputy Inspector-General of Police, Ráwalpindi.

There are no tribes proclaimed under the Criminal Tribes Act. The results of police enquiries during the last five years are shown in Table No. XLI.

Jails.

There are two jails in Multan, the District and the Central Jail. Statistics regarding them will be found in Statement No. XLII, below.

The District Jail at headquarters contains accommodation for 742 prisoners; the average daily population for the five years ending 1898-99 was 628 males and 9 females. The jail receives prisoners sentenced to terms not exceeding three years from the Multan district, and also from Muzaffargarh, and in the hot weather from Bhakkar, Leiah and Miánwali. It is under

Chapter V. A.

General Administration.

Jails.

the control of the Civil Surgeon, who acts as Superintendent, and under him is managed by a Jailor with Clerks and Warders. The annual cost of maintenance and guarding of prisoners in the five years ending 1898-99 was Rs. 34,654, and the average profits of convict labour Rs. 4,718, giving an average net cost per prisoner of Rs. 47. The chief industries followed by the prisoners in the jail are paper-making, lithographic printing, carpet-making, and manufacture of articles for use in the jail. There is also a jail garden maintained by convict labour, the produce of which is consumed by the prisoners.

The Central Jail was started as a temporary structure some twenty years ago on the completion of the Sirhind Canal, and the consequent dismantlement of the jail at Rupar. The buildings have since been put on a quasi-permanent footing: there is accommodation for 1,068 prisoners, and arrangements are being made for extending this so as to meet the wants of 1,500 prisoners. The jail is situated some four miles south-east of Multán on the Basti-Maluk road, and is in charge of a special Superintendent, who lives on the premises, and who has under him a staff of 1 Jailor, 1 Deputy Jailor, 2 Assistant Jailors, 2 Muharrirs and several Warders. The average daily population in the five years ending 1898-99 was 885. The average cost of maintenance in the four years ending 1899 was Rs. 55,842, and the average value of prison labour Rs. 5,314, giving an average net cost per prisoner of Rs. 57-1-0. The industries pursued are of much the same character as in the District Jail, and there is also a garden attached. The jail contains male prisoners from the district of Multan and its neighbourhood, whose sentence does not exceed four years, and also convalescents from all jails in the Punjab. It is provided with tent accommodation for prisoners in case of cholera; and an area of 27 acres of Government land, with a well, has been reserved in the neighbourhood for use as a site for a camp in case of an outbreak of this disease.

Registration.

The Deputy Commissioner is the Registrar of the District; the Tahsíldar of each of the outlying tahsils is Sub-Registrar for his tahsíl, and the Cantonment Magistrate is Sub-Registrar for the cantonments. The Tahsíldar of Multán is Joint Sub-Registrar; there being also a non-official Sub-Registrar at Multán for the registration of documents relating to the Multán tahsíl. The number of deeds registered at each registration centre during the last twenty years is shown in Table No. XXXII A, and details regarding the character and value of the transactions in Table No. XXXIII. It will be seen that the number of deeds registered was more than doubled in twenty years and their value more than trebled.

Chapter V. A.

General Administration.

Stamps.

The income from the sale of stamps in the district for the last 22 years is given in Table No. XXXIII. The number of stamp vendors in each tahsíl in 1900 was :—

	Court-fee stamps.			Non-judicial stamps.
Multán ...	4	...	...	17
Cantonment	1	...	...	3
Shujabad ...	1	...	...	7
Lodhran ...	2	...	...	4
Mailsi ...	1	...	...	3
Kabírwala	3	...	...	8
Total ...	12	...	...	42*

Income-tax.

The number of persons assessed to income-tax as having a net income derived from other sources than land, exceeding Rs. 500 per annum, was in 1898-99, 2,258, and the amount of tax assessed was Rs. 50,911. From the figures given in Table No. XXXIV, it will be seen that since the tax was first imposed in 1886-87 the income and the number of assessees has nearly doubled. Taking the figures for 1898-99 as a basis, the annual gross income subjected to the tax is about 25 lakhs of rupees, and the average income so assessed about Rs. 1,100. Nearly half the assessment is, as might be expected, from the Multán tahsíl. The number of incomes exceeding Rs. 1,000 which came under assessment in 1898-99, was 718, of which 255 were in the Multán tahsíl.

Statistics of land revenue.

Table No. XXIX gives figures for the principal items and the totals of all- land revenue collectious under the three recognized heads of fixed, fluctuating and miscellaneous. Table No. XXXI gives details of balances, remissions and agricultural advances for the last 30 years. Table No. XXX shows the amount of assigned land revenue. Further details regarding the assessment and working of the land revenue will be found in Section B of this Chapter.

Within the municipal limits of Multán and minor municipalities the management and expenditure of local funds is vested in the town or municipal committee ; and in the town of Dunya-

* These figures include 12 court-fee-stamp vendors.

Chapter V. A.

General Administration.

District Board.

pur, which is a 'notified area,' a committee of two members controls the local income. Detailed notices of these committees and their working will be found in Chapter VI, below. Outside the limits above described all local funds are vested in the District Board, a body of 46 members, under the *ex-officio* presidency of the Deputy Commissioner. The Board consists of 12 official members and 34 non-official, the latter being nominated from among the more prominent landholders in the district. The business of the Board is carried on in an office adjoining the district kutcherry, and meetings are supposed to be held once in three months. The Board exercises control over the construction and maintenance of roads; the establishment and management of hospitals, dispensaries, sarais, rest houses and schools; the planting and preservation of trees; the management of cattle pounds and public ferries; and other measures for the promotion of the health, comfort and convenience of the public. The annual income and expenditure of the Board in past years is shown in Statement No. XXXVI. The income is mainly derived from a cess of Rs. 10-6-8 per cent. on the land revenue of the district, and fluctuates with the land revenue. The expenditure in 1898-99 was distributed roughly as follows:—Education, 15 per cent.; Medical, 11 per cent.; Public Works 34 per cent.; Contributions from Local to Provincial for general services, 20 per cent.; other heads, 20 per cent.

Education.

Table No. XXXVII gives figures for the District Board, Municipal Board or Committee, and aided, high, middle and primary schools in the district. There are three high schools at Multan city and one at the cantonments. Of the former, one is managed by the Municipal Board of Multan, another by the Church Missionary Society, and the third is an unaided public school (Anglo-Sanskrit) managed by the members of the Arya Samáj. The high school in the cantonment is managed by the Cantonment Committee.

The Anglo-Vernacular middle schools are at Shujabad, Kahror and Multán. That at Shujabad is managed by the Municipal Committee there, and that at Multán by the Anjuman-i Islámia. Of the Vernacular middle schools, one is at Kahror and another at Sarai Siddhu, both under the management of the District Board. There are two more at Tulamba and Jalálpur Pírwála, both managed by their respective Municipal Committees. There is a European and Eurasian school near the railway station at Multán cantonment maintained by private subscription and by grant-in-aid-from Government.

There are 62 primary schools, including 5 zamindari schools where special concessions are made for the purpose of

Chapter V, A.

General Administration.

Education.

extending education to the agricultural classes. These primary schools were in 1900 located at the following places :—

List of Schools in the Multán District.

No.	Names of schools.
	PRIMARY SCHOOLS.
	Multan Tahsil.
1	Thatta-Paulian.
2	Makhdúm Rashíd.
3	Luthar.
4	Kadirpur Rawan.
5	Jhok Wains.
6	Bosan.
7	Lábar.
8	Nawábpur.
9	Sura Miani.
10	Arjwan Sharif.
11	Sher Sháh.
12	Muzaffarabad.
13	Sultánpur.
14	Kasba.
15	Kotla Sadát.
16	Traggar.
17	Budhla Sant.
	Shujabad Tahsil.
18	Sikandrábad.
19	Shahpur.
20	Chak.
21	Soman.
22	Wains.
23	Bagren.
24	Matotli.
25	Jalálpur Kháki.
26	Bet Kech.
27	Jahánpur.
28	Ghazipur.
29	Khan Bela.
30	Theh Kalan.
31	Khoja.
32	Bahadurpur.

List of Schools in the Multan District—concld.

No.	Names of schools.
	PRIMARY SCHOOLS—*concld.*
	Lodhrán Tahsil.
33	Gogran.
34	Lodhrán.
35	Dánwaran.
36	Amírpur.
37	Dunyapur.
38	Kahror (Municipal Board School).
39	Salsaddar.
40	Jhámbewáhan.
41	Chauki Rangu Khan.
	Mailsi Tahsil.
42	Nurabba.
43	Drúbarwáhan.
44	Fatehpur.
45	Jallah.
46	Karampur.
47	Khanpur.
48	Mailsi.
	Kabírwála Tahsil.
49	Jiwandsinghwala.
50	Kabírwála.
51	Makhdúmpur.
52	Nawáb Bhuti.
53	Mansa Manglani.
54	Jodhpur.
55	Sham Kot.
56	Khánewál.
57	Sardárpur.
58	Mamdál.
59	Salárwáhan.
60	Sháh Dhanyál.
61	Thul Najib.
62	Mubarakpur.
63	Narhál.

There is one girls' school at Multán with a total number of about 141 pupils. This is maintained by a grant-in-aid from Government and from municipal funds. This is the only public institution for females in this district.

Chapter V, A.

General Administration.

Education.

In addition to the schools above mentioned, there is a normal school for training of schoolmasters and a model school attached to it. Both these are supported from provincial revenues.

Besides the Government schools there are a large number of private or indigenous schools in the district. The number of these schools in the end of 1899, in which the number of scholars did not fall below 6, was 157, and the facts regarding these schools are tabulated as follows :—

Class of Schools.		Number of Institutions.	Number of pupils.				Pupils learning.	
			Hindus.	Sikhs.	Muhammadans.	Total.	A Classical language.	A Vernacular language.
1. Teaching Arabic books with translation ...		6	...	...	71	71	71	...
2. Do. Persian		8	6	...	93	99	87	12
3. Do. Sanskrit books with translation ...		9	89	...	...	89	89	...
4. Do. Urdu	For Boys	18	56	...	336	392	10	382
5. Do. Gurmukhi	For Boys	9	142	5	...	147	...	147
6. Do. Hindi	For Boys	8	192	...	...	192	...	192
7. Do. Lande, Mahajani, etc.	For Boys	7	676	...	...	676	11	665
8. Do. the Koran by rote ...	For Boys	76	4	...	927	931	910	21
	For Girls	11	...	...	109	109	107	2
9. Do. Sanskrit books by rote	For Boys	5	57	...	...	57	57	...
Total ...	...	157	1,222	5	1,536	2,763	1,342	1,421

Chapter V. A.

General Administration.

Education.

The district lies in the Derajat educational circle, and the Inspector of that circle has his head-quarters at Multan. Table No. XIII gives statistics of education collected at the census, and the general state of indigenous education has been described in Chapter III above.

Medical.

At Multán itself there is a civil hospital, a female hospital, called the Victoria Jubilee Hospital, a female branch dispensary in the city, and a male branch dispensary. In the district there are eight dispensaries, *viz.*, at Shujabad, Jalalpur, Lodhran, Kahror, Mailsi, Kabirwála, Serai Sidhu and Tulamba. One formerly at Luddan was closed in 1899.

The civil hospital, which dates from 1854, is situated outside the city wall in the suburbs of the town of Multán at no great distance from the Bohar Gate, and consists of a central block, which contains the dispensing and operating room, two blocks for surgical and medical cases, and five small rooms built for the use of patients who have their families with them. There is another block, which is partly used as a store-room and partly for the reception of infection cases. Attached to the hospital is an Assistant Surgeon, who lives in a house close to the hospital itself, and belonging to the hospital. The staff includes also 3 compounders, 2 ward coolies and 6 menials. The accommodation is for 52 in-patients. The hospital has recently been practically rebuilt, the old wards being replaced by new and loftier rooms.

Adjoining the civil hospital, but separated from it, is the Victoria Jubilee Hospital erected in 1887. It contains two wards capable of accommodating 24 patients, and 4 separate rooms for better class people, including European and Eurasian females. A female Assistant Surgeon is in charge, who is assisted by 1 compounder, 1 dresser and 5 menials.

At the Kup, in the centre of the City, is situated the branch male and female hospitals, but under one roof, and both for out-door patients only. The male branch is under the charge of a Hospital Assistant, assisted by 3 compounders and 2 menials. In charge of the female branch there is a female Hospital Assistant, assisted by 1 compounder and 2 menials. There is also a Mission Hospital for females in the cantonments.

All the dispensaries in the district receive in-patients, with the exception of that at Tulamba, which treats out-door patients only. All are in charge of Hospital Assistants, assisted by 1 compounder and 2 menials.

Chapter V, A.

General Administration.

Vaccination.

The following table gives the number of vaccinations for the last five years :—

Year.	Vaccinations.	Re-vaccinations.	Total.
1895	19,679	6,833	26,512
1896	24,769	1,828	26,597
1897	20,811	637	21,448
1898	21,127	7,331	28,458
1899	25,126	11,540	36,666

Buffalo lymph is chiefly used, vaseline paste being employed when procurable. The vaccination establishment, excluding 1 vaccinator employed exclusively in the city, consists of 2 native Supervisors, 1 first class Vaccinator, 4 second class Vaccinators, 7 third class Vaccinators, and a vaccination Muharrir and Clerk. The expenditure is met by the District Board. The Vaccinators are supposed to do the vaccinating, while the native Supervisors check their work. The method employed is for the Vaccinators in a body to divide the villages in a zail among them, and when these are finished to move into an adjoining one When the work in one tahsil is finished another tahsil is taken in hand.

Ecclesiastical.

There is a large Anglican Church in cantonments, where parade services are held, and also a small Anglican Church in the civil lines. The Mission Church of the Church Missionary Society is outside the Husain Gahi, between the fort and the city. There is also a soldiers prayer-room in cantonments, where parade services for non-conformist troops are held under the guidance of the clergyman of the American Methodist Episcopalian Mission. Roman Catholic parade services are held in the Roman Catholic Chapel in cantonments, to which a Chaplain is attached. In 1899 a convent of nuns was opened, by whom a school is conducted.

Troops and Cantonments.

Multán Cantonment lies 613 miles from Karachi and 202 miles from Lahore. It is in the Lahore district of the Punjab Command, and is commanded by a Colonel on the staff. The normal garrison in 1900 consisted of 1 Field Battery, 1 Heavy Battery, 1 Battalion of British Infantry, 1 Regiment of Native Cavalry, and 1 Battalion of Native Infantry.* Of the above the Heavy Battery and one company of British Infantry were located in the defensible fort; and the Native Infantry furnished a guard for the old

* A second battalion of Native Infantry has since been added.

Chapter V, A.

General Administration.

Troops and Cantonments.

fort, which is still in charge of the Military. The staff consists of a Station Staff Officer of the first class, an Executive Commissariat Officer, Senior Medical Officer, Chaplain and Cantonment Magistrate.

The Volunteers at Multán are part of "B" Company of the N.-W. Railway Volunteer Rifles; other parts of the company being at Khanpur, Montgomery, Rojhanwali and Samasatta. The company musters some 100 strong, and is composed entirely of enrolled Railway employés. Its parade ground is opposite the Railway Institute outside the Cantonment Station, and the rifle range is situated about a mile south-west of the same station.

Head-quarters of the Departments.

The head offices of the N.-W. Railway are at Lahore, but Multán is the head-quarters of an Executive Engineer, a District Traffic Superintendent and a Loco. Superintendent. The Telegraphs are under the Telegraph Superintendent at Lahore, and the Post Offices under the Superintendent of Post Offices, Multán. The public buildings in the district are in charge of an Assistant Engineer, who is under the control of the Executive Engineer, Dera Ghází Khan. The canals of the district are divided into two charges: one known as the Multán Canals Division, is held by the Executive Engineer, aided by three Assistants, who are stationed at Sidhnai head-works, at Rashida and at Multán, respectively; the other, known as the Lower Sutlej Canals Division, is held by an Executive Engineer, aided by an Assistant stationed at Kahror. The head-quarters of both charges are at Multán, which is also the head-quarters of the Deraját Canal Circle. The Inspector of Schools for the Educational Deraját Circle also has his head-quarters in this station; and so has Assistant Conservator of Forests for the Multán Forest Division.

Excise.

The Excise administration concerns itself with (1) imported European spirits and fermented liquor; (2) fermented liquors manufactured at licensed breweries in India; 3) spirits passed from distilleries in India worked according to the European method; (4) country spirits or spirits manufactured after the native method; (5) opium; (6) hemp drugs. These are sold wholesale or retail. On the wholesale vend of spirits or liquors a low fixed fee is charged. The fees for retail sale are generally fixed by competition; shops are allowed to be opened wherever they appear to be wanted and no objection exists, and the lease of right to sell spirits, liquor or drugs at each shop, as the case may be, for the term of one year, is sold by auction. Sometimes tenders for leases of certain shops or groups of shops are accepted, and the auction system is dispensed with. The numbers of retail shops for sale of country spirits, European liquors, opium and other drugs that have been maintained in this district during

Chapter V, A.

General Administration.

Excise.

the last ten years are shown in Table No. XXXV. The opium and drug licenses have always been granted together; a shop licensed to sell the one is licensed to sell the other. Of the European liquor shops a small proportion are licensed to sell rum only. In addition to the license fees for their sale, rum and country liquor are also charged with still head duty, the former paying Rs. 4 an imperial gallon of proof liquor, and various special rates on a sliding scale for liquor under proof. The rum is principally manufactured at the Rosa distillery of the Shahjahánpur district of the North-West Provinces.

The country spirits are manufactured in the central distillery at Multán, and the total amount so manufactured in 1899-1900 was 11,939 gallons, of which 2,544 gallons were in hand at the end of the year, 5,590 gallons went to shops in Multán city and cantonments, 105 gallons to villages of the Multán tahsil, 430 to villages in Shujabad, 171 to villages in Lodhran, 183 to villages in Mailsi and 186 to villages in Kabírwala, and the rest to the Dera Gházi Khan and Muzaffargarh districts. This country liquor was formerly manufactured by a number of separate wholesale dealers working under Government supervision in an old building outside the Delhi gate; but in 1898 a new distillery was built outside the Daulat gate, and a new system introduced, under which the sole right of distillation in Multán was granted to the firm of Messrs. Edulji Dinshast and Company for two years from 1st April 1899; the object of the grant of this license being the introduction of improved appliances for the distillation of 'country spirit.' The licensees were required, among other things, to keep a reserve stock of plain uncoloured can-spirit of not less than 300 gallons and 75 gallons at Dera Gházi Khan and Rajanpur tahsil head-quarters respectively. The Multán district being mainly populated by Muhammadans, and containing few or no Sikh inhabitants, is a very small contributor to the Excise revenue.

There are four kinds of opium at present consumed in the Multán district: (1) Ghazipur opium, supplied from Bengal to the Government of the Punjab at a cost of Rs. 8-8-0 per ser, *plus* cost of carriage to the Punjab, and sold here at Rs. 15 a ser from the Government Treasury; (2) Malwa opium, of which a limited quantity is bought annually at Ajmere for about Rs. 6 or Rs. 7 a ser, and at present pays Rs. 3 per ser duty on importation into the Punjab; (3) hill opium imported free of duty from Kashmir and the Hill States round Simla; (4) Punjab-grown opium, which pays an average duty varying from Rs. 2 to Rs. 4 an acre in different districts. The cultivation of the poppy, which used to be carried on to a certain extent, has in this district been absolutely prohibited since 23rd February

Chapter V, B.

Land and Land Revenue.

1897. The kind of opium most in favour among opium consumers is the Ghazipur opium, but, as noted in Chapter IV above, the consumption is small.

Excise.

The hemp drug concoction known as *charas* is imported from Yarkand under regulations enforced by a system of passes. *Charas* is imported across the north-western portion of the Punjab, chiefly by the Kulu route. A smaller quantity is brought down through Kashmir and Rawalpindi. *Bhang* is an infusion prepared by soaking the dried hemp-leaf for a time in water, and the kind of hemp used for this purpose is mainly imported, though a certain amount is also locally cultivated in small patches for their own use by fakírs and others.

SECTION B.—LAND AND LAND REVENUE.

Assessments under native rule.

The systems of land revenue assessment prevalent under the various native Governments previous to annexation were of much the same general types. The theory throughout was that the Government were entitled to a share of the gross produce. This share was known as the *mahsúl*, and it might be taken in kind or in cash. The methods usually employed may be classified under four heads—(i) *jinsí*, (ii) *nakdí jinsí*, (iii) *zabti*, and (iv) *karárí*.

Produce.

(i). *Jinsí.*—The standard method and that most ordinarily employed was the assessment of a share in the actual crop (*jinsí*, *batái*, *bhaoli*). The share was taken after deduction of ordinary menials' dues and of crops actually used for fodder. What the rates actually taken were it is difficult to say, as these varied immensely, not only with the soil and position of the land, but also with influence and power of resistance enjoyed by the land-owners. Sir Charles Roe's opinion was that 'putting aside fear or favouritism, it may be said generally that one-third was the rate for sailáb lands; one-fourth for good well lands, and one-sixth and one-seventh for inferior wells.' If, however, the rates of previous assessments recorded in the village records of the second Settlement are to be trusted, the rates would seem, as a whole, to have been somewhat lower on sailáb lands, while on canal aided wells the kharíf or nahri rate would be usually one-fourth, the rabi being one-fifth. The grain was not allowed to leave the threshing-floor until it had been inspected by a Government official, and it was then conveyed at the

Chapter V, B.

Land and Land Revenue.

expense of the landholder to the nearest State grauary. Remains of these old granaries can still be seen at Lodhran, Kotla Chákar and other places.

Valuation of produce.

(ii) *Nakdi jinsí.*—A *nakdi jinsí* or cash-kind assessment indicated the first step towards a cash revenue, and the form of assessment became more common under Díwan Sawan Mal than formerly. The *mahsúl* was still at a certain rate and was set aside at the division of the produce. But instead of its being carried off by a Government official, the landholder was made to purchase it at a rate fixed by Governmnt which generally was something above the actual market price of the neighbourhood.

Fluctuating cash rates.

(iv) *Zabti*—The next stage towards a cash assessment was indicated by the assessment of cash rates per acre cultivated. These rates (known as zabtí rates) were applied mainly to the better class of crops, such as indigo, sugarcane, etc., which it was difficult to divide; but they were also employed freely for all crops in tracts like the Ravi riverain, which were too far away from head-quarters to make the removal of the grain profitable to the Government. Where these rates were applied to cultivation generally, it was usual to exempt all crops used for fodder.

Fixed lease.

(iv) *Karárí* —The three classes of assessment above mentioned were most commonly employed on sailáb land and on lands receiving canal water only. They all represented more or less directly the original theory that the Government, as over-lord of the land, was entitled to a share in the produce, and the lands paying them were often spoken of as 'sirkárí' In contradistinction to these lands were the areas, in which the landholder had himself, by constructing a well or otherwise, provided the means of cultivation, and in such areas (known as ikrárí or karári areas) it was very common for the Government to grant a fixed assessment at a lump sum of money.* Such assessments were known as karárí or ikrárí (or sometimes as patái, the assessment being fixed by a deed known as a patta). The amount ordinarily assessed for a well was Rs. 12, and was spoken of as the 'sath hunála panj siála,' because Rs. 7 was taken in the kharíf and Rs. 5 in the rabi. Assessments higher than Rs. 12 were, however,

* A survival of the old distinction between ikrárí and sirkárí lands is to be found in mauza Ferozpur, tahsíl Multán, where the payments made by the chakdars to the actual revenue payers or malguzars (a Multani Pathán family) differ in the two classes of land.

Chapter V, B.

Land and Land Revenue.

Fixed leases.

not uncommon. No period was assigned for the rate, and it was presumed to last as long as the ruler who fixed it remained in possession; but it was of course possible for the ruler to vary the actual demand by his control over the cesses. The demand, too, appears to have been remitted when the wells went out of use. The karárí jama, however, covered not whatever land might be irrigated from the well but only the land mentioned in the patta, generally 15 to 20 acres per well. All extra cultivation was separately assessed at jinsi or zabti rates, and the better classes of crops, such as sugar, rice and indigo, were separately assessed, whether they were grown in excess of the fixed area or not. These cash lump assessments per well in the Utar and Rawa tracts received a considerable impetus from Díwán Sawan Mal, who settled with hundreds of landholders in new lands in this way.

Another special method of assessment sometimes employed for wells in the heart of the Rawa, more especially on the borders of the present Multán and Lodhran tahsils, was to take a certain sum (generally Rs. 2 or Rs. 3) per yoke of cattle in use on the well. The assessment was thus lightened in bad seasons when the well went partially out of use.

Confusion and instability of the system adopted.

The above gives a much more orderly idea of the systems pursued than was actually the case in practice. The zabti rates, for instance, differed enormously from village to village. In village *A* tobacco paid Rs. 3 and cotton Rs. 2-8-0 per acre; in *B* tobacco and cotton both paid Rs. 2-8-0; in *C* tobacco paid Rs. 10 and cotton Rs. 4; in *D* cotton paid Rs. 4 and tobacco Rs. 2; and so forth. Nor were the various systems applied uniformly throughout a tract or a village. Even in single holdings two or three different systems might be in force. At the end of this gazetteer are appended specimens of deeds granted to landholders at various periods of native rule, from which can be gathered, far better than from any general description, the character of the assessments levied. And in regard to these assessments, a point to be remembered is that none of them was established with any degree of permanency, each being liable to be changed at any time for another at the request of the revenue payer or at the caprice of the ruler. Special exemptions by way of mafi or light assessments held good only for the life of the grantee and only for the life of grantor: and they were doubtless only renewed for a consideration. Nothing is more remarkable about the written sanads of native rulers than the persistence with which powerful native Governors seem to have disregarded them, and the insistence with which each new grant especially declares that the local authorities were not to

Chapter V, B.

Land and Land Revenue.

call constantly for its renewal : 'dar har fasl sanad mujaddad talab na dárand.'

Extra cesses.

The charges above noticed constituted the revenue demand proper. They may be termed the ordinary charges ; but besides downright exaction there were many other items which were levied as a matter of course. The landholder had to pay *malba*, and the continuance of his karári lease depended on his fully keeping up the cultivation of his jinsi lands. In some places Rs. 8 per maund were charged as *moghala* or royalty on all indigo sold ; in some tracts sums were levied as *shukrána* or thank offerings ; in others *nazrána* was demanded : this might take the form of an additional Rs. 2 or Rs. 3 on the cash jama, or it might be realized in the form of a horse or a lump sum of money. Sometimes, too, Rs. 2 or Rs. 4 per well were levied as *chári* or pasturage dues, and sometimes the crops used for fodder, such as gram, methra and china, were charged at special rates. The grants given in Moghal times almost always contained a clause specially exempting the grantee from these cesses, and the scribes of those days delighted in letting their pens run on through the enumeration of these 'takálif' (as they were suitably called): the mubligh-i-báládasti, faujdári, lawázima, tappadárí, mohassilí, chára filán, peshkash, fasláua, moharrirí, kánúngoí, chaudhri, sabíl muchalka, farmaish káh wa paikár wa hema wa hashrí, thánadarí, mihmání, talabána wa juramána wa ámilána, wa jaríbána, wa zábitána, wa dároghána, kharch dabír, tahrir diwáni, wakáia nawísi, tafrík chanda, begár wa shikár, etc., etc. After annexation Mr. Edgeworth found the following cesses in force in the Multán tahsil : nazarcháhi, malba (the same as our talabána), dabíra, mohassilí, farohí, juft nargáo, ábiána, hissábána, kadam kash, dharat, goat tirni, orderly, guzrána and bhatti níl. All these cesses were not, of course, exacted from every holding, but their bewildering number and detail indicates clearly the immense effect which they must have had in altering the character of the nominal revenue demand.

First move towards fixed cash assessments.

When the Punjab came under the political control of the British Government in 1844, the assessments of the Multán tract were left untouched, but elsewhere efforts were made to introduce by degrees the principle of a fixed cash assessment. When Sirdár Kahn Singh was sent on the ill-fated mission of 1848 to take over charge from Díwán Múlráj, he was ordered by the Lahore Darbar to make tentative experiments in this direction. The instructions given to him, which are interesting in other ways also, are reproduced below :—

Orders of the Lahore Darbar to Sirdar Kahn Singh Man, March 31, 1848.

1st, regarding the Land Revenue—You will receive the revenue arising from the rubbee harvest of 1905 according to the regulations in force under Díwán Múlráj's Government, whether it be by a fixed rate ("mushakhsa") or by "chaslie," or by "kunkoot," and in accordance with the existing practice, through

Chapter V, B.

Land and Land Revenue.

his old kardars. If you think proper, appoint three or four clever men, and, after taking security from them, employ them to look into the collection of the land revenue and enquire whether it be too high or too low, and to prevent embezzlement, so that no loss may accrue to the Government.

First move towards fixed cash assessments.

Of the khureef harvest. With a view to the future settlement, first obtain from the Díwán all papers connected with the last ten years' jumma from the rubbee of 1895 to the khureef of 1904, and assume one-tenth of the total as the jumma for one year. Should there be any suspicion as to the accuracy of these papers after instituting a careful inquiry fix a suitable assessment, assemble all the zamindars, and after devising the speediest method of collecting the revenue from them and from the malgoozars carry it into practice.

Draw up books for each village, for it will often be found that the zamindars are content with the old methods, and are averse to a fixed assessment ("mushakhsa"). With a view to fixing a proper and equitable jumma take security from the Kutrees of the village, and make the contract assessment with them. In making the settlement of any district, should any inconvenience arise, or should it appear that the old system of collecting the revenue be more for the advantage of the State and the good of the people; after mutual consultation continue to act according to the old system. When you have made the settlement, arrange for the appointment of tahsildars and treasurers after consultation and for their salaries. (Page 174 of Parliamentary Blue Book No. 41, 1849, Punjab).

Summary Settlements.

Immediately after annexation orders were issued for the introduction of fixed cash assessments throughout the district. These orders were carried out by Lieutenant James for the Shujabad, Lodhran and Mailsi tahsíls, and by Mr. Edgeworth, the Commissioner, for the greater part of Multán and Sarai Sidhu. This Settlement is commonly known as the Chársálá, having been based on the estimated value of the average collections of the four years previous to annexation. From the estimates so made the cesses and extra charges were deducted, and some further reductions were also made in some groups of villages in consideration of their general cicrumstances. The cultivation of the period cannot be ascertained, but on that of the Regular Settlement the rate of the assessment imposed would be Rs. 1-5-0 per acre.

The First Summary Settlement was sanctioned in 1850 for a period of three years, but though carefully constructed on the data available it broke down before its term was concluded. The people felt severely the change from kind assessment to cash, more especially as the price rates assessed for the cash assessments were far higher than those actually prevailing during the Settlement; and they also felt very severely the sudden fixity of the demand in the canal and sailáb areas. The assessment was found to be especially severe in the Shujabad tahsíl, remissions and reductions had to be granted, and a new Settlement was ordered. The Second Summary Settlement was carried out by Major Hamilton, Deputy Commissioner, for the Shujabad and Lodhran tahsíls in 1853, and by his successor, Mr. H. B. Henderson, in 1854 for the other tahsíls. This Settlement was carried out with some elaboration. Though no field maps were made, the cultivation was measured, assessment circles framed, soils classed, produce estimates made, and the value of the

Chapter V, B.

Land and Land Revenue.

Summary Settlements.

Government share at certain prescribed fractions of the gross produce worked out. Reductions were granted in the tahsíls Shujabad and Lodhran, where the former assessment had fallen hardest; but enhancements were taken elsewhere, and the total assessment fell only a little short of the previous demand. The fluctuating system, which at the First Settlement had only been tentatively retained in parts of the Mailsi tahsíl, was now extended in the form of a dialluvion assessment to all the areas directly affected by the river.

The total assessment thus imposed was not a heavy one, but, like its predecessor, this Settlement failed to give satisfaction. On the canal lands a fixed revenue continued to be taken in spite of the great variations in cultivation, and on the river areas the proposed varying system fell through, owing partly to the dislike of the zamindars to annual measurements, and partly to an unfortunate arrangement by which all new cultivation was assessed, not at any general or circle rate, but at the average rate at which the Settlement assessment happened to fall on the cultivation of the village at Settlement.

First Regular Settlement.

It was to remedy these defects that the Regular Settlement was undertaken in 1857—1860 by Mr. Morris, afterwards Sir John Morris and Chief Commissioner of the Central Provinces. The fields were measured and soils classified, but many of the elaborations of the previous Settlement were discarded and no produce estimates were framed. Average rates per acre for each class of soil and average rates per well for each well area were fixed on general considerations fortified by common sense and a fairly intimate knowledge of the district. The system of annual assessments for sailáb lands was given up, and on canals the old fixed system was maintained; but in order to admit of a fixed revenue being taken from such varying conditions of cultivation Mr. Morris had to assess very low, and the result was a reduction of some 16 per cent. on the previous assessment.* Even with this low revenue, however, he recognized that special arrangements must be made to meet bad years; and in each village a certain portion of the revenue (averaging some 54 per cent. of the whole) was ear-marked as 'remissible' in case of any great and *general* failure of sailáb or canal irrigation. The scheme met with the fate that attends most schemes devised at Settlement which cannot afterwards be carried out automatically, in that it was never brought into action; and though there were some years in which the scheme of remission might have reasonably been utilized, yet, owing to the extreme lightness of the demand, no serious hardship was caused by this oversight.

* The exceedingly low assessment in the Regular Settlement was also largely due to the Settlement having been made in the year of the mutiny, during which the zamindars of this district had, as a whole, shown themselves extremely loyal.

Chapter V, B.

Land and Land Revenue.

Second Regular Settlement.

Mr. Morris's assessment was sanctioned for ten years only; but no revision of his Settlement was ordered till 1873, when Mr. Roe (afterwards Sir Charles Roe and Chief Judge of the Punjab Chief Court) commenced the Second Regular Settlement, which has just expired. Mr. Roe adopted the same assessment circles and the same classes of soil as were used in the First Regular Settlement. In pursuance, moreover, of the orders then in force, he prepared a half net assets estimate, and proposed soil rates, more or less based upon this estimate, but checked by the various other estimates then prescribed. For canal lands a special check was devised in the shape of 'crop rates' by which the village assessments could be differentiated according to the quality of the crops grown. The produce outturns assumed for the half net assets estimate were distinctly full ones, but the prices assumed were very low, and the estimate, as a whole, was a lenient one; but this estimate, although not treated very seriously, sufficed to show that a very substantial increase in the revenue was called for, and a very substantial increase was taken, amounting, in the district as a whole, to no less than 41 per cent. This increase was necessitated to some extent by an extension of cultivation amounting to 16 per cent., but it was mainly caused by the need for making up the deficiencies of the previous assessment. The large increase was distributed over the villages with care and discretion, and the resulting assessment met with general approval in the district.

The question of fluctuating assessments had in this Revised Settlement to be once more faced; and a great step forward was made (chiefly on the initiative of the Financial Commissioner, Mr. Egerton) by introducing in the areas subject to the direct action of the rivers a system of absolute fluctuation. For canal lands a system of differential fluctuating crop rates was for a long time mooted in connection with the question of the abolition of chher labour, but it was ultimately held that our arrangements for crop measurements, as then organized, were not sufficiently trustworthy to justify the adoption of a fluctuating system against the wishes of the zamindars; and a scheme put forward by Mr. Lyall, Settlement Commissioner, for the remission of revenue on failed areas was ultimately adopted. This scheme took up the 'remissible' system of Mr. Morris and extended it from villages to holdings, so that for each holding irrigated by a canal at Settlement the revenue was divided into 'canal' or 'remissible' and 'non-remissible'. If in such a holding canal irrigation ceased or ran short, the owner could on application receive under certain rules a fitting amount of remission, limited, however, to the extent of the 'remissible' revenue imposed on his holding at Settlement. If, on the other hand, canal irrigation were extended to holdings not irrigated at Settlement, it would pay a light canal advantage rate (known as *beshi nahri*) of 8 annas per acre.

Chapter V, B.

Land and Land Revenue.

Second Regular Settlement.

The land revenue demand of the Second Regular Settlement (excluding malikana and date revenue) compares as follows with the previous assessments :—*

		Rs.
First Summary Settlement ..	... =	5,94,151
Second Summary Settlement	... =	5,87,835
First Regular Settlement ...	... =	4,85,835
Second or Revised Settlement	... =	6,85,016

The new demands were introduced in the riverain circles of Kabírwála from rabi 1877, and in the rest of that tahsil from kharíf of the same year. In the rest of the riverain circles and in the tarafs of Multan the new assessments came into force from rabi 1879, and in the remainder of the district from kharíf 1879.

Third Regular Settlement.

The 'canal-remissible' system then introduced however, not being automatic, was entirely neglected and failed to relieve in any way the general fixity of the demand. Out of a total remissible revenue of Rs. 2,74,609, the average annual remissions prior to 1897 affected some Rs. 2,000 only, and out of some 90,000 holdings entitled to claim remission some 58 holdings only obtained on an average any kind of remission in the year. In 1885 the Financial Commissioner, Colonel Wace, toured through the district, and strongly urged the early extension of a purely fluctuating system to the tracts under fixed revenue. In 1886 the Sidhnai canal was opened, and the assessment on the areas irrigated by it was made entirely fluctuating In 1888 fluctuating water rate charges were introduced on the Hajíwah canal. In 1890 the assessment of the chher or statute labour demand was altered so as to fluctuate in accordance with the area irrigated in each year. And in 1893 the old system of leasing to middlemen the bár-báráni cropping in the Mailsi bar was abolished and a fluctuating cash assessment substituted for it. When, therefore, the Third Regular Settlement was commenced in October 1896 things were ripe for a considerable extension of the fluctuating system.

The general plan of the assessment now in force (there are local exceptions which need not be detailed here) is briefly as follows. On every well is imposed a lump assessment, which is classed as fixed revenue, and which is paid irrespective of the area from time to time irrigated by the well : if, however, the well falls out of use for any cause this lump assessment is remitted. All kinds of cultivation other than that irrigated by well water alone—that is to say, all cultivation dependent on river, canal or rain water—pays at fluctuating rates assessed per acre matured

* The figures given are those now made up from the village totals. Owing to changes in boundaries and other reasons, they differ somewhat from those entered in Mr. Roe's Settlement Report, which are respectively Rs. 5,80,601, Rs. 5,78,163, Rs. 4,82,928 and Rs. 6,72,527. The figures above given are taken from those quoted in the Assessment Reports of the Third Settlement after adding figures for the eight villages received from Jhang in 1898.

Third Regular Settlement.

in each harvest. For the inundation canals and for rain cultivation these rates are uniform for all crops: in the sailáb areas and on the Sidhnai canal they are differentiated according to the class of crop grown. The well assessments being remitted when the wells are out of use and all other assessments being purely fluctuating, there is no longer any fear of revenue being exacted from lands which have no produce to pay it with.

Further details regarding the character of the new assessments are given in the Assessment and Settlement Reports prepared by the Settlement Officer. The general aspect of the various assessments made in the district since annexation is shown briefly in the following table:—

	Estimated increase in cultivation per cent.	Land revenue assessed.*	Increase or decrease in land revenue per cent.	Probable incidence of land revenue per cultivated acre.	Percentage of estimated half net assets taken.	Percentage of estimated total produce taken.	Percentage of land revenue which is fluctuating.
		Rs.		Rs. a. p.			
First Summary Settlement, 1849	...	5,94,151	...	1 5 0	...	...	...
Second Summary Settlement, 1854	...	5,87,835	−1	1 4 11	...	...	...
First Regular Settlement, 1858	...	4,85,835	−18	1 1 9	...	...	...
Second Regular Settlement, 1880	16	6,85,016	+41	1 5 0	86	12	13
Average of 5 years preceding Third Settlment.	33	10,31,636	+51	1 7 1†	...	...	46
Third Regular Settlement 1901	33‡	13,39,844	+30§	1 10 6†	92	15	76

* Excluding dates and malikana.
† On matured area.
‡ Since Second Regular Settlement.
§ Since preceding 5 years.

Chapter V, B.

Land and Land Revenue.

Third Regular Settlement.

The new assessments came into force in the Kabírwála tahsil in kharíf 1899, and in the rest of the district in kharíf 1900; and the Settlement will probably be sanctioned for a period of twenty years. The land revenue is payable in two instalments as follows:—

Kharif	...	15th December and 15th January.
Rabi	...	15th June and 15th July.

Assigned Land Revenue.

The formal assignment of land revenue was a practice little resorted to by Sáwan Mal, and a large number of the old jágírs of Moghal times were resumed by that ruler, so that when the district came under British rule there were not as many cases of assignments to be considered as in most districts of the Province, and a fair proportion of the existing assignments especially those to Multani Pathán families, are the creations of British rule. The present assigned land revenue of the district is shown in the following table:—

	Land revenue assigned.			Date revenue assigned.
	Fixed.	Estimated fluctuating.	Total.	
Grants in perpetuity ...	5,131	644	5,775	66
Life grants	6,951	1,574	8,525	464
Grants for maintenance of institutions ...	3,832	5,962	9,794	463
Total ...	15,914	8,180	24,094	994

Out of the above a sum of Rs. 9,826 is received by assignees in the form of fixed deductions from the land revenue; and, as noted in Chapter III above, a further sum of Rs. 3,158 is spent annually in the shape of zamindari ináms to deserving landholders.

Cesses.

The land revenue proper (including also the date revenue) in subject to an extra charge in the form of cesses. These at the First Regular Settlement amounted to Rs. 10-2-0 per cent. of the revenue, and at the Second Settlement to Rs. 13 per cent. This again was raised a few years later to Rs. 20-14-8, and at the present Settlement the figure has been put at Rs. 21-10-8, of which the following are the details:—

	Rs.	a.	p.
Local rate	10	6	8
Lambardari	5	0	0
Patwari	6	0	0

Chapter V. B.

Land and Land Revenue.

Date revenue.

The date-trees in the district have always in theory been the property of the Government, but for practical purposes they are assessed as though they were the property of the zamindars in whose lands they grow. When they grow in Government land (as along the Sidhnai reach) the assessment on the trees is paid by the neighbouring zamindars, who in such cases are entitled to the fruit, but not to the trunks, etc., of the palms. The assessment on the dates is imposed, like other fixed land revenue, by a lump sum on the village, and this is distributed over the holdings by means generally of a uniform rate per female tree. The assessments made at the Second and Third Settlements are shown in the following table:—

	At Second Settlement.	At Third Settlement.
Number of trees*	2,35,522	3,15,055
Assessment	Rs. 14,366	Rs. 24,521
Average rate per tree	1 anna.	1 anna 3 pies.

As a general rule (with some few exceptions) the date revenue on máfi lands is also assigned.

Leased lands.

Lands leased on long terms from Government are known in this district as 'ta'ahhud-khwáhi' lands, and are of two classes, *viz*, (*i*) those granted under the ordinary rules, and (*ii*) those given in connection with the Sidhnai colonization scheme.

(*i*) Darkhwasts.

Grants of the ordinary type (usually spoken of as *darkhwásts*) were originally granted for the most part under orders issued by the Board of Administration in 1850; after some misunderstanding and correspondence, it was decided in 1875 that the lessees holding under those orders should receive proprietary rights.

New rules were issued in 1868, by which persons receiving leases of waste land were entitled at the termination of the lease to the pre-emption of the proprietary right at a fair and reasonable price. Lessees who were holding under these rules at the Second Settlement (1877—1888) were granted proprietary right on payment of Re. 1 per acre. Government, however, continued to give leases under the rules of 1868 until new rules appeared in 1885.

* Excluding villages in which no assessment was made,—that is to say, villages in which the assessment would have come to less than Rs. 5, and villages in which the assessment, though more than this, would have been very small in comparison with the extent of the village.

Chapter V, B.

Land and Land Revenue.

(i) Darkhwásts.

The rules of 1885 originally allowed lessees to purchase, at any time, on payment of five times the maximum amount of annual revenue and málikána assessed on them, and several leases were given under these conditions. But shortly after the issue of these rules it was determined to cancel in future leases the condition regarding purchase, and thus to leave the lessees at the mercy of Government in this matter.

Excluding, therefore, the cases in which lessees were entitled to purchase under the unaltered rules of 1885, the leases found in existence at the recent Settlement were practically all of a class in which the Government was under no obligation to sell, and it was decided by Government in 1900 that no offer of sale should be made to any of the lessees.

At the same time an alteration was made in the manner of assessing such leases. They had previously been assessed to a somewhat severe fixed land revenue, with or without a small additional charge as málikána ; but the assessment was not very even, and the systems followed at various times varied. It was now decided that, with regard to the land revenue part of the assessment, the leases should be treated in all respects on a level with proprietary lands, and that apart from the land revenue assessment each lease should be assessed to a malikána which should represent, as nearly as might be, 4 per cent. of the selling value of the land.

The areas of the lands thus held on lease at the time of the recent Settlement were :—

Tahsils.	Total area.	Cultivated area.	Málikána imposed.
			Rs.
Kabírwála	10,867	1,015	2,721
Multan	3,342	1,263	925
Shujabad	284	106	159
Lodhrán	3,349	173	760
Mailsi	8,026	3,135	1,345
Total	25,868	6,592	5,910

(ii) Sidhnai canal leases.

The Sidhnai canal which was opened in 1886, irrigated a large extent of Government waste, which was given out to

Chapter V, B.

Land and Land Revenue.

(iii) Sidhnai canal leases.

settlers on lease in plots averaging about 90 acres each. Under the original form of lease the lessee was entitled to purchase his land at the rate of Rs. 3 per acre if he had fulfilled certain conditions, the most important of which was that he should by the end of five years have brought under cultivation two-thirds of his land, after deducting 20 per cent. from the total as representing roughly the unculturable portion of the lease. The lease was at the same time liable to resumption if these terms were not fulfilled. In 1896 it was found that an enormous number of lessees had failed to fulfil these conditions, and it was decided that they should be then called upon to cultivate one-third of their lands within one year, one-half within two years and the full two-thirds within three years, on pain of confiscation. To those who failed to reach the prescribed limit within the first and second years, further grace was freely given up to the termination of the third year: and when at the conclusion of the third year it was found that a large number of leases remained in which the lessees had still failed to cultivate the required amount, it was decided to treat them on the following system:—

(*i*) All lessees who had cultivated as much as three-fourths of the required amount were held to be entitled to purchase at Rs. 3 per acre.

(*ii*) All lessees who had cultivated one-half of the required amount, but less than two-thirds, were held to be entitled to receive occupancy rights from Government.

(*iii*) The lessees of certain small plots adjoining proprietary lands were allowed to purchase at Rs. 12 per acre, although they had not cultivated three-fourths of the required amount.

The above relates mainly to the leases originally given out between 1886 and 1896. In the latter year it was decided that in fresh leases of Sidhnai land no promise of proprietary right should be given, but that lessees should be entitled, on fulfilment of the terms, to occupancy rights only. When, therefore, the Rawan rájbaha was extended in 1898-99 to the Government waste lying north-east of Multán city, the new leases were all given on these terms, and all lands in the formerly colonized area, which owing to confiscation or otherwise became available for re-grant, were also given out on these later conditions.

The málikána or rent payable under the original leases was a fixed sum determined at the rate of Rs. 10 per holding of

Chapter V. B.

Land and Land Revenue.

(ii) Sidhnai canal leases.

90 acres. In 1900, however, a system of fluctuating *málikána* was introduced at the following rates :

(*a*) For lessees on the Rawan extension—

	Per matured area. Re. a. p.
For the first 2 years	*Nil.*
" " next 3 "	0 6 0
" " " 5 "	0 12 0
After 10 years	1 8 0

(the enhanced rate after the fifth and tenth year to take effect only after the sanction of the Financial Commissioner).

(*b*) For lessees on the old Sidhnai area :—

	Re. a. p.
If the lessee holds on a tenure allowing eventual purchase ...	0 12 0
If the lessee holds on a tenure not allowing of eventual purchase...	As in (*a*) above, but the full rate of Re. 1-8-0 not to be taken till Kharíf 1904.

Bárbáráni.

The only part of the district in which there is much cultivation dependent on rain alone is the Mailsi bár, where in years of good rainfall there is a good deal of rain cultivation (*kásht báráni*) in the hollows or *dhoras* in the Government waste. The collection of revenue from these scattered and distant plots had always been a difficult matter, and it was customary, up to 1893, to give out to the bigger neighbouring landowners the contract for the collection of this revenue : the contractors paid in a fixed sum per annum to Government, and were in return entitled to realize a share of the produce from the actual cultivators. By 1893 the village record agency had been sufficiently organized to enable annual measurements and direct assessments by Government to be made, and it was decided to abolish the contract system. A survey was made of the lands ordinarily cultivated under the bár-báráni arrangements, and the cultivators who had held their lands for a reasonable period were made tenants of Government, some with an occupancy status and some without. The cultivation was measured annually and assessed at certain determined rates per matured acre. At the third settlement it was decided to assess such lands at the fluctuating rates prescribed for the circle *plus* a málikána of 4 annas per matured acre.

Harvest cultivation.

Government land is also given out on leases for cultivation for a single harvest. This cultivation is known as khám kásht or kásht khám tahsíl, and the rates at present prescribed for such cultivation are the same as for proprietary lands except that *cháhi* crops pay Re. 1 per acre. A málikána of 4 annas per matured acre is also taken and 2 annas are charged for each acre applied for but not cultivated.

Chapter V, B.

Land and Land Revenue.

Harvest cultivation.

The average matured area held on such leases in the five years preceding the Third Settlement was 2,816 acres, yielding a revenue of Rs. 4,177 ; but the grant of these harvest leases is now much restricted, and the income derived from them is likely to decrease considerably.

Tirni.

We have no detailed information regarding the taxation of cattle under native rule ; but it appears that under the Nawábs camels and goats were liable to the tax. Sáwan Mal added female buffaloes and cows, but allowed liberal exemptions. Theoretically the tax was levied on all animals grazing in the Government waste, but (as noted in Chapter III above) all waste was then looked upon as in a sense the property of Government, so that the tax virtually amounted to a capitation tax on all cattle of the descriptions noted which were possessed by the people.

At annexation the old system was continued, except that collection of the tax was given out to lambardars or other contractors in return for fixed payments. In 1853 Mr. Edgeworth, the Commissioner, drew up rules on the subject, and certain further rules, proposed by Colonel Hamilton, were sanctioned in 1860. Between 1860 and 1870 the tirni-guzars (*i.e.*, practically the village headmen) supplied lists of assessable cattle of their villages; rates were fixed for each class of animal, and an assessment based on the result, but not necessarily following it exactly, was fixed by the Deputy Commissioner ; the village paid this assessment, and the cattle of the village were then free to graze in any Government waste in the district. The lambardars supplied fresh lists every year, and the villages were nominally liable to alterations of assessment, but as a matter of fact the old assessment usually ran on. In 1870 an attempt was made to introduce a system of farming out the pasturage by 'chaks,' but the system was so manipulated as to leave the old arrangements practically unchanged. The rates, however, were somewhat altered, and the assessments were gradually enhanced.

In 1882 certain changes were introduced at the instance of the Settlement Officer, Mr. Roe, the chief of which was that the assessments were fixed for terms of five years, subject to certain special adjustments to meet the case of transfers from one village to another. The assessment, moreover, though based on certain uniform rates applied to the cattle enumerated, was differentiated more than formerly in dealing with the various villages, regard being had, *inter alia*, to the condition of the village and its position as regards the Government waste. This system remained in force until 1901, and four different assessments were made under it, the last being sanctioned for a two years' term only.

Chapter V, B.

Land and Land Revenue.

Tirni.

The sums fixed at each of these assessments were as follows :—

Years.	Tirni assessed.		Total.
	Cattle.	Camels.	
	Rs.	Rs.	Rs.
1882	63,221	21,956	85,177
1887	54,694	23,225	77,919
1892	46,557	22,674	69,231
1899	51,321	21,230	72,551

The system started in 1882, though an improvement on the previous arrangements, was still open to the objection that in practice it imposed a considerable burden on a large number of villages which very seldom used the Government waste, and thus remained to some extent a capitation tax on animals rather than a charge for the use of the Government pasturage. Accordingly arrangements were arrived at in 1900 by which, so far as regards cattle, a distinction was made between villages adjoining the Government waste and villages at a distance from it. The former, which could with certainty be said to make free use of the Government waste, were assessed as before to fixed contract sums for five years, in return for which they were entitled to free use of the waste. The latter were not assessed to tirni at all, but could only use the Government pasture on payment of fees at prescribed rates to farmers appointed by Government. As regards camels, the old system of quinquennial assessments was left undisturbed. The rates described for the collection of fees by farmers were :—

	Rs.	a.	p.
For each buffalo, male or female, over one year old	0	14	0
" " cow or ox, over one year old	0	6	0
" " sheep or goat, over six months old	0	1	0

and farmers were appointed for each of the six 'chaks' into which the district was divided, *viz.*, (*i*) Trans-Rávi, (*ii*) Cis-Rávi Kabírwála, (*iii*) Multan, (*iv*) Lodhrán, (*v*) Mailsi West, (*vi*), Mailsi East. For camels, male or female, the standard rate prescribed for the contract assessments was Re. 1-4-0. The result of the arrangements arrived at in 1901 was :—

Tahsils.	*Fixed contract assessments.*		Farms of cattle fees.	Total.
	On camels.	On cattle.		
Kabírwála	4,070	2,433	1,200	7,703
Multan	4,025	2,177	545	6,747
Shujabad	3,105	2,389	...	5,494
Lodhran	2,121	5,300	300	5,085
Mailsi	5,249	...	1,000	11,549
Total ...	18,570	...	3,045	36,578

SECTION C.—THE CANALS.

Chapter V, C.

The Canals.

The Government canals of the district are of three kinds, *viz* :—

(*i*) The old Inundation canals.
(*ii*) The Hájíwah canal.
(*iii*) The Sidhnai canal.

They are all under the control of the Superintending Engineer, Deraját Circle, whose head-quarters are at Multan. The Sidhnai canal and those inundation canals which take out of the Chenab are under the Executive Engineer, Multan Canals; while the Hájíwah canal and the other inundation canals which take out of the Sutlej are under the Executive Engineer, Lower Sutlej Canals.

I.—THE OLD INUNDATION CANALS.

(i) The old Inundation Canals.

A full report of the system of the Inundation canals as it existed in 1858 was prepared by Mr. Morris, the Settlement Officer. A reprint of his general description is to be found in Appendix B of the former edition of this Gazetteer, and a reprint of his detailed accounts of the various canals in Appendix I of the Completion Report (1895) of the Multan Canals. In the following account of the canals free use has been made of this useful report, and little has been done except to bring it up to date with the aid of the Completion Report above referred to.

All the inundation canals are, comparatively speaking, of recent formation, the most ancient of them not having been dug more than one hundred and sixty years ago. They would appear to owe their existence to the drying up of the Beás and to the change in the course of the river Rávi which rendered it incumbent on the inhabitants to devise some other mode of providing water for their lands.

The question has sometimes been raised how far these canals are State property and how far they may be looked on as owned by private persons. The bed of the canals is in many places recorded as the property of the adjacent owners, no compensation having been paid for it; and this record has been regularly maintained even in cases where the Government has been in possession for forty years or more. But the management and control of the canals is entirely in the hands of Government, and all the main canals owe their origin to the direct or indirect support of the Government in power for the time being; some having been dug by the former rulers of the country, and others by powerful zamindars or associated village communities aided by Government. The majority of Chenáb canals were made by the Patháns when holding the position of rulers in

Chapter V, C.

The Canals.

(i) The old Inundation Canals.

Multan and Shujabad; whilst those on the Sutlej were chiefly dug by the Daudpotras, a powerful tribe, who on the extinction of Mughal power completed the conquest of this part of the country, and continued in possession until its acquisition by Ranjít Singh. One of the largest, however, of the Sutlej canals —the Diwánwah of tahsil Mailsi—was excavated by Diwán Sáwan Mal, who also enlarged and improved several others, and showed great liberality in making grants for the re-excavation and improvement of the canals in general.

The canals forty years ago were thirty-four in number, fourteen issuing from the Chenáb and twenty from the Sutlej. It has, however, been the policy of Government to link up the canals as far as possible, so as to avoid the expense and loss of irrigating power entailed by a number of separate heads. The number of canals is now generally returned as fourteen (eight on the Chenáb and six on the Sutlej), but the number of heads is at present (1900) nine only (four on the Chenáb and five on the Sutlej) and proposals are under consideration for still further reducing the number of heads. The separate canals as now ordinarily returned are described briefly below:—

THE CANALS FROM THE CHENAB.

Canals from the Chenab.

The *Matital canal* has its head in mauza Mamdal. It was built in 1830 by one Yar Muhammad, a zamindar. Owing to the head of the canal being not far below the confluence of the Rávi and the Chenáb rivers, the head silts badly, and the canal has generally closed earlier than other canals on the Chenab. Proposals are under consideration for bringing the greater part of the area irrigated by it within Sidhnai limits.

The *Wali Muhammad Khan Canal*, made in 1755 by Wali Muhammad or Ali Muhammad Khan, Khakwani, Governor of Multan. It formerly had its head in mauza Ran Labi Darya, but now takes out in mauza Jamálke. The same channel from the river to the head regulator also supplies the Khádal with its branches, the Tahirpur and the Durána Langána.

The *Khádal* branch, originally a separate canal, made in 1815 by one Sheo Das, a munshi, under the orders of Nawáb Muzaffar Khan. Between 1891 and 1899 this branch was worked as a branch of the Matital, but in the latter year was joined to the Wali Muhammad.

The *Tahirpur* branch, made originally from a separate head in Gagra Kalandar Jahánian, for the benefit of the Tahirpur village by Sayad Rahman Shah of Shahpur in 1815. This branch now takes out of the Khádal.

From shortly above Multan takes out:—

The *Khairpur* rájbaha made in 1880 mainly for the better irrigation of the village of Khairpur, which had formerly been dependent for irrigation on a water-course passing through the Cantonment of Multan.

At or near the tail of Wali Muhammad are three long water-courses—the Kassi Kasba, Lar Khoja and Lar Chhaddar, which are, however, not, cleared by Government.

The *Durána Langána* canal has now the same head as the Wali Muhammad, having been amalgamated with that canal in 1896. The canal was originally a small cut dug about 1760 A.D. by one Kaim, a zamindar; but it was much improved and extended by the British Government soon after annexation, and is often spoken of as the 'Angrezi nála.' Proposals are under consideration for the construction of three rájbahas from the lower part of the canal to irrigate lands on the right bank. At present there is only one branch of this canal subsequent to its separation from the Wali Muhammad at the Bosan regulator, namely :—

Chapter V, C.

The Canals.

Canals from the Chenáb.

The *Shahpur* branch.—This was originally a separate canal made in 1780 by Wali Muhammad Khan, Khakwani, Governor of Multan. It used to take out from the river at Ran Labi Darya, but has for many years been worked as a branch of the Durána Langána, and it tails off into the Wali Muhammad canal. just behind the house usually occupied by the Deputy Commissioner in Multan. The branch takes off at present from the right bank of the Durána Langána, about 1½ mile below the Bosan regulator, but a proposal to change the head to the regulator has been sanctioned.

The *Sikandrabad* canal.—This canal was made in 1777 by Nijabat Khan, the ancestor of the Khokhar family, and its original head was in Bhakhri, from which it was afterwards changed to Nawábpur, and then again to Gagra Kalandar Jahánian, where its present head is. The Sikandarabad has a few small branches at or near its tail, such as the Lar Khandar, Lar Kamandi, Lar Daudsher and Rájbaha Shahpur.

The *Gajjuhatta* canal.—This canal was made originally in the time of Muzaffar Khan by Daim and Mithu, zamindars of the village of Gajjuhatta. It had a separate head taking off just above the N.-W. Railway bridge on the Chenáb near Sher Shah, but in 1899 it was linked up to the Sikandarabad at Muzaffarabad. This canal now includes the irrigation of the area formerly served by the Dhundun canal, which appears to have been abandoned about 1886. It has now three main branches, *viz* :—

The *Bakhtuwah*, made originally as a single separate canal in the time of Nawáb Shuja Khan by one Bakhtu, zamindar of Todarpur. It is now divided into two branches, the Upper and the Lower Bakhtuwah, each of which takes off from the main canal and from which spring a large number of smaller branches such as the Lar Jhangiwah, Lar Kasturiwah, Lar Mubárikwah, Lar Mir Kadri, Lar Waryámwah, Lar La'natwah, Lar Halálwaja, Lar Núr Fakir, Lar Sheikhpur and Lar Choti.

The *Nángewah-Panjáni* branch, irrigates the eastern part of the Gajjuhatta area. The Nángewah was originally a Kassi and was extended and improved in 1892 by chher labour. In 1900 a further extension was made to link up the Panjani canal, which formerly had a separate head in mauza Panjani, having been made in the time of Nawáb Baháwal Khan by Paira Lál, Kardar. This extension also supplanted the irrigation formerly carried out by two small private canals—the Wilayat Shah and Kaurewah : these canals now run as water-courses from the Punjani.

The southernmost canals of the series are the *Sikandarwah* and *Bilochanwah*, which have since 1898 had a single head but were previously two separate canals. The Sikandarwah was made in 1775 in the time of Nawáb Bahawal Khan by Sikandar Khan, Channar, a kardar; and the Bilochanwah was dug at some period not known by the Biluches of Bet Kesar.

THE CANALS FROM THE SUTLEJ.

Canals from the Sutlej.

The *Diwánwah*, a large canal made in 1831 in the time of Diwán Sáwan Mal by Ghulám Mustafa Khan, Khakwani. Edwardes in his 'Year on the Punjab Frontier,' gives the following account of its origin : 'Diwan Sáwan Mal offered one day in open Darbar to give ten thousand rupees down and to permanently raise the pay of any of his servants to forty rupees a day if he would increase the revenue of the barren district of Khai, by irrigation, from six thousand to forty thousand rupees a year. Mustafa Khan accepted the offer, and received the district in farm for five years on the following terms .....For the first and second year Mustafa Khan rather lost by the bargain; but the canal which he had cut worked better every year, and in the third year the district yielded thirty-two thousand rupees. Now comes the point of the joke. Sáwan Mal seeing the

Chapter V. C.

The Canals.

Canals from the Sutlej.

canal now complete and reproductive cancelled the canal cutter's lease; and when asked for the promised reward, laughed heartily.' This canal has usually worked well; and since 1878 it has included the irrigation of the area formerly served by a small separate canal called the Sultánwah Khurd (made in 1775 by Karam Khan, Daudpotra), which irrigated the villages about Burana and Alampur. Since 1899, also, the Jámwah Khurd has formed part of Diwánwah system.

The *Jámwah Khurd* originally made in 1755 by Jám Khan, Daudpotra, in the time of Nawáb Sádik Muhammad Khan. It was linked up in 1899 to the Diwánwah at Karampur. It had a branch called the Chattarwah, which was taken over by Government in 1870 and amalgamated with the Jámwah Kalán in 1883-84. From 1892-93 it had again been worked as a branch of the Jámwah Khurd, and it has itself a sub-branch known as the Lar Chattarwah.

The *Jámwah Kalán*, also made in 1775 by Jám Khan, Daudpotra, in the time of Nawáb Sádik Muhammad Khan. With this canal have been amalgamated since 1894 the Kábilwah and Sádikwah branches. These were originally separate canals; the former having been made in 1755 by Kábil Khan, Daudpotra, and latter, also in 1755, by one Sádik Khan. The Sádikwah is now a branch of the Kábilwah; they were both amalgamated with the Bahawalwah Mailsi in 1886, but were transferred to the Jámwah Kalán in 1894. The Kábilwah has a branch called the Naukábilwah, and the Sádikwah has a branch called the Uchhalwah.

The *Baháwalwah Mailsi*, made in 1753 by Nawáb Bahawal Khán. This has now a branch, the Sultánwah, from which the Abbánwah, Jamrániwah and Nazarwah take out. All these, except the last were at one time separate canals.

The *Sultánwah* was made in 1797 by one Sultán Khan, kardar, in the time of Nawáb Sádik Muhammed Khán. It was (with its branches) amalgamated with the Baháwalwáh Mailsi in 1894. Another small branch of the Baháwalwah Mailsi is called the Barádarwah.

The *Abbanwah*, originally made by Abban Khan, Daudpotra, in the time of Nawáb Baháwal Khan, and repaired afterwards by Diwán Sáwan Mal. It was amalgamated with the Sultánwah in 1860-61.

The *Jamrániwah* made by Sikandar Khan, Daudpotra, in 1745. It was afterwards amalgamated with the Sultánwah, but the date of the amalgamation is not known.

The *Muhammadwah-Sardárwah*. These were until 1893-94 two separate canals. The Muhammadwah originally was made about 1740 by Muhammad Khan, Daudpotra, but fell into decay, and was restored about 1840 by Diwán Sáwan Mal; the lower part of this canal below Basantpur, representing the extension made by the Diwán, is often spoken of by the people as the Diwánwah. The Sardarwah again, one of the earliest, if not the earliest, of the present system of inundation canals, was made in 1739 by Sirdar Muhammad Khan, Daudpotra, of Khairpur. It was in 1893-94 amalgamated with the Muhammadwah. At the tail the Sardárwah splits into two branches known as the Lar Dozakhi and Lar Bihishti. An attempt was made in 1892-93 to reduce the length of the water-courses towards the tail by the construction of a rájbaha, called the Chajjuwah after one Chajju Singh, a canal subordinate; and a further set of minors, etc., was constructed with the same object in 1901 and 1902.

The last of the Sutlej canals is the *Baháwalwah-Lodhrán*, a canal originally excavated by Nawáb Baháwal Khan of Baháwalpur, and now including the irrigation of a series of other canals of which each had formerly a separate head, *viz.*:—

The *Sheikhwah Sharkia*, made in A.D., 1739, by Sheikh Hamid Ganj Bakhsh, a feudatory of the Baháwalpur State. This canal was finally amalgamated with the Baháwalwah-Lodhrán in 1880. This branch runs by the tahsil head-quarters at Lodhran and has three main sub-branches—the Aliwah, Kádirwah and Jami.

The *Mubárikwah*, made in 1767 by Nawáb Mubárik Khan of Baháwalpur. It had formerly a separate head at Gudpur, but has since 1880 been worked as a branch of the Baháwalwah.

Chapter V, C.

The Canals.

Canals from the Sutlej.

The *Khanwah*, made in 1777 by Nawab Baháwal Khan. It had formerl ya separate head at Jagir Kikri, but has since 1880 been worked as a branch of the Baháwalwah.

The *Sheikhwah Gharbia*, made in 1802 by Sheikh Makbúl Muhammad, Wazír of Baháwalpur. It had formerly a separate head at Jhok, but has since 1890-91 been worked as a branch of the Baháwalwah.

The *Bahádurwah*, made in 1742 by Bahádur Khan, kardar of the Baháwalpur State. It had formerly a separate head in Betowahi, but it has for some time been worked as a branch of the Háfizwah.

The *Háfizwah*, made about 1810 by Háfiz Abdurrahmán, a kardar in Baháwalpur. It formerly issued from the river at Jhambu, but has since 1891-92 been treated as a branch of the Baháwalwah.

The upper reach of the Baháwalwah-Lodhrán canal near the head is often spoken of locally as the 'Chhár.'

The following are the average areas matured on these canals during the five years ending 1898-99 :—

Canal	Acres.	Canal	Acres.
Matital	9,357	Diwánwah	21,952
Durána Langána ...	24,199	Jamwah Khurd ...	14,431
Wali Muhammad ...	36,971	Jámwah Kalán ...	18,434
Sikandrabad ...	43,873	Baháwalwah-Mailsi	21,776
Gajjuhatta	31,460	Muhammadwah-Sardarwah	34,616
Panjáni	3,276	Baháwalwah-Lodhrán	27,671
Sikandarwah ...	5,433		
Bilochanwah ...	4,394		
Total ...	158,963	Total ...	138,770

The heads of the canals.

Wherever such a thing is possible, the heads of inundation canals should take off from creeks, but in the case of the Chenáb canals the heads are mostly in the main-stream, it being impossible, owing to the course and nature of the river, to take the canals off from a side creek except in the case of the Sikandarwah. This very often leads to the heads being silted up early owing to erosion of the banks above, the silt from the erosion of the banks being washed into the canal head. It also often occurs that the river wipes out a large portion of the head of the canal, and nothing short of expensive training works would prevent this.

The canals may be divided into two main portions—the portion above the regulator and the portion below. The former is generally termed the *supply channel,* and is frequently a natural channel left by the river after it has moved away. The portion below the head regulator is mainly artificial, though in the case of the Sikandarabad canal the first six miles were originally, for the most part, a creek which is now being canalised. The head regulator is combined with an escape, so that surplus water coming down the supply channel may be passed off. In the case of the Sikandarabad canal a large

Chapter V, C.
The Canals.
The heads of the canals.

masonry regulator has been provided as the head to an escape channel which leads back into the river. In the case of other Chenáb canals the surplus water is effectively passed off by a cut in the bank above the regulator, the surplus water not being so great as in the case of the Sikandarabad canal. Before the construction of the head regulators the canals were at the mercy of the river and the only way to dispose of the surplus water in the flood season was to cut the banks, make *tals* as they were called. This of course was a very clumsy and unsatisfactory way of dealing with the surplus water. In order to prevent the river water in the flood season pouring over the canal irrigated land, which is much lower than the river water surface in July and August, and to prevent this water forcing its way into the canals below the head regulator, the outer bank of the canals nearest the river is strengthened or special marginal embankments made. In this way there is a chain of protection extending from a point some 26 miles north of Multan down to Jalálpur Khaki, south of Shujabad, a total length of over 80 miles.

The Chenáb river is much less liable to violent changes than the Sutlej, and within the last six or seven years or more no change in the course of the river Chenáb has taken place such as would necessitate cutting a new head for the canals taking off from this river. As stated above, there has been a certain amount of loss in the length of supply channels, but, comparatively speaking, the damage done has been insignificant. It is of course quite possible this happy state of things will not last, and there is also the fear that at some future time the river may threaten to cut into the supply channels at some distance from the head, or even sever the channels below the head regulator.

Chief differences between these canals and perennial canals.

A description of the method of cultivation on these canals has been given in Chapter IV above; the figures showing the irrigation accomplished by them from 1868-1869 onward will be found in Chapter I, and the present position of the question of the irrigation rights of the people is described in Chapter III. It will suffice to note here a few of the points on which working of these canals differs from that of the permanent canals with which most Government officers are acquainted :—

(*i*). In the first place, the alignment is not straight but sinuous, having, as a rule, been originally designed so as to avoid splitting up properties, and without the same careful regard for levels which is now customary. These sinuosities are perhaps more unsightly than harmful, but some of the worst bends on the Chenáb canals have been removed and in course of time more improvements will be carried out in this direction.

Chapter V. C.

The Canals.

Chief differences between these canals and perennial canals.

(*ii*). A further essential difference lies, of course, in the fact that these canals are, as a rule, open only while the natural water level in the river is higher than the bed level of the canal head—that is, for about four or six months in each year. The constant variation in supplies makes an adequate distribution very difficult.

(*iii*). There is much waste in the distribution owing to the absence of any system of rájbahas and minors. On the one hand the villages furthest off from the canal receive their supplies through very long and expensive water-courses, sometimes extending for as much as 13 or 14 miles and costing many thousands rupees each year to clear. And, on the other hand, the villages adjacent to the canals are supplied to a large extent direct from the canal by a number of independent outlets in the bank, very many of which are not of masonry; and a further result of this system is that it is often impossible to ride for any distance along the canal banks during the irrigating season. The defect of long water-courses (*kassis*) is found mainly in the Sutlej canals; that of direct outlets mainly in the Chenáb canals. A great deal has been done and more is being done year by year to provide the heads of the water-courses with masonry outlets, but as the cost of such outlets is considerable the work can only be done very gradually.

(*iv*). Another peculiarity of these canals is that the bed and banks of the canal are often the property of private persons, though they have been occupied by Government for a long series of years. As, however, the full control of the bank is necessary for the management of the canals, it is everywhere the rule that where Government is responsible for the maintenance of the bed of any canal or branch (*lar*) it is entitled to control the vegetation of all kinds growing on the banks, whether it is recorded as owner or not.

(*v*). Another point which is sometimes lost sight of is that as the rabi crops on these canals receive no canal water after the beginning of October, the amount of water utilized for rabi sowings before the closure of the canals must necessarily be much larger than that customary for the corresponding period in perennial canals.

(*vi*). Finally, from the financial standpoint, the fact that these canals were constructed under native rule and by statute labour, renders it impossible to estimate the relation of the annual profits to the capital account. The figures available are given in the Completion Report of 1895; but they mean little or nothing.

Another point in which the management of the inundation canals has hitherto differed from that of the perennial canals deserves separate mention, and that is the system of silt clearances.

Chapter V, C.

The Canals.

Silt clearances.

The frequent alterations in the river channels sometimes render heavy cuttings through large sandbanks, or the construction of new canal heads, necessary to secure the required supply of water. In addition, however, to this, an annual clearance of the silt, which regularly accumulates each year in every canal, is also indispensable; otherwise the canal bed would in the course of a few years become so choked up as almost entirely to prevent the ingress of any water at all, except during the very highest floods.

Since the formation of the canals, their annual repair and clearance, the stoppage of breaches, preservation of banks, and all other expenses, were until recently borne by the zamindars benefiting from their irrigation. Under the Pathán and Sikh Governments occasional grants were made for extending and improving the canals, but these were regarded as matters of favour, not right; whilst, on the other hand, all ordinary expenses of every description were borne by the people themselves, who were, moreover, especially called on to furnish labourers for the annual clearance. The labourers thus furnished were commonly named *chhers*; and hence this system of clearance is technically known as the *chher* system.

The *chher* system under the Sikhs may be briefly described as follows. When the time of clearing the canals arrived, the kardar of each pargana demanded as many labourers as he considered necessary for the season, according to the state of the canal and extent of clearance required. The number to be furnished by each village and proprietor was then determined on, some furnishing according to the number of their wells or yokes, and others according to the produce of their lands in the past season, a certain number of labourers being fixed for each Rs. 100 worth of produce. The labourers thus furnished were paid by the parties furnishing them; and it was incumbent on them to be present during the entire season of clearance, non-attendance being punished by a fine called *nágha*, which varied from two to three annas a day. The proceeds of these fines were used in providing hired labourers in the room of the absentee *chhers*, and also in the payment of a small establishment, consisting of a darogah, a muharrir and some mirabs whose duty it was to keep the *chhers* at work and generally look after the canal. The balance, if any, remaining, after the payment of the hired labourers and establishment, was carried to the credit of Government. *Chhers* were furnished by all villages receiving water, with the exception of the six suburbs of the city of Multan, and a few small estates in their vicinity, from whom, however, a water rent, varying from Rs. 1 to 4 and 5 per jhalár, was levied in lieu of *chher* labour.

From the above it will be seen that the annual clearance and whole expense of maintaining the canals was borne by the

Chapter V, C.

The Canals.

Silt clearances.

community; and although the system was liable to abuses, still there can be no doubt but that, on the whole, it was popular with the people, especially under Diwán Sáwan Mal, whose entire system of canal management is even now never mentioned or referred to but in terms of the highest commendation. The chief aim of the Diwán was to secure an early and plentiful supply of water. To effect this he well knew that a thorough annual clearance of the canals was absolutely necessary, and only obtainable by the regular attendance of the *chhers*. Their attendance, therefore, was rigorously *enforced;* and although in some few instances the *nágha* fine was levied from absentees, still these were the exceptions, the real fact being that *chhers* were not allowed to absent themselves. In short, the system under Sáwan Mal was one of forced labour: the *chhers* were forced to come, and forced to work, and hence the canals were dug. If any zamindar failed to furnish his quota of *chhers*, he was beaten till he did, and the *chhers* once obtained, stringent measures were taken to keep them at their work. Again, the kardars and principal headmen in charge of the canals were made personally responsible for their proper and early clearance, which was consequently well and effectually done.

In short, the success of the Diwán's system may be ascribed to two principal causes. First, that the system was essentially one of forced labour, thus ensuring an effectual and timely clearance; and, secondly, that the superintendence of this clearance was chiefly in the hands of those most interested in its being fairly carried out, so as to secure for each village on the canal an amount of water proportionate to its wants.

Chher system under British rule.

The system of working clearances by *chher* labour has been modified from time to time under British rule. The chief stages through which it has passed are described chiefly below:—

(*i*). The system in force for the assessment of the labour previous to 1859 differed on the two sets of canals. On the Chenáb the *chhers* were provided at a certain proportion to the land revenue; on the Sutlej the canal lands were measured annually and a *chher* provided for every 15 acres irrigated.

(*ii*). In 1859 it was arranged that the number of *chhers* required for the clearance of each canal should be fixed; the distribution of the number over the villages should be determined by a *panchayat;* and the distribution within each village should be left to the lambardars.

(*iii*). In 1880 the rules were again revised, and minor improvements were effected, but the system of assessment remained practically unchanged.

(*iv*). In 1886 a new set of rules was issued, retaining the old system of fixing the total number of *chhers* required for each canal, but distributing this demand strictly according to the area irrigated. The area matured in the kharíf and half the

Chapter V, C.

The Canals.

area irrigated for the rabi were calculated for each holding, and demand distributed on this basis.

Chher system under British rule.

The system on which the *chher* labour was assessed and utilized under the latest rules may be described briefly as follows:—For each canal was fixed (subject to triennial revision) the total number of days' labour required for the purposes of clearance and maintenance. After the kharíf girdáwari of each year the total matured canal-irrigated kharíf area was totalled up for each canal, and to this was added half the area irrigated by the canal for the ensuing rabi. The required labour was then distributed over the area thus obtained, so that each *chher* payer knew how many days' labour he had to provide. The work commenced on the 15th December and continued for some three months. If the *chher* payer was unable or unwilling to provide the labour himself, he was allowed to pay Government in its place a sum of 8 annas for each day's labour to which he was assessed; and the proceeds of these sums went to form a fund, known as the *zar-i-nágha*, from which Government could provide labour for the completion of the clearance and maintenance work.

Introduction of cash occupier's rates.

The abolition of the system of statute labour and the substitution of a system of cash payments had been several times mooted, but it was first seriously considered at the second Settlement in 1874—1879. It was at that time proposed to abolish the *chhers* and to levy from the owners fluctuating cash rates which would cover both canal land revenue and clearance charges; but the annual measurements required for this system were found to be both inefficient and unpopular, and the proposal, for this and other reasons, ultimately abandoned. In 1888 a further effort was made, at the instance of Major Hutchinson, the Deputy Commissioner, to introduce a cash assessment by consent of the irrigators on the Gajjuhatta canal, but the irrigators were found to be unwilling, and this proposal had also to be dropped. The question was taken up again in 1898-99, and it was then decided that the *chher* system should be gradually done away with, and that in its place a system of occupier's rates should be introduced. The rates prescribed were as follows:—

	Rate per acre of matured crop.					
	Flow.			Lift.		
	Rs.	a.	p.	Rs.	a.	p.
Class I. Rice, gardens, and pepper	2	4	0	1	11	0
" II. Cotton, sugarcane and til	1	12	0	1	5	0
" III. Other kharíf crops	1	8	0	1	2	0
" IV. Rabi crops	0	14	0	0	10	0

Irrigation on grass lands to be assessed at half rabi rates at the discretion of the Deputy Commissioner.

Chapter V. C.

The Canals.

Introduction of cash occupier's rates.

These rates are not fixed for the term of Settlement, but are liable to alteration at the discretion of Government. They have been fixed with due regard to the estimated cost of the maintenance of the canals, but it has been definitely laid down that they are not intended to be in any way limited by the actual cost of maintenance, and that Government is at liberty to use them, like the occupiers' rates on other canals, so as to obtain for itself the full price of the water supplied. They were introduced for the first time on the Gajjuhatta, Sikandrabad, Bilochanwah and Sikandarwah canals in the kharif of 1900, and on the Matital, Wali Muhammad and Durána Langana in the kharif of 1901.

II.—Hajiwah Canal.

Hajiwah. Origin and history.

The Hájiwah canal owes its origin to the enterprise of a Khakwani Pathán, Ghulám Mustafa Khan, who was one of Sáwan Mal's kardars, and afterwards Tahsildar of Mailsi. In the Regular Settlement he held the contract for the revenue on the *lár* lands in the east of the tahsíl, and, with the sanction of Government, built the Hájíwah canal to irrigate a portion of those lands. At the Second Settlement, his son, Ghulám Kádir Khan, received from Government in proprietary right a tract of 60,000 acres irrigated by the canal, and the grant was formally confirmed by a deed executed in 1886.

In 1888 Ghulám Kádir died, leaving four sons, who immediately began to quarrel among themselves, to the great detriment of the canal irrigation. In December 1888 the canal was placed by the civil court in charge of the Deputy Commissioner, and shortly afterwards the Government took over the canal on the authority of a clause in the deed of 1886. Between 1890 and 1892 it was administered as a provincial work, but in 1892 it was transferred to the Imperial head, and since that date the accounts of the Hájíwáh canal have been amalgamated with those of the other Sutlej inundation canals of the district. The Government administration of the canal was contested by the three younger sons of Ghulám Kádir Khán and the suit was finally decided by the Privy Council in 1901. The bed of the canal was declared to be the property of the four sons of Ghulám Kádir, but in other respects the Government was left unfettered in its action.

Rates in force.

In 1893 the Government imposed certain charges on Hájíwah irrigation and at the present Settlement these charges were amended, so that at present the system is as follows:—

(*a*) on lands owned by the descendants of Ghulám Kádir Khan and certain of their relations within the original grant a maintenance rate of 12 annas per acre matured is charged, the rest of the revenue being fixed;

Chapter V. C.

The Canals.

(b) on other lands irrigated by this canal the ordinary canal advantage land revenue and occupier's rates prescribed for the rest of the inundation canals of the tahsil are assessed.

III.—The Sidhnai Canal.

Sidhnai. History of the Project.

The history of this canal is given in full in the Completion Report (1894) prepared by Mr. T. Higham, from which it appears that the first proposal for a canal from the Sidhnai reach of the river Rávi was made by Lieutenant (afterwards Colonel) J. Anderson, R. E., Superintendent, Inundation Canals. The proposal was to re-open as "a navigable canal of irrigation" a channel known as the old Ravi, extending from the town of Sarai Sidhu to Multan, to be supplied by means of a dam across the Rávi at the up-stream end of the straight and permanent reach known as the "Sidhnai," which extends for 7 miles below Tulamba. The Bári Doáb canal was at that time designed to terminate at or near Tulamba, and it was supposed that the tract intervening between the terminus and Multan might eventually be irrigated by means of some such canal as had been proposed by Lieutenant Anderson. The question was first regularly investigated in the course of the surveys of the Lower Bári Doáb undertaken in 1870—75, in the last of which years two alternate estimates were submitted by Mr. E. C. Palmer for a permanent and for an inundation canal from the Sidhnai reach, which amounted to Rs. 16,68,317 and Rs. 5,85,289, respectively, exclusive of indirect charges. The project, however, remained in abeyance owing to the increased expenditure on other large schemes then in progress, and to the doubts that were entertained as to the reliability of the data on which these estimates were based.

In 1882 the Government of India invited the Punjab Government to submit proposals for new Irrigation Works to be constructed out of loan funds, and the scheme for the Sidhnai canal was then reconsidered, with the result that a General Estimate, amounting to Rs. 7,74,480, was forwarded to the Government of India in 1883, to which sanction was accorded in 1884. The work was for the most part carried out by Mr. MacLean, Executive Engineer, and by his assistant Mr. Johnston. Work was started in December 1883, and the canal was opened for irrigation on the 27th May 1886, in the kharif of which year 5,976 acres were matured, which were followed by 20,479 in the succeeding rabi, making a total area of 26,455 acres of crops brought to maturity in the first year after opening. The canal as originally designed was practically completed in the following year, when the irrigated area rose to 75,284 acres, although in the estimate of 1883 the maximum area anticipated after the irrigation had been fully developed was 48,000 acres only.

Subsidiary Canals.

The success of the canal was thus immediate and complete, but during the course of its construction it was found necessary

Chapter V, C.

The Canals.

Subsidiary Canals.

to propose a slight extension of the scope of the project. As early as 1884 the zamindars of the villages situated on the right and left banks of the Rávi below the site of the weir, then under construction, took alarm, and submitted petitions regarding the probable effect of the new channel on their existing irrigation from the river, which was effected from open cuts in the banks. The question was promptly investigated, and it was found that these cuts were placed at such a high level that they were only effective when the river was in high flood, at which times they would be practically unaffected by the canal works. It appeared probable, however, that there might be some decrease in the area below the weir, which had previously been covered by high floods, and that the prosperity of the villages concerned would be affected by the emigration of the cultivators to the more favoured tracts commanded by the new canal; and as it was undesirable that these villages, which were not at their best in a very flourishing condition, should be reduced to greater straits by the opening of the Sidhnai canal, it was proposed to provide irrigation for such of their lands as could be commanded by two subsidiary canals taking out from the right and left banks above the weir. It was at the same time pointed out that a third canal might be usefully taken out from the left bank of the river about 3½ miles above the weir which would command a small tract that could not be reached from the Sidhnai canal. Estimates were accordingly prepared for—

1st, the Kuranga canal, to take out from the right flank of the Sidhnai weir;

2nd, the Fazal Sháh canal, to take out from the left flank of the weir, and between it and the head of the Sidhnai canal;

3rd, the Abdul Hakim canal, to take out from the left bank of the river, about 3½ miles above the weir.

The conditions upon which the construction of these three canals was proposed were:—

(*a*) that the requirements of the Sidhnai canal should be first supplied in full;

(*b*) that any surplus water in the river should first be equally distributed between the Kuranga and Fazal Sháh canals;

(*c*) that any balance should go to the Abdul Hakim canal.

The Kuranga and Fazal Sháh canals were opened for irrigation in the months of June and July 1890, respectively, and the Abdul Hakim in the kharíf of the following year.

Head-works.

The head-works of the canal consist of a weir built right across the channel of the river and at right angles to its axis, the distance between the right and left flank walls being

Chapter V, C.

The Canals.

Head-works.

737·5 feet, and the actual width of the Sidhnai reach at this point being about 800 feet. The crest of the weir is at the general level of the river bed, or R.L. 453·5, the level of the floor of the canal regulator immediately above it being 1 foot higher, or R. L. 454·5. The weir is divided into 32 bays of 20 feet each by piers 7·5 feet in height and 3 feet in width. The tops of these piers are connected at their upstream ends by timber beams 18 inches in width and 12 inches deep, and the vents thus formed are closed by wooden needles placed nearly vertically, so that their lower ends abut against the crest of the weir, while they are supported at the upper ends by the beams over the piers.

Since the weir was first built it has been considerably strengthened, a 3 foot platform has been added at the level of the timber beam for greater convenience in working the needles, and a timber roadway has been added out of reach of the highest floods, so that it is possible to go from bank to bank in all seasons.

With a low river the vents are entirely closed by the needles, which are gradually removed as the supply rises and are taken out before the advent of a flood. Floods are telegraphed from Mokaisar above the head of the Bári Doáb canal, from Shahdera near Lahore and from Chichawatni, so that ample warning is given of the approach of flood. The water is now ordinarily held up to the level of the needle-beam or R. L. 462·0; but in order to pass supplies into the canals when these are silted the water is headed up to R. L. 462·5, and in light floods the piers are submerged to a depth of 2 feet.

General Statistics.

The following table gives particulars of the four canals which constitute the Sidhnai system :—

Name of Canal.	Length in canal miles of 5,000 feet.	Capacity in cusecs.	Gross area commanded.	
			Square miles.	Acres.
Sidhnai canal	31·2	1,820	490·0	313,600
Kuranga canal	14·6	235	40·2	25,740
Fazal Sháh canal	11·31	200	49·0	31.360
Abdul Hakim canal	9·5	150	26·0	16,640
Total	66 7	2,405	605·2	387,340

Chapter V, C.

The Canals.

Main Line.

The main line of the Sidhnai canal extends from the head at Sidhnai to a point about 200 feet below the Lahore road, a distance of 31·2 canal miles. Beyond this point, called Rangho, two tail rajbahas take off; the Ráwan, which has now a total commanded area of 67,300 acres, takes off on the right bank, and the Mákhdúm Rashíd, with a total commanded area of 67,500 acres, takes off in continuation of the canal alignment. These two rájbahas are in fact the largest distributaries in the Sidhnai, taking together 30 per cent. of the total supply entering the canals. The canal is thus of very short length in comparison with the area commanded and irrigated. The first rájbaha takes off two miles only below the head. The very short lead through which the supply has to be carried before irrigation commences is a peculiar characteristic of this canal, and one of the causes of its financial success. The main line was originally constructed with a bed width of 80 feet and a full supply depth of 5 feet, with a bed slope of 1 in 8,000, the estimated full supply being 800 cusecs. The canal banks have been much strengthened and improved, and the full supply depth increased. Operations were commenced in the cold weather of 1900-01 with the object of regrading the canals throughout, and the maximum supply allowed at the head is now 1,820 cusecs with a bed width varying from 90 feet at the head of the canal to 32 feet at the tail, and a full supply depth varying from 7·0 at the Sidhnai to 5·8 feet at Rangho.

On the Sidhnai there are 13 distributaries (rájbahas), which are named as follows:—

Right bank—Choparatta.	*Left bank*—Makhdúmpur.
Hashmat Mirali.	Határan.
Kotli Bhutta.	Vanoi.
Kukarhatta.	Kabírwála.
Munganwala.	Cháwan.
Tail—Makhdúm Rashíd and Ráwan.	Mahni Syál.

Recent extensions.

Since the Completion Report was prepared in 1894 there have been several small extensions, *viz.* :—

(*i*) in 1898 an extension of the Kotli Bhutta and Kukarhatta rájbahas, so as to include within irrigation limits a tract of land extending up to the Chenáb *band* and the Matital canal ;

(*ii*) in 1899 an extension of the tail of the Kuranga canal, so as to irrigate eight villages lying to the north of the lower course of the Rávi.

(*iii*) in 1899 an extension of the Ráwan rájbaha, so as to include some 32,700 acres of land, largely Government waste, lying between the Makhdúm Rashíd rajbaha and the railway ;

(*iv*) in 1902 an extension of the Munganwála, Kukarhatta and Ráwan rájbahas, so as to include certain areas east of the Chenáb *band* hitherto irrigated by the Matital canal.

Chapter V, C.

The Canals.

Uncertainty of supply.

A very noticeable feature of this canal is the great irregularity of the supply. The rabi supplies of the river Rávi fall far short of the capacity of the Bári Doáb canal, and into that canal every drop of water available in the river is passed whenever the demand exceeds the supply. Owing to percolation, however, through the boulder and shingle bed, water reappears in the bed of the river at some distance below the Bári Doáb canal head-works at Mádhopur, but this exiguous supply cannot be expected to reach the Sidhnai, which is more than 300 miles distant; and it frequently happens, therefore, that the Sidhnai reach is absolutely dry for many consecutive weeks or months. In spite, therefore, of the fact that the head-works permit the utilization of every drop in the river, the conditions of the Sidhnai canal in some respects resemble those of the Inundation canals on the Sutlej, Chenáb, and Indus, although the liability to failure is not due, as in those cases, to want of control at the head but to the absolute failure of the source of supply.

The areas irrigated and matured by the canal since it was started are as follows:—

Year.	Kharíf.	Rabi.	Total.	Year.	Kharíf.	Rabi.	Total.
1886-87 ...	5,976	20,479	26,455	1893-94 ...	58,947	92,480	151,427
1887-88 ...	45,320	29,964	75,284	1894-95 ...	48,529	95,868	144,397
1888-89 ...	47,989	52,727	100,716	1895-96 ...	65,803	50,624	116,427
1889-90 ...	52,601	32,336	84,937	1896-97 ...	79,416	52,038	149,454
1890-91 ...	53,775	59,561	113,336	1897-98 ...	108,376	77,333	185,709
1891-92 ...	54,502	59,917	114,419	1898-99 ...	57,113	27,193	84,306
1892-93 ...	54,815	83,471	138,286	1899-00 ...	14,331	11,934	26,265

The number of days for which the main canal was in flow and the percentage of the sown area which failed have in each year been as follows:—

	Days in flow.	*Percentage of kharába.*
1887-88	251	13
1888-89	272	8
1889-90	208	22
1890-91	234	7
1891-92	226	27
1892-93	204	9
1893-94	348	9
1894-95	349	4
1895-96	230	8
1896-97	233	6
1897-98	221	7
1898-99	108	33
1899-1900...	114	79
1900-1901...	260	...

Chapter V, C.

The Canals.

Colonization.

The greater portion of the area commanded was, prior to the construction of the canal, Government waste, which in the absence of water could not be profitably brought under cultivation, and from which only an insignificant revenue was realized in the form of grazing dues. While the canal officers were engaged in providing water for this considerable area, the duty of introducing colonists into the waste lands and making suitable arrangements for the new settlements devolved on the civil officers. A similar duty was simultaneously imposed on them in connection with the new Sohag-Para canal, which was also under construction at the same time; but the settlement of both these comparatively small tracts was but a prelude to the colonization, on a far larger scale, of the vast area of the Crown waste which was afterwards to be undertaken on the Chenáb canal. The great importance of these pioneer experiments was from the first fully realized by the late Colonel Wace, who, as Financial Commissioner, took a deep personal interest in the scheme; the general principles and main details of which were formulated by him on so sound a basis that, as regards the Sidhnai canal, success had been assured even before his lamented death in 1889. The colonization of the waste lands covered by the original scheme was carried out from first to last by Major Hutchinson, Deputy Commissioner of Multan. The lands were for the most part given out in 90-acre plots, and of the new lessees about half came from districts other than Multan. The immigrants included Kambohs and Aráín Jats from Chunian, Bhadechas from Amritsar, Rájpúts from Jullundur, etc.; and the colonization of this canal is noteworthy as the first successful instance in the history of the province of the transfer of considerable bodies of agriculturists from the central Punjab to other and less thickly populated tracts. The terms on which the lessees on this canal have at various times obtained their grants have been explained in Section B of this Chapter.

Financial results.

The marked success of the canal as a financial concern is shown by the following figures:—

	1894-95.	1895-96.	1896-97.	1897-98.	1899-1900.
	Rs.	Rs.	Rs.	Rs.	Rs.
Net revenue less interest charges.	1,26,426	2,02,673	1,52,306	1,92,394	1,01,868
Net revenue up to end of year.	7,08,599	10,43,215*	11,95,521	13,87,915	14,89,783
Capital outlay to end of year.	10,21,940	10,93,592	11,24,106	11,64,409	11,98,977
Profit per cent.	16·16	22·28	17·37	20 33	12·32

* Includes Rs. 1,31,943 on account of arrears of share of land revenue (málikána) due to the end of 1893-94.

Chapter V. C.

The Canals.

The canal sung in verse.

The canal has not wanted its sacred bard, as the following verses from a poem by one Wazira Máchhi of Zorkot will show :—

Wáh nahr ajúbí ái,	Wáh ! the wonderful canal has come,
Páni píwen sab Khudáí.	All God's people will receive water.
Ai Lát Sáhib ki akhbárí,	The Lieutenant-Governor's order came
'Nawin nahr dí karo tiyárí.	'Build a new canal.
Nahin to mardí ho khalkat sári.	Else all the folk will die,
Mínhán kíti he bewáfái.'	The rains have played us false.'
Wáh nahr ajúbí ái.	Wáh ! the wonderful canal has come.
Rajj kháwín sab Khudáí.	All God's people will eat their full.
Charh Jánsan Sáhib jo áyá,	Johnston Sáhib came,
Jis ne nahr kúu khatáyá.	Who had the canal dug.
Kul mihntián rajj kháyá,	All the workers ate their full,
Zálin mardán tokri chái.	Women and men lifted baskets.
Wáh nahr ajúbí ái.	Wáh ! the wonderful canal has come,
Páni píwin sab Khudáí.	All God's people will receive water.
Páni Kukarhatta nún áyá.	The water came to Kukarhatta,
Jithe Sáhib banglá pawáyá.	Where the Sáhib built a bungalow.
Zilladár makán banáyá,	Zilladars constructed houses,
Kánúngoián kitáb khíndhái.	Kanungos opened their books.
Wáh nahr ajúbí ái.	Wáh ! the wonderful canal has come,
Rajj kháwín sab Khudáí.	All God's people will eat their full.

Considerations of space alone prevent the quotation of the whole poem, which paints in a most vivid manner the impression made by the canal on the people, and their joys and troubles during the early days of the new irrigation.

Private Canals.

Small cuts.

There are in the district a certain number of small cuts from the river which can scarcely be looked on as of sufficient importance to be called canals. There are a number of these in the Rávi on and above the Sidhnai reach, and there is one in the village of Chauki Muhan. The Government does not interfere with the working of these cuts and the irrigation from them is classed as sailab.

One large cut of this nature is the Barkat Ali Khan canal, made in 1887 by Khan Bahahur Muhammad Barkat Ali Khan, Extra Assistant Commissioner, to irrigate a grant of land held by him near Tulamba. It proved a failure, and in 1893 he sold it to Government. The Government has since given up all attempts to keep the canal in order, and such irrigation as is done from it is assessed as sailáb.

There were also in the Shujabad tahsil till lately several cuts known as the Wilayat Sháh, Kaurewah, Gurang, etc., which were of the nature of private canals. These have now all disappeared by reason either of their being abandoned or of their being amalgamated in the Government canal system.

Chapter V. C.

The Canals.

The Ghulámwah.

There now remains in the district only one private canal, properly so called, *viz.*, the Ghulámwah in tahsil Mailsi, a canal excavated from time to time between the First and Second Regular Settlements by Ghulám Muhammad Daulatána of Luddan, who is the sole owner of the canal. The lands irrigated by this canal at the Second Settlement were assessed in the same way as lands irrigated by Government canals; but the clearance was left entirely to the owner, and no *beshi nahri* rate was assessed on subsequent extensions of irrigation from the canal. The clearance is done by the cultivators, who are assessed by the owner to *chher* at the uniform rate of one *chher* for 30 acres of irrigation, and the owner of the canal receives from the land-owners a cash rate, which is usually 10 annas an acre for flow and 8 annas for lift; the rates being subject to deductions in certain cases, such as those of relations, Syads, etc. The average area irrigated in the five years ending 1898-99 was 7,936 acres, and of this 5,403 acres belonged to Ghulám Muhammad himself, either as sole proprietor or lessee or in conjunction with his brother. Irrigation from this canal is now assessed by Government at 8 annas per acre for lift and 6 annas for flow, and the canal owner also pays to Government a royalty of Rs. 500 per annum for the use of the river water.

Canal terminology.

It may be useful to note here some of the local terminology in connection with the canal arrangements. Land which is easily commanded is spoken of as 'lahú,' and land hard to command as 'otar': these terms are applied also to the water in either case as well as to the land. An aqueduct is called a 'sandlá' and an escape 'tál'; a dam or regulator on a canal or large water-course is called 'thokar'; a temporary dam on a small water-course is a 'chháp'; and a dam of earthwork at the end of a water-course is a 'súkband.' A large branch of a canal is known as 'lar'; a smaller branch as 'kassí' or 'wáhí'; and the small water-courses as 'paggu.' The head of a canal or water-course is 'mundh' and the tail 'pánd.' English terms, such as 'minor,' 'regulator,' 'escape,' 'berm,' 'syphon' etc., are also not uncommonly used by the zamindars.

CHAPTER VI.

TOWNS, MUNICIPALITIES AND CANTONMENTS.

Chapter VI.

Towns, Municipalities and Cantonments.

At the census of 1901 all municipalities and cantonments and all continuous collections of houses, possessing urban characteristics and inhabited by not less than 5,000 persons, were classed as towns. Under this rule the following places were returned as towns in the Multan district:—

TAHSIL.	TOWN.	Persons.	Males.	Females.
Multán	Multán	87,394	49,328	38,066
Shujabad ...	Shujabad ...	5,880	3,236	2,644
	Jalálpur	5,149	2,704	2,445
Lodhrán ...	Kahror	5,552	2,878	2,674
	Dunyapur ...	2,150	1,012	1,134
Kabírwála... ...	Tulamba... ...	2,526	1,272	1,254

The distribution by religion of the population of the towns and the number of houses in each town are shown in Table No. XLIII, while particulars regarding births and deaths in towns are given in Table No. XLIV. The remainder of this chapter consists of a detailed description of each town, with a notice of its history, the increase and decrease of the population, its manufactures, commerce, municipal government, institutions, public buildings, and so forth.

Multan City.

History: Foundation.

The date of the founding of the city of Multan is unknown. It is only probable, but not historically established, that Multan was the city of the Malli which Alexander stormed, and where Alexander was wounded*; and the first real appearance of the town in history is in the middle of the 7th century A.D., when it was seized by the Chach Dynasty of Sindh.

Name.

The original form of the name is difficult to discover. Hiuen Tsang, who was in the city in 741 A.D., calls it 'Mu-lo-san-pu-lu,' which is said to be a transliteration of

* Natives interested in history will sometimes mention Alexander's attack on Multan: but there is no separate tradition. They have merely picked up the somewhat loose speculations of Europeans on the subject.

Chapter VI.

Towns, Municipalities and Cantonments.

Multan-Name.

'Múlasthánapura.' Albirúni, writing in the beginning of the 11th century, quotes (as will be seen below) a Kashmirian author, who calls the town, apparently, Múla-tána; and Munshi Hukm Chand, in his vernacular History, says that an early name of the town was Múla-tráng or Múlatáran. In present conventional Sanskrit usage both Múla-tráua and Múlaisthána seem to be used.

In this uncertainty as to the original form of the name, it is perhaps superfluous to inquire into its meaning. Writers of all kinds have, however, leapt into the breach; and we are told (*a*) that Múla represents the Malli, the tribe which fought Alexander; or (*b*) that Múla means 'origin,' and Multan means 'the original abode'; or (*c*) that Múla means 'centre,' and Multan 'the centre of the world'; or (*d*) that Múla is an equivalent of another word, and that other word is an equivalent of the sun: so that Multan is 'the place of the sun-god.'*

Albirúni quotes from Utpala, a native of Kashmir, who in his commentary on Viráhamihra's Sanhita is said to write: 'The names of countries change, and particularly in the yugas. So Multan was originally called Kasyapapura, then Hansapura, then Bágapura, then Sámbhapura, and then Múlasthána, *i.e.*, the original place, for múla means root, origin, and tána means place.' (Sach. Alb., i. 298) † The same legend is reproduced in a couplet known among the pandits of the city, which runs:—

Hanspur; Bhágpur; Shámpur; chautha pur Multán;
Pánchwan pur pahájkar thísí Arepur Sultán.

Hanspur is said to have been outside the Bohar gate, and Bhágpur near Bíbí Pákdáman, south of the city railway station; while Arepur, or the City on the High Ground, which is ultimately to be the Ruler, is said to represent the present cantonments.

The Arabs had further stories as to the city and its name. Ibn Khurdadba (died 912 A.D.) says Multan was called 'the Farj of the house of gold'; and Masúdi (died 956 A.D.) writes that the word Multan means 'the boundary of gold'. (Ell. Hist., i. 14, 21). 'Farj', according to Dowson, is here used in the sense of 'frontier'; but Raverty reads 'Farkh' or temple (J. B. A. S., 1892, p. 190). The references to gold are explained by the account of the old temple given below.

Visits of European travellers.

The general history of Multan city is much the same as that of the district at large (see Chapter II above). The city was from time to time visited by European travellers, and it is of some interest to read their various descriptions:—

Still and Crowther, who were here on 22nd May, 1614, say that Multan 'is a great and ancient citie within three course (kos) of Indus, but poore; for which cause they detain the caravans there divers dayes, eight, ten or twelve to benefit the citie.'

De Laet's description in his compilation is as follows:—'Multan provincia amplissima est et imprimis fertilis et mercimoniis valde opportuna, ob tria flumina quae illam rigant, et haud longe a metropoli confluunt. Metropolis

* These guesses are noted in Hukm Chand, p. 42, and Cunningham's Anc. Geog., pp. 233-4.

† Cunningham has an explanation for all these names, see his Anc. Geog., pp. 232-3. On the strength of the name Kasyapapura, he even goes so far as to identify Multan with the Kaspapuros of Hekataeus, the Kaspaturos of Herodotus and the Kaspeira of Ptolemy (Arch. Repts., v., 129. *cf.* Dr. M. L. Stein in J. A. S. B. 1899., 'Anc. Geog. of Kashmir,' pp. 9—12.

Chapter VI.

Towns, Municipalities and Cantonments.

Multan.

Visits of European travellers.

illius est Multhan, sive Moltan, quae distat à regia urbe Lohore centum et viginti cosas, per illam iter est mercatoribus, qui e Persia per Kandahar in provincias Indiae descendunt. Tria ista flumina sunt Raveo, Babat sive Behat, et denique Sind sive Indus,quae rapido cursu hanc provinciam secant. Precipuae hujus provinciae merces sunt saccharum, quod magna copia secundo flumine Indo versus Tattam navibus deportatur ; atque adeo adversus Lahorem Item gallae et opium, sulfur quoque et magna copia pannorum lineorum et gossypinorum ; plurimi denique hic aluntur cameli, et industria incolarum in arcubus conficiendis imprimis celebratur.*—(India Vera., p. 96.)

Tavernier in his Travels (Vol. ii., p. 57, ed. 1676) gives the following description of the place :—' Multan est une ville on il se fait quantité de toiles et on les transportoit toutes à Tata avant que les sables eussent gaté l'embouchure de la riviere : mais depuis que la passage a esté fermé pour les grands vaisseaux on les poste à Agra, et d' Agra à Surate, de même qu 'une partie des marchandises qui se font à Lahor. Comme cette voiture est fort chere il va maintenant peu de marchands faire des empletes tant à Multan qu'à Lahor, et même plusieurs ouvriers ont deserté, ce qui fait que les revenus du Roy sont aussi beaucoup diminuez en ces Provinces. Multan est le lieu ou sortent tous les Banianes qui viennent negocier dans la Perse, ou ils font le même métier des Juifs comme j 'ay dit aillieurs, et l'encherissent sur eux par leurs usures. Ils ont une loy particuliere qui leur permet en certains jours de l'année de manger des poules, et de ne prendre qu 'une femme entre deux on trois freres dont l'aîné est censé le pere des enfans. Il sort encore de cette ville—là quantité de baladins et de baladines qui s'epandent en divers lieux de la Perse.'

Thevenot in his Travels (Part iii, 1687, p. 55) describes Multan as follows :—' Multan is watered with many rivers that make it fertile. The capital town, which is also called Multan, was heretofore a place of very great Trade, because it is not far from the river Indus ; but seeing at present Vessels cannot go up so far, because the channel of that river is spoilt in some places, and the mouth of it full of shelves, the Traffick is much lessened, by reason that the charge of Land carriage is too great : However the Province yields plenty of Cotton, of which vast numbers of Cloaths are made. It also yields Sugar, Opium, Brimstone Galls and store of Camels, which are transported into Persia by Ghazna or Candahar or into the Indies themselves by Lahore ; but whereas the commodities went heretofore down the Indus at small charges, to Tatta, where the merchants, of several Countries came and bought them up, they must now be carried by land as far as Surrat, if they expect a considerable price for them.

'The town of Multan is by some Geographers attributed to Sinde, though it makes a Province by itself. It lies in twenty-nine degrees forty minutes North Latitude, and hath many good towns in its dependance, as Cozdar or Cordar Candavil, Sandur and others. It furnishes Hindustan with the finest Bows that, are to be seen in it, and the nimblest Dancers. The Commanders and Officers of these Towns are Mussulmans ; and by consequence, it may be said that most of the inhabitants are of the same Religion : But it contains a great many Banians also, for Multan is their chief rendezvous for trading into Persia, where they do what the Jews do in other places ; but they are far more cunning, for nothing escapes them and they let slip no occasion of getting the penny, however small it be . . . . . The richest merchants of the Indies are of them and such I have met in all places where I have been in that country. They are commonly very Jealous of their wives, who at Multan are fairer than the Men, but still of a very brown complexion, and love to Paint.

'At Multán there is another sort of Gentiles whom they call Catry. That town is properly their country, and from thence they spread all over the Indies ; but we shall treat of them when we come to speak of the other sects ; both the two have in Multan a Pagod of great consideration because of the affluence of people that come there to perform their devotion after their way ; and from all places of Multan, Lahore and other countries they come thither in pilgrimage. I know not the name of the idol that is worshipped there : the face is black, and it is cloathed in red leather ; it hath two pearls in place of eyes ; and the Emir or Governor of the country takes the offerings that are presented to it. To conclude, the town of Multan is but of small extent for a Capital, but it is

---

*** There is a quarter of the city still well known as the Mohalla Kamángran.**

Chapter VI.

Towns, Municipalities and Cantonments.
Multan.

pretty well fortified; and is very considerable to the Mogul, when the Persians are masters of Candahar as they are at present.

'What the Great Mogol receives yearly from this Province amounts to seventeen millions five hundred thousand livres.'

Visits of European travellers.

Elphinstone, who arrived here with his Kabul Mission on the 11th December 1808, writes:—'The city of Multan stands about four miles from the left bank of the Chenab or Acesines. It is above four miles and a half in circumference. It is surrounded with a high wall, between forty and fifty feet high, with towers at regular distances. It has also a citadel on a rising ground and several fine tombs, especially two with very high cupolas, ornamented with the painted and glazed tiles already noticed. The tombs are seen from a great distance all round the town. Multan is famous for its silks, and for a sort of carpet, much inferior to those of Persia. The country immediately round the city was very pleasing, fertile, well cultivated, and well watered from wells. The people were like those at Baháwalpur, except that there were more men, who looked like Persians, mixed with them; these, however, were individuals and chiefly horsemen.

'The mission remained for nineteen days in the neighbourhood of Multan, and as most of the party were out almost every day from seven or eight to three or four, shooting, hunting or hawking, we had good opportunities of observing the country. The land was flat and the soil excellent, but a large proportion of the villages were in ruins, and there were other signs of a well cultivated country going to decay; about a half was still cultivated and most abundantly watered by Persian wheels: the produce was wheat, millet, cotton, turnips, carrots, and indigo. The trees were chiefly neem and date, with here and there a peepul tree. The uncultivated country near the river was covered with a thick copse wood of tamarisk, mixed with a tree like a willow, about 20 feet high: at a distance from the river it was bare, except for scattered tufts of long grass, and here and there a date tree. The country abounded in game of all kinds. The weather was delightful during our stay: the thermometer, when at the lowest, was at 28° at sunrise: there were slight frosts in the night, but the days were rather warm.'—(Caubul i, 27-8).

Elphinstone's description of his meeting with the Nawáb has been already quoted in Chapter II above.

Masson, who was here twice in about 1827 A.D., writes (Travels, i, 394):—'It cannot be less than three miles in circumference and is walled in. Its bazars are large, but inconveniently narrow, and, I thought did not exhibit that bustle or activity which might be expected in a place of much reputed commerce. The citadel, if not a place of extreme strength, is one on which more attention seems to have been bestowed than is usual, and is more regular than any fortress I have seen, not constructed by European Engineers. It is well secured by a deep trench, neatly faced with masonry; and the defences of the gateway, which is approached by a drawbridge, are rather elaborate. The casualties of the siege it endured have not been made good by the Sikhs, consequently it has become much dilapidated since that period. It can scarcely be said to have a garrison, a weak party of soldiers being merely stationed as gurads at the entrance. Within the citadel are the only buildings of the city worth seeing—the battered palace of the late Khan and the Mahomedan shrine of Bahawal Hak. The latter,* with its lofty gumat or cupola, is the principal ornament of the place.

'Multan is said to have decreased in trade since it fell into the hands of the Sikhs, yet its bazars continued well and reasonably supplied with all articles of traffic and consumption. There are still numerous bankers, and manufacturers of silk and cotton goods. Its fabrics of shawls and lunghis are deservedly esteemed, and its brocades and tissues compete with those of Bahawalpur. It still supplies a portion of its fabrics to the Lohani merchants of Afghanistan, and has an extensive foreign trade with the regions west of the Indus.

* This refers evidently to the shrine of Rukn-i-Alam.

Chapter VI.

Towns. Municipalities and Cantonments.

Multan.

Visits of European travellers.

'The ruins around the city spread over a large space; and there is an amazing number of old Musalman graves, tombs, masjids and shrines; and, as all of them are held sacred, they would seem to justify the popular belief that one lakh or one hundred thousand saints lie interred within the hallowed vicinity. Many of these are substantial edifices, and, if not held to establish the saintly pretensions of the city, may be accepted as testimonies of its prosperity under the sway of the Mahomedan dynasties of India. North of the city is the magnificent and well preserved shrine of Shams Tabrezi. . . . . . . The gardens of Multan are abundant and well stocked with fruit trees, as mangos, oranges, citrons, limes, &c. Its date groves also yield much fruit, and vegetables are grown in great plenty. The inundations of the Ravi extend to the city, but it * is three miles distant, and has what is called a bunder, or port, in this instance expressive of a boat station, whence there is communication with the Indus, and, consequently, with the sea.

'The area enclosed within the walls being compactly built over, the city may be supposed to contain not less than eight or nine thousand houses, or from forty to forty-five thousand souls. At present a Brahman, Soband Mal,† resides at Multan as governor for Ranjit Singh, with the title of Subahdar; and his jurisdiction is extensive, comprising the southern parts of the Sikh kingdom from the Sutlej to the Indus. He has at his command a force of eight hundred Sikhs, under Gandar Singh, besides the governors sprinkled over the country. He is a popular ruler; and many anecdotes are related of his liberality and indulgence, even on matters connected with religion. The Sikh authority over the conquered provinces held by the Subahdar being firmly established, the administration is mild, owing partly, perhaps, to his personal character: and two Sikhs are located at every village and hamlet on the part of the Government. The peasantry make over a third of the produce of their lands; neither do they complain.'

Masson again halted at Multan on his way back from Lahore to Sindh: halting 'near the ziarat of Shams Tabrezi.'

Multan was visited on the 15th June 1831, by Lieutenant Alexander Burnes, who gives the following account of his visit (Travels in Bokhara, etc., i, 94-8):—'On the 15th we came in sight of the domes of Multan, which look well at a distance; and alighted in the evening at the Hoozooree Bagh, a spacious garden enclosed by a thin wall of mud, a mile distant from the city. The ground is laid out in the usual native style: two spacious walks cross each other at right angles, and are shaded by large fruit trees of the richest foliage. In a bungalow at the end of one of these walks, we took up our quarters, and were received by the authorities of the city in the same hospitable manner as at Shoojuabad. They brought a purse of 2,500 rupees, with 100 vessels of sweetmeats, and an abundant supply of fruit; we felt happy and gratified at the change of scene and civilities of the people.

'The city of Multan is described in Mr. Elphinstone's work on Cabool, and it may appear foreign to my purpose to mention it; but his mission was received here with great jealousy, and not permitted to view the interior of the town, or the fort. I do not hesitate, therefore, to add the following particulars drawn up after a week's residence. The city of Multan is upwards of three miles in circumference, surrounded by a dilapidated wall, and overlooked on the north by a fortress of strength. It contains a population of about 60,000 souls, one-third of whom may be Hindus: the rest of the population is Mahomedan, for though it is subject to the Seiks, their number is confined to the garrison, which does not exceed 500 men. The Afghans have left the country since they ceased to govern. Many of the houses evidently stand on the ruins of others; they are built of burnt brick, and have flat roofs: they sometimes rise to the height of six stories, and their loftiness gives a gloomy appearance to the narrow streets. The inhabitants are chiefly weavers and dyers of cloth. The silk manufacture of Multan is "kais," and may be had of all colours, and from the value of 20 to 120 rupees per piece; it is less delicate in texture than the "loongees" of Bhawulpoor. Ranjit Singh has with much propriety en-

* This refers doubtless to the Chenab.

† The Khatri Sáwan Mal is evidently intended.

Chapter VI.

Towns, Municipalities and Cantonments.

Multan.

Visits of European travellers.

couraged this manufacture since he captured the city; and by giving no other cloths at his court, has greatly increased their consumption; they are worn as sashes and scarfs by all the Seik Sardars. They are also exported to Khorasan and India, and the duties levied are moderate. To the latter country, the route by Jaysulmeer and Beecaneer is chosen in preference to that by Sinde, from the trade being on a more equitable footing. The trade of Multan is much the same as at Bhawulpoor, but is on a larger scale, for it has forty shroffs (money-changers), chiefly natives of Shikarpoor. The tombs of Multan are celebrated: one of them, that of Bawulhuq, who flourished upwards of 500 years ago, and was a contemporary of Sadee, the Persian poet, and is considered very holy; but its architecture is surpassed by that of his grandson, Rookn-i-Allum, who reposes under a massy dome sixty feet in height, which was erected in the year 1323 by the Emperor Tooghluck as his own tomb. Its foundation stands on higher ground than the summit of the fort wall; there is also a Hindoo temple of high antiquity, called Pyladpooree, mentioned by Thevenot in 1665.

'The fortress of Multan merits a more particular description; it stands on a mound of earth, and is an irregular figure of six sides, the longest of which, towards the north-west, extends for about 400 yards. The wall has upwards of thirty towers, and is substantially built of burnt brick, to the height of forty feet outside; but in the interior the space between the ground and its summit does not exceed four or five feet, and the foundations of some of the buildings overtop the wall, and are to be seen from the plain below. The interior is filled with houses, and till its capture by the Seiks in 1818 was peopled; but the inhabitants are not now permitted to enter, and a few mosques and cupolas, more substantially built than the other houses, alone remain among the ruins. The fortress of Multan has no ditch; the nature of the country will not admit of one being constructed; and Ranjit Singh has hitherto expended great sums without effect. The inundation of the Chenab, and its canals together with rain, render the vicinity of Multan a marsh, even in the hot weather, and before the swell of the river has properly set in the waters of last year remain. The walls of the fortress are protected in two places by dams of earth. The modern fort of Multan was built on the site of the old city by Moorad Bukhsh, the son of Shah Jehan, about the year 1640, and it subsequently formed the jagheer of that prince's brothers, the unfortunate Dara Shikoh and the renowned Aurungzebe. The Afghans seized it in the time of Ahmad Shah, and the Seiks wrested it from the Afghans, after many struggles, in 1818. The conduct of its governor during the siege deserves mention. When called on to surrender the keys, and offered considerate treatment, he sent for reply that they would be found in his heart, but he would never yield to an infidel; he perished bravely in the breach. His name, Moozuffur Khan, is now revered as a saint, and his tomb is placed in one of the holiest sanctuaries of Multan. The Seiks threw down the walls of the fort in many places, but they have since been thoroughly renewed or repaired; they are about six feet thick, and could be easily breached from the mounds that have been left in baking the bricks, which are within cannon range of the walls.

'The climate of Multan differs from that of the countries lower down the Indus; showers of rain are common at all seasons, and yet the dust is intolerable. For nine successive evenings we had a tornado of it from the westward, with lightning and distant thunder. Such storms are said to be frequent: they appear to set in from the Sooliman mountains, between which and the Indus the sand or dust is raised. The heat and dust of Multan have grown into a proverb, to which have been added, not unmeritedly, the prevalence of beggars, and the number of the tombs, in the following Persian couplet—

"Chuhar cheez hust, toohfujat-i-Multan,
Gird, guda, gurma wu goristan."

As far as I could judge, the satire is just: the dust darkened the sun; the thermometer rose in June to 100 of Fahrenheit in a bungalow artificially cooled, the beggars hunted us everywhere, and we trod on the cemeteries of the dead in whatever direction we rode.'

From the 6th to the 16th April, 1836, the traveller Vigne visited Multan, being entertained in the Bagh Begi, near the present city railway station.

Chapter VI.

Towns. Municipalities and Cantonments.

Multan.

Visits of European travellers.

'Upon my arrival in Multan,' he writes, 'I was domiciled in a Bara deri (twelve doors), or summer house, in the Bhagh-i-Begi, made by the Nawáb Sorfuras Khan, about thirty years ago; it was cool, well-shaded with orange trees, and laid out in the usual manner with reservoirs and fountains. The walks, intersecting each other at right angles, were raised above the parterres and flower-beds, that they might be dry when the latter are covered with water. There are numerous gardens in the environs of Multan, often formed around the shrine of some Mussulman faquir; and no man will quarrel with the fanaticism which has procured him shade and shelter in the climate of India. In the Hazuri Bagh, or the garden of the Presence, on the north side of the fort, I saw a large tree, the Mowul-Siri, grown, as they told me, from a cutting, which was originally brought from Mecca; but I do not vouch for the truth of the story. The principal shrine is that of the Faquir Shums-i-Tabriz.

'Multan supposed to be the capital of the Malli, of Alexander's historians, is a dusty and slovenly-looking city, containing about forty-five thousand inhabitants. The streets are narrow and the houses are two, three and four stories high; flat-roofed of course, and built of sun-burnt brick, with a washing of mud over them. The city wall, about five and thirty feet high, is of the same material, but in a decayed state. Around Multan, in various directions, are numerous hollow ways of no depth, connected by a short cut or hole through the bank when necessary. In the hot weather these are filled by means of a deep canal which communicates with the river Chenáb. The fort was built by Buran Bey, the son of the Emperor Jehan Guire upon a mound that rises in the north part of the city, of which it occupies a considerable portion: the city is about three miles in circumference.

'There are four gates, one of which is closed up by the order of the Maharajah Ranjit Singh. The walls of the fort, which in some places are sixty feet in height, with bastions at intervals of about seventy yards, are in good repair, but mounted with a total of only six or seven ill-cast native guns. They have been surrounded by a ditch, in many places entirely destroyed. In the interior of the fort is the shrine of Nar Singhpureo, a Hindoo saint, and two lofty and spacious buildings erected over the tombs of two Mussulman saints of great celebrity—Bhawul-Huk and Shah Allum. The ground plan of one is an octagon with a diagonal of about eighteen yards, and buttresses at the angles. The lower part of the building is surmounted with another octagon and a dome rising to the height of a hundred feet. The whole of the outside is tastefully ornamented with coloured tiles, chiefly blue, in imitation of those of China. They were originally used in ornamenting the public buildings of Multan, and were made there; but there is now no other manufactory of them nearer than Delhi. Ranjit Singh's cannon appear to have told with great effect upon the roofs of the principal mosques. Most of the buildings of the fort were destroyed after the capture of the city, with the exception of these shrines and the house of Mozuffer Khan, which stands on the most elevated part of it and commands an extensive view. This brave man, the last independent Nawáb of Multan, lies buried in the vestibule of Bhawul-Huk. For twelve years he resolutely opposed the inroads of the Sikhs; but the fort was at last taken in the year one thousand eight hundred and eighteen by Kurruk Singh, the only son of Runjit, and present ruler of the Punjab. Mozuffer Khan fought in person at the Koderi gate of the fort, and at last fell mortally wounded, after a desperate resistance. When Ranjit Singh visited his tomb afterwards, he is reported to have made a speech somewhat of the same nature with that uttered by Napoleon at the tomb of Frederick of Prussia.

'Multan is famous for its silk manufactures. I visited the house of a weaver; it presented a very different appearance from the atelier of a shawl-maker in Kashmir. There I have seen twenty men at work in one room; here there are seldom more than three, who sit in a hollow in the ground, by which means their hands are brought down even with the tanee or woof, which is extended near the floor and fastened to a post not more than a foot in height. This apparatus takes up a great deal of room whereas the frame of the shawl-worker, which is perpendicular, does not occupy a space of more than six square yards. Seven hundred maunds of raw silk are brought to Multan every year by the Lohanis chiefly from Bokhara and Turkistan: these are manufactured in one hundred and fifty workshops. One man will finish an ordinary kaish or piece of silk in

Chapter VI.

Towns, Municipalities and Cantonments.

Multan.

Visits of European travellers.

six days, perhaps three yards long and a foot and a half wide, taking eight days previously for the arrangement of the weaving apparatus. A very handsome kaish is finished in sixteen days. That of the red colour is most valuable : it is dyed with cochineal, which is brought from either Bombay or Bokhara ; that from Bombay is one rupee a seer, about a shilling a pound. Multan is also famous for its carpets and embroidery.

'There are from a thousand to fifteen hundred maunds of tobacco produced around Multan annually. The best, which is called suruk, or the red, is sold for six annas, equal to about nine pence a seer. Inferior kinds are sold from four to two annas a seer.

'I exchanged visits with Sáwan Mal, the Governor of Multan. Runjit Singh has been heard to say that he was one of the best officers in his service. Whilst I was at Multan, he sent me a kilaat, or dress of honour, together with an elephant and a couple of horses for my use, as an especial mark of his favour. He is a thin man, with a good tempered and, for a native, a superior expression of countenance, and is said to have distinguished himself at the taking of the city. His government was well spoken of by the Lohani merchants who gave him an excellent character for justice in his dealings with them. He is the arch opponent of the minister, Rajah Dhihan Singh, and his brothers, Gulab and Sucheyt Sing, whose influence at the court of Runjit is usually all powerful.

'On the eleventh of April, the Besak, a Hindoo festival, took place in the morning. I rode to the river, about three miles distant. The country which intervenes between the city and its banks was looking very green and picturesque, considering it is entirely flat: a great deal of land was under cultivation and bearing very fine crops of wheat. Well-planted gardens were always in sight ; and date and palm trees standing singly or in groups were frequently seen amongst the numerous topes or clumps of mulberry, mango, banian, peepul, and acacia trees. By the roadside were the vendors of wreaths and fans made from the flags that grew on the water's edge. In the afternoon there was a fair in the Bagh Ali Akber, a garden with a shrine of a fakir of that name. I saw the Multanis returning, every species of conveyance had, of course, been put in requisition : horses, mules, donkeys, carrying one or two persons ; camels, each bearing seven or eight women and children, disposed on either side in trucks ; and unlicensed bullock carts, with cargoes of giggling dancing girls. The number of persons who will stow themselves in these vehicles is quite astounding ; all were in their holiday dresses. The Hindoo was to be distinguished by his caste-mark on his forehead, his rose-coloured turban, and red flowing trousers. The Multan Mussulman usually wore a white dress of the same kind of pattern. The Sikh, generally a Sepahi, was recognised by his sword, matchlock and accoutrements, his scanty turban, his earrings, his would-be knee-breeches, or his close-fitting ill-made trousers.' (Ghazni, p. 14).

In June 1837, Lieutenant Robert Leech, of the Bombay Engineers, and Dr. Percival Lord, who were attached to Burnes' Kabul Mission, came over to Multan on their way from Dera Ghází Khan to Dera Ismail Khan. At Multan they gathered much important information ; and although 'they experienced some difficulties, their stay there was by no means disagreeable.'—(Burnes' Cabool, 1842, p. 88 ; Wood's Oxus, 2nd edition, p. 51.)

After this Multan seems to have been somewhat sparingly visited by Europeans until the siege of 1848-49, which has been already described in Chapter II, above.

Multan, it may here be mentioned, has the honor of being the birth-place of three distinguished men in history. The Delhi Emperor Muhammad Tughlak Sháh is said to have been born about the end of the thirteenth century in a hamlet now lying between the Lohari gate and the civil lines church, which is still known by the name of 'Toleh Khan'—a corruption, it is said, of 'Tughlak Khan.' Early in the fifteenth century, too, was born,

Chapter VI.

Towns, Municipalities and Cantonments.

Multan.

Visits of European travellers.

at a house known as the 'Khizánawala Makán,' near the Hussain Gáhí. the Emperor Bahlol Lodi, and his birth, it is said, was prematurely occasioned by a house falling upon, and, at the same time, killing his mother. Lastly, it was in the Saddozái Kirri, in the suburbs of Multan, as nearly as may be in the spot nowocupied by the house facing the Sessions Court, that Ahmad Sháh Abdáli, the first of the Durani sovereigns of Afghanistan, is said to have been born somewhere towards the end of the 17th or beginning of the 18th century.

The chief features of the town will now be noticed under three heads, according as they lie (*i*) in the fort, (*ii*) in the city, and (*iii*) outside the city.

(I).—The Fort.

The fort.

The fort is built on a detached mound of earth separated from the city by the bed of an old branch of the Rávi river. As regards the date of the foundation of the fort, we have no historical evidence, and our conclusions can be based only on the results of a well sunk by Sir Alexander Cunningham when he was here in 1853. The well was just outside the walls of the temple of Prahladpuri, and the results are thus given in a tabular form :—

Depth, feet.	*Probable date.*	*Discoveries.*
1, 2	1700	Upper stratum ; English broken bottles ; pieces of iron shells ; leaden bullets.
3	1600	......
4, 5	1500	Glazed pottery and glazed tiles.
6	1400	Small bricks, 6″ × 4″ × 1″.
7, 8	1300	......
9	1200	......
10, 11	1100	* Coin of Muiz-ud-din Kaikobad, A.D. 1286-89. Glazed blue chiragh or oil lamp.
12	1000	Coin of Sri Samanta Deva, Circa A.D. 900.
13, 14	950, 900	Bricks 11″ × 6½″ × 2″. Glazed tiles and pottery ceased.
15, 16, 17	800, 700	Red ashes 2 feet deep. } Bricks 11″ × 6½″ × 2″.
18	600	Black ashes 6 to 9 inches. } Bricks 11″ × 6½″ × 2″.
19, 20	500	......
21	400	Fragments of large bricks 14″ × 11″ × 2½″.
22, 23	300	......
24	200	......
25, 26	100	......
27	B.C.	......

* *Sic.* in orig.

The fort.

Depth, feet.	*Probable date.*	*Discoveries.*
28 } 29 }	100	......
30	200	2 feet of ashes and burnt earth. Silk-spinner's ball. Shoemaker's sharpening stone. Copper vessel with some 200 coins.
31 } 32 }	300	
33	400	... ..
34 } 35 }	500	......
36	600	Natural soil unmixed.
37 } 38 }	700	
39	800	
40		......

—(See *Arch. Sur. Reps.*, v, 127.)

The ashes in the 8th century A.D. may, according to Cunningham, represent the capture of Multan by Mahomed Kasim in A.D. 702, and those in the 4th century B.C. the supposed capture by Alexander in B.C. 326.

While it was intact the circuit of the fort was 6,600 feet, or 1¼ miles, and it had 46 bastions, including two flanking towers at each of the four gates. The four gates were (i) the De or Deh gate on the west, which is the one usually entered by visitors. The name is said by Cunningham to represent 'Dewal,' the gate having in former times led straight to the Dewal or temple inside the fort, which will be described below.* (ii) The Khizri gate, on the north-east, so called because it led most directly on to the river, which, like other water, is under the protection of the saint Khwaja Khizr.† (iii) The Sikhi gate on the south-east. The name of the gate may or may not be connected, as has been suggested, with the neighbouring town of Sikha, so often mentioned by the early Arab Historians; but it is as likely to mean merely the 'Spiked gate.' It is said that the doors of the gate were armed with projecting spikes to prevent their being battered by elephants. It was at this gate that the murderous attack was made on Mr. Agnew in 1848. The gate has now disappeared, but a road leads past it to the shrines of Prahladpuri and Bahawal Hakk. (iv) The Rehri gate opposite the Hussain Gáhi, so called because of the deep depression below it; this has now practically disappeared. There is now an inner wall in the fort, and the enclosure formed by this wall is accessible only by the Det gate and by a new gate leading towards the tomb of Bahawal Hakk.

For a year or two after annexation, and until the present cantonment was laid out, the greater part of the garrison was

* It should, at the same time, be observed that none of the gates is so far from the site of the old temple as this one. One of the drains in the centre of the fort is still known as Mámú De's drain.

† *Cf.* the Khizri gate of Lahore City. Cunningham suggests that the gate was named after Khizr Khan, a governor of the 14th Century mentioned in chapter II above.

Chapter VI.

Towns, Municipalities and Cantonments.

Multan.

The fort.

stationed in the fort: but the fort has now lost its military importance. The British troops were withdrawn from it, and the fort handed over to the civil authorities in March 1891. It was, however, again taken over by the military in January 1893, and is still under military control; the main buildings being kept up by the Military Works Department.

The sun temple.

The earliest and most celebrated of the buildings in the fort is one of which there is now not a trace remaining, *viz.*, the temple known to the early Mahomedans as the Temple of the Sun. This temple is mentioned by Hiuen Tsang in 641 A.D. It was apparently destroyed in the 11th century, but it was again restored, and it seems to have been still standing in Theve not's time (after 1666 A.D.) It appears to have been shortly afterwards destroyed by Aurangzeb, and its place seems to have been taken by a Jama Masjid. This in its turn was made by the Sikhs into a powder magazine, and this magazine was blown up by a shell from the British batteries in the siege of 1848. Its ruins were seen by Cunningham in 1853 'in the very middle of the fort.' According to the map attached to the Archæological Survey Report of 1872-73, the building must have been just to the west of the place where the obelisk in memory of Agnew and Anderson now stands. The following are the accounts given of the temple by the several writers who mention it:—

Hiuen Tsang, who was in Multan in 641 A.D., writes:—

'The country is about 4,000 li in circuit; the capital town is some 30 li round. It is thickly populated. The establishments are wealthy. This country is in dependence on the Kingdom of the Cheka (Tso-Kiá). The soil is rich and fertile. The climate is soft and agreeable. The manners of the people are simple and honest; they love learning, and honour the virtuous. The greater part sacrifice to the spirits; few believe in the law of Buddha. There are about ten sangharamas mostly in ruins; there are a few priests, who study indeed, but without any wish to excel. There are eight Deva temples, in which sectaries of various classes dwell. There is a temple dedicated to the sun, very magnificent and profusely decorated. The image of the Sun-deva is cast in yellow gold and ornamented with rare gems. Its divine insight is mysteriously manifested, and its spiritul powers made plain to all. Women play their music, light their torches, offer their flowers and perfumes to honour it. This custom has been continued from the very first. The kings and high families of the five Indies never fail to make their offerings of gems and precious stones (to the Deva). They have founded a home of mercy (happiness), in which they provide food and drink, and medicines for the poor and sick, affording succour and sustenance. Men from all countries come here to offer up their prayers; there are always some thousands doing so. On the four sides of the temple are tanks with flowering groves, where one can wander about without restraint.'—(BEAL: *Records of Western Countries*, HIUEN TSANG, ii, 274).

Wilford in As. Res., xi, 70, quotes a story from the Bhavishya Purana to the effect that Samba, son of Krishna, crossed to the north of the Chenab, and soon after erected a golden statue to the sun.

Abu Zaid (about 916 A.D.) mentions 'the idol called Multan' which, he says, is situated 'in the environs of Massura'; and says that aloes from Kamrun (Assam) are used by the ministers of the temple as incense.—(ELL. i, 11.)

Chapter VI.

Towns, Municipalities and Cantonments.

Multan.

The sun temple.

According to the Chach-náma (written originally before 750 A.D.) Muhammad Kasim, when he took Multán in 712 A.D., was told of a hoard buried in old times by Jibawín (v.l Jaswin, Jasúr), a chief of the city and a descendant of the Rai of Kashmir, who 'made a reservoir, on the eastern side of Multan, which was 100 yards square. In the middle of it he built a temple 50 yards square, and under it a chamber in which he concealed 40 copper jars, each of which was filled with a fine gold dust. 'Over it there is a temple in which there is an idol made of red gold, and trees are planted round the reservoir.' Kasim went there and found 'an idol made of gold, and its two eyes were bright red rubies. He had it taken up and obtained 13,200 mans of gold.—(ELL., i, 203.)

Al Biladuri (883-4), in speaking of Muhammad Kasim's expedition, says he captured the temple ministers. 'The Mussulmans found there much gold in a chamber 10 cubits long by 8 broad, and there was an aperture above through which the gold was poured into the chamber... The temple (budd) of Multan received rich presents and offerings, and to it the people of Sind resorted as to a place of pilgrimage. They circumambulated it and shaved their heads and beards. They conceived that the image was that of the prophet Job.—God's peace be on him!'—(ELL. i, 122.)

Istakhri (about 951 A.D.) mentions the idol and the number of pilgrims who went to worship it. 'The temple of the idol is a strong edifice situated in the most populous part of the city in the market of Multan below the bazar of the ivory dealers and the shops of the copper-smiths. The idol is placed under a cupola in the midst of the building, and the ministers of the idol and those devoted to its service dwell round the cupola. In Multan there are no men, either of Hind or Sind, who worship idols except those who worship this idol in this temple. The idol has a human shape and is naked, with its legs bent in a quadrangular posture on a throne made of brick and mortar. Its whole body is covered with a red skin like morocco leather, and nothing but its eyes are visible. Some believe that the body is made of wood, some deny this, but the body is not allowed to be uncovered to decide the point. The eyes of the idol are precious gems, and its head is covered with a crown of gold. It sits in a quadrangular position on the throne, its hands resting upon its knees with the fingers closed, so that only four can be counted. When the Mahomedans make war upon them and endeavour to seize the idol, the inhabitants bring it out, pretending that they will break it and burn it, upon this the Mahomedans retire, otherwise they would destroy Multan."—(ELL. i, 27.)

Masudi (died 957 A. D.) says Multan contains the idol known by the name Multan; and mentions the pilgrimages to it and the rich present of aloes made to it. 'When the unbelievers march against Multan, and the faithful do not feel themselves strong enough to oppose them, they threaten to break the idol and their enemies immediately withdraw.'—(ELL. i, 23.)

Ibn Haukal (976 A. D.) copies Istakhri word for word.—(ELL. i, 35.)

Abu Rihan Albiruni (970-1038) writes:—

'A famous idol of theirs was that of Multan, dedicated to the sun and therefore called Aditya. It was of wood and covered with red Cordova leather: its two eyes were two red rubies... When Mahomed Ibn Alkasim Ibn Almunabbih conquered Multan, he inquired why the town had become so very flourishing and so many treasures had there been accumulated; and then he found out that this idol was the cause, for there came pilgrims from all sides to visit it. Therefore he thought it best to leave the the idol where it was, but hung a piece of cow's flesh on its neck by way of mockery. On the same place a mosque was built. When then the Karmatians occupied Multan, Jalaun Ibn Shaiban, the usurper, broke the idol into pieces and killed its priests. He made his mansion, which was a castle built of brick, on an elevated place, the mosque instead of the old mosque, which he ordered to be shut, from hatred against anything that had been done under the Caliphs of the house of Umayya. When afterwards the blessed prince Mahomed swept away their rule from these countries he made again the old mosque the place of the Friday worship, and the second one was left to decay. At present it is only a barn floor where branches of Hinna (*Lawsinia inermis*) are bound together.'—(SACHAU, i, 116.)

Again, talking of places of Hindu pilgrimage, the author says: 'They used to visit Multan before its idol temple was destroyed.'—(SACHAU, i, 148.)

Chapter VI.

Towns, Municipalities and Cantonments.

Multan.

The sun temple.

Idrisi (about 1103 A.D.) copies a good deal from Istakhri. He says, however of the idol: 'It is in the human form, with four sides, and is sitting on a seat made of bricks and plaster. . . It is, as we have said, square, and its arms below the elbows seem to be four in number. The temple of the idol is situated in the middle of Multan, in the most frequented bazar. It is a dome-shaped building. The upper part of the dome is gilded, and the dome and the gates are of great solidity. The columns are very lofty, and the walls coloured. . . . . Being ignorant of the name of the man who set it up, the inhabitants content themselves with saying it is a wonder.—(ELL. i. 81)

Kazwini (about 1275 A.D.) says of Multan: 'The infidels have a large temple there and a great idol (budd). The chief mosque is near this temple . . . . All this is related by Misar bin Mahallil . . . The same author says the summit of the temple is 300 cubits, and the height of the idol is 20 cubits. The houses of the servants and devotees are round the temple, and there are no idol worshippers in Multan besides those who dwell in those precincts. . . . Ibn-ul-Fakih says that an Indian came to this idol and placed upon his head a crown of cotton daubed with pitch: he did the same with his fingers, and having set fire to it stayed before the idol until it was burnt.'—(ELL. i, 96.)

No other mention of the idol is made before that of Thevenot, the French traveller, who wrote in 1687, and whose description has been quoted above.

The Prahladpuri temple.

On the north edge of the fort is the temple of Prahládpuri, which takes its name from Prahlád, the hero of the story of the Lion or Narsingh Avatár of the god Vishnu. The story tells how this country was at one time under the sway of a Raja named Harnákhash (Hiranya Kasipu), a local Mezentius, who contemned the gods and forbade the doing of homage in their name. His son, the pious Prahlád Bhagat, refused to obey his orders, and the tyrant ordered a pillar of gold to be heated with fire, so that the son might be bound to it. When, however, twilight came, and the servants attempted to bind the pious Prahlád to the pillar, the pillar burst in twain, and out sprang the god Vishnu in the form of a Man-Lion, who at once proceeded to lay the king across his knees and rip him open with his claws, in the manner which we see at times so vividly portrayed in the pictures which adorn the walls of Hindu shops and dwellings.*

The temple, lying, as it does, so close alongside the shrine of Baháwal Hakk, is probably an old one, † but it possesses no proper Mahatmya, or sacred chronicle, to show its previous history, the only book of the kind owned by the priests being the Narsing-puran, which is said to contain no local allusions. The temple is noticed by Burnes in his account of Multan quoted above. It was unroofed, and otherwise damaged, by the explosion of the magazine during the siege of 1848. When Cunningham was in Multan in 1853, it was 'quite deserted,' but subsequently it was repaired by subscription, and a new

* This king had, after the style of Balder, received a promise that he would be killed neither in heaven nor on earth, neither by night nor by day, &c.

† Some say that the original Narsingh temple was here, and that the Emperor Sher Shah replaced it by a mosque known as the 'bara-thambawala' from its 12 columns. This mosque having fallen in, the Prahládpuri temple was built on its ruins.

Chapter VI.

Towns, Municipalities and Cantonments.

Multan.

The Prahládpuri temple.

image of the Narsingh Avatár was set up in it. It appears that there was formerly an entrance to the temple through the shrine of Baháwal Hakk, but during the years in which the temple was disused this was closed. In 1810 the Hindús raised the height of the spire of the temple, a proceeding which led to protests from the guardians of the neighbouring shrine, and subsequently to a good deal of ill-feeling, which ultimately ended in a serious riot in the city.

The shrine was well supported by the Sikh Government, and still retains some mafi lands. The mohant also receives, or till lately received, an annual contribution from every shop in the city. There is a fair at the Narsingh Chaudas in Jeth (in May), which lasts from 3 to 6 P.M.: towards end of the fair the people used to throw cucumbers at each other, and the proceedings used to be a bit noisy, but of late years they have become more decorous.

Immediately to the west of the Prahládpuri temple is the shrine of Baháwal Hakk.

Shrine of Baháwal Hakk.

Shaikh Baha-ud-din Zakaria, otherwise known as Baháwal Hakk, was, according to Abdul Fazl (Jarret iii., 362), 'the son of Wajih-ud-din Muhammad-b-Kamál-ud-din Ali Shah Kurayshi, and was born at Kot Karor,* near Multan, in A.H. 565 (A.D. 1169-70). His father died when he was a child: he grew in wisdom, and studied in Túrán and Irán. He received his doctrine from Shaykh Shihab-ud-din Suhrawardi at Baghdad, and reached the degree of vice-gerent. He was on terms of great friendship with Shaikh Farid Shakkarganj, and lived with him for a considerable time. Shaikh (Fakr-ud-din) Iráki and Mir Husayni were his disciples.' Baháwal Hakk was for many years the great saint of Multan, and has still a very extensive reputation in the South-West Punjab and in Sindh. One of his miracles was the preservation of a sinking boat, and the boatmen of the Chenab and Indus still invoke Baháwal Hakk as their patron saint in times of difficulty. His death is thus described by Abulfazl: 'On the 7th of Zafar A.H. 665 (7th November 1266), an aged person of grave aspect sent in to him a sealed letter by the hand of his son Sadr-ud-din. He read it and gave up the ghost; and a loud voice was heard from the four corners of the town: "Friend is united to friend" (Dost ba dost rasid).†

The shrine is said to have been built by the saint himself, and according to Cunningham, there is only one other specimen of the architecture of this exact period, and that is at Sonepat. The tomb is thus described. 'The lower part of the tomb is a square of 51 feet 9 inches outside. This is surmounted by an

* This is Karor in the Leiah Tahsil of Mianwali.

† Ferishta also gives an account of the saint.

Chapter VI.

Towns. Municipalities and Cantonments.

Multan.

Shrine of Baháwal Hakk.

octagon, about one-half of the height of the square, above which there is a hemispherical dome. The greater part of the building is a mass of white plaster; but on the eastern side there are still existing some fairly preserved specimens of diaper ornaments in glazed tiles.'* The tomb was so much damaged during the siege of 1848 as to become an almost complete ruin. A proposal was made in 1850 by the Local Government that 10,000 rupees should be granted for the repair of this tomb and that of Rukn-i-Alam, but the proposal was not sanctioned, and the shrine was repaired by means of subscriptions collected by the then Makhdum, Shah Mahmud.†

The shrine contains, besides the tomb of the saint and many of his descendants, that of his son Sadr-ud-din. The story is that Baháwal Hakk left enormous sums of wealth to his son, but that Sadr-ud-din, on coming into possession of it, at once distributed the whole of it to the poor, saying that, although his father had sufficiently conquered himself to have no fear of an improper use of it, he himself, not being so advanced in sanctity, dreaded the temptation.‡ According to Abdul Fazl he died in A.H. 709 (A.D. 1309).§

Opposite the door of the shrine is a small grave adorned with blue tiles, which covers the body of the brave Nawab Muzaffar Khan, who died sword in hand at the gate of the shrine in 1818, defending himself against the assault of the Sikh invaders. On the tomb is the following fine inscription (now nearly obliterated):—

Shujá' was ibn-us Shujá' wa Hájí
Amír-i-Multán zahe Muzaffar.
Ba roz-i-maidán ba tegh o bázú
Che hamla áwurd chún ghazanfar.
Chú surkh-rú shud ba súe jannat
Baguft Riswán 'Biyá Muzaffar.' (*i. e.*, A. H. 1233.)

Of which the following (though missing some of the points of the original) may be given as a translation:—

The brave, son of the brave, and Háji,
Amir of Multan, O brave Muzaffar,
In the day of battle—with arm and sword—
How lion-like was his onslaught;
When, with face aflame, he set out for Paradise.
The porter of Heaven's gate cried; 'Come, O! Muzaffar.'

---

* Archæological Survey Reports, v, 131.

† See Griffin's Punjab Chiefs, new edition, ii, 87.

‡ Ferishta, quoted by Jarret.—Ain iii, 362.

§ Jarret.—Ain iii, 365.

Chapter VI.

Towns, Municipalities and Cantonments.

Multan

Shrine of Bahawal Hakk.

In these precincts are buried also Shahnawaz Khan, son of Muzaffar Khan, who was killed with his father; the celebrated Makhdum Shah Mahmud, the late Makhdum Baháwal Bakhsh, and most of the eminent members of the Koreshi family. On the eastern wall of the shrine is an inscription commemorating the repair of the dome by one Pir Mahomed, of Thanesar, and over the western gateway is an interesting inscription regarding the exemption of grain from taxation in the year 1762-63 by Ali Mahomed Khan, Khákwani, then Subadár of Multan. The inscription may be translated as follows:—

In the days of the Duráni Emperor,
When every man's hunger was satisfied with bread,
In every place was bread cheap in price,
Nor was there famine save in Multan alone. *
No one dieth save from hunger,
And exaction of grain dues hath made high the price of food.
Now for God's sake and for the sake of the friend of God,
By the aid of the Syads, his noble offspring
And by the grace of the countenance of the great Pir Mahbúb Subháni,
Who in saintness exceedeth all other saints;
By the aid of the countenance of the great Makhdum Bahá-ud-din
And for the sake of Rukn-i-Alam (know this):
And for the praise of Ahmad Shah Abdáli,
From whom the kings of the earth receive their crowns;
Alí Mahomed Khan, the servant of God,
Hath remitted the dues upon grain.
If any Subadár take any due on grain
May his wife be three times utterly divorced.
A voice from heaven cried, in the name of the All-Pure God,
'The year of this event is The eternal Giver of Treasure.'

(*i. e.*, A.H. 1176.)

Shrine of Rukn-i-Alam.

On the south-west side of the fort is the magnificent tomb of Rukn-i-Alam, *alias* Rukn-ud-din Abul Fatteh, the grandson of the saint Baháwal Hakk. Rukn-i-Alam was a man of great religious and political influence in the days of the Tughlak sovereigns, and was in Multan when the city was visited by the traveller Ibn Batuta, in 1334. 'Shaykh Rukn-ud-din,' says Abul Fazl (Jarret, iii, 365), 'was the son of Sadr-ud-din Arif, and the successor of his eminent grandfather. At the time when Sultan Kutb-ud-din (Mubarak Shah Khilji (A.H. 717, A.D., 1317) regarded Shaykh Nizám-ud-din with disfavour, he summoned Shaykh Rukn-ud-din from Multan in the hope of disturbing his influence. On his arrival near Delhi he met Shaykh Nizam-ud-din. Kutb-ud-din, on receiving the Shaykh (Rukn-ud-din), asked him "Who among the people of the city was foremost in going out to meet him?" He replied: "The most eminent person of his age." By the happy answer he removed the king's displeasure.'

* The people in the Punjab generally having apparently recovered from the great famine of A. D. 1759-60.

Chapter VI.

Towns, Municipalities and Cantonments.

Multan.

As regards the teaching of the saint, Griffin writes: 'From what remains of his doctrines, scattered through the works of his disciples, it appears that he taught a modified form of metempsychosis. He asserted that at the day of judgment the wicked would rise in bestial forms suitable to the characters which they had borne on earth: the carnal man would rise a leopard; the licentious man a goat; the glutton, a pig; and so on through the animal kingdom.'—(*Punjab Chiefs*, new edition, ii, 85.)

Shrine of Rukn-i-Alam.

The shrine is thus described by Cunningham *:—'This fine building is an octagon of 51 feet 9 inches diameter inside, with perpendicular walls 41 feet 4 inches high and 13 feet 3 inches thick, supported by sloping towers at the angles. This is surmounted by a smaller octagon of 25 feet 8 inches exterior side, and 26 feet 10 inches in height, which leaves a narrow passage all round the top of the lower story for the Muazzin to call the faithful to prayers from all sides. Above this is a hemispherical dome of 58 feet exterior diameter. The total height of the tomb, including a plinth of 3 feet, is just 2 inches over 100 feet. But as the building stands on the high ground on the north-western edge of the fort, its total height above the country is 150 feet. This great height makes it one of the most striking objects on approaching Multan, as it can be seen for a distance of 12 or 15 miles all round.

'The Rukn-i-Alam is built entirely of red brick, bounded with beams of sisam wood, which are now much decayed. The whole of the exterior is elaborately ornamented with glazed tile panels, and string courses and battlements. The only colours used are dark blue, azure, and white, but these are contrasted with the deep red of the finely polished bricks; and the result is both effective and pleasing. These mosaics are not like those of later days,—mere plane surfaces—but the patterns are raised from half an inch to two inches above the back ground. This mode of construction must have been very troublesome; but its increased effect is undeniable, as it unites all the beauty of variety of colour with the light and shade of a raised pattern. In the accompanying plate I have given a few specimens of these curious and elaborate panels.

'The interior of the Rukn-i-Alam was originally plastered and painted with various ornaments, of which only a few traces now remain. The sarcophagus of Rukn-ud-din is a large plain mass of brick-work covered with mud plaster. About one hundred of his descendants lie around him under similar masses of brick and mud, so that the whole of the interior is now filled with rows of these unsightly mounds.

'There are several curious stories about this tomb, some of which would appear to have originated in the fact that it was first built by Tughlak for himself, and was afterwards given up by his son, Mohammad Tughlak, for the last resting-place of Rukn-ud-din. Tughlak first began to build close to the tomb of Baháwal Hakk, when a voice was heard from the tomb of the saint saying. "You are treading on my body." Another site was then chosen at a short distance when again the saint's voice was heard, saying, "You are treading on my knees." A third site, still farther off, was next taken, when a third time the voice was heard, saying, "You are treading on my feet." Tughlak then selected the present site at the very opposite end of the fort; and as the voice was not heard again, the tomb was finished. Some say that the voice was heard only once, exclaiming, "You are treading on my feet."

'Another story is, that Rukn-ud-din, who was originally buried in the tomb of his grandfather Baháwal Hakk, removed himself to his present tomb after his burial. It would appear from the account of Ibn Batuta that the mysterious death of Tughlak was really planned by his son Mohammad, and carried out by Malik Záda, the inspector of buildings, who afterwards became the chief Wazir of Mohammad, with the title of Khwaja-i-Jahan. The Multan saint was present at the catastrophe, and Ibn Batuta's account was obtained direct from him. His words are: "Shekh Rukn-ud-din told me that he was then near the Sultan, and that the Sultan's favourite son Mahmud was with them. Thereupon Mohammad came and said to the Shekh: 'Master, it is now time for afternoon

---

* Archæological Reports, v. 132-4.

Chapter VI.

Towns, Municipalities and Cantonments.

Multan.

Shrine of Rukn-i-Alam

prayer, go down and pray.' 'I went down,' said the Shekh, 'and they brought the elephants upon one side, as the prince and his confidant had arranged; when the animals passed along that side, the building fell down upon the Sultan and his son Mahmud. I heard the noise,' continued the Shekh, 'and I returned without having said my prayers. I saw that the building had fallen. The Sultan's son Mohammad ordered pickaxes and shovels to be brought to dig and seek for his father, but he made signs for them not to hurry, and the tools were not brought till after sunset. Then they began to dig, and they found the Sultan, who had bent over his son to save him from death."

'Here we see the anxiety of Mohammad for the safety of Rukn-ud-din, as testified by the saint himself, and at the same time we learn from his trustworthy eye witness that Mohammad made signs to the people not to hurry in bringing tools to extricate his father. His anxiety for the safety of the saint betrays his guilty intentions towards his father; and I think that the people of Multan are right in their belief that the great tomb at Multan was given by Mohammad to Rukn-ud-din as a bribe to keep him quiet regarding the death of Tughlak Shah.'

This shrine and that of Baháwal Hakk are enlivened at times by the visits of bands of pilgrims from Sindh and elsewhere, who march in with flags, crying out in chorus : "Dam Baháwal Hakk! Dam Baháwal Hakk!" The official custodian of the shrines is the Makhdum, Hassan Bakhsh, a viceregal darbari, an account of whose family is given in Chapter III above. Although the fort is closed to outsiders at night, the 'Mujawars' are allowed to reside at the Rukn-i-Alam shrine, and the Makhdum has a license to come in at any time of the day or night. There are considerable tracts of country held in jagir for the benefit of the shrines, and these buildings, more than any others, have contributed to the fame of Multan in Mussalman countries.

Memorial obelisk.

In the centre of the fort is an obelisk erected to the memory of Messrs. Agnew and Anderson, who were murdered at the Idgah in 1848 (see Chapter II above). The obelisk is about 50 feet high, with five steps to a pedestal 5 feet high. On a white tablet, on the west face of the pedestal, there is an inscription written by Sir Herbert Edwardes in the taste of the time, which runs as follows :—

Beneath this Monument
Lie the Remains
of
PATRICK ALEXANDER VANS AGNEW,
of the Bengal Civil Service, and
WILLIAM ANDERSON,
Lieutenant, 1st Bombay Fusilier Regiment,
Assistants to the Resident at Lahore,
Who being deputed by the Government to
Relieve, at his own request,
Diwan Mulraj, Viceroy of Multan,
Of the fortress and authority which he held
Were attacked and wounded by the Garrison
On the 19th April, 1848,

Chapter VI.

Towns, Municipalities and Cantonments.

Multan.

Memorial obelisk.

And, being treacherously deserted by the Sikh Escort,
Were on the following day,
In flagrant breach of national faith and hospitality,
Barbarously murdered
In the Edgah under the walls of Mooltan
Thus fell
These two young public servants
At the ages of 25 and 28 years,
Full of high hopes, rare talents,
And promise of future usefulness,
Even in their death
Doing their Country honour.
Wounded and forsaken
They could offer no resistance,
But hand in hand calmly awaited
The onset of their assailants;
Nobly they refused to yield,
Foretelling the day
When thousands of Englishmen should come
To avenge their death,
And destroy Mulraj, his army, and fortress.
History records
How the prediction was fulfilled.
Borne to the grave
By their victorious Brother Soldiers and Countrymen
They were buried with Military honors,
Here,
On the summit of the Captured Citadel,
On the 26th January, 1849.
The annexation
Of the Punjab to the Empire
Was the result of the War,
Of which their assassination
Was the commencement.

To the east of the obelisk are three large sepulchral monuments, with the following inscriptions:—

SACRED to the Memory of Major GEORGE SHEAFE MONTIZAMBERT killed in action in Command of H. M. 10th Regiment, on the 12th September 1848, aged 34 years; and of Captain HOLLINGSWORTH, of the same Regiment, who died of a wound received in the action of the 9th September 1848, aged 30 years.

To the Memory of Second-Lieutenants J. THOMSON and C. T. GRAHAM, Bengal Artillery, who fell at the siege of Multan, 1849.
Erected by their Brother Officers.

In Memory of 1 SERGEANT and 13 GUNNERS, Bengal Foot Artillery, who fell at the siege of Multan, 1848-9.
This Tomb is erected by their Comrades.

in the open space to the west of the obelisk is the tomb of Syad Darbar Shah, Bukhari; a small structure with an attendant in charge.

Chapter VI.

Towns, Municipalities and Cantonments.

Multan.

Memorial obelisk.

II.—The City.

The City proper of Multan is bounded on the north by the depression lying between it and the fort, and on all other sides by a brick wall.

'The walled city,' writes Cunningham,* 'is 4,200 feet in length and 2,400 feet in breadth, with the long straight side facing the south-west. Altogether the walled circuit of Multan, including both city and citadel, is 15,000 feet, or very nearly three miles; and the whole circuit of the place, including the unwalled suburbs, is from four and a half to five miles. This last measurement agrees exactly with the estimate of Hiuen Thsang, who makes the circuit of Multan 30 "li," or just five miles. It agrees also with the estimate of Elphinstone, who, with his usual accuracy, describes Multan as above four miles and a half in circumference. The fortress had no ditch, when it was seen by Elphinstone and Burnes, but a broad deep ditch, which could be readily filled by the waters of the Ravi canals, was shortly afterwards added by Sawan Mall, the energetic Governor of Multan, under Ranjit Singh. The walls are said to have been built by Murad Bakhsh, the youngest son of Shah Jahán, who was Governor of Multan for a few years towards the close of his reign. But the work of Murad Bukhsh must have been confined to repairs, including a complete facing of the greater part; for when I dismantled the defences of Multan in 1854, I found that the brick walls were generally double, the outer wall being about four feet thick, and the inner walls from 3½ to 4 feet. The whole was built of burnt bricks and mud mortar, excepting the outer courses, which were laid in lime mortar to a depth of 9 inches.

The city has six gates, which are placed in the following order:—The Lahori or Lohárí gate at its north-western corner; the Bohar gate at its south-western corner. Next to the Bohar gate, on the south, comes the Haram gate; then the Pák gate.† On the eastern side is the Delhi gate, and at the north-eastern corner is the Daulat gate.‡ The bastion at the south-eastern corner is the Khuni Burj, or Bloody Bastion, where the British troops, on January 2, 1849, stormed the city. On the northern side is a wide approach to the city, rising from the old bed of the Ravi and known as the Husain Gahi.§ From the Husain Gahi, a wide paved street runs for about half a mile in a southerly direction into the heart of the city. This is known as the chauk, and at two-thirds of its length from the Husain Gahi it sends out a broad street to the Delhi gate on the east, and another to the Lahori on the west. The chauk ends at the mosque of Wali Muhammad, at which point three broad streets branch off to the Bohar, Haram and Pák gates, respectively. The other streets are narrow and tortuous, often ending in *culs de sac*. The central portion of the city near the Wali Muhammad Mosque is known as the "Kup."

The Gardezí shrine.

Of the Mahomedan buildings in the city, the most remarkable is the shrine of Shekh Muhammad Yusaf Gardezi, near

---

* Archæological Survey Reports, v. 124.

† The Pák gate is so called from the adjoining shrine of Musa Pák Sháhíd and the Haram gate, from the fact that the zanana of the Gilání descendants of the same saint (Musa Pák Shádíd) was there situated.

‡ So called because the Moghal court and cantonments were outside this gate in the neighbourhood of the Am Khas. The suburb of Aghapura, to the south of this, was the residence of the Moghal lords or aghas.

§ Said by some to be called after a grass-seller of the name of Husain, the grass market having once been in this neighbourhood. Others derive the name from a Syad Husain Agahi, whose tomb is shown in the neighbourhood.

Chapter VI.

Towns. Municipalities and Cantonments.

Multan.

The Gardezi shrine.

the Bohar gate. This is a rectangular domeless building, plentifully decorated with glazed tile work of considerable beauty. In the same courtyard are several graves; an imambara some 30 years old, a mosque, also modern, and a new building for ablutions; also a small shrine covering a footprint of the Caliph Ali; but the effect of the buildings is a good deal spoilt by their being closely surrounded by houses. Muhammad Yusaf was a descendant of the prophet through the Imam Hassan, and was born in A.H. 450 (A.D. 1058) at Gardez, near Ghazni, in Afghanistan, to which his grandfather is said to have emigrated from Baghdad. The saint came to Multan, it is said, in A.D. 1088, in the reign of Ala-ud-din Bahram Shah, of the Ghaznavi dynasty. There is at that time a great gap in the history of Multan, and it is very likely, as the family history of the Gardezis states, that the invasion of Sultán Modud in 1042 (see Chapter II above) had entirely obliterated the old city. We are told that the Multan of Modud's time lay to the south of the present city near the tomb of Mulla Manj, south of Mai Pákdaman, and that Shekh Muhammad Yusaf, by taking up his abode on the site of the present shrine, then near the banks of the Ravi. induced the people to colonise the present city and fort of Multan. The story probably, in some dim way, represents a change in the course of the Ravi river; and we find the saint's descendants enjoying for many centuries large properties and jagirs along the old banks of the Ravi between Multan and Kabírwala. Shekh Muhammad Yusaf was a specially gifted man: he could ride tigers and could handle snakes: and for 40 years after his death his hand would occasionally come out of his tomb.

Shrine of Musa Pák Sháhíd.

Another well-known shrine in the city is that of Musa Pák Sháhíd inside the Pák gate. Shekh Abulhassan Musa Pák Sháhíd, a descendant of Abdul Kadir Gilani, was born at Uch in 1545 A.D., and was killed in A.D. 160 in a skirmish with some raiders near Mangehatti in the south of the Multan tahsil. His body was brought into Multan by his successor in A.D. 1616: it is said that the body was not decomposed at all, and was brought in sitting on a horse. Among his descendants were Hamid Ganj Bakhsh (buried near Musa Pák Sháhíd), Yahya Nawab (buried between the Pák and Haram gates), Inayat Wilayat (buried near the Haram gate in a somewhat conspicuous tomb), and Jan Muhammad (buried at Delhi). The shrine of Musa Pák is largely frequented by Pathāns, and there is a small mela on Thursday evenings. Part of the village of Hafizwala in Shujabad is held in jagir by the guardians of the shrine.

Shrine of Sháhdná Sháhíd.

Another Mahomedan shrine which may be noted is that of Sháhdná Sháhid, near the Delhi gate. When this saint was 10 months old, his mother made accusations against the great Baháwal Hakk, similar to those which Potiphar's wife made against Joseph. The infant child gave miraculous evidence in favour of the accused, and was accordingly done away with by his mother. He was, however, restored to life by Baháwal Hakk, whose faithful attendant he became for the rest of his life. There is a couplet which says :—

Shrine of Shádná Sháhíd.

Andar Ghaus Baháwal-hakk ; báhar Kutb Faríd ;
Je tou bahut utáwali mang Shádí Sháhíd.

('Within is Baháwal-hakk ; outside is Kutb Faríd ; but if you wish a thing done in a great hurry, call on Shádná Shahíd ')

Mosques.

The Wali Muhammad Mosque in the Godri bazar, in the very centre of the town, was built by the Pathan Governor, Ali Muhammad Khan, Khákwani, in 1758, and exhibits a good specimen of the enamelled tiled work of the district. During the Sikh supremacy, the Nazim held his kutcherry in the court of this mosque, and a copy of the Granth was kept inside. The use of the mosque was restored to the Mussulmans with the advent of British power.

The Phulhattanwali Mosque in the Chopar bazar, on the western side of the city, is said to have been built by the Emperor, Farukh Siyar. It is said that while the Emperor was here a fakir foretold the birth of his son, and when the son was born the Emperor built this mosque as a memorial. The mosque derives its name from the flower-sellers' shops at the door.

There is also a mosque known as the Darswala, near the Daulat gate, where the attendants have previously had, and still to a large extent retain, a reputation for learning. It is said to have been patronised by Baba Faríd.

Nao-gajas.

The names of 15 'nao-gaja' tombs (*i e.*, tombs of saints, 9 yards long or thereabouts) were supplied to Cunningham when he was in Multán. Most of these were in or immediately adjoining the city. They were :—

(a) By the fort (these were all buried under the dismantled parapets before 1853) :—

(1) Near the Sikki gate, the tomb of Lal Husain Bairagi, a converted Hindu.

(2) Near the De gate, tomb of Miran King Samar (?), 4 gaj in length.

(3) Near the Kehri gate, tomb of Sabz Ghazi, 3½ gaz in length.

(4) Near the Jama Masjid, tomb of Kazi Kutb Káshàni.

(b) In and about the city :—

(5) Near the Bohar gate, and inside the city, tomb of Pir Adham.

(6) Near the Bohar gate and outside the city, tomb of Pir Dindar, 54½ feet long.

(7) Above Husain Gahi, in the Nand Mohalla, tomb of Pir Ramzan Ghazi, 21 feet 3 inches long;

Chapter VI.

Towns, Municipalities and Cantonments.

Multan.

Nao-gajas.

(8) Outside the Delhi gate, 450 feet distant, tomb of Pir Gor Sultan. This tomb is 35½ feet in length. Beside it there is a large circular stone 27 inches in diameter and 8 inches thick, with a hole through the middle 9 inches in diameter. The stone is of a chocolate colour, with many marks of light yellow. It is called Manka. Some say the saint wore it round his neck, but the general belief is that it was his thumb-ring. This tomb is said to be 1,300 years old.

(9) and (10). Near Sagar, two tombs, each 3½ gaj in length. Names not known.

(11) and (12) At Shádna Shâhíd, two tombs, of the Shádna himself and of some unknown martyr, each 3½ gaj in length.

(13). In Sajjika Mohalla, unknown tomb.

(14). In Mangar ka mohalla, unknown tomb.

Hindus as well as Mahomedans pay their devotions at these tombs, and place lights before them on Fridays,

Narsinghpuri temple.

Of the Hindu buildings in the city the most celebrated is the Narsinghpuri temple, which is situated in the Sabz Mandi. The original Narsinghpuri temple mentioned in the histories has been described above, and was situated in the fort. No trace now remains of the old temple, and a new one was built about 1872 A D by the Prahládpuri Mohant on the site of a thakurdwara, known as Fateh Chand Tanksâlia's. This again was to be lately in ruins and has only recently been reconstructed by subscription.

Other Hindu shrines.

In the Kanak Mandi, or wheat market, in the Bharthianwala Mohalla, is a dharmsála built in the time of the Pathán supremacy. It contains two copies of the Granth, and is especially frequented by Shikárpuri sahukars.

In the Haram gate bazar is a shrine known as Dwara Banarsi Bhagat, built in honour of a holy man called Banarsi who came to Multan 300 years ago from Girot in the Shahpur district. Cunningham (Archæological Survey, v, 126) mentions some fragments of statues in a temple near the Haran or Haram Darwaza, which are said to have been made by Adu, the father of Adam.

In the north-east of the city is a building known as Bhai Dyal Singh's Dharmsála, which is kept by a respectable group of Nirmala Sadhus, and which is patronised by several of the better class of Hindus in the city. It contains a fine open hall, in which the Granth is suitably installed.

Mohallas.

The mohallas or quarters in the city are known chiefly after the name of the tribes or professions which inhabit them, such as the Kamángars, the Kumhárs, the Gardezis, the Gilanis, and so forth. Generally speaking, the quarters adjoining the city walls are inhabited by Mussulmans ; while those in the centre of the city and towards the fort (the quarters which in former days were the safest) are inhabited by Hindus.

Chapter VI.

Towns, Municipalities and Cantonments.

Multan.

III.—OUTSIDE THE CITY.

The Idgah.

About a mile to the north-east of the city is the Idgah, which was built in 1735 by Nawab Abdussamad Khan, Governor of Lahore. It was employed in Sikh times for military purposes, and it was here that the ill-fated Agnew and Anderson were massacred in 1848 (see chapter II above). After annexation, the building was for some years used as the Deputy Commissioner's kutcherry; but in 1863 it was restored to the Mussalman community on their entering into engagements to preserve the tablet, which was placed under the central dome to the memory of Messrs. Agnew and Anderson. The inscription on the tablet, which is still accordingly preserved, runs: 'Within this dome, on the 19th of April 1848,* were cruelly murdered Patrick Vans Agnew, Esquire, Bengal Civil Service, and Lieutenant William Anderson, 2nd Bombay Fusiliers, Assistants to the Resident at Lahore.' The Idgah before annexation suffered from an explosion of powder while it was used as a powder magazine by the Sikhs. It was also in some disrepair as late as A.D. 1891, when it was restored at the instance largely of Mr. H.C. Cookson, the Deputy Commissioner, and of Nawab Muhammad Hyat Khan, the Divisional Judge, some Rs. 10,000 being collected by subscriptions and Rs. 10,000 being subscribed by Government on condition of the maintenance of the tablet above mentioned. The proportion of real tile work on the outside to imitation paint or plaster is not sufficiently large to dissipate a certain impression of tawdriness, but in other respects the mosque is a fine building. It is 240 feet long by 54 feet broad, and has one central dome, with open chambers on either side. It is faced by a fine brick paved courtyard with a small brick wall along side.

Bákirabadi Mosque.

Some two miles east of the Idgah, near the Durána Langána Canal, is the Bákirábádi Mosque, built by Bákir Khan, who was Subadar of Multan about the year 1720. In Diwán Sáwan Mal's time it was common for parties in a suit to be sent to this mosque to take oaths on the matter in dispute, the oaths taken in this mosque being held peculiarly sacred. The building is now in ruins.

Baba Safra.

South of the Idgah is the shrine of Baba Safra, round which in Sikh times the army used to be cantoned. There is a camping-ground here which is known in the route books as the Am Khas, and opposite it a small European cemetery.†

---

* A curious mistake. The real date was the 20th.

† This cemetery contains the graves of the following persons:—Captain John Inglis, 11th Bengal Light Cavalry, died 16th February 1849 in his 44th year. William eldest son of Sergeant-Major and Catherine Reid, Bombay Rifles, deceased 14th June 1849, ætat 2 years and 10 months. G. M. Barker, Esquire, Indus Flotilla, died 16th June 1849 aged 29 years. W. H. Anderson, Lieutenant, Bombay Artillery, who departed this life at Multan, June 22nd, 1849, aged 20. Captain W.G.C. Hughes, 4th Bombay Rifles, died 1st July 1849, age 30 years. Edwin Charles Fuller, the beloved child of Lieutenant and Mrs. Stevens, 11th Regiment N. I., who departed this life 25th February 1850, aged 4 months and 18 days. Catherine Barfoot, wife

Chapter VI.

Towns, Municipalities and Cantonments.

Multan.

Shams Tabrez.

To the south of this lies the shrine of Shams Tabrez. The shrine is said to be named after one Shams-ud-din, of Sabzawar, in Afghanistan, a descendant of the Imam Jafar, who was born in A.D. 1165. This saint raised from the dead the son of the ruler of Ghazni, and afterwards came to Multan, which at that time was full of holy men. The chief of these, the holy Baháwal Hakk, sent to the new arrival a lota full of milk, indicating thereby that there was no room for him in the city, where there were already as many saints as could be supported. Shams-ud-din, however, returned the lota, after placing a rose leaf on the surface of the milk, and the delicate reply was appreciated. His death is said to have taken place in A. D. 1276, and the shrine was first built by his grandson in A.D. 1330. It was, however, practically rebuilt, at great expense, by one of the saint's followers as late as A.D. 1780. The guardians of the shrine are Shias, and they declare that the Shams, after whom the shrine is named, is called Shams Tabrez by mistake, the real cognomen being Tap-rez or Heat-giving.* The legends connecting the saint with the sun are thus described by Cunningham :—

'There are several legends about Shams Tabrez, but they all agree in attributing the great heat of Multan to the direct influence of the saint, in causing the sun to approach nearer to Multán than to other parts of the earth. One of the stories is related by Burnes, who calls him "Shams-i-Tabrezi, a saint from Bagdad, who is believed to have performed many miracles, and even raised the dead. This worthy, as the story is told, was flayed alive for his pretensions. He had long begged his bread in the city, and in his hunger caught a fish, which he held up to the sun, and brought that luminary near enough to roast it. This established his memory and equivocal fame on a firmer basis. The natives to this day attribute the heat of Multan, which is proverbial, to this incident." According to another version, the saint had begged for food through the city in vain, and when he was dying from hunger he prayed to the sun in his anger : 'O sun, your name is Shams, and my name is Shams, come down and punish the people of Multán for their inhumanity." The sun at once drew nearer, and the heat of Multan has ever since been greater than that of any other place. Another version attributes the prayer of the saint to the persecution and taunts of the people, who used to disturb and worry him when he was at his devotions.'

A similar tale is given in Malcolm's History of Persia (1829, ii, 282), but without special reference to Multan ; and Malcolm describes this saint as one of the sect of Sufis. The attendants at the shrine of Ram Tirath, it may be noted, have similar tales

---

of Sergeant J. A. Barfoot, 2nd Company, 1st Battery Artillery, who departed this life in childbirth on the 28th September 1851, aged 22 years 2 months and 2 days; also of Catherine Sophia Barfoot, infant child of the above, who departed this life on the 5th May 1852, aged 7 months and 20 days. John Conlon, Patrol Preventive Service, Sutledge Line, who died on his way from Sultanpur to Multán on 21st June 1852, aged 34 years. Ellen and Denis, the beloved children of Ellen and Corns O'Leary, Cattle Sergeant, Multan ; the former died 11th September 1852, the latter on 3rd July 1853. Percy James, infant son of Mr. and Mrs. William Ellison, Barí Doab Survey, who died at Shoojabad, 14th December 1857, aged 20 days. Hugh Bernard Biggen, the beloved son of M.A. Biggen and Sergeant, died 10th May 1861, at the age of 3 months and 3 days. Mary Anne Eleanor Biggen, daughter of M. A. Biggen and Sergeant H. Biggen, Ordnance Department, who departed this life at Multan on the 11th August 1861, aged 2 years and 11 months. Mrs. B. S. Chakrabarti, beloved wife of Mr. K. D. Chakrabarti, died 20th June 1872, aged 36 years. Jane Laura, infant daughter of Wm. and Mary K. Chand, aged 10 months and 7 days (no date).

* Curzon's Persia, Vol. 1, p. 519.

Multan.

regarding Keshpuri and connect the Hindu and the Mahomedan saints together. The building of Shams Tabrez is thus described by Cunningham :—

Shams Tabrez.

'The main body of the tomb is a square of 34 feet side, and 30 feet in height, surrounded by a verandah with seven openings on each side. Above this it takes an octagonal shape, and is surmounted by a hemispherical dome covered with glazed sky-blue tiles. The whole height is 62 feet. I could not learn the date of Shams-i-Tabrez himself, as the people of Multan are profoundly ignorant of everything, except certain silly miraculous stories of their saints. But the building itself cannot be earlier than the time of the Mughals; and the people themselves say it is not quite 200 years old. Portions of the walls are ornamented with patterns in glazed tiles, but the colours are chiefly blue and white, with a perfectly even surface, which betrays a late age. There are, however, many fragments of glazed tile work of an earlier age let into the gateway and walls of the surrounding court-yard, which, according to the people, belonged to the old original tomb of the saint, which is referred to the time of "Tughal Padshah" (Tughlak) by some, and to a much earlier date by others.'

Mr. Eastwick in Murray's Handbook adds:—

'To the left of the entrance is a small square building, dignified with the name of the Imambarah. Low down in the wall is inscribed : "The slave of God Mian died 7th of Muharram 1282, A.H." (A.D.1865). On one of the alcoves in the corridor is a heart of a deep blue colour, with "O God" in the centre and near it a *panja*, or hand, well painted There are two inscriptions on the door of the tomb in Persian of 12 and 14 lines, respectively, in praise of the saint.'

Am Khas and neighbourhood.

South of the tomb of Shams Tabrez is the Am Khas garden, so called, because in the days of Shahzada Murád Bakhsh, son of Sháh Jahán, the public receptions were held here, private receptions being held in the fort. This was a very favourite place of Diwán Sáwan Mal, who used to hold his kutcherry here, and who did a good deal to beautify the surroundings. It was here that Sáwan Mal was assassinated, and it was to this place that his son Mulráj fled when Agnew was attacked outside the Sikhi gate of the fort. The old buildings have been made into the tahsil, and a large part of the grounds are now a public garden, maintained by the municipality. North of the tahsil are the stallion stables and the ground on which the annual horse fair is held. To the west are the remains of a Wahábi mosque. To the south is the Zabardast Khán garden, which includes a disused swimming bath, and is also maintained by the municipality.

To the east of the tahsil, on the north side of the Lahore road, is the samádh, or cenotaph of Diwán Sáwan Mal, which is maintained by the family with the aid of a small grant of revenue. To the south of this and east of the tahsil is the khankah of Háfiz Muhammad Jamál, a holy man, who died in 1811 A.D. There is a curious legend which identifies the disciples of this saint as the spiritual counterparts of the temporal power for the time being. In 1848-9, for instance so long as Munshi Ghulam Husain, the disciple of Muhammad Jamál, was alive the rule of Diwán Mulráj prevailed ; but when this man had been shot by a British soldier, the city capitulated to the English next day. A little to the north of Shams Tabrez is a curious shrine in a garden known as the shrine of Sakhi Shah Habíb. Sháh Habíb is said to have been the *alias* of no less a

Chapter VI.

Towns, Municipalities and Cantonments.

Multan.

person than Sultan Sháh Shuja, the son of Shah Jahán, who when he disappeared from public life is said to have settled down in Multan as a fakir. The shrine is connected with the somewhat disreputable Rasúl Sháhi sect of fakirs.

Am Khas and neighbourhood.

On the road round the city, to the east of the Daulat gate and opposite the new distillery (built in 1898), lie the quarters of the potters, and prominent among them the quarters and shops of the 'Káshígars,' who make the enamelled tile work for which Multan is so famous. Further on, down a street to the left, opposite the Delhi gate, is the tomb of Pir Gor Sultán, already mentioned. Further on, at the south-east corner of the city, is the Khúni Burj, or Bloody Bastion, where the besiegers in 1849 effected their breach and stormed the town. Turning here to the east one goes through the suburb of Aghapura and past the celebrated Mandi Awa, or large mound, near which was fought the action of December 27th, 1848 (see Chapter II). Further to the east is the open space where the Dasehra is held, and beyond that again the 'Barsáti band,' or rain-water dam, which was built in the days when Multan was liable to floods, and the repair of which afforded occupation to the destitute during the famine of 1896-97.

Ram Tirath.

From this point the Mailsi and Budhla Sant roads branch off to the left, and the Dunyapur road to the right. Following the latter, one passes on the left the shrine of Ram Tirath, or Rama Kund, a small tank where Rama is said to have halted when he visited Multan in the days of the Narsingh Avatár. The present buildings are by Ranjit Singh and the place is a favourite resort for Hindus on Sundays. Closely adjoining is the shrine of Keshopuri, who is the Hindu equivalent of Shams Tabrez, the saint who was skinned alive and from whom Multan acquired one of its early names. The building contains only a few samadhs, three rude images of Bhairon, Kali and Hanuman, and a 'gúfa,' or grotto, where fakirs sit in the hot weather to get cool. To the west of these buildings, and on the same side of the railway, is the Hindu burning-ground (obviously at one time like most Hindu burning-grounds on the bank of the river) and the so-called Dharmsala, where was fought the terrible affair of the 12th September 1848 (see Chapter II above).

Central Jail.

Crossing the railway we come, further to the south, to the Central Jail. In this neighbourhood the British troops were encamped during a large part of the time occupied by the siege of Multan in 1848-49, and there are memorials of their presence in the shape of three Christian graveyards.*

---

* One of these is at the Daya Ramwala well to the south of the road leading from the city Railway Station to the Central Jail, and it contains the following inscriptions :—

'In memory of Captain C. Keith Erskine, Bombay Lancers, who died January 12th, 1849, age 49': and 'In memory of Captain Brooke Bailey and men of the Bombay Artillery who fell during the siege of Multan, 22nd January 1849.'

Chapter VI.

Towns, Municipalities and Cantonments.

Multan.

Suraj Kund.

To the south of the railway lie a large number of cotton ginning factories. At the western end of the line of factories runs the road from the city to Suraj kund, a celebrated tank and shrine, which lies some 4 miles south of Multan. Although the brickwork of the tank was built by Diwan Sawan Mal, and the adjoing building even later, the spot itself has been one of considerable sanctity from a very remote period, and the legends regarding it interweave in a curious way the stories of the two forms of Hindu worship for which Multan has been so famous, *viz.*, that of the Sun and that of Vishnu in the form of Narsingh. The tale is that when Vishnu appeared as a Man Lion to tear up the tyrant Hirnákhash, his anger was so hot that all the gods came down to earth to appease him, and the place where they alighted was an old haunt of the Sun deity, situated where the tank of Suraj kund now stands. The mohant and his disciples are Bairagis, and they have tales connecting the site with Keshopuri, the Hindu Shams Tabrez, to whom reference has been made above. There is a very fine garden attached to the shrine, and the place is maintained partly by the aid of a perpetual grant of land revenue from Government. It is a common resort of Hindus from the city, and there are two large annual fairs here in winter and one in summer.

Jog maya.

On the road between Suraj Kund and the city one crosses the Wali Muhammad canal by a bridge, which was a strategic point of some importance during the operations of 1848-49. Further on, to the west of the road, is a *kacha* tank, known as Chandar Kund, or the Moon's tank. Near this also, but on the west of the road, is the mound of Mulla Mauj, who is said to have been the first Muhammadan saint to come to Multan. Nearer the city, on the east side of the road, is the shrine of Jogmaya, which marks the spot where Devi tarried when the gods came down to appease the angry Narsingh. In Aurangzeb's time there was only a platform here, where goats were offered ; but new buildings were made in the Pathan times, and these were much improved in the days of Sawan Mal. There is a story that when the shrine of Totla Mai was destroyed (see below), the lights of that shrine moved over of themselves to the shrine of Jogmaya, and these lights are the chief object of devotion at Jogmaya at the present day.

Totla Mai.

The shrine of Totla Mai used to stand on the west side of the Suraj Kund road, on the immense mound, which there

---

The other two graveyards are at the well known as Sher-Khan-ka-bagh, a little south of the Railway line and west of the Kahror road. The northern one has no inscription, but the southern one, near the well, has the following :—

'In memory of Thomas Cubitt, Lieutenant, 49th Regiment, Native Infantry, who was killed in action September 12th, 1848,' and 'Major John Gordon, Her Majesty's Rifles, both killed in action before Multan on the 27th December 1848.'

Chapter VI.

Towns, Municipalities and Cantonments.

Multan.

marks one of the early traditional sites of Multan city. There is an old couplet which runs—

> Hingláj pachham Shástri, Totla ghar Multan
> Nagarkot Dukh-bhanjni, tínon deo pardhán;

Totla Mai.

which is being interpreted: 'There are three goddesses of fame: Shastri in Hinglaj of the west; Totla whose home is Multan, and Dukh-bhanjni in Nagarkot

In the days of Aurangzeb an attempt was made to turn the temple into a mosque, whereupon the goddess walked out and jumped into the adjoining well, still known as the Múrat-wala well. The pujári of the shrine was, however, somewhat of a physician, and having cured the king's son of an internal pain, he got leave to take the image out of the well and convey it to a small house in the city. The present shrine, which is near the Haram gate, inside the city, was begun in Sikh times when Badan Hazari was kardar.

Mai Pakdaman.

Immediately to the south of the old site of Totla Mai is the Muhammadan shrine of Mai Pákdáman, the wife of Sheikh Sadr-ud-din, the son of the great Baháwal Hakk. This is a striking rectangular building faced with fine coloured tiling, but somewhat concealed from view by a surrounding wall. Females alone are allowed inside the enclosure.

Sidi Lal.

At the level-crossing, by the city railway station, there lies, immediately to the north, the mound known as Sidi Lal-ka-bhir, which formed the objective of one of the attacks made by the British force on the 27th December 1848, and which is surmounted by a small shrine where Hindus and Mussulmans alike pay their devotions. To the north of this again is the site of the Bagh Begi, the garden where, in the Pathan and Sikh times, strangers were entertained; the baradari in the middle is still extant and the remains of a picturesque mosque.

The Pathan suburbs.

On the road between the Haram gate and the cantonments lies the Shish Mahal, which marks the place where the earliest Saddozai settlers in the end of the 17th century took up their abode It is even said that the house to the north of the road, opposite the Divisional Court, is on the exact site of the house in which Ahmad Shah, Abdali, was born. The Shish Mahal garden was built by Shakir Khan, Saddozai, and the shrine to the west is in memory of Shah Husain, the first of the family to immigrate to India. To the same family belonged Lánge Khan, who made the Lánge Khan garden, now used as a public garden, and Abid Khan, who made the Abid Khan garden, on the Sikandrabad canal, north of cantonments.

The Pathans were for the most part allowed to settle outside the city walls only, and when they went inside the city they were only allowed to frequent the eastern half, the western portion being reserved for the Mughal or official class. Of the Pathan settlements or 'kirris' several are still well known, such as the

Chapter VI.

Towns, Municipalities and Cantonments.

Multan.

The Pathan suburbs.

Kirri Jamundon, near the city railway station; the Kiri Afghán—án round the dispensary: Kiri Misri Khan on the an canal east of the Lánge Khan garden; and the Khudakka Kotla near the station cricket ground. It may be noted also that the quarter round the present Municipal Hall was known in Mughal times as the Sultanganj, and is still spoken of as the Ganj: and it was here that octroi was taken on imports. Traders importing goods from Afghanistan were stopped by the officials a little further from the city, and the place of their detention—still much frequented in the winter by vagrant Pathans—is known as the Chehelyak Sarai, from the rate—one in forty—at which the tax was levied from them.

To the immediate north-west of the city, between the Behar gate and the Lánge Khan garden, lies the shrine of Mai Mihrbán, the wife of Sheikh Hasan, who is said to have come to Multan shortly after the time of Sheikh Yusaf Gardezi. Immediately south of the Lánge Khan garden, on the banks of the Wali Muhammad canal, lies the Shivala of Sawan Mal, built by that ruler in 1837. Just outside the Lohari gate is the Jubilee Municipal Hall surmounted by a clock tower. The low land lying north of the fort in this vicinity is known as Luludharan, and the story is that when the Ravi was flowing here Shekh Rukn Alam (or, as others say, Sheikh Yusaf Gardezi) threw into the river a pearl which a disciple had presented to him. Seeing the disciple vexed at this treatment, the saint bade him close his eyes and look again; when he did so, he said that the whole river was one mass of pearls.

Civil Lines.

To the north-west of the city, and at the distance of something over half-a-mile, are the district offices built in 1861; and about a mile further on is the district jail. The jail is said to cover the spot once occupied by General Ventura's house when he was Governor in Multan. Round the district kutcherry lie the houses of civil officers and others. In the early days of annexation, when the district offices were in the Idgah, the civil station was mainly confined to that neighbourhood, but the attraction of cantonments is gradually causing the houses on the eastern side of the station to be deserted in favour of houses nearer cantonments. The most remarkable of the old houses on the west of the station is the Hazúri Bagh, a garden house built in the time of Shahzáda Murád Bakhsh. In this garden Elphinstone and Burnes halted during their stay in Multan, and this was the spot originally intended for the accommodation of the ill-fated Agnew and Anderson in 1848. It afterwards became the Commissioner's residence, but was again deserted by the Commissioner in favour of the bungalow opposite the dâk bungalow, now owned by the Nawáb of Bahawalpur.

Chapter VI.

Towns, Municipalities and Cantonments.

Multan.

Sura Miani.

A short distance to the north of the civil station, on the Rajghat Road, is the shrine of Shah Ali Akbar in Sura Miani. The two buildings at the shrine are finely situated amidst a grove of trees, and are profusely decorated with coloured tiles. The saint was a descendant of Shah Shams-ud-din; and his disciples and descendants inhabit the adjoining village. There was a good deal of commerce between this village and Kabul in the days of Durani sovereignty, and this is said to be reflected in the architecture of the houses, which so resembles that of Kabul, that Sura Miani is often spoken of as 'a mohalla of Kabul.' There is a considerable fair in the neighbourhood on the day of the Baisakhi.

Multan Municipality.

The Municipality.

The Municipality of Multán was first constituted in 1867 and it is now a municipality of the first class. The boundaries of the municipal control as laid down in 1885, are—

East.—Kutcha road from north-east corner of 'Woodlands' to 'Edgah;' thence along Barsati bund to junction with road leading from Daulat gate, and thence along that road to railway line.

West.—Cantonment boundaries from railway line as far as pillar No. 10 at north-west corner of dák bungalow compound; thence the road to the front of the jail gate.

North.—Road from front of jail gate to the bridge across the Wali Muhammad canal on the police line road; thence in a straight line to the junction of the roads at the north-east corner of 'Woodlands.'

South.—Railway line.

The boundaries, for purposes of octroi, are the same as the municipal boundaries, but the octroi system also includes the area within the cantonment boundaries.

Constitution.

The constitution of the Municipal Committee has differed at different times. Between 1885 and 1899 it consisted of 36 members, of whom 24 were elected and 12 nominated; but since 1899 it has been composed of 24 members only, of whom 16 are elected and 8 nominated. Of the elected members, 8 are Muhammadans and 8 Hindus, and there are now eight election wards only as against nineteen formerly, and proposals for further reducing these to four are under consideration. The nominated members comprise 4 Europeans, 3 Muhammadans and 1 Hindu.

Income and expenditure.

The income of the Municipality for the last thirty years is given in Table No. XLV. Taking the figures for the year 1899

Chapter VI.

Towns, Municipalities and Cantonments.

Multan Municipality.

Income and expenditure.

as an example, the normal incomings and outgoings may be summarized as follows :—

Income.	Rs.	Expenditure.	Rs.
Octroi	1,41,394	Administration and Collection,	24,588
Conservancy fees	6,596	Police	27,075
Education fees	11,350	Conservancy	29,813
Other sources	14,310	Dispensaries and Vaccination,	15,917
		Public Works	26,253
		Schools	20,663
		Contributions	14,774
		Other expenditure	21,920
Total ...	1,73,659	Total ...	1,81,003

Drainage, etc.

The outfall of the sewage of the city is at present at three sites outside the city walls, the city drainage being collected by open drains converging on a large open drain outside the city walls, which in its turn conducts the sewage to certain neighbouring wells. A scheme for the introduction of a better system is, however, at present under consideration. Street sweepings are removed by cultivators on licenses which are given at the rate of Re. 1-8-0 and Re 1-0-0 per bullock per mensem ; the lower rate being taken from the cultivators living outside municipal limits. Human excreta are collected in enclosures outside the city walls, whence they are removed to three different centres to be worked into poudrette and then sold by auction.

Water.

The water supply is dependent on wells in the streets and in private houses, and it is belived to be on the whole good and sufficient.

Paving.

Most of the streets in the city are paved. A sum of Rs. 6,000 is spent annually on maintaining and extending the paving, and a sum of Rs. 10,000 on repairing the municipal roads.

Hackney carriages.

There are about 175 hackney carriages, mostly tum-tums' which are licensed at Rs. 7 each per annum (including the driver's license of Re. 1).

Chapter VI.

Towns, Municipalities and Cantonments.

Multan Municipality.

Octroi.

The chief source of income, as will be seen from the figures above quoted, is the octroi. This branch of the administration is superintended by an octroi tahsildar, a head darogha, an assistant darogha and fifty muharrirs, and the collections are made at 14 posts, men being also posted at each of the six city gates. The cantonments are included in the octroi system, but both the railway stations are just outside the octroi boundary.

The incidence of the octroi taxation in 1898-99 was Re. 1-13-2 per head of the population. The chief articles taxed and the rates of taxation on each are as follows :—

Articles.	Rate.
Rice, all kinds	2 annas per maund.
Wheat, barley, moth, gram, múng, másh, etc. ...	1 anna ,, ,,
Sawank, chino, kangni, masur	6 pies ,, ,,
Ghi	1 rupee ,, ,,
Oil	3 annas ,, ,,
Sugar, refined	2 ,, ,, ,,
Gur and sugar, unrefined	1 anna ,, ,,
Mangoes	4 annas ,, ,,
Native fruits	2 ,, ,, ,,
Building wood of *deodar*, *shisham* and *tun*, bricks, hemp and flax	6 pies ,, rupee
Tobacco and snuff	8 annas ,, maund.
Native and European cloth	Re. 1-4-0 per cent.
Gold embroidered cloth and shoes	Re. 1-8-0 ,, ,,
Vegetables and sugarcane	6 pies ,, maund.
Fruits, such as *sawagi*, *manaka*, etc.	6 ,, per rupee.
Spices of all kinds, *chini*, *maraba*, *kariana*, medicines (native), perfumes	6 ,, ,, ,,
Sheep and goats	1 anna per head.
Firewood, coal and sajji	3 pies per rupee.
Sesamum, rape and ussún	1 anna per maund.
Brass and brass articles, iron and iron articles, copper and copper articles, and metals of all kinds ...	Rs. 1-8-0 per cent.

The chief articles exempted from taxation are—

Indigo, cotton, colours of all kinds, *majith*, *wakam*, keroaine oil, ivory, leather, horse harness, sowing thread, silk (raw), shora, sulphur and sulphuric articles, mill wheels, exciseable articles, postins, stationery and books, clocks and watches, tea of all kinds, silk and golden ornaments, cane and cane sticks, salt, umbrellas, arms, tables, and chairs, grass of all kinds, and agricultural produce grown within municipal limits.

The following table shows the articles subject to octroi which were imported into Multan city and cantonments in 1897-98 to 1899-00 :—

Details.	Weight.			Value.		
	1897-98.	1898-99.	1899-00.	1897-98.	1898-99.	1899-00.
	Mds.	Mds.	Mds.	Rs.	Rs.	Rs.
Articles of food, etc.						
Rice (husked and unhusked)	55,867	52,709	53,313	1,86,104	1,31,211	1,53,862
Wheat	382,323	438,817	391,048	11,46,919	10,42,190	13,68,668
Other cereals and pulses	185,151	158,420	136,399	6,65,355	3,01,527	4,40,110
Ghi	13,836	19,421	15,022	4,42,760	6,21,469	5,40,786
Sugar, refined ...	84,415	59,387	62,113	8,44,154	5,34,479	6,21,125
Gur	46,097	49,761	54,002	1,84,389	1,74,165	2,16,007
Fruits	33,208	32,485	44,029	1,51,625	1,80,173	1,77,611
Fish	1,843	1,968	1,335	9,213	5,890	6,774
Sugar cane	11,260	11,987	17,032	22,521	5,994	8,516
Potatoes	11,064	11,429	12,105	44,254	22,859	30,263
Vegetables, etc. ...	172,479	127,876	71,942	1,74,564	97,252	73,384
Bhusa	115,439	147,276	239,536	41,657	53,438	88,860
Animals for slaughter	28,907	30,042	34,960	1,74,862	1,88,825	2,21,027

Chapter VI.

Towns, Municipalities and Cantonments.

Multan Municipality.

Octroi.

Details.	Weight.			Value		
	1897-98.	1898-99.	1899-00.	1897-98.	1898-99.	1899-00.
	Mds.	Mds.	Mds.	Rs.	Rs.	Rs.
Lighting materials						
Oil and oil seeds ...	94,943	151,218	117,536	4,58,544	5,65,192	5,63,342
Soap, sajji, etc.	17,820	28,973	38,825	31,223	42,318	48,487
Charcoal	14,174	17,160	21,576	14,174	21,450	26,970
Firewood	435,097	520,432	487,637	1,08,774	1,30,108	1,21,909
Building materials ...	83,786	120,773	124,646	1,61,096	2,01,142	1,61,126
Spices and perfumes ...	18,051	16,198	15,256	1,57,056	1,45,593	1,41,101
Tobacco	3,107	2,748	3,511	37,286	21,983	35,170
Piece-goods, etc.						
Cloth, Native	1,591	1,647	2,110	63,724	65,896	84,413
" European	18,255	21,353	19,126	18,25,502	21,35,278	19,12,581
Woollen cloth	585	298	284	23,138	12,666	28,440
Silk "	25	21	32	8,590	13,431	19,161
Gold embroidered cloth ...	14	32	34	27,493	30,308	36,466
Slippers	71	72	84	4,541	5,133	7,242
Sacking	1,313	1,677	469	17,722	11,455	14,064
Native twist and yarn ...	619	756	594	15,481	18,915	14,850
Metals	9,279	10,078	8,477	1,05,064	99,144	82,628
Total ...	1,840,709	2,035,000	1,973,253	71,47,788	63,88,484	72,44,952

Trade.

The trade of Multan city constitutes the main feature of the trade of the district, which has already been described in Chapter IV above. The following statement, however, which is based on figures furnished by the Municipality, is of interest in showing the changes which have come over the trade of the town during the last twenty years :—

Chapter VI.
Towns, Municipalities and Cantonments.
Multan.

Trade.

Statement showing export and import of articles in the Multan Municipality and Cantonment (in maunds).

Articles.	Imports.			Exports.			Imports.			Exports.		
	1880-81	1881-82	1882-83	1881-82	1882-83	1883-84	1897	1898	1899	1897	1898	1899
Raw cotton	17,853	23,891	26,455	14,057	17,926	15,586	23,835	28,608	32,438	120	50	...
European twist and yarn ...	2,122	2,065	1,872	59	107	73	3,628	1,248	1,200	...	...	...
" piece-goods	21,687	17,708	15,607	12,991	14,109	10,976	18,255	21,353	19,120	...	5,022	2,042
Indigo	12,248	24,071	15,027	9,480	12,334	11,971	3,888	3,796	3,860	784	456	150
Wheat	255,582	213,695	293,637	13,515	10,880	26,215	382,323	438,817	391,048	1,480	2,360	500
Gram and pulse	64,560	52,405	86,778	8,375	4,024	4,465	105,464	85,797	73,530	700	1,396	44
Rice	25,563	29,366	24,365	5,763	6,655	4,068	24,790	20,042	18,231	...	32	...
Ghi	12,400	11,278	15,689	1,060	377	170	13,836	19,420	15,021	...	...	...
Lahori salt	11,389	10,569	11,488	1,363	875	1,113	7,144	4,346	2,404	228	112	20
Seeds, all kinds	93,922	107,964	109,255	15,647	14,573	19,197	69,147	121,557	82,706	...	...	...
Silk, raw	1,235	847	1,169	416	215	135	616	360	388	5	7	...
Sugar, refined	55,138	57,503	58,918	20,620	20,486	18,754	84,415	59,386	62,112	228	150	95
Sugar, unrefined	59,598	94,849	42,781	33,134	43,809	19,188	46,097	49,711	54,100	204	...	...
Indian tea	...	23	46	...	...	...	1,100	100	1,300	...	...	...

Chapter VI.

Towns, Municipalities and Cantonments.

Multan.

Population.

The population of Multan, as ascertained at the various enumerations, is shown in the margin. In 1855 the population was returned at 55,999, but this seems to have included not only the cantonments but also the agricultural population of those areas of the 'tarafs' which lie outside the municipality. It is difficult also to ascertain the precise limits within which the enumerations of 1868 and 1875 were taken; the figures for the population within municipal limits, according to the census of 1868, are taken from the published tables of the census of 1875; but it was noted at the time that their accuracy was doubtful. The figures quoted for the 'whole town' in 1881, 1891 and 1901 include merely the cantonments and the municipality, and the difference between the upper and the lower figures quoted represents the population of the cantonments. As regards the population within municipal limits, this also is divided into two groups, *viz.*, the population living in the city proper and that living in the suburbs. The details of the groups at the last three enumerations were as shown in the margin. The details for the chief suburbs were worked out in 1881, and will be found in the Report of the Census of that year but they were not taken out separately at subsequent enumerations.

Limits of enumeration.	Year of census.	Persons.	Males.	Females.
Whole town.	1868 ...	54,652	31,830	22,822
	1881 ...	68,674	38,988	79,686
	1891 ...	74,562	41,953	32,609
	1901 ...	87,394	49,328	38,066
Municipal limits.	1868 ...	45,602	...	...
	1875 ...	50,878	...	...
	1881 ...	57,471	31,088	26,383
	1891 ...	64,265	34,595	29,670
	1901 ...	74,627	40,527	34,100

Municipal limits.	1868	1881	1891	1901
City proper ...	27,683	31,878	35,381	39,705
Suburbs ...	19,919	25,593	28,884	34,922
Total ...	45,602	57,471	64,265	74,627

The constitution of the people by religion is shown in Table No. XLIII. The proportion of Hindus and Musalmans within municipal limits was in 1901 as shown in the margin. These figures are unfortunately of more than merely statistical interest, as from time to time the feeling between the two religions has run somewhat high. The chief occasion on which the feeling has become prominent was on the 20th September 1881, when a riot took place between the Hindus and Muhammadans regarding the sale of beef in the city, and the additions then recently made to the Prahladpuri temple. Property

In 1901	Hindus and Sikhs	... ...	43·
,,	Muhammadans	... ...	56·6

Chapter VI.

Towns, Municipalities and Cantonments.

Multan.

estimated at Rs. 50,000 was destroyed. The city was occupied by troops from the 20th to the 30th September ; and a punitive police post, costing Rs. 8,500, was imposed on the city for one year. The feeling also breaks out occasionally in a milder form on the occasion of the annual Muharram processions.

THE CANTONMENTS.

The Cantonments.

Position and population.

The Sikh cantonments used to be at Baba Safra near the site now covered by the encamping ground known as the Am Khas, north of the tahsil. After annexation the British troops were for a time stationed in the old fort, but subsequently cantonments were found in the high stretch of land lying to the south-west of the town, and the whole of the troops in the district, are now stationed in these cantonments. To the cantonments was added some ten years ago a defensible post, situated on the southern side near the railway. On the side of the cantonments towards the city lie the commissariat lines and a sadr bazaar of the usual type.

The population of the cantonments varies naturally from time to time according to the number of the tropps stationed in them. The figures given at the various enumerations are as follows :—

Year.	Persons.	Males.	Females.
1881	11,203	7,900	3,303
1891	10,297	7,358	2,939
1901	12,767	8,801	3,966

The constitution by religion also varies somewhat with the class of regiments composing the garrison. In 1901 fifty per cent. of the population were Hindus or Sikhs, 37 per cent. Musalmans and 12 per cent. Christians, one per cent. Jains and others.

Authorities.

The cantonment is commanded by a Colonel on the staff. The staff consists of a Station Staff Officer of the first class, an Executive Commissariat Officer, Senior Medical Officer, Chaplain and Cantonment Magistrate.

The cantonment authority is the Cantonment Committee, of which the Commanding Officer of the cantonment is the President, and the Cantonment Magistrate the Secretary. The

Chapter VI.

Towns, Municipalities and Cantonments.

Multan cantonment.

Authorities.

committee meets monthly and consists, in addition to the President and Secretary, of the following members :—A Magistrate of the first class, being also a Joint President appointed by the District Magistrate to represent him; such Commanding Officers in the cantonment as may be appointed in station orders to be members; the Sanitary Officer; the Executive Engineer; the District Superintendent of Police. One non-official member has also been appointed a member by the General Officer of the Command.

Income and expenditure.

The average yearly income of the cantonment fund is about Rs. 34,000. The chief sources of revenue and the amount under each head were in 1899-00 as follows:—

	Actuals for 1899-00. Rs.
Octroi collected by the Municipality who pay a share of one-tenth to the cantonment authority ...	12,465
House tax ...	6,201
Conservancy tax ...	5,155
Land revenue ...	2,606
Slaughter house and markets ...	2,025
Sale of manure ...	1,144
Miscellaneous ...	4,991

The chief items of expenditure were as under—

Conservancy ...	9,683
Police ...	4,929
Maintenance of roads and bridges ...	3,462
Gardens and tree tending... ...	3,417
Road watering ...	2,956
Cantonment General Hospital ...	2,976
Lighting ...	698
Collection of Revenue and Office Establishment ...	3,253
Miscellaneous ...	2,153

The night-soil and rubbish is put up to public auction, and is usually taken by the grass farm committee at the highest bid. The night-soil is carted at the cost of the cantonment fund to the grass farm lands, where it is disposed of according to what is known as the Allahabad system. This work is done under European supervision.

There is no system of drainage in the sadr bazar, and consequently cesspools are a necessity. The dirty water from these is sold by auction. Little inconvenience is caused by these cesspools, which are also under European supervision, and the health of the bazar, and in fact of the cantonment generally, is excellent.

Chapter VI.

Towns, Municipalities and Cantonments.

Multan Cantonment.

Income and expenditure.

There are some 455 acres of grass farm, which yield an outturn as follows: green grass 4,000 maunds, hay 10,000 maunds, bedding grass 4,500 maunds, green chari 6,700 maunds, green khasil 2,600 maunds. The grass farm is managed by a committee consisting of the Officer Commanding the Cantonment as President, and the Officers Commanding the Royal Artillery and Native Cavalry as Members. The Secretary is usually an officer of the Native Cavalry.

The public buildings are few in number, and for the most part insignificant in style. There are two Churches, Protestant and Roman Catholic. The Cantonment General Hospital is situated to the east of cantonments, and is under the medical charge of one of the Medical Officers quartered in cantonments.

The defensible post was completed in 1890-91, but was garrisoned by a detachment from the 2nd Battalion, Warwickshire Regiment, in 1889.

Multan is a sub-division of the Military Works Service, and is under the Garrison Engineer, Lahore District, Mian Mir. The repair and maintenance of all cantonment fund roads is carried out by the Military Works Department; the cost being borne by the cantonment fund.

European cemeteries.

The main cemetery at Multan is that in cantonments situated north of the Native Infantry Lines. There are also round the city the cemetery of the Am Khás, and the three cemeteries in the direction of the Central Jail, constructed during the siege of 1848, to which reference has been made above.*

Shujabad Town.

Shujabad town.

Shujabad (often spoken of as Shuja da Kot, or Tal Kot or merely as Kot) is situated about five miles east of the Chenab river, and two miles west of the Shujabad Railway station on the N.-W. Railway. The town is chiefly built of brick, and it is surrounded by a wall, with four gates; the Multani gate on the north, the Mári Mori gate on the east, the Rashid Shah gate on the south, and the Chautáka gate on the west. A broad bazar runs from the Multani to the Rashid Shah gate, and is crossed at right angles by another straight bazar running from

* At Adamwahan there is a cemetery containing the tombs of railway employés and others who died there during the construction of the Empress bridge in the years preceding 1878. At Shujabad there is the tomb of an unknown European; and at Lodhran the tomb of a Mr. Leeson, dating from before 1858. In the canal bungalow compound at Kahror, a Mr. Greene, Assistant Engineer, is buried, and just outside the old customs bungalow in the same place there are two small tombs of an oriental type, which are said to have been constructed by a Mr. Wright, an officer of the Customs Preventive Service, in memory of two of his children. There are European tombs also at Bagren, in Shujabad, and at Kádirpur Ran, on the Lahore road: those at Bagren are said to be tombs of officials of the Customs Preventive Service.

Chapter VI.

Towns, Municipalities and Cantonments.

Shujabad town.

the Mári Mori to the Chautaka gate. The city was founded in A.D. 1750 by Nawab Shuja Khan, who built the present walls in 1767 to 1772. The town was a favourite residence of the Nawab and great pains were taken by him to induce Hindus of wealth to live and trade in it. Under Nawab Muzaffar Khan the prosperity of the town was still further advanced. Besides eight large houses,* one for each of his sons, this Nawab built at considerable cost the Mubarik Mahal, the Samman Burj and the Jaház Mahal. The two former were on the city walls, and have since been destroyed, but the Jaház Mahal is now used as a tahsil, and a part of it was, until A.D. 1900, used as a police station. The building received its name either from the fact that it was built more or less in the form of a ship, or as a corruption of 'Hajáz,' its construction having been undertaken immediately after Muzaffar Khan returned from Mecca †; and in the western room there are still to be seen some curious frescoes, which are said to represent Arabian cities. In one of the halls there used to be a beautiful marble floor; which, however, was removed some time ago, and is now to be seen in a somewhat mutilated state in the Multan Subscription Library in the Lánge Khan Garden, which was formerly a small local museum. The traveller Masson, who passed Shujabad on his way from Sindh to Lahore, apparently in 1827, wrote of this place ('Travels, i, p. 394)—

> 'Shujah Kot or Shujabad is a considerable fortified town, and its lofty battlements, irregularly built, have a picturesque appearance. It has a very excellent bazar, and is the seat of some cotton manufactures, besides being famous for its turners in wood. There is a small garrison, and a few guns are mounted on the walls; near it are several good gardens, particularly one bearing the name of Muzaffar Khan, The town stands in a highly cultivated tract, and for two or three *cosses* to the south there were immense fields of sugarcane The cotton plant is also abundantly grown.

Shujabad capitulated to Edwardes in 1848 immediately after the action at Kineri, and throughout the seige at Multan it was the site of a considerable Commissariat Depôt. A little outside the town, at its north-west side, is a Christian tomb without inscription, which is said to commemorate an English soldier who died here during that period. The town was seriously threatened by heavy floods in 1893 and 1894, and in 1894 a dyke or *band* was made round the town partly at the expense of the Municipal Committee, and partly from public subscription.

---

* One of them is now used as a dispensary.

† A few miles south of Shujabad is an old garden, known as the Mubarik Bagh, from the fact that this was the place to which the inhabitants of Shujabad went to meet and to congratulate Nawab Muzaffar Khan on his return from the Hajj.

Chapter VI.

Towns, Municipalities and Cantonments.

Shujabad town.

The population of Shujabad at the various enumerations is shown in the margin. The constitution of the population by religion is given in Table No. XLIII, from which it will be seen that in 1901 sixty-five per cent. of the population were Hindus. The place inside the walls is almost exclusively devoted to Hindus, the Muhammedans being found mainly in the suburban hamlets outside the walls. The Municipal Committee consists of fifteen members (ten elected and five nominated) under the presidency of the Tahsildar.

	Year.	Persons.	Males.	Females.
Municipal limits.	1868...	6,095	3,180	2,915
	1875...	6,280	...	...
	1881...	6,458	3,420	3,038
	1891...	6,329	3,439	2,880
	1901...	5,880	3,236	2,644

The income of the Municipality for the last thirty years is shown in Table No. XLV. The present incomings and outgoings, taking the year 1899 as an example, are as follows :—

Income.	Rs.	Expenditure.	Rs.
Octroi	7,406	Police	1,509
Other sources	2,480	Conservancy	1,659
		Dispensaries	1,639
		Public Works	90
		Schools	2,538
		Miscellaneous	2,273
Total	9,886	Total ...	9,708

The city has a certain reputation for the manufacture of the sweet confections known as *pápar* and *reorian*, for the production of which the sugarcane grown in the vicinity used to afford special advantages.

Jalalpur Pirwala.

Jalalpur.

This town is situated on the banks of an old river bed, known as the Bhatari, which still receives a backwater flooding from the Chenab in good years. The town is said to have been founded by Sultan Ahmad Kattál a descendant of Syad Jalál; but it is also stated that a Langáh or Awán of the name of Jalál founded the town, and that Sultan Ahmad Kattál settled here subsequently. It is known in old documents as Jalalpur Ahmad Kattálwah or Jalálpur Sádát, but is generally now known as Jalálpur Pirwala. The town used to be celebrated for its manufactory of native paper, of a good and durable type, which was largely used for shopkeepers' books and other purposes; but the extension of railways has much injured this industry, and it is now moribund. The wells, as a rule, are

Chapter VI.

Towns, Municipalities and Cantonments.

Jalalpur Pirwala

bitter, and such wells as are sweet (*e.g.*, that outside the thana) are thronged night and morning. The centre of attraction in the town is the fine shrine of Sultan Ahmad Kattál. This saint was a descendant of Syad Jalal of Uch, a native of Bokhara, who died in A.H. 690 (A.D. 1291). Pir Kattál himself was born at Uch in A.H. 949 (A.D. 1542), and at an early age set out on his travels with Sanniasis and other holy men of both religions. At Kahror he attended on Pir Ali Sarwar, and one day, when Ali Sarwar was asleep and some sparrows began to twitter, Ahmad Kattál, fearing that they would wake the saint, slew them by a single word. Pir Ali Sarwar on waking and seeing what had happened, said: 'You are a great killer' (*kattál*); for which reason the saint was known thereafter as Ahmad Kattál. After travelling to Mecca, Baghdad and Karbala, he returned to Multan, and for some time preached in the Bar country among the Lakhwera and Saldera tribes, whom he converted to Islam. He took up his abode in 990 A.H. (A.D. 1582) in Jalalpur, and died in A.H. 1041 (A.D. 1631) in the odour of great sanctity. The present tomb was built by one of his descendants in A.H. 1158 (A.D. 1745), and though not very striking in outline it presents a magnificent field of coloured tile work of a good kind.

There is a large fair here every Friday in the month of Chet (March-April), which is celebrated for the practice, which prevails of exorcising evil spirits from women. The practice is known as '*jinn khelna*,' and the Musalman women are exorcised by day and the Hindus by night. There is a good deal of scandal connected with the business; it is openly said that women feign possession in order to make assignations at the fair, and the better class of zamindars look on the matter with a certain amount of disgust.

Masson who visited this town (apparently in 1827) writes (Travels, vol. i, p. 392). :—

"Leaving Uch I directed my course to the river Garra, eight *cosses* from it and, crossing at a ferry, came two or three *cosses* further on to a large cut, or arm, probably derived from it. I might have been perplexed as to the mode of crossing it, but fortunately I saw a person, before I reached it, strip himself of his clothing, and, placing it on his head, pass to the opposite side. I had therefore only to imitate him, and waded through the stream some fifty or sixty yards in breadth, with the water of uniform depth, and up to my mouth, which I was compelled to keep closed. The water was tepid, whence I inferred that it was a canal I was crossing.* About a *coss* beyond it I found the small town of Pir Jalalpur, which contains the shrine of a Musalman saint; a handsome building covered with painted and lacquered tiles and adorned with minarets and cupola. The bazar was a good one, and in the neighbourhood of the town were decayed brick buildings, proving that the site was formerly of importance.

* Not a canal but the Vehary or Bhatari, which Masson probably crossed at the usual place near Shujaatpur village. A bridge has recently been built at this crossing.

Chapter VI.

Towns, Municipalities and Cantonments.

Jalalpur.

The town is the head-quarters of a thana, and its population at the various enumerations is shown in the margin. It is difficult to ascertain the precise limits within which the enumerations of 1868 and 1875 were taken. The figures for the population within municipal limits, according to the census of 1886, are taken from the published tables of the census of 1875, but it was noted at the time that their accuracy was doubtful.

Limit of enumeration.	Years of census.	Persons.	Males.	Females.
Whole town.	1868 ..	3,585	1,822	1,763
	1881 ...	3,875	1,965	1,910
	1891 ...	3,884	1,866	1,918
	1901 ...	5,149	2,704	2,445
Municipal limits.	1868 ...	3,596	...	...
	1875 ...	3,525	...	...
	1881 ..	3,875	1,965	1,910
	1891 ...	3,884	1,966	1,918
	1901 ...	5,149	2,704	2,445

The constitution of the population by religion is set forth in Table No. XLIII. The Municipal Committee consists of 12 members (9 elected, 2 *ex-officio* and 1 nominated), with the Tahsildar as President. Its income for the last 26 years is shown in Table No. XLV. The income and expenditure, taking the year 1899 as an example, now stands as follows:—

Income.	Rs.	Expenditure.	Rs.
Octroi	3,630	Police	815
Other sources	1,293	Conservancy	813
		Dispensaries	400
		Public Works	15
		Schools	1,444
		Micellaneous	1,625
Total ...	4,923	Total ...	5,112

DUNYAPUR TOWN.

Dunyapur town.

The town of Dunyapur was formerly watered by irrigation from the Bias, and now receives a certain amount of water from the Jámwah Kalán Canal; but it is generally approached through a stretch of desert, and presents a somewhat weird appearance in the middle of so much surrounding desolation. Whether the name implies its previous size (sc. World city), or whether one Duni Chand was its founder, is uncertain; but the tales which ascribe its foundation to the Joyas in Aurangzeb's reign are obviously wrong, as the town is mentioned in the 'Ain-i-Akbari,' and it was at the beginning of the 16th century the scene of a great fight between the Bhatti Ráwal

Chapter VI.

Towns, Municipalities and Cantonments.

Dunyapur town.

Chachik of Jaisalmir and the Langáh Princes of Multán. The event is described as follows by the inimitable Tod :—

'Two years after this Chachik made war on Thirr-raj Khokur, the Chief of Pilibunga, on account of a horse stolen from a Bhatti. The Khokurs were defeated and plundered; but his old enemies, the Langahs, taking advantage of this occasion, made head against Chachik, and drove his garrison from the new possession of Dhuniapur. Disease at length seized on Ráwal Chachik after a long course of victorious warfare, in which he subdued various tracts of country, even to the heart of the Punjab. In this state he determined to die, as he had lived, with arms in his hand, but having no foe near with whom to cope, he sent an embassy to the Langah Prince of Multán, to beg, as a last favour, *jood-dan*, or gift of battle, that his soul might escape by the steel of foemen, and not fall a sacrifice to slow disease. The Prince, suspecting treachery, hesitated; but the Bhatti messenger pledged his word that his master only wished an honourable death, and that he would only bring five hundred men to the combat. The challenge being accepted, the Rawal called his clansmen around him, and on his recounting what he had done, seven hundred select Rajputs, who had shared in all his victories, volunteered to take the last field, and make *sunkluf* (oblation) of their lives with their leader . . . . . . Meanwhile Rana Chachik marched to Dhuniapur 'to part with life.' There he heard that the Prince of Multán was within two *coss*. His soul was rejoiced; he performed his ablutions, worshipped the sword and the gods, bestowed charity, and withdrew his thoughts from this world. The battle lasted four *gharris* (two hours), and the Jadun Prince fell with all his kin after performing prodigies of valour. Two thousand Khans fell beneath their swords; rivers of blood flowed in the field, but the Bhatti gained the abode of Indra, who shared his throne with the hero.'—(*Tod, Rajasthan, Calc. Edition of* 1894, ii, pp. 212-13.)

The houses of the town are almost all of brick, and there are traces of two forts, one in the city itself and one to the north. There is a half ruined mosque on the north side of the city, adorned with the remains of some enamelled tile work, and a somewhat picturesque Jama Masjid in the middle of the town. Half-a-mile or so to the north-west is the *samadh* of Jamna Nath, a *sanniási* of the XVIth century, whose guru immigrated from Bahawalpur to this place. The holy man's rosary, conch and other instruments of worship are said to be preserved here. The places where he and his disciples buried themselves alive are still shown, and immediately adjoining are small temples to Shiv and Devi. The place is locally known as the 'Marhián.'

The figures on the margin show the population of the town at the various enumerations. It is difficult to ascertain the precise limits within which the enumerations of 1868 and 1875 were taken. The figures for the population within municipal limits, according to the census of 1868, are taken from the published tables of the census of 1875; but it was noted at the time that their accuracy was in many cases doubtful.

Limits of enumeration.	Years of census.	Persons	Males.	Females.
Whole town.	1868 ...	2,687	1,310	1,377
	1881 ...	2,041	935	1,106
	1891 ...	2,101	901	1,200
	1901 ...	2,150	1,012	1,138
Municipal limits.	1868 ...	2,708	...	...
	1875 ...	2,054	...	...
	1881 ...	2,041	935	1,106
	1891 ...	2,101	901	1,200
	1901 ...	2,150	1,012	1,138

Chapter VI.

Towns, Municipalities and Cantonments.

Dunyapur town.

The excess of females over males is due to the fact that numbers of the male population are employed in Government service as patwaris, etc., outside the town, both in British and in Bahâwalpur territory. The constitution of the population by religion is shown in Table No. XLIII, from which it will be seen that nearly two-thirds of the inhabitants are Hindus.

There was a Municipal Committee here till 1893. On 6th December 1893 the town was made a "notified area" under Act XX of 1891, and its internal administration is now looked after by a committee of two members and the Tahsildar as President. The chief income is from octroi, and the amount of the receipts for the past 26 years will be found entered in Table No. XLV below. Taking the figures for 1899 as an example the accounts of the town are as follows :—

Income.	Rs.	Expenditure.	Rs.
Octroi	675	Police	204
Other sources	204	Conservancy	160
		Miscellaneous	422
Total ...	929	Total ...	786

KAHROR TOWN.

Kahror.

Kahror (also spelt Karor, and pronounced in the neighbourhood Kirhûr;) is situated on the south bank of an old river bed. The local legend is that it was founded by one Kehr, a Bhatti, dependant of the Delhi sovereigns ; and that when Kahror revolted it was retaken by the Joyas, who, till lately, were the most prominent Muhammadan landowners in the place. Tod, in his account of Jaisalmir history in the fourteenth or very beginning of the fifteenth century, writes that " Kailun (Chief of Jaisalmir) built a fort on the Beyah, called after his father Kerroh or Kerore.*"

The most remarkable building in the town is the shrine of Ali Sarwar, which is a domed *khankah,* visible for many miles round. Ali Sarwar was a Syad of Delhi, who came to Kahror A.H. 600 (A.D. 1204)†, and married a Pathan wife ; for which reason his descendants are known as Pathans. He spent many years in Baghdad and elsewhere, and, visited Mecca six times, but ended his days in Kahror. The shrine was built by his son, and his descendants are men of position at the present day.

* As will be seen by a reference to Chapter II above, Kahror is mentioned by historians of a much earlier date, but the Kahror there referred to is probably Kot Karor in the Dera Ismail Khan district.

† The legend of Sultan Ahmed, Kattâl, given in the account of Jalâlpur above, ascribes to Ali Sarwar a date three centuries later.

Chapter VI.

Towns, Municipalities and Cantonments.

Kahror town.

They intermarry only among themselves and not with either Syads or Pathans.

Another building of note is the shrine of Pír Badhan, which lies about half-a-mile to the east of Kahror. This commemorates the rule of one Pír Badhan, a governor of Kahror in Moghal times, who used to give away to the poor not only his money, but the Government treasure as well. But when he remitted broken bricks and potsherds to Delhi instead of treasure, these were changed on the way to Ashrafis, so that no evil results followed the pious ruler's liberality. At the shrine both Hindus and Muhammadans have their childrens' heads shaved.

Near the canal bungalow on the south-west of the town are four brick obelisks, which are said to mark the *samadhs* of Sanniasis. In the bungalow compound, surrounded by a thick hedge, is the tomb of a canal officer with an iron head-mark, on which is inscribed: "G Green, Assistant Engineer, died 6th July 1867."

The town itself has a good paved bazar running through it, which was made after the British occupation, and it consists mainly of brick houses, some of which are of a peculiar type, being like ranges of factories without windows. The ground on which the town is built is undulating, which makes the appearance of the town more picturesque than that of most Indian towns. The town is the centre of the trade of the Sutlej tahsils of this district, dealing especially in wool, piece-goods and wheat, and it has a local reputation for the manufacture of stamped coverlets (palang-poshes). The inhabitants of Kahror are satirised in the following verses:—

> Ayá yár Kahrori
> Lash pash ghaní, mohabbat thori,
> Vikháien darwáza, te langháien mori;

which means that a friend from Kahror is full of protestation but has little real affection; what seemed a wide door turns out to be a narrow wicket.

The population of the town at the different enumerations is shown in the margin. It is difficult to ascertain the precise limits within which the enumerations of 1868 and 1875 were taken; the figures for the enumeration in 1868 of the population within municipal limits are taken from the published returns

Limits of enumeration.	Year of census.	Persons	Males.	Females.
Whole town.	1868 ...	5,024	2,662	2,362
	1881 ...	4,804	2,532	2,272
	1891 ...	5,498	2,861	2,637
	1901 ...	5,552	2,878	2,674
Municipal limits.	1868 ...	5,069	...	...
	1875 ..	4,650	..	...
	1881 ...	4,804	2,532	2,272
	1891 ...	5,498	2,861	2,637
	1901 ...	5,552	2,878	2,674

Chapter VI.

Towns. Municipalities and Cantonments.

Kahror town.

of 1875, but it was noted at the time that the figures were in many cases of doubtful accuracy. The constitution of the population by religion is shown in Table No. XLIII below, from which it will be seen that in 1901 sixty-five per cent. of the inhabitants of the municipality were Hindus.

The town is managed by a Municipal Committee of 14 members (10 elected, 2 nominated and 2 *ex-officio*), with the Tahsildar as President. The income for the last thirty years is shown in Table No. XLV. The figures for income and expenditure in 1899, which may be taken as a fair illustration of the position of the municipality, are as follows :—

Income.	Rs.	Expenditure.	Rs.
Octroi	3,733	Police	99
Other sources	187	Conservancy	744
		Dispensaries	825
		Public Works	118
		Schools	1,372
		Miscellaneous	1,008
Total ...	3,920	Total ...	4,062

Tulamba Town.

Tulamba.

The present town of Tulamba appears to have been preceded by at least two previous sites, one of which was at the huge mound known as "Mamu Sher," a mile or so to the south-east of the present town, and the other among the ruins which extend immediately to the west. Local tradition ascribes the foundation to one Raja Tal, a descendant of Raja Saliváhan of Sialkot, from whom the fort was called 'Tal Ubha" (or Northern Tal) ; others, with a shade less of improbability, say "Tul Ubha" (the Northern Fort). Whether Tulamba is, as Cunningham suggests, the "χωρίον ὀχυρὸν καὶ τετειχισμένον," taken by Alexander, or, as Masson suggests, the "Βραχμάνων πόλις" also taken by the same conqueror (see Chapter II above), is a question somewhat difficult of solution ; the distances given being rather in favour of the former conjecture, while the fact that the city is still a stronghold of Brahmans is to some extent in favour of the latter. There is a tradition that it was taken by Mahmud of Ghazni, but its first appearance in actual history is during the invasion of Tamerlane, who himself in his Memoirs gives the following account of his capture and sack of the city (October 1398) :—

"When I arrived at the city of Tulamba I pitched my camp at the bank of the river. Tulamba is about seventy miles from Multan. On the same day the Saiyids, and 'Ulama, and Sheikhs, and chief men and rulers of Tulamba came out to meet

Chapter VI.

Towns, Municipalities and Cantonments.

Tulamba town.

me, and enjoyed the honour of kissing my stirrup. As sincerity was clearly written on their foreheads, every one of the them, according to his rank, was distinguished by marks of my princely favour. Marching forward I halted on Saturday, the 1st of the month Safar, in the plain which lies before the fortress of Tulamba. My Wazirs had fixed the ransom of the people of the city at two lakhs of rupees, and appointed collectors; but as the Saiyids, who are family and descendants of our Lord Muhammad, the chosen, and the 'Ulama of Islam, who are the heirs of the prophets (upon him and upon them be blessings and peace), had always in my court been honoured and treated with reverence and respect, I gave orders now that a ransom was about to be levied from the citizens of Tulamba, that whatever was written against the names of the Saiyids and 'Ulama should be struck out of the account, and I sent them away, having filled their hearts with joy and triumph by presents of costly dresses of honour and Arab horses. A reinforcement of troops arrived about this time, so that my troops became more numerous than the tribes of ants and locusts, causing scarcity of provisions, so that there was a dearth of grain in my camp, though the people had quantities. Since a part of the ransom, consisting of coin, had not yet been callected, and since my troops were distressed on account of the scarcity of provisions, I ordered that the citizens should make payment in grain instead of money; but they persisted in storing up their corn, totally regardless of the sufferings of my troops. The hungry Tatars, making a general assault upon them like ants and locusts, plundered an enormous number of granaries, so numerous, indeed, as to be incalculable, and according to the text, "Verily kings when they enter a city utterly ruin it," the hungry Tatars opened the hands of devastation in the city till a rumour of the havoc they were making reached me. I ordered the Saiyids and Tawachis to expel the troops from the city, and commanded that whatever corn and other property had been plundered should be taken as an equivalent for so much ransom. At this time it was represented to me that some of the chief zamindars of the environs of Tulamba, at the time when Prince Pir Muhammad was marching on Multan, had presented themselves before him, walking in the path of obedience and submission, but when they had received their dismissal, and returned to their own home, they planted their feet on the highway of contumacy and rebellion. I immediately gave orders to Amir Shah Malik and to Sheikh Muhammad, the son of Aiku, Timur, to march with their tumans and kushuns against these rebels, and to inflict condign punishment upon them. Amir Shah Malik and Sheikh Muhammad taking a guide with them, instantly commenced their march, and having arrived at the jungles in which these wretches, forsaken by fortune, had taken refuge, they dismounted, and entering the jungle slew two thousand of these ill-fated Indians with their remorseless sabres, carrying off captives their women and children, and returned with a great booty of kine, buffaloes, and other property. When on their victorious return they displayed in my sight the spoils they had won, I ordered to make a general distribution to the soldiery. When my mind was satisfied with the extermination of these wretches, on Saturday, the 7th of Safar, I set my foot in the stirrup and marched from Tulamba.'

The statement made in Dow's translation of Firishta (i., 487) that the fort was left untouched because its capture would have delayed Tamerlane's progress does not seem to be supported by the original. The city, however, seems to have continued in existence, and its removal to its present, or at any rate to another, site is ascribed to a change in the course of the river in the days of Mahmúd Khán, Langáh, at the beginning of the sixteenth century. Tulamba appears in the Sikh legends as the scene of adventure experienced with a thag by Guru Nanak. The city is mentioned as one of the mahals of Multan Sirkar in the days of Akbar, and in Shah Jahan's time it was the site of one of the sarais on the road between Lahore and Multan. This sarai is said to have been cut away by the river in A.D. 1750. The city was looted by Ahmad Shah, Abdali, in one of his incursions, but recovered prosperity under Sharif Beg, after-

Chapter VI.

Towns, Municipalities and Cantonments.

wards. Naib-Názim of Multan, who built (about 1759 A.D.) the striking enclosure (said to have been a serai), which still stands on the south-west edge of the town, and in which are situated the thana, school, post office and other Government buildings.

Tulamba town.

The site of the old city at Mámú Sher is thus described by Cunningham, who visited it twice :—

"It consisted of an open city, protected on the south by a lofty fortress 1,000 feet square. The outer rampart is of earth, 200 feet thick, 20 feet high on the outer face, or *faussebraie*, with a second rampart of the same height on the top of it. Both of these were orginally faced with large bricks, 12 by 8 by 2¼ inches. Inside the rampart there is a clear space or ditch, 100 feet in breadth, surrounding an inner fort 400 feet square, with walls 40 feet in height, and in the middle of this there is a square tower or castle, 70 feet in height, which commands the whole space. The numerous fragments of bricks lying about, and the still existing marks of the courses of the bricks in many places on the outer faces of the ramparts, confirm the statements of the people that the walls were formerly faced with brick.

The traveller Masson, who was here about 1827 A.D., writes—

"Another march brought us to the neighbourhood of Tulamba, surrounded by groves of date trees and, to appearance, a large, populous and walled-in town. I did not visit it, for, although we stayed three or four days in its neighbourhood, I fell sick. Close to our camp was, however, the ruins of a mud fortress with walls and towers unusually huge and thick. I cannot call to mind the name it bears."

And he proceeds to identify the fortress (the Mámú Sher mound) with the Brahman city of Arrian.

The population of the area within municipal limits as ascertained at the various enumerations is given in the margin, and from these figures it will be seen that the population of Tulamba is subject to more fluctuations than that of any other town in the district.

		Persons.	Males.	Females.
Municipal limits.	1868 ...	3,152	1,762	1,390
	1875 ...	1,948	...	...
	1881 ...	2,231	1,214	1,017
	1891 ...	2,792	1,532	1,260
	1901 ...	2,526	1,272	1,254

The cause of the variations is the dependence of the prosperity of the town on the irrigation from the Ravi, which is now extremely uncertain in its action. The town has also lost a good deal of such importance as it once possessed since the railway supplanted the river route to and from Lahore. The constitution of the population by religions is given in Table No. XLIII, which shows that more than half the inhabitants are Hindus.

The town is a considerable centre of the local date trade, and has also a reputation for the stamped floor-cloths (*tak*) manufactured here. Its affairs are managed by a Municipal Committee consisting of 9 members (7 elected, 1 nominated and 1 *ex-officio*); with the Tahsildar as President.

Chapter VI.

Towns, Municipalities and Cantonments.

Tulamba town.

The income of the municipality for the last twenty-six years is shown in Table No. XLV. The accounts of the municipality taking the year 1899 as an example, now stand as follows :—

Income.	Rs.	Expenditure.	Rs.
Octroi	1,630	Police	248
Other sources	728	Conservancy	252
		Public Works...	14
		Schools	1,349
		Miscellaneous...	627
Total ...	2,358	Total ...	2,490

APPENDIX TO CHAPTER II.

BALLAD OF THE MULTAN CAMPAIGN, 1848-49.

By Sobha, son of Fazil, Biloch, of Wahi Tajewala, Tahsil Shujabad, who died about 1870 *A.D. at the age of* 60.*

1.	**Angrezán wí cháre ní kíte, Charh Multán wí áyá.**	The English made an attempt, They marched to Multan.
2.	**Wich mutábiat háizr thiye, Wanj Múle sís niwáyá.**	Múla presented himself humbly, He went and bowed his head.
3.	**Bát kahí Angrez ihá, Phir nál Diwán aláyá.**	The Englishman spoke thus, Addressing the Diwán :
4.	**Súbe kul Panjábí Sáhib chá mauqúf karáyá.**	'All the Governors in the Panjab Have the Sáhibs had dismissed.
5.	**Ghin sipáh uthá tamámí, Sat ghat mulk paráyá.**	Take away all thy troops, Yield up the realm which is no longer thine.'
6.	**Akhyus nahín adúl mekon til jittí. Sáhib jiwen farmáyá.**	He said to them : 'I cannot but obey, Even as the Sáhib hath spoken.'
7.	**Hukm kitá Angrezán Múle charh kar shahr phiráyá.**	The English gave the order Múla mounted and showed them the city.
8.	**Dekhan nál khánqáhán de Sáhib Múle kanún puchhwáyá.**	On seeing the shrines The Sáhibs made enquiry of Múla.
9.	**Eh gumbad kibán nishánián? Ithán kain eh naqsh banáyá?**	'What signify these domes? Who made these wonderful buildings?'
10.	**Akhyus eh hin khánqáhán pírán dián Jinhán he Multán banáyá.**	He said to them : 'They are the shrines of the pírs Of them that made Multán.
11.	**Gaí he khák chumendí har kai Jo Súbá ithe áyá.**	All that have come hitherto as Governors Have kissed the dust before them.
12.	**Akhyus khákí khám karesán gumbad Jo main hik gurz chaláyá.**	The Englishman answered : 'I shall beat the domes to dust With one sweep of my mace.'
13.	**Díwán há aswár pakhí dá Rakhke qadam sawáyá.**	The Díwán rode on a fiery horse Which moved forward before the rest.
14.	**Angrez ulárivá chábak Ghorá Múle dahon dauráyá.**	The Englishman raised his whip, (1) Thereon Múla spurred on his horse.
15.	**Barchhí már sipáhí dauriyá Wendá nazar ná áyá.**	A soldier struck the Englishman with his spear and ran And become lost to sight.
16.	**Thí zakhmí Angrez giyá. Wal dere dahon sidháyá.**	The Englishman was wounded And returned quickly to his camp.
17.	**Díwán áya wich kháne de Jain musaddí kul sadáyá.**	The Díwán entered his home And called all his ministers.
18.	**Akhyus bandobast badho kái changí. Iwen ghamzade farmáyá.**	Said he : 'Give me good counsel,' So spake he in his dejection.
19.	**Wer rakhán main shibán nál, Bhárí jang ghazab da cháyá.**	'I have a feud with liens, I have provoked a terrible war.

*** It may be noted here that the transliteration and translation of this ballad are only in the rough, and could doubtless be much improved by an expert in the local dialect.**

(1). This version of the origin of the outbreak is, I believe, entirely legendary. At his trial Múlráj had every opportunity of stating his own case, and this story was nowhere hinted at throughout the proceedings.

No.	Text	No.	Translation
20.	Hathún chhut giyán dorán, Oh welá báth ná áyá.	20.	The reins have slipped from my hands, I have let go the opportunity.'
21.	Musaddí ral saláh ditti, Díwán kún samjháya.	21.	His ministers gave counsel together, They spake thus to the Diwán.
22.	Kití baras khazána terá, Khutde nahín khutáyá.	22.	'Thy treasury, if opened, Will last out many years.
23.	Kôt qilá gadh yákí, Na de mul ajáyá.	23.	Thy towns and forts are strong and powerful, Cast them not away in vain.'
24.	Pakke the hamráh Gorkhe, Roheláin bhárá cháya.	24.	The Gurkhas promised to remain firm by him, The Rohelas (Pathans) took up the load (of responsibility. (2)
25.	Hindú Singh topán de utte Badh kamar kar áyá.	25.	Hindu Singh girded up his loins And came to his guns.
26.	Gole gird maresán girdún Je tháin sáit bacháya.	26.	'I shall fire shot on shot,' Quoth he, 'while life lasts.'
27.	Ahá samán age da Múle Behad bahún karáyá.	27.	Múla had made beforehand Many preparations.
28.	Dárú, loh, patthar te sikká, Undá ant na páyá.	28.	Powder, iron, stone, money There was no limit to them.
29.	Atá, ghiú, mithái, arzán, Beshumár anáyá.	29.	Flour, ghí, sweetmeats, He had collected beyond count.
30.	Qalam jári wich lashkar de. Mawájib chá wadháyá.	30.	He issued orders to the army, He raised their allowances.
31.	Sun sun áwan sipáhí, Chhik Azráil ghin áyá.	31.	As they heard it the soldiers crowded in. The Angel of Death dragged them on.
32.	Pahli ránd rasi itháin, Chá Angrezán kún bhuláya.	32.	At the first rush people collected together. They forgot the power of the English.
33.	Trut gai sipáh sabhá, Jinhán khar Sardár kuháyá.	33.	In the end their whole force was dispersed, They saw their Chiefs seized and killed before them.
34.	Mang amán sipábí chhutte, Thi naukar jí chhurwáyá.	34.	The soldiers asked for pardon, They took service and saved their lives.
35.	Jin kin chhutíán dákán, Kágbaz Kalkatte dáhon pucháya.	35.	Letters were sent out on all sides, A message was sped to Calcutta.
36.	Sun Angrez hairán thae, Parh likhiá pur máyá.	36.	As they heard the news, the English were distressed. As they read what was written, they were full of astonishment.
37.	Is dhotí ban karár utte Kahín nahín itbár thahráya.	37.	No one could believe it of, This dhoti-wearing kirár!
38.	Takkar jhaleso bádsháhán dí, Jain chá fatúr khindáyá.	38.	You shall find you have offended kings. You that have raised this trouble.
39.	Jin kin chhútián dákán, Har mulkán wich sunáyá.	39.	Letters were sent out on all sides, The news was spread in every country.
40.	Likhiá Sáhib lokán dá Khán chum chat akhín te láyá.	40.	The Khan (of Bahawalpur) kissed and licked and put to his eyes The message of the Sáhibs.
41.	Bakhsh dewe jágírán, Jain kul ráje kún sadwáya.	41.	The Government will give jagirs, Having summoned all the Chiefs.
42.	Baí bhí bahún sipáh kharái, Khazána Khán haláyá.	42.	Other troops he collected, Much treasure did the Khán spend.
43.	Toman mil smále thae Sad kolun Khán balháyá.	43.	The tumans were collected together. The Khán called them to his side.
44.	Hukm bajá ándone Jo parh Khán munh aláyá.	44.	They obeyed the order Which the Khan spake unto them.
45.	Wich lashkar de bakhshí Fateh Muhammad Khán thahráyá.	45.	He made Fateh Muhammad Khan The Bakhshí (commander) of the army.
46.	Lashkar langh pawe satwíwín Wáda Khán Sáhib farmáyá.	46.	The Khán Sáhib promised That the army would cross the river on the 27th of the month.

---

(2) The Gurkhas were those of Agnew's guard who deserted him. The Rohelas were the Multáni Patháns.

47.	Chhikián áyan sab berián Te kul maláh sadwáyá.	47.	All the boats were seized, And all the boatmen summoned.
48.	Tarfún wí Angrez de Langh Pír Bráhim áyá.	48.	Pir Ibrahim also came From the side of the English.
49.	Sarwar Sháh Pír kún Urwárún Khán sadwáyá.	49.	The Khán called over from this side Sarwar Sháh Pír.
50.	He oh mard zoráwar Jaindá ho shihán te sáyá.	50.	That man was powerful As he was feared by lions.
51.	Lare waráin na rahsí hargiz Kolun phir tikáyá.	51.	There was doubt that he would never refrain from opposing the English, So the Khán kept him at his side.
52.	Alipur jang jhalli, Tibbi Sayadan Thi Shahíd dikháyá.	52.	At Alipur there was a fight, at Tibbi Syadan (3) He became a martyr.
53.	Maut piyála ajalwála Chum chat akhin te cháyá.	53.	The fateful cup of death He accepted it with zeal.
54.	Pahla derá kúch kitone, Tán wanj Gawen qadam aráyá.	54.	Marching thence they pitched their first camp, Then went they and halted at Gaven.
55.	Topán chhute ghubáre, Tán wanj Shujabád kambáyá.	55.	The guns began to roar, They struck terror in Shujabad.
56.	Fikr piyá karárán kún Langh Dádpotra áyá.	56.	The Kirárs were filled with distress At the oncoming of the Daudpotras.
57.	Bhanná Mohan Multán dahen Jain lashkar jald anáyá.	57.	Mohan ran speedily to Multan, (4) And fetched quickly thence an army.
58.	Dunián desan be sir bahún, Je qismat Kot bacháyá.	58.	'I will give you,' he said, 'much wealth; If fate shall preserve Kot.' (5)
59.	Rám Rakhiá te Jábar Singh Thí mukhtári áyá.	59.	Ram Rakhia and Jowáhir Singh Went as his emissaries.
60.	Wanj laran parere Kot kanún Eh Mohan Rám aláyá.	60.	'Go and fight beyond Kot,' Quoth Mohan Rám.
61.	Charh dal Singhan dá Tán jiwen Kot Hassan de áyá.	61.	Marched forth the army of the Singhs, Then came it to Kot Hassan. (6)
62.	Di kirár Nonárán di Phir Geje áu sunáyá.	62.	Thereon came Geja and gave news (to the Khán's army) That the Kirárs were at Nunar.
63.	Rátín án charhione topán Singhán dá bhiráya.	63.	At night they brought up their guns And opposed the Singhs.
64.	Gawen kanún charh thee ráwána Naqárá kúch wajáyá.	64.	Forth from Gawen marched the army To the roll of kettledrums.
65.	Naqárá wajje Din da Har mulkán wich sunáyá.	65.	The roll of the drums of the Faith Was made to be heard in all lands.
66.	Súhin na hin zamínán de, Chá Kháwand mulk dikháyá.	66.	They (the Sikhs) know not the country, God shewed them the land.
67.	Hik mard Bukhári dhro kitá, Chit chárá rare ghin áya.	67.	One man, a Bukhari Syad, deceived them, He led them astray in a wilderness.
68.	Án dhako han wich topán Gard ghubár utháya.	68.	They came within range of the guns, The guns filled the air with dust.
69.	Hik sáre dhup malúkán kún, Dúja páni bin sukáya.	69.	Not only did the heat scorch their tender bodies, But it also parched them from want of water.
70.	Hik dính qahr dá táman tattá, Dújá bhá munjháyá.	70.	Not only was the day one of terrific heat (like a copper vessel), But the fire of the guns also distressed them.

(3). The present village of Basti Sayadan. The Alipur mentioned is the village of that name in the Shujabad Tahsil.

(4). Mohan was Mohan Lal, a prominent member of the Babla family, after whom the village of Mohanpur is named.

(5). By 'Kot' is meant Shujabad.

(6). *i.e.*, Gurdezpur,

71.	Trut gián mihr dián táráu Rukh Azráil dikháyá,	71.	Broken were all the cords of love, The Angel of Death displayed his countenance.
72.	Kehre sar de pakhí áhe Kithe jamán jayá	72.	Of what grove were they the birds ? In what birth-place were they born ?
73.	Haddán nál na had ralle Phir jún jangal dá áyá.	73.	Their bones lay not with their fathers' bones, Their souls passed into the jangal.
74.	Was kanún be was hoe Anchittá wadá páyá.	74.	Their strength became as no strength, Great and unthought of was the calamity.
75.	Sift karán Angrezan dí, Itbit mulk lattárí áyá.	75.	Let me speak the praise of the English, Of Itbit (7) that came by forced marches.
76.	Már Tíwána tábe kitus, Jain wanj Sayál niwáyá.	76.	He had smitten and subdued the Tiwánas, He had made the Syáls to bow their heads.
77.	Agún táb na áudi Dere, Jain wanj hoká Sangarh páyá.	77.	Dera could not stand against him, The terror of his name reached Sanghar.
78.	Langh pawe oh jaldí Jekún top awáz sunáyá.	78.	He crossed the river in haste When he heard the roar of the guns.
79.	Jaldi dauriá Singhán te, Jald pahr wich áyá.	79.	He rushed in haste on the Singhs, In haste he came without delay.
80.	Weráh kitone Singhán kún, Jún machhi jal phahaya.	80.	They surrounded the Singhs on all sides, They caught them like fish in a net.
81.	Án imán badhone jinhán Morchá án aráyá.	81.	They came on in confidence, And erected their batteries.
82.	Fateh Khán Gori top utte Badh kamar kar áyá.	82.	Fateh Khan Gori girt up his loins, And came to the gun.
83.	Kar ke shist chaláus gola Topán wich raláyá.	83.	He aimed and fired a shot, He made it fall among the enemy's guns.
84.	Wanj dabáyus top Singhán dí kún To golamdáz udáya,	84.	He caused the Singhs' gun to fall, He blew up the gunner.
85.	Sikh pawan kar tikh laran da Munsif nahín wanjáyá.	85.	If truth be told, The Sikhs fought and laid on gallantly.
86.	Bál gashtán bandúqán márián Wáh wáh lar dikháya.	86.	They plied their guns and muskets, A glorious fight they showed.
87.	Bhaj bhaj laran Pathán uthán Jinhán mehná piyá mokháyá.	87.	There rushed the Pathâns to the fight, Disdaining to flee.
88.	Wáh wáh laran Baloch Chándie, Jinhán kar insáf dikháyá.	88.	The Chándia Biloches (8) also fought valiantly, They showed their power of fighting.
89.	Topán wich márin talwárin, Tán gawáh karendá áyá.	89.	They smote with their swords amid the guns, So that they convinced the bystanders of their courage.
90.	Bhái Dád Potre wi Bhár wangún tarkáyá.	90.	The Daudpotras also Made the enemy spring like gram in a parching pan.
91.	Jíwen baghyár bhodán wich pawe Már agún chá láyá,	91.	As a wolf among the sheep, So did they chase the enemy before them.
92.	Maut khumár karárán kún, Bhaj Singh dá lashkar áyá.	92.	Death and senselessness came on the Kirárs, When the army of the Singhs came fleeing.
93.	Mil sahúkárí Kotwale Ral ibo pak pakáyá.	93.	The sahukars of Kot met together, And came to this decision :
94.	Sáhibí tán Singhán dí wich, Asán wadá lod ludáyá.	94.	' In the rule of the Singhs,' they said, ' We have had much favour shown us.
95.	Chal milún Sáhib lokán kún, Je qismat chá bacháya,	95.	' Come, let us meet the Sahibs If fate should spare us.'
96.	Kunjián án hazúr rakhione, Piyá badshábi sáyá.	96.	They brought forward the keys of the town, And laid them before the conquerors.

(7) *i.e.*, Edwardes.
(8) The poet's tribute to his own tribe.

97. Kot kanún charh thai rawána,
Mushkil pendá áyá.
98. Pakká Derá burd kitone
Suraj Kund jamáyá.
99. Nikal pawe Multánún Múla
Ura án kharáyá.
100. Akhyus hargaz jí jí marná
Chá hírá hathán wich páyá.
101. Topán wich ghatái chhare
Kare fareb sawáyá.
102. Wal bhái Dádpotre wí
Bhár wangún tarkáyá.

103. Bande te qatal ám húi,
Jo khás qalam te áyá.
104. Derá wiún hatione,
Tán wanj qile wich pháyá.
105. Sirkarde bahún kam ái
Main kehra gin sunáya.
106. Muhammad Dulle Shah Mír dá—
Sir Khán dahún pahuncháya.
107. Parahn seti is kágaz de,
Pír Jání múnhún aláyá.
108. Pálíus prit Farangi di,
Sir bhár safar dá cháyá.
109. Záidá kul phirá Khán,
Jang tamám charháyá
110. Pakre úth hazárán,
Tán har mulkán tún pakráyá.
111. Bhún kakh sukká tandá
Gádiwánán cháyá
112. Chhikiá giyá sabho dáná
Kál rukh dikháyá.
113. Dánewále karde máná
Chá Qádir agh láyá.
114. Rozí bhí ghal desí úho
Jain mihrún menh wasáyá.

115. Jarnel kítá charh mel Singhán te.
Ayá daur tikhái,
116. Akhyus turat maresán bilkul,
Gharián wich adhái.
117. Sámán kítus Multán utte
Ae roz siyáda lái.
118. Likhiá Sahib lokán de
Wanj pauhncha já ba jái
119. Súrsat dewán hákim,
Aín mane har kái
120. Fauján kul Panjábí dián
Giyá pichhán hatái.
121. Aganbút wich daryáwán de,
Giyá hikmat nál luráhí
122. Wanj pauhte shahr de nere,
Sakht kítus werábí
123. Dharí lagí topan dí
Dính rát na kadhan sábí
124. Gole pae pawan dugáre
Wanjan ghubáre chái.
125. Gole bhanan khánqáhán kún
Baní razá Iláhí.
126. Hath hathyár talwár pharan
Jo akhián disc latái.
127. Qarábínián tamanche chhute
Topán kamí na kái.
128. Barchhián te oh sángán márin
Wich wadh kar sipáhí.

97. The army marched from Kot,
It came a weary stage.
98. They halted finally,
And encamped at Suraj Kund.
99. Múla came out from Multan
And pitched his camp on the hither side.
100. He said he would fight to the death,
He wore a diamond on his hand.
101. He discharged shot from his gun,
He tried every device in his power.
102. Then the Daudpotras also
Made the enemy spring like gram in a parching-pan.
103. Many were captured and slain,
Which was clear to all.
104. They moved away then camp,
And entered into the fort.
105. Many leaders ware slain,
Whom shall I enumerate?
106. Muhammed Dule Shah Mír—
The Khán sent his head.
107. As he read this paper,
Pir Jáni spake as follows.
108. He made promise to the Farangis,
He willingly undertook the journey.
109. He collected all his tribesmen,
He sent them to the war.
110. Thousands of camels were seized,
They were seized from every country.
111. Straw, grass, and dried jowár
Were taken up by the cart-drivers.
112. All the grain was impressed,
Famine showed its face.
113. The grain-dealers grew proud,
The Almighty raised for them the price.
114. He who sends His rain on the earth,
He will send food also.
115. The general marched on the Singhs,
And rushed fiercely against them.
116. He said he would utterly destroy them,
In the twinkling of an eye.
117. He made preparations against Multan,
He came after much delay.
118. The letters of the Sahibs
Had reached every quarter.
119. The rulers provided supplies,
Every one obeyed their orders.
120. All the troops of the Panjabis
Were sent back.
121. Steamboats in the rivers,
Did he bring with his skill.
122. He advanced near the city,
And strictly surrounded it.
123. There was a continual succession of guns,
Day nor night had they rest.
124. The shot fell in showers,
On came the shrapnel.
125. The shot struck the shrines of the saints,
Such was the will of God.
126. Seizing their arms and swords,
Their eyes grew red with anger.
127. Carbines and pistols were discharged,
There was no lack of guns.
128. They strike bayonets on spears
Rushing in, the soldiers.

No.		No.	
129.	Taqdír masít udái dárún, Silhán thián bawái.	129.	Fate exploded the powder in the mosque The bricks flew in the air,
130.	Gore wí lar pawan zore Kítí wanjan adái.	130.	The white soldiers too fought valiantly. They paid their due to the full.
131.	Bhaj bhaj pawan agáhán te Jíwen kare patang tikhái.	131.	Fiercely did they rush on their opponents As swiftly as a kite mounts in the air.
132.	Luk chhap koi ná chhuttá, Jo munh Gorián de ái.	132.	None escaped by hiding, Who came before the white soldiers.
133.	Thaí kharáb khalqat Multání. Rullí já bajái.	133.	The people of Multan were ruined, They wandered from place to place.
134.	Sabha sakht were Múle kún baithe Qile wich phalái.	134.	Mula was strictly surrounded, And enclosed in his fort.
135.	Zaidá kul bhirá Mule kun baithe Sab sipáh sadái,	135.	Mula sent for all his brothers, He called all his troops.
136.	Akhyus was kitum bahtere, Har gaz chali ná kái.	136.	He said: 'I have made much effort, But with no success.
137.	Saat harí do wele. Tán hún kaun kare hamráhí.	137.	In this hour of adversity, Who will now be my comrade?'
138.	Sáf jawáb sipáhian dittá, Kalhe sir te ái.	138.	The soldiers refused absolutely, Retribution came on his head alone.
139.	Tháí saláh kufar wichh íwen, Milan jihán nahín kai.	139.	In their faithlessness this was the decision, That there was naught save surrender.
140.	Wanj khare Sahib de agún, Gal wich kapra pái.	140.	He went and stood before the Sahib, With his cloth round his neck.
141.	Bakhsh Alláh de lekhe mekon, Main hán pur taqsír gunáhí	141.	'For the sake of God," he said, 'Forgive: I have sinned and committed wrong.
142.	Eh mulk terá, eh mulk terá, Tun hain mulkán da sáin.	142.	This land is thine, this land is thine, Thou art the Lord of all lands.
143.	Thí bandá jalesán terá, Je tún qaidún jind bachái.	143.	I shall be thy slave, If thou save me from prison,'
144.	Jarnel te Lek Sáhib Phir gal íhá farmái.	144.	The General and Lake Sahib (9) Then spake as follows:—
145.	Gídí thí kiyon milyon Múla, Karen há pher larái.	145.	'Why hast thou surrendered, Mula? Thou shouldst have fought again'
146.	Akhyus nahi munásib mekon Sahib Lokán nál karan larái.	146.	He said: 'It is not fitting for me, To fight with the Sahibs.
147.	Wazír Amír mere tan íwen Phúk limbí ag lái.	147.	It is my Wazirs and Amirs, Who have blown up this fire.'
148.	Jarnel kítá chá zail Múle kún, Gal íhá farmái.	148.	The General imprisoned Mula, And spoke as follows:—
149.	Mál khazána daulat duníán, Lekha de ithain.	149.	'Of thy goods and treasures wealth and stores, Give herewith an account.'
150.	Akhyus main ham bichára Súba. Ahí Ranjít dí badshahí.	150.	He said: 'I was only a poor Governor, The Kingdom was Ranjit's.
151.	Mulk áhá wich ijáre, Daulat sál basál puchái.	151.	The country was on lease, I paid the revenue year by year.
152.	Baí Daulat áí kam hathyarán de Mihanat ghinan sawái	152.	What else there was, on purchase of arms, Was it all spent in addition.
153.	Jo isbáb sipahián de Oh gai hin ithan lutái.	153.	And the goods of the soldiers, These have here been plundered.
154.	Kaí rathe kaí bhane, Kaí ladhe nahín kitháin.	154.	Some have fled, some have escaped, Of others there is no trace.
155.	Kar áe ban bahána rozída, Oh gai hin sir marái.	155.	They came to earn a livelihood, And they have earned death.'
156.	Akhyus bahún gunáh hin sir tere. Múlá chhute kahín adái.	156.	The General replied: 'Great is thine offence: Mula, how canst thou be pardoned?
157.	Likh bhejiá hisse Landan, Walsí nál tikhái.	157.	I have written to London, Answer will come speedily.

(9) Lieutenant Edward Lake, afterwards Financial Commissioner, was then attached to, and practically in command of, the Bahawalpur Contingent.

158. Jo Kampaní da ásí likhíá,
Nán jánesan til táín.
159. Táng rakhe Multán di Kampaní,
Bhále nit idáhín.
160. Jíndá án dikhálo Mulá,
Ik wár ithàín.

161. Dhotí ban Karár wanjáyá,
Ande Ahl Kitáb ni Sáín.
162. Dekho khel ih dádhe Rab dí,
Wasdíán ujar gián ni jáín.
163. Hun aman zamána áyá he,
Ral khedan shíuh te gáín.
164. Jo kuchh guzriá mulke andar,
Sobha ákh sunaín.

158. Whatever order the Company gives,
I shall not know for a time.
159. The Company is in expectation of news from Multan,
It is always looking in this direction.
160. ' Bring Mula and show him to us alive,
For once here."

161. God has destroyed the dhoti-wearing Kirar,
He has brought us People of the book.
162. Behold this sport of the Almighty,
How our populous cities are laid waste.
163. Now hath come the age of peace,
The lion and the cow play together.
164. Whatsoever happened in this land,
That has SOBHA set forth.

APPENDIX TO CHAPTER V.

SPECIMENS OF SANADS.

The following grants are printed here as specimens of the manner in which favourable rates of land revenue were fixed at various periods under native rule.

SANAD GRANTED BY MUHAMMAD DARA SHIKOH, DATED A.D. 1650.

Chún dar abádání wa mámúri-i-pargana Alampur Panáh ihtimám-i-tamám ast, binábarán mauza-i-Yúsufpur wa Gardezpur muta'lliqa marhúme maghfúre Shaikh Abdul Jalíl az qarár-i-nakdí sar-i-bíga do rupaye dar kharíf Kúel wa yak ním rupaye dar rabi' Bijel ba 'amal darámada wa az áyanda fasli kharif Bijel siyádat wa nakábat-panah Shaikh Muhammad Rájú wa Sayad Muhammad wald Sayad Fateh Muhammad muta'llíqe rá guzáshtand; chunánchi tamassuk ba muhr-i-khud nawishta dádand; wa chún ba qazáe Rabbáni tughiání-i-áb zamín-i-muáziát mazkúr gharqába shuda wa muzárián az bedilí aksar mutafarrika gashta wa ba'ze ki mánda ánár níz rúhe ba firár ma nihádand; binábar baqa-e--abádání wa kifáyat--i-sirkár wa tasalli r'iáyá hawále khádimán-i-asmatí panáh iffat-dastgáh mahal-i-kalán koch Abdul Jalil bint Sháh Abulfatteh Gardezi az ibtidáe fas-kharif Bíjel hawála namúda shud; ki ba imdád-i-tukhm wa taqqávi mawáziat rá ábád sázad wa ba kirár-i-baháwali chaháram hissa yak hissa díwán wa se hissa riáyá wa chakdár muqarrar namúda shud, wa naishakar wa pamba sar-i-biga do rupaya wa mauza Jalílpur waghaira aml-i-mamúl ba hál dáshta shud; báyad ki ba khátir jama' dar taraddud wa abádání saí' balígh namáyand ki fasl ba fasl wa sál ba sál muáfiq-i-kirárdád-i-sadr bázyáft namúda khwábad shud, wa ba illat-i-kankút wa topa bakhshi wa hech waja' muzáhimat na khwábad shud, muáfiq hast búd ba amal khwáhad darámad—Insha'alla ta' alla az ín kaul wa qirár tafáwat wa tajáwaz na khwáhad hud. Tahrír ul tárikh 21 Shahre Muharram ul-harám San 30.

Translation

As we are anxious for the extension of cultivation in the pargana of Alampur Panh, and the villages of Yusafpur and Gardezpur belonging to the late Sheikh Abdul Jalil were assessed at a cash rate of Rs. 2 per bigha in the kharif of the Turkish year of the Sheep and Re. 1-8-0 per bigha in the rabi of the year of the Ape, and as the right reverend Sheikh Raju and Syad Muhammad, son of Syad Fateh Muhammad, have resigned the said lands with effect from the kharif of the "year of the Ape" and have written a deed to this effect and signed it with their seal, and as God has pleased to flood the said villages with excessive inundations, and the tenants have mostly fled in despair, and they that remain are ready for flight; therefore, in order to establish cultivation and to benefit the Government and to comfort the subjects of Government, the said villages are entrusted to the honorable widow of the said Abdul Jalil with effect from the kharif of the "year of the Ape" so that she may bring the said lands into cultivation by grants of seed and takavi; and a fourth share of the produce shall be due to Government and three shares to the cultivators and the chakdár; and sugarcane and cotton shall pay Rs. 2 per bigha, and in Jalilpur, &c., the present arrangements shall continue. The grantees should, therefore, exert themselves confidently in bringing the land under cultivation. Payment shall be made every harvest and every year according to the above agreement, and no kind of exaction shall be made in the form of appraisement, or the patwárí's "topa," or any other cess: payment shall be according to the actuals. Please God there shall be no deviation of any kind from the above deed and agreement. Written on the 21st Moharram in the 30th year of the reign [of Shah Jahan].

SANAD GRANTED BY ZABARDAST KHAN, A.D. 1781.

Hazrat Makhdúm Shekh Muhammad Rajú wa Mián Bagh Shah Gardezi.

Chún darbáb-i-mazid-i-ábádi wa mámúrí-e-muázi'-i-pargana Balda Sarkár wa Súba-i-Multán ihtimám tamám ast, darinwila wakíl-i-khándán-i-qudsínishán mashíkhat wa syádat martabat sifwat wa nijábat manzilat hakái wa muárríf manqibat silálal e-auliá-e-kirám zubda-e-masháikh, azam Shekh-ul-Islám Makhdum-ul-ánám-w'ul ikrám bandagi ——— —— istidá namúd ki mauzi' Raipur wa Núrpur Kalán waghaira ta'alluqa milkí murúsi manakkal az muddat wírán wa kamtaraddud as o manfa'at dar Sarkár á'id hech nest; agar patta-e-ahsán ba sígha-e-istimrár naqdí kamqarárí sar-i-dahna amlí wa aima siwáe ábádi sábika iná'yat shawad, ba imdád i tukhm wa taqqavi az muzárián-i qadim wa jadid ábá az mazrúa' mitawánem sákht : chún izdiád-i-ábádi ba har unwán aulatar ast, liháza nazar bar kifávat i-mál sárkár wa rifáyiat-i-riáyá dáshta min ibtidá-e-fasl kharif Udel Sau 1189 fasli chunán kirár yáft ki khádimán-i-mausúf ba khátir jama ' wa istiqlál-i-tamám ba imdád-tukhm wa taqqávi taraddud-i-kisht-kár-i-mazru'át i-amli wa aima az muzari'án-i-qadím wa jadid qarár wáqi' kunánad, ki kásilát-i-áurá ba mújib-i-zimn ba sharat i-ábádi hama jihat sar i-dahna fasl ba fasl dar sarkár bázkhwást tawánad namúd wa siwá-e-án ba ráhi izáfa wa peshkash wa nazrána wa kharch-i-darbár wa taurír i-diwáni wa sursat wa ámilána wa waqai-nigári wa muhassili wa fasláná wa farmáisn-i kár sirkár wa tafríq chánda waghaira kul takálif ba wajhin mini'l wajún muáka iza ba myán na kawánad awurd. Insha'alla ta'alla az in qaul wa qirár tafáwat wa tajáwaz ráh na khwáh-hand yáft. Taurír ba tárikh paujam shahr i-Rabí'-us-sáuí Sau 1195 Hijri.

Zimn siwái chábán-i-ábád-i-sábiq ba hama jihat ba sharat-i-ábádi sar-i dahna R. 20 sál tamám wa rasúm.

Fasl Kharif R. 9.		Fasl Rabí R. 11.	
Amli Sar i dahna R. 6.	Aima R. 3.	Amlí sar i dahna R. 8.	Aima R. 3.

Translation.

As we are anxious for the extension of cultivation in the villages of Pargana Balda in the Sirkár and Suba of Multan, and as the agent of the right reverend (etc., etc.) Gardezis represents that the villages of Raipur and Núrpur Kalán, etc., belonging to the hereditary property of his principals have remained long uncultivated, without in any way benefiting the Government, and that, if a favorable grant were made to them at fixed low cash rate per well (unassigned and assigned), exclusive of the previous cultivation, they would be able to bring the land under cultivation by cultivators, old and new, with grants of seed and takavi ; and whereas the increase of cultivation is our foremost care, therefore, out of consideration for the increase of the Government revenue and the prosperity of the Government's subjects, it is hereby determined, with effect from kharif of the Faslí year 1189, the Turkish year of the Ox, that the grantees shall in all confidence bring into cultivation the said lands, unassigned and assigned, by tenants, old and new, with grants of seed and takavi, and that if the said lands be cultivated their produce shall be paid to the Government every harvest in the form of a fixed sum per well according to the endorsement appended; and, saving the above, no manner of cess shall be exacted by way of izáfa, or peshkash, or nazrana, darbár expenses, or court writing-expenses, or military supplies, or officials' fees, or news-writers' fees, or muhassil's fees, or harvest fees, or Government order, or distribution of benevolence, or any other due. Please God there will be no deviation in any way from this deed and agreement. Written on the 5th of Rabí-us-sáni, 1195 Hijri.

Endorsement.

Exclusive of wells, already cultivated, the payment per well (on condition of cultivation) will be Rs. 20 annually, excluding fees—

Kharif Rs. 9 { Unassigned, Rs. 6 per well.
Assigned, Rs. 3 „

Rabí Rs. 11 { Unassigned, Rs. 8 per well.
Assigned, Rs. 3 „

PATTA GRANTED BY DIWAN CHAND (A KARDAR OF THE NAWAB OF BAHAWALPUR) IN A.D. 1816.

Chún darbáb mazid wa afzúni taraddud ta'alluqát muta'llaqa Khálsa Lálwáh ihtimám tamám ast, darin waqt Rai Mul Chand Monghia wa Isra Mal Gajwáni darkhwást namúdand ki agar patta yak dahna cháh ba sigha istamrár dar zamín banjar ghairábád wáqi'a Kot Hájí muta'lliqa Nála Baháwalwáh az Sirkár daulat-madár marhamat shawad, mashár-un-ilen ba kharch mubligh az khud yak dahne cháh dar zamín i mazkúr nau ihdás kunánida ábádi i án ba amal árad ; liháza hasb ul hukm hazúr álá wa afzúni mahsúl sirkár i alá wa rafáhiyat riáyá madd i nazar dáshta min ibtidái fasl i rabi Sijkánel sál 1223 fasli chunán qirár yáft ki mubligh 14 rupaye istamrár sál tamám cháh mazkúr chunánchi 9 rupaye dar fasl i rabi wa 5 rupaye dar fasl i kharíf bábat pamba dánadár ba sharat ábádi cháhi wa búdand 25 bigha mazru'át dar fasl i rabi wa 5 bigha dar fasl i kharíf bábat pamba dánadár dar Sirkár i álá báz yaft khwáhad shud. Agar mazrú át cháh mazkúr ziáda az sharah marqúm ul sadar az rúe zabtí baráyad, waja taufir i án mújib sharah ta'alluqa nála Sirdárwáh dar Sirkár i álá bazyáft khwáhad shud. Wa ma'malat jawárí waghaira har ijnás sailába wa jhalár dar zamín ahta cháh mazkúr ábád shawad, sailába ba qirár 5 hissa wa jhalár ba qirár shahsam hissa, ba'd waza' rahkám nisfí kasúr dar iwaz taraddudí ba ma' abwáb... kharch wazan ba masharun ileh mujawwaz; nisfí kasúr wa mahsúl ba ma' abwáb kharch waghaira dafa'át mújib shara bar bast ta'alluka mazkúr dar sirkar i álá bázyáft khwáhad shud. Bayad ki masha ileh ba khátir jama' ábádí i cháh ba 'amal árad. Insha'alla ta'alla az in qaul wa iqrár tafawaz zarra na khwáhad yáft. Tahrir ba tárikh ghurra máh i Snábán, 1231 Hijri.

Translation

With a view to the extension of cultivation in the territories of Lálwáh, and whereas at this time Rai Mul Chand, Monghia and Amra Mul Gajwání represent that, if a patta be granted to them by Government for one well in perpetuity in the uncultivated land of Kot Haji appertaining to the Bahawalwah Canal they will at their own expense construct and bring into use a well in the said land; therefore, in accordance with superior orders, and in view of the increase of the Government revenue and the comfort of the lieges, it is hereby determined, with effect from the rabi of the year of the Mouse, *i.e.*, the Fasli year 1223, that there shall be paid in perpetuity to Government a sum of Rs. 14 per annum,—Rs. 9 in the rabi and Rs. 5 in the kharif (for cotton)—on condition of the cultivation being by well alone and of there being 25 bighas of cultivation in the rabi and 5 bighas of cotton in the kharif. If the cultivation of the said well exceed by measurement at any time the abovementioned limits, the excess portion shall pay to Government at the rates [of batai] fixed for the Sirdarwáh territory. And such jowar, etc., as may be cultivated on the said well by flow or lift from the canal shall pay to Government at the rate of one-fifth for flow and one-sixth for lift. After deducting the tenant's share, half kasúr shall be taken by the lessee in return for his expenses on cultivation, together with the cesses and deductions on crops other than grain crops. The other half of the kasúr and the owner's share shall go to Government, together with cesses, deductions, dues, etc., according to the established rate prevailing in the said territories. Let the lessees, therefore, set themselves confidently to bring the well into use; and please God there shall be no deviation whatever from the terms of this deed and promise. Dated the 1st of Shaban, A.H. 1231 (A.D. 1816).

PATTA GRANTED BY DIWAN MULRAJ (A.D. 1846).

Chún tawajjuh khátir sirkár-i-álá baráhi mazid ábádí ta'alluqa Shujá'ábád mutasarraf shud darinwila Chaudhri Mohan Lal ámada záhir karda ki qitta zamín mutasil Chah Khandawala wáqia' mauza Bangála wírán wa banjar mutlaq uftáda; agar patta istamrári ba sigha ihsán az sarkár marahmat shawad ánjá dar zamín mazkúr cháh nau ihdás karda ábád tawánam sakht. Chun dar mazíd ábádi intifá sirkár ast nazar barán dáshta mubligh 12 rupaye sál tamám siwái nílsiyáh wa naishakar waghaira istamrár mújib zail jáiz karda; agar árázi bar cháh mazkúr siwái ziraiat gandam wa jawár bájri waghaira raqba qirárí ziráiat nil siyáh wa naishakar kásht kunad, tháwali i án ba qirár haftam hissa, kharch ba shará mauza'wa ghalla shálí ba qirár shasham hissa mujawwaz karda; báyad ki árázi ba khátir jama' cháh nau ihdás karda ábádí dar posh namáyad; ba mújib hamin nawishta ba 'amal khwáhad ámad; wa chhera ihdásí ba mújib nau ábádán muqarrar shud, chhera sál awwal muáf, áyanda ním chhera muqarrar namúda shud.

Istamrár Rs. 12 { Dar rabí' Rs 7, asl Rs. 6, siwá Re. 1
Dar kharíf Rs, 5, asl Rs. 4, siwá Re. 1

Rakba qarár { Dar rabí' 25 bigha
Dar kharíf—az ghalgi 13 bigha; az kásht vanwár 7 bigha
muáf

Kásht sabzí tarkárí ba qarár panjam hissa bilá kharch.

Tahrir 4 máh Jeth, Sambat 1902.

Translation.

Whereas the Government is anxious for the increase of cultivation in the taluka of Shujabad and whereas Chaudhri Mohan Lal has come and declared that a certain plot of land near the Khandawala well in Mauza Bangála is deserted and entirely uncultivated, and that, if a fixed lease were granted by the Government on favorable terms, he would be able to bring the land into cultivation by building a new well therein, and as the extension of cultivation is the profit of Government, in consideration thereof a fixed rent of Rs. 12 per annum, exclusive of indigo and sugar, is hereby sanctioned; and it is hereby laid down that if the lessee, in addition to the cultivation of wheat, jowar, bajra, etc., shall in the area covered by the lease, cultivate indigo and sugar, he shall pay batái thereon at the rate of one-seventh; and the deductions for cultivation expenses shall be at the ordinary village rate ; and rice will be divided at the rate of one-sixth. The lessee should start fearlessly on the cultivation of the land by constructing the well, and this present lease shall come into operation The scale of forced labour for canals is fixed at the rate adopted for new cultivation *i.e.*, the first year *nil*, and afterwards half rates.

Fixed payments Rs. 12 per annum. { Rabi Rs. 7, revenue Rs. 6, cesses Re. 1.
Kharif Rs. 5, revenue Rs 4, cesses Re. 1.

Area covered by the lease { In the rabi 25 bigahs.
In the kharif 13 bighas of grain crops, 7 bigas of cotton

Vegetables to pay one-fifth batai after deducting expenses.

Written on the 4th Jeth, Sambat 1902.

STATISTICAL TABLES

APPENDED TO THE

GAZETTEER

OF THE

MULTAN DISTRICT.

(INDEX ON REVERSE.)

STATISTICAL TABLES.

Table No. IA LIST of COMMISSIONERS and DEPUTY COMMISSIONERS.

No.	Name.	Period of office. From	To
	Commissioners.		
	(*a*).—Multan Division.		
1	Mr. P. M. Edgeworth	May 1849	May 1855.
2	Lt.-Col. Hamilton	May 1855	21st October 1862.
3	Mr. Ford	21st October 1862 ...	24th March 1868.
4	Lt.-Col. Cripps	24th March 1868 ...	5th March 1869.
5	Mr. Brandreth	11th March 1869 ...	18th April 1871.
6	Col. Graham	25th June 1871 ...	4th March 1873.
7	Cols. Hall, Young, Coxe, Tighe	4th March 1873 ...	21st October 1874.
8	Mr. Brandreth	27th October 1874 ...	7th February 1876.
9	Col. Graham	7th February 1876 ...	20th September 1878.
10	Mr. Cordery	21st October 1878 ...	October 1879.
11	,, R. T. Burney	October 1879	February 1880.
12	,, J. G. Cordery	February 1880	April 1880.
13	Major E. L. Ommanney	April 1880	November 1880.
14	Lt.-Col. F. M. Birch	November 1880... ...	January 1881.
15	Mr. J. G. Cordery	January 1881	March 1881.
16	Major R. T. M. Lang	March 1881	April 1881.
17	Mr. D. G. Barkley	April 1881	August 1881.
18	,, G. R. Elsmie	August 1881	September 1881.
19	,, D. G. Barkley	September 1881 ...	December 1881.
20	,, H. E. Perkins	December 1881	January 1883.
21	Col. E. P. Gurdon	January 1883	30th October 1884.
	(*b*).—Lahore Division.		
1	Col. C. A. McMahon	1st November 1884 ...	4th February 1885.
2	Mr. G. R. Elsmie	5th February 1885 ...	7th February 1887.
3	,, W. Coldstream	8th February 1887 ...	23rd July 1887.
4	,, C. M. Rivaz	24th July 1887	12th April 1889.
5	Col. C. Beadon	13th April 1889... ...	12th July 1889.
6	Mr. C. M. Rivaz	13th July 1889	23rd February 1890.
7	Col. G. G. Young	24th February 1890 ...	7th April 1890.
8	,, C. Beadon	8th April 1890	5th October 1890.
9	Mr. G. M. Ogilvie	6th October 1890 ...	31st October 1891.
10	Lt.-Col. J. B. Hutchinson	1st November 1891 ...	30th November 1891.
11	Mr. C. M. Rivaz	1st December 1891 ...	17th October 1892.
12	Lt.-Col. J. B. Hutchinson	18th October 1892 ...	6th April 1893.
13	Mr. G. M. Ogilvie	7th April 1893	10th July 1893.
14	,, J. R. Maconachie	11th July 1893	19th November 1893.
15	Lt.-Col. J. B. Hutchinson	20th November 1893 ...	8th July 1895.
16	Mr. J. R. Maconachie	9th July 1895	8th October 1895.
17	Lt.-Col. J. B. Hutchinson	9th October 1895 ...	25th April 1898.
18	Mr. J. McC. Douie	26th April 1898	15th July 1898.
19	Lt.-Col. J. B. Hutchinson	16th July 1898	29th August 1898.
20	Mr. J. McC. Douie	30th August 1898 ...	19th December 1898.
21	Lt.-Col. J. B. Hutchinson	20th December 1898 ...	21st March 1899.
22	Mr. J. McC. Douie	23rd March 1899 ...	15th March 1900.
23	,, R. Clarke	16th March 1900 ...	8th November 1901.
	(*c*).—Multan Division.		
1	Lt. Col. Leigh	9th November 1901 ...	...
	Deputy Commissioners.		
1	Lt. James	March 1849	August 1849.
2	Capt. Morrison	September 1849 ...	March 1850.
3	Mr. H. F. Fane	April 1850	30th December 1851.
4	,, W. Ford	31st December 1851 ...	1st February 1853
5	Major Hamilton	2nd February 1853 ...	17th May 1854.
6	Mr. H. B. Henderson	26th May 1854	28th January 1856.
7	Major Voyle	29th January 1856 ...	13th December 1861.
8	Genl. Van Cortlandt, C.B.	14th December 1861 ...	10th March 1863.

Table No. IA LIST of COMMISSIONERS and DEPUTY COMMISSIONERS—concluded

No.	Name.	Period of office. From	Period of office. To
	Deputy Commissioners—concld.		
9	Major Maxwell	11th March 1863 ...	4th November 1863.
10	Genl. Van Cortlandt, C.B.	5th November 1863 ...	23rd March 1868.
11	Mr. D. G. Barkley	24th March 1868 ...	24th September 1868.
12	„ R. T. Burney	7th April 1869	2nd December 1869.
13	Major R. G. Shortt...	3rd December 1869 ...	September 1870.
14	Col. Ferris	15th November 1870 ...	13th April 1873.
15	Capt. Lang	14th April 1873 ...	14th April 1875.
16	Col. Mercer	15th April 1875 ...	28th February 1876.
17	Lt.-Col. Birch	29th February 1876 ...	3rd April 1877.
18	Mr. A. H. Benton	4th April 1877	20th December 1877.
19	Capt. Lang	21st December 1877 ...	28th March 1880.
20	„ A. S. Roberts	29th March 1880 ...	29th November 1880.
21	Major Lang	30th November 1880 ...	25th March 1881.
22	Mr. C. A. Roe	26th March 1881 ...	1st June 1882.
23	„ E. O'Brien	2nd June 1882	27th February 1885.
24	„ T. Troward	28th February 1885 ...	31st March 1885.
25	Major J. B. Hutchinson	1st April 1885	14th July 1887.
26	„ A. DeC. Rennick	15th July 1887	31st July 1887.
27	„ J. B. Hutchinson	1st August 1887 ...	30th August 1887.
28	„ A. DeC. Rennick	31st August 1887 ...	2nd October 1887.
29	„ J. B. Hutchinson	3rd October 1887 ...	19th July 1888.
30	„ A. DeC. Rennick	20th July 1888	19th October 1888.
31	„ J. B. Hutchinson	20th October 1888 ...	18th May 1889.
32	Lt. C. G. Parsons	19th May 1889	29th October 1889.
33	Mr. G. L. Smith	30th October 1889 ...	1st December 1889.
34	„ E. B. Steedman	2nd December 1889 ...	15th January 1890.
35	„ W. Chevis	16th January 1890 ...	12th February 1890.
36	„ H. C. Cookson	13th February 1890 ...	31st October 1890.
37	„ J. C. Brown	1st November 1890 ...	3rd February 1891.
38	„ C. E. F. Bunbury	4th February 1891 ...	5th February 1891.
39	„ H. C. Cookson	6th February 1891 ...	6th October 1891.
40	„ H. W. Gee	7th October 1891 ...	20th October 1891.
41	„ J. R. Maconachie	21st October 1891 ...	18th November 1892.
42	„ A. Meredith	19th November 1892 ...	4th August 1893.
43	„ H. A. Casson	5th August 1893 ...	4th October 1893.
44	„ A. Meredith	5th October 1893 ...	30th August 1894.
45	„ H. W. Gee	31st August 1894 ...	30th November 1894.
46	„ A. Meredith	1st October 1894 ...	28th February 1895.
47	„ T. J. Kennedy	1st March 1895 ...	25th April 1896.
48	„ R. Love	24th April 1896 ...	7th June 1896.
49	„ T. J. Kennedy	8th June 1896	17th October 1896.
50	„ C. H. Atkins	18th October 1896 ...	8th November 1896.
51	„ J. G. M. Rennie	9th November 1896 ...	25th February 1897.
52	„ E. D. Maclagan	26th February 1897 ...	19th March 1897.
53	„ J. G. M. Rennie	20th March 1897 ...	30th June 1897.
54	„ E. D. Maclagan	1st July 1897	12th August 1897.
55	„ J. G. M. Rennie	13th August 1897 ...	4th April 1898.
56	Capt. C. P. Egerton	5th April 1898	23rd June 1898.
57	Mr. E. R. Abbott	24th June 1898	24th July 1898.
58	Capt. C. P. Egerton	25th July 1898	27th June 1899.
59	Mr. C. A. Barron	28th June 1899	4th July 1899.
60	„ E. A. Estcourt	5th July 1899	25th September 1899.
61	Capt. C. P. Egerton	26th September 1899 ...	13th February 1900.
62	Mr. A. M. Stow	14th February 1900 ...	2nd March 1900.
63	„ C. H. Harrison	3rd March 1900 ...	18th November 1900.
64	Capt. C. P. Egerton	19th November 1900 ...	20th April 1902.
65	Mr. M. L. Waring	21st April 1902... ...	...

Table No. II showing DEVELOPMENT.

1	2	3	4	5	6	7	8	9	10	11
DETAILS.	1853-54	1858-59	1863-64	1868-69	1873-74	1878-79	1883-84	1888-89	1893-94	1898-99.
Population	...	...	...	472,266	...	555,964	551,964	551,964	631,434	631,434
Cultivated acres	..	...	...	624,434	624,640	799,360	518,622	657,313	700,479	1,004,291
Irrigated acres	...	...	...	505,750	540,657	410,054	423,789	527,540	623,837	693,138
Ditto (from Government works)	...	...	...	303,627	192,733	339,644	326,057	357,125	446,439	568,352
Assessed land revenue, rupees ...	...	...	...	5,33,404	5,41,760	5,43,895	5,67,340	9,13,125	10,63,076	10,15,605
Revenue from land, rupees ...	...	...	...	5,09,405	6,70,171	5,25,125	5,62,695	5,52,607	5,30,006	5,49,875
Gross revenue, rupees	...	...	...	7,19,420	9,81,066	8,91,260	10,27,153	10,50,524	11,68,521	10,76,256
Number of kine	...	...	...	182,411	167,174	168,809	199,395	299,253	166,961	152,342
Do. sheep and goats ...	...	...	...	313,087	311,589	326,130	369,648	459,594	413,488	667,528
Do. camels	..	...	...	11,942	15,050	23,854	10,491	18,774	17,156	26,316
Miles of metalled roads	...	...	...	1,467	59	51	51	51	51	68
Do. unmetalled roads ...	...	...	...		1,430	907	1,122	1,143	1,214	1,220
Do. railways	...	...	...	64	81	130	130	130	130	130
Police staff	...	...	837	906	817	854	905	875	820	798
Prisoners convicted	1,037	1,337	988	1,338	2,709	4,035	1,053	1,798	1,162	2,120
Civil suits,—number	1,255	1,107	1,680	3,010	3,970	5,451	8,432	8,581	7,198	8,116
Do. value in rupees ...	90,989	1,07,926	1,53,157	2,19,832	3,31,369	2,61,514	4,53,404	7,03,215	11,56,114	8,29,707
Municipalities,—number	...	...	...	...	3	6	6	6	6	6
Do. income in rupees	...	...	...	93,566	81,828	91,802	1,17,667	1,42,338	1,80,385	1,95,666
Dispensaries,—number of ...	...	...	...	3	3	5	6	7	11	11
Do. patients	...	...	...	9,511	20,100	28,123	39,933	57,246	116,864	112,365
Schools,—number of	...	...	55	58	47	57	...	...	82	94
Do. scholars	...	...	1,165	1,085	3,099	2,866	...	...	7,124	7,978

Table No. III ANNUAL RAINFALL in inches from April to March.

1	2	3	4	5	6	7	8	9	10	11	12	13
Stations.	Average 1858 to 1900.	1890-91.	1891-92.	1892-93.	1893-94.	1894-95.	1895-96.	1896-97.	1897-98.	1898-99.	1899-1900.	Average 1890-91 to 1899-1900.
Multan ...	5·89	9·69	2·24	18·59	12·70	6·57	10·84	1·26	11·92	2·40	3·42	7·96
Shujabad ...	5·37	5·49	2·47	13·71	7·05	4·54	6·39	3·25	10·89	1·77	2·10	5·76
Lodhrán ...	4·53	4·04	3·95	12·80	4·58	2·74	5·73	2·83	11·70	1·88	·35	5·12
Mailsi ...	4·19	7·35	6·03	9·05	8·32	4·05	5·46	3·37	10·39	2·67	2·31	5·90
Kabirwála ...	5·97	6·34	6·30	14·58	9·01	6·46	6·15	3·03	7·33	5·26	1·96	6·64

NOTE.—These figures are taken from the District Agricultural Registers.

Table IIIA showing RAINFALL at HEAD-QUARTER.

1	2	3	4	5	6	7	8	9	10	11	12	13
MONTH.	Average, 1885-1890.	1890-91.	1891-92.	1892-93.	1893-94.	1894-95.	1895-96.	1896-97	1897-98.	1898-99.	1899-1900.	Average, 1890-91 to 1899-1900.
April	·06	...	·25	...	·41	...	·23	...	·42	...	·02	·13
May	·44	...	·85	·08	·96	...	...	..	·03	·08	...	·20
June	·58	·22	...	1·49	...	·40	2·27	...	·19	·14	1·16	·59
July	1·20	1·98	·14	9·78	5·66	1·24	·11	·15	1·62	1·48	·87	2·30
August	1·78	2·89	·29	4·23	...	2·76	6·82	·71	7·75	...	·65	2·61
September	..	...	·15	...	2 32	·24	...	·06	·03	·42	...	·32
Total hot months ...	4 06	5·09	1·68	15·58	9·35	4·64	9·43	·92	10·04	2·12	2·70	6·15
October	...	...	...	...	...	...	...	...	...	...	·06	·01
November	12	·91	...	...	...	...	...	·01	...	...	·01	·09
December	·04	1·67	...	·64	·80	·60	·07	...	·48	·01	...	·43
January	·38	·74	·26	1·34	·77	·61	·27	...	·15	...	·23	·44
February	·38	·50	·30	1·03	·68	·10	·72	·21	1·25	·22	·32	·53
March	·44	·78	...	...	1·10	·62	·35	·12	...	·05	·10	·31
Total cold months ...	1·36	4·60	·56	3·01	3·35	1·93	1·41	34	1·88	·28	·72	1·81
Total year ...	5·42	9·69	2·24	18·59	12·70	6·57	10·84	1·26	11·92	2·40	3·42	7·96

NOTE.—These figures have been taken from the Agricultural Registers of the District.

Table IIIB showing RAINFALL at TAHSILS.

1	2	3	4	5	6	7	8	9	10	11	12	13
	SHUJABAD.			LODHRAN.			MAILSI.			KABIRWALA.		
YEAR.	Hot months—April to September.	Cold months—October to March.	Total year.	Hot months—April to September.	Cold months—October to March.	Total year.	Hot months—April to September.	Cold months—October to March.	Total year.	Hot months—April to September.	Cold months—October to March.	Total year.
1890-91 ...	2·36	3·13	5·49	2·65	1·99	4·64	3·26	4·09	7·35	1·55	4·79	6·34
1891-92 ...	2·06	·41	2·47	3·58	·37	3·95	5·80	·23	6·03	6·01	·29	6·30
1892-93 ...	11·15	2·56	13·71	11·12	1·68	12·80	7·30	1·75	9·05	12·83	1·75	14·58
1893-94 ...	5 13	1·92	7·05	3·03	1·55	4·58	6·58	1·74	8·32	6·82	2·18	9·00
1894-95 ...	2·68	1·86	4·54	1·81	1·43	2·74	2·37	1·68	4·05	4·38	2·08	6·46
1895-96 ...	4·97	1·42	6·39	3·92	1·81	5·73	4·15	1·31	5·46	4·93	1·22	6·15
1896-97 ...	1·78	1·47	3·25	2·68	·15	2·83	2·85	·52	3·37	2·31	·72	3·03
1897-98 ...	8·85	2·04	10·89	9·16	2·54	11·70	8·21	2·18	10·39	5·58	1·75	7·33
1898-99 ...	1·63	·14	1·77	1·70	·18	1·88	2·64	·03	2·67	5·26	...	5·26
1899-1900 ...	1·64	·46	2·10	·35	...	·35	2·04	·27	2·31	1·16	·80	1·96
Average of ten years ...	4·22	1·54	5·76	3·95	1·17	5·12	4·52	1·38	5·90	5·08	1·56	6·64

NOTE.—These figures are taken from the Agricultural Registers of the District.

Table No. IV showing TEMPERATURE.

1	2	3	4	5	6	7	8	9	10
	Temperature in shade (in Degrees Fahrenheit).								
	May.			July.			December.		
Year.	Maximum.	Mean.	Minimum.	Maximum.	Mean.	Minimum.	Maximum.	Mean.	Minimum.
1868-69	121·0	...	...	115·0	...	...	84·0	58·15	30·0
1869-70	124·0	94·18	68·0	114·75	93·25	72·0	79·0	56·94	40·0
1870-71	...	...	...	..	...	...	...	...	...
1871-72	121·0	94·69	72·0	117·0	94·61	74·0	105·0	...	...
1872 73	119·7	...	...	114 5	95·08	75·0	90·0	60·85	35·7
1873-74	116	87·65	60	117	96·88	76	88	57·54	85·
1874-75	120·0	92·37	62·0	125·0	96·0C	74·Ͻ	83·0	57·17	31·0
1875-76	119·0	94·03	67·0	115·0	95·47	73·0	77·0	59·18	37·0
1876-77	119·0	94·9	66·0	113·0	94·2	78·0	76·9	57·0	32·1
1877-78	109·9	87·3	65·1	109·0	93·2	76·2	77·9	59·3	39·0
1878-79	110·9	89·3	66·2	113·9	95·1	75·2	93·9	55·8	30·0
1879-80	115·9	91·7	67·2	111·9	95·0	77·2	75·9	55·3	33·0
1880-81	114·9	70·2	92·5	108·9	75·2	91·9	78 9	38·0	57·9
1881-82	112·9	91·6	61·1	109·9	92·3	74·2	79·9	59·2	36·0
1882-83	113·5	87·7	63·0	106·9	89·0	76·4	81·9	60·3	38·0
1883-84	111·9	87·5	68·2	105·9	90·2	75·4	75·9	56·6	37·0
1884-85	110·9	89·3	64·1	108·9	94·9	74·2	80·4	59·0	40·0
1885-86	102 9	81·9	66·0	108·9	92·7	74·9	81·4	56·9	38·1
1886-87	114·3	91·0	67·2	114·8	93·2	74·2	81·1	58·5	33·4
1887-88	115·6	91·6	70·2	106·1	93·4	77·2	82·6	59·0	36·4
1888-89	116·6	91·9	63·3	111·6	94·8	75·2	79·3	59·5	39·2
1889-90	113·8	91·1	68·2	112·3	94 3	76·2	81·3	61·0	40·8
1890-91	120·3	93·5	65·2	111·2	94·1	78·2	75·3	57·6	39·2
1891-92	113·3	88·3	67·7	116·8	96·1	78·2	80·3	60·6	38·2
1892-93	118·3	95·7	69·2	115·3	94·3	76·2	81·3	59·2	39·1
1893-94	113·4	91·6	67·1	105·9	92·0	75·1	78·3	61·4	43·2
1894-95	114·5	94·6	72·1	106·4	92·9	76·1	81·3	59·0	40·6
1895-96	120·5	98·0	70·6	112·4	94·9	76·6	81·3	61·1	43·7
1896-97	117·5	96·3	73·1	112·9	...	...	81·8	58·7	37·0
1897-98	115·5	95·5	73·0	113·4	95·2	75·5	84·8	60·2	42·9
1898-99	117·0	92 9	70·0	115·0	95·8	78·0	84·3	59·3	37·5

Note.—The figures previous to 1882 are taken from the last edition of the Gazetteer; the remaining figures are taken from Table No. II of the Administration Report

Table No. V showing the DISTRIBUTION of POPULATION.

1	2	3	4	5	6	7	8	9	10	11	12	13	14	15	16	17	18	19	20	21	22	23	24
										Towns and villages.								Occupied houses.		* Unoccupied houses.		* Resident families.	
	Total square miles according to village papers.	Cultivated square miles according to village papers.	Culturable square miles according to village papers.	Square miles under matured crops (average).	Total population.	Urban population.	Rural population.	Total population per square mile.	Rural population per square mile.	Over 10,000 souls.	5,000 to 10,000.	3,000 to 5,000.	2,000 to 3,000.	1,000 to 2,000.	500 to 1,000.	Under 500.	Total.	Towns.	Villages.	Towns.	Villages.	Towns.	Villages.
District—																							
1881	5,880	1,249	4,247	730	551,964	88,083	463,881	93	78	1	1	6	11	88	189	997	1,293	16,235	77,364	7,495	16,004	24,264	91,583
1891	...	...	...	...	631,434	59,166	536,268	106	90	2	2	5	10	108	210	1,060	1,397	20,127	98,895	...	...	21,307	109,208
1901	5,948	1,569	3,830	1,144	710,626	108,651	601,975	120	101	1	3		26	132	240	955	1,357	23,826	108,744	...	...	...	...
Tahsils (1901)—																							
Multan	953	364	...	...	232,126	87,394	144,732	243	152	1	...		10	29	49	201	290	20,086	25,723	...	...	...	...
Shujabad	679	264	...	...	124,907	11,029	113,878	183	160	..	2		8	29	51	60	150	2,095	21,285	...	...	...	...
Lodhrán	1,056	264	...	...	113,359	7,702	105,657	107	100	...	1		2	23	46	192	264	1,263	18,706	...	...	...	...
Mailsi	1,657	312	...	...	109,727	...	109,727	66	66	...	...		4	23	33	272	332	...	19,777	...	...	...	...
Kabírwála ...	1,603	315	...	...	130,507	2,526	127,981	81	79	...	...		2	28	61	230	321	382	23,253	...	...	...	...

NOTE.—Figures for 1881 have been copied from the old Gazetteer; those for 1891 from Tables Nos. I and III of the Census Report, 1891, and those for 1901 from Tables I and III of the Census Report, 1901, except cultivated, culturable and crop areas, which have been taken from the Settlement Report.

* These data are not available in the Census Records of 1901.

Table No. VI showing MIGRATION.

1	2	3	4	5	6	7	8	9	10	11	12	13	14
District.	Immigrants.			Emigrants.			Males per 1,000 of both sexes.						
							Immigrants.			Emigrants.			
	1881.	1891.	1901.	1881	1891.	1901.	1881.	1891.	1901.	1881.	1891.	1901.	
Amritsar	1,532	2,226	3,854	148	303	329	728	668	638	676	660	587	
Siálkot	1,375	1,528	2,451	47	83	106	746	714	658	617	602	472	
Lahore	2,328	3,677	5,099	578	848	747	634	602	577	612	581	660	
Gujránwála	1,076	1,502	1,616	98	230	198	721	691	670	536	635	596	
Jhang	10,944	24,751	25,439	1,478	1,877	9,383	614	589	572	571	471	560	
Montgomery	3,480	7,230	6,136	1,838	2,592	2,206	602	580	566	558	547	565	
Muzaffargarh	4,073	7,414	8,091	5,901	8,843	8,0[illegible]	603	561	565	669	548	532	
Dera Ismail Khan ...	1,245	1,479	2,385	375	41[illegible]	45[illegible]	720	689	645	610	543	597	
Native States of the Punjab.	9,767	10,658	8,931	4,209	...	7,962	589	562	552	...	...	893	
N.-W. P. and Oudh ...	7,434	4,582	4,027	...	...	570	688	679	666	...	...	554	
Rájpútána	1,061	990	4,498	...	...	89	585	605	557	...	...	674	
Afghanistán	1,021	786	856	...	...	...	926	943	833	...	...	...	
Europe, etc.	1,278	1,465	1,312	...	...	...	893	876	925	...	...	...	

Note.—Figures for 1881 have been copied from the old Gazetteer; those for 1891 from Table No. XI of the Census Report, 1891; and those for 1901 from Table XI of Census Report of 1901, with the exception of Emigrants to N. W. P. and Oudh and Rajputana, which have been supplied by the Superintendents of the Census Operations of those Provinces.

Table No. VII showing RELIGION and SEX.

1	2	3	4	5	6	7	8	9	10	11	12	13	14	15	16
	DISTRICT.									TAHSILS.					Villages.
	Persons.			Males.			Females.			Multán.	Shujabad.	Lodhrán.	Mailsi.	Kabirwála.	
	1881.	1891.	1901.	1881.	1891.	1901.	1881.	1891.	1901.						
Persons	551,964	631,434	710,626	...	...	...	...	...	...	232,126	124,907	113,359	109,727	130,507	
Males	...	...	...	304,517	347,158	388,570	...	...	...	129,031	67,954	61,221	59,676	70,688	
Females	...	...	...	...	...	...	247,447	284,276	322,056	103,095	56,953	52,138	50,051	59,819	
Hindus	112,001	122,714	133,560	62,942	68,508	74,326	49,059	54,206	59,234	55,117	20,882	20,871	16,296	20,394	
Sikhs	2,085	2,832	4,662	1,480	1,939	2,983	6[illegible]5	893	1,679	2,224	586	169	146	1,537	
Jains	47	24	134	34	12	72	23	12	62	134	...	...	...	...	
Buddhists	...	...	...	...	...	...	...	...	...	...	...	...	...	...	
Zoroastrians	63	...	52	39	...	28	24	...	24	50	...	2	...	...	
Mussalmans	435,901	503,962	570,254	238,591	275,183	309,592	197,310	228,779	260,662	172,679	103,432	92,303	93,285	108,555	
Christians	1,861	1,892	1,964	1,436	1,508	1,569	425	384	395	1,922	7	14	...	21	
Others and unspecified	6	1	...	5	1	...	1	...	...	...	...	...	...	...	
European and Eurasian Christians	1,819	1,851	1,766	1,418	1,485	1,445	401	366	321	1,731	6	10	...	19	
Sunnis	431,656	495,679	...	236,322	270,561	177,109	195,334	225,118	...	56,607	31,446	28,285	29,110	32,261	
Shiahs	3,830	5,787	...	2,031	3,243	2,153	1,799	2,544	...	1,139	122	81	65	846	
Wahábis	79	...	...	44	...	123	35	...	...	49	14	2	8	55	

NOTE—Figures for 1881 have been taken from the old Gazetteer; those for 1891 from Table No. VII of the Census Report, 1891, those for 1901 from Table VI of the Census Report of 1901.

Figures of sects for 1901 represent population of males over 14 only, and the figures for the rest of the population are not available.

Table No. VIII showing LANGUAGES.

1	2	3	4	5	6	7	8	9
Languages.	District.			Distribution by Tahsils (1901).				
	1881.	1891.	1901.	Multan.	Shujabad.	Lodhrán.	Mailsi.	Kabírwála.
Hindustáni	10,446	8,635	7,933	7,412	192	150	63	86
Bágri	864	997	60	38	12	1	...	9
Panjábi	160,578	87,102	113,536	29,641	1,971	921	3,209	77,794
{ Jatki	375,097	530,338	41	38	3	...	...	...
{ Multáni	...	...	565,108	185,698	119,479	111,118	97,042	51,771
Bilochi	11	20	163	163	...	...	...	...
Pashtu	1,260	1,255	1,288	961	155	71	57	44
Pahári	22	32	224	209	...	3	...	12
Kashmíri	59	72	16	9	4	2	...	1
Sindhi	1,018	674	872	592	225	36	4	15
Nepalese	1	1	3	3	...	...	...	...
Persian	25	53	55	52	2	1	...	...
English	1,794	1,810	1,734	1,699	6	10	...	19

Note.—Figures for 1881 have been copied from the old Gazetteer; those for 1891 from Table No. X of the Census Report; those for 1901 from Table X of Census Report of 1901.

Table No. IX showing MAJOR CASTES and TRIBES.

1	2	3	4	5	6	7	8	9	10
	Total Numbers.			Sexes, 1901.		Strength by Religions, 1901.			
Caste or Tribe.	1881.	1891.	1901.	Males.	Females.	Hindus.	Sikhs.	Mussalmans.	Proportion per mille of 1901.
Total Population ...	551,964	631,431	710,626	388,570	322,056	133,560	4,662	570,254	...
Arain	23,981	28,582	32,410	17,428	14,982	...	...	32,410	45·6
Arora	76,842	82,331	88,987	49,183	39,804	88,293	613	81	125·2
Biloch	18,547	21,603	24,438	13,535	10,953	...	...	24,488	34·5
Brahmans (including Muhiáls	4,183	5,310	5,579	3,334	2,245	5,571	8	...	7·9
Charhoa	11,452	9,299	14,682	7,852	6,830	430	...	14,252	20·6
Chuhra	29,489	32,026	11,187	6,037	5,150	8,991	...	2,196	15·7
Jats—									
Langáhs ...	2,190	2,402	2,927	1,546	1,381	...	...	2,927	4·1
Langrials ...	...	2,375	3,174	1,787	1,387	2	1	3,171	4·5
Sumras ...	2,214	1,730	1,460	874	586	2	...	1,458	2·1
Tahims ...	2,821	4,300	4,540	2,356	2,184	...	...	4,540	6·4
Others ...	...	135,275	128,214	68,712	59,502	321	2,271	125,622	180·4
Total ...	102,952	146,082	140,315	75,275	65,040	325	2,272	137,718	197·5
Julaha	23,753	28,545	27,232	15,146	12,086	44	1	27,187	38·3
Kharral	2,492	4,750	4,748	2,535	2,213	1	1	4,746	6·7
Khatri	9,798	9,694	10,877	6,065	4,812	10,669	204	4	15·3
Khoja	5,640	8,772	9,776	5,262	4,514	...	...	9,776	13·8
Khokhar	9,696	17,612	11,666	6,359	5,247	24	...	11,582	16·3
Kumhhar	13,716	12,478	18,827	10,149	8,678	70	4	18,753	26·5
Lohar	2,768	2,553	3,774	2,013	1,761	39	57	3,678	5·3
Machhi	9,610	8,436	12,429	6,566	5,863	...	...	12,429	17·5
Mahtam	4,193	3,802	5,127	2,781	2,346	1,869	2	3,256	7·2
Mallah	6,011	5,916	7,745	4,321	3,425	1	...	7,745	10·9
Mirasi	7,510	7,699	10,767	5,850	4,917	19	...	10,748	15·2
Mochi	16,596	14,503	24,144	12,923	11,221	283	...	23,861	34·
Mughal	4,601	10,843	8,038	4,556	3,482	...	...	8,038	11·3
Nai	6,035	6,149	8,438	4,651	3,787	80	3	8,355	11·9
Od	3,459	2,362	3,782	1,901	1,881	3,769	...	13	5·3
Pathán	9,067	7,069	8,251	5,040	3,211	...	...	8,251	11·6
Qassáb	5,914	4,978	3,817	2,257	1,560	...	...	3,817	5·4
Rajputs—									
Bhattis ...	14,890	30,675	25,951	13,943	12,008	195	81	25,675	36·5
Chaubáns ...	2,134	4,552	3,498	1,928	1,570	186	29	3,283	4·9
Dhudhis ...	1,356	2,227	1,704	903	801	16	1	1,687	2·4
Joyas	5,059	5,649	7,212	3,947	3,265	3	62	7,147	10·1
Panwárs ...	4,995	5,192	5,666	3,105	2,561	221	...	5,445	8·
Syáls	23,037	30,999	30,995	16,787	14,208	...	...	30,995	43·6
Others... ...	8,156	38,951	16,490	9,292	7,198	1,538	214	14,738	23·2
Total ...	59,627	90,637	91,516	49,905	41,611	2,159	387	88,970	128·8
Saiyad	8,908	15,392	10,567	5,701	4,866	...	...	10,567	14·9
Sheikh	12,649	12,234	6,826	3,947	2,879	...	...	6,826	9·6
Tarkhán	11,915	10,427	17,356	9,459	7,897	76	104	17,176	24·4

NOTE.—Figures for 1881 have been copied from the old Gazetteer; those for 1901 from Table No. XVI of the Census Report, and those for 1901 from Table XIII, Part II A, pages 104-06, of the Census Report of 1901 without omitting any figures as done in the Table.

Table No. IXA showing MINOR CASTES.

1	2	3	4	5	6	7
	Total number.			Sexes 1901.		
Caste or Tribe.	1881.	1891.	1901.	Males.	Females.	Remarks.
Agari	...	12	...	...	...	
Aheri	...	44	5	5	...	
Ahír	887	822	495	333	162	
Arab	475	81	...	...	...	
Arya	199	8	...	...	...	
Awán	2,899	3,267	3,600	2,812	1,288	
Bádhla	...	8	...	...	...	
Bághbán	20	5	17	12	5	
Bahrupia	...	7	...	...	...	
Bangáli	8	9	2	6	3	
Banjára	457	394	539	287	252	
Banya	562	236	324	204	120	
Barara	...	31	195	104	91	
Barwála	2	167	1	1	...	
Batwál	...	9	2	2	...	
Bawaria	...	14	...	...	...	
Bázigar	130	527	224	123	101	
Bhábra	248	429	613	282	331	
Bhand	506	268	93	44	199	
Bharai	930	644	1,300	697	603	
Bharbhúnja	82	8	...	...	...	
Bhat	336	207	537	275	262	
Bhatia	1,995	1,478	2,718	1,540	1,178	
Bhátra	...	126	...	...	...	
Bhatyára	1,964	873	2,216	1,193	1,023	
Bisati	...	5	...	...	...	
Bishnoi	1	9	...	...	...	
Bodla	54	2	29	18	11	
Bohra	...	101	127	63	64	
Chamar	1,946	1,361	750	447	303	
Changar	79	317	74	88	86	
Chhímba	484	830	18	6	7	
Dabgar	69	88	...	...	...	
Dági	...	30	...	...	...	
Dárugar	...	31	...	...	...	
Darzi	532	446	1,885	1,000	885	
Daúdpotra	1,315	942	670	394	276	
Dhai (Sirkiband)	...	294	2	2	...	
Dhobi	...	9,299	14,682	7,852	6,830	
Dhogri	...	4	...	...	...	
Dhund	...	6	8	8	...	
Dhunsar	8	11	...	...	...	
Dogar	186	138	24	16	8	
Dogra	...	28	...	...	...	
Dumna	83	40	...	...	...	
Fakír	2,324	2,711	4,541	2,596	1,945	

Table No. IXA showing MINOR CASTES—*contd.*

1	2	3	4	5	6	7
	Total Numbers.			Sexes, 1901.		
Caste or Tribe.	1881.	1891.	1901.	Males.	Females.	Remarks.
Gadbi	...	6	...	...	...	
Gagra	...	20	...	...	...	
Gakkhar	...	64	186	99	87	
Garri	...	14	3	3	...	
Ghirath	4	34	...	...	...	
Ghosi	332	1	38	10	28	
Ghulam	99	3	87	43	44	
Gorkha	6	3	3	2	1	
Gujar	604	1,056	764	428	336	
Hesi	...	44	...	...	...	
Hijra	...	1	...	...	...	
Jaiswara	226	329	669	379	290	
Jhabel	1,868	1,154	2,954	1,625	1,329	
Jhinwar	303	1,553	858	620	238	
Jogi	691	676	704	440	264	
Kachhi	...	6	19	9	10	
Kahut	22	14	21	14	7	
Kalál	580	857	366	231	135	
Kamboh	687	1,318	1,953	972	981	
Kanera	109	74	1,397	854	543	
Kanet	...	44	...	...	...	
Kangar	...	7	...	...	...	
Kanjar	...	957	*1,313	513	800	* Kanchan.
Karral	...	27	1	1	...	
Kashmiri	92	128	139	79	60	
Kayath	84	205	664	361	303	
Kehal	232	27	78	37	41	
Khakha	...	134	833	473	360	
Kharasia	...	5	...	...	...	
Khatik	18	99	37	24	13	
Khunma	...	5	...	...	...	
Kochi	...	1	...	...	...	
Koral	...	78	...	...	...	
Kori	578	789	733	444	289	
Kurmi	33	25	16	13	3	
Labana	307	475	222	119	103	
Lilari	442	231	199	42	157	
Lodha	378	105	587	329	258	
Mahajan	...	21	...	...	...	
Mali	49	31	76	58	18	
Maniar	...	53	41	14	27	
Maratha	...	53	2	2	...	
Megh	...	60	13	13	...	
Meo	3	...	7	4	3	
Mina	...	74	...	...	...	
Nat	369	337	928	484	444	
Nungar	2,303	99	...	...	...	
Nyaria	...	110	47	27	20	

Table No. IXA showing MINOR CASTES—*concld.*

1	2	3	4	5	6	7
Caste or Tribe.	Total Numbers.			Sexes, 1901.		Remarks.
	1881.	1891.	1901.	Males.	Females	
Pakhiwára	727	866	1,053	587	466	
Parácha	7	1	...	...	...	
Pársi	63	31	52	28	24	
Pási	...	19	62	37	25	
Patwa	264	1	56	43	13	
Penja	91	36	4,209	2,167	2,042	
Perna	130	49	223	103	120	
Pujári	...	1	...	...	...	
Púrbia	55	57	425	192	233	
Qalandar	16	35	10	10	...	
Ráj	...	171	...	...	...	
Rangrez	...	107	785	508	277	
Rathi	...	95	...	...	...	
Saini	53	136	47	34	13	
Sánsi	115	56	23	8	15	
Sapela	...	197	8	8	...	
Sarera	...	72	6	6	..	
Sud	...	79	...	...	...	
Surár	2,044	2,140	2,821	1,493	1,328	
Tagah	...	8	...	...	...	
Tamboli	...	6	32	20	12	
Teli	484	1,228	1,119	645	474	
Thákar	52	66	48	30	18	
Thathera	274	97	152	91	61	
Tori	..	38	...	...	...	
Toba	201	106	139	79	60	
Turk	1	115	17	14	3	
Ulma	2,211	1,299	118	60	58	
Native Christian	42	41	198	124	74	
European, English		1,529	666	532	134	
" Scotch	945	38	33	21	12	
" Irish		84	71	44	27	
" Welsh		25	5	2	3	
" Spanish		1	...	...	...	
" French		4	...	...	...	
" Italian		2	...	...	...	
" Greek		1	2	2	...	
" German	764	1	...	...	...	
" Others		...	864	791	73	
American		1	...	...	...	
Canadian		3	1	1	...	
Australian		1	...	...	...	
Eurasian	110	162	124	52	73	

NOTE.—The figures of the Census, 1881, are taken from Table VIIIA of that Report; those of 1891 from Table No. XVI of the Census Report, 1891; and those for 1901 from Table No. XIII, Part IIA, pages 104-106, of the Census Report of 1901.

Table No. X showing CIVIL CONDITION.

1	2	3	4	5	6	7	8	9	10	11	12	13	14	15	16	17	18	19
Detail.	Single.						Married.						Widowed.					
	Males.			Females.			Males.			Females.			Males.			Females.		
	1881.	1891.	1901.	1881.	1891.	1901.	1881.	1891.	1901.	1881.	1891.	1901.	1881.	1891.	1901.	1881.	1891.	1901.
Actual figures for religion.																		
All religions.	176,047	199,687	224,999	103,639	122,089	142,430	110,585	127,241	141,905	108,044	124,419	140,118	17,885	20,230	21,666	35,764	37,768	39,508
Hindus	34,868	37,659	40,475	17,876	26,309	22,237	24,097	26,523	29,062	21,838	24,426	27,136	3,977	4,326	4,789	9,345	9,471	9,861
Sikhs	646	905	1,538	213	339	716	764	932	1,334	322	452	835	70	102	111	70	102	134
Jains	12	4	28	7	4	19	9	7	40	10	8	32	3	1	4	6	...	11
Musalmans.	139,321	159,807	181,566	85,329	101,241	119,244	85,457	99,590	111,286	85,669	99,362	111,935	13,813	15,786	16,740	26,312	28,179	29,483
Christians	1,178	1,308	1,373	204	195	208	238	185	175	192	170	170	20	15	21	29	16	17
Distribution of every 10,000 souls of each age.																		
All ages	5,781	5,752	5,790	4,189	4,299	4,422	3,631	3,665	3,652	4,366	4,381	4,351	587	582	558	1,445	1,319	1,227
0—9	9,991	9,985	9,988	9,956	9,945	9,958	9	15	12	43	53	41	...	...	...	1	2	1
10—14	9,664	9,528	9,728	8,151	7,439	8,596	330	459	268	1,818	2,521	1,386	6	13	4	31	40	18
15—19	8,155	7,192	8,260	2,533	1,611	3,135	1,789	2,705	1,693	7,311	8,158	8,728	55	103	47	155	231	137
20—24	5,811	4,371	5,635	548	358	642	4,023	5,318	4,187	9,078	9,182	9,074	166	281	178	374	460	284
25—29	3,701	2,532	3,301	195	197	245	5,976	6,982	6,336	9,090	8,874	9,223	322	486	363	715	929	532
30—39	1,949	1,340	1,487	127	115	147	7,395	7,811	7,837	8,292	7,669	8,559	656	819	676	1,581	2,216	1,294
40—49	1,119	877	850	101	106	134	7,638	7,534	7,950	6,319	5,432	6,617	1,243	1,589	1,200	3,580	4,462	3,249
50—59	855	758	731	90	68	103	7,238	6,736	7,297	4,195	3,225	4,346	1,907	2,506	1,972	5,715	6,707	5,551
60 over	822	718	709	91	101	109	5,741	5,393	5,831	1,873	1,667	1,938	3,437	3,889	3,460	8,036	8,232	7,953

Note.—Figures for 1881 are copied from the old Gazetteer; those for 1891 from Table No. VIII of Census Report; and those for 1901 from Table VII, Part II, of the Report of 1901.

Table No. XI.—showing BIRTHS and DEATHS.

1	2	3	4	5	6	7	8	9	10	11
	Total Births registered.			Total Deaths registered.			Total Deaths from			
Year.	Males.	Females.	Persons.	Males.	Females.	Persons.	Cholera.	Small-pox.	Fever.	Remarks.
1880	8,531	6,814	15,345	6,529	5,163	11,692	...	203	8,030	
1881	9,481	7,884	17,365	8,096	6,748	14,844	...	250	10,687	
1882	9,694	8,348	13,042	10,928	9,202	20,130	...	92	14,997	
1883	10,115	8,820	18,935	9,113	7,417	16,530	...	40	11,568	
1884	12,408	11,095	23,503	10,647	9,309	19,956	...	184	13,486	
1885	10,211	9,382	19,593	9,493	7,795	17,288	105	129	11,373	
1886	14,106	8,473	22,579	7,463	6,363	13,826	...	72	8,620	
1887	11,415	10,423	21,838	7,917	6,802	14,719	1	274	9,267	
1888	12,079	10,543	22,622	7,982	7,074	15,056	4	782	9,703	
1889	12,179	10,568	22,747	9,396	8,215	17,611	...	99	12,281	
1890	11,952	10,399	22,351	10,371	9,070	19,441	11	12	14,173	
1891	11,431	10,118	21,549	10,011	8,803	18,814	9	10	14,191	
1892	11,647	10,110	21,757	18,858	16,145	35,003	1,939	96	25,874	
1893	10,855	9,393	20,248	9,950	8,340	18,290	...	53	11,649	
1894	18,318	11,574	24,892	9,648	8,371	18,019	...	39	11,852	
1895	14,702	13,248	27,950	10,269	8,969	19,238	...	329	12,375	
1896	15,059	13,430	28,489	8,570	7,383	15,953	...	751	9,289	
1897	15,718	14,420	30,138	10,464	10,350	20,814	...	203	14,285	
1898	12,691	11,495	24,186	9,422	8,310	17,732	...	33	12,266	
1899	17,120	15,563	32,683	9,021	8,243	17,264	117	114	11,191	
1900	15,503	13,868	29,371	9,306	8,420	17,726	216	174	12,270	

Note.—These figures are taken from the Sanitary Reports.

Table No. XIA,—showing MONTHLY DEATHS from all CAUSES.

Months.	1895.	1896.	1897.	1898.	1899.	Average.	Remarks.
January	1,674	2,540	1,221	2,439	1,717	1,918	
February	1,331	1,452	920	1,492	1,506	1,340	
March	1,358	1,292	836	1,343	1,410	1,248	
April	1,448	1,148	902	1,137	1,219	1,171	
May	1,680	1,138	930	1,515	1,483	1,349	
June	1,224	1,182	939	1,309	1,260	1,183	
July	970	996	979	1,048	1,170	1,032	
August	995	1,135	1,088	996	1,120	1,067	
September	1,120	1,114	1,345	1,070	1,234	1,177	
October	1,504	1,292	3,226	1,535	1,727	1,857	
November	1,995	1,353	4,825	1,968	1,590	2,350	
December	3,939	1,311	3,603	1,860	1,828	2,508	
Total ...	19,238	15,953	20,814	17,732	17,264	18,200	

NOTE.—These figures are taken from the Sanitary Reports.

Table No. XIB,—showing MONTHLY DEATHS from FEVERS.

Months.	1895.	1896.	1897.	1898.	1899.	Average.	Remarks.
January	1,074	1,801	649	1,835	1,156	1,303	
February	877	874	492	1,043	1,005	858	
March	937	770	492	916	962	815	
April	952	664	530	788	871	761	
May	1,080	643	566	1,150	1,002	888	
June	769	704	512	980	811	755	
July	544	527	481	728	686	593	
August	467	589	507	632	626	564	
September	592	584	764	600	747	657	
October	829	708	2,397	1,008	1,076	1,203	
November	1,268	707	4,011	1,386	1,028	1,680	
December	2,986	718	2,884	1,200	1,221	1,801	
Total ...	12,375	9,289	14,285	12,266	11,191	11,878	

NOTE.—These figures are taken from the Sanitary Reports.

Table No. XII,—showing INFIRMITIES.

1		2	3	4	5	6	7	8	9	10
Detail.		Insane.		Blind.		Deaf and Dumb.		Lepers.		Remarks.
		Male.	Female.	Male.	Female.	Male.	Female.	Male.	Female.	
District	1881 ...	361	165	1,485	1,290	423	191	44	23	
	1891 ...	184	80	767	665	368	217	23	7	
	1901 ...	328	186	1,041	859	605	330	39	24	

A.—By age (1901).

Age.	Population afflicted.			Insane.			Deaf-mutes.			Blind.			Lepers.		
	Persons.	Males.	Females.	Persons.	Males.	Females.	Persons.	Males.	Females.	Persons.	Males.	Females.	Persons.	Males.	Females.
1	2	3	4	5	6	7	8	9	10	11	12	13	14	15	16
Total ...	3,331	1,964	1,367	514	328	186	(a) 935	605	330	(b) 1,900	1,041	859	(c) 63	39	24
0 and under 1 ...	6	3	3	...	...	...	3	1	2	3	2	1	...	...	...
1 „ „ 2 ...	5	2	3	...	...	...	2	1	1	3	1	2	...	...	...
2 „ „ 3 ...	12	8	4	3	2	1	6	5	1	4	2	2	...	...	...
3 „ „ 4 ...	28	18	10	7	5	2	9	6	3	15	8	7	...	...	...
4 „ „ 5 ...	29	19	10	6	5	1	15	10	5	8	4	4	1	1	...
Total 0 and under 5	80	50	30	16	12	4	35	23	12	33	17	16	1	1	...
5 and under 10 ...	227	138	89	63	43	20	121	75	46	53	28	25	2	2	...
10 „ „ 15 ...	273	178	95	82	44	38	133	93	40	67	42	25	5	4	1
15 „ „ 20 ...	224	151	73	72	49	23	93	68	25	64	38	26	3	1	2
20 „ „ 25 ...	186	121	65	52	31	21	81	55	26	52	33	19	10	7	3
25 „ „ 30 ...	215	129	86	54	33	21	86	51	35	72	44	28	6	2	4
30 „ „ 35 ...	245	147	98	44	26	18	83	51	32	114	67	47	7	4	3
35 „ „ 40 ...	178	107	71	40	23	17	40	24	16	98	59	39	4	3	1
40 „ „ 45 ...	248	138	110	30	22	8	60	36	24	160	82	78	5	3	2
45 „ „ 50 ...	163	94	69	20	14	6	44	28	16	97	52	45	3	1	2
50 „ „ 55 ...	247	134	113	19	13	6	43	26	17	184	96	88	6	3	3
55 „ „ 60 ...	122	61	61	3	2	1	14	7	7	104	52	52	2	1	1
Total 60 and over ...	923	516	407	19	16	3	102	68	34	802	431	371	9	7	2
60 and under 65 ...	342	190	152	8	7	1	36	22	14	298	160	138	2	2	...
65 „ „ 70 ...	95	57	38	4	3	1	12	9	3	79	45	34	1	1	...
70 „ „ 75 ...	209	118	91	4	3	1	26	18	8	177	95	82	4	3	1
75 „ „ 80 ...	50	27	23	1	1	...	3	2	1	45	24	21	2	1	1
80 „ „ 85 ...	144	82	62	1	1	...	7	6	1	137	76	61	...	...	...
85 „ „ 90 ...	13	9	4	...	...	...	1	1	...	12	8	4	...	...	...
90 „ „ 95 ...	28	13	15	...	...	...	10	6	4	19	8	11	...	...	...
95 „ „ 100 ...	16	7	9	1	1	...	2	1	1	13	5	8	...	...	...
100 „ „ 105 ...	17	9	8	...	...	...	1	1	...	17	8	9	...	...	...
105 „ „ 110 ...	2	1	1	...	...	...	1	...	1	1	1	...	...	...	...
110 and over ...	7	3	4	...	...	...	3	2	1	4	1	3	...	...	...

(a) Column 8 (935) includes 53 persons (31 males and 22 females), who are also insane.
(b) Column 11 (1900) includes 7 persons (3 males and 4 females) who are also insane and 19 persons (14 males and 5 females) who are also deaf-mutes.
(c) Column 14 (63) includes 2 persons (1 male and 1 female) who are also deaf-mute.

Table No. XII,—showing INFIRMITIES—*continued.*

1	2	3	4	5	6	7	8	9	10
Detail.	Insane.		Blind.		Deaf and Dumb.		Lepers.		Remarks.
	Male.	Female.	Male.	Female.	Male.	Female.	Male.	Female.	
	B.—By caste (1891). *								
Caste—									
Abír	...	...	4	1	1	1	...	...	
Aráín	10	2	43	41	14	11	2	..	
Arora	24	4	111	81	37	25	4	2	
Awán	1	...	5	6	...	1	...	...	
Biloch Dasti	...	...	...	1	...	...	...	...	
„ Hot	...	...	...	...	...	...	1	...	
„ Korai	1	...	...	9	4	...	1	...	
„ Kulachi	1	...	...	1	...	...	...	...	
„ Lishari	...	...	...	1	...	...	...	...	
„ Maghassi ...	3	1	...	...	...	...	...	...	
„ Miscellaneous ...	...	...	19	8	1	...	...	...	
Banya	...	...	1	1	...	...	...	...	
Barar	...	...	1	...	...	...	...	...	
Bazigar	...	...	2	1	...	...	...	...	
Bhabra	...	...	3	1	1	2	...	...	
Bhand	...	...	...	1	...	...	...	...	
Bharai	...	...	...	1	...	...	...	...	
Bhat	...	...	1	...	...	...	...	...	
Bhatia	...	...	...	1	...	...	...	...	
Bhatyara	...	...	1	1	...	...	...	...	
Brahman	...	2	5	3	4	2	...	...	
Chamar	...	...	3	1	...	...	...	...	
Changar	...	...	...	1	2	...	...	...	
Charhoa	...	1	...	...	...	...	...	...	
Chishti	...	...	...	...	...	...	...	...	
Chuhra	8	...	45	30	16	10	...	...	
Dhobi	1	2	5	15	5	2	...	...	
Fakir	...	...	7	4	1	...	...	...	
Gadaria	...	...	1	...	...	...	...	...	
Gujar	...	...	1	1	...	...	...	...	
Gusain	...	...	1	...	...	...	...	...	
Husaini	...	...	1	...	...	...	...	...	
Jat Bhutta	...	2	4	6	1	5	...	...	
„ Deswal	...	...	...	...	1	...	...	...	
„ Dhankar	...	...	...	...	...	2	...	...	
„ Gil	...	...	...	...	...	1	...	...	
„ Hinjra	...	...	2	...	4	...	...	...	
„ Langáh	...	...	5	...	1	2	...	...	
„ Sidhu	...	...	...	...	1	...	...	...	
„ Sipra	1	...	...	...	...	...	...	...	
„ Tahim	1	...	2	3	...	5	...	...	
„ Viraich	...	...	...	...	1	...	...	...	
„ Virk	1	...	...	...	...	...	...	...	
„ Miscellaneous ...	34	20	139	147	80	49	4	2	
Julaha	6	4	28	17	14	10	1	...	
Jhabel	...	...	2	1	...	1	...	...	
Jhinwar	...	...	2	4	...	1	...	...	
Kalal	...	...	2	...	...	1	...	...	
Kamboh	...	...	1	2	...	2	...	...	
Kanera	...	1	1	1	...	...	...	...	
Kanjar	...	...	2	2	...	...	...	...	
Kori	...	...	2	2	..	...	...	...	
Kehal	...	...	1	..	...	...	...	...	

* Not compiled by caste in 1901.

Table No. XII,—showing INFIRMITIES—*concluded*.

1	2	3	4	5	6	7	8	9	10
Detail.	Insane.		Blind.		Deaf and Dumb.		Lepers.		Remarks.
	Male.	Female.	Male.	Female.	Male.	Female.	Male.	Female.	
Caste—concluded.									
Kharral	...	2	5	2	4	...	...	...	
Khatri	7	1	18	12	8	4	...	...	
Khokhar	8	5	24	22	12	6	1	...	
Khoja	17	4	9	16	8	4	...	...	
Kumhar	11	5	24	12	17	10	1	...	
Labana	4	5	1	...	...	...	...	...	
Lodha	...	...	...	...	1	...	...	...	
Lilari	1	...	1	4	...	...	...	...	
Lohar	4	3	1	4	1	...	...	...	
Machhi	4	1	15	20	3	1	...	2	
Madari	...	...	1	...	...	...	...	...	
Mahtam	...	...	7	3	2	1	...	...	
Mallah	2	...	10	10	8	2	...	...	
Mali	...	...	...	...	...	1	...	...	
Mirasi	1	1	11	9	7	2	...	...	
Mochi	...	6	17	16	10	3	...	...	
Mughal	1	...	10	16	9	5	...	...	
Nai	1	...	10	4	2	4	1	...	
Nangar	...	...	1	...	...	...	...	...	
Od	1	...	7	3	...	...	...	...	
Pathan Afridi	...	...	...	...	1	...	...	...	
„ Ghilzai	...	...	1	...	...	...	...	...	
„ Lodi	...	...	1	...	...	...	...	...	
„ Musa Khel ...	...	...	1	...	...	...	...	...	
„ Tarin	...	...	1	...	...	...	...	...	
„ Yusafzai ...	...	...	...	1	...	...	...	...	
„ Miscellaneous ...	2	1	6	4	4	1	...	...	
Pali	...	...	...	2	...	...	...	...	
Qassab	1	1	8	4	6	3	...	...	
Raj	...	...	1	...	...	...	...	...	
Rajput Bagri	...	...	3	1	...	...	...	...	
„ Bhatti	9	4	31	36	14	5	...	...	
„ Chauhan ...	...	...	4	8	4	2	...	...	
„ Dharwal ...	...	...	1	...	...	...	...	...	
„ Dudhi	...	...	1	...	...	1	...	...	
„ Joya	...	...	5	6	4	2	...	...	
„ Khichi	...	...	3	...	2	3	...	...	
„ Manhas	...	...	...	1	...	1	...	...	
„ Panwar	5	1	2	5	1	3	1	...	
„ Syal	5	2	25	18	19	6	1	...	
„ Wattu	1	...	...	...	...	...	...	...	
„ Miscellaneous ...	1	1	2	2	...	1	...	...	
Saini	...	...	...	1	...	...	...	...	
Saiyad	10	2	19	6	4	4	1	...	
Shekh	3	1	15	4	7	2	3	...	
Sirkiband	...	..	...	1	4	1	...	...	
Sunar	1	...	4	6	7	...	...	...	
Tarkhan	3	1	9	9	6	4	...	1	
Teli	...	...	2	2	...	1	...	...	
Ulama	...	...	...	1	1	2	...	...	

Table No. XIII,—showing EDUCATION.

1	2	3	4	5	6	7	8	9
Detail.	Year.	All religions.	Hindus.	Sikhs.	Jains.	Musalmans.	Christians.	REMARKS.
Learning ...	1881	7,241	3,443	49	1	3,490	254	
	1891	5,880	3,371	64	1	2,317	127	
Literate ...	1881	21,653	15,602	320	6	4,343	1,340	
	1891	29,042	20,634	583	5	6,231	1,586	
	1901	40,533	28,437	1,054	38	9,358	1,609	

TAHSILS.

Detail.	Year.	Multan.	Shujabad.	Lodhran.	Mailsi.	Kabirwala.	
Literate ...	1901	17,735	5,546	6,701	4,213	6,338	

NOTE.—Figures for 1881 have been copied from the old Gazetteer; those for 1891 are taken from Table No. IX of the Census Report, and those for 1901 from Table VIII, Part II, pages 43 and 44 of the Census Report of 1901.

Figures for 'learning' were not compiled in 1901 and the figures of the 'literate' in 1901 include the literate of all ages.

Table No. XIV,—showing detail of SURVEYED and ASSESSED AREA.

1	2	3	4	5	6	7	8	9	10	11	12
	Cultivated.				Uncultivated.						
	Irrigated										
Year.	By Government Works.	By private individuals.	Unirrigated.	Total cultivated.	Grazing lands.	Culturable.	Unculturable.	Total uncultivated.	Total area assessed.	Gross assessment.	Unappropriated Government waste the property of Government.
1868-69	303,627	202,123	118,684	624,434	2,053	715,441	2,422,260	3,139,754	3,764,188	533,404	1,880,489
1873-74	192,733	347,924	83,983	624,640	100,000	777,081	2,291,559	3,168,640	3,793,280	541,760	1,879,906
1878-79	339,644	70,410	389,306	799,360	100,000	2,618,080	245,760	2,963,840	3,763,200	543,895	1,214,485
1883-84	326,057	97,732	94,833	518,622	103,815	2,917,462	245,462	3,266,739	3,785,361	587,842	1,357,278
1888-89	426,001	156,495	74,817	657,313	118,596	1,234,410	258,579	1,611,585	3,866,468	913,125	1,522,899
1893-94	452,963	162,178	125,633	740,774	118,841	1,178,322	257,111	1,554,274	3,781,580	1,055,972	1,480,018
1898-99	388,838	141,376	93,576	623,790	113,339	1,015,406	240,115	1,368,860	3,795,023	891,746	1,433,706

Tahsils detail by measurements of new Settlement.

1	2	3	4	5	6	7	8	9	10	11	12
Multán	...	...	18,995	225,335	340	146,641	47,186	194,167	...	...	164,996
Shujabad	..	...	37,157	163,558	7,915	185,283	48,520	241,718	...	...	25,398
Lodhran	...	...	13,078	184,756	2,834	237,957	48,483	289,274	...	...	205,022
Mailsi	...	...	50,955	207,423	28,940	243,319	54,836	327,095	...	...	527,929
Kabírwala	...	...	26,048	224,701	61,186	193,464	39,817	294,467	...	...	521,198
Total	...	...	146,233	1,005,773	101,215	1,006,664	238,842	1,346,721	...	...	1,444,543

Note.—The figures for the District are taken from the Revenue Reports; those for the tahsils from the Assessment Reports. The term 'cultivated' bears a somewhat different meaning in the two sets of figures.

Table No. XV,—showing TENURES held direct from Government as they stood in 1898-99.

1	2	3	4	5	6	7	8
Description of villages according to revenue paid by them.	Tenure.	Number of estates.	Number of villages.	Number of holders or shareholders.	Gross area.	Average area of each estate.	Average assessment of each estate.
Villages paying Rs. 5,000 to Rs. 50,000.	1. Zamindari ...	...	...	...	...	...	...
	2. Pattidari and Bhayachara	9	9	2,293	75,030	8,337	6,609
Villages paying Rs. 100 to Rs. 5,000.	1. Zamindari ...	75	75	803	94,247	1,256	427
	2. Pattidari and Bhayachara	1,005	1,005	65,849	2,170,606	2,160	727
Villages paying less than Rs. 100.	1. Zamindari ...	134	134	1,093	268,681	2,005	37
	2. Pattidari and Bhayachara	206	206	3,884	306,304	1,487	49
	Leases from Government without right of ownership.	11	11	2,112	130,317	11,847	4,463
	Total	1,440	1,440	76,034	3,045,185	2,115	615

ADDENDA.

	3	4	5	6		7	8 (Revenue.)
A. Holdings included in the above held wholly or partially free of revenue, *viz.*:—							
1. In perpetuity free of conditions ...	...	...	227	22,211		...	8,997
2. " subject to conditions ..	...	...	176	16,129		...	3,082
3. For life or lives	...	...	58	12,467		...	4,022
4. At pleasure of Government	...	...	126	1,491		...	10,853
5. Up to the time of Settlement...	...	...	14	18		...	566
Total of these holdings	...	..	601	52,316		...	27,520
				Total.	Of which cultivated.		
B. Lands included in the above of which the ownership is encumbered by usufructuary mortgages.			13,498	277,299	104,101		

NOTE.—These figures are taken from Table No. XI of Land Revenue Report, 1898-99.

Table No. XVI, showing TENURES not held direct from Government, as they stood in 1898-99.

1	2	3	4	5	6	7	8	9	10	11	12	13
Detail.	Number of holdings.	Area.	Number of holdings.	Area.	Number of holdings.	Area.	Number of holdings.	Area.	Number of holdings.	Area.	Number of holdings.	Area.
	District.		Tahsil Multán.		Shujabad.		Lodhran.		Mailsi.		Kabírwala.	
Total cultivated area	111,152	918,305	18,967	225,335	30,258	168,062	19,752	153,064	17,216	140,919	24,959	230,926
Area cultivated by owners	31,149	230,033	4,605	52,889	11,506	57,013	6,297	34,036	2,412	20,762	6,329	65,333
Area cultivated by tenants free of rent or at nominal rent.	1,031	2,633	582	1,234	127	923	130	138	98	177	94	161
Area cultivated by tenants paying rents — With right of occupancy — paying at revenue rates with or without malikana.	1,161	6,733	232	2,427	291	1,127	15	73	501	1,989	122	1,107
Area cultivated by tenants paying rents — With right of occupancy — paying other cash rents ...	41	152	6	36	2	13	1	1	18	54	14	48
Area cultivated by tenants paying rents — With right of occupancy — paying in kind with or without an addition in cash.	2,224	17,026	501	7,046	356	3,817	722	3,876	419	1,345	166	942
Area cultivated by tenants paying rents — Without right of occupancy — paying at revenue rates with or without malikana.	1,167	4,719	33	467	680	1,716	14	66	262	1,361	178	1,109
Area cultivated by tenants paying rents — Without right of occupancy — paying other cash rents ...	2,192	21,996	1,198	13,998	252	2,557	407	862	101	719	234	3,860
Area cultivated by tenants paying rents — Without right of occupancy — paying in kind with or without an addition in cash.	72,187	635,014	11,750	147,238	17,044	100,896	12,166	114,012	13,405	114,502	17,822	158,366
Total held by tenants paying rent ...	78,972	685,640	13,780	171,215	18,625	110,126	13,325	118,890	14,706	119,980	18,536	163,432

Table No. XVI, showing TENURES not held direct from Government, as they stood in 1898-99—concld.

1			2	3	4	5	6	7	8	9	10	11	12	13
Detail.			Area.											
			Irrigated.	Unirrigated.	Irrigated.	Unirrigated.	Irrigated.	Unirrigated.	Irrigated.	Unirrigated.	Irrigated.	Unirrigated.	Irrigated.	Unirrigated.
Detail of rents and area on which paid by tenants-at-will.	Rents in kind.	(1) Zabti rents	217	...	1	...	50	...	166	...	...	...	...	...
		(2) Half produce or more ...	220,270	39,068	55,836	13,031	11,616	8,070	10,180	889	14,742	73	127,896	17,005
		(3) Two-fifths and less than half.	76,148	5,689	14,482	51	24,813	3,260	15,221	1,522	14,809	829	6,823	27
		(4) One-third and less than two-fifths.	209,021	35,322	40,704	335	38,134	9,111	73,190	3,349	51,431	22,346	5,562	181
		(5) Less than one-third ...	47,955	965	22,435	194	5,379	286	9,381	103	9,890	382	870	...
		(6) By fixed amount of produce.	344	15	168	1	163	14	11	...	...	...	2	...
		(7) Total area under rents in kind.	553,955	81,059	133,626	13,612	80,155	20,741	108,149	5,863	90,872	23,630	141,153	17,213
	Cash rents.	(8) Total paying at revenue rates with or without malikana.	2,511	2,208	137	330	568	1,148	60	6	702	659	1,044	65
		(9) Total paying other cash rents.	20,262	1,734	13,527	471	2,420	137	414	448	665	54	3,236	624
		(10) Total cash rents paid on area entered in column 9.	133,930	1,812	92,373	...	13,981	1,317	1,030	175	236	8	26,304	312

Table No. XVII,—Showing GOVERNMENT LANDS in 1899-1900.

1	2	3	4	5	6	7	8	9	10	11	12	13	14
			Area included in columns 2, 3, let for cultivation.		*Area of unclassed forests under the Forest Department let for cultivation.*				*Income for the year ending 31st September 1900.*				
DETAIL.	Area of unclassed forests and Government waste lands under the control of Deputy Commissioner.	Area of nazúl lands leased for agricultural purposes and consequently subject to the waste land lease rules.	Cultivated in the year.	Uncultivated.	Cultivated in the year.	Uncultivated.	Area of Government land held by Government tenants under Act III of 1893 or under any Colonization Scheme.	Total of columns 2, 3, 6, 7, 8.	Land revenue on lands included in columns 4, 5, 6, 7, 8.	Málikána on lands included in columns 4, 5, 6, 7, 8.	Other income.	Total income.	REMARKS.
District	1,498,331	144	4,848	12,889	...	...	104,357	1,602,832	22,012	7,723	1,08,766	1,38,501	
Tahsil Multan	189,983	142	1,141	1,968	...	...	32,890	223,015	9,297	1,363	25,714	36,374	
„ Shujabad	32,922	2	106	126	...	...	...	32,924	120	42	13,764	13,926	
„ Lodhrán	206,843	...	191	1,555	...	...	...	208,843	497	167	15,533	16,197	
„ Mailsi	551,576	...	3,374	9,225	...	...	...	551,576	4,644	392	23,873	28,909	
„ Kabírwála	515,007	...	36	15	...	...	71,467	586,474	7,454	5,759	29,882	43,095	

NOTE.—These figures are taken from Statement No. XXII of the Land Revenue Report as noted in Chapter V a large part of the unclassed forests have since been protected.'

Table No. XVIII,—Showing RESERVES.

1	2	3	4
Tahsil.	Name of Reserve.	Area in acres by Settlement measurement.	Remarks.
Kabírwála	Makhdúm Vanoi ..	24,641	
	Akil	16,142	Measured together and named Bura Kotla Akil.
	Dangra		
	Bura Kotla		
	Pakka Háji Majíd ...	2,072	
	Rajuana	3,847	
	Pír Mahal	14,494	
Multan	Arbi	354	
Shujabad	Shujatpur	996	
	Ubaora	650	
	Kot Walik	507	
	Nauraja Bhutta	1,178	
	Jalálpur	1,475	
Lodhrán	Khanwah	1,278	
	Lodhrán	1,440	
Mailsi	Sharaf	5,196	
	Tajuana	2,039	
	Chak Kaura	1,578	
	Sahuka	20,963	

Note.—Figures taken from Settlement Records.

Table No. XIX,—Showing LAND acquired by Government (total of 10 years 1889-90 to 1898-99).

1	2	3	4	5
Purposes for which acquired.	Acres acquired.	Compensation paid in rupees.	Reduction of revenue in rupees.	Remarks.
Roads	3	75	...	
Canals	239	6,925	58	
State Railways	...	...	...	
Buildings and Miscellaneous Works ...	18	955	5	
Total ...	322	10,608	72	

Note.—These figures are taken from Statement No. XXIV of the Land Revenue Reports.

Table No. XX, showing Acres under CROPS.

1	2	3	4	5	6	7	8	9	10	11	12	13	14	15
Year.	Rice.	Wheat.	Barley.	Jowar.	Bajra.	Gram.	Oil-seed.	Sugar-cane.	Cotton.	Indigo.	Tobacco	Carrots and Turnips.	Total cropped.	Remarks.
1888-89	12,178	277,677	11,389	77,840	21,134	11,202	34,210	2,665	52,383	39,664	2,260	42,925	658,134	
1889-90	15,855	280,838	11,201	82,860	23,698	8,285	42,771	2,365	60,161	58,036	1,279	41,275	699,961	
1890-91	13,507	314,558	13,159	85,642	25,540	16,560	47,445	1,695	51,967	29,331	2,134	48,277	741,293	
1891-92	17,907	324,817	12,311	83,392	17,431	25,409	34,524	1,877	52,142	29,607	1,654	45,555	721,104	
1892-93	7,267	343,032	11,889	80,622	37,168	36,885	69,447	1,683	27,642	17,053	2,370	42,579	766,580	
1893-94	11,511	355,705	15,391	5,549	14,486	32,243	41,054	1,175	56,709	24,311	2,403	47,045	740,774	
1894-95	11,071	362,120	9,355	64,572	7,873	27,021	32,352	1,163	66,903	40,742	2,204	45,765	756,942	
1895-96	14,861	280,709	6,556	68,931	5,611	13,831	29,044	2,241	72,884	34,695	2,115	47,428	659,741	
1896-97	17,075	262,047	8,908	77,249	11,201	12,718	28,145	2,846	87,484	33,099	2,169	44,211	679,412	
1897-98	32,669	352,294	13,984	56,943	19,556	26,910	45,521	1,790	85,181	81,993	1,970	46,277	830,003	
1898-99	20,428	285,032	9,802	52,790	22,517	14,974	41,939	903	22,267	10,960	1,514	44,021	623,791	

Tahsil averages of five years from 1894-95 to 1898-99.

1	2	3	4	5	6	7	8	9	10	11	12	13	14	15
Multán	6,370	68,743	2,045	14,882	3,904	7,445	9,768	467	21,342	7,771	599	10,558	179,632	
Shujabad	7,553	74,863	1,915	5,245	1,478	1,766	2,743	836	10,115	8,971	339	7,134	146,179	
Lodhran	1,827	55,103	1,980	12,963	2,190	2,028	7,184	3	7,040	8,788	298	10,468	120,493	
Mailsi	201	56,923	1,591	14,202	4,463	2,788	9,096	4	6,835	4,152	281	8,553	122,699	
Kabirwala	3,329	54,504	2,403	18,980	879	5,290	8,351	450	21,743	599	482	8,060	144,966	
Total District ...	19,280	310,136	9,934	66,272	12,914	19,317	37,142	1,760	67,075	30,281	1,999	44,773	713,969	

Note.—These figures are taken from the Revenue Reports.

Table No. XXI, showing AVERAGE YIELD per acre harvested in maunds.

1	2	3	4	5	6	7	8	9	10	11	12	13	14	15	16	17	18	19	20
		HITHAR.					UTAR.					RAWA.							
Crop.	Soil.	Multán.	Shujabad.	Lodhran.	Mailsi.	Kabírwala.	Multán.	Shujabad.	Lodhran.	Mailsi.	Kabírwala.	Multán.	Shujabad.	Lodhran.	Mailsi.	Kabírwala.	Sidhnai Circles.	Tarafs of Multán.	REMARKS.
Rice (unhusked) ...	Nahri	10	10	...	...	...	11	11	12	...	...	...	...	...	...	...	9	12	
	Cháhi Nahri ...	...	...	...	...	...	...	12	...	...	...	...	...	...	...	...	...	...	
Jowár	Nahri	5	5	6	5	...	5	5	6	½	...	...	5	5	5	...	6	...	
	Cháhi Nahri ...	...	...	...	...	...	...	...	...	...	...	...	...	...	...	...	...	...	
	Sailáb	...	...	...	...	6½	...	...	...	...	...	...	...	...	...	...	...	...	
Til	Sailáb	2⅓	...	...	...	2¾	...	...	...	...	2⅓	...	...	...	...	...	...	...	
	Nahri	...	3	3	3	...	...	...	3½	3½	...	...	3¾	3½	...	...	3⅓	...	
	Báráni	...	...	...	...	...	...	...	...	2	...	...	...	...	2	...	...	...	
Sathri	Nahri	...	...	...	...	...	...	...	...	...	...	...	...	...	...	...	5	...	
Bájra	Nahri	...	...	...	...	...	...	...	6	5½	...	...	...	...	5½	...	6	...	
	Cháhi Nahri ...	...	...	...	...	...	...	...	...	...	...	...	...	...	...	...	...	10	
	Sailáb	5	...	...	...	...	...	...	...	...	...	...	...	...	...	...	...	...	
	Báráni	...	...	...	...	...	...	...	...	...	...	...	...	...	5	...	...	...	
Maize	Cháhi Nahri ...	...	...	...	...	...	...	...	...	...	...	...	...	...	...	...	...	40	
Chína	Nahri	...	...	...	...	...	6	...	...	...	...	...	...	...	...	...	7	...	
	Cháhi Nahri ...	...	...	...	...	...	8	...	...	...	...	...	...	...	...	...	...	...	
Sugarcane	Nahri	...	...	...	...	...	...	...	...	...	...	...	...	...	...	...	60	...	
	Cháhi Nahri ...	...	18	...	...	...	...	...	...	...	...	...	...	...	...	...	...	...	
Cotton	Cháhi	...	...	...	3¾	4½	3¼	...	...	...	4½	...	...	...	...	4½	...	...	
	Nahri	3	3	3½	3	...	4½	3¾	3¾	3½	...	3	2½	3¾	3½	...	4	...	
	Cháhi Nahri ...	...	3¼	...	...	...	...	4	4	...	...	...	3¼	...	...	...	4½	...	
	Abi	...	...	...	3¼	...	...	...	...	...	...	...	...	...	...	...	...	...	

Table No. XXI, showing AVERAGE YIELD per acre harvested in maunds.

1	2	3	4	5	6	7	8	9	10	11	12	13	14	15	16	17	18	19	20
		Hithar.					Utar.					Rawa.							
Crop.	Soil.	Multán.	Shujabad.	Lodhran.	Mailsi.	Kabirwala.	Multán.	Shujabad.	Lodhran.	Mailsi.	Kabirwala.	Multán.	Shujabad.	Lodhran.	Mailsi.	Kabirwala.	Sidhnai Circles.	Tarafs of Multán.	Remarks.
Indigo (sérs)	Nahri	...	10	10	...	...	11	11	10	10½	...	...	11	11	...	...	10	...	
	Cháhi Nahri ...	...	...	...	...	...	...	...	...	...	...	...	...	...	...	...	...	...	
Wheat	Cháhi	...	...	8	8	7½	7½	7½	8	9	7½	7½	8	9	9	8	8	10	
	Cháhi Nahri ...	9½	9½	10	9	...	9½	10	10	10½	...	...	10	11	...	...	11	12	
	Nahri	...	...	...	6½	...	...	...	...	7	...	...	...	...	...	...	8½	...	
	Cháhi Sailáb ...	9	9¼	...	...	10	...	...	...	...	9½	...	...	...	...	...	...	...	
	Abi	...	...	8	...	...	...	...	...	...	...	...	...	...	...	...	...	...	
	Sailáb	7	6¾	6	7	7¾	...	...	...	...	7½	...	...	...	...	...	...	...	
	Báráni	...	...	...	...	...	...	...	...	...	...	5	...	...	5	6½	...	...	
Barley	Cháhi	...	...	...	...	...	...	...	8	...	...	...	...	...	...	...	...	...	
	Cháhi Nahri ...	...	...	...	...	...	...	9½	9	...	...	...	...	...	...	...	...	...	
	Nahri	...	...	...	...	...	...	...	...	...	...	...	...	...	...	...	8½	...	
	Sailáb	...	6½	...	...	...	...	...	...	...	...	...	...	...	...	...	...	...	
Ussun	Cháhi Nahri ...	...	...	...	...	...	...	...	...	...	...	...	4½	...	...	...	...	...	
	Nahri	...	...	...	...	...	...	...	...	3	...	3	...	...	...	...	...	...	
	Báráni	...	...	...	...	...	...	...	3	2½	...	3	...	...	2½	...	...	...	
Gram	Sailáb	5	5	4½	...	5¼	...	...	...	...	5	...	...	...	...	...	...	...	
	Nahri	...	...	5½	...	...	...	...	5½	5½	...	...	...	...	...	...	6	...	

Note.—These figures are taken from the Assessment Reports.

Table No. XXII, showing Number of STOCK.

1	2	3	4	5	6	7	8	9	10	11	12	13	14
	WHOLE DISTRICT FOR THE YEAR.							TAHSILS FOR THE YEAR 1898-99.					
Kind of Stock.	1868-69.	1873-74.	1878-79.	1883-84.	1888-89.	1893-94.	1898-99.	Multán.	Shujabad.	Lodhran.	Mailsi.	Kabirwala.	REMARKS.
Bulls and buffaloes						166,961	186,645	43,243	36,439	35,289	30,789	40,885	
Cows						143,256	154,918	34,876	31,074	23,522	25,478	39,968	
Male buffaloes	182,411	167,174	168,809	199,395	335,720	4,673	6,606	1,397	1,354	317	411	3,127	
Cow buffaloes						30,225	38,765	10,167	7,097	4,621	6,902	9,978	
Young stock, calves or buffaloes' calves.						40,089	152,226	37,214	28,343	25,750	23,589	37,330	
Sheep						152,666	318,972	76,233	50,574	56,778	59,887	75,500	
Goats	313,087	311,589	326,130	368,648	459,594	260,822	374,236	73,767	43,646	85,676	103,705	67,442	
Horses and ponies	3,141	3,219	1,672	1,729	9,091	9,945	11,635	3,770	2,397	1,291	1,580	2,597	
Mules and donkeys	11,659	9,465	10,350	12,196	28,903	30,114	32,115	7,422	6,667	6,827	5,219	5,980	
Camels	11,942	15,050	23,854	19,491	18,774	17,156	25,858	4,638	2,145	3,241	7,987	7,847	
Ploughs	55,474	54,742	55,653	53,293	66,192	79,317	77,346	17,313	15,570	14,393	12,425	17,645	
Carts	99	124	105	110	107	982	1,162	486	65	352	213	46	
Boats	106	114	82	78	101	101	119	48	23	12	16	20	

Table No. XXIIA, showing HORSE and MULE BREEDING in the Multan District.

Year.	Number of horse stallions.	Number of donkey stallions.	Number of new branded mares.	Total number of branded mares in the district.	Number of mares served by Government horse stallions.	Number of mares served by Government donkey stallions.	Number of fillies and colts out of branded mares.	Number of mules foaled.	Number of castrations effected.	REMARKS.
1893-94	6	6	56	515	182	346	67	62	150	
	2	**1**			**28**	**47**	**8**	**18**		
1894-95	7	6	49	536	185	310	63	62	118	
	2	**1**			**27**	**53**	**7**	**15**		
1895-96	8	7	105	476	256	468	48	32	358	
	2	**1**			**89**	**33**	**35**	**8**		
1896-97	7	8	29	446	244	536	77	56	248	
	3	**1**			**141**	**51**	**50**	**15**		
1897-98	6	9	79	501	237	410	67	73	124	
	3	**1**			**138**	**56**	50	**15**		
1898-99	6	9	102	579	251	489	65	64	134	
	3	**1**			**198**	**62**	55	**16**		

NOTE.—This Statement has been supplied by the Superintendent, Civil Veterinary Department. [illegible] figures in antique show the operations paid for by the District Board.

Table No. XXIII, showing the OCCUPATIONS of the POPULATION in the Multan District (according to the Census of 1901).

1	2	3	4	5
No.	Name of occupation.	Actual workers. Males.	Actual workers. Females.	Dependents, both sexes.
1	Total population	231,834	19,736	459,056
2	Civil administration	4,240	14	7,654
3	Army	3,244	...	1,355
4	Foreign, etc., Service	45	...	271
5	Live-stock	7,873	144	12,114
6	Land-owners (non-cultivating)	3,219	765	7,451
7	Do. (cultivating)	24,992	413	62,206
8	Mafidars and Jagirdars	...	...	...
9	Mortgagees (cultivating)	47	...	208
10	Do. (rent-receivers)	32	4	158
11	Tenants	53,874	433	119,331
12	Sharers	216	...	293
13	Agricultural labourers	7,122	96	6,837
14	Growers of special produce and trees	199	10	338
15	Agricultural training and supervision	65	...	117
16	Barbers	2,445	...	5,026
17	Washerman	1,696	115	3,974
18	Water-carriers	620	91	889
19	Cooks and other servants	5,124	461	5,889
20	Non-domestic service	11	2	12
21	Sweepers and scavengers	653	106	1,064
22	Sanitary officers, etc.	1	...	7
23	Dealers of milk, ghi, cheese and fish, etc. (provision of animal food).	1,439	91	2,952
24	Grain and flour merchants	10,573	212	19,495
25	Grain parchers and bakers	561	598	1,272
26	Grinding and preparing flour and pulse	160	3,335	2,373
27	Sweets, fruits and vegetables, etc., sellers	1,600	133	2,992
28	Ice, soda, sugar, salt grocers and general shop-keepers	674	7	1,388
29	Oil pressors and kerosine-oil sellers, etc.	427	10	988
30	Firewood and grass gatherers and dealers, etc.	887	177	1,143
31	Brick and lime burners and sellers, etc.	840	39	1,577
32	Masons, builders, etc.	3,430	97	7,484
33	Railway mechanics	...	...	...
34	Preparation and supply of material substances (arms, &c.)	36	...	80
35	Wool and fur spinners and dyers, etc.	112	66	156
36	Silk carders, spinners and dyers, etc.	1,385	284	2,232
37	Workers in cotton and cotton cloth, weavers, etc.	14,646	4,389	30,312
38	Workers in jute, flax, coir, etc.	700	257	1,422
39	Tailors and darners, etc.	967	318	1,647
40	Piece-good dealers	654	1	1,548
41	Gold and silver dealers and makers	1,725	10	3,310
42	Brass and copper vessel workers and sellers	201	...	813
43	Tin, zinc, lead and quicksilver workers and sellers	34	...	107
44	Blacksmiths and ironsmiths, &c.	900	...	1,902
45	Potters, glass and chinaware dealers and sellers, etc.	3,286	87	7,855
46	Wood-cutters and sawyers, etc.	580	...	863
47	Carpenters, etc.	763	...	1,627
48	Mat-makers and sellers, etc.	2,055	245	6,092
49	Chemists and druggists, antimony preparers and sellers, etc.	313	1	552
50	Workers and dealers in leather and grease, etc.	6,843	205	14,940
51	Money-lenders and money-changers and testers, etc.	432	25	1,229

Table No. XXIII—*concluded.*

1	2	3	4	5
No.	Name of occupation.	Actual workers.		Dependents, both sexes.
		Males.	Females.	
52	General merchants	805	2	1,721
53	General shopkeepers and pedlars, etc.	1,581	29	3,174
54	Brokers and commission salesmen	843	...	1,964
55	Miscellaneous contractors and farmers, etc.	99	...	164
56	Superior officers, station masters and guards (Railway service).	1,659	...	2,910
57	Cart and carriage owners and drivers, etc.	71	...	138
58	Boat owners, boatmen, etc.	466	1	947
59	Pack camel, elephant, donkey owners and drivers, etc. ...	5,194	58	11,098
60	Postmasters and postal messengers, etc.	172	...	303
61	Telegraph officers	16	...	50
62	Watchmen, etc. (storage)	517	...	1,478
63	Religion—(*a*) priests and ministers, (*b*) subsidiary religions services.	3,299	219	7,128
64	Principals, professors and teachers in colleges, etc. ...	383	29	729
65	Public scribes and copyists	25	...	43
66	Petition-writers and pleaders	180	...	628
67	Practitioners, medical, European and Native system, etc. ...	230	224	643
68	Compounders, etc.	95	6	170
69	Engineering and inspection officers	45	...	60
70	Painters and other services	32	...	65
71	Players on musical instruments and dancers	998	112	1,964
72	Polo, shikaries and acrobats, etc.	60	...	90
73	Well-sinkers, road, canal and Railway labourers, etc. ...	881	2	1,474
74	General labourers	21,573	2,426	38,613
75	Prostitutes and others unspecified	771	593	2,153
76	House-rent sharers and other property not being land ...	175	83	539
77	Mendicancy (not being affiliated to a religious order, etc.)	11,758	2,493	16,432
78	Pension, Civil and Military services, and pensions undefined	106	3	243
79	Prisoners, etc.	2,080	7	...

Note.—These figures are taken from Table XV, Part II, of the Census Report of 1901.

Table No. XXIV, showing working of FACTORIES.

1	2	3	4	5	6	7	8	9	10	11	12	13	14
					Average daily number of operatives employed.								
					Adults.			Children.					
Factories.	Name and locality of factory.	Nature of industry.	Name of moving power.	Amount of moving power.	Males.	Females.	Total.	Males	Females.	Total.	Total columns 8 and 11.	Whether the factory is worked mainly (1) by shifts, or (2) by mid-day stoppages, or (3) otherwise.	Whether a general holiday generally given (1) on Sundays, or (2) on varying week days, or (3) whether the factory is exempted under Section 5, B, 2 (c) or (4) under Section 5, B, 2 (d) of the Act, or (5) otherwise worked.
				Horses.									
1. Raja Wallabb Deo & Co. ...	Beyond City Railway Station.	Cotton Press	Steam ...	40	75	...	75	...	...	...	75	Stoppages.	Sundays or varying week days instead.
2. French Press & Co.		Ginning ...		45	59	48	107	...	...	...	107		
3. S. Choith Ram & Co.				20	30	12	42	...	...	...	42		
4. Tek Chand, Chiman Das & Co.				25	46	27	73	6	11	17	90		
5. Jetha Nand & Co.				35	25	76	101	15	12	27	128		
6. Hira Lal, Rallia Chand & Co. formerly called Sukhdeo Das & Co.				25	35	40	75	...	...	...	75		
Railway Workshop	Cantonment Railway Station.	Repairing Engines.	Steam and labour.	...	235	...	235	...	...	...	235		
8. Gurdit Singh & Co.				16	12	14	26	...	...	...	26		
9. Nibban Das & Co.	City Railway Station.	Ginning ...		7	12	40	52	...	...	...	52		
10. Danji Maharaj & Co.				20	15	12	27	...	...	...	27		
11. Cotton Factory at Mailsi ...	Mailsi ...			7	17	11	28	...	...	...	28		

NOTE.—These figures are taken from the District Factories Report of 1898-99.

Table XXV, showing RIVER TRAFFIC.

1	2	3	4	5	6
Trade.		Principal merchandise carried.	Average duration of voyage in days.		Distance in miles.
From	To		Summer or floods.	Winter or low water.	
Sakkhar	Ferozepore	Iron and sajji	90	120	400
Ferozepore	Sakkar	Wheat, gram, til, rope and wool	30	45	400
Ditto	Kotri	Ditto ditto	40	50	600
Akhnur	Mithankot	Grain of all kinds, sugar, salt, spices, ghi, country cloth, silks and wool	20	30	450
Mithankot	Multan	Dhán, rice, dhanya, peas, string, sajji, zira, ajwain, methra	30	60	120
Wazirabad	Do.	Wheat, gur, ghi, country cloth, wool, cotton, kupas, horns, halela, balela, awla, sarna, timber	20	30	230
Ramnagar	Do.	Ditto ditto ditto	18	25	210
Pindi Bhattian	Do.	Ditto ditto ditto	14	20	180
Wazirabad	Mithankot	Ditto ditto ditto	25	45	350
Ramnagar	Do.	Ditto ditto ditto	22	36	330
Pindi Bhattian	Do.	Ditto ditto ditto	18	30	300
Multán	Wazirabad	Iron, cocoanuts, dates, black pepper, munj, sajji	30	45	230
Do.	Ramnagar	Ditto ditto ditto	24	40	210
Do.	Pindi Bhattian	Ditto ditto ditto	21	35	180
Mithankot	Wazirabad	Ditto ditto ditto	50	60	350
Do.	Ramnagar	Ditto ditto ditto	45	52	330
Do.	Pindi Bhattian	Ditto ditto ditto	40	45	300
Jhelum	Multán	Gram and oil-seeds	20	35	250
Do.	Sakkhar	Ditto	45	60	500
Do.	Kotri	Ditto	60	90	750

NOTE.—These figures are copied from the old Gazetteer.

Table No. XXVI, showing PRICES of WHOLESALE PRODUCE.

1	2	3	4	5	6	7	8	9	10	11
	Wholesale Prices of Agricultural Produce per maund of $82\frac{2}{7}$ lbs.									
Year.	Rice.	Wheat.	Barley.	Jowár.	Bájra.	M[illegible]ze.	Gram.	Moth.	Múng.	Másh.
	Rs. a. p.	Rs. a. p.	Rs. a. p.	Rs. a. p.	Rs. a. p.	Rs. a. p.	Rs. a. p.	Rs. a. p.	Rs. a. p.	Rs. a. p.
1895-96	5 5 11	2 9 1	2 2 8	2 11 1	2 12 8	2 1 9	2 3 7	...	...	...
1896-97	5 11 9	3 4 4	2 10 0	3 14 10	3 15 3	4 2 9	3 9 0	...	...	...
1897-98	5 4 9	2 8 6	1 11 10	2 2 3	1 14 8	2 0 11	2 0 6	2 0 10	3 6 6	3 3 10
1898-99	4 9 0	2 1 1	1 11 0	1 9 4	1 15 3	1 7 11	2 0 10	1 13 5	2 11 5	2 5 2

1	12	13	14	15	16	17	18	19	20
	Wholesale Prices of Agricultural Produce per maund of $82\frac{2}{7}$ lbs.—*concld.*								
						Fodder			
Year.	Linseed.	Til.	Sugar.	Cotton (cleaned).	Ghi.	Grass.	Straw.	Jowár and Bájra.	Remarks.
	Rs. a. p.	Rs. a. p.	Rs. a. p.	Rs. a. p.	Rs. a. p.	Rs. a. p.	Rs. a. p.	Rs. a. p.	
1895-96	4 7 1	5 2 8	4 4 8	12 1 0	34 9 11	0 7 1	0 8 6	0 7 1	
1896-97	5 0 0	5 5 0	4 11 11	12 10 10	31 3 10	0 5 5	0 8 0	0 6 5	
1897-98	4 3 5	4 10 7	4 4 7	10 2 0	36 9 5	0 5 1	0 6 5	0 4 0	
1898-99	4 1 8	3 15 6	3 6 4	9 12 7	32 13 5	0 5 4	0 7 6	0 3 4	

Note.—These figures are taken from Statement No. IX of the Land Revenue Reports.

Table No. XXVIA, showing RETAIL PRICES.

Number of Sers and Chattaks per Rupee.

1	2		3		4		5		6		7		8	
Year.	Wheat.		Barley.		Gram.		Indian corn.		Jowar.		Bajra.		Rice (fine).	
	S.	C.	S.	C.	S.	C.	S.	C.	S.	C.	S.	C.	S.	C.
1861-62	15	10	19	9	15	3	...	...	16	5	15	4	8	...
1862-63	20	6	32	12	21	4	...	..	28	2	25	9	9	...
1863-64	20	13	32	15	25	8	...	...	31	10	30	5	9	2
1864-65	13	11	13	15	19	15	...	...	17	13	16	15	7	9
1865-66	12	12	20	8	19	8	...	...	16	5	17	12	7	6
1866-67	15	14	19	4	21	11	...	...	18	4	19	4	6	13
1867-68	13	4	19	15	17	6	...	...	20	1	18	9	7	4
1868-69	13	7	19	6	14	12	...	...	14	15	16	14	6	6
1869-70	9	11	16	3	9	15	...	...	13	10	13	5	5	6
1870-71	12	5	17	13	14	6	...	...	17	12	14	12	6	2
1871-72	17	12	26	8	17	...	17	...	27	...	24	...	6	...
1872-73	19	...	24	...	17	...	25	...	26	...	28	...	8	...
1873-74	16	...	22	...	22	...	24	...	25	...	22	...	8	...
1874-75	20	..	29	...	9	...	26	...	27	...	25	...	7	...
1875-76	18	8	26	...	23	...	23	...	24	..	24	...	7	...
1876-77	23	...	40	...	40	...	28	...	28	...	27	...	6	...
1877-78	14	8	23	...	17	...	20	...	20	...	20	...	7	8
1878-79	9	12	15	...	13	...	13	...	12	...	15	...	7	8
1879-80	12	4	17	...	14	8	16	...	17	..	16	...	6	...
1880-81	12	...	17	12	16	8	17	...	19	...	14	...	6	...
1881-82	16	...	23	...	21	8	22	...	22	...	23	...	6	...

1	9		10		11		12		13		14		15		16	
Year.	Urd Dal.		Potatoes.		Cotton, cleaned.		Sugar, refined.		Ghi, cow's.		Firewood.		Tobacco.		Salt, Lahori.	
	S.	C.	S.	C.	S.	C.	S	C.	S.	C.	S.	C.	S.	C.	S.	C.
1861-62	11	4	...	..	3	4	2	7	1	13	149	5	5	9	11	11
1862-63	15	...	...	...	2	12	2	6	1	14	147	12	4	10	10	1
1863-64	15	13	...	...	1	6	2	4	2	4	130	10	4	10	9	10
1864-65	12	12	...	...	1	2	2	5	1	14	130	10	4	10	9	1
1865-66	15	2	...	...	3	9	2	7	1	6	111	15	4	11	9	13
1866-67	16	1	...	...	2	3	2	9	1	5	97	15	4	...	9	12
1867-68	13	12	...	...	2	8	2	4	1	5	105	13	3	9	10	1
1868-69	10	5	...	...	2	2	2	5	1	4	107	5	3	12	10	1
1869-70	8	11	...	...	1	12	2	4	1	6	93	5	3	13	9	11
1870-71	12	15	...	...	2	3	2	4	1	5	100	...	3	...	11	...
1871-72	15	...	9	...	2	4	2	14	1	8	80	...	4	...	10	12
1872-73	13	8	13	...	2	6	2	12	1	13	100	...	4	...	10	12
1873-74	16	...	14	...	2	12	3	...	1	12	100	...	5	...	10	8
1874-75	18	...	14	...	3	2	2	12	1	11	100	...	3	...	10	12
1875-76	15	8	12	...	2	12	2	12	1	9	90	...	4	...	10	...
1876-77	18	...	15	...	2	12	3	...	J	8	56	...	4	...	10	12
1877-78	10	8	12	...	2	8	2	8	1	7	70	...	3	8	10	4
1878-79	8	...	9	...	3	2	2	...	1	6	70	...	3	8	11	...
1879-80	12	...	9	...	2	9	2	8	1	6	70	...	3	8	11	...
1880-81	13	...	10	...	2	6	2	4	1	6	90	...	4	...	12	...
1881-82	14	8	12	...	2	14	2	6	1	8	90	...	3	...	12	8

Note.—Figures up to 1881-82 have been copied from the old Gazetteer; those for 1882-83 to 1899-1900 from the District and Tahsil Multán Register of Prices for 1st January of each year.

Table No. XXVIA, showing RETAIL PRICES—*concld.*

1	2		3		4		5		6		7		8		9		10		11		12		13		14		15		16	
	NUMBER OF SERS AND CHATTAKS PER RUPEE.																													
YEAR.	Wheat.		Barley.		Gram.		Indian corn.		Jowar.		Bajra.		Rice (fine).		Urd Dal.		Potatoes.		Cotton, cleaned.		Sugar, refined.		Ghi, cow's.		Firewood.		Tobacco.		Salt, Lahori.	
	S.	C.	S.	C.	S.	C.	S.	C.	S.	C.	S.	C.	S.	C.	S.	C.	S.	C.	S.	C.	S.	C.	S.	C.	S.	C.	S.	C.	S.	C.
1882-83	Not available.																													
1883-84	18	...	28	8	28	...	29	...	27	...	25	8	6	8	13	8	10	...	2	14	3	...	1	8	80	...	4	...	14	...
1884-85	19	...	31	...	28	...	21	...	27	...	24	...	6	...	15	...	13	...	2	14	3	4	1	7	80	...	3	...	15	...
1885-86	17	...	27	...	23	8	19	...	24	...	20	...	6	...	15	8	13	...	2	14	3	4	1	8	80	...	3	...	14	12
1886-87	12	...	17	...	21	...	16	...	16	...	15	...	6	4	16	...	12	...	2	8	3	12	1	8	100	...	3	...	15	...
1887-88	11	...	17	...	16	...	20	...	18	...	16	...	6	...	15	...	13	...	2	8	3	12	1	6	100	...	3	...	15	...
1888-89	14	...	22	...	17	...	22	...	20	...	17	...	6	...	15	...	11	8	2	8	3	8	1	3	100	...	4	...	12	...
1889-90	16	...	27	...	22	...	25	...	25	...	22	...	6	4	16	...	13	...	2	8	3	4	1	4	100	...	4	...	12	...
1890-91	15	...	24	...	18	...	24	...	26	...	23	...	5	4	15	...	14	...	2	9	4	...	1	10	100	...	4	...	13	...
1891-92	12	...	20	...	17	...	18	...	16	8	15	...	6	...	12	...	14	8	2	12	3	12	1	1	100	...	3	...	12	4
1892-93	10	12	14	8	17	4	12	...	16	...	15	8	5	8	13	4	14	...	2	9	3	4	1	3	90	...	3	...	12	4
1893-94	18	...	30	...	27	8	12	...	24	...	26	...	5	...	19	...	15	...	2	...	3	12	1	5	80	...	3	8	12	4
1894-95	17	8	28	...	23	8	16	...	24	...	22	...	5	8	13	...	16	...	2	13	3	12	1	7	90	...	3	8	12	...
1895-96	14	...	20	...	16	4	14	...	19	8	16	...	5	...	12	4	14	...	3	...	2	12	1	3	80	...	3	8	12	8
1896-97	9	6	11	4	9	...	9	4	11	...	9	12	5	...	10	4	12	...	2	9	3	4	1	4	90	...	3	...	12	8
1897-98	11	...	16	...	10	4	12	...	15	6	15	6	5	...	11	...	13	8	3	...	3	...	1	4	100	...	3	8	12	4
1898-99	16	...	26	...	19	8	20	...	28	...	23	...	5	...	...	...	17	...	3	4	3	...	1	4	90	...	3	8	13	...
1899-1900 ...	11	4	14	4	11	8	18	...	13	...	11	...	5	...	...	...	17	...	3	4	3	...	1	4	100	...	3	8	12	8

NOTE.—Figures up to 1881-82 have been copied from the old Gazetteer; those for 1882-83 to 1899-1900 from the District and Tahsil Multán Register of Prices for 1st January of each year.

Table No. XXVII,—Showing PRICE OF LABOUR.

1	2	3	4	5	6	7	8	9	10	11	12	13
Year.	Wages of labour per day.				Carts per day.		Camels per day.		Donkeys per score per day.		Boats per day.	
	Skilled.		Unskilled.									
	Highest.	Lowest.	Highest.	Lowest.	Highest.	Lowest.	Highest.	Lowest.	Highest.	Lowest.	Highest.	Lowest.
	Rs. a. p.	Rs. a. p	Rs. a. p.	Rs. a. p.	Rs. a. p.		Rs. a. p.		Rs. a. p.			
1868-69	0 8 0	0 4 0	0 4 0	0 2 0	2 0 0		0 6 0		3 4 0		Rates according to tonnage and distance.	
1873-74	0 10 0	0 6 0	0 4 0	0 2 0	2 0 0		0 8 0	0 6 0	5 0 0	1 4 0	4 0 0	1 0 0
1878-79	0 10 0	0 7 0	0 4 0	0 2 0	1 0 0	0 8 0	0 10 0	0 7 0	5 0 0	1 4 0	2 8 0	1 0 0
1879-80	0 10 0	0 7 0	0 4 0	0 2 0	1 0 0	0 8 0	0 10 0	0 7 0	5 0 0	1 4 0	2 8 0	1 0 0
1880-81	0 10 0	0 7 0	0 4 0	0 2 0	1 0 0	0 8 0	0 10 0	0 7 0	5 0 0	1 4 0	2 8 0	1 0 0
1881-82	0 10 0	0 7 0	0 4 0	0 2 0	1 0 0	0 8 0	0 10 0	0 7 0	5 0 0	1 4 0	2 8 0	1 0 0
1888-89	0 12 0	0 8 0	0 5 0	0 4 0	1 4 0	0 1 0	0 8 0	0 5 0	5 0 0	3 12 0	5 0 0	2 0 0
1893-94	1 0 0	0 10 0	0 5 0	0 4 0	0 10 0	0 6 0	0 8 0	0 6 0	5 0 0	3 12 0	7 0 0	2 8 1
1898-99	0 14 0	0 8 0	0 5 0	0 4 0	0 12 0	0 8 0	1 0 0	0 4 0	6 4 0	2 8 0	10 0 0	2 0 0

NOTE.—The figures for 1868-69 to 1881-82 are taken from the old Gazetteer; those for other years from the Administration Report.

Table No. XXVIII,—Showing REVENUE collected.

1	2	3	4	5	6	7	8	9
					Excise.			
Year.	Fixed land revenue.	Fluctuating and miscellaneous land revenue.	Tribute.	Local rates.	Spirits.	Drugs.	Stamps.	Total collections.
1868-69 ...	5,09,405	87,771	...	...	24,876	23,681	60,708	7,06,441
1869-70 ...	5,23,307	82,689	...	...	19,849	21,597	64,118	7,11,569
1870-71 ...	5,20,284	1,07,981	...	...	19,041	19,253	49,622	7,61,181
1871-72 ...	5,15,199	1,25,725	...	33,530	22,485	23,341	68,257	7,88,539
1872-73 ...	5,16,991	1,35,367	...	34,767	24,019	22,700	59,556	7,93,400
1873-74 ...	5,22,697	1,45,950	...	35,042	23,759	19,841	70,448	8,17,737
1874-75 ...	5,27,862	1,25,996	...	36,659	23,743	22,890	65,564	8,02,714
1875-76 ...	5,15,186	1,23,482	...	39,186	26,656	22,188	75,810	8,02,508
1876-77 ...	5,12.133	1,33,069	...	39,176	27,496	23,047	78,924	8,13,845
1877-78 ...	5,18.578	1,33,911	...	40,042	29,452	25,043	84,662	8,31,688
1878-79 ...	5,25,125	1,17,634	...	51,535	26,822	23,395	91,409	8,35,920
1879-80 ...	5,52,418	1,53,879	...	55,425	28,671	20,837	90,704	9,01,934
1880-81 ...	5,65,139	1,96,308	...	59,479	32,399	21,445	97,158	9,71,928
1881-82 ...	5,61,052	1,84,302	...	59,241	30,350	20,341	98,122	9,53,408
1882-83 ...	5,64,861	1,96,680	...	64,596	33,557	22,521	1,01,561	9,83,776
1883-84 ...	5,62 823	2,29,483	...	64,441	35,000	25,539	1,09,867	10,27,153
1884-85 ...	5,68,735	1,83,181	...	81,956	32,258	23,823	1,06,896	9,96,849
1885-86 ...	5,60,027	2,08,865	..	82,144	30,231	29,399	1,06,038	10,16,704
1886-87 ...	5,69 489	1,94,768	...	83,753	32,611	24,021	1,11,361	10,16,003
1887-88 ...	5,54,449	2,10,560	...	1,02,198	35,037	24,723	1,19,445	10,46,412
1888-89 ...	5,52,607	2,03,528	...	1,06 815	41,059	23,843	1,22,672	10,50,524
1889-90 ...	5,53,557	2,28,249	...	1,00,585	46,963	23,333	1,20,420	10,73,107
1890-91 ...	5,50,590	2,75,142	...	1,09,443	47,286	29,872	1,15,634	11,27,967
1891-92 ...	5,47,567	2,18,325	...	1,05,471	47,653	24,670	1,14,338	10,58,024
1892-93 ...	5,47,802	3,01,564	...	1,19,905	50,856	25,485	1,25,355	11,70,967
1893-94 ...	5,30,006	3,20,815	..	1,21,139	52,536	25,572	1,18,453	11,68,521
1894-95 ...	5,38,854	3,21,125	...	1,19,837	57,811	26,558	1,20,476	11,84,661
1895-96 ...	5,66,972	3,08,404	...	1,11,442	59,545	26,781	1,26,361	11,99,505
1896-97 ...	5,61,196	3,20,758	...	1,19,131	61,896	25,245	1,54,692	12,42,918
1897-98 ...	5,61,782	3,53,809	..	1,33,071	60,488	26,323	1,48,056	12,83,529
1898-99 ...	5,49,875	1,96,791	..	98,410	59,181	27,663	1,44,332	10,76,252

Note.—The figures up to 1882-83 are taken from the old Gazetteer; those for subsequent years from the Revenue Reports.

Table No. XXIX,—Showing REVENUE derived from Land.

1	2	3	4	5	6	7	8	9	10	11	12	13
			FLUCTUATING REVENUE.					MISCELLANEOUS REVENUE.				
								Grazing dues.				
YEAR	Fixed land revenue (demand).	Fluctuating and miscellaneous land revenue (collections).	Revenue of alluvial lands.	Revenue of waste lands brought under assessment	Water-advantage revenue.	Fluctuating assessment of river lands.	Total fluctuating land revenue.	By enumeration of cattle.	By grazing leases.	Sale of wood from rakhs and forests	Sajji.	Total miscellaneous land revenue.
District figures :—	Rs.	Rs.	Rs.	Rs.	Rs.	Rs.	Rs.	Rs.	Rs.	Rs.	Rs.	Rs.
Average of five years: –												
1868-69 to 1872-73	5,32,874	1,07,907	4,505	3,904	342	...	8,924	22,1[illegible]7	46,589	17,982	6,911	98,983
1872-73 to 1877-78	5,32,241	1,32,331	5,051	7,521	...	...	12,749	7,371	83,512	16,055	7,333	1,19,582
1878-79 to 1882-83	5,62,336	1,69,310	776	1,569	1,192	46,277	58,841	...	82,823	13,193	7,916	1,10,471
1883-84 to 1887-88	5,67,912	2,02,825	...	918	9,926	82,222	94,363	...	65,116	18,162	8,902	1,03,311
1888-89 to 1892-93	5,52,883	2,45,647	... 27	2,029	25,487	1,03,072	1,48,481	53,073		9,126	6,476	92,171
1893-94 to 1898-99	5,61,808	3,03,617		482	13,522	1,07,699	1,70,163	46,292		103	1,939	1,23,977
Tahsils for 1899-1900 :—												
Multan	1,29,120	51,476	...	39	5,182	28,509	33,691	6,624		...	...	48,957
Shujabad	1,62,892	46,169	...	...	1,857	31,457	33,314	5,634		...	...	39,648
Lodhrán	1,39,821	21,195	...	20	1,664	4,780	6,444	600		...	...	8,327
Mailsi	83,139	36,016	...	56	2,423	11,991	14,414	3,979		...	...	21,437
Kabírwála	47,457	60,293	...	59	6,800	26,212	33,012	4,037		...	83	50,214

NOTE.—The figures up to 1892 have been copied from the old Gazetteer, those for subsequent years from Statements Nos. XVIIIA and XX of Land Revenue Report.

Table No. XXX,—Showing LAND REVENUE ASSIGNMENTS for 1898-99

1	2	3	4	5	6	7	8	9	10	11	12	13	14	15	16	17	18	19	20	21	22	23	24	25	26
Total area and revenue assigned.								Distribution of area and jama.												Number of holders.					
Village.		Fractional portions of villages.		Plots.		Total.		In perpetuity free of conditions.		In perpetuity subject to conditions.		For life or lives.		At pleasure of Government.		For term of settlement.		Pending orders of Government.		In perpetuity free of conditions.	In perpetuity subject to conditions.	For life or lives.	At pleasure of Government.	For term of settlement.	Pending orders of Government.
Area.	Jama.	Area.	Jama.	Area.	Jama.	Area.	Jama.	Area.	Jama.	Area.	Jama.	Area.	Jama.	Area.	Jama.	Area.	Jama.	Area.	Jama.						
16,734	6,107	11,021	6,808	5,167	19,808	33,522	23,723	18,632	9,435	7,016	3,711	7,701	3,606	173	6,971	...	...	...	...	217	141	47	85	...	...

NOTE.—These figures are taken from District Revenue Report.

Table No. XXXI,—Showing BALANCES, REMISSIONS and TAKAVI.

1	2	3	4	5	6
	Balance of Land Revenue in Rupees.				
YEAR.	Fixed.	Fluctuating and Miscellaneous Revenue.	Reduction of Fixed Demand on account of bad seasons, deterioration, etc., in Rupees.	Takávi advances in Rupees.	REMARKS.
1868-69	8,658	...	112	4,600	
1869-70	4,754	...	328	10,150	
1870-71	8,161	...	5	800	
1871-72	3,643	...	10,890	10,946	
1872-73	3,969	..	...	1,880	
1873-74	4,479	...	416	1,250	
1874-75	5,910	...	671	472	
1875-76	20,348	535	671	251	
1876-77	22,630	1,990	129	1,430	
1877-78	15,497	555	362	2,145	
1878-79	6,739	...	523	1,137	
1879-80	15,209	2,601	...	520	
1880-81	12,960	...	54	1,592	
1881-82	11,965	...	213	1,909	
1882-83	3,884	164	3,862	71,845	
1883-84	4,654	1,783	438	1,28,685	
1884-85	5,704	56	15	1,61,029	
1885-86	14,308	4,540	104	38,350	
1886-87	13,959	280	60	66,421	
1887-88	10,406	2,552	5,016	1,01,025	
1888-89	3,207	945	3,888	16,208	
1889-90	3,271	993	...	17,822	
1890-91	6,001	101	...	17,780	
1891-92	4,280	12,990	...	29,140	
1892-93	4,560	9,241	...	40,799	
1893-94	22,193	11,822	...	40,430	
1894-95	10,800	9,553	...	20,115	
1895-96	2,632	5,437	...	21,840	
1896-97	8,199	8,146	...	11,679	
1897-98	7,831	12,939	...	11,350	
1898-99	17,217	47,782	...	37,345	

NOTE.—Figures up to 1881-82 have been taken from the old Gazetteer, and the remainder from Statements Nos. XVIIIA, XIX, XX and XXVI of the Land Revenue Reports.

Table No. XXXII,—Showing SALES and MORTGAGES of Land.

1	2	3	4	5	6	7	8	9	10	11
	Sales of land.			Mortgages of Land.			Redemptions of mortgaged Land.			
Year.	Number of cases.	Area of land in acres.	Purchase-money.	Number of cases.	Area of land in acres.	Mortgage-money.	Number of cases.	Area of land in acres.	Mortgage-money.	Remarks.
District figures—			Rs.			Rs.			Rs.	
Average of 6 years 1868-69 to 1873-74 ...	205	7,399	94,764	131	8,820	80,241	...	...	...	
" " 5 " 1874-75 to 1878-79 ...	366	10,641	1,74,803	333	12,701	1,58,875	21	1,259	1,980	
" " 5 " 1879-80 to 1883-84 ...	686	15,345	2,55,050	684	22,529	3,77,729	111	4,643	1,57,517	
" " 5 " 1884-85 to 1888-89 ...	1,486	29,636	5,27,268	1,094	41,689	5,25,627	265	12,281	1,29,617	
" " 5 " 1889-90 to 1893-94 ...	1,380	23,364	7,31,989	794	21,302	4,93,333	709	18,817	4,07,954	
" " 5 " 1894-95 to 1898-99 ...	1,758	42,310	9,74,886	1,276	26,874	8,51,000	881	21,532	4,46,222	
Average Tahsil figures for—										
Multan ... 1877-78 to 1881-82 ...	101	2,993	51,443	129	4,316	67,769	13	800	6,166	
Multan ... 1894-95 to 1898-99 ...	381	11,877	3,62,809	352	8,904	3,55,283	264	7,766	1,71,397	
Shujabad .. 1877-78 to 1881-82 ...	72	1,135	44,233	114	1,961	73,892	8	156	4,195	
Shujabad .. 1894-95 to 1898-99 ...	412	2,942	1,72,227	277	2,812	1,34,325	179	2,155	77,970	
Lodhrán ... 1877-78 to 1881-82 ...	146	2,372	37,782	105	1,803	29,633	5	100	959	
Lodhrán ... 1894-95 to 1898-99 ...	483	6,154	1,54,859	288	5,922	98,561	207	3,533	47,972	
Mailsi ... 1877-78 to 1881-82 ...	104	5,024	43,366	79	7,530	38,399	12	820	6,354	
Mailsi ... 1894-95 to 1898-99 ...	200	6,087	1,24,948	112	3,563	75,914	95	4,634	50,583	
Kabírwála ... 1877-78 to 1881-82 ...	46	1,229	11,718	58	2,143	21,515	6	259	1,917	
Kabírwála ... 1894-95 to 1898-99 ...	316	13,370	1,59,544	268	5,774	1,87,716	185	3,453	63,080	

Note.—Figures up to 1881-82 are taken from the old Gazetteer; those for remaining years from the Revenue Reports.

Table No. XXXIII,—Showing SALES of STAMPS and REGISTRATION of DOCUMENTS.

1	2	3	4	5	6	7	8	9	10	11	12	13	14
	INCOME FROM SALE OF STAMPS.				OPERATIONS OF THE REGISTRATION DEPARTMENT.								
	Receipts in Rupees.		*Net income in Rupees.*		*Number of Deeds registered.*				*Value of Property affected in Rupees*				
YEAR.	Judicial.	Non-judicial.	Judicial.	Non-judicial.	Touching immoveable property.	Touching moveable property.	Money obligations.	Total of all kinds.	Immoveable property.	Moveable property.	Money obligations.	Total value of all kinds.	REMARKS.
1877-78	59,375	18,294	58,520	17,749	1,148	266	224	1,638	6,41,393	13,646	91,873	7,46,912	
1878-79	65,453	25,956	56,690	24,811	1,373	200	222	1,795	7,44,316	5,920	1,11,371	8,61,607	
1879-80	62,076	28,626	55,189	27,146	1,598	56	160	2,020	9,62,740	12,377	60,097	10,36,735	
1880-81	64,104	33,054	58,123	31,259	1,850	60	178	2,298	12,57,435	25,872	1,14,313	13,99,116	
1881-82	67,181	30,941	60,556	29,350	1,621	44	141	2,034	10,10,117	22,506	71,085	11,05,755	
1882-83	69,377	32,184	62,524	30,702	1,707	43	134	2,120	10,70,984	35,177	55,078	11,65,742	
1883-84	75,829	34,038	67,981	31,921	1,808	63	148	2,313	11,79,343	21,027	81,318	12,86,324	
1884-85	73,747	33,149	66,281	31,489	1,829	59	131	2,355	13,02,772	23,951	1,13,731	14,48,963	
1885-86	69,384	36,654	62,424	34,988	1,936	56	126	2,446	15,54,340	24,333	69,264	16,48,062	
1886-87	75,599	35,762	66,968	34,074	2,101	54	146	2,659	13,33,111	16,201	77,743	14,28,892	
1887-88	79,900	39,545	71,395	37,484	2,359	47	175	2,909	15,20,027	37,541	89,141	16,51,132	
1888-89	79,754	42,918	77,155	39,352	2,248	30	150	2,801	15,12,531	10,796	76,144	16,07,239	
1889-90	79,489	40,931	77,384	37,957	2,200	43	179	2,759	17,08,784	14,347	1,11,372	18,74,962	
1890-91	78,631	37,003	76,875	34,988	2,221	39	125	2,688	13,60,566	15,788	72,932	14,55,247	
1891-92	75,912	38,426	73,900	36,266	2,092	46	127	2,565	15,49,082	18,277	85,938	16,62,215	
1892-93	79,407	45,948	77,188	43,511	2,416	53	112	2,889	21,83,368	16,049	64,598	22,72,913	
1893-94	76,168	42,285	73,635	39,608	2,238	28	134	2,723	16,03,284	18,986	1,08,731	17,35,541	
1894-95	77,683	42,793	75,368	40,274	2,285	32	103	2,756	17,08,669	13,108	81,568	18,12,145	
1895-96	82,343	44,018	80,497	41,668	2,324	23	81	2,765	16,96,334	13,886	99,437	18,18,890	
1896-97	1,02,036	25,539	98,644	49,837	2,785	47	180	3,370	23,71,544	23,792	1,52,373	25,58,375	
1897-98	99,165	48,734	95,691	45,907	2,763	34	116	3,241	22,65,460	24,832	88,520	23,94,772	
1898-99	91,607	52,668	88,931	48,777	2,959	33	116	3,389	23,70,344	15,522	83,137	24,80,454	

NOTE.—These figures have been taken from Appendix A of Annual Stamp Reports and from Statements Nos. II and VII of Registration Reports. Figures before 1882-83 have been copied from the old Gazetteer.

Table No. XXXIII A,—Showing REGISTRATION.

1	2	3	4	5	6	7	8	9
	Number of Deeds registered by							
Year.	Registrar, Multan.	Sub-Registrar, Multan.	Sub-Registrar, Multan Cantonment.	Sub-Registrar, Shujabad.	Sub-Registrar, Lodhrán.	Sub-Registrar, Mailsi.	Sub-Registrar, Kabirwála.	Total.
1880-81 ... Compulsory	48	959	23	282	108	190	61	1,671
Optional	1	87	3	21	19	25	21	177
Total	49	1,046	26	303	127	215	82	1,848
1881-82 ... Compulsory	26	771	54	259	131	135	79	1,455
Optional	1	89	11	19	19	11	16	166
Total	27	860	65	278	150	146	95	1,621
1882-83 ... Compulsory	28	839	43	267	181	151	46	1,555
Optional	3	96	10	8	10	17	8	152
Total	31	935	53	275	191	168	54	1,707
1883-84 ... Compulsory	57	911	47	266	138	194	59	1,672
Optional	2	95	13	6	3	12	13	144
Total	59	1,006	60	272	141	206	72	1,816
1884-85 ... Compulsory	46	613	37	257	143	186	46	1,327
Optional	...	105	7	10	8	11	17	158
Total	46	718	44	267	151	197	63	1,485
1885-86 ... Compulsory	59	662	28	342	161	119	35	1,406
Optional	...	119	17	13	24	9	14	196
Total	59	781	45	355	185	128	49	1,602
1886-87 ... Compulsory	16	972	44	378	170	119	69	1,768
Optional	...	193	6	25	12	8	2	246
Total	16	1,165	50	403	182	127	71	2,014

Table No. XXXIII A,—Showing REGISTRATION—*contd.*

1	2	3	4	5	6	7	8	9
	Number of Deeds registered by							
Year.	Registrar, Multan.	Sub-Registrar, Multan.	Sub-Registrar, Multan Cantonment.	Sub-Registrar, Shujabad.	Sub-Registrar, Lodhrán.	Sub-Registrar, Mailsi.	Sub-Registrar, Kabírwála.	Total.
1887-88 ... Compulsory	3	1,244	31	382	178	153	79	2,070
Optional	...	206	13	26	20	7	10	282
Total	3	1,450	44	408	198	160	89	2,352
1888-89 ... Compulsory	...	1,116	34	398	190	177	83	1,998
Optional	...	184	10	21	16	12	7	250
Total	...	1,300	44	419	206	189	90	2,248
1889-90 ... Compulsory	11	1,168	46	368	178	148	55	1,974
Optional	...	167	10	23	12	10	3	225
Total	11	1,335	56	391	190	158	58	2,199
1890-91 ... Compulsory	14	1,206	31	307	203	132	71	1,964
Optional	...	184	11	24	17	15	3	254
Total	14	1,390	42	331	220	147	74	2,218
1891-92 ... Compulsory	32	1,196	44	295	183	110	53	1,913
Optional	...	144	5	12	10	4	3	178
Total	32	1,340	49	307	193	114	56	2,091
1892-93 ... Compulsory	44	1,321	46	294	226	150	95	2,176
Optional	...	151	7	14	18	4	8	202
Total	44	1,472	53	308	244	154	103	2,378
1893-94 ... Compulsory	33	1,296	37	208	218	133	78	2,003
Optional	...	182	5	5	23	5	12	232
Total	33	1,478	42	213	241	138	90	2,235

Table No. XXXIII A,—Showing REGISTRATION—*concld.*

1		2	3	4	5	6	7	8	9
		Number of Deeds registered by							
Year.		Registrar, Multan.	Sub-Registrar, Multan.	Sub-Registrar, Multán Cantonment.	Sub-Registrar, Shujábad.	Sub-Registrar, Lodhrán.	Sub-Registrar, Mailsi.	Sub-Registrar, Kabírwála.	Total.
1894-95 ...	Compulsory	56	1,317	71	260	206	123	79	2,082
	Optional	...	165	7	12	12	5	5	206
	Total	56	1,482	78	272	218	128	84	2,288
1895-96 ...	Compulsory	58	1,235	55	243	257	120	91	2,059
	Optional	...	141	3	6	25	11	7	193
	Total	58	1,376	58	249	282	131	98	2,252
1896-97 ...	Compulsory	62	1,526	48	250	314	173	161	2,534
	Optional	...	191	6	9	26	10	6	248
	Total	62	1,717	54	259	340	183	167	2,782
1897-98 ...	Compulsory	51	1,662	56	275	285	98	133	2,560
	Optional	1	151	6	8	21	10	6	203
	Total	52	1,813	62	283	306	108	139	2,763
1898-99 ...	Compulsory	27	1,782	35	350	228	126	221	2,769
	Optional	1	145	10	11	19	2	2	190
	Total	28	1,927	45	361	247	128	223	2,959
1899-1900	Compulsory	24	1,704	45	342	232	116	231	2,694
	Optional	...	119	13	13	34	2	13	194
	Total	24	1,823	58	355	266	118	244	2,888

Note.—These figures have been supplied by the Registration Office.

Table No. XXXIV,—Showing INCOME TAX COLLECTIONS.

1	2	3	4	5
Year.	Number of assessees.	Amount of tax.	Total collections.	Remarks.
1886-87	1,384	26,749	26,799	
1887-88	1,387	26,872	26,894	
1888-89	1,566	29,613	29,613	
1889-90	1,829	36,018	36,018	
1890-91	1,976	38,175	38,175	
1891-92	1,984	38,968	38,942	
1892-93	1,937	38,827	38,757	
1893-94	1,991	40,447	40,565	
1894-95	1,979	40,975	40,965	
1895-96	2,206	45,269	45,229	
1896-97	2,170	48,412	48,432	
1897-98	2,142	48,544	48,642	
1898-99	2,258	50,911	50,911	
Tahsil details for 1898-99 :—				
Multan	733	20,451	20,451	
Multan Cantonments	153	3,262	3,262	
Shujabad	380	8,846	8,846	
Lodhrán	359	6,561	6,561	
Mailsi	335	6,637	6,637	
Kabírwála	298	5,154	5,154	

Note.—The figures have been taken from the Income Tax Reports.

Table No. XXXV,—Showing EXCISE STATISTICS.

1	2	3	4	5	6	7	8	9	10	11	12	13	14	15
	Fermented Liquors.					Intoxicating Drugs.						Excise Revenue from		
		Number of retail shops.		Consumption in gallons.		Number of retail licenses.		Consumption in maunds.						
Year.	Number of central distilleries.	Country spirits.	European liquors.	Rum.	Country spirits.	Opium.	Other drugs.	Opium.	Charas.	Bhang.	Other drugs.	Fermented liquors.	Drugs.	Total.
1877-78	2	36	9	1,270	5,680	111	111	33	24	465	...	29,430	25,035	54,465
1878-79	2	36	11	1,260	5,202	111	111	27	13	278	59	26,822	23,395	50,217
1879-80	2	35	11	1,211	6,245	106	106	26	13	277	...	28,671	20,826	49,497
1880-81	2	37	14	1,147	6,442	107	107	28	15	348	...	32,341	21,242	53,783
1881-82	2	37	14	1,151	6,123	107	107	31	15	459	...	30,350	20,341	50,691
1882-83	2	38	15	1,264	6,285	108	108	29	12	434	...	33,557	22,521	56,078
1883-84	2	39	19	928	6,518	111	108	27	14	463	...	35,000	25,539	60,539
1884-85	2	39	20	527	6,327	108	108	26	12	405	...	32,258	23,823	56,081
1885-86	2	39	18	853	5,942	108	108	25	12	367	...	30,301	29,399	59,700
1886-87	2	39	20	975	6,552	108	108	23	16	342	...	32,611	24,021	56,632
1887-88	2	39	20	885	6,866	108	108	24	17	582	...	35,037	24,723	59,760
1888-89	1	40	21	909	7,475	108	108	23	17	548	...	41,059	23,843	64,902
1889-90	1	47	20	956	8,358	108	108	26	16	536	...	46,959	23,333	70,292
1890-91	1	49	19	1,007	7,898	108	108	19	13	410	...	47,128	29,872	77,000
1891-92	1	60	17	1,126	8,357	76	76	22	12	462	...	47,447	24,668	72,115
1892-93	1	52	17	1,290	9,027	76	76	19	12	427	...	50,896	25,495	76,391
1893-94	1	51	17	1,379	9,733	75	75	22	15	335	...	54,221	25,572	79,793
1894-95	1	53	17	1,214	11,442	75	75	26	17	390	...	59,729	26,374	86,103
1895-96	1	53	17	1,372	12,102	75	75	23	20	443	...	61,632	26,781	88,413
1896-97	1	53	12	998	10,751	70	71	43	48	596	...	58,314	25,245	83,559
1897-98	1	53	12	1,266	9,671	72	69	29	19	483	...	60,488	26,324	86,812
1898-99	1	53	6	1,070	9,332	72	69	30	22	503	...	59,181	27,663	86,844
	Licensed distillery.													
1899-1900	1	53	7	1,313	8,657	72	69	30	26	555	...	58,810	30,637	88,947

Note.—These figures are taken from the Annual Excise Reports. The figures up to 1881-82 have been copied from the old Gazetteer.

Table No. XXXVI,—Showing DISTRICT FUNDS.

1	2	3	4	5	6	7	8	9	10	11	12
	ANNUAL INCOME IN RUPEES.			ANNUAL EXPENDITURE IN RUPEES.							
YEAR.	Provincial rates.	Miscellaneous.	Total income.	General administration.	Police.	Education.	Medical.	Other minor departments.	Other miscellaneous.	Public Works.	Total expenditure.
1882-83	63,787	4,086	68,473	...	...	15,352	7,157	3,429	18,797	23,284	68,019
1883-84	Not available.										
1884-85	65,631	3,320	68,951	6,422	...	17,579	7,309	6,600	7,310	29,053	59,053
1885-86	Not available.										
1886-87	63,130	8,093	71,223	3,060	821	19,205	8,300	4,342	13,636	10,895	65,909
1887-88	73,912	7,724	81,636	2,612	822	17,672	8,185	5,211	6,791	2,918	72,549
1888-89	76,217	6,238	82,455	2,040	1,082	20,153	9,884	4,061	17,495	32,744	87,459
1889-90	81,764	7,595	89,359	1,938	2,085	17,102	10,986	3,976	16,547	38,647	91,281
1890-91	80,104	7,237	87,341	2,637	1,194	17,794	9,448	3,536	16,934	30,313	81,856
1891-92	88,323	9,129	97,452	2,802	1,433	17,854	13,030	4,559	22,218	43,002	1,04,898
1892-93	86,313	20,108	1,06,421	2,672	1,479	18,814	12,026	6,958	34,234	36,501	1,12,684
1893-94	95,464	11,484	1,06,948	3,622	1,499	18,829	14,069	5,166	25,836	30,729	99,750
1894-95	95,087	13,827	1,08,914	4,393	1,417	18,892	13,982	5,241	30,480	40,043	1,14,448
1895-96	1,00,775	11,009	1,11,784	4,342	1,335	18,919	13,596	7,040	27,949	31,702	1,04,883
1896-97	96,039	31,216	1,27,255	3,664	1,538	19,714	12,481	6,426	36,525	44,868	1,25,216
1897-98	98,720	22,001	1,20,721	3,631	1,447	19,721	12,946	6,790	43,088	44,851	1,32,474
1898-99	94,450	24,438	1,18,888	3,212	1,508	19,258	13,454	5,300	39,997	41,811	1,24,540

NOTE.—These figures are taken from Appendices A and B to the Annual Review of the District Fund Accounts.

Table No. XXXVII,—Showing GOVERNMENT, AIDED and UNAIDED SCHOOLS, including DIS[illegible]RICT and MUNICIPAL BOARD SCHOOLS.

1		2	3	4	5	6	7	8	9	10	11	12	13	14	15	16	17	18	19	20	21	22	23	24	25	26	27	28	29	30	31	32	33
		HIGH SCHOOLS.										MIDDLE SCHOOLS.								PRIMARY SCHOOLS.													
		ENGLISH.						VERNACULAR.				ENGLISH.						VERNACULAR.		ENGLISH.								VERNACULAR.					
		D. B. or M. B.		Aided.		Unaided.		D. B. or M. B.				D. B. or M. B.		Aided.		Unaided.		D. B. or M. B.		Government.		D. B. or M. B.		Aided.		Unaided.		D. B. or M. B.		Aided.		Unaided.	
		Schools.	Scholars.	Schools.	Scholars.	Schools.	Scholars.	Schools.	Scholars.	Schools.	Scholars.	Schools.	Scholars.	Schools.	Scholars.	Schools.	Scholars.	Schools.	Scholars.	Schools.	Scholars.	Schools.	Scholars.	Schools.	Scholars.	Schools.	Scholars.	Schools.	Scholars.	Schools.	Scholars.	Schools.	Scholars.
Boys	1896-97	1	655	2	445	1	161	...	...	...	...	1	256	...	...	2	245	4	539	1	76	...	...	...	...	...	...	67	2,503	13	349	205	2,355
	1897-98	1	668	2	436	1	209	...	...	...	...	1	260	...	...	1	103	4	537	1	80	...	...	...	...	...	...	68	2,481	12	341	191	3,235
	1898-99	1	670	2	437	1	163	...	...	...	...	1	259	...	...	1	110	4	522	1	71	...	...	...	...	...	...	68	2,470	12	343	188	3,243
	1899-1900	1	671	2	435	1	153	...	...	...	...	1	255	...	...	1	119	4	495	1	77	...	...	...	...	...	...	68	2,630	11	320	157	2,763
	1900-01	1	703	2	421	1	248	...	...	...	...	1	266	...	...	1	101	4	558	1	49	...	...	...	...	1	8	67	2,448	10	286	166	2,629
Girls	1896-97	...	...	...	...	...	...	...	...	...	...	...	...	...	...	...	...	...	...	...	...	...	...	...	...	...	...	1	106	...	...	...	...
	1897-98	...	...	...	...	...	...	...	...	...	...	...	...	...	...	...	...	...	...	...	...	...	...	...	...	...	...	1	132	...	...	...	...
	1898-99	...	...	...	...	...	...	...	...	...	...	...	...	...	...	...	...	...	...	...	...	...	...	...	...	...	...	1	103	...	...	...	...
	1899-1900	...	...	...	...	...	...	...	...	...	...	...	...	...	...	...	...	...	...	...	...	...	...	...	...	...	...	1	139	...	...	...	...
	1900-01	...	...	...	...	...	...	...	...	...	...	...	...	...	...	...	...	...	...	...	...	...	...	...	...	...	...	1	141	...	...	...	...

NOTE—(1) There is no Government School in the District, except one Government Primary School known as the Model School.
(2) D. B., District Boards; M. B., Municipal Boards
These figures have been supplied by the District Inspector.

Table No. XXXVIII,—Showing the working of DISPENSARIES.

1	2	3	4	5	6	7
	NUMBER OF PATIENTS TREATED.					
YEAR.	Men.	Women.	Children.	Total.	Indoor patients.	Expenditure in Rupees.
For whole district :—						
1877	16,301	4,670	3,736	24,707	1,235	9,858
1878	17,709	5,644	4,770	28,123	1,215	8,926
1879	15,527	4,550	3,729	23,806	1,098	10,814
1880	16,248	6,492	4,748	27,488	1,215	9,555
1881	23,557	8,447	6,290	38,294	1,639	10,125
1882	28,679	10,654	8,785	48,118	1,760	12,571
1883	24,786	8,661	6,486	39,933	1,926	15,250
1884	Not available.					
1885	27,708	9,152	8,251	45,104	1,629	14,696
1886	25,805	7,903	7,047	40,755	1,502	11,863
1887	29,119	9,153	8,829	47,101	1,620	12,936
1888	35,871	10,316	11,059	57,246	1,760	16,400
1889	Not available.					
1890	40,875	10,997	12,826	64,698	1,915	15,780
1891	49,439	14,951	14,434	78,824	2,236	21,539
1892	65,888	22,641	24,836	113,365	2,301	24,350
1893	65,522	24,976	25,866	116,364	2,412	21,548
1894	68,515	25,863	28,851	123,229	2,726	22,676
1895	65,511	21,848	25,111	112,470	2,550	20,200
1896	71,319	20,432	26,257	118,008	2,571	18,237
1897	75,405	25,467	34,156	135,028	2,581	20,281
1898	64,679	21,897	25,789	112,365	2,461	21,612
1899	68,673	25,579	27,614	121,866	2,385	32,599
Detail by dispensaries for 1899 :—						
Name of dispensary—						
Civil Hospital class I...	6,261	1,164	2,315	9,740	585	14,404
V. J. Hospital „ II...	...	3,065	1,492	4,557	185	3,527
City Branch { Male, Class II,	13,535	3,505	5,368	22,403	*Nil.*	2,238
City Branch { Female „	*Nil.*	3,278	1,879	5,157	*Nil.*	1,456
Shujabad class II ...	9,689	4,077	4,926	18,642	411	1,947
Jalálpur „ ...	6,550	1,952	1,963	10,465	278	1,278
Lodhrán „ ...	4,692	1,152	1,255	7,099	110	1,458
Kahror „ ...	5,560	1,342	1,572	8,474	155	1,458
Mailsi „ ...	6,695	1,960	3,035	11,690	198	1,541
Tulamba „ ...	3,248	647	515	4,410	*Nil.*	474
Kabírwála „ ...	5,793	1,104	1,836	8,733	61	1,118
Sarai Sidhu „ ...	5,725	2,142	1,353	9,220	386	1,242
Luddan „ ...	975	191	110	1,276	16	553

Table No. XXXIX,—Showing CIVIL AND REVENUE LITIGATION.

1	2	3	4	5	6	7	8	9
	NUMBER OF CIVIL SUITS CONCERNING.				VALUE IN RUPEES OF SUITS CONCERNING.			
YEAR.	Money or moveable property.	Rent and tenancy rights.	Land and revenue and other matters.	Total.	Land.	Other matters.	Total.	Number of revenue cases.
1878 ..	4,965	120	1,243	6,337	17,234	2,44,280	2,61,514	5,204
1879 ...	5,414	274	1,112	6,800	32,209	3,11,806	3,44,015	5,294
1880 ...	5,755	172	797	2,724	38,588	3,34,236	3,72,774	8,108
1881 ...	5,155	126	603	5,884	55,234	4,66,350	5,21,584	8,074
1882 ...	5,168	52	1,049	6,269	72,296	3,97,863	4,70,159	8,697
1883 ...	Not available.							
1884 ...	7,604	159	669	8,432	51,082	4,02,322	4,53,404	16,347
1885 ...	8,834	119	204	9,157	16,231	4,45,099	4,61,330	3,008
1886 ...	8,039	109	336	8,484	40,039	4,72,992	8,73,031	2,964
1887 ...	9,035	83	299	9,417	1,52,511	5,62,917	7,15,428	6,875
1888 ...	8,204	96	281	8,581	81,646	6,20,569	7,02,215	7,829
1889 ...	7,675	73	299	8,047	3,75,757	4,92,289	8,67,986	7,826
1890 ...	6,795	89	382	7,266	1,90,850	5,98,496	7,89,346	7,456
1891 ...	6,402	104	367	6,873	2,48,879	4,58,898	7,06,777	7,597
1892 ...	6,495	88	318	6,901	8,40,155	4,58,389	12,98,544	7,591
1893 ...	6,821	82	295	7,198	1,35,271	10,20,843	11,56,114	8,765
1894 ...	6,255	86	321	6,662	2,18,167	4,89,836	7,08,003	8,330
1895 ...	6,450	92	437	6,979	1,96,502	5,59,387	7,55,889	7,933
1896 ...	6,834	102	456	7,392	1,77,908	5,34,231	7,12,139	9,410
1897 ...	7,644	84	486	8,214	2,60,621	6,89,844	9,50,465	6,222
1898 ...	7,622	113	381	8,116	2,23,725	6,05,982	8,29,707	15,099
1899 ...	7,243	83	388	7,714	1,53,734	5,39,264	6,92,998	15,741

NOTE.—Figures up to 1882 have been taken from the old Gazetteer, and those for subsequent years from Statements Nos. II and III of the District Civil Reports.

Table No. XL,—Showing CRIMINAL TRIALS.

	1	2	3	4	5	6	7	8	9	10	11	12
	Details.	1878	1879	1880	1881	1882	1883	1884	1885	1886	1887	1888
Persons tried.	Brought to trial	6,292	5,843	5,076	5,496	5,914	6,259	5,751	5,265	6,204	6,822	6,817
	Discharged	1,318	1,276	1,539	1,353	1,597	1,866	1,475	1,383	1,770	2,197	2,635
	Acquitted	904	957	774	1,083	752	890	867	721	1,000	1,068	1,240
	Convicted	4,031	3,504	2,752	2,948	3,483	6,166	5,117	5,228	6,142	6,774	4,761
	Committed or referred ...	31	22	13	49	66	58	111	46	52	74	45
Cases disposed of.	Summons cases (regular)	...	...	...	1,585	1,653	1,782	1,645	1,362	1,484	1,373	1,398
	,, (summary)	...	...	...	9	4	158	...	4	13	109	267
	Warrant cases (regular)	...	...	...	1,346	1,343	1,461	1,438	1,569	1,653	1,964	1,723
	,, (summary)	...	...	...	13	19	84	2	8	10	239	12
	Total cases disposed of ...	3,060	3,466	3,010	2,953	3,019	3,493	3,095	2,950	3,167	3,700	3,416
Number of persons sentenced to	Death	4	2	3	2	1	4	4	2	15	7	10
	Transportation for life ...	2	1	...	...	4	9	11	4	8	5	18
	,, for a term...	1	...	...	...	...	...	...	...	2	5	1
	Penal servitude	...	...	...	...	...	...	...	...	...	...	...
	Fine under Rs. 10 ...	2,907	2,496	1,964	1,951	1,802	2,076	2,035	2,274	503	1,897	1,845
	,, 10 to 50 Rupees...	575	314	248	430	522	584	486	285	58	574	299
	,, 50 to 100 ,, ...	35	28	14	13	35	33	21	12	...	14	17
	,, 100 to 500 ,, ...	3	...	4	3	7	17	13	3	...	5	1
	,, 500 to 1,000 ,, ...	...	1	...	...	...	2	...	...	...	...	...
	Over 1,000 Rupees ...	...	...	...	...	...	...	...	...	...	...	...
	Imprisonment under 6 months.	437	390	460	449	578	597	499	478	37	600	586
	Imprisonment 6 months to 2 years.	274	338	278	264	248	198	229	168	...	306	294
	Imprisonment over 2 years.	80	41	26	10	39	25	17	14	...	12	9
	Whipping	192	137	139	195	118	94	72	63	...	72	60
	Find sureties of the peace.	3	...	7	14	6	43	77	18	...	38	37
	Recognisance to keep the peace.	40	23	23	16	...	4	49	20	...	1	11
	Give sureties for good behaviour.	53	213	139	93	733	296	338	170	...	455	166

Table No. XL,—Showing CRIMINAL TRIALS—*concluded.*

1	13	14	15	16	17	18	19	20	21	22	23
Details.	1889	1890	1891	1892	1893	1894	1895	1896	1897	1898	1899
Persons tried.											
Brought to trial	6,278	6,750	8,163	7,558	8,369	8,973	8,751	8,960	8,954	9,022	9,911
Discharged	2,432	2,486	3,580	3,586	3,590	4,676	3,556	4,273	4,183	4,127	4,314
Acquitted	1,090	1,196	1,045	968	1,281	1,104	1,262	1,138	1,714	1,428	1,887
Convicted	6,221	6,661	8,040	7,440	8,137	8,854	8,561	8,758	8,771	8,628	9,702
Committed or referred ...	30	56	45	93	83	49	34	60	83	56	28
Cases disposed of.											
Summons cases (regular)	1,197	1,094	1,259	1,258	1,579	1,104	1,325	1,317	1,007	1,058	1,232
,, (summary)	268	375	681	319	211	536	258	656	692	732	799
Warrant cases (regular)	1,851	2,011	2,270	2,305	2,367	2,707	2,609	2,467	2,573	2,291	2,676
,, (summary)	2	...	1	7	5	2	12	1	15	11	50
Total cases disposed of ...	3,330	3,494	4,228	3,901	4,170	4,362	4,212	4,455	4,294	4,095	4,171
Number of persons sentenced to											
Death	11	9	10	4	11	5	14	14	11	17	7
Transportation for life ...	14	11	7	9	10	7	15	9	8	10	13
,, for a term ...	2	6	7	...	...	1	6	11	...	...	...
Penal servitude	...	...	...	...	...	...	...	...	...	...	...
Fine under Rs. 10 ...	1,705	1,942	2,511	1,868	1,838	1,689	1,776	2,162	1,748	2,020	2,114
,, 10 to 50 Rupees...	398	312	284	216	384	300	445	486	250	289	391
,, 50 to 100 ,, ...	12	18	16	12	28	39	29	25	5	13	16
,, 100 to 500 ,, ...	3	1	2	1	5	3	7	7	2	...	5
,, 500 to 1,000 ,, ...	1	...	...	...	...	1	...	...	1	1	6
Over 1,000 Rupees ...	...	...	...	...	...	...	...	...	1	...	...
Imprisonment under 6 months.	496	503	506	622	525	435	437	585	480	534	639
Imprisonment 6 months to 2 years.	272	251	325	230	355	178	313	378	294	234	294
Imprisonment over 2 years.	12	10	21	28	16	17	35	20	20	48	47
Whipping	55	79	74	111	109	81	128	142	141	149	142
Find sureties of the peace.	20	13	36	43	22	37	43	30	4	31	43
Recognisance to keep the peace.	...	8	3	2	25	3	3	...	16	...	...
Give sureties for good behaviour.	130	197	151	89	469	324	367	163	93	60	141

Table No. XLI.—Showing POLICE INQUIRIES.

1	2	3	4	5	6	7	8	9	10	11	12	13	14	15
NATURE OF OFFENCE.	Number of Cases inquired into.													
	1877.	1878.	1879.	1880.	1881.	1882.	1883.	1884.	1885.	1886.	1887.	1888.	1889.	1890.
Rioting or unlawful assembly	10	8	11	8	19	20	17	67	38	63	86	15	10	12
Murders and attempts to murder	15	10	7	5	5	11	8	14	6	12	21	14	12	12
Total serious offences against the person	30	24	31	20	26	104	131	176	133	142	137	84	68	102
Abduction of married women	...	...	...	...	...	12	15	22	18	29	23	6	4	11
Total serious offences against property	500	499	489	402	354	424	481	451	456	581	552	496	477	519
Total minor offences against the person	184	130	113	58	58	72	9	25	21	28	33	4	2	10
Cattle theft	272	309	334	272	263	270	171	230	233	345	392	261	280	237
Total minor offences against property	1,114	1,220	1,076	864	955	981	954	1,117	1,021	1,148	1,298	914	828	775
Total cognizable offences	1,921	1,959	1,787	1,407	1,467	1,611	1,612	1,857	1,685	1,978	2,135	1,561	1,416	1,442
Rioting, unlawful assembly, affray	...	1	8	4	1	1	1	3	4	3	...	...	...	1
Offences relating to marriage	13	9	4	2	14	6	7	7	8	8	6	8	8	...
Total non-cognizable offences	163	156	152	99	137	192	251	151	189	182	180	163	81	47
Grand Total of offences	2,804	2,115	1,939	1,506	604	1,803	1,863	2,008	1,874	2,160	2,315	1,724	1,497	1,489

Table No. XLI.—Showing POLICE INQUIRIES—*continued.*

	16	17	18	19	20	21	22	23	24	25	26	27	28	29
NATURE OF OFFENCE.	*Number of Cases inquired into*—concld.										*Number of persons arrested or summoned.*			
	1891.	1892.	1893.	1894.	1895.	1896.	1897.	1898.	1899.		1877.	1878.	1879.	1880.
Rioting or unlawful assembly	30	19	14	11	17	37	23	44	34		81	57	53	100
Murders and attempts to murder	17	12	9	14	13	20	17	17	21		18	17	10	6
Total serious offences against the person	102	111	84	77	90	106	129	164	188		93	80	75	124
Abduction of married women	12	10	8	2	7	8	17	20	35		...	...	...	...
Total serious offences against the property	536	628	450	395	486	784	695	688	830		189	202	239	259
Total minor offences against the person	4	10	8	2	8	5	11	5	19		253	192	156	99
Cattle theft	295	300	239	212	279	443	349	360	356		156	240	289	239
Total minor offences against property	936	920	796	626	724	1,119	960	1,070	1,090		675	1,025	1,050	842
Total cognizable offences	1,621	1,705	1,373	1,125	1,340	2,059	1,831	1,986	2,184		1,352	1,711	1,647	1,425
Rioting, unlawful assembly, affray	1	2	...	...	2	1	2	1	1		...	3	43	10
Offences relating to marriage	210	262	229	297	270	245	472	346	325		14	4	2	4
Total non-cognizable offences	1,607	1,611	1,644	1,696	1,940	1,968	1,431	3,144	2,460		305	238	203	138
Grand Total of offences	3,228	3,316	3,017	2,821	3,280	4,027	3,262	5,130	4,644		1,657	1,949	1,850	1,563

Table No. XLI,—Showing POLICE INQUIRIES—*continued.*

Nature of Offence.	30	31	32	33	34	35	36	37	38	39	40	41	42	43
	Number of persons arrested or summoned—contd.													
	1881.	1882.	1883.	1884.	1885.	1886.	1887.	1888.	1889.	1890.	1891.	1892.	1893.	1894.
Rioting or unlawful assembly	248	85	127	173	75	185	170	230	230	295	603	851	732	882
Murders and attempts to murder	5	11	19	15	5	14	25	25	18	16	31	20	20	16
Total serious offences against the person	267	114	145	150	121	124	140	181	131	136	219	285	218	220
Abduction of married women	...	16	11	...	12	16	19	18	17	14	37	47	47	15
Total serious offences against property	294	225	281	225	204	274	312	308	281	277	406	415	347	325
Total minor offences against the person	85	133	20	14	27	18	34	17	31	32	39	38	31	110
Cattle theft	209	170	137	154	174	252	289	280	277	207	232	307	240	195
Total minor offences against property	907	796	775	769	670	849	1,007	897	766	766	1,012	1,156	1,192	1,113
Total cognizable offences	1,659	1,359	1,374	1,361	1,110	1,478	1,688	1,649	1,469	1,570	2,302	2,767	2,554	2,686
Rioting, unlawful assembly, affray	13	9	8	5	...	16	9	...	5	451	3	4	...	...
Offences relating to marriage	15	...	5	4	...	1	6	445	376	420	186	698	724	923
Total non-cognizable offences	239	221	343	355	244	210	168	2,862	2,338	4,747	4,185	3,836	4,320	4,326
Grand Total of offences	1,898	1,580	1,717	1,716	1,354	1,688	1,856	4,511	3,807	6,317	6,487	6,603	6,874	7,012

Table No. XLI,—Showing POLICE INQUIRIES—*continued*.

Nature of Offence.	44	45	46	47	48	49	50	51	52	53	54	55	56	57
	Number of persons arrested or summoned—concld.						*Number of persons convicted.*							
	1895.	1896.	1897.	1898.	1899.		1877.	1878.	1879.	1880.	1881.	1882.	1883.	1884.
Rioting or unlawful assembly	786	816	167	330	206		62	32	35	87	93	44	75	121
Murders and attempts to murder	30	29	15	21	25		2	10	5	3	3	6	3	8
Total serious offences against the person	309	299	177	166	247		69	51	52	100	101	75	81	78
Abduction of married women	59	65	20	37	49		...	...	...	...	...	10	8	12
Total serious offences against property	348	441	380	371	427		144	205	180	189	152	159	222	152
Total minor offences against the person	102	36	45	14	33		198	146	105	63	67	117	12	6
Cattle theft	297	396	326	305	361		90	161	205	172	152	141	95	103
Total minor offences against property	1,101	1,254	904	901	1,058		470	774	752	615	659	630	587	525
Total cognizable offences	2,679	2,865	1,687	1,794	1,993		969	1,234	1,156	1,033	1,059	1,031	995	901
Rioting, unlawful assembly, affray	5	2	2	1	1		...	3	37	8	7	7	7	...
Offences relating to marriage	804	617	532	497	450		9	1	...	2	9	...	1	2
Total non-cognizable offences	5,122	4,530	5,458	3,987	3,790		208	199	146	104	178	158	249	251
Grand Total of offences	7,801	7,395	7,145	5,781	5,783		1,177	1,433	1,302	1,137	1,237	1,189	1,244	1,152

Table No. XLI,—Showing POLICE INQUIRIES—*concluded.*

	58	59	60	61	62	63	64	65	66	67	68	69	70	71	72	73
NATURE OF OFFENCE.	*Number of persons convicted*—concld.															
	1885.	1886.	1887.	1888.	1889.	1890.	1891.	1892.	1893.	1894.	1895.	1896.	1897.	1898.	1899.	
Rioting or unlawful assembly	47	78	64	51	114	36	115	52	28	48	59	96	80	158	72	
Murders and attempts to murder	1	5	3	7	10	8	6	6	6	5	3	6	3	6	5	
Total serious offences against the person ...	57	67	61	69	51	62	58	78	69	43	80	64	64	60	80	
Abduction of married women	4	5	51	6	2	2	4	4	3	1	1	4	11	15	10	
Total serious offences against property ...	118	175	212	190	179	198	190	183	179	154	150	173	232	207	233	
Total minor offences against the person ...	15	6	13	2	..	5	...	8	10	1	1	5	10	3	9	
Cattle theft	104	165	182	208	180	145	133	165	117	87	145	168	180	158	190	
Total minor offences against property ...	453	543	636	578	473	461	502	536	469	337	380	491	516	488	582	
Total cognizable offences	698	883	1,002	903	835	741	876	868	773	597	683	830	913	925	993	
Rioting unlawful assembly, affray	...	16	9	...	5	...	3	...	...	...	5	2	2	1	1	
Offences relating to marriage	...	...	...	17	205	...	9	27	20	15	20	29	22	25	26	
Total non-cognizable offences	172	161	118	778	1,157	...	722	511	646	390	469	568	648	473	478	
Grand Total of offences	870	1,044	1,120	1,681	1,992	741	1,598	1,379	1,419	987	1,152	1,404	1,561	1,398	1,471	

NOTE.—The figures up to 1882 are copied from the old Gazetteer; and those for subsequent years from District Police Statement A.

Table No. XLII, showing CONVICTS in the District Jail.

1	2	3	4	5	6	7	8	9	10	11	12	13	14	15	16	17	18	19	20	21	22	23	24	25	26
	Number in Jail at beginning of the year.		Number imprisoned during the year.		Religion of Convicts.			Previous occupation of male Convicts.						Length of sentence of Convicts.							Previously convicted.			Pecuniary results.	
Year.	Males.	Females.	Males.	Females.	Musalman.	Hindu.	Buddhist and Jain.	Official.	Professional.	Service.	Agricultural.	Commercial.	Industrial.	Under 6 months.	6 months to 1 year.	1 year to 2 years.	2 years to 5 years.	5 years to 10 years.	Over 10 years and transportation.	Death.	Once.	Twice.	More than twice.	Cost of maintenance.	Profits of Convict labour.
1877-78	608	14	820	39	1,116	211	...	37	...	43	728	...	...	756	314	289	64	39	18	1	63	23	10	29,722	4,183
1878-79	564	18	873	48	1,184	236	...	31	...	148	627	...	...	751	402	318	93	27	9	3	94	23	21	30,529	5,545
1879-80	794	22	1,020	30	623	50	...	31	7	...	430	7	...	187	253	165	82	23	4	...	87	23	12	44,762	6,550
1880-81	691	23	886	41	557	70	...	11	9	124	345	22	...	92	119	230	181	53	3	...	87	23	12	33,402	2,366
1881-82	657	21	928	31	542	90	...	15	5	12	410	81	...	53	150	169	224	60	8	1	64	16	10	34,688	8,252
1882-83	644	21	1,030	37	787	67	...	22	6	20	597	2	...	222	202	224	181	55	6	...	44	18	9	32,545	2,620
1883-84	871	19	1,248	55	798	141	...	33	20	61	325	3	...	589	100	116	45	11	1	1	111	31	21	34,598	4,360
1884-85	564	19	753	47	602	123	...	44	...	25	289	3	25	512	92	120	51	18	7	...	106	21	15	24,539	2,797
1885-86	468	18	638	22	518	112	...	27	2	13	291	23	15	353	154	95	52	5	1	...	75	22	17	23,919	5,052
1886-87	407	4	836	22	720	101	...	37	...	20	412	12	77	548	183	76	39	4	2	6	77	17	10	24,769	3,396
1887-88	523	5	974	36	867	115	...	24	3	21	489	23	115	637	186	128	45	9	3	2	104	39	11	30,163	4,094
1888-89	702	9	863	19	799	83	...	18	6	27	401	24	83	549	141	136	42	6	7	1	107	28	13	34,891	5,060
1889-90	717	10	939	20	868	88	...	27	2	19	469	1	75	588	140	158	48	10	10	5	96	25	21	33,519	3,675
1890-91	718	8	1,260	19	1,140	159	...	34	2	14	757	1	80	727	263	186	79	11	8	5	102	34	18	32,835	2,712
1891-92	704	12	1,362	20	1,246	126	...	13	...	28	1,035	18	13	762	277	237	82	9	9	6	139	44	27	36,826	8,919
1892-93	561	16	1,536	30	1,325	241	...	33	1	126	1,171	118	23	923	381	127	79	14	8	2	226	60	30	35,061	4,303
1893-94	730	13	1,798	29	1,602	225	...	31	...	445	1,080	98	30	866	604	247	82	15	8	5	424	155	106	37,428	7,822
1894-95	661	11	1,040	12	940	110	...	587	283	113	45	16	...	587	283	113	45	16	6	2	245	50	40	27,125	6,516
1895-96	491	2	1,287	26	1,181	131	...	36	5	138	773	56	70	688	265	227	99	14	13	7	209	46	44	26,664	6,325
1896-97	467	5	1,514	36	1,377	170	...	34	18	32	849	48	69	875	329	253	71	10	7	5	234	57	32	34,155	1,791
1897-98	556	11	1,615	36	1,458	191	...	23	29	42	858	55	83	928	372	241	93	10	4	3	146	51	69	49,052	4,490
1898-99	589	...	1,387	...	1,745	139	...	17	12	55	1,140	70	74	1,103	428	250	69	19	7	11	161	63	38	36,276	4,467

NOTE.—The figures up to 1881-82 have been taken from the old Gazetteer; those for subsequent years from the Administration Report, Statements Nos. 28, 29, 30—33, 34.

Table No. XLII A,—Showing CONVICTS in Central Jail.

1	2	3	4	5	6
Year.	Number in Jail at beginning of the year.		Pecuniary Results.		Remarks.
	Males.	Females.	Cost of maintenance.	Profits of convict labour.	
1877-78	...	...	...	...	
1878-79	...	...	...	...	
1879-80	...	...	...	...	
1880-81	...	...	...	...	
1881-82	...	...	...	...	
1882-83	...	...	...	...	
1883-84	582	...	67,247	7,769	
1884-85	648	...	51,140	3,291	
1885-86	...	...	...	...	The Jail was closed during these years.
1886-87	...	...	...	...	
1887-88	...	...	...	...	
1888-89	...	...	...	...	
1889-90	549	...	55,848	3,286	
1890-91	837	...	54,875	444	
1891-92	896	...	55,117	4,674	
1892-93	983	...	58,905	2,040	
1893-94	862	...	53,962	51	
1894-95	876	...	45,323	1,916	
1895-96	578	...	51,540	7,698	
1896-97	744	...	56,580	10,057	
1897-98	969	...	68,716	809	
1898-99	970	...	65,947	5,273	

Note.—These figures have been supplied by the Superintendent, Central Jail.

Table No. XLIII,—Showing the POPULATION of Towns.

1	2	3	4	5	6	7	8	9	10	11
Tahsil.	Town.	Census.	Total population.	Hindús.	Sikhs.	Jains.	Musalmáns.	Other religions.	Number of occupied houses.	Persons per 100 occupied houses.
Multan	Multan City	1881	57,471	29,962	661	46	36,294	1,711	12,617	514
		1891	64,265	27,486	462	17	36,087	213	...	...
		1901	74,627	31,272	796	97	42,202	260	15,913	469
	Multan Cantonment.	1881	11,203	...	...	...	...	...	...	...
		1891	10,297	4,644	499	7	3,678	1,469	...	...
		1901	12,767	5,675	792	37	4,697	1,566	4,173	306
	Total	1881	68,674	29,962	661	46	36,294	1,711	12,617	544
		1891	74,562	32,130	961	24	39,765	1,682	...	...
		1901	87,394	36,947	1,588	134	46,899	1,826	20,086	435
Shujabad.	Shujabad	1881	6,458	3,970	9	1	2,476	2	1,477	437
		1891	6,329	3,937	12	...	2,880	...	...	...
		1901	5,880	3,810	74	...	1,995	1	1,312	448
	Jalálpur	1881	3,875	1,613	5	...	2,257	...	622	623
		1891	3,884	1,699	...	...	2,185	...	...	...
		1901	5,149	2,021	23	...	3,105	...	783	658
Lodhrán	Dunyapur	1881	2,041	1,396	...	...	645	...	302	676
		1891	2,101	1,454	...	...	647	...	...	...
		1901	2,150	1,406	8	...	736	...	324	664
	Kahror	1881	4,804	2,967	5	...	1,832	...	848	567
		1891	5,498	3,440	2	...	2,056	...	...	...
		1901	5,552	3,606	22	...	1,924	...	939	591
Kabírwála	Tulamba	1881	2,231	1,282	2	...	947	...	369	605
		1891	2,792	1,578	12	...	1,202	...	...	...
		1901	2,526	1,407	4	...	1,115	...	382	661

NOTE.—The figures for 1901 are taken from Table No. V of the Census Report of 1901.

Table No. XLIV,—Showing BIRTHS and DEATHS for Towns.

1	2	3	4	5	6	7	8	9	10	11	12	13
Town.	Sex.	Total population by the Census of 1891.	*Total Births registered during the year.*									
			1890.	1891.	1892.	1893.	1894.	1895.	1896.	1897.	1898.	1899.
Multan ...	Males...	34,595	1,344	1,401	1,426	1,246	1,603	1,534	1,598	1,591	1,376	1,605
	Females	29,670	1,280	1,363	1,283	1,170	1,477	1,516	1,466	1,533	1,321	1,509
Multan suburbs...	Males...	Not available	1,269	1,294	1,436	1,352	1,662	1,744	1,887	2,062	1,786	2,163
	Females		1,087	1,168	1,122	1,073	1,407	1,660	1,739	1,938	1,517	2,041
Kahror ..	Males...	2,861	120	102	67	90	116	86	114	91	71	170
	Females	2,637	81	76	60	69	77	64	84	59	43	103
Shujabad	Males ..	3,439	97	126	120	70	95	102	128	125	76	136
	Females	2,890	101	105	98	93	98	102	116	134	77	117
Jalálpur...	Males...	1,966	120	167	107	109	108	116	100	126	80	133
	Females	1,918	102	107	186	88	97	86	116	132	59	106
Tulamba...	Males ..	1,532	53	67	74	43	71	73	55	77	62	75
	Females	1,260	58	55	66	30	63	64	67	63	55	67
Dunyapur.	Males ...	901	...	...	...	...	43	48	56	41	44	74
	Females	1,200	...	...	...	...	36	37	41	55	37	152

1	2	14	15	16	17	18	19	20	21	22	23
Town.	Sex.	*Total Deaths registered during the year.*									
		1890.	1891.	1892.	1893.	1894.	1895.	1896.	1897.	1898.	1899.
Multan	Males ...	1,102	892	1,830	997	1,015	1,284	926	1,079	972	1,182
	Females	978	907	1,678	944	943	1,207	924	1,072	920	1,065
Multan suburbs ..	Males ...	1,157	1,001	1,948	1,142	1,082	1,408	1,051	1,282	1,354	1,252
	Females	1,007	822	1,483	934	901	1,266	854	1,269	1,104	1,210
Kabror	Males ...	80	141	180	88	80	62	60	67	65	90
	Females	76	131	177	103	72	55	55	59	44	90
Shujabad ...	Males ...	167	123	204	146	130	128	109	132	105	93
	Females	150	98	248	156	114	120	78	147	91	73
Jalálpur	Males ...	102	106	115	84	90	82	70	93	75	61
	Females	90	95	110	87	84	83	63	107	81	64
Tulamba	Males ...	51	141	191	67	66	47	42	36	28	45
	Females	53	131	177	56	13	45	55	51	20	41
Dunyapur ...	Males ...	...	...	...	...	37	47	33	51	41	30
	Females	...	...	...	...	19	47	24	54	31	32

Table No. XLV,—Showing MUNICIPAL INCOME.

1	2	3	4	5	6	7
Year.	Multan.	Shujabad.	Kahror.	Tulamba.	Jalálpur.	Dunyapur.
	Class I.	Class III.	Class III.	Class III.	Class III.	Class III.
1870-71 ...	44,507	4,941	2,875	...	...	...
1871-72 ...	71,213	7,077	3,150	...	...	...
1872-73 ..	67,165	6,547	2,853	...	...	...
1873-74 ...	67,195	6,088	2,633	...	...	...
1874-75 ...	87,831	5,937	2,563	1,309	2,131	750
1875-76 ...	82,409	6,567	2,852	1,071	2,813	689
1876-77 ...	76,965	6,791	3,286	1,599	2,887	853
1877-78 ..	81,709	7,039	2,840	1,118	2,850	761
1878-79 ...	76,888	6,635	2,974	1,553	3,056	696
1879-80 ...	82,485	6,330	3,456	1,392	3,479	886
1880-81 ...	88,435	6,652	3,328	957	3,255	695
1881-82 ...	86,585	7,299	3,582	1,221	3,025	896
1882-83 ...	1,10,038	6,785	3,148	1,052	2,405	843
1883-84 ...	1,02,142	7,243	3,519	1,147	2,693	923
1884-85 ...	1,03,686	6,625	3,305	1,491	2,751	752
1885-86 ...	1,07,510	7,124	3,232	1,547	3,361	703
1886-87 ...	1,23,063	8,641	4,724	1,633	3,222	1,424
1887-88 ...	1,20,343	7,852	4,716	3,840	1,523	1,310
1888-89 ...	1,21,786	8,697	3,932	2,297	4,401	1,225
1889-90 ...	1,21,900	9,359	3,858	1,925	4,584	1,377
1890-91 ...	1,27,763	9,890	3,733	1,347	4,698	1,117
1891-92 ...	1,62,143	10,336	4,184	2,235	5,807	...
1892-93 ...	1,36,406	10,552	3,771	1,697	5,116	...
1893-94 ...	1,59,102	9,945	4,270	2,415	4,566	...
1894-95 ...	1,78,520	10,031	4,003	1,942	4,317	...
1895-96 ...	1,76,557	10,199	4,196	2,245	4,630	...
1896-97 ...	1,63,807	9,694	4,251	1,857	4,953	...
1897-98 ...	1,62,275	10,629	3,718	2,389	5,464	...
1898-99 ...	1,73,659	9,886	3,920	2,358	4.923	...

Note.—These figures are taken from Statement No. XXXIX of the Administration Reports.

Table XLVI,—Showing WORK down by Government Post Offices.

Description of work.	1891-92.	1892-93.	1893-94.	1894-95.	1895-96.	1896-97.	1897-98.	1898-99.
1. Letter mail articles received for delivery ...	862,108	812,448	888,758	959,010	937,456	913,666	997,542	948,402
2. Registered articles received for delivery ...	42,900	37,180	40,868	47,606	48,126	55,666	58,526	58,058
3. Insured letters received for delivery	158	182	338	208	130	208	130	156
4. Parcels registered received for delivery	6,904	6,782	7,826	7,826	8,086	8,138	8,164	8,996
5. Parcels unregistered received for delivery ...	...	...	...	...	364	806	910	1,066
6. Insured parcels received for delivery	832	572	1,066	624	1,066	728	910	806
7. Value payable articles and other registered articles received for delivery ...	2,678	2,600	3,822	3,978	3,978	4,602	5,720	4,888
8. Money orders, numbers issued	(A) 27,294	(B) 26,800	...	(D) 7,850	48,088	(A) 59,578	62,143	64,563
9. Money orders, numbers paid	(A) 8,971	(B) 9,024	(C)	(D) 2,083	17,550	(A) 20,857	28,430	26,746
10. Savings Bank, number of accounts open on 31st March	1,801	2,078	2,201	2,444	2,573	2,841	2,950	3,030
11. Savings Bank, account of credit of depositors on 31st March	Rs. a. p. 3,64,159 5 5	Rs. a. p. 3,93,359 13 10	Rs. a. p. 4,43,872 12 7	Rs. a. p. 4,93,830 3 5	Rs. a. p 4,90,680 15 0	Rs. a. p. 58,869 1 10	Rs. a. p. 5,31,249 4 2	Rs. a. p. 5,47,747 4 1

(A) Represents figures for 11 months. (B) Represents figures for 9 months. (C) Information not available. (D) Represents figures for 2 months.

XLVII.—POLYMETRICAL TABLE of DISTANCES of the MULTAN DISTRICT.

* *viâ* Multan.

	Multan	Adi Bágh	Shujabad	Gawen	Jalálpur	Koreishiwála	Sher Shah *	Shini	Lár	Basti Malúk	Aliwála	Lodhrán	Matti Tal	Mahtamán	Narúl	Fázal Shah	Kádarpur Rán	Kabírwála	Makhdúmpur	Tulamba	Serai Sidhu	Khánewála	Channú	Pakhi Mián	Makhdúm Rashíd	Tibba	Mittru	Karampur	Luddan	Sahuka	Mailsi	Dunyapur	Kahror	Ranewáhan	Dhanot	Meeranpur	Adamwáhan	Garha Tahil Singh	Fattehpur
Multan ...																																							
Adi Bágh ...	14																																						
Shujabad ...	26	12																																					
Gawen ...	39	25	13																																				
Jalálpur ...	53	39	27	14																																			
Koreishiwála ...	67	53	41	28	14																																		
Sher Shah ...	14	25	37	50	64	78																																	
Shini ...	63	49	37	24	10	24	74																																
Lár ...	14	*28	27	40	54	48	25	72																															
Basti Malúk ...	26	27	15	28	50	35	37	60	12																														
Aliwála ...	38	39	27	40	38	23	49	48	24	12																													
Lodhrán ...	49	44	32	39	27	13	60	37	35	23	11																												
Matti Tal ...	15	29	41	54	68	82	26	78	29	41	53	64																											
Mahtamán ...	25	39	51	64	78	92	36	88	39	51	63	74	10																										
Narúl ...	29	43	55	68	82	96	40	92	43	55	67	78	14	4																									
Fázal Shah ...	35	49	61	74	88	102	46	98	49	61	73	84	20	10	6																								
Kádarpur Rán ...	15	29	41	54	68	82	26	78	29	41	53	64	3	13	17	23																							
Kabírwála ...	29	43	55	68	*82	88	40	92	*43	*55	67	75	17	14	10	16	14																						
Makhdúmpur ...	41	55	67	80	94	94	52	104	*55	67	79	81	29	26	22	24	26	12																					
Tulamba ...	53	67	79	92	106	106	64	126	*67	79	91	93	41	38	33	27	38	24	12																				
Serai Sidhu ...	44	58	70	83	97	103	55	107	*58	*70	*82	90	30	20	16	10	29	15	14	17																			
Khánewála ...	37	51	63	76	94	80	48	104	*51	63	75	67	25	22	18	34	22	8	14	26	24																		
Channú ...	62	76	88	101	113	99	73	251	*76	88	99	86	50	47	42	36	47	33	21	9	26	33																	
Pakhi Mián ...	63	77	75	88	94	80	92	104	*77	60	92	67	69	66	61	55	66	52	40	28	45	42	19																
Makhdúm Rashíd	14	*28	*40	53	*67	65	25	*77	*28	*40	*52	52	18	*28	*43	48	15	28	40	52	43	26	58	49															
Tibba ...	31	*45	*43	56	62	48	42	72	*45	28	40	35	*35	*45	*49	65	32	40	46	68	65	37	51	32	17														
Mittru ...	43	*57	55	68	74	60	54	84	*57	40	52	47	*58	*68	*48	64	44	38	44	56	54	30	49	30	29	12													
Karampur ...	61	*75	73	86	80	66	72	90	75	58	61	53	76	70	66	82	62	56	52	62	72	48	53	34	47	30	18												
Luddan ...	73	*87	85	98	92	78	84	102	87	70	73	65	77	82	78	77	84	68	62	50	67	60	41	22	59	42	30	12											
Sahuka ...	93	*107	105	118	112	98	104	122	*107	90	93	85	97	102	98	97	104	88	82	70	87	80	61	42	79	62	50	32	20										
Mailsi ...	53	*67	65	78	63	52	64	76	*67	50	47	39	57	66	62	78	54	52	58	70	68	44	63	44	39	22	14	14	26	46									
Dunyapur ...	33	40	28	41	47	33	44	57	25	13	52	20	*48	*58	*62	*68	*48	65	71	83	*72	57	76	47	32	15	27	45	57	77	37								
Kahror ...	49	46	44	57	45	31	60	55	41	29	25	18	*64	*74	*70	*84	*61	71	79	91	89	65	84	65	48	31	35	35	47	67	21	16							
Ranewahan ...	59	56	54	67	55	41	70	65	51	39	35	28	74	*84	*80	*94	*74	70	76	88	99	62	81	62	43	41	32	32	44	64	18	26	10						
Dhanot ...	57	62	40	47	35	21	68	46	43	31	19	8	72	*82	*86	*92	*72	83	89	101	99	75	94	75	43	43	45	45	57	77	31	26	10	20					
Meeranpur ...	62	59	57	70	58	44	73	68	58	42	38	31	*66	*87	*83	97	63	61	67	79	77	53	72	53	48	31	21	23	35	55	9	29	13	23	23				
Adamwáhan ...	55	50	38	47	33	19	66	43	41	29	17	6	70	80	84	90	70	81	87	99	97	73	92	73	58	41	53	59	71	91	45	26	24	34	14	37			
Garha Tahil Singh	45	*55	57	70	76	62	54	86	59	42	54	49	43	40	36	52	46	26	32	44	41	18	42	23	39	14	21	26	38	58	26	29	45	57	55	35	55		
Fattehpur ...	66	63	61	74	62	48	77	72	58	46	42	35	81	77	37	87	56	63	69	81	79	55	74	55	50	33	25	25	37	57	11	33	17	7	27	8	41	37	

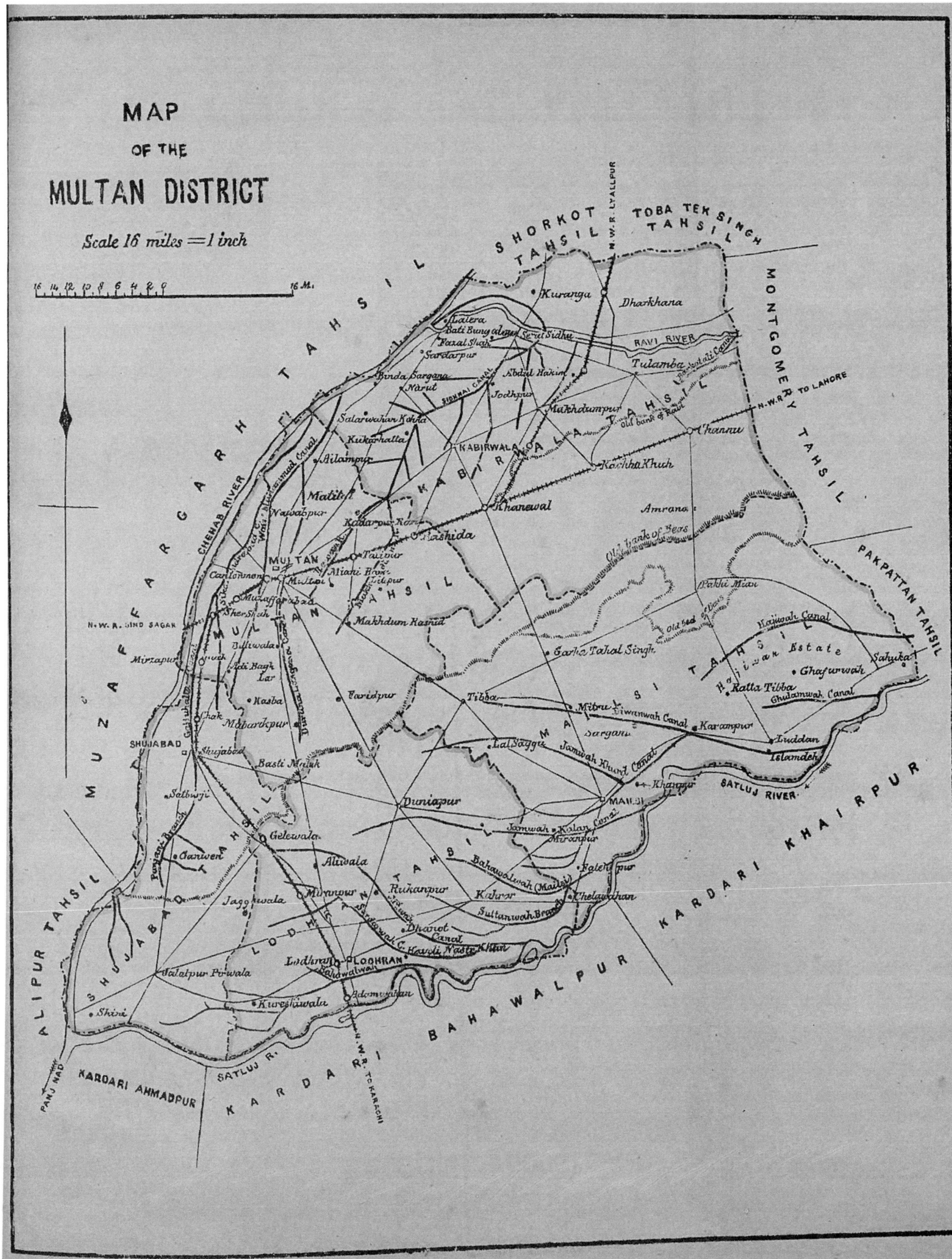

Nasir Ahmad L. Press Lahore 12-4-01